AF600596

TRANSFORMATION ON THE SOUTHERN UKRAINIAN STEPPE

Letters and Papers of Johann Cornies

TRANSFORMATION ON THE SOUTHERN UKRAINIAN STEPPE

Letters and Papers of Johann Cornies

VOLUME I: 1812–1835

Translated by Ingrid I. Epp

Edited by Harvey L. Dyck, Ingrid I. Epp, and John R. Staples

UNIVERSITY OF TORONTO PRESS
Toronto Buffalo London

Toronto Buffalo London
www.utppublishing.com

ISBN 978-1-4426-4506-6

Tsarist and Soviet Mennonite Studies

Library and Archives Canada Cataloguing in Publication

Cornies, Johann, 1789–1848
[Works. Selections. English]
Letters and papers of Johann Cornies.

(Tsarist and Soviet Mennonite studies)
Translated from the German.
Includes bibliographical references and index.
Contents: Volume 1: 1812–1835. Transformation on the southern Ukrainian steppe / translated by Ingrid I. Epp ; edited by Harvey L Dyck, Ingrid I. Epp, and John R. Staples.
ISBN 978-1-4426-4506-6 (v. 1 : bound)

1. Cornies, Johann, 1789–1848 – Correspondence. 2. Germans – Ukraine, Southern – Correspondence. 3. Mennonites – Ukraine, Southern – Correspondence. 4. Germans – Ukraine, Southern – History – 19th century. 5. Mennonites – Ukraine, Southern – History – 19th century. I. Dyck, Harvey L. (Harvey Leonard), editor II. Staples, John Roy, 1961–, editor III. Epp, Ingrid I. (Ingrid Ilse), translator, editor IV. Title. V. Series: Tsarist and Soviet Mennonite studies

DK508.425.G47C67 2015 947.7'300431 C2015-903579-1

University of Toronto Press acknowledges the financial assistance to its publishing program of the Canada Council for the Arts and the Ontario Arts Council, an agency of the government of Ontario.

Canada Council for the Arts Conseil des Arts du Canada

Funded by the Government of Canada Financé par le gouvernement du Canada

Contents

Maps

Preface

The eighteenth and nineteenth centuries saw the grasslands of the world open to agricultural settlement. In places as diverse as Argentina, the United States, Canada, South Africa, and Russia, people travelled to "promised lands" dreaming of peace, plenty, and escape from their overcrowded homes. They came with the urging and support of governments that viewed the grasslands as both a groundspring of national wealth and a tabula rasa upon which to create new moral orders and shape new national identities.

Russia's expansion east to Siberia and south onto the steppe was born of this vision, but in the south – "New Russia" as Catherine the Great named it – the Russian imperial project intersected with geopolitical realities that gave it unique shape. Beyond New Russia lay the Ottoman Empire, a powerful competitor with its own imperial ambitions. Expansion towards the Black Sea and Balkans meant certain conflict between the two great powers.

Geopolitics shaped the contours of Russia's colonial project, and southward expansion was a carefully managed affair, constrained by the need to create communities that could support the Russian military. The clearest examples were the "military colonies" of peasant conscripts, relocated with their families to the New Russian frontier and ordered to build their own villages and grow their own food, all under harsh military discipline.

The Russian administrative ideal was cameralism, a theory of centralized planning and tight control, administered through an obedient and well-trained bureaucracy. It relied in part upon providing models of proper behaviour to the Russian and Ukrainian peasants who moved to the empire's new territories. Russia actively recruited settlers from the German states as "model colonists" who could teach their progressive agricultural methods by example. Prussian Mennonites, renowned for their hard work and agricultural successes, became a central target for such recruitment.

The Mennonites who immigrated to the Russian Empire in the late eighteenth and early nineteenth centuries brought little with them beyond a deep-rooted Christian Anabaptist faith and a tradition of hard work. Settled in New Russia, they built villages, ploughed the rich prairie, and established model farmsteads. They built farm machinery, milled grain, and manufactured cloth, creating a bustling, prosperous community that, in the late nineteenth century, led the way in Russia's nascent industrial revolution.

By 1914, Mennonites were also the target of Russian nationalist resentment, singled out for their German language, their unorthodox religious beliefs, and their prosperity. The First World War, and then the Revolution, brought confiscations and persecution. Those who could, fled; those who remained were impoverished and – when they clung to their faith – harried, imprisoned, and killed. By 1991, the Mennonites had become a "blank page" in Russian and Soviet history, unknown even to the people who occupied the homes they had once built. The survivors in Siberia and Central Asia well knew to keep their beliefs to themselves.

The Russian Mennonite story remained alive in the émigré communities that left Russia in successive waves beginning in the 1870s and continuing into the 1940s. They settled in Canada, the United States, and South America, built new villages, and transplanted their Russian successes – and religious disputes – to their new homelands.

The story that these Mennonites preserved was mainly one of faith and suffering. Filtered through their late Russian and Soviet experiences, it stressed their religious values and sense of community. It ignored (or did not understand) their role in the larger Russian story of colonization and economic development. This was true even in the work of secular historians, who were almost exclusively dependent on in-group Mennonite accounts.

This document collection addresses the first period of Mennonite settlement. It reveals the foundations of Russian Mennonite prosperity in their hard work, self-discipline, and entrepreneurial spirit. It likewise reveals the fermentation of religious beliefs in their community. Significantly, it depicts a sometimes contentious, sometimes cooperative, constantly evolving relationship to surrounding peoples and the Russian state.

The collection unveils the Russian colonial world through the eyes of Johann Cornies and his many correspondents. Cornies was the leading figure in his community – an ambitious, entrepreneurial, and energetic reformer. He accrued great wealth and power, and he devoted himself to transforming New Russia. In Moscow, St. Petersburg, and the West, his keen mind and tremendous work ethic brought him acclaim. In the Mennonite community, it brought him respect, but also deep hostility as his reform plans – and his imperious manner – created controversy.

Johann Cornies' correspondence and studies offer a rich and varied feast. They depict a Russian colonial world where colonists could play a key role in shaping their own fate, and even gain influence in the highest levels of imperial power. They reveal a Mennonite community in which money and political connections sometimes competed with, but sometimes worked hand-in-hand with, tradition and religious authority. Not least, they open a window onto the personal life of a remarkable man.

This Volume

The selection, translation, and editing of Johann Cornies' papers has posed a series of significant challenges. Copies of Cornies' personal and business correspondence, along with the correspondence of the Molochnaia Forestry Society and Agricultural Society, are preserved in the Ukrainian State Archives of the Odessa Region, intermingled with other Mennonite records. Originally gathered by the Molochnaia Mennonite Peter J. Braun, the collection was seized by the Soviet government in 1929 and then disappeared. It was rediscovered in 1990 and microfilmed and distributed as *The Peter J. Braun Russian Mennonite Archive* to selected Western depositories in the mid-1990s by the University of Toronto's Research Program in Tsarist and Soviet Mennonite Studies.[1] Between the time of the Soviet seizure of the documents and their rediscovery, some documents disappeared (primarily during Germany's Second World War occupation of Ukraine), some were damaged beyond repair, and some were destroyed. Although what remains is not a complete collection, the tens of thousands of surviving pages provide a remarkable and coherent record of tsarist Mennonite life. In this published collection, the material of the Braun archive has been supplemented with documents from other archives, collections in the

Former Soviet Union and elsewhere,[2] and articles by and about tsarist Mennonites in the pages of the biweekly *Unterhaltungsblatt fuer deutsche Ansiedler im südlichen Russland.*

The vast majority of the documents are written in German Gothic script, often as copies of originals hurriedly recorded by Cornies' various secretaries, but sometimes in Cornies' own crabbed hand. Reading the documents is sometimes difficult and occasionally almost impossible; their translation represents more than a decade of painstaking work by Ingrid I. Epp, whose knowledge of the contents of the collection (and of nineteenth-century Mennonite German orthography) is unequalled.

Not everything that Cornies wrote is insightful, interesting, or revealing, and not all of it merits publication. The editors have tried to select documents that reveal:

- administrative policies and practices of Cornies, and of local, regional, and central governments and organizations;
- religious beliefs and practices of Cornies himself, of tsarist Mennonites, and of their neighbours and contacts at home and abroad;
- influences on Cornies, whether religious, philosophical, administrative, or practical, and Cornies' religious, philosophical, administrative and practical influence on people and organizations he came into contact with; and
- Cornies' personal life, including his interactions with friends and family.

Frequently Cornies wrote what amounted to form letters reporting on his activities and offering advice and recommendations to his friends and superiors. For example, Cornies' letters to Samuel Contenius and Andrei Fadeev are often very repetitive. One of the major tasks of the editors has been to select for publication what they regard as the most informative or clearest versions of such letters.

A second major challenge has been to select and include representative examples from the correspondence of the Forestry and Agricultural Societies, of which only a small percentage survives. Cornies chaired and actively administered these societies, and their correspondence clearly represents his activities and attitudes, so there can be no question that they belong in this collection. However, they are often highly repetitive, sometimes, for example, consisting of identical letters sent to each village in the Molochnaia settlement. The editors have selected representative samples of this correspondence that elucidate important society policies and initiatives and document significant events.

The documents selected for inclusion in the collection have been rigorously edited. The editors' first principle has been to retain the literal meaning of the documents at all cost. Beyond this, significant editing has been necessary. German syntax does not translate easily into English, and nineteenth-century tsarist Mennonite syntax – sometimes constructed by writers with little formal education – is often tortuous. Consequently, long sentences have been shortened and confusing syntax has been simplified in the interests of clear communication. One of the greatest challenges has been to retain the documents' original tone. Cornies was painfully aware of the social and political hierarchies within which he operated, and his correspondence with those whom he recognized as his superiors is frequently couched in terms of fawning obeisance. This is particularly apparent in the paragraph-long salutations that begin many of Cornies' letters, and their length and repetitively formulaic nature have led us to sharply abbreviate them, while retaining titles and attempting to replicate the signifiers of rank and status that appear in the body of the letters. Those readers for whom such signifiers are essential will have to turn to the originals.

Most of the correspondence is presented in strict chronological order, based on the date that it was written. The significant exception is the series of ethnographic studies written by Cornies that are grouped together separately in the second part of the first volume.

The division of the collection into three volumes is necessitated by its sheer size. The dividing points are partly based on the quantity of correspondence, but they are not otherwise arbitrary. Volume 1 ends in February 1836, on the eve of the creation of the Molochnaia Mennonite Agricultural Society. Volume 2 ends in 1841 with Cornies' report on the Mennonite administration, which marks the full maturation of Cornies' world view. The last of the four ethnographic studies published in volume 1 is undated, but was certainly written after May 1836. It is included in volume 1 in order to keep Cornies' major ethnographic writings together.

Acknowledgments

This project was made possible by the 1990 opening to scholarly study of previously secret collections in Soviet archives. One such collection in the Ukrainian State Archive of the Odessa Region, entitled "Mennonite Society in the County of Berdiansk," contained a rich collection of letters and papers of Johann Cornies, a leader in the settlement and transformation of the New Russia frontier (today southern Ukraine). A selection from this and other sources constitute the basis for the three volumes of this project.

We are deeply grateful to Vladimir Malchenko, then director of the Odessa Archive, and Olga Konovalova, his associate, for drawing to our attention the existence of these sources, for guiding us through their intricacies and organization, and for agreeing to and overseeing their microfilming.

For their encouragement and assistance at every stage of our work, and for providing space, we thank Carol Moore, past chief librarian, University of Toronto Libraries, and her colleagues: Larry Langford, head of access and information; Karen Turko, head of microtext; and Jim Ingram, microtext specialist. Richard Ratzlaff, our editor at the University of Toronto Press, cheerfully oversaw the appearance of this volume into print.

Translator's Note

The source of most of the Johann Cornies correspondence, and of his other documents, is the Peter J. Braun Russian Mennonite Archive, housed in the Ukrainian State Archives of the Odessa Region. They were gleaned by checking the microfilm of the somewhat disorganized files of the first half of the Braun Archive, and cover the years 1812 to 1848, the period of Cornies' activity.

All of the German documents are written in the German Gothic script then in use, many of them in a careful, regular hand. Others were obviously dashed off or written by someone with limited practice in writing. The documents themselves show many personal styles and personalities and it is regrettable that these cannot be conveyed adequately without turning the translations into quaint documents.

Translation methods have been as direct as possible. The German umlaut has been translated using the conventional method of adding the letter "e" after the vowel with the umlaut. The spelling of German names has not been changed, but Russian names have been spelled in the Library of Congress style of transliteration from Russian into English. The reference for the spelling of Mennonite village names is the map reproduced in Franz Issac's *Die Molotschnaer Mennoniten*. Names of organizations have been translated into English, for example, "Agricultural Society" rather than "Wirtschaftlicher Verein." Titles of German publications are given in German with the literal English translation following in brackets. Sometimes translations could not be found for individual terms – often either terms of local application, or terms transferred from Russian – and in these cases the translator has made an attempt to convey the sense of the sentence, sometimes including the term in the document in square brackets.

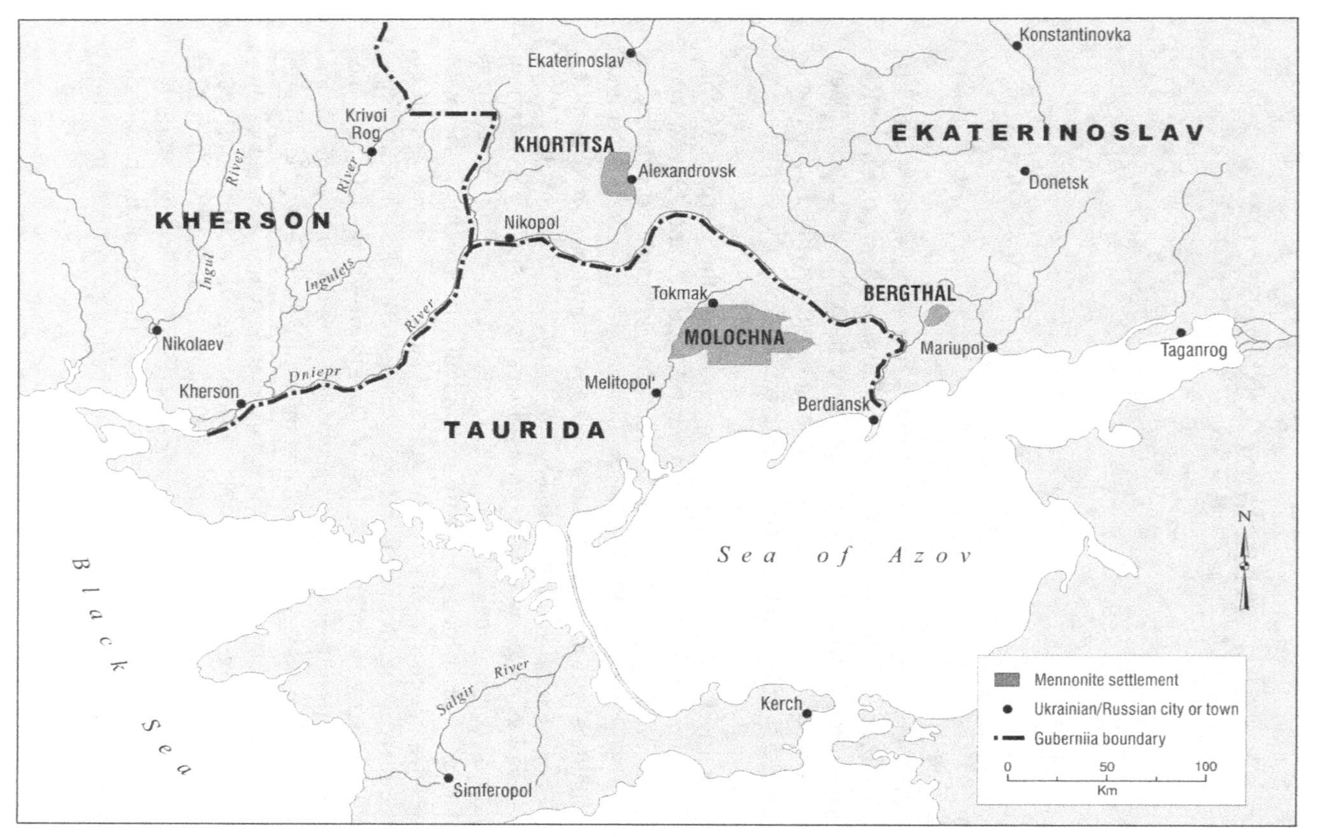

Map 1: Mennonite Settlements in New Russia, circa 1880. Harvey L. Dyck, trans. and ed., *A Mennonite in Russia: The Diaries of Jacob D. Epp, 1851–1880,* University of Toronto Press, 1991.

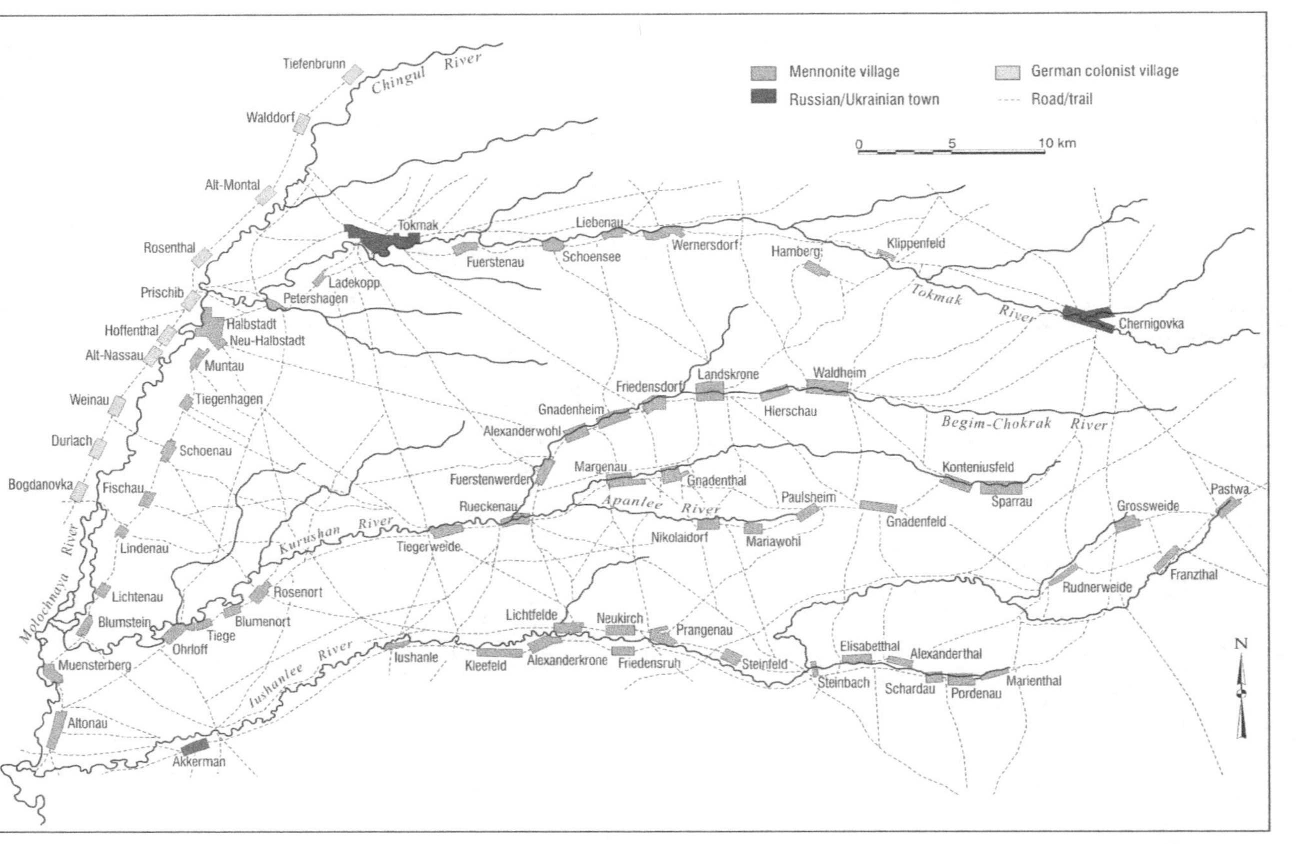

Map 2: The Molochnaia Mennonite Settlement. William Schroeder and Helmut Huebert, eds., *Mennonite Historical Atlas*, 2nd ed., Springfield Publishers, 1996. Used with permission.

Introduction

John R. Staples

Johann Cornies was born in Prussia in 1789, just as revolution swept away the Old Regime in France and threw open the door to decades of turmoil in Europe. He immigrated to New Russia (now southern Ukraine) with his parents in 1805, as the Napoleonic Wars threatened the survival of the European monarchies. He died in New Russia as the Revolutions of 1848 shook the Old Regimes to their core.

In the context of such cataclysmic events it may be hyperbole to call Cornies a revolutionary. After all, he accepted the God-given authority of the Russian tsar without question as essential to orderly government and to the well-being of his own Mennonite people. Yet within the tsarist Mennonite world of New Russia, Cornies was indeed a revolutionary. His cause was economic modernization: he was determined to rationally order the economic life of his people, and if this required methods that were extreme – and indeed revolutionary for Mennonite society – then he was more than willing to oblige.

Thrust into a leadership role by a combination of circumstance, aptitude, and ambition, Cornies emerged as a visionary reformer within Mennonite society, as well as the main intermediary between Mennonites and the tsarist state. The world around the Mennonites was changing, and Cornies sometimes forced his community to take part, but he equally sheltered it from excessive state intrusions when the need arose. In the process, he became a towering figure in the affairs of New Russia. At the height of his powers in the 1840s, Cornies was fully alive to the currents of local, regional, national, and international events that affected his region and his country. No one in the tsarist Mennonite community – and few people anywhere – were so engaged, so informed, and so determined as he. From the Ministry of State

Domains in St. Petersburg to the smallest petty merchants in local villages, people sought his advice, his opinions, and his patronage. The shabby treatment of Russian peasant apprentices was no more beneath his concern than the religious disputes of Mennonites in Prussia. He addressed himself equally to economic management in the Caucasus and to primary school curriculum in Khortitsa villages.

Employing all of his energy, determination, and intelligence, Cornies fundamentally changed the tsarist Mennonite world. Whether the changes were positive or negative is a controversial subject. He has sometimes been glorified and sometimes reviled, and there is little agreement about his personality or his role in Mennonite and Russian history. The 1990 discovery of a vast cache of his personal and business papers in the Ukrainian State Archives of the Odessa Region – selectively translated and published for the first time in these volumes – will help resolve these disagreements, providing a view deep into the private and public life of a remarkable and complex man.[3]

The story these papers tell not only lays bare the Russian Mennonite world; it is equally revealing of Russian imperial policy and of life on the empire's southern frontier in the early nineteenth century. While valuable comparative scholarship is emerging on the Russian imperial project, it focuses almost exclusively on the unequal relationship between central and regional authorities. Emblematic of this central focus, leading scholar Michael Khodarkovsky, in his important study of Russia's southward expansion, altogether dismisses the "recent fashion of seeing in almost every colonial encounter a 'middle ground,'" and insists that, in Russia, "the government's ideology allowed no room" for negotiation.[4] In dismissing regional influences, such scholarship equally ignores the general relationship between religion and empire in Russia. Traditional Mennonite scholarship has tended to support this imperial perspective, viewing Mennonite attempts to carve out an independent identity in the centralizing Russian Empire as a lost cause, leading inevitably to the tragic repressions that befell Mennonites in the twentieth century.

In contrast to this centrist focus, some recent scholarship has posited that the Russian Empire functioned as an "empire state," where "difference among groups was accepted by all as the normal way of being."[5] This revisionist argument suggests that the distinct status of regional minorities carried with it distinct rights that the central government accepted and benefited from. Johann Cornies' role in the Mennonite and Russian communities, revealed in this collection of documents, lends support to the "empire state" thesis. In Cornies' activities there is important evidence of how a non-indigenous, non-elite frontier minority could assert substantial influence over their own lives, and even come to influence imperial policy.

The Mennonites provide a rare regional perspective on the Russian Empire, for they occupied a unique position in tsarist Russia's colonial hierarchy in the first half of the nineteenth century. Their European-wide reputation as industrious, efficient agriculturists had provoked Catherine the Great and Tsar Alexander I to invite them to emigrate from Prussia to New Russia. The Russian state looked to Mennonites to become model colonists who, by their example, would encourage improvements in agriculture, afforestation, trade, and industry in Russia's newly acquired southern territories. Mennonites were to become agents of the tsarist colonial administration, and the state eagerly tried to exploit this status, believing that Mennonites offered the state an opportunity to extend central control to the peripheries of the empire. Mennonites were, in this sense, "insiders" in the administration.

But Mennonites were not only agents of tsarist colonial policy; they were at the same time subjects of it. As tsarist policy evolved, the state expected its Mennonites to evolve, too, and become models for the latest colonial fashions from St. Petersburg. Yet Mennonites had religious and cultural traditions that they would not lightly abandon, and they preferred to walk the imperial stage in their own plain-cut cloth. Mennonites, as "outsiders," employed Russia's traditional local self-administrative system to defend their religious and cultural freedoms, and in the process forced the state to clearly define the relationship between the rights and obligations of its colonial subjects.

Through Cornies' eyes, we gain the unique perspective of a literate, insightful outsider who never held a Russian administrative post and who lived his life as a member of a frontier community, but who nonetheless became an important informant and adviser to imperial insiders. There is no other comparable record of the Russian imperial project, and Cornies' papers consequently provide a singular opportunity to understand the Russian Empire.

The Polish Legacy[6]

Johann Cornies was a Mennonite, and this above all else defined his existence. Mennonites are pacifist Christian Anabaptists (i.e., believers in adult baptism). Their religion originated in Switzerland and the

Netherlands in the sixteenth century, and owes its name to one of its founders, Menno Simons. They were harshly persecuted for their religious beliefs in the sixteenth and seventeenth centuries, causing many Mennonites to flee to the Vistula River delta of Poland, where they prospered in the relatively tolerant Polish state.

Poland's unique political situation made it possible for Mennonites to settle and prosper there, but at the same time the shifting political, economic, and religious forces in Poland also placed constant pressures on the Mennonite community. In an early modern age of growing monarchical absolutism in Europe, Poland was a sharp exception to the trend, emerging in the sixteenth century as a highly decentralized state with a notoriously weak monarchy. This was a consequence of Poland's geographical position at a crossroads in Central Europe where Germanic, Slavic, and Jewish peoples and Protestant, Catholic, Uniate, and Orthodox religions intersected. In order to unite this diverse group and build a state that could protect them from the surrounding Austrian, Ottoman, Swedish, and Russian states, the Polish Crown was forced to grant unparalleled levels of autonomy to its various constituents. The Crown required the consent of the Polish nobility – granted in the *Sejm,* or noble assembly – to institute any new law, and any single member of the nobility could veto legislation in the *Sejm* by employing the notorious *liberum veto*. As a consequence of this political arrangement, the nobility enjoyed substantial autonomy on its own land, and the Catholic Church, and several major cities, enjoyed equal autonomy on its land.

Because there was no strong central government capable of dictating policy, Poland was in a constant state of negotiation among its various constituents. At times, such "negotiations" devolved into brute force, and many of the great Polish noble magnates retained large private armies to defend and extend their interests. More often, the negotiations addressed economic issues and found economic solutions. The Polish economy was largely agricultural, focused on the Baltic grain trade. Grain flowed down the Vistula River to Danzig and Elbing, and from there on to Western European markets. To prosper, Polish landowners needed reliable tenants to work their land, and because Poland was far less densely populated than Western Europe, good tenants could negotiate favourable lease terms.

Mennonites were very good tenants, and from the outset they were able to negotiate long-term leases on land, particularly in the areas of Danzig and Elbing. Most Mennonites who migrated to Poland settled in the Vistula delta within sight of the walls of Danzig, a Hansa city with a bustling trade and craft economy. The Cornies family lived in one such village, Baerwalde. The Mennonites came to Poland as artisans, traders, and farmers who had little trouble in adapting to local economic circumstances. Their skills, whether in draining swampy delta land for farming or as craftsmen, ensured that they would be welcome additions to their new homeland, although their sectarian religious beliefs – while more tolerated in Poland than in the Netherlands – nevertheless caused them to be forbidden from living within the city walls.

Because Mennonites leased their land, and because the attitudes of their landlords, and the landlords themselves, changed over time, Mennonites had to learn how to constantly negotiate their position in Poland. By the eighteenth century, Mennonites were deeply integrated into the Vistula's economic and political life. Economic necessity ensured that they attuned their economy and society to local and international political and market forces. They were also well represented in the dike societies and other organizations that coordinated regional life, and this introduced them to the complexities of official bureaucracies, complete with the infighting and patronage networks that always accompany them. Mennonite religious beliefs forbade them from taking oaths, and this meant that they could not hold high political offices, so for them negotiation meant playing various external interest groups against each other, including the Catholic Church, the Crown, city governments, and foreign interests. Often this meant the judicious use of monetary "gifts" to government and Catholic Church officials.[7] This experience of negotiating their existence in the convoluted Polish political, ethnic, and religious milieu would help shape the internal administrative culture that Mennonites later fostered in Russia, as well as their relations with the Russian imperial bureaucracy.

All Vistula Mennonites shared a set of basic religious doctrines, including adult baptism, congregational autonomy, and pacifism, and when circumstances demanded it, they presented a united front to the larger administrative world. But internally, Mennonites were divided between the liberal "Frisian" and the conservative "Flemish" congregations. Flemish congregations dominated the Vistula delta, including the Cornies' village of Baerwalde, while Frisian congregations dominated the higher regions of the Vistula River valley, where Mennonites only comprised a small percentage of the population. Overall the Frisians were a distinct minority.

The most significant point of discord between the two congregations revolved around the application of the ban, that is, the practice of excommunicating members who violated congregational or community rules. Frisians favoured a relatively lenient application, not demanding, for example, that spouses shun their banned mates, while the Flemish were far more strict. Frisians were also open to dialogue with, and even intermarriage between, members of other religious confessions, and this openness permitted pietism to gain powerful influence in the Frisian communities in the late eighteenth century. The Flemish, meanwhile, strongly opposed religious dialogue with other confessions, and particularly the emotionalism and universalism of the pietist movement.

Pietism, which emphasizes inner spiritual regeneration and evangelical activities, emerged as a significant force in Prussia and other German states in the eighteenth century. Originating as a reform movement within the Lutheran Church, pietism promoted the cultivation of personal piety through an individual exploration of faith, and it consequently challenged the authority of the established Church. At the same time, because of the centrality of Bible-reading to this individual exploration, pietism promoted literacy and education. Beginning with the establishment of Philipp Jakob Spener's *Ritterakademie* in Halle in 1694, systematic pietist education cast its net across East-Central Europe, harvesting generations of literate, numerate, *very* serious young men to fill the ranks of the Prussian bureaucracy.[8] Under Frederick the Great, they became key players in Prussia's highly disciplined bureaucracy.[9]

The pietist emphasis on evangelism was particularly controversial to conservative Mennonites, whose traditional beliefs tended to promote separation from the secular world. Their goal was to live ascetic lives in imitation of early Christian communities, in anticipation of securing their future in the next life. Their early history of martyrdom had given emphasis to this belief, for Mennonites had learned to keep their heads down if they wanted to survive. In contrast, pietism demanded engagement with the larger world, leading implicitly towards the creation of the Kingdom of God on Earth. By the late eighteenth century, pietism was becoming a major influence, but also a point of contention, within Mennonite society.

Whatever their internal differences, Vistula Mennonites faced the 1774 partition of Poland and their consequent subjection to Prussian rule as a common threat to their religious rights and economic security. The militarist Prussian state had little tolerance for pacifist Mennonites, and the reign of Frederick Wilhelm II (1786–97) in particular saw a concerted attack on Mennonite rights. Prussia linked official permission for the Mennonites to purchase land to military service, impeding expansion of Mennonite landholdings. This was a policy that Mennonite leader Heinrich Donner characterized as a "secret persecution against both our means of livelihood and our religious freedom."[10] Coupled with Russia's aggressive recruitment of Mennonite immigrants, the new Prussian laws stimulated the Mennonite migration to Russia that began in 1789. The migrants, drawn by the promise of plentiful land and religious freedom, looked to Russia as a refuge.

Mennonite migration from Prussia to Russia continued in fits and starts for over fifty years, with a total of some 30,000 departing for the tsarist Empire. Those Mennonites who remained in Prussia were forced to adapt to the aggressive Prussian brand of nationalism that culminated in the creation of the modern German state in 1871. Left with little choice, many Prussian Mennonites accepted conscription and military service, and slowly integrated into German society. In retrospect, it seems apparent that whatever the hardships that Russia imposed upon Mennonites in the long term, in the short term it provided greater opportunities than did Prussia for them to preserve their culture and beliefs and to play a role in deciding how these matters would evolve in reaction to the forces of modernization and nationalism.[11]

The Russian Option

In the late eighteenth century, Russia seemed as eager to lure the Mennonites as Prussia was to get rid of them. During the reign of Catherine the Great (1762–96), Russia expanded to encompass southern Ukraine. Catherine justified southern expansion by a mixture of security concerns and imperial ambitions. Before 1783, the Khortitsa and Molochnaia regions, where the first Mennonite migrants settled, were on the hostile frontier with the Crimean Khanate, a vassal state of the Ottoman Empire. The Ottoman Empire was Russia's major competitor for power on the southern steppe as well as in the Balkans and Caucasus. Catherine viewed herself as rightful protector of the Orthodox peoples of the Ottoman Empire. She openly acknowledged her ambition to wrest control of the Balkans from the Turks, and in 1779, she famously hinted at her desire to capture Constantinople itself when she christened her grandson Constantine.[12]

By the time of Catherine's reign, Russia was beginning to gain the upper hand in its long series of wars with the Ottoman Empire. In the Russo-Turkish War of 1768–74, Russia seized the city of Azov and the Black Sea coastline between the Dnieper and Bug Rivers, and gained formal Ottoman recognition of the independence of the Crimean Khanate, including the Molochnaia region. In 1783, Catherine annexed the Crimea, ultimately provoking the Russo-Turkish War of 1788–91. Catherine's victory in that war cemented Russian control of the Crimea and helped start the Ottoman Empire down the long road to its twentieth-century demise. She labelled the newly gained territories "New Russia," a powerful metaphor of her imperial ambitions. Catherine saw the south as a blank slate where Russia might create a modern economy and people that, in turn, would help her transform the interior of the Empire.

Military subjugation of the south did not yet constitute enlightened administration: Catherine's goal was to exploit the agricultural and commercial potential of her new territories in the interests of the state. A devotee of the physiocratic belief that national wealth was rooted in population size, Catherine set out to populate her new domains.[13]

Russia did not have enough peasants to populate its vast new territories, and the problem was further complicated by Russia's serf and state-peasant economy, which sharply restricted peasant mobility and made the type of spontaneous settlement of the prairies that occurred in North America impossible. Catherine therefore looked to foreign immigrants, creating in 1793 a special Chancellery for the Guardianship of Foreigners and issuing an open invitation for immigrants to populate the southern steppe on attractive terms. She commissioned recruiting agents to lure Western European immigrants with promises of money, tax exemptions, and large land grants.

Peasants from the German states became prime targets of this recruitment campaign. Catherine knew that Germanic peasants were skilled agriculturists and, equally important, experienced crafts- and tradespeople; they constituted an ideal population for Catherine's grand project, and she hoped that they would provide a model for the Russian and Ukrainian peasants she intended to settle alongside them. Mennonites figured prominently in these plans, for Catherine and her most able administrators were well aware of the Mennonites' reputation as sober, hard-working, prosperous, and progressive agriculturists.[14] Catherine and her successors founded Germanic peasant settlements across Russia. The most extensive were along the Volga River and in New Russia, where, by the early nineteenth century, the German language could be heard in cities and villages stretching from Odessa to Ekaterinoslav.

In 1789, the first cohort of Vistula Mennonite immigrants arrived in New Russia, founding the Khortitsa Settlement on the banks of the Dnieper River, near present-day Zaporizhzhe; in 1803–6, a second cohort founded the first eighteen villages of the Molochnaia settlement along the Molochnaia River, just north of present-day Melitopol. The Cornies family – Johann, with his father, Johann Sr., his mother, Maria, and his brothers, Peter (b. 1791) and David (b. 1794) – came at the tail end of this second wave, arriving in Khortitsa in 1805 and moving on to the Molochnaia village of Ohrloff in 1806. Johann's youngest brother, Heinrich, was born in Ohrloff in 1806. Subsequent waves of Mennonite settlers came to the Molochnaia in 1818–22 and 1835–8, before the emergence of Russian nationalist attitudes, Tsar Nicholas I's fear of liberal Western ideas, and concerns about the emerging German state caused Russia to slow and finally stop immigration in the latter half of the nineteenth century. By 1914, Mennonite settlements, springing from these original settlements, had spread across European Russia, Siberia, the Caucasus, and Central Asia, and the tsarist Mennonites numbered over 100,000.[15]

The Mennonites' status in Russia was spelled out in the *Privilegium,* promised to the first immigrants by Catherine in 1787 and finally granted by Tsar Paul I in 1800. Mennonites regarded the *Privilegium* as a fundamental, God-willed guarantee of their rights and privileges in Russia.[16]

The privileges that Paul I awarded the Mennonites can be divided into two categories: religious and economic. The *Privilegium* granted Mennonites "the liberty to practise their religion according to their tenets and customs," and – crucially important to their pacifist beliefs – a complete exemption from military service. Economically, besides temporary tax exemptions shared by all settlers in New Russia, the *Privilegium* granted each Mennonite family "incontestable and perpetually inheritable possession" of a sixty-five *desiatina* (one *desiatina* = 1.09 hectares, or 2.7 acres) allotment, the right to build factories, to enter trade guilds, and to engage in commercial activities.

In the *Privilegium*'s concluding clause, Paul I ordered "all our military and civil authorities and government offices not only to leave these Mennonites and their descendants in unmolested enjoyment of their houses, lands, and other possessions, not to hinder them in the enjoyment of the privileges granted to them, but also to show them in all cases every assistance and protection." This seemed to guarantee very significant freedoms, but they came at a price, for Russia was in pursuit of its own modernization agenda and the Mennonites were part of it. As the *Privilegium* made clear in its opening phrases, the Mennonites received their special status because their "excellent industry and morality may … be held up as a model to the foreigners settled [in New Russia]."[17]

Russia assumed that Mennonites would, by their example, promote improvements in agriculture, afforestation, trade, and industry in Russia's newly acquired southern territories; in essence, the state was rewarding Mennonites with religious freedoms in payment for economic services. The problem was that there persisted among some Mennonites a religious ideal of withdrawal from secular entanglements. Mennonites possessed a foundation myth of agricultural life as the ideal expression of this withdrawal, for life in their agricultural villages permitted physical withdrawal to match the ideal of spiritual withdrawal.[18] This religiously inspired tendency towards isolation was reinforced by a series of other factors. The late eighteenth and early nineteenth centuries were a time of enormous social, economic, and religious upheaval in Europe. The Enlightenment with its secularizing undercurrents, the countercurrents of pietism, the aggressive expansion of Prussia, the French Revolution, and the Napoleonic Wars all provided a strong stimulus for some Mennonites to seek escape into religiously sanctioned isolation. Clearly this ideal of withdrawal could not sit easily with playing the role of model settlers as promoted in the Russian *Privilegium*, and from the outset it seemed certain that tensions would arise among the Mennonites about their relationship to the state.

Yet alongside the isolationist tradition, a practical need for economic and political engagement had penetrated deeply into the Mennonite world view by the late eighteenth century. The Mennonites who migrated to Russia were not unanimous in their attitudes towards the tsarist state and society. Countervailing forces pushed Mennonites to engage with the tsarist government, society, and economy. Most importantly, in Poland and Prussia, Mennonites had been integrated into a market economy.[19] Their basic understanding of their own economic existence was founded on the relatively mature market conditions of the Vistula, where their agricultural and craft production found ready buyers in the cities of Danzig and Elbing, and in export markets in Western Europe. Families like the Cornies' lived side by side with Lutherans and Catholics in their Prussian villages, quickly embracing their Low German language and trading (and undoubtedly socializing) with their neighbours. Probably many of the Mennonite migrants came to Russia, not to isolate themselves but to find new and better economic opportunities. The Cornies family fit comfortably into this latter group; what little we know of Johann Cornies' father, Johann Sr., suggests that he had worked as a merchant seaman, travelling far beyond the confines of Prussian Mennonitism, and certainly his eldest son harboured no desire to be cloistered in an isolated community.[20]

The existence of this outward-looking element among the Mennonite migrants is apparent from the activities of the advanced parties sent by Mennonites to survey potential settlement sites in New Russia. They focused on finding economically viable locations, and the *Privilegium* they negotiated sought not to isolate Mennonites, but to define the terms of their engagement with Russia. It was a document that reflected all of their experience in the complex Polish state that they had left behind. Mennonites undoubtedly favoured exclusively Mennonite settlements – in contrast to being scattered among other religious denominations as they had been in the Vistula – and the establishment of such exclusive settlements was at any rate mandated by the Russian state. But there was no explicit attempt by the Mennonites to cut these settlements off from the surrounding world.[21] This was less isolationism than it was community-building: Mennonites were willing to engage the tsarist state, economy, and society, but they wanted a say in the terms of engagement. It was precisely the willingness of the tsarist "empire state" to negotiate conditions that made the emigration attractive to Mennonites. The *Privilegium* was a first step in this engagement, but as the forces of modernization and nationalism emerged in Russia, the terms of the relationship would have to be continuously adjusted in the future.

Mennonites modelled the communities they established in New Russia on their Vistula communities, which were governed internally by church congregations. All members of a congregation were subject to its ethical rules, enforced by an elected elder (*Ältester*) assisted by elected ministers (*Lehrer*) and deacons (*Diakonen*). These internal structures are the thing that most clearly set Mennonites apart from other Germanic immigrants to Russia. Catholic and Lutheran immigrants, who had a passive relationship to their churches, were accustomed to accepting church and state as part of a single social and political system. By comparison, Vistula Mennonites had been separated legally and religiously from their neighbours and state, and this separate existence helped build a strong sense of community identity that survived and flourished in Russia.

When two Moravian Brethren emissaries visited the Molochnaia settlement in 1806, they recorded how fully and quickly the Mennonite community had transplanted itself from Poland to New Russia:

> They have made such good use of their first two years here that there is little left to do to fully complete their establishment. One can see how much work they have put into each of their buildings, their stables, barns, gardens, homes and farmyards with the surrounding ditches. The yard of each fullholding is forty *faden* wide [one *faden* = 1.9 meters] and each is separated from the neighbouring yard by a fourteen *faden* strip of uncultivated land. The houses stand ten *faden* back from the street. All of the buildings and everything inside them is in very good order. They also have very beautiful windmills, fitted out with storage bins, which make a very fine flour of a quality that cannot be found outside of this Settlement. They have sent a man to Taganrog with butter, which immediately found a buyer, so others will soon also be sending butter there. Indeed, the Mennonites are already so firmly established here that, as an indication of their confidence, each of the eighteen villages is separated from the others by several *verstas* [one *verst* = 1.07 kilometres], in order to leave ample land for the increasing numbers of their descendants.[22]

The challenge for Molochnaia Mennonites would be to adapt the imported practices described here to their new Russian circumstances.

The Russian state required Mennonites to adopt the district (*volost*) administration system, created by Tsar Paul I in 1797, of elected village mayors (*sels'skii vybornyi*) and ten-men (*desiatskie*). The Mennonite equivalent of a *volost* was the *Gebietsamt* (district), and just as Ukrainian and Russian state peasants had an elected *volost* mayor (*volost'naia golova*), the Mennonites had an elected *Gebietsamt* mayor (*Oberschulz*).[23] The existing congregational system would come to coexist with the Russian administrative system, with elders, ministers, and deacons exercising significant influence on the election of local secular officials, and secular officials relying on the support of congregational officials in the enforcement of regulations.

The state charged local officials with publicizing new laws, encouraging church attendance, taking measures against epidemics and fires, ensuring maintenance of roads and bridges, and arbitrating minor disputes. It also gave them authority over important economic functions, including agricultural practices and grain reserves.[24] They were, in other words, representative of secular authority over economic affairs in the Mennonite villages.

The state agency that directly oversaw Mennonites and other foreign colonists was the Guardianship Committee for Foreign Settlers in New Russia, which in turn answered to the Ministry of Internal Affairs before 1836 and to the Ministry of State Domains after its creation in 1836. The Guardianship Committee became a gathering place for some of the most reform-minded bureaucrats in the Ministry of State Domains, and Cornies' association with such people strongly affected him. The Committee was headquartered in Kishinev until 1834, when it relocated to Odessa. Until 1834, a local Guardianship Committee Bureau in Ekaterinoslav oversaw New Russian Mennonite affairs with considerable autonomy from Kishinev; after 1834, the Molochnaia and Khortitsa Mennonites answered directly to the central offices in Odessa. This administrative system survived virtually unchanged until the Great Reforms of the 1860s, which attempted to fully integrate Mennonites into the larger Russian state system.[25]

While the Russian state did not intend to isolate Mennonites, and Mennonites were divided in their attitudes towards self-isolation when they arrived in southern Ukraine, the conditions they encountered upon arrival inevitably shaped their subsequent development. Their new frontier home was exotic and foreboding, filled with the babble of unfamiliar languages (Russian, Ukrainian, Tatar, Yiddish, and multiple versions of Low German) and unfamiliar customs and religious practices. There were no cities like Danzig and Elbing to provide them with markets, and the nearest ports were too distant to support the market-oriented crop agriculture that many had practised in the Vistula. The howling blizzards that sometimes decimated Mennonite livestock, and the summer "black blizzards" – moisture-sapping dust storms – had no precedent in their Vistula lives. While the Molochnaia region provided rich agricultural soil, it was a semi-arid zone where inconsistent precipitation made crop agriculture a boom-or-bust proposition and where careful land management was a significant prerequisite for future prosperity. The understaffed Russian bureaucracy was a distant influence, quite unlike the intrusive Prussian bureaucracy of their final Vistula years. At first, the Mennonite migrants had in practice little choice but isolation as they struggled for survival in their new homeland.[26]

This moment of relative isolation contributed to a strong sense of community identity that emerged among tsarist Mennonites in the nineteenth century and ultimately took shape in their self-image as a distinct Russian-Mennonite people. But forces of integration were equally central to the tsarist Mennonite story from almost the moment of their arrival. Mennonites experienced their greatest isolation at the very start of their settlement. With each subsequent year, the immigration of both Slavic and Germanic peasants to New Russia, the evolution of regional and national markets, the establishment of nearby ports, the influx of new religious currents, and the growth of the tsarist bureaucracy (in size and competence) pressed in upon the Mennonites. After the briefest period of frontier isolation, they moved beyond the gates of their tightly knit Mennonite home into a larger Russian world through their encounter with, and integration into, a complex and changing multi-ethnic and multi-cultural empire. Their experiences in Poland had provided them with important tools to begin the process of negotiating their relationship with their new neighbours and the state, but they would also have to learn new lessons. It was through this process of negotiation and learning, as much as through the experience of isolation, that their collective identity developed. Johann Cornies emerged in the first half of the nineteenth century as their lead negotiator, the principal political and economic intermediary between Mennonites and the tsarist state, and, most of all, as the leading Mennonite innovator and advocate of modernization.

Johann Cornies

We know almost nothing of Cornies' youth, and nothing at all of the period before his arrival in Russia as a sixteen-year-old. He moved with his parents and family to Ohrloff in 1806, and lived there, and at his nearby estate of Iushanle, until his death in 1848. What little we do know about the first years after Cornies' arrival comes from a handful of early Mennonite histories, including most notably David Epp's 1909 biography of Cornies, Franz Isaac's 1908 history of the Molochnaia Settlement, and P. M. Friesen's 1911 history of the Mennonite Brethren. The image that emerges out of these sources is one of Cornies as a kind of Mennonite Horatio Alger, carting cheese and butter across the wild steppes to markets, fleeing marauding Tatars, and simultaneously educating himself by voraciously reading everything he could lay his hands on.[27]

The hagiographic tone of these accounts was only adopted by Mennonites in the early twentieth century. At the time of his death, Cornies was unpopular in his own community, and it was only in official Russian accounts, such as the long biographical appreciation that appeared in the *Journal of the Ministry of State Domains* shortly after his death, that Cornies appeared in such heroic shades.[28] Such official accounts would ultimately inform Mennonite historians like Friesen, Isaac, and Epp, who adopted Cornies as a Mennonite "superman" (to use Epp's term). This late-tsarist Mennonite glorification of Cornies is a reflection of a Mennonite community that, following the Great Reforms of the 1860s and 1870s, felt threatened by the social, economic, and political upheavals that their Russian world was experiencing, and most particularly by the rising tide of Russian nationalism with its anti-German overtones. Russian Mennonites, in the early years of the twentieth century, *needed* a superman, and Johann Cornies was the obvious choice.[29]

Whatever the exaggeration of these accounts may be, the few documents we do possess from the first years of Cornies' Russian life reveal an unusual figure, leading the way beyond the gates of the Mennonite community at a very young age. Already in 1812, at the age of twenty-three, he rented large swathes of pasture land from the state. Located on the Iushanle River just east of Ohrloff, some of this land would ultimately become Cornies' private estate and the headquarters for all of his activities.

Johann Cornies married Anganetha Klassen in 1811, and they moved onto their own fullholding in Ohrloff in 1812. He and Anganetha would have an atypically small family: a son, Johann Jr., born in 1812, and a daughter, Agnes, born in 1818. We know relatively little about Cornies' home life; there are no surviving letters between Johann and his wife, while just two letters survive from daughter Agnes to her father, and none from him to her. The letters between Johann and his brothers are disappointingly impersonal and deal mainly with business, and his correspondence with Johann Jr., though more revealing of Cornies' attitudes, provides sparing evidence of family relations. These family letters imply – as much from what they do *not* say as what they do – that Cornies was a stern, intimidating, authoritarian patriarch to the entire extended family. At the same time, there are tantalizing hints that Cornies was more than a typical nineteenth-century Mennonite family patriarch, most significantly in his decision to permit his teenage daughter Agnes to travel to Moscow in 1836, and in his doting accounts of his grandson in the 1840s.

For the period 1812–17, a handful of records reveal Cornies' business affairs. It is unfortunate that these records are not more extensive, for the wealth Cornies accrued at this time, and the respect he gained in his community, was essential to his future success. Most of the extant evidence pertains to his Iushanle lease land, but we also know that by 1817 he had partnered with Wilhelm Martens – Cornies' closest friend and, by Martens' death in 1845, probably the richest Mennonite in Russia – in leasing from the state the brandy monopoly for the Molochnaia Mennonite district. This brandy monopoly allowed Cornies and Martens to broker all brandy sales in the region, and it contributed substantially to their wealth. They also worked together in commercial sheep-raising, purchasing and leasing land, and other business ventures.

Despite the incomplete record, it is certain that by 1817 Johann Cornies was, at the age of twenty-eight, a man of wealth and consequence in his community. In that year, the Molochnaia Mennonite district appointed him as its official land surveyor, and in 1818, it made him a member of the Mennonite Settlement Commission that oversaw the establishment of new villages in the Molochnaia for new immigrants from Prussia.

The 1818 immigration was a watershed moment in the Molochnaia Mennonite Settlement, introducing dynamic tensions into the established community. The new immigrants had lived through the defeat of Napoleon and the rapid growth of Prussian-German nationalism with its accompanying processes of economic and political modernization. Not only were the immigrants primarily Frisian, pietist Mennonites, but their experiences under Prussian rule had made them better educated and more open to progressive economic reforms than were the first settlers. They were even linguistically distinct, for some among them had begun to prefer High German to their traditional Mennonite Low German. In sum, they brought to the Molochnaia an impetus for economic, religious, and cultural change.

The year 1818 was as critical a juncture for Johann Cornies as it was for his community, for it was then that he emerged at the fulcrum point of the diverse internal and external forces that played upon the tsarist Mennonites over the coming thirty years. His appointment as a member of the Settlement Commission symbolized the respect he had already earned from the established Molochnaia Mennonite community. The new settlers gave him access to new Western ideas, and stimulated in him a thirst for greater knowledge, while at the same time offering a potential base of community support for his own reform plans. As a community representative, he found himself in direct contact with Mennonites who remained in Prussia, and they would become valuable informants about ongoing developments in the West. He was likewise placed in direct and continuous contact with the tsarist state through the Guardianship Committee, and this opened the way to his role as the principal intermediary between the Mennonites and the state. Following Mennonite patterns established in Poland, he quickly found patrons in the colonial administration to support him and his reforms against opponents in his community and promote community and personal interests at the highest levels of the tsarist administration.

Cornies' relationship to the chief figures in the Ekaterinoslav Bureau of the Guardianship Committee, Samuel Contenius and Andrei Fadeev, had a profound impact on his own life and that of his community (and, it is worth noting, the Mennonite successes he engineered equally served the career ambitions of his benefactors). The elderly Contenius was the chairman of the Ekaterinoslav Bureau, and consequently the most important state administrator for Molochnaia Mennonite affairs.[30] Born in Silesia, Contenius was an energetic proponent of agricultural modernization, and his wide contacts with the central Guardianship Committee administration in Kishinev, and with senior governmental authorities in St. Petersburg, often allowed him to bypass administrative red tape and push through reforms among the foreign colonists under his supervision. Contenius was a domineering bureaucrat who adhered to the cameralist precepts that defined the imperial perspective of his age. Cameralism promoted highly centralized planning and tight control, administered through an obedient and well-trained bureaucracy. It reached its highest form in Prussia, which the nineteenth-century tsarist autocracy looked to as a model. Contenius placed enormous demands on everyone he commanded, and Cornies both feared and admired him. Although Contenius officially retired in 1818, he retained an office and staff in Ekaterinoslav until his death in 1830, and continued to be a driving force in colonist affairs until almost his last days. Cornies modeled strategic aspects of his own economic agenda and administrative practices on Contenius' example.

Andrei Fadeev, Contenius' successor as chairman of the Ekaterinoslav Bureau, is an equally interesting figure.[31] Born (like Cornies) in 1789, he married Princess Elena Pavlovna Dolgorukha, a member of one of Russia's most powerful aristocratic families. This gave Fadeev unusual measures of influence. First as Contenius' deputy, and then as his replacement as chairman, Fadeev became Cornies' friend and mentor, helping Cornies to enlarge his economic vision and to navigate the channels of officialdom even after Fadeev was posted away to a new position in the Caucasus in 1836. Fadeev's willingness to use his influence to promote Cornies and his various projects helped open the way to Cornies' success. Together, Fadeev and Contenius recognized Cornies' potential, recruited him, employed him for their own interests, and ultimately became powerful patrons for him in Mennonite community disputes as well as in negotiations with the state. While they imposed upon Cornies, they also offered him leverage with which to pursue personal and community interests.

Cornies' contact with leaders in the Prussian Mennonite community who oversaw the Prussian end of the 1818 immigration was also important. In future years, these Prussian contacts helped inform Cornies about changes in the broader world and served as agents in his personal and community business interests in the West. Through his access to Western ideas about things ranging from agricultural techniques to administrative practices, Cornies became the main conduit for Western ideas into the Molochnaia, and an important conduit for such ideas into the tsarist state.

These contacts also brought with them significant controversy, for many of them were associated with pietism, a lightning rod for controversy among Mennonites. Pietism arrived late to the Molochnaia, for the original immigrants were drawn almost entirely from the Flemish congregation. The 1818 migration opened the door to religious controversy by introducing a large group of pietist Frisians.[32] In 1820, the newcomers spearheaded the creation of the Christian School Association, which in 1822 opened a school in Ohrloff.[33] As noted above, education was one of the primary tools of pietism. In Prussia, pietism's influence had been secured by providing the foot soldiers of the state bureaucracy, that is, the educated men that were necessary to fill the administrative ranks and permit cameralism to function efficiently.

Mennonite villages already provided their children with a basic education, but its purpose was limited to rudimentary literacy and numeracy. While all Mennonites needed to be able to read the Bible, conservatives feared that any further education would encourage children to question traditional beliefs. Moreover, religious education was the prerogative of ministers, and the creation of an independent Christian school seemed to challenge this prerogative. The opening of the Ohrloff school was clearly a significant innovation.[34]

A second innovation came in 1821, when representatives of the Russian Bible Society visited the Molochnaia, stimulating the formation of a Molochnaia chapter of the Society dedicated to the distribution of Bibles in the settlement and surrounding communities. This again angered some Flemish congregationalists, who disapproved of any affiliation with non-Mennonite Christian organizations and distrusted the administrative system of the Molochnaia branch of the Bible Society, which was not under congregational control.[35]

The final straw for Flemish congregationalists came in 1822 when, against all tradition, the Flemish congregation's Elder Jacob Fast permitted a visiting non-Mennonite missionary to address a prayer meeting and take communion in Ohrloff. Although Fast quickly acknowledged his mistake and apologized, conservative leaders could not be placated, and beginning in 1824, they formed a new congregation, the Large Flemish Congregation, under the leadership of Altonau minister Jacob Warkentin. Roughly three-quarters of the members of the original Flemish congregation joined it.[36] The formation of this congregation, and the process of obtaining its formal recognition from the state in 1828, caused bitter disputes in the Molochnaia.

Warkentin, as leader of the Large Flemish Congregation, represented a conservative Mennonite world view closely linked to the eighteenth-century rural Prussian communities from which most of the first Molochnaia settlers had come. He promoted a quietist theology of strict withdrawal from the secular world, and by the 1830s, he would encourage his followers to extend the religious autonomy that they already enjoyed in the tsarist empire to include economic autonomy. But at first his movement was primarily a reaction against the pietist religious innovations that had arrived with the 1818 migrants.[37] Almost from the outset, Johann Cornies became a focus of Warkentin's opposition to pietism, for he identified Cornies – a leading member of the Settlement Commission, treasurer of the Bible Society, and chairman of the School Society – as a leading figure of the Molochnaia pietist movement.

Cornies' personal religious beliefs are a subject of controversy among historians, and they cannot be fully explored here. What is clear, however, is that his role in the 1818 immigration provided him with contacts in a national and international pietist community that was important to his future reform activities. Several of these Western pietists figure prominently in his correspondence. Daniel Schlatter, a Swiss Separatist missionary to the Nogai Tatars and a nephew of Anna Bernet-Schlatter, one of the leading figures of European pietism, came to the Molochnaia in 1824 and spent much of the next three years there, living for long stretches in Cornies' home.[38] A fast friendship formed between the two men, and Schlatter provided Cornies with important contacts, particularly among the Moravian Brethren. Another friend and frequent correspondent of Cornies emerging from the 1818 immigration was

David Epp. He was one of the two most important pietist Mennonite ministers in Prussia, and his correspondence throughout the 1820s and early 1830s kept Cornies informed about developments in the Prussian Mennonite Church. It was Epp who served as intermediary for the immigration of the reform-minded pietist Gnadenfeld community to the Molochnaia Settlement in 1835. Jacob Van der Smissen of Danzig, the other leading pietist Mennonite minister in Prussia, played a similar role. A member of a noted Swiss pietist family, Van der Smissen also corresponded warmly with Cornies, and both he and Epp were visited by Cornies in 1827.[39] Finally, Cornies formed one of his strongest and most lasting friendships with Traugott Blüher, a Moscow wool merchant. Cornies met Blüher in 1824 while he was on his way to St. Petersburg to buy sheep, and though we have no account of their first acquaintance, it seems that they quickly developed a close bond. The two men corresponded steadily for over two decades, discussing business and personal affairs in a manner that reflects a warm friendship. Blüher was the head of the Moscow trading house of the Moravian Brethren, and his advice about changing Russian markets for wool and grain was invaluable to Cornies and his community.

The decade following Cornies' rise to community prominence in 1818 was a period of public engagement and personal exploration. While his circle of friends, and his wealth, grew rapidly, he also experienced serious controversies within the Molochnaia Mennonite community. One such controversy deeply marked him. In the summer of 1825, the *Gebietsamt* asked Cornies to travel through the Nogai district to try to locate stolen Mennonite horses.[40] Cornies quickly recovered two stolen horses and turned the thieves over to Nogai authorities. The horses were entrusted to Cornies personally, in exchange for his promise that the Mennonite *Gebietsamt* would follow up with a formal statement to the Nogai district administration describing the theft and identifying the owners of the horses.

This seemingly minor matter embroiled Cornies in a major dispute. In April 1826, rumours spread throughout the Mennonite Settlement and neighbouring colonist and Ukrainian communities that Cornies was buying stolen horses from the Nogais. Cornies blamed the *Gebietsamt* for failing to squelch the rumours and demanded that it investigate and punish the culprits for what he characterized as "criminal" behaviour. At the same time, he resigned from his position as land surveyor and renounced all further work for the *Gebietsamt*.[41]

The dispute between Cornies and the *Gebietsamt* was exacerbated in 1826, when Contenius proposed that Cornies travel to Saxony on behalf of the Settlement to buy merino sheep as breeding stock for Mennonite flocks. Contenius had been promoting the introduction of high-quality merino sheep into New Russian colonist herds since he first came to the Guardianship Committee in 1800, and after his retirement as chairman of the Ekaterinoslav Office of the Committee in 1818, he made the improvement of sheep-breeding the main focus of his Office for Special Projects.[42] Cornies refused to take up the project unless the *Gebietsamt* directly asked him to. Still angered by the horse-theft accusations, he wanted to force the *Gebietsamt* to swallow its pride and invite him back into community service. Over the following months, Cornies and the *Gebietsamt* took turns denouncing one another to Contenius, each blaming the other for their inability to come to agreement about the Saxony trip. Finally, when the *Gebietsamt* flatly refused to sponsor the trip, Cornies announced to Contenius that he would go to Saxony at his own expense. The embarrassed *Gebietsamt*, under pressure from Contenius, reluctantly agreed to buy sheep from Cornies upon his return, though only on generous credit terms.

The resulting 1827 journey to Saxony was the longest and most influential trip of Cornies' life, taking him to Poland, Prussia, and Saxony. Curiously, though Cornies was the foremost Mennonite modernizer, he found the relatively modern Polish and German states lacking as he compared them to his own Russia. He admired the order and prosperity he encountered in the West, but what is most striking is his final conclusion that Prussia and Saxony were overcrowded and over-regulated. Russia, by comparison, was a land of opportunity for young, hard-working, entrepreneurial people.

Cornies returned home in October 1827, where six weeks later he fell gravely ill. From this illness emerges a set of letters almost unique within the Cornies collection for their frankness and passion. Writing to friends and family in Prussia and Russia, he described his illness and, most importantly, his faith. The letters show a Cornies who believed that God demanded not just passive, inwardly focused faith, but action addressing the needs of the whole of humanity. Out of 1827 – the year of both the trip west and the illness – emerged in Cornies a growing sense of mission. He became an activist, determinedly involved in community affairs, in the affairs of neighbouring peoples, and in the affairs of the Russian state. For him, progress was now essential to survival, and he would throw himself into transforming the Mennonite community and the world around it.

The decade following the Saxony trip was a time of experimentation for Cornies. Stimulated in part by state initiatives and in part by his own sense of mission, he launched himself into the economic reforms that would be his greatest legacy. In this period, he became increasingly close to Fadeev, who, deploying the authority of the Guardianship Committee, was a guiding force in reforming the Mennonite economy. It is in these years that the claim of some scholars that Cornies was principally an agent of the state – and therefore a traitor to his Mennonite community – finds the most support.[43] Yet the present publication of Cornies' correspondence and studies must inevitably bring about a reconsideration of this contention, for even in the period 1827–36, Cornies was already beginning to put his own stamp on Guardianship Committee projects within the Mennonite community. Cornies recognized that Mennonite and state interests frequently converged, and so far as the state was an agent of modernization, he was happy to broker its programs; but where state programs threatened important Mennonite values, Cornies was equally ready to use his influence to protect Mennonite religious and cultural autonomy.

That autonomy was in grave danger in the 1830s and 1840s, for the tsarist state was in the midst of a wholesale effort to extend and secure its control of all areas of the Empire. The expansion of state influence in the Molochnaia in this period must be understood within the context of broader developments in Russia. The 1834 transfer of the Guardianship Committee offices from Ekaterinoslav to Odessa was part of a pattern of Russian administrative reform that reflected attitudes that had gripped Russian officialdom since Tsar Alexander I's death in 1825.[44] Partially stimulated by the Decembrist Revolt of 1825, in which a small group of military officers attempted to seize control of Russia and impose a constitution, and partly in reaction against the general currents of romantic nationalism in Western Europe, Tsar Nicholas I endorsed an ideology of "Official Nationality," which promoted orthodoxy, autocracy, and nationality as the essential characteristics of loyal tsarist subjects. Determined to tighten autocratic control of his domains and prevent Western constitutional influences from weakening his power, Nicholas instituted administrative reforms intended to strengthen central authority and impose strict cameralist rule throughout the Empire. As Western European monarchies faced growing threats to their power in the 1840s, Nicholas redoubled his own efforts to isolate Russia from baleful Western influences and assert close autocratic control.

One of the unique values of Cornies' collected correspondence is that it provides insight into how Nicholas' policies played out on the imperial frontier. While they constrained frontier communities, they also continued to offer opportunities for effective engagement with the state. Mennonites could not opt out of the new policies, but unlike many ethno-cultural and ethno-religious minority communities in the Empire, the Mennonites had already experienced similar developments in Poland, and they employed their experience to position themselves to be allowed to self-administer the Russian reforms, moderating their worst effects. They gained this privilege because Cornies was himself the source of many reform projects and had earned the trust of the state. But to retain that trust, Cornies would have to successfully institute both his own reforms and those of the state in the face of strong opposition from some quarters of his community.

The most visible elements of Nicholas' reforms in the Molochnaia were economic "societies." Contenius had created a first, the Sheep Society, in 1824, before Nicholas' ascension to the throne. It provided a model for the much more powerful Forestry Society, created at the state's behest in 1831, and, most importantly, the Agricultural Society, created in 1836.[45] The latter society was established in conjunction with what was undoubtedly the most critical reform for the Mennonites, that is, the 1836 creation of the Ministry of State Domains. Nicholas charged this new ministry with improving the administration of the state peasants, a legal classification that defined roughly 40 per cent of Russia's population, including the Mennonites and almost all of their neighbours in the Molochnaia. Under the direction of P.D. Kiselev, the new ministry undertook sweeping investigations of peasant affairs.[46]

Contenius personally created the Sheep Society and provided detailed instructions on its structure and activities. He hand-picked Cornies as its chair-for-life and insisted that Cornies report extensively on his activities and successes. The Forestry Society was also Contenius' idea, although by the time it was created he had died, and Fadeev played the central role in formulating its charter. Again, the state was the architect of this society's mission and its intended activities, although this time the Guardianship Committee consulted with Cornies and his closest associates about the Society charter, signalling Cornies' emerging role as political broker for his community.[47] The Agricultural Society had much greater authority than the Forestry Society, the former governing all the economic activities of Molochnaia Mennonites. Cornies was allowed virtually free rein in defining the Agricultural Society's authority in internal Mennonite economic affairs.[48]

It was in his role as chair of the Forestry Society from 1830–6 that Cornies' managerial style fully emerged. At first, Cornies worked hard to cooperate with the elected Mennonite authorities in the *Gebietsamt*. Modelling himself on Contenius and Fadeev, he consulted with the *Gebietsamt*, asked for its approval and support, and even recruited its members into the society. While these efforts could not satisfy everyone in his community, they did build a constituency of support without which Cornies' eventual successes could not have been realized. By the time the Agricultural Society superseded the Forestry Society in 1836, Cornies was exercising ever greater personal control, micromanaging the activities of the Forestry Society. He issued orders, expected compliance (to be documented in endless reports), and seldom consulted with anyone outside of a small group of confidants.

Changing state demands, and Cornies' role in developing and promoting them, did not occur in a static Mennonite community. Expectations of Mennonite success, voiced by Russian and foreign visitors in the first years of their settlement, were clearly being realized by the 1830s. The growth of European and English cloth production had provided Mennonites with a ready market for their wool, and when the tsarist state opened an international port at nearby Berdiansk in 1835, exports rose exponentially, from a value of 112,000 rubles in 1836 to over 4 million rubles in 1840.[49] As wool demand peaked and then dipped in the 1840s, Mennonite grain began to replace it on international and domestic markets, and there was no slowing of the economic growth. Fuelled by the Molochnaia Mennonite economy, by the early 1850s the annual fair at the local peasant village of Bolshoi Tokmak grew to become one of the largest 100 fairs in all the tsarist empire.[50]

This economic success was reflected in the visible prosperity of the Mennonite villages. Large, neat homes appeared, with ornate gates and painted windows and doors, where meals were served on German-made china, sometimes by German maids. New churches and other public buildings sprang up, and charitable organizations such as the Orphans' Fund grew so wealthy that they became the focus of community disputes. Such ostentation did not sit easily with some Mennonites. In 1833, Heinrich Balzer famously denounced the "pride, ostentation, vanity, greed for money and lust for wealth, avarice, drunkenness, luxury, vicious life, masquerades, obscene songs, gambling, and above all the miserable smoking of tobacco" that had emerged in his community.[51] Balzer alerts us to tensions in the Molochnaia Mennonite Settlement, but at the same time, the publication of his pamphlet was itself a sign of prosperity and of an emerging culture. After all, writing, publishing, and political debates all demand free time, and consequently, prosperity.

Balzer was the harbinger of Cornies' greatest political fight. In the 1830s, the most conservative religious elements of the Molochnaia Mennonite community, whose suspicion of state authority was grounded in both religious belief and historical experience, began to see Cornies as a representative of state authority. They resented his intrusion into their personal lives and household economies, and, because the village elders were expected to enforce Cornies' regulations, they equally resented the resultant intrusion into village and district politics.

Opposition to the reforms hardened among some Molochnaia Mennonites. At times fullholders resisted Cornies' demands, and some villages turned against their mayors, rejecting efforts to implement Forestry Society and Agricultural Society orders. Cornies and his societies responded by demanding that those who failed to obey orders be fined and punished by community service, and, in the most extreme cases, be forced to sell their land to more able (or tractable) persons.

The disputes between conservatives and reformers culminated in the late 1830s in a major crisis in the Molochnaia Mennonite community.[52] Jacob Warkentin, elder of the Large Flemish congregation, was the leading defender of the internal autonomy of the Mennonite community from tsarist administrative influence. Following the 1836 creation of the Agricultural Society, Warkentin urged Molochnaia Mennonites to refuse to cooperate with Cornies' reforms. In the 1838 district mayoral election, he attempted unsuccessfully to unseat presiding mayor (and Cornies ally) Johann Regier and replace him with a conservative candidate.

In the 1841 elections, Warkentin's mayoral candidate, the widely respected Peter Toews, won the election by a narrow margin. When Cornies claimed voting irregularities and refused to accept the results, Warkentin travelled to Odessa and protested to Evgenii von Hahn, the newly appointed deputy to General Inzov, the aging head of the Guardianship Committee. In early 1842, Hahn ordered a new election, and Toews won a landslide victory.[53] Cornies, it seemed, had demanded too much and lost the support of both his community and the state.

Warkentin and his supporters believed themselves the clear victors in this struggle for political supremacy in the Molochnaia Mennonite Settlement, and rumours even circulated that Hahn intended to exile Cornies to Siberia.[54] However, what Warkentin had failed to understand was that Cornies' reforms were part and parcel of a larger tsarist reform movement that Mennonites would not be allowed to reject. The most they could hope for was to moderate state influence, and Cornies was the only likely agent of such moderation because of his status in the eyes of the state. Cornies was equally essential to the state, which relied upon his status in the Mennonite community to push through reforms. During an inspection tour of the Molochnaia, Hahn accused Warkentin of meddling in official matters and dismissed him from his position as congregational elder. At the same time, Hahn dissolved the Large Flemish congregation, creating in its place three smaller congregations.[55]

Though some leading adherents to the Large Flemish congregation were not fully silenced for several more years, the 1842 dissolution of the congregation brought its real political power – and the most significant events of what is known to Mennonites as the "Warkentin affair" – to an end.[56] It was a major political victory for Cornies, who would now dominate the Molochnaia Mennonite Settlement until his death in 1848, and even extend his authority to the Khortitsa Mennonite Settlement when he was made head of the Khortitsa Agricultural Society in 1846.[57]

Triumphant in this political struggle, Cornies now entered the years of his most dramatic and far-reaching reforms. It is in this period that he earned his reputation as a severe and authoritarian figure, relentlessly pursuing his economic modernization agenda with the full authority of the now-dominant Agricultural Society. Leaving the management of his personal business affairs to his brothers, Cornies guided Molochnaia society through wholesale changes. With obsessive attention to detail, he turned his energies to reforming agriculture, industry and crafts, trade, education, and administration. At the same time, his authority expanded as the state pressed him to oversee projects in other communities, both colonist and Russian.

The most important of Cornies' agricultural reforms was the transition from sheep-raising to crop agriculture. Cornies revolutionized Molochnaia agriculture by forcing his community to adopt a four-field crop rotation. While surrounding communities continued to practise long-fallow – using the same piece of land for years at a time and then abandoning it to regenerate on its own – Mennonites introduced a disciplined field rotation system that sharply increased crop productivity, and at the same time, brought more land under crops. This prepared the way, psychologically and institutionally, for the rapid expansion of crop agriculture in the 1860s and beyond. As international wool markets declined and grain markets grew in the 1840s, Mennonite fullholders began to emerge as the prosperous farmers of later reputation, and some among them began to establish the great estates that would be such a distinguishing characteristic of Russian Mennonite society in the late nineteenth and early twentieth centuries.[58]

Rapid increases in crop production led to high profits for Molochnaia fullholders, and, in turn, this newfound wealth, along with Cornies' determined guidance, contributed to the beginning of diversification of the Molochnaia Mennonite economy. Cornies' role in settling new immigrants had taught him early on that the Mennonites' Molochnaia land grant had a limited agricultural capacity, and in 1838, he began to promote the establishment of a village for craftsmen. This led to the founding in 1842 of Neu-Halbstadt (the present-day city of Molochansk), which eventually became the industrial capital of the region. Cornies also actively promoted Mennonite inventors and manufacturers of agricultural equipment, helping to stimulate an industry that became central to the Mennonite industrial economy in the latter half of the century.

Following Evgenii von Hahn's 1842 inspection of the Molochnaia Settlement, Cornies was also charged with reforming the Mennonite education system. In 1843, Hahn ordered the Agricultural Society to take full control of all Mennonite schools, and Cornies threw himself into the task, not only intervening in the hiring and supervision of teachers, but even personally selecting textbooks. The quality of Mennonite education improved dramatically, helping produce the literate, numerate society that was a vital prerequisite of the industrialization processes of the late nineteenth century.[59]

As Cornies' authority in his Mennonite community grew, his national reputation as an expert in forestry, agriculture, and administrative matters, also grew. Tsar Nicholas I was determined to better administer his peasants, and beginning in 1836, this manifested itself in extensive surveys of their condition. While these surveys had little immediate impact on imperial policy, in the long term they would provide vital groundwork for the Great Reforms of the 1860s. Cornies had long been an informant to the Guardianship Committee, and, through it, to higher authorities about conditions in southern Ukraine. His 1826 study of the Nogais was written at the request of the Guardianship Committee, as were his 1830s studies of the Doukhobors, Molokans, and German colonists. Fadeev, as he prepared himself to move on to the Caucasus in 1834, began to promote Cornies as an expert on all New Russian things, and it is probably through Fadeev's efforts that in 1836 the Nogai study was published in the important Moscow journal *Teleskop*.[60]

Cornies' growing reputation earned him the attention of Petr Keppen, a well-known Russian historian and statistician, as well as a prominent figure in the new Ministry of State Domains.[61] Keppen, the son of a transplanted Baltic German official, was raised and educated in the southern Ukrainian city of Kharkiv and began his government career in the Crimea before moving on to prominence in St. Petersburg. When Keppen returned to southern Ukraine in 1836 to conduct an economic survey for the new ministry, he immediately recognized in Cornies an invaluable ally, turning to the Mennonite for detailed information about the Molochnaia region. Cornies made such a strong impression on Keppen that in 1837 Cornies was recruited to take part in a similar ministry survey in the Kuban region.[62] In the following years, Cornies – recruited by Keppen as a corresponding member of the Learned Committee of the Ministry of the State Domains – published myriad reports in Russian journals and newspapers, mainly on agricultural subjects, but also on the archeological digs he conducted at Keppen's behest and on peasant administration.

Cornies' 1841 study of peasant administration is among his most influential written works.[63] This is emphatically *Cornies'* vision of what constituted an efficiently run peasant society. It describes, in idealized terms, the Molochnaia Mennonite administrative system, and promotes that system as a model for all peasant administration in Russia. This study, written for the Ministry of State Domains and widely circulated to ministry offices around the empire, described Cornies' Agricultural Society as the central administrative office overseeing every aspect of Molochnaia Mennonite life. It claimed that the society's authority, once based on the authority of the Mennonite *Gebietsamt* and congregational officials, was now explicitly based on the authority of the Guardianship Committee, and it characterized *Gebietsamt* officials as little more than liaisons between the Agricultural Society and individual householders. Even village and district elections were supposedly vetted by the society.

In his final years, Cornies' influence spread far beyond his own community. As the state sought to extend Mennonite success into other communities, it naturally turned to Cornies for help. Beginning in 1839, he accepted young men from Ukrainian and Nogai villages as apprentices at his Iushanle estate, where he trained them in forestry, sheep breeding, and other agricultural pursuits.[64] In 1846, he helped plan the creation of the *Judenplan* villages, which were to be shared by Mennonites and Jews. The state's intention was to transplant Jews from overcrowded *shtetls* to vacant New Russian land, where Mennonites would, by example, teach them to become agriculturists.[65] The Ministry of State Domains consulted him constantly on plans to grow trees, potatoes, rice, and whatever else came into fashion.

Cornies' role as a Mennonite publicist, trumpeting Mennonite accomplishments in Russian journals and in reports to the Guardianship Committee and Ministry of State Domains, was one of his most important contributions to his community. In an empire ruled by an autocrat determined to centralize power, standardize administration, and integrate his subjects, Cornies was building a case that Mennonite privileges were justified by their successes, and, indeed, that Russia should become more Mennonite. It is here most distinctly that Cornies is revealed as a promoter and defender of Mennonites to the tsarist state. From the perspective of broader imperial history, he reveals how the "Empire State" relied upon regional authorities for support, and how such regional figures could in turn influence the shape of the policies that affected them.

Conclusion

While Cornies undoubtedly exaggerated Agricultural Society authority in his 1841 account, there is no doubt that, under the society's guidance, the Molochnaia settlement was, by the 1840s, maturing into one of Russia's most economically advanced regions. In 1843, the noted German scholar Baron August von Haxthausen visited the Molochnaia and claimed that there was nowhere else in Russia that had attained "such a uniformly high level of agricultural and social development." He was equally certain that the credit for this development belonged to Johann Cornies, whom he called one of the "most influential personalities of southern Russia."[66] This sentiment was widely echoed in official Russian publications and by other influential European writers.

It was not a sentiment that found much sympathy in Cornies' own community. As the 1842 elections show, he had lost the support of large parts of his community, and in reaction, he was becoming increasingly authoritarian. Only eight of the forty-eight extant Molochnaia village histories written on the order of the state shortly after Cornies' death in 1848 have anything positive to say about him. Yet perhaps the greatest indication of Cornies' final success in overseeing the transformation of his community's economy came during the harvest failures of 1848. In that year, southern Ukraine experienced a severe drought and harvest failure, accompanied by epidemic diseases in livestock. A comparable 1833 drought had devastated the Mennonite community, but while surrounding communities suffered again in 1848, the Molochnaia Mennonites passed through the year with barely a concern. Grain reserves from the bountiful crops of the previous decade ensured that everyone was fed; livestock suffered, but this was already a secondary consideration in the increasingly crop-based Molochnaia economy. Through Cornies' reforms, Molochnaia Mennonites had left behind their earlier tenuous peasant economy and become a modern farming community, far in advance of most of their Ukrainian and Russian neighbours.

When Cornies died, the Mennonite community was economically prosperous, internally stable, and well respected by the tsarist state. The early expectations for this immigrant community had been fully realized. The world around it was less fortunate. The European revolutions of 1848, the Crimean War of 1852–5, and Russia's Great Reforms of the 1860s and 1870s were all looming external challenges to Mennonites. Internally, rapid demographic growth leading to the creation of a large landless group of Mennonites, and religious perturbations born of pietism, threatened the community.

Mennonites could not avoid these problems any more than they had avoided the problems of their first half-century in Russia. The landlessness crisis of the 1860s forced Mennonite society to find ways to placate the disaffected landless and prompted the establishment of daughter settlements across Ukraine, European Russia, Siberia, and Central Asia. The creation of the Mennonite Brethren in 1860 saw pietism enter into the mainstream of tsarist Mennonite society. Though at first deeply controversial, in time the Brethren became an accepted part of Mennonite life. The Great Reforms brought an end to many Mennonite privileges and forced the Mennonites to renegotiate their position, accepting work in the tsar's forestry service as an alternative to military service. To escape these crises, some Mennonites chose a new migration, this time to North America. Most stayed, negotiating new terms with the state and continuing their economic success down to the time of the revolution.

In all of these processes the hand of Johann Cornies can be seen. The status that Mennonites had gained, as the most progressive and economically successful foreign colonists in Russia, gave them leverage in negotiations with the state. The experience of earlier negotiations helped them succeed in reaching a new deal with the tsar after the Great Reforms. The Mennonites' wealth helped them to resolve the landlessness problem and the religious problem by establishing daughter settlements. It equally allowed some Mennonites to reject the state's new demands and choose emigration.

Cornies' legacy of economic and political reform and religious controversy has long been the subject of disputed interpretations. Those who would see him as an agent of the Russian state will find support in these papers, but they will also find contradictions, for Cornies shaped state policy to fit Mennonite needs as he perceived them. Those who would see him as an enemy of traditional Mennonite beliefs will also find support, but even here, the question is of *which* Mennonite tradition. Cornies' religious views were mainstream: they were clearly shared by a significant minority in his own community, and were consonant with evolving Mennonite religious beliefs in Western Europe. It is equally clear that his economic policies enjoyed the support of many Molochnaia Mennonites.

The documents published here open the door to a much fuller appreciation of Johann Cornies. He was a person driven by religious belief, personal experience, ambition, state demands, and all of the other forces that humans are subject too. His correspondence provides a remarkable window onto his public life, the life of his community, and the relationship of this frontier community with the imperial tsarist state.

NOTES

1 Harvey L. Dyck and Ingrid I. Epp, *The Peter J. Braun Russian Mennonite Archive: A Research Guide* (Toronto: University of Toronto Press, 1996).

2 Ibid.

3 The rediscovery of the collection, and its contents, are described in ibid.

4 Michael Khodarkovsky, *Russia's Steppe Frontier: The Making of a Colonial Empire, 1500–1800* (Bloomington: Indiana University Press, 2002), 227–8. For a similar conclusion, see Willard Sunderland, *Taming the Wild Field: Colonization and Empire on the Russian Steppe* (Ithaca, NY: Cornell University Press, 2004).

5 Jane Burbank and Mark von Hagen, "Coming into the Territory: Uncertainty and Empire," in Jane Burbank, Mark von Hagen, and Anatolyi Remnev, *Russian Empire: Space People, and Power, 1700–1930* (Bloomington: Indiana University Press, 2007), 10.

6 The standard English-language work on Polish Mennonites is Peter J. Klassen, *Mennonites in Early Modern Poland and Prussia* (Baltimore: Johns

Hopkins University Press, 2009). Klassen provides a brief history in *A Homeland for Strangers: An Introduction to Mennonites in Poland and Prussia* (Fresno: Center for Mennonite Brethren Studies, 1989). Mark A. Jantzen provides an important account of the nineteenth-century Polish Mennonite experience in *Mennonite German Soldiers: Nation, Religion, and Family in the Prussian East, 1772–1880* (Notre Dame: University of Notre Dame Press, 2010). An important early account is H. G. Mannhardt, *The Danzig Mennonite Church: Its Origin and History from 1569–1919,* trans. Victor G. Doerksen, ed. Mark Jantzen and John D. Thiesen (Mishawaka, IN: Bethel College, 2008). For an overview of Polish history, see Norman Davies, *God's Playground,* 2nd ed., 2 vols. (New York: Columbia University Press, 2005).

7 Klassen, *Mennonites,* chap. 5.

8 For a general introduction to Pietism, see W.R. Ward, *The Protestant Evangelical Awakening* (Cambridge: Cambridge University Press, 1994), particularly 57–63.

9 Historians such as Benjamin Marschke, Klaus Depperman, Mary Fulbrook, Carl Hinrichs, and perhaps most emphatically Richard L. Gawthrop have begun to place pietism at the centre of the development of the cameralist Prussian state model – see Klaus Depperman, *Der hallesche Pietismus und der preussische Staat unter Friedrich III* (Goettingen: Vandenhoeck & Ruprecht, 1961), Mary Fulbrook, *Piety and Politics: Religion and the Rise of Absolutism in England, Wuerttemberg and Prussia* (New York: Cambridge University Press, 1983); Carl Hinrichs, *Preussentum und Pietismus: Der Pietismus in Brandenburg-Preussen als religioes-soziale Reformbewegung* (Goettingen: Vandenhoeck & Ruprecht, 1971); Richard L. Gawthrop, *Pietism and the Making of Eighteenth-Century Prussia* (Cambridge: Cambridge University Press, 1993). On Prussia, see Marc Raeff, *The Well-Ordered Police State: Social and Institutional Change through Law in the Germanies and Russia, 1600–1900* (New Haven, CT: Yale University Press, 1983).

10 Cited in Mark Jantzen, *At Home in Germany? The Mennonites of the Vistula Delta and the Construction of a German National Identity, 1772–1880* (Notre Dame, IN: University of Notre Dame, 2002), 65.

11 Ibid.

12 On Catherine's imperial ambitions, see Isabel De Madariaga, *Russia in the Age of Catherine the Great* (New Haven, CT: Yale University Press, 1982), and Harvey L. Dyck, "Pondering the Russian Fact: Kaunitz and the Catherinian Empire in the 1770s," *Canadian Slavonic Papers* 22, no. 4 (1980): 451–69.

13 Catherine's views on immigration are detailed in Roger Bartlett, *Human Capital: The Settlement of Foreigners in Russia, 1762–1804* (Cambridge: Cambridge University Press, 1979).

14 See, for example, the letter of the Duc de Richelieu to Samuel Contenius, 19 August 1804, published in *Pis'ma gertsoga Armana Emmanuila de Rishel'e Samuilu Khristianovichu Konteniusu 1803–1814*, ed. O. Konovalova (Odessa: Institut germanskikh i vostochnevropeiskikh issledovanii Goettingen, 1999), 50.

15 For an introduction to tsarist and Soviet Mennonite history, see John B. Toews, *Czars, Soviets and Mennonites* (Newton, KS: Faith and Life Press, 1982). The standard history of the first hundred years of Mennonite life in southern Ukraine is James Urry, *None But Saints: The Transformation of Mennonite Life in Russia, 1789–1889* (Winnipeg: Windflower Communications, 1989).

16 The *Privilegium* and its role in tsarist Mennonite society are detailed in John R. Staples, "Religion, Politics, and the Mennonite Privilegium: Reconsidering the Warkentin Affair," *Journal of Mennonite Studies* 21 (2003): 71–88. On the larger history of such *Privilegiums*, see James Urry, *Mennonites, Politics, and Peoplehood: Europe-Russia-Canada 1525–1980* (Winnipeg: University of Manitoba Press, 2006).

17 The *Privilegium* is reproduced in translation in Urry, *None But Saints*, 282–4.

18 Ibid., 36–8.

19 See Klassen, *A Homeland for Strangers*, and Jantzen, *Mennonite German Soldiers*.

20 On Johann Sr., see David H. Epp, *Johann Cornies* (Winnipeg: Canadian Mennonite University Press, 1995).

21 The initial surveys are described in Peter Hildebrand, *From Danzig to Russia: The Emigration of Mennonites from the Danzig Region to Southern Russia*, trans. Walter E. Toews and Adolf Ens (Winnipeg: CMBC Publications and Manitoba Mennonite Historical Society, 2000). See also Urry, *None But Saints*.

22 "Diarium des Johann Eck von seine u. des Br. Carl Jacob Loretz von Sarepta gemachten 7. Monatlichen Reise ueber Taganrok, Odessa, Pultawa, Charkoff, Woronesch im Jahre 1806," transcribed by Harvey L. Dyck from microfilm of manuscript in Archive of the Moravian Brethren in Herrnhut, Germany.

23 George Bolotenko, "Administration of the State Peasants in Russia before the Reforms of 1838" (PhD diss., University of Toronto, 1979), 195–209.

24 Ibid., 209.

25 On Mennonite experiences after the Great Reforms, see Toews, *Czars, Soviets and Mennonites.*

26 On the environmental and administrative challenges the Mennonites faced in their first years of settlement, see John R. Staples, *Cross-Cultural Encounters on the Ukrainian Steppe: Settling the Molochnaia Basin, 1784–1861* (Toronto: University of Toronto Press, 2003).

27 Epp, *Johann Cornies*; Franz Isaac, *Die Molotschnaer Mennoniten* (Halbstadt, 1908); P.M. Friesen, *The Mennonite Brotherhood in Russia (1789–1910)* (Fresno, CA: Board of Christian Literature, General Conference of Mennonite Brethren Churches, 1978).

28 For an English translation of this biography, see Harvey L. Dyck, trans., "Agronomist Gavel's Biography of Johann Cornies (1789–1848)," *Journal of Mennonite Studies* 2 (1984): 29–41.

29 On Mennonite and non-Mennonite perceptions of Cornies, see Harvey L. Dyck, "Russian Servitor and Mennonite Hero: Light and Shadow in Images of Johann Cornies," *Journal of Mennonite Studies* 2 (1984): 9–28.

30 *Pis'ma gertsoga Armana Emmanuila de Rishel'e Samuilu Khristianovichu Konteniusu 1803-1814*, O. Konovalova, ed. (Odessa: Institut germanskikh i vostochnevropeiskikh issledovanii Goettingen, 1999), 5–20.

31 A. M. Fadeev, "Vospominaniia Andreia Mikhailovicha Fadeeva," *Russkii Arkhiv* (1891), books 2, 3, 4, 5, 9, 10, 11, 12.

32 Urry, *None But Saints*, 34–49, 99–100.

33 Ibid., 105.

34 Ibid., 105–6.

35 Ibid., 101.

36 Ibid., 102.

37 Historian John B. Toews summarizes the religious position of the conservative Flemish congregation in the Molochnaia as quietist, formalistic, and liturgically rigid. See *Czars, Soviets and Mennonites*, 18–21.

38 On Anna Schlatter, see *Starke fromme Frauen: Begegnungen mit Erdmuthe von Zinzendorf, Juliane von Krüdener, Anna Schlatter, Friederike Fliedner, Dora Rappard-Gobat, Eva von Tiele-Winckler, Ruth von Kleist-Retzow* (Giessen: Brunnen Verlag, 1997). Daniel Schlatter described his experiences in the Molochnaia in *Bruchstuecke aus einigen Reisen nach dem Suedlichen Russland* (St. Gallen: Huber, 1830).

39 John Friesen, "Education, Pietism and Change among Mennonites in Nineteenth-Century Prussia," *MQR* 66 (April 1982): 155–66; Peter J. Klassen, "Faith and Culture in Conflict: Mennonites in the Vistula Delta," *MQR* 57 (July 1983): 194–205; Robert Friedmann, "Anabaptism and Pietism," *MQR* 14 (April 1940): 90–128.

40 Cornies to District Office, 10 September 1825, document 29.
41 The horse theft controversy is described in documents 55, 57, 58, and 62.
42 See document 55, Samuel Contenius to Johann Cornies, 4 January 1826.
43 This position is most cogently argued by anthropologist James Urry, whose *None But Saints* is the most influential study of the Russian Mennonites. Urry gives full credit to Cornies for the progressive nature of his reforms (labelling Cornies the "Prophet of Progress"), but he stresses the arbitrary nature and divisive character of the reforms. This is not an unfair focus; Urry properly sets aside the hagiographic Mennonite historiography that continues to dominate in-group Mennonite accounts of Cornies and returns to the words of Cornies' contemporaries, who clearly document a deeply divided Molochnaia Mennonite world. Still, Urry's *None But Saints* was written before the discovery of the Cornies papers, so it was impossible for Urry to look beneath the public record at Cornies' motivations and his keen understanding of the Russian situation.
44 W. Bruce Lincoln, *In the Vanguard of Reform: Russia's Enlightened Bureaucrats, 1825–1861* (DeKalb: Northern Illinois University Press, 1982).
45 The state established comparable societies in other colonial communities in New Russia, and it pursued a parallel administrative policy among state peasants in the region, but there is no evidence of comparable results in other communities. This is partially a tribute to Mennonite record keeping, which makes the implementation of the policy visible, but it also reflects the fact that Mennonites – and particularly Molochnaia Mennonites – far outstripped other colonial communities in their economic development. This success can be attributed to Mennonite order and industry, but also to the extraordinary contributions of Cornies, who chaired each successive society. The Mennonite economic success story is the subject of much recent interest in Ukrainian scholarship. See, for example, N.V. Venger, *Mennonitskoe predprinimatels'stvo v usloviakh modernizatsii iuga Rossii: mezhdu kongregatsiei, klannom i rossiiskim obshchestvom (1789–1920)* (Dnepropetrovsk: Izdatelstvo Dnepropetrovskogo natsionalnogo universiteta, 2009); and Marina V. Belikova, "The Mennonite Colonies of Southern Ukraine, 1789–1917" (PhD diss., Zaporizhzhe State University, 2005).
46 The standard history of the Ministry of State Domains is M.N. Druzhinin, *Gosudarstvennye krest'iane i reforma P. D. Kiseleva*, 2 vols. (Moscow: Nauka, 1946 and 1958).
47 Fadeev to Cornies, document 225.
48 On the role of these societies, see Staples, *Cross-Cultural Encounters*.
49 Staples, *Cross-Cultural Encounters*, table 5.2, 133.
50 Ibid., 134.

51 Heinrich Balzer, "Understanding and Reason: Simple Opinions Regarding the Difference between Understanding and Reason, Discussed According to Their Teachings of the Gospel," in Delbert F. Plett, *The Golden Years: The Mennonite Kleine Gemeinde in Russia (1812–1849)* (Steinbach: By Author, 1985), 244.
52 This dispute is described in detail in Staples, "Religion, Politics, and the Mennonite Privilegium in Early Nineteenth-Century Russia."
53 Urry, *None But Saints*, 128.
54 Ibid.
55 Ibid., 129.
56 Ibid., 133–4.
57 Ibid., 135.
58 On the economic record, see Staples, *Cross-Cultural Encounters*, and Venger, *Mennonitskoe predprinimatels'stvo.* Venger provides an excellent account of Mennonite wealth in the late imperial period. On Mennonite estates, see Al Reimer, "Peasant Aristocracy: The Mennonite Gutsbesitzertum in Russia," *Journal of Mennonite Studies* 8 (1990): 76–88; and James Urry, "Through the Eye of a Needle: Wealth and the Mennonite Experience in Imperial Russia," *Journal of Mennonite Studies* 3 (1985): 7–35.
59 On Mennonite education, see I.V. Cherkazianova, *Nemetskaia natsionalnaia shkola v Sibiri, XVIII v.-1938 g.* (Moskva: Obshchestvennaia akademiia nauk rossiiskikh nemtsev, 2000).
60 Cornies, "Kratkii obzor polozheniia Nogaiskikh tatar, vodvorennykh v Melitopolskom uezde Tavricheskoi gubernii," *Teleskop* 33 (1836). The article appeared in the same issue of the journal as Petr Chaadaev's famous "Apology of a Madman," earning Cornies far wider circulation than he could ever have otherwise achieved.
61 F.P. Keppen, *Biografiia P.I. Keppena* (St. Petersburg: Tip. Imp. akademii nauk, 1911).
62 The invitation, Cornies' report, and related correspondence are located in *PJBRMA*, File 414.
63 Cornies, "Po otnosheniiu Departmenta Sel'skago Khoziaistva o vvedenii u russkikh pereselentsev khoziastva i poriadka upravleniia menonitov," Russian State Historical Archive, *fond* 383, *opis* 10, *delo* 7164.
64 Staples, *Cross-Cultural Encounters*, 145–7.
65 Harvey L. Dyck, "Landlessness in the Old Colony: The *Judenplan* Experiment, 1850–1880," in *Mennonites in Russia 1788–1988: Essays in Honour of Gerhard Lohrenz,* ed. John Friesen (Winnipeg: CMBC Publications, 1989), 183–202.
66 Cited in Dyck, "Russian Servitor and Mennonite Hero."

PART ONE

Correspondence, 1812–1836

1812–1823

1. Inspector for Molochnaia Colonies, Sieter, to Johann Cornies. 1 January 1812. State Archive of the Odessa Region (SAOR) 89-1-7/4.[1]

Contract:

On 1 January 1812, the following contract to lease part of the land designated for Mennonite settlement was concluded by inspector for the Molochnaia colonies, Mr. Sieter, with the undersigned, the Mennonite Johann Cornies Jr. of Ohrloff.

1. Johann Cornies Jr., Ohrloff, will lease whatever land remains after the Mennonites are settled, designated as tracts number sixty-two and fifty-eight on the Uezd map, plus whatever land remains after land belonging to the Crown village Bolshoi Tokmak and to Fuerstenau and Rueckenau villages has been subtracted. If it is decided to transplant the Schoensee community to one of the above numbered tracts, the area remaining after land designated for this community has been subtracted is also included, as well as land traded with the Nogai land district, east of the Iushanle [stream] as far as the border of tract number fifty-six. J. Cornies Jr. will assume the lease for the combined land described above for one year, from 1 January 1812 until 1 January 1813.

2. To ensure that accounts are in order, leaseholder Johann Cornies will pay the Honourable Inspector 300 rubles rent for the land listed

1 This is the original lease of Cornies' land at Iushanle. Beginning in 1820, he would repeatedly request that the state cede him ownership of this land; he finally received a land grant of 500 desiatinas at the Iushanle site in 1836. See documents 1, 5, 152, 177, 178, 185, 531, 535, and additional documents in volume II.

above for the specified time, 100 rubles when the contract is concluded, 100 rubles at the beginning of the second third of the lease period, and the last 100 rubles at the beginning of the last third.

3. The Honourable Inspector will determine the exact boundaries specified and inform the leaseholder, Johann Cornies, accordingly.

4. If a settlement is begun on this land during the year of the lease, or if the Imperial government should make other provisions for the leased land, the leaseholder, Johann Cornies, must surrender the land without disagreement. The latter must, however, pay rent for the surrendered part for the period in which he has used the land. Rent for the remaining leaseland must be adjusted pro rata.

5. Neither the Mennonite community nor any person may impede the leaseholder in his unfettered use of the leased land. Should, however, impediments arise, the inspector is obliged to provide Cornies with the support needed to remove them.

6. The leaseholder must ensure that his own and any other livestock are not pastured outside the boundaries of the leased land designated in this contract. If this rule is not observed, and such livestock cause damage to the Mennonite community or to other neighbours, the leaseholder must make good the damage as determined by an inspection and forfeit his lease. He will also forfeit his lease if he does not pay the rent at the time specified.

7. If the leaseholder permits or tolerates persons who lack passes or otherwise appear suspicious to stay on the leased land, he will forfeit his lease.

8. To affirm the undertaking that the stipulations contained in this contract will be carried out, the leaseholder, Johann Cornies Jr., as well as his guarantor, the landholder David Penner of Ohrloff, sign in person.

2. Molochnaia Mennonite District Office (hereafter District Office) to Johann Cornies. 11 November 1817. SAOR 89-1-21/55.

Honourable Johann Cornies,

General-Surveyor in the Ekaterinoslav Survey Bureau, Titular Counsellor Ilin, has arrived in Melitopol Uezd to investigate disputes in regard to ownership of land. Since our properties located in this Uezd have become the subject of disputes with neighbours on our boundaries, we authorize you to determine our boundaries with our Doukhobor neighbours for the General-Surveyor. You must be present when this is done, conduct the matter in a friendly manner, and state the reasons for your views in an agreeable way.

Should the Doukhobors seek unjustly to take possession of some of our land, you must state your objections and, where possible, reach agreement in a friendly manner. Where absolutely necessary, you may also submit appropriate petitions. We further authorize you to sign whatever is required, to be present constantly throughout this process, and to act or not act as you consider advisable. We promise not to question or protest against your actions in the future. We confirm this undertaking with the signing of our names.

[twenty names]

3. Agreement between Johann Cornies and Molochnaia individuals. 1 April 1818. SAOR 89-1-17/1.

On 1 April 1818, agreement on the following terms was reached between persons whose signatures appear below: the leaseholder of Crown lands Johann Cornies, and his Molochnaia subtenants. The meadows and ploughland of the strip of land surveyed as a *chumak* [carters'] road are to be divided into four equal parts. Each of the Molochnaia subtenants is to be allowed exclusive use of one of these parts, according to his own judgment. The leaseholder will assign use of the fourth part at his discretion.

The tenants agree:

1. To maintain the dwellings they take over, making the required repairs and doing the appropriate caulking and whitewashing inside and out.

2. To maintain the road leading over the dam, making the required repairs. Should the dam be damaged by water or ice, or its sides crumble, the leaseholder will restore it to its former condition at his own expense.

3. If wells now situated on these segments have insufficient water for use by [the chumak] trekkers, the tenants are obligated to dig wells in the Iushanle [area] as needed.

4. Each tenant will work for the leaseholder for eighteen days: six days during the hay harvest, six days during the grain harvest, and six days carting grain.

5. If any strange livestock take shelter with the tenants, they must immediately report this to the leaseholder.

6. Tenants must not accept foreign livestock or allow them to graze on their lands. If such livestock are found, fifty kopeks must be paid to the leaseholder for every horse or head of cattle and twenty-five kopeks for each sheep thus found.

7. Tenants must not permit persons lacking passes to lodge with them. If such suspicious persons are found, they must be apprehended and the leaseholder informed without delay.

8. If a tenant sells brandy, he must pay an additional ten rubles in cash annually.

9. If disputes with travellers arise, tenants must seek agreement and diligently endeavour to live peaceably with one another and with the travellers. If travellers or chumaks injure tenants without cause, the latter must apprehend the guilty and turn them over to the leaseholder. A tenant will use his influence in the appropriate place to ensure that these disturbers of the peace are dealt with according to the law.

10. In all cases referred to in this contract, tenants must obey their superior who is appointed by the leaseholder. This individual is obliged to give the leaseholder a complete accounting.

To affirm all matters referred to above, which we have discussed and agreed upon, we sign personally,

[No signatures]

4. Authorization for Johann Cornies by village mayors. 19 May 1820. SAOR 89-1-21/16.

Authorization:

On behalf of our village communities, we the undersigned Molochnaia Mennonite village mayors hereby declare and make known our authorization of the esteemed Johann Cornies of Ohrloff to survey and define our outer and inner boundaries, seeking to settle such boundaries for the well-being of the whole community, and to notify the District Office of all such decisions. To attest to this, we have signed this document in the District Office on 19 May 1820.

Isaac Fast, Claas Dueck, […], Peter Fast, David Loewen[?], Peter[?] Heidebrecht, Aron Schellenberg, Isaac Tiessen[?], David Warkentin, Peter Wiens, Franz Klassen, Heinrich Friesen, Jacob Wiens, […], Peter Bergman, […] Fehr, Jacob Warkentin, Johann Martins.

That the above village mayors have signed personally,

Witnessed and certified by District Chairman Toews, Deputy Enns.

5. Johann Cornies to Ivan N. Inzov. 24 June 1820. SAOR 89-1-820/2.[2]

To his Excellency, Lord Head Curator and President of the Guardianship Committee for Colonists in Southern Russia, Lieutenant General Inzov,

---

2 Regarding Cornies' efforts to gain a permanent land grant at Iushanle, see also documents 1, 152, 177, 178, 185, 531, 535, and additional documents in volume II.

A most respectful petition from the Molochnaia Mennonite Johann Cornies, in the village of Ohrloff:

With deepest respect, I take the liberty of submitting a petition to Yr. Excellency on a matter of some urgency that arises from the fact that [public] interest in unsettled land [in our area] is steadily rising. I humbly request that Yr. Excellency graciously take this matter under advisement.

In 1812, I established a small khutor on the south bank of the Iushanle stream, close to the chumak road leading from the Crimea to the city Alexandrovsk, on land that had been exchanged with the Nogai Tatars. My principal purpose was to improve sheep breeding. Initially, former colonial inspector Sieter encouraged me in the hope that high-ranking authorities would grant me, in perpetual ownership, an area sufficient for my livestock holdings in return for the payment of legal land taxes. This expectation was based on a promise in the pamphlet, "Encouragement for the improvement and refining of sheep breeding in Russia," by M.L. Friebe (Riga, 1809), that had been commissioned by His Highness, the Interior Minister. It was addressed to persons who were establishing farms with a view to improving sheep raising in the southern provinces of the Russian Empire.

With ceaseless effort and at considerable cost, I have sought to enlarge and refine my livestock holdings and to construct buildings essential for such an establishment. The latter consist of the following:

1. One dwelling and barn, forty-eight fut long and eighteen fut wide.
2. One small dwelling, thirty-three fut long and eighteen fut wide.
3. One sheep barn, sixty-six fut long and eighteen fut wide.
4. An enclosure, fenced with boards, for sheep, cattle, and horses, two hundred forty fut long and forty-eight to sixty fut wide.

My livestock holdings at present consist of:

1. 1,425 refined sheep, including pure Spanish and refined rams.
2. 100 head of cattle of various breeds.
3. 180 horses.

In the year 1813, on orders of the former colonial inspector Sieter, the line separating tract fifty-nine from tracts sixty-two and fifty-eight was extended across the above-mentioned land exchanged with the Nogai Tatars to the Nogai Tatar boundary, and marked off with two furrows. An area of approximately 3,800 desiatinas was severed, and I established my khutor on this land. The land is divided by two chumak roads, each two verstas wide, leading from the Crimea to the cities of Alexandrovsk and Bakhmut. What remains of the above total is only about 2,000 desiatinas of usable and unusable land, divided into three pieces. None are suitable for the founding of future settlements. None have flowing water, which can only be obtained from wells. With the exception of a small piece, the entire area has soil of only moderate quality.

With deepest humility, I ask Yr. Excellency to bestow on me your high favour by granting me the perpetual ownership of the above-mentioned land in exchange for the payment of the legal land taxes. This would permit me to continue the undertaking I have begun and to pursue it with ever greater zeal. I have considered purchasing land for this purpose, but my financial position does not permit me to do so without falling into considerable debt. Even if I were eventually able to accumulate the required sum of money to purchase this land, my resources would be insufficient to enable me to continue the endeavour I have begun and to improve and refine my livestock at the same time. And were I to suffer misfortune, I would find it impossible to recover my former economic position.

I therefore rely on the hope that Yr. Excellency will graciously consider my humble request and benevolently bless me with an early resolution of this matter. I have the honour to call myself, with the deepest respect, Yr. Excellency's completely obedient servant,

Johann Cornies

Ohrloff, 24 June 1820[3]

6. Andrei M. Fadeev to Johann Cornies. 7 July 1820. SAOR 89-1-21/1.

To the authorized representative of the Molochnaia Mennonites, Johann Cornies,

I need detailed information about the 1815 sale of state lands by the Tavrida Financial Department to several private persons. Are any of these designated in the enclosed notes?

3 Several versions of this petition exist in the Braun archive, but this is the best organized one. Another version is entered in the Cornies correspondence journal for 1825 (SAOR 89-1-63/26v) and dated 14 November 1825.

I hereby authorize you to travel around the areas located on the enclosed map,[4] to inspect their general nature, the depth of wells, and if, in your view, there are a sufficient number of sites available for settlement. Is the border located correctly on this map? If you find mistakes, note these, and also the location of the border on the 83,000 desiatinas of land sold in 1815. According to the lists included here, there are accounted for only 74,165 desiatinas of usable land and 1,689 of wasteland, for a total of 75,854 desiatinas. Some 8,000 desiatinas are missing. Please make an effort to find where these 8,000 desiatinas are located, whether they belong to private persons, and who these persons are.

I authorize you to investigate these matters without informing the present owners of these lands of your purpose. You might make it appear that you intend to buy a portion of the land, or have other intentions. Try to send me these lists by 12 July.

Senior Member, Fadeev

7 July 1820. Carried out.

7. Andrei M. Fadeev to Johann Cornies. 1 July 1821.
SAOR 89-1-21/27.

To the authorized representative of the Molochnaia Mennonites, Cornies,

I hereby request that you notify the elders of the two colonial districts resident on the Molochnaia, the Prussian as well as the Wuertemberg colonists, that in keeping with a preliminary notification from His Excellency [Ivan N. Inzov], Lord Head Curator and President of the Guardianship Committee for Colonists in Southern Russia, the survey of the land for their settlement has already been confirmed at the highest level and assigned by you. This refers to the 24,000 desiatinas, listed as tracts number fifteen and sixteen known to you, and also the 8,946 desiatinas, in two parts, referred to as Nogai lands, which you inspected last year.

I am travelling to Kishinev today to see His Excellency, and I will not fail to ask him to make the appropriate request that this land be

4 The map is not extant.

surveyed as soon as possible. I may also stop off in Simferopol on my return journey because of this. I intend to return to Ekaterinoslav through the Molochnaia villages.

1 July 1821.

Senior member Fadeev

Carried out.

8. Werner to Johann Cornies. 20 May 1822. SAOR 89-1-36/3.

Most highly honoured Mr. Cornies,

Last Monday, I visited your sheep farm but did not find you there. I wanted to describe to you how impossible it is for me to fulfil the promise I made to you. I am grieved that you, Mr. Cornies, may feel justified in entertaining a bad opinion of me. Your friendship is of great importance to me, not simply because I am in your debt, but also because your philanthropic character inspires my respect, love, and friendship. I am convinced that if you could understand my situation, you would sooner pity me than be angry at my insolvency.

I would like to borrow the money that I have collected for your Bibles, but the interest of 10 per cent is too high, too severe, for my meagre income. Would you allow me to make a claim on your kind heart? I count on it. You will, for some time, as I hope, treat my insolvency with forbearance.

You would undoubtedly prefer that I carry out my promise. As an upright man, I too would prefer to discharge my duty so that your good opinion of me would grow stronger and my zeal to serve you in future could be strengthened. I must forego this honour until I can find another opportunity to convince you that my goal is to increase the well-being of humanity, even if I personally derive no advantage, but only pain, from it.

The villages of Reichenfeld and Alt Monthal have not yet paid for six Bibles. Since they have no money, I advised the buyers to request the forbearance of Mr. Cornies in Ohrloff. They informed me that you had extended their term until after the harvest, when they will pay. I may soon be fortunate enough to speak to you personally about what must be done and to give testimony. With all respect, love, and trust, I remain your honourably disposed, and eager to be of service,

Werner

Rosenthal, 20 May 1822

9. Samuel Contenius to Johann Cornies. 18 October 1822. SAOR 89-1-36/1.

Dear honoured Johann Cornies,

I am sorry that we failed to meet when you were here recently. I hope business matters will bring you back again soon and give me another opportunity to see you.

Our honoured friend and benefactor, William Allen in London, has again sent me seeds for distribution to good tree growers. He urgently wishes to obtain detailed information about the Doukhobor sect's specific way of thinking, about their system and dogma. His conversation with some Doukhobors in Simferopol seemed to confirm some of his own views. He and his American travelling companion, Stephen Grellet, feel the sect may resemble their own, the Quakers, in a number of ways.[5]

We must now ask if the written confession of faith delivered to me is a real declaration of their principles of faith or if it simply consists of hypocrisy. Do they all accept it, or only a few? What can a closer acquaintance with them teach us? Are they closer to Christianity or to Judaism?

What is the name of the Doukhobor to whom you, dear Cornies, introduced me last June in Ohrloff, and with whom our friend Allen is said to have had a number of discussions in Simferopol? My experiences among the Prussian colonists last June filled my head so full that I remember little of what this man said about the subject in question.

Please, dear Cornies, assist me, since you are more closely acquainted with these matters and have greater experience with the sect's opinions and principles of belief than I have. This would enable me to share the information with my friend in London, who will send it on to America. Do not forget to include the name of the person who spoke the most with friend Allen in Simferopol.

My friendliest greetings to your dear father and the rest of your family. With the most excellent esteem, I remain your honestly respectful,

S. Contenius.

Ekaterinoslav, 18 October 1822

5 William Allen and Stephen Grellet were Quakers who visited New Russia in 1819. For Allen's account of the trip, see *Life of William Allen, with Selections from His Correspondence*, 2 vols. (Philadelphia: Henry Longstreth, 1847).

P.S. I hereby send you, dear Cornies, four almonds ripened in the local Crown plantation, to be planted according to written instructions from District Chairman Ens. It is my desire that you will in time have the satisfaction of picking fruits of this kind in your own garden.

N.B. Will the Molokans, or whatever they may call themselves, settle on the land assigned to them in your neighbourhood, or go elsewhere?

1824

10. Guardianship Committee to Johann Cornies. 1824. SAOR 89-1-58/41.

To Johann Cornies, Mennonite from Ohrloff village, the Mennonite community's authorized representative to purchase merino sheep for the improvement of the community's herds,

High authorities have approved a plan to meet an urgent need in both the Molochnaia and Khortitsa communities by purchasing merinos to perfect sheep breeding in the villages. You are being dispatched to St. Petersburg, to His Imperial Majesty's agricultural establishment called Tsarskoe Selo, to execute exactly and deliberately the following commission:

1. Together with the Mennonite Gerhard Martens, who is associated with you in order to carry out the present plan, and with Christian Schmidt, the community's sheep master, you should leave for St. Petersburg without delay and complete the journey without interruption.[1] The merinos must be examined before sheep shearing begins and brought to this area before autumn. Enclosed is a pass permitting free, unhindered travel for you and your companions.

1 There appear to have been two important Gerhard Martens in Cornies' life. One (probably the one referred to here) was Johann Cornies' personal secretary, who accompanied him to St. Petersburg in 1824 and Saxony in 1827, and continued to work for him until at least 1833. The other, who lived in Halbstadt, was the secretary of the Molochnaia Mennonite District Office. Cornies regarded him as a friend and relied upon him to forward correspondence.

2. Upon arrival in St. Petersburg, you should present the enclosed report at the Department of the Imperial Economy under its director, His Excellency the Acting State Counsellor, Stepan Semenovich Dzhunkovskii.[2] There you should request a communication that you will present to the administrator at Tsarskoe Selo. This will ensure that the merinos in question will be exhibited and that you will be able to take possession of them. You will receive the necessary support and help for the speedy dispatch and favourable completion of your commission.

3. According to an announcement sent from Acting State Counsellor Mr. Dzhunkovskii to the Head Curator for Colonists in southern Russia, this year eighty rams and forty ewes are to be sold in Tsarskoe Selo. His Excellency Mr. Dzhunkovskii has been given advance notice that the colonial communities will purchase thirty rams and probably all forty ewes. The enclosed report explains why a larger number of ewes is considered necessary to more quickly advance the refinement of sheep in your communities. You should therefore work with the administrators to ensure that you may lay claim to the entire quantity of ewes being sold this year.

4. Having secured detailed information about the merinos for sale in Tsarskoe Selo, you should try to purchase rams as advantageously as possible, considering not only the quality of their wool, but also their age and health. Do not act hastily, but observantly and carefully. After the merinos are purchased, you must take [wool] samples from each animal, as prescribed, and mail them to the Committee.

5. You must give scrupulous deliberation to the arrangements you make to move these sheep to their destination safely and well. You must decide carefully on the means of transport to ensure the lowest possible loss. Take scrupulous care to protect their health. Their Excellencies, the Head Curator and Mr. Dzhunkovskii, are of the opinion that special cages or containers are best suited to this end, despite the view of the District Offices and the Sheep Society that it is better and safer to drive them on foot. This matter can only be resolved after local circumstances, and the convenience of driving them on foot or carrying them in containers, are considered on the spot. Please take this matter in hand and decide what is best. In particular, consideration should

2 Dzhunkovskii's full title was Director of the Department of the Imperial Economy and Public Buildings of the Ministry of Internal Affairs [*Departament gosudarstvennogo khoziastva i publichnykh zdanii MVD*]. He was also the editor of the highly influential journal, the *Works of the Imperial Free Economic Society*.

be given to the advantages of driving them to Smolensk or to Orsha and then transporting them by water on the Dnieper in a serviceable barge or several flat-bottomed vessels with dependable boatmen and workers.

6. After you have taken possession of the merinos and decided on the means of transport and prepared everything for the journey, you must again report to the Department of the Imperial Economy. There you will receive money to pay for the return journey and for the merinos. A total of 17,000 rubles, for thirty rams, estimated at a cost of 250 rubles per head, and for forty ewes at 125 rubles per head, has been mailed to the Department for this purpose. You should then immediately leave on your return journey.

7. While on your way, you and your people should exercise constant vigilance to ensure that none of the merinos are injured or lost en route because of sickness, death, overly-vigorous driving, or bad fodder and water. Obtain the needed medical remedies that may be needed en route, as well as instructions [on the care of the sheep] published in books on Spanish sheep breeding.

8. Enclosed is a book for running accounts to record all income and expenses relating to this commission. You are obligated to watch for any possible savings, note all expenditures exactly, and submit the book to the Committee for checking and auditing on your return.

9. Report in detail to the Committee from every guberniia capital and several uezd cities en route, on your arrival in St. Petersburg, and again during your return journey. A detailed travel journal regarding all matters affecting your commission must be kept en route.

10. The Committee has tested your intelligence and experience and is firmly convinced that you will demonstrate the greatest zeal in caring for the herd entrusted to your care, fulfilling all obligations and keeping costs low. We are confident that as you make your own intelligent and cautious decisions in all foreseeable matters, you will justify the confidence the administration and the colonial communities have invested in you.

11. Khortitsa District Office to Johann Cornies. 8 April 1824. SAOR 89-1-58/49.

Official authorization No. 33:

The Khortitsa District Office hereby officially authorizes Johann Cornies, Mennonite from the Molochnaia Mennonite village of Ohrloff, to purchase Spanish sheep, ewes, and rams for the whole community from His Imperial Majesty's herd at Tsarskoe Selo and to transport them to this District. You should proceed according to your own best judgment and make all necessary expenditures. You will be compensated for your efforts and for your expenditures after your accounts have been presented. We undertake to be satisfied with all services rendered and not to reproach you in any way. To attest to the foregoing, this official authorization from the District Office is signed personally and has the imperial seal affixed.

8 April 1824.

District Chairman Toews, Deputy Penner, Deputy Loepky, Secretary Heese

12. District Office to Johann Cornies. 9 April 1824. SAOR 89-1-58/50.

Official authorization No. 69:

We, officials of the Molochnaia Mennonite District Office, have signed below to explicitly authorize you, Johann Cornies from Ohrloff village, our local authorized representative for land surveying, to purchase merino sheep for the entire Molochnaia community as designated by the District Administration. We request that you travel to Tsarskoe Selo, near St. Petersburg, and there purchase merino sheep required for our local sheep breeding at the cost of the community treasury. We undertake to compensate you completely, as our authorized representative, for the travel costs required for this purpose.

Given in the Halbstadt District Office, on 9 April 1824.

Deputy Warkentin, Deputy Fast, Substitute Toews

13. Guardianship Committee to Johann Cornies. 16 April 1824. SAOR 89-1-58/38.

From the Ekaterinoslav Guardianship Committee,

To Johann Cornies, Mennonite from Ohrloff colony, the Mennonite community's authorized representative to purchase merinos that will help to refine the colonial herds. Directive. The office supplies necessary for the work of the Ekaterinoslav Guardianship Committee office in 1824 are estimated as follows: holland paper, No. 1, 15 reams, No. 2, 35 reams, No. 3, 45 reams and one ream postage paper; also 15 pounds of No. 1 seals and 20 pounds of No. 2 seals. Since your journey to St. Petersburg leads through Moscow, where all these materials can be bought more cheaply than they can be here, the Ekaterinoslav

Guardianship Committee directs you to purchase the listed materials. They should be of the best quality, bought at the most favourable prices and forwarded to the Committee with an accounting of the expenditures.

The Committee advances 1,000 rubles from its treasury. Should this amount be insufficient, you may expend your own money, if you deem it desirable.

16 April 1824

Same meaning as the original, translator Goern.

14. Johann Cornies to Guardianship Committee. [July, 1824]. SAOR 89-1-58/30.

To the Ekaterinoslav Bureau for Foreign Settlers,
Respectful request by Authorized Representative Johann Cornies:

I intend to arrive in Ekaterinoslav with the merinos between 12 and 15 August. If no accidents have occurred, or unusual obstacles arisen along the way, I would then like to relinquish my management of the transport of merinos to the Molochnaia so that I could spend several days in Ekaterinoslav to accurately settle my accounts.

I request that the worthy Committee for Foreign Settlers instruct the three District Offices to send one member from each district, accompanied by the Molochnaia and Khortitsa community shepherds, to Ekaterinoslav. They should arrive at a specific time. They will take receipt of the merinos from me and divide them among themselves. Should the worthy Committee not find my request contrary to its purpose, I ask it most respectfully to allow my request.

I continue, submissively, as the worthy Bureau's dutiful,
Johann Cornies

15. Johann Cornies to Tsarskoe Selo administrator. August 1824. SAOR 89-1-58/20.

Dear Sir,

To fulfil my promise, I report our safe arrival with the merinos in Ekaterinoslav. As you know, we left Tsarskoe Selo on 14 June and the transport of the merinos reached Ekaterinoslav on 11 August, healthy and strong. The consistently good health of the sheep and the cool weather for most of the journey contributed to its speedy conclusion. I can assure you, however, that I would hesitate to undertake a second journey over the same route. Without considering the other difficulties, on such a journey one can find no rest during day or night for fear that an animal might die, despite our vigilance and care. How easily we could have been discredited for failing in the duties entrusted to us.

From Tsarskoe Selo to some 200 verstas from Ekaterinoslav, the merinos were in the same robust condition in which I had received them from you in Tsarskoe Selo. Then, however, we were struck by a terrible heat wave and a plague of grasshoppers that devoured everything in their path, so that the sheep had great difficulty on the last leg of their journey to Ekaterinoslav.

His Excellency, the acting State Counsellor, Contenius, was not at home when I arrived, having gone to the Crimea for health reasons. Officials in the Guardianship Committee told me that His Excellency was satisfied with the quality and fineness of all but two of the wool samples sent from St. Petersburg.

My family was well and happy when, to their great delight, I arrived home on 19 August. I send greetings to you and your dear brother with many thanks for your kindness during my stay in Tsarskoe Selo.

I sign myself as your willing Cornies.

16. Johann Cornies to Traugott Blueher. 12 August 1824. SAOR 89-1-58/23v.

Sincerely beloved Mr. Blueher,

My travelling companions and I arrived safe and sound in Ekaterinoslav from St. Petersburg on 11 August. I would be pleased to learn that you and your dear life's companion are also well.

Forgive me, my dear friend, if I burden you with a task. Through Mr. Graff, the book dealer, His Honour, Mr. Fadeev, senior member of the Ekaterinoslav Committee, ordered several hundred books from Germany about the economies of local communities. They were to be delivered from Moscow to Ekaterinoslav when transportation became available. But Mr. Fadeev knows no one in Moscow who can receive the books and forward them to merchant Chelkov in Kharkov. I have therefore taken the liberty of directing Mr. Fadeev to you as an obliging and efficient forwarding agent. Please forward these books and advance money to the carters. Upon receipt of the invoice, you will be reimbursed by our [Guardianship] Committee.

I send cordial and sincere greetings to you and your family, with many thanks for the love and support you showed me during my stay in Moscow. May the Lord bless you, and give you His peace. This is the heartfelt wish of your honest friend and brother in Christ,

Johann Cornies

17. Johann Tihlmann to Johann Cornies. 1 October 1824. SAOR 89-1-76/1.

Most valued Mr. Johann Cornies,

May the peace of God our Lord, our Creator of heaven and earth, be with you in all eternity even as the Lord has granted me in His grace. My heart would be ungrateful were I to fail to drop you a few lines, since you kindly provided me with money that enabled me to attend school here, where I am taught the Word of God. Otherwise, I might have been lost for all eternity. I must thank you again and again. I pray that our loving God give you earthly and spiritual riches in abundance that continue into eternity. Earthly riches will disappear when the Son of Man descends in heaven's clouds and calls forth the remains of the dead. In this school, it is important to speak about God's Word. Writing and calculation are most important in other schools.

Dear Mr. Johann Cornies, last year you promised me a winter outfit, though you actually said this to my dear teacher, Mr. Voth, who told me. Please, because I need it so badly, let me have the garment now.

I thank you from my heart for your love and kindness in providing the wood for the wooden foot I needed and desired. At first I thought I would not be able to use the foot, but the dear Lord healed my knees. I can now use the foot in whatever way I like, although my knees hurt when I ride a lot.

In closing my letter, I hope that you will grant my request. I wish you the peace of God which is higher than all human understanding. I remain your faithful friend,

Johann Tihlmann

18. Johann Cornies to Traugott Blueher. December 1824. SAOR 89-1-58/10.

Very dear Mr. Blueher, treasured friend and brother in Christ,

After I had taken my unforgettable leave from you and your dear life's companion, I set out from Moscow for St. Petersburg with my travelling companions and, with God's wondrous guidance, reached St. Petersburg safely after a thirteen-day journey. There I reported to public officials in the Department of Imperial Economy who provided me with the necessary documents. With these I set out for Tsarskoe Selo to purchase thirty rams and forty ewes from the Tsar's sheep farm. There I was told that no more than fifteen ewes, but more than forty rams, were for sale this year. My instructions, however, referred mainly to ewes and my understanding was that our flocks could not be refined as quickly using only rams.

I therefore applied to His Excellency, Minister Buskoi.[3] Through his mediation and after much running around, I eventually obtained an agreement to purchase fifteen of this year's female lambs in addition to fifteen old ewes from His Imperial Majesty's flocks. In addition to the thirty rams already ordered by our authorities, I bought another five, bringing the total to sixty-five genuine merinos, all of good quality with fine wool. To enable you to judge their quality, I enclose a sample from one ram.

On 13 June, after spending three weeks in and around St. Petersburg, we set out on our return march with the merinos. All of the sheep, in good condition, arrived in Ekaterinoslav on 11 August. We thank the Lord for the speedy journey and His guidance and preservation that exceeded our expectations. As our guide and helper on the entire journey, His be the glory, praise, and honour.

We paused in Ekaterinoslav for eight days to settle orders and accounts in connection with our trip. All items I purchased in Moscow with your kind assistance had arrived in good order, except for the tea, which cannot be located anywhere despite questions directed to the merchant, Mr. Chelkov in Kharkov. Please make inquiries with the merchant from whom we bought the tea, since it may have been left behind. If this is the case, please forward the tea to me with the packages of books. Also tell me what the letters that you forwarded to me cost so that I might reimburse you immediately.

This year's harvest on the Molochnaia is very poor, as it is also in the guberniias of Ekaterinoslav and Kherson. Grasshoppers consumed virtually all the grass, and what remained was burned by scorching heat and ceaseless winds. We thought that great black clouds in the distance were rain, but when we drew nearer, we realized they were clouds of dust darkening the sun. God's judgments are just and merciful and only [as we accept them] can we resist the bitterness and delusion of human understanding. And as we experience such trials, God's word in the Bible acquires greater strength and light.

I found my whole family healthy and contented, praise God.

3 It is not clear who "Minister Buskoi" might be. At the time, Vasily Lanskoi was the Minister of the Interior, while Egor Kankrin was already the Minister of Finance.

1825

19. Andrei M. Fadeev to Johann Cornies. 16 January 1825. SAOR 89-1-77/3.

Ekaterinoslav
Most valued Cornies,

I received a letter from the Minister, Mr. Kochubei, in Odessa, dated 11 January.[1] His Lordship informs me that there is an opportunity for the purchase of the best merinos from Saxony. What they need is a dependable man with practical knowledge of sheep breeding to select and transport the sheep. His Lordship has asked me to make a proposal to you in this regard. Would you be willing to accept this commission, and if so, please let me know what you would require for your efforts?

The Minister goes further to say that, should you accept this commission to undertake this trip, he would like to send you to Saxony with an official from Odessa late in March or early in April. All preparations are already in place. They have been made by knowledgeable people. It would be your business to select the sheep and supervise their care en route. Shepherds from Saxony would accompany the sheep to the border.

Please think carefully about this proposal and give me your decision as soon as you can. I understand that your own household may suffer greatly as a result of such frequent journeys, yet do not lose sight of

1 Viktor Kochubei (1768–1834), a prominent Russian statesman and diplomat, was Minister of the Interior from 1802–12 and again from 1819–25, and chairman of the State Council and the Committee of Ministers from 1827–34.

this journey's purpose. It might also turn out to be useful for you in a number of ways, including the opportunity to perfect the knowledge needed to breed your own sheep. Similarly, your acquaintance with Mr. Kochubei might allow you to gain his support for the acquisition of several thousand desiatinas of land as a number of Frenchmen have managed to do.

Should your economic circumstances permit, the best thing would be to come to Ekaterinoslav to reach an appropriate agreement that also includes Mr. Contenius. I leave this to your own consideration. Please enable me to give the Count a definite answer soon. I remain forever,

Your benevolent A. Fadeev.

P.S. When you have time, please let me know about the number of Doukhobor and Molokan villages, families, and souls [living in your area]. What is the real difference between these two sects? What are the peculiar characteristics of their morality and character, etc.? If you do not have time for this yourself, the writing could, on the basis of your information, be done by Bartram.

Received 19 January 1825.[2]

20. Johann Cornies to Andrei M. Fadeev. 27 January 1825. SAOR 89-1-63/2.

The Honourable Senior Member of the Ekaterinoslav Guardianship Committee, Fadeev,

Your Honour's letter of 16 January that I received on 19 January, informed me of the honoured proposal that I take charge of the Spanish merino sheep His Highness, the Minister of the Interior, Count Kochubei, is intending to buy in Saxony. I am well able to appreciate the value of this highly honoured commission and deem it an obligation to willingly carry out orders and commissions from our superiors.

Because of the distressing conditions currently prevailing in our villages, however, and our anxieties about our daily bread, there is a real threat that a majority of our inhabitants may lose the courage to continue with their industrious and useful activities. The education and

2 A letter of 24 January 1825 from Samuel Contenius (SAOR 89-1-77/24), almost identical to this letter and so not included in this collection, makes the same proposal to Johann Cornies, stressing also the knowledge and experience Cornies would gain about sheep breeding and the wool trade.

further well-being of the growing generation might, as a result, suffer irreparable loss. I have many responsibilities in this respect and think that my absence on a long journey might result in the serious neglect of these duties.

Since I enjoy the confidence of my community, it is my inescapable duty to seek the well-being of every single individual and the entire community according to my best understanding. The Lord, with His gentle hand, has blessed me with such temporal riches that I am free of troublesome worries about survival. This makes it even more important for me than for many another upright man to carry out my obligations and responsibilities and to serve the general well-being.

Since returning from St. Petersburg and Odessa, internal community matters have so occupied me that I have almost no time left to attend to my own business. Moreover, current misfortunes have greatly complicated internal matters in our community. Many of our existing arrangements require supervision that is long and firm. Much is needed if we are to prevent the further neglect and deterioration of our situation.

Over the past seven or eight years, I have given almost unlimited time and effort to the settlement's concerns through community appointments and commissions from the Honoured Committee. Many responsibilities rest on me. At present, I do not have the time to properly undertake my own business and, at the same time, carry on my correspondence with patrons, friends, and acquaintances. Still, were my local obligations to be delegated to someone else, I would not hesitate to take on this commission and use all of my diligence and strength to earn the cherished trust placed in me.

Your Honour knows well that I have willingly taken on every commission I have been given. I would therefore ask Yr. Honour, in this case, to graciously excuse me to His Highness, the Honourable Minister. Not my convenience or interests, but only the situation, make my long absence from the settlement impossible.

I would have visited Ekaterinoslav to explain this matter to you personally, but the continuing severity of this winter has resulted in a serious fodder shortage over a wide area around our settlement. I have purchased fodder from the Nogais, not far from the Wuertemberg settlement, and my horses have been sent to this area.

I will gladly send Your Honour the information you request about the Doukhobors and the Molokans after I receive answers to my queries.

Your Honour's obedient servant.

21. Johann Cornies to Samuel Contenius. 30 January 1825. SAOR 89-1-63/3v.

His Excellency, Acting State Counsellor, Contenius,

Yesterday I received Your Excellency's valued letter of 24 January. It expresses confidence in me by proposing that I travel to Saxony for His Honour, Minister Kochubei. As I have already written to the Chief Judge, I hasten respectfully and honestly to reply that under present circumstances, I cannot accept Your Excellency's generous invitation to visit Ekaterinoslav. Given our grave shortage of fodder, it is necessary for me to stay here to find means that would sustain our livestock.

I would draw Your Excellency's attention to my letter to the Chief Judge explaining in detail why it is not possible for me to leave home for such a long period of time without serious damage to my own establishment and to community affairs. I am convinced that I must decline your flattering invitation, though not for superficial or disrespectful reasons. My refusal has caused me great pangs of conscience. I am convinced, however, that your generosity and knowledge of my situation will permit you to graciously accept my reply. Please believe me when I say that I am flattered by the request from His Excellency, the Minister, from Your Excellency, and from the Chief Judge. I am thankful and honoured by your confidence in me and it would give me pleasure to demonstrate my devotion and faithfulness to you in deed, as my circumstances and my humble abilities allow.

My conscience does not, however, permit me to leave the community for such a long time under these dismal circumstances. Members of the community come to me daily and I thank God that I am able to assist them with advice and in practical ways. Many general matters of business accumulated during my long absence last year, and I was able to assume responsibility over my own business affairs from my brother only recently. I am now putting my accounts in order and catching up on what was neglected, restoring the damage as best I can. Meanwhile, as the community's business has increased markedly, I have also recognized how my own economic management could serve the community as an example. The choice I have made is thus not the easier, but the more difficult one. I am aware, of course, that the honour, enjoyment, and advantage of accepting such an exceptional proposal is very appealing.

May Your Excellency graciously consider my circumstances, and accept my conviction that the community's business and my own affairs are my first obligation, at least for this year.

With respect and devotion,

Johann Cornies

22. Johann Cornies to Andrei M. Fadeev. 5 February 1825. SAOR 89-1-63/5.

To the Honourable Senior Member of the Ekaterinoslav Guardianship Committee, Mr. Fadeev,

Obedient request from the Mennonite community's authorized representative, Johann Cornies:

Over the past two years, an almost total crop failure in our region has plunged many residents in our settlement into extreme poverty. Even people who previously had considerable means have suffered significant reverses. Many who earlier helped and supported others in need, can now not help themselves. Private money has been exhausted, winter persists, and the harvest was so poor that the problem of maintaining people and their livestock seems insurmountable for many. The scanty summer pasturage meant that our livestock was already extremely thin. They are now emaciated because of the poor, limited fodder. Many villagers are already totally without fodder and some are using thatch on their roofs to extend somewhat the lives of their livestock. Many find themselves in a situation where they are without money, bread, and fuel. Every day several people come asking me for help but I cannot, even with the best intentions, help everyone. The distress grows daily.

My love and compassion for humankind prompts me to ask that Your Honour permit the extension of assistance from the community treasury for those suffering extreme need. This could save many from total penury. I would suggest that a local community committee be named to investigate the matter, to support those suffering extreme want, and to supervise this work. I know of no other remedy. I feel strongly that I should come to Ekaterinoslav to put this urgent matter of our need before your worthy Committee, but the severe winter compels me to go out in search of fodder for my own considerable livestock.

Within the next few days, two District Office members will arrive in Ekaterinoslav in support of this proposal. On behalf of those suffering extreme need, I dutifully beg Your Honour to make expeditious arrangements in keeping with your wise and well-intentioned administration. Hunger permits no delay. Please do not receive this well-meaning initiative ungraciously.

Your Honour's most obedient servant,
J.C.

23. Johann Cornies to Andrei M. Fadeev. 4 March 1825. SAOR 89-1-63/8v.

Yr. Honour, Senior Member of the Ekaterinoslav Guardianship Committee Fadeev,

Early in February, I received several parcels from Kharkov, sent on from St. Petersburg. One was addressed to Your Honour. I gave it to the local District Office to be forwarded to you, but was unable to inform Your Honour of this fact because of strong winds and a driving snowstorm. These forced me to stay on my sheep farm and tend to my livestock. Fate, as wind and snow, has now struck me a hard blow. Because of the scarcity of winter fodder, I had constructed a sheepfold on the steppe, a *koshara* that permitted me to graze my sheep on good pasturage in moderate weather. But during the night of 14 February, a powerful wind arose that set the snow into violent motion. The day grew dark. Visibility was reduced to twenty sazhen. Objects above ground were transformed into mountains of snow. The storm filled every yard with snow and almost completely cut communications between houses. It scattered my sheep. I have lost more than 700 head. Additionally, I lost around 100 horses and a number of cattle. They were in the yard, near the threshing floor and covered with snow. All this has caused me much work and hardship that will continue.

The community's shortage of fodder has increased greatly. Much livestock has fallen and no fodder can be bought in the surrounding region at any price. Mr. Stiglitz' horses suffered a like fate. When his herd passed through here several days ago, it left behind a trail of dead horses. Mr. Granobarskii had 1,105 horses. Now, fewer than 100 remain. There are similar misfortunes everywhere. Many, many thousands of animals have been lost to hunger, wind, and snow.

24. Johann Cornies to Traugott Blueher. SAOR 89-1-63/11. 25 June 1825.

Honoured Mr. Blueher,

I received your letter of 4 May and the enclosed 500 R.B.A. ["assignation rubles", i.e. paper money] advance to purchase a quantity of wool.

I tried to purchase for you 200 or 300 puds of wool of the quality you specified, or to have someone else do it for me, but I have failed in this endeavour. The local sheep breeders have never sold their wool sorted for the factory in this way. Sales here involve only a general sorting of whole fleeces into three categories. For example, the sheep breeder sorts a herd of 1,000 head at shearing time into three groups, according to the quality of the whole pelt. Purchasers inspect each category to see if there are great variations among them, set their prices, and bargain with sellers accordingly, either for the entire quantity or for each category separately.

To enable you to acquire accurate knowledge about our wool and about local purchases and sales, I have tried to persuade the community to send you 200 puds of unwashed wool from the community sheep farm for sale on commission. This would enable you to judge its quality and to determine whether better prices can be obtained for washed or unwashed wool. If this transaction produces a higher sale price than the local price of wool on the spot (after commission, freight, and other costs are deducted), you will undoubtedly receive a large quantity of local wool for sale on commission next year.

This year's shipment will give you a more accurate knowledge about the fineness and quality of our local wool than is possible in letters and small samples, while you will assume no risks. I have pointed out to our community that our purchase of constantly more refined merino rams and ewes will improve the quality and quantity of our wool from year to year so that you could sell it in Moscow, should you so wish. Even if you do not wish to continue such a commission, you will in the process have obtained better knowledge of the wool produced here, and can make your own purchases more effectively in future.

Members of the Molochnaia Mennonite District Office and some villagers are now packing the wool carefully, to have it sent to you in Moscow by trustworthy carters. Very little wool has been produced here. Our local community sheep farm did not produce a full 200 puds because it lost about 1,500 sheep in the great snowstorm. The [Molochnaia] Colonist District has offered to send fifty puds of their wool, and their office will inform you accordingly.

Wool prices are very different here this year, with little specific attention to fineness. In Kharkov, Mr. Cholkov paid an average of twenty-one to twenty-three R.B.A. for unwashed wool, and an average of thirty-one R.B.A. for washed wool, but obtained little at this price. Our local merchants sent about 2,000 puds of wool on consignment to the Romen [market]. The esteemed Gerhard Enns from Altonau bought more than

2,000 puds for the Ekaterinoslav state factory for 20 to 25 rubles, second and third quality, unwashed.[3] Washed was from 30 to 34 R.B.A. per pud. Mr. Shokin, a merchant of the first guild from Moscow, bought the Khoritisa community sheep farm wool, unwashed, at an average price of 32 R.B.A. On private sheep farms, first and second qualities of wool, washed, sold at 35 R.B.A., third quality at 27 R.B.A. An Englishman from Kherson (I do not know his name) paid from 25 to 28 R.B.A. on average for private wool, unwashed. An average of 28 R.B.A. was offered here for the wool now given to you on consignment.

I should have written you long ago about our local wool trade and whether your proposed wool purchase could be realized. However, I continued to hope that I could obtain the quantity of wool you specified to be purchased at your risk, but I was in no position to let you know definitely until now. Difficult though this delay is for you, please do not ascribe it to indifference or negligence on my part, but simply to the great distances here and my own numerous business matters. Please send me instructions about your 500 R.B.A. that I still have. Should I return the money to you or give it to the local District Office immediately for the wool being sent to you?

The weather this summer is as glorious and splendid as it was sad and difficult last year. The steppe grass, with its variegated flowers, has not grown so well since our settlement here twenty-one years ago. Mounds of grass were mowed in spots where there was only sparse pasturage for livestock in other years. The crops on the ploughed fields look very promising. Although summer crops will not be the most productive, winter grains are growing well. They promise an end to the shortages suffered in most homes.

The shortage of money remains dire, however. It seems that livestock still surviving after last winter cannot be sold at any price. The price for the best Ukrainian cows was twenty rubles at the annual markets in

3 Gerhard Enns of Altonau was one of Cornies' closest allies in the Molochnaia. He was deputy chair of the District from 1818–22 and chair from 1822–6. One of the wealthiest Molochnaia Mennonites, he was the foremost wool merchant in the Molochnaia. In 1831, he became one of the original members of the Forestry Society, and in 1836, he took the same role in the Agricultural Society. In the 1840s, Enns became one of the two biggest silk manufacturers in the Molochnaia. He was also one of Cornies' most prominent supporters during the "Warkentin Affair" that marked the climax of the Molochnaia political crisis of the 1830s and 1840s. See also documents 225 and 549.

May, but there were still not enough buyers. Thousands of head were left unsold and their poor owners were forced to return to their children, who were waiting painfully for the bread their father was going to buy when he sold his livestock. Starvation caused scurvy in Russian villages, and many deaths. Thank God, over the last month people are again healthy, and such illnesses are no longer mentioned.

A few weeks ago, I was honoured with a visit from the esteemed Governor of Tavrida, His Excellency Naryshkin.[4] The local Melitopol Uezd head reported that 124,900 head of livestock perished in the snowstorm in his uezd. If livestock from German settlements and those belonging to the Nogais and nomadic peoples are added, the number would be much greater. I know that 10,000 sheep, 1,800 head of cattle, and 1,200 horses died in the Mennonite community alone, a small number compared to the losses among Nogais and nomads.

After my last report to you on 4 March 1825, another snowstorm occurred on 8 March and killed another 100 or more horses from my breeding herd. My total loss this winter is more than 30,000 rubles. However, He who owns everything left me a considerable quantity of livestock for my future stewardship, and I am overwhelmed by His goodness and grace. Many of my fellow men and my brothers lost all their livestock, and find themselves in desperate circumstances, while I still have a great abundance of everything. *What God does is well done.* Even when He does not give us what we want, I am absolutely certain that He gives us whatever contributes to our salvation. At this moment, I am convinced that if I had only the slightest bit more, it would be too much. If it were less, it would be insufficient. So precisely has God, our beloved Father, measured everything out. It is our fault if we are not satisfied. My prayer is only thanks! thanks! thanks! Physically we are, thank God, in very good health.

Brother Schlatter is still living with his Nogais. He was in Odessa and in the Crimea for more than two months, and returned only a few days ago. He sends warm and heartfelt greetings to you, with the sincere wish that our beloved Saviour keep you in body and soul. May He grant you His blessings on earth and in eternity. In the hope that we will one day embrace one another in the purity of transfiguration, I say adieu.

Your C.

---

4 Dmitriy V. Naryshkin, governor of Tavride guberniia, 1823–9.

P.S. If it is not too inconvenient or does not involve too many errands, kindly buy for me in Moscow, at my expense, two or three bottles of *Lebensessenz* ["Essence of life," possibly aquavit] according to the enclosed description and send it by mail addressed to Gerhard Martens, District Office secretary in Halbstadt on the Molochnaia, to be forwarded to me. Because I seldom get to Orekhov, goods sent to my address there frequently stay at the post office for a long time.

Please write to me about anything you want to know concerning this area or how I can be of service to you. I hope that next time it will not take so long to reply, except when I am away on a trip.

I would like to know what a good surveyor's astrolabe costs in the booths at the Galanteria or in the stores, and also a compass, known as a box compass, with not too small a compass card. A few book catalogues from the best German bookstore would be very welcome. Please inform me about my debts with you, so that I can remit the correct amount. Heartfelt thanks for all good things,

Cornies

25. Johann Cornies to District Office. 23 July 1825. SAOR 89-1-870/7.[5]

To the esteemed District Office in Halbstadt,
From the authorized representative, Johann Cornies,

Declaration:

In response to summons No. 674, of 20 July, from the esteemed District Office, I respond briefly that I have conscientiously surveyed the land apportioned to the Alexanderwohl village community according to my best insights, taking into consideration the nature of the site and the possibility that a village might be settled next to it in future. At the time, the leaders of the Alexanderwohl community confirmed in writing: "We, the Alexanderwohl community leaders, are satisfied with the land apportioned to us."

Therefore, if the Alexanderwohl community believes that it will be completely ruined because of this survey, this is not the fault of the authorized representative. It is due to the spirit of our times, with its generally dissatisfied disposition, or to our many hardships and our own human inability to direct events. They depend not on me but on a higher hand.

5 Regarding the Alexanderwohl land dispute, see also documents 26, 30, 31, and 95.

I found it quite remarkable that after their earlier written declaration of satisfaction, the Alexanderwohl community should now be unable to survive on this apportioned land, and also that the settlement Commission members, H. Ba[lzer] and S. Edi[ger] in Grossweide, accepted, considered, and confirmed their complaint without carrying out an effective investigation.

This Commission will have to justify its remarks to the higher authorities (to whom the complaint is actually directed), and suggest ways in which Alexanderwohl can be assigned land closer to village homes without encroaching upon a neighbouring village community or damaging future settlers. It should demonstrate that it is impossible for the Alexanderwohl village community to survive with its present land and show that they are in a less advantageous situation in comparison to other village communities, such as Gnadenheim, Friedensdorf, etc. (which have not complained).

To enable me to act appropriately in such situations in future, I request that the esteemed District Office inform me about the obligations of the above-mentioned Settlement Commission and what my duties as authorized representative are to be.

26. District Office to Johann Cornies. 29 July 1825. SAOR 89-1 870/5.[6]

No. 892. Report to the Authorized Representative Johann Cornies in Ohrloff:

On 23 July, you inquired about the extent of your responsibilities to the appointed Settlement Commission with respect to the authorization for surveying given to you by the community. The District Office hereby notifies you that the Settlement Commission's sole purpose is to ensure that the assistance money released for settlement by the esteemed Crown is used appropriately. Thorough checking is needed to ensure that whatever was ordered is carried out to the letter. The Committee ordered the District Office to explain this to you and it was also reported today to the two members of the Settlement Commission, Heinrich Balzer and Salomon Ediger in Grossweide.

Halbstadt District Office, 29 July 1825
Chairman Klassen

6 Regarding the Alexanderwohl land dispute, see also documents 25, 30, 31, and 95.

27. Johann Cornies to Guardianship Committee. 24 August 1825. SAOR 89-1-63/19.

Report to the Committee:

I respond to the esteemed Committee's Order No. 2,200, of 14 August, asking whether I have carried out directive No. 297, of 29 January. I was to investigate water levels and find suitable locations for village sites in Tashchenak ravine, Melitopol Uezd, on the two tracts of land designated as numbers fifteen and sixteen on the map. Wells were to be dug, the positions of the colonies marked with a plough, etc. If this was not done, I was to report on the reasons why.

I obediently report to the esteemed Committee that I did not neglect these duties, nor cause them to be delayed. The only reason for the delay was simply the local food shortage. Persons to be hired for this work could not be found anywhere. I tried to hire workers who would provide their own food, but found none. The hay harvest here arrived early this year, and the grain harvest followed immediately thereafter, so that everyone was busy with his own work.

I also waited to survey the land missing from tract number sixteen to avoid a conflict with its present occupant, not wanting to undertake investigations on land not yet surveyed and marked off with ploughed furrows.

Now that most work on the land has been completed, I have taken measures to investigate tract numbers fifteen and sixteen in early September, in accordance with instructions. I will not neglect to inform the honoured Committee of my findings.

Cornies

28. Johann Cornies to Traugott Blueher. 27 August 1825. SAOR 89-1-63/20.

On 16 August, I received your letter of 3 August, informing me that you had filled the requests I sent you. I sincerely thank you for your cooperative assistance.

As the District Office reports, the community's wool must already be in your hands. According to my last letter, fifty puds of wool from the [German] colonist district were also to be included on commission. However, two agents from the trading firm Thomson, Bauar and the company from St. Petersburg bought it here for thirty-four R.B.A. This occurred because of our pressing shortage of money.

We thank God that when large swarms of grasshoppers passed through our district, His Almighty hand prevented them from devouring anything. Our grain was harvested without damage.

However, God has many means to test us and we again became the object of His frightful lash. This punishment, a message from Job, has greatly disheartened our community. Four members of our community travelled to the annual market in Romen to purchase supplies for their retail trade. Several community members also entrusted them with 2,000 puds of wool to be sold on commission. On arrival in Romen, they purchased their supplies, loaded them onto twenty-three chumak carts [ox wagons] and sold the wool at forty-five rubles per pud.

As news of their departure had already arrived here, the return of the men was awaited eagerly as was the return of the carters bringing the supplies. The carters stated that the men passed them thirty verstas on this side of Romen. It was assumed that they might have driven to the annual market in Kharkov, but it is now assumed that they were murdered. One of their wagons was found in Pishol near Kremenchuk on the Dnieper, but nothing else is yet known. A merchant from Kharkov states that he travelled with them to Iadiech, fifty-four verstas on this side of Romen. When he took the road to Kharkov, our people turned off to Poltava, passing through seven verstas of forest with difficult sand. It is assumed that they were murdered there. Several local men were sent to the area to see if more definite traces of their murder could be discovered.[7]

Four young men of consequence and a twelve-year old boy have thus suffered anguished, terror-filled deaths. They are estimated to have had 80,000 to 100,000 rubles cash with them, and the loss of the men and money is a huge setback for our community. The women and children left behind are suffering great pain and deep sorrow. How unfathomable and yet how glorious are God's ways, even when our eyes see only darkness in His sublime resolutions. Our faith is still the anchor of our hopes. Nothing happens by chance. While His judgment may be difficult to understand, it always works to our advantage. His will is holy and true and we must pray without ceasing that it be carried out on earth as it is in heaven. Amen.

We send heartfelt greetings to you and your life's companion. Please give my sincere greetings to brothers Dietrich and Haass, Mr. Pastor

---

7 Regarding this robbery and the murders, see also documents 49, 79, and 84.

Kohlreif, and his dear family. I commend myself to your further loving remembrance,

Cornies

P.S. Brother Daniel Schlatter is healthy and well and works as a servant for his Nogai employer, Ali, where he is so comfortable that I believe it would break his heart if the two had to separate. He visits us every Sunday dressed like a Tatar, and we take heartfelt pleasure together in the Lord. He sends many greetings to you, your dear wife, and brothers Dietrich and Haass, and asks for your prayers to our beloved Saviour.

29. Johann Cornies to District Office. 10 September 1825. SAOR 89-1-63/23.

To the District Office in Halbstadt,

On 9 and 10 September, I travelled around among the Nogais looking for horses stolen from our community. I found:

1. With Nogai Zirkle Begeboro in the Nogai village Iantoran, a five-year-old mare, small in stature, with a white spot on its forehead. It was branded MK on its left rear shank, and A on the front shank of the same side.

2. With Nogai Bokale Kaipov in the Nogai village Nekus, a brown gelding of medium size, five-years-old, the right hind foot white to the knee, a small white spot below the forehead, branded MK on the left back shank, and A on the front shank of the same side.

I immediately had these two Nogais arrested by the village police and sent to the Nogai Molochnaia District Office in Akuiau, as is shown on the enclosed receipt.

The Nogai District Office released these two horses to me upon my promise that the Mennonite District Office would send a detailed statement by 12 September as to who, by name, owns the horses, when and where they were stolen, and a precise description of their markings. Without this statement, the two Nogai suspects cannot be sent to their commanding officer. To avoid accusation of delay against us, I request that the esteemed District Office act to determine the owner of these horses as quickly as possible. The horses are here, on my property. Judging by the markings, I think the mare belongs somewhere in the five villages above Steinbach and was bought from Germans. There is no doubt that the gelding comes from Altonau.

The statement should be dated 9 September, the day the Nogai suspects were delivered to the Nogai District Office. Iaachsekilde and his associates are free, travelling around, speculating, and are seldom home.

30. Alexanderwohl Village Office to Johann Cornies. 12 September 1825. SAOR 89-1-870.[8]

To the Authorized Representative, Johann Cornies, Ohrloff,

Petition:

Need compels us, the village community of Alexanderwohl, to seek help from you because our land problem is well known to you. Our land is very narrow, and most of it is too far from the village to be of use, and we cannot survive on the usable land located close to the village.

We did declare to the government in writing that we were satisfied with this land, but at that time we were unfamiliar with it and did not wish to appear as dissatisfied inhabitants. Now, however, we realize that we have been nearly ruined, our livestock is dying, we do not have enough pastureland, and the livestock cannot be adequately watered at the far end of our allotment. During the summer of 1824, we suffered a considerable loss. We are now in danger of losing the small means we brought from Prussia and also our assistance grant. We fear we will be removed from our hearth-sites and will be left with nothing.

Should you still have the sympathetic attitude you expressed to us on 29 January 1824, we would seek your help. At that time, you kindly advised us to establish a sheep farm and to petition the District Office to find water in this area. We did as you suggested, but a resolution of the matter remains outstanding.

We ourselves looked for water on our land and then in the Gobotko ravine, but found none. This cost us much money, money inhabitants in other villages can apply to [the construction of] their buildings. Now we are cut off from the ravine by the village founded between us and Tokmak, and our hopes of getting water and establishing a sheep farm have been lost forever.

We humbly request that you give careful consideration to our situation, show us your neighbourly love, and rescue us from total

8 Regarding the Alexanderwohl land dispute, see also documents 25, 26, 31, and 95.

destruction. If this cannot be done without reporting to the Committee, we humbly request that you represent us before that body and seek a solution for us. We are convinced that the high authorities would not settle people on land they cannot use.

In the firm hope that you will assist us in finding an early resolution to our sad situation, we obediently sign ourselves,

Mayor Heinrich Kroeker, Deputy Schmidt, Deputy Heinrich Block
Alexanderwohl, 12 September 1825

31. Johann Cornies to Alexanderwohl Village Office. 22 September 1825. SAOR 89-1- 63/24.[9]

To the Alexanderwohl Village Office,

Report:

I reply to your petition of 12 September as follows. In my judgment, and despite my goodwill, I cannot improve the location of your village without causing injury to your neighbours. Complaints that your livestock died of hunger last summer cannot be taken into consideration. Otherwise, three times as much land and more would have to be assigned for your village. Even this would not be sufficient during a drought (whom God wishes to punish). The cause of your ruin is not what you have described.

As is my duty, I will present your request to the District Office, asking it to review your situation on the map as well as on location. If your situation can be improved without injury to another village, this will be considered by the District Office and by me.

Cornies

32. Johann Cornies to Andrei M. Fadeev. 29 September 1825. SAOR 89-1-63/25v.

To Fadeev,

Report:

Yr. Honour, I am pleased to report that last week I was able to begin my authorized task of searching for water by drilling in the Taschenak ravine and to locate suitable sites for village settlements there, etc.

9 Regarding the Alexanderwohl land dispute, see also documents 25, 26, 30, and 95.

There are convenient locations for settlements in the Tashchenak, the first for 180-fut (thirty-faden) hearth-sites in two rows, and the second for the same.

In the Orta Otluk, the first location can provide 80-by-180-fut hearth-sites in two rows, or in a cruciform layout, while in the second site there are twenty 180-fut hearth-sites, partly in one row, partly in two rows.

In the Ovrakh of the Orta Otluk, and at its peak, there are forty to fifty 180-fut hearth-sites, partly in two rows and then in one row.

In the Ahis Otluk there are twenty 180-fut hearth-sites in one row.

All of these locations are surveyed and provisionally marked with mounds, because it cannot yet be ascertained whether water will be found in each. This report must also be considered provisional. Once a search for water is done, I will be able to provide more definitive information as to whether water is present by drilling at shallow or greater depths, and will report the information to Your Honour in detail.

Johann Cornies

33. Johann Cornies to Semenov. 29 October 1825. SAOR 89-1-63/25.

The Honourable Deputy of the Ekaterinoslav Guardianship Committee, Mr. Semenov,

According to a communication of 29 October from the [Molochnaia] Mennonite District Office, I am to send Jacob Olinskii, a colonist in my employ, to you in Orekhov by 30 October.

It is impossible for me to do this by the date specified. Olinskii is at present the manager of land I lease at the Baden settlement in Mariupol District. I am having him summoned now, but I request that Yr. Honour not be angered if Olinskii arrives in Orekhov several days late.

I further request that Yr. Honour regard Olinskii's matter before the court positively and extend your protection to him. Olinskii has been in my service for the past two years and has at all times behaved in an honest, sober, and orderly fashion. For this reason, I have put an important part of my establishment under his management. I urgently request that you release him as quickly as possible. Otherwise, I will suffer losses.

In the hope that Yr. Honour will grant my request,

Cornies

34. Johann Cornies to Andrei M. Fadeev. 4 November 1825. SAOR 89-1-63/26.

Your Honour,

I have the honour to report that I found water at no great expense, using a ground auger built of wood, which can be moved from place to place with little difficulty. It can be operated by eight men and can drill ten to eleven sazhen on a day as short as is normal for this time of year. The government's heavy iron auger, on the other hand, requires at least twenty-five men to operate with great additional effort and expense.

Using the auger I invented, I found water in the Tashchenak in two spots at a depth of ten arshins: at thirteen arshins on site No. 1, and at nine arshins in one spot of site No. 2. In Orta Otluk, the levels were thirteen arshins at site No. 1, twenty-six arshins at site No. 2, and twenty-one arshins at site No. 3. In the Ovrakh of the Orta Otluk, at its peak, water was found in three spots at thirty-three arshins at site No. 1, fifteen at site No. 2, and forty-one at No. 3.

The Ahis Otluk is an uncomfortable location for a village site, and the ground is so rocky it is impossible to look for water with the ground auger. Therefore, I did no sampling in this ravine and turned my attention to the Ovrakh of the Orta Otluk. From its peak, the Ahis Otluk can be used easily and comfortably by settlers.

We now need the land surveyor, with whom I can divide, lay out, and mark the village with ploughed furrows. Following instructions, I can then determine the village centres, proceed to dig wells, and divide the village land into sixty desiatina hearth-sites, marking them with ploughed furrows.

Wells cannot be lined with wood this autumn because of a wood shortage. Especially thick planks are needed to make deep wells durable and long-lasting. A simple inexpensive pump could be constructed to provide settlers and livestock easier access to water.

35. Johann Cornies to Samuel Contenius. 5 December 1825. SAOR 89-1-63/29.

Mr. Contenius,

I have the honour to send Your Excellency two small wool samples. They are supposed to have come from the finest and best merinos in Switzerland and France.

I obtained these samples with the assistance of a trading firm in Basel, and also the two letters (the originals are enclosed) from the owners of these Spanish merinos. Your Excellency will see the degree of fineness of the wool and the prices of the wool itself, of cloth manufactured from it, and the sale price of merinos on the spot, etc.

Over the past several years, I have made the acquaintance of this trading firm in Basel through an exchange of letters. Recognizing the firm's honesty, I ventured to request their services in obtaining several small wool samples from the very finest and most genuine merinos in Switzerland and France, and also information on the price of the merinos and their wool on the spot, etc. I pursued these inquiries because I was interested in discovering how our development here compares to sheep breeding in France, where it has been cultivated with great attention and zeal for the last twenty-five years. I wanted to obtain a clear, correct concept of what the specific term "super-fine" wool actually signifies, and the degree to which wool from our best sheep remains inferior to that grade.

I presume to ask Your Excellency to kindly return the wool samples and letters after examining them as requested. If it is not too much of an imposition, you might measure the wool with your gauge (cirometer). This could establish a benchmark for us.

Cornies

36. Johann Cornies and Wilhelm Martens to Peter Wedel, Franz Goerz, and Bernhard Fast. 11 December 1825. SAOR 89-1-63/31.

Esteemed Elders Peter Wedel, Franz Goerz, and Bernhard Fast,

We take this opportunity to respond to your gracious proposal of 13 November for a new edition of the church hymnbook. We are prepared to underwrite the costs of a new edition to meet the needs of our community, and to conduct the needed correspondence until all the books have arrived. You, our esteemed elders, will however understand our just requirement that the capital sums we invest be secured. Our concerns are about the risks involved in the large edition that will undoubtedly be required. The same edition of the book could be published in Prussia at the same time, in numbers that would make the sale price there cheaper. Members of our own community would then be able to obtain this book more cheaply from visiting travellers and immigrants, or order a larger number of copies directly from Prussia. Where would that leave us with our small, special edition of the book? If our books remained unsold, how would we recover our capital investment and interest? We could well be risking the loss of a considerable amount of money.

We obediently submit these doubts for your gracious consideration and deliberation. Please discuss the security you can offer that would enable us to employ our capital in support of a basic need without risking losses. The esteemed elders will not consider these concerns unreasonable, since it is the duty of every person to practise good housekeeping with his property and not be negligent with what has been entrusted to his care.

We are convinced that the esteemed church elders will provide us with the security requested. With respect and obedience, we sign ourselves as humble and willing members of your community.

Wilhelm Martens, J. Cornies

37. Johann Cornies to District Office. December 11, 1825. SAOR 89-1-63/31v.

Report to the District Office in Halbstadt:

This report to the esteemed District Office is a response to a summons from Titulary Counsellor Semenov to appear at Abitochna by 13 December, for an investigation in regard to stolen horses. I spent considerable time among the Nogais this summer looking for stolen horses. My own establishment suffered considerably because I felt obligated to do my part. I am now disinclined to devote even more time to this matter, especially in winter when stormy weather demands my presence here. I handed the horse thieves over to the Nogai commanding officer with dependable and incontrovertible evidence.

I request that the esteemed District Office decline this instruction from Mr. Semenov and allow me to remain peacefully at home and attend to matters I have neglected to do. I am willing to participate in investigations in neighbouring Nogai villages for a day, but I simply will not take part in the entire matter.

Requesting that a report be made to Mr. Semenov on this matter, I respectfully remain,

Johann Cornies

38. Johann Cornies to David Epp, Prussia. 13 December 1825. SAOR 89-1-63/32v.[10]

Dear brother David Epp,

We have not exchanged letters for more than two years and I hope that this is not for reasons that might be considered disagreeable. For my part, it was simply because of the weight of my official duties.

I have now been officially commissioned to write to our community in Prussia. Since I do not know whom to approach, I am so bold as to inform you, dear brother, about a proposal I received on 19 November 1825 from the Lord Chief Curator of the Guardianship Committee for the Colonists in southern Russia, Lieutenant General Inzov. He visited me to discuss, among other things, a settlement in Bessarabia. He considered my proposal to found a new Mennonite settlement in the aforementioned province and responded positively.

I am now asking you, my good friend, if emigrants might be found in Prussia who were interested in settling in Bessarabia, to live under the same administration and rights that we enjoy on the Molochnaia. The settlers would have to be good, economically successful farmers, able to pay for their own transportation to the new location, and to finance their own construction and development. No financial assistance could be expected from the Imperial Crown. Such support has also ended here on the Molochnaia. This area has advantages over the Molochnaia area in that the soil is of better quality and it is also closer to Odessa, an export centre. There are no forests on the land chosen for settlement, but they are not far away. There is sufficient water of good quality.

The number of families might range from fifty to one hundred. The Russian Imperial Embassy in Prussia would assist their departure, but a detailed declaration of the settlers' monetary and other wealth must first be sent here to show their serious intentions. If enough families are found – certainly no fewer than fifty – and they request more detailed information, I am prepared to visit Bessarabia this coming summer (unless important events intervene) to inspect the land, travel across it, and make accurate maps to send to Prussia. This would give those interested in settling an exact idea of the nature of this area.

10 The Bessarabian settlement project discussed in this letter occupied Cornies for three years, before it ultimately foundered as a result of the Russo-Turkish war (1828–9): see also documents 61, 64, 66, 80, 81, 85, 86, 104, and 148.

This is an important subject that needs reflection and deliberation. I would advise potential immigrants to first select a dependable man to conduct a thorough correspondence, to make detailed inquiries, and to demand information, but this should under no circumstances be done simply to satisfy one's curiosity. Experience has taught me that permitting everyone the freedom to write letters and ask questions wastes time and accomplishes nothing.

Please consider this proposal and make it public. I will certainly provide thorough and accurate information as required. To begin, I would like to know if there is an interest in this proposal. Please respond as quickly as you can so that I can make more detailed inquiries, etc.

39. Johann Cornies to Koshani. 20 December 1825. SAOR 89-1-63/33v.

Esteemed Mr. Koshani,

Please forgive me for taking the liberty of inquiring about the agricultural operations at Tsarskoe [Selo]. Given the sheep farm's good management, I am interested in knowing how the physical structure of the merinos is maintained and improved, and also in the fineness of their wool. Do climate and locality have a marked influence on them? Have they increased in number? Will you be selling merinos this coming year? How many rams and ewes? What was this year's selling price for their wool and the return per head? I would appreciate answers to these questions. Please let me know if you have established an Institute for Shepherds, how many apprentices it takes on, what they must pay, etc.

Several of the merinos I purchased in 1824 from the Tsarskoe [Selo] sheep farm for our communities died of anthrax immediately upon arrival at home. I know that only four of the ten rams, and six of the ten ewes, are still alive on our sheep farm. More have survived on the Khortitsa and Gruenthal sheep farms, which each obtained the same number of merinos.

When I arrived home on 11 August 1824, it was extremely hot and dry here. Grasshoppers had ravaged the area, consuming everything in sight, and no blade of grass, green or dry, could be found anywhere. This great change devastated the organisms of these animals, even though they survived the march well. Those still alive today are healthy and robust. This area and climate apparently suit them well. For this reason, I regret that we could not obtain a larger number of these same merinos.

The summer of 1824 was dry and grasshoppers consumed everything still growing. Grain and fodder shortages soon followed. Winter started with the worst snowstorm any of our oldest inhabitants could remember and many thousands of livestock died. I myself lost 1,000 head of improved Spanish sheep, 200 horses from my stud farm, and forty head of cattle. I estimate my loss at no less than 30,000 rubles. Thank God, everything turned out well again this past summer. Grasshoppers did not cause any damage, and we again have sufficient food for humans, and fodder for our livestock.

We had the good fortune to welcome His Majesty, the Tsar, to our villages on 22 October. His Majesty deigned to enter my home as well, to speak with me, and to enjoy a cup of tea.

Your love and friendship remain unforgettable in my memory. I respectfully await an early answer and remain your servant,

J.C.

P.S. How is your esteemed brother? Please give him many greetings, and also greet Mr. Ude in the Tsarskoe ribbon factory, if this is not too difficult. I would very much like to know how they are.

40. Johann Cornies to Diedrich Warkentin. 27 December 1825. SAOR 89-1-63/36v.

To Diedrich Warkentin, Altonau,

The active, honest zeal on behalf of the general well-being that animates your sensitive nature motivates me to write to you about an idea I have to establish a generally useful emergency assistance fund for the Molochnaia Mennonite community.

The impulse for this idea came to me when we spent a night together in Gnadenheim while travelling around the villages. I have been developing this proposal ever since. I sincerely value your solid reasoning and zeal to improve life in our community, and I hereby send you a copy of my idea, which you may keep. Please consider possible changes and amend it as required. Even if the result is not precisely this idea, something similar may emerge that is of general benefit.

To the extent that we seek the general good and not our own self-interest, we have no right to bury our capital. We must increase it as best we can in the general interest, so that our capital will also appear as positive on the great judgment day.

Let me faithfully and candidly declare to you that my overall goal is to help promote everything that is generally useful, according to my best insights. Nothing frightens me from pursuing this objective, be it ridicule, scorn, or contempt to the greatest degree. With God's benevolence, I will continue to devote myself to working energetically and actively for whatever advances the general well-being, and is to the best advantage of the state in which we live.

Were I permitted to explain to our community, briefly or in detail, the dispositions of many high officials to limit the freedom of the Mennonites, the community would complain about injustice. Yet, it could be demonstrated that nothing less is taking place. Therefore, my good friend, to the extent that it lies in our power, let us seek to avert anything that does not serve the general and individual good. This should not be out of fear, but out of love for our fellow man, so that, when we are old and at our gravesides, we will be calm in the knowledge that we have always worked, or intended to work, according to our best judgment.

With heartfelt greetings and sincere love, I remain your honest friend,
Cornies

1826

41. Daniel Schlatter to Johann Cornies. Undated [probably 1826]. SAOR 89-1-84/11.[1]

Beloved friend,

Thank you for your faithful love that has provided me with so much, and heartfelt thanks to my Heavenly Father and provider. I am grateful for the short conversation I had with the Governor General about continuing my undisturbed life among the Nogais (at least as far as humans can foresee). He was gracious, approved my plan, and assured me of his protection. May his few words have fruitful results for the Nogais. In the past, God has done more for me than I could ask and everything is in his hands. I am especially obliged to Mr. Fadeev, who kindly introduced me to His Excellency. Please use every opportunity to assure him of my gratitude, respect, and devotion.

---

1 This letter is oblique and difficult to interpret without additional context. Schlatter had come to New Russia without any formal sponsorship, and his religious views were too eccentric for any of the main missionary organizations to accept him. Before coming to New Russia, he had applied for membership in the Basel Missionary Society, but he was refused. At the time he wrote this letter, he was contemplating becoming a Baptist, and thereby gaining financial support from the British Baptists, but the Baptists also rejected his application. Without direct financial support, he was reduced to appeals to private benefactors; he received gifts of money from the Basel Missionary Society, an unnamed missionary society in Berlin, and he borrowed significant sums from Cornies. In this letter, he suggests that his solution might be to return to Switzerland and take up his old job at a Swiss trading house.

My love for the Tatars is great, as is, especially, my love for my good Ali and his family. I suffer at the thought of being parted from them, even for a short time. How he continues to struggle and cannot find peace.

I am astonished to learn that the letter I wrote to London was delayed. This was not blind fate. At the time, my heart was in turmoil after getting a few letters from my dear mother. The last one, in particular, was full of worries. Even worse, she cannot dare complain. She must bear her worries secretly in her heart, and runs the risk of being misjudged by her friends. Matters are partly hidden even from my two brothers, although they give her their support. I am happy to provide her with a little comfort and some happiness. This is my greatest duty as a child. If I thought it would make any difference, I would gladly make every sacrifice, abandoning my own wishes and returning to the position I previously occupied. The main reason for her suffering is what led me in the first place, after years of waiting, to live among heathens or Muslims, as I wished. If I were now to return to be with her, she would be mortified, and there would be much disunity and evil in our family. Only God can help. But He who today imposes a heavy cross on my dear Mother will help tomorrow, as His word promises. Of this I am confident [rest of sentence illegible].

I am troubled at the thought that I am neglecting my duties. Perhaps I could best support her by making her less dependent on me, more self-sufficient. Since reading the last letter from my beloved mother, I cannot forget the words of scripture: "He who does not provide for his own, especially for the people in his house, has denied his faith and is worse than a heathen. It is a clean and undefiled worship of God to visit widows and orphans in their distress. A widow's tears may well run down her cheeks as she cries out against the one who has caused this suffering. A believing widow must have support in order that a righteous widow may not suffer want."

Imagine, dear friend, her tender, her sensitive heart. Surely you know the obligations that a child owes his mother. Put yourself in my position and my state of mind. My mother does not deserve to suffer shortage, because she is, as scripture describes, a righteous widow: "A righteous widow in her loneliness puts her hope in God and continues her prayers and supplications day and night." These words best and most truly depict my mother. You know what it means to live within a community, and also how oppressive hidden poverty can be. My mother does not suffer from a want of food, clothes, and shelter. It is impossible to describe the pressures upon families when they have lost their wealth but continue to live in the same style and circumstances in order that they might maintain their previous position. Still, I must admit that my mother, who has lived a spendthrift and luxurious life, could well do without many things.

Should a child try to change the failings and weaknesses of an otherwise pious mother if God gives him the means to do so? Why does God give him these means? It is especially hard on my dear mother when she cannot be charitable to the poor, as she would like. In the past she could easily provide unlimited help, which she no longer does because she suffers shortages herself.

I cannot expect more from my brothers than what they are already doing. And even if they could do more, it would give me sweet pleasure to at least do my part. The fact of the matter is that she lives in someone else's home, and to spare herself greater grief, cannot reveal her shortages even to her two brothers. They are quite different from her in character and viewpoint. Given our great friendship, I can tell only you about these matters in writing. Were this knowledge to fall into the hands of certain of my relatives, my mother's position would worsen a lot. But could I write about all of this openly, I would soon find sufficient support for my mother. A few rich friends who are a little acquainted with these circumstances always give her support. However, her last letter, among other things, reads: "Because of certain comments by N.N.N. that I am not in any need, these sources are disappearing. I continue to trust in the Lord. He will not forsake me." Money could not eliminate her greatest suffering, but would provide the means to alleviate many of her physical sufferings and those of her household.

Missionary associations work on the principle of supporting the missionary himself and not his relatives. Were I to accept money, part of which would go to my mother, I would then have to answer to demands made on me that I cannot fulfil because of my inner vocation. I cannot be designated a missionary for the sake of money. It should also be mentioned that I do not have the vocation, the anointing, nor the ability to teach things that are in agreement with the agency providing the money. I would like to discuss my own and my mother's situation with dear Angas and several other friends in England.[2] I hope to acquire means from a dear friend in Germany and from others in

2 "Angas" is W.H. Angas, the prominent British Baptist missionary organizer, who encouraged the British Baptists to recruit Schlatter as a missionary and who personally provided Schlatter with financial support. See Angas' letter dated 24 September 1823, printed in *Baptist Magazine*, 1824, 490–1.

England that would, if it is God's will, provide her with regular support in future.

There are many things that do not surprise me, but there is also much that I cannot find out. The letter from Angas prepared me for this, but it might be better not to give advance notice. I mentioned to the Governor General that I was thinking of travelling to England and then to establish myself in Russia, provided I were granted permission. He kindly promised me his help, saying that he himself was travelling to London. Secretary Levchime gave me his own address in Odessa so that I might turn to him should His Excellency have left before I reach Odessa.

My journey to London has another important purpose, to join a Baptist congregation (not in secret but without drawing attention to myself).[3] My decision is not yet totally firm. Once I have made detailed inquiries and investigated matters personally, I will decide on the spot. I do not owe anyone an accounting. I am happy to inform you about my thoughts, however, for my own benefit, since you are my confidant, and in order that you might give me your response to the following propositions:

1. My principle is that I cannot openly acknowledge a church or have people consider me as a member of a church that has a confession of faith, teachings, and arrangements for worship that offend my principles, or if I find that I disagree with individuals in the church.

2. I am not trying to find the one true Christian church in any existing temporal church or congregation. I think that many different churches and congregations include members of Christ's church who consider Christ to be their head, as God became flesh, who died to pay for their guilt and their sins. They consider him to be sitting on the right hand of God, a living intermediary and saviour. They can only come to God and find justification and holiness through Him. Still, I consider it proper (though nothing is perfect) to join a church that I can accept as better and to acknowledge this openly.

3. I do not therefore consider the Baptist church to be the only one that provides salvation, but I feel that its congregational structure and administration, as well as its articles of faith and its teachings, are generally more in agreement with God's word and with the teachings and structures of the first Christian church, than those of other churches. Although I prefer other churches regarding some individual matters or on certain points, I have long found myself in agreement with

3 The Baptists rejected Schlatter due to his undoctrinaire religious beliefs, detailed in the present letter. See *Baptist Magazine*, 1827, 344.

[the Baptists] on several very important issues. I have actually never belonged to the Reformed Church (into which I was born, though it was not my choice). Therefore the step that I take cannot be called a withdrawal from a congregation, but simply my public admission to a church to which I have belonged ever since I understood God's word, and whose principles I have long acknowledged.

4. As a member of human society, living on earth as flesh and blood, subject to vanity, but also subject to many useful and highly necessary measures taken by the state, I see that my own writing induces me to acknowledge one of the temporal churches now in existence. If this is the case, and as long as I have the freedom to do so, why should I not acknowledge the church I consider to have the best confession of faith and organization? It would, on the other hand, only be indifference to religion and the church to allow myself to be considered a member of a church whose principles I do not accept, from whose precepts I have distanced myself, and against which I must openly speak.

5. It is probable that I will settle in Russia forever. If I wish to pursue my main purpose, I will establish myself in Russia and no longer live as a foreigner in the country of my choice. Then, however, I will no longer be able to join another church or community. My membership will be what is listed in my papers and I must remain there and be treated according to its rules of conduct – for example, military service, and swearing of oaths. I cannot claim to belong to the Reformed Church. My deeds must testify to what I believe, and I should live by them as best I can. I can now have my registration changed from Reformed to Baptist without scrutiny in England, and in this way prevent many evil consequences (at least from a human perspective). Granted, this is a human viewpoint, but it is applied human intelligence.[4]

42. Biography of Daniel Schlatter (draft in secretary's hand with revisions in Cornies' hand). Undated [probably 1826]. SAOR 89-1-873/1.[5]

Daniel Schlatter, a merchant's son from St. Gall in Switzerland, received a Christian upbringing and education from his parents and became an outstanding youth in his city and surroundings. As the senior trading

4 The letter ends here. It was probably written in 1826, because Cornies received a letter from Schlatter in 1827 that refers to his visiting in Switzerland at the time.

5 This biographical sketch is appended to the preceding letter from Schlatter.

official and bookkeeper in an important merchant firm in St. Gall, he conducted the business of his employer for fifteen years until it became a matter of conscience for him. He heard about the Molochnaia area in Russia and got the idea of going to work there among the nomadic Nogai Tatars. Not to his own advantage, but only out of sympathy for these poor people, he tried to introduce among them moral behaviour through his exemplary lifestyle and the use of his own limited powers, even though he could not help more than one family.

He was sent to me by the Mennonite trading firm van der Smissen, in Altona, near Hamburg, to be commended further to the Nogais. I suggested that he seek employment with an energetic Nogai agriculturalist, Ali-Ammetov, in the Nogai village of Second Burkut. Although he did not understand their language, he was able to gain their love and trust through his own good conduct. Dressing like a Nogai to avoid offence, he was better able to observe them. He worked faithfully as a servant for his Nogai master, making a great effort to assist the neglectful Nogais. He attended the church service in Ohrloff almost every Sunday, or else kept company with Germans, who could give him no other testimony than as a good, faithful, industrious, and accountable man.

He devotes whatever time he can spare from the above activities to the study of the Nogai language. One sees him at this business, happy and contented. He does no proselytizing among the Nogais. He is not a missionary nor is he dependent upon a missionary organization. He rarely gets letters, except from his family. He is not concerned with the state or anything otherwise extraneous, but only to be useful. He is making considerable progress with the language, but since he does not wish to neglect his duties in agriculture, the time he has for study is limited. In general, he endeavors to understand the external order of the Nogais in a practical way: the obstacles to moral living and morality their culture represents, what the Muslim influences represent, and how he can influence Muslim people and their rulers and lead them to true culture.

43. Daniel Schlatter to Ali. Undated [probably 1826]. SAOR 89-1- 84/15.

My dear Ali,

How are you and yours? I love you all very much and hope that you are well, spiritually and physically. I will be thinking of you especially when I am in Stambul [Istanbul], that was once your home, but I think of you every day.[6] My heart was in shreds when we said our farewells. Partings from Christian friends are painful, but it is even more painful to part from a Muslim whose well-being is so close to my heart and whom I love like a father. Over the last four years I have come to recognize that, in the midst of life's sufferings, the poor human heart can find no peace in your beliefs and no true solace or joy in looking towards a future life. It tears at my heart that you are not at peace, not happy. You blame others, but I am asking you to examine yourself. God will show you that you are not on the right path. I pray to God daily that I might be united with you forever, and with your wife and children, and that not one of you will be lost. May God grant it.

With 1,000 greetings for you, dear Ali. Adieu!

44. Samuel Contenius to Johann Cornies. 4 January 1826. SAOR 89-1-88/44.

Honoured Johann Cornies,

I have received samples of two kinds of wool you obtained from abroad. Your effort is praiseworthy. These samples are essential to forming a correct concept of "very fine" and "extremely fine" wool. The value of this wool is six to ten times greater than the wool now produced in our settlements.

The sample from the Raz sheep farm near Croissy is finer than any wool I have ever seen. I must point out that prices for such wool are almost as high as those for silk. It is remarkable that a kilogram (or two funt) sells for twenty-five francs or twenty-five rubles. This is enlightening for anyone who knows that cloth can be manufactured at a price of six rubles per arshin, or at thirty rubles.

I consider it necessary that you, honoured Cornies, endeavour to obtain wool samples from full-grown, extremely fine Saxon "electoral" merinos.[7] It is well known that the enlightened Saxons have made clear-eyed observations of the natural processes in the refinement of

---

6 "Stambul" is probably Istanbul, through which Schlatter passed on his journey home to Switzerland.

7 "Electoral" merino sheep refers to the merino sheep imported from Spain to the electorate of Saxony in the eighteenth century. They produced an extremely fine wool, regarded as the best quality wool produced in the German states. See Peter Horst and Wolfgang Leucht, "Quality Measurements in Old and Recent Fine Wool Merino Breeds," *EFFN News* 1 (August 1997), 8–12.

wool. Their many experiments in cross-breeding various types of rams and ewes have reached the point where Saxon wool now ranks near the top with respect to fineness and quality. Wool from France is ranked second, and Spanish wool third, in quality.

What purpose does the acquisition of such wool samples serve? It is none other than to arouse a desire for a breed to refine our herds to the level where a pud of our wool is valued at prices of 100 to 150 rubles. This is surely possible if the correct viewpoint is taken on this matter. How can this be accomplished? Income from the brandy lease and from the community sheep farm should no longer be irresponsibly dispersed or wasted. Also, half the community herd should not be allowed to die of hunger or incurable illness. Instead, an honest and serious effort must be made, in accordance with our august government's benevolent intention, to obtain a profitable and enduring advantage from sheep breeding for every single inhabitant in the District.

Many will object that a large sum of money is needed to purchase the merino breed essential for such high refinement, and correctly so. There is no doubt that at least 30,000 rubles are required for the first purchase, and another 3,000 ducats after several years. I hear people say that they cannot possibly raise such a monstrous sum. Those who think in this way must examine their consciences and admit that profits from the brandy lease are 15,000 rubles, and those from the community sheep farm almost 14,000. The total is therefore about 30,000 rubles annually. They must further admit that a well-regulated administration could increase this income from year to year, improving the community's well-being and that of every single inhabitant in the District. I challenge anyone to find my opinion erroneous or false, and let it be a well-founded and reasonable refutation. I will thank anyone who can convince me of my error.

What is there to lose by purchasing highly refined merinos for 30,000 rubles? The illegal, useless squandering of 800 or 900 pails of brandy annually must be stopped. Brandy purchases must be increased as much as possible in the community and the proceeds applied to the advancement of the general well-being according to government laws.

What could be gained in this way? Annual incomes of the poorest family heads would rise by 300 to 400 rubles, for those with more insight and energy by 800 to 900 rubles and for those best able to calculate the advantages, by several thousand rubles. I recommend to everyone who believes himself to be truly concerned with the community's well-being that he reflect on this matter. I would therefore charge you,

Johann Cornies, to ensure that the contents of this letter are understood by the Wool Improvement Society at its next meeting and that they are added to the minutes.

Since I assume that you do not understand these two interesting French letters, I am sending you translations of both on condition that you return them to me after you have made copies. I need the originals and the wool samples for a little while longer. I hope you will come to pick them up yourself.

After wishing you a Happy New Year, made joyful through God's blessings, I remain your honestly affectionate,

S. Contenius.

4 January 1826, Ekaterinoslav. Received January 9

45. Johann Cornies to Andrei M. Fadeev. 10 January 1826. SAOR 89-1-82/3v.

Observation:

There are several good, authentic Dutch cows in our villages, and each produces no fewer than nine to ten puds of good butter, or fifteen to sixteen puds of cheese in one year, under conditions of correct, efficient milking, and clean, tidy management of the milk itself. This assumes the cow has a good, regular build, is healthy, is at the best and strongest age, and has ample pasture and healthy, nutritious winter fodder.

Naturally, such an average cannot be counted on from ten or more cows, because among ten cows, there will also be some that are younger or older and organically varied to some degree. These would give less butter on average. It is obvious that illness produces great changes in the flow of milk. Variations can be expected from the cows in question, when they may give insufficient milk for days or weeks, even with the best attention and handling.

46. Johann Cornies to Samuel Contenius. 4 February 1826. SAOR 89-1-82/6v.

His Excellency, the Acting State Counsellor, Mr. Contenius,

I am honoured to return to Your Excellency the copies you kindly sent me of two French letters translated into German. At the same time, I report that on 2 February, a general meeting of the Wool Improvement Society and the District Office was held at the Kurdushan community sheep farm. After the meeting was opened, I slowly and clearly read Your Excellency's honoured letter of 5 January, and explained its contents as best I could. I made clear the great disadvantage for the community that arises from the free distribution of 800 pails of brandy. Money produced by selling it could be added to the general treasury and be used, with other savings, to purchase pure-bred and extremely fine merino sheep, ewes, and rams, to the advantage of individuals and the community in general.

The Society and District Office members unanimously affirmed that they understood these matters and everyone showed his willingness to make every effort to persuade the community to end the free distribution of brandy. It was agreed that these and similar sums should be directed to the treasury in order to make important purchases of extremely fine merinos abroad for the community's well-being. I am sufficiently familiar with the thinking of Society and District Office members to believe that they can be depended upon to carry out their declarations.

I also report to Your Excellency that Johann Wiens' wife in Ohrloff has recovered completely from her illness. The box of vetches Your Excellency kindly sent me is of the same kind as ours. We have had little snow until now and winter seeding has not suffered to date.

With the most complete respect I remain, to the end of my life, Your Excellency's obedient servant,

Johann Cornies

47. District Office to Johann Cornies. 11 February 1826. SAOR 89-1-88/27.

No. 173.

The Ekaterinoslav Guardianship Committee has instructed this District Office to notify you of its directive No. 263, of 26 January, in response to your petition regarding the collection of money owed you by the Nogais Atvbirir Musaka and Ialabat Manuambet for horses you sold them, plus the accrued interest. It has asked the Nogais' chief commanding officer to order the above to pay the money owed without delay. This will help to maintain the trust that Mennonites have until now had in their neighbours. He is to inform the Committee about the results.

You are herewith notified of this instruction.

District Office in Halbstadt, 11 February 1826

District Chairman Klassen

48. Johann Cornies to Heinrich Heese. 13 February 1826. SAOR 89-1-82/7v.

Dear brother Heese,

I hasten to answer your communication of 3 February in regard to the forwarding of your community's Spanish wool to the Moscow merchant firm for sale on consignment. This firm is known for its honesty and promptness in business affairs. It accepts sound merchandise on consignment and promotes its sale at the highest price in return for a very reasonable commission. The agent is prompt and orderly in the conduct of his correspondence.

Should your community decide to entrust its wool to the above firm on consignment, I think it advisable to correspond with the firm first (as you mention in your letter) and obtain its agreement. I have already explained how the quality of the Khortitsa community wool compares to other wool. Therefore, only a letter to the firm asking it to sell your wool on consignment is needed. You should further seek the firm's advice as to whether the wool should be washed or unwashed, sorted by quality or by the fleece, so that it can be sold most advantageously. Details on the preferred way to pack the wool for transport and sale must also be requested.

I advise you not to correspond with the firm until it is definite that you will be able to send in your wool. As you will understand, the firm begins to bargain with a consignment of wool as soon as you reach an agreement. If you fail then to send it in, you might have great difficulty in winning the trust of the firm. This would also embarrass me.

I would naturally have liked to drop in on the district chairman when I passed through your area, but it was not God's will. Please do not apologize for my friend not being at home. How could he have known that I was coming? He has a lot of important business to look after without paying attention to things that are of no significance. Please give my greetings and sincere love to him and his dear wife.

We offer our sincerest good wishes on the birth of your child. We ask God, our Father, for your wife's early recovery. Might he keep mother and child in his boundless care.

May He, out of his abundance, pour out his blessings over you, keep you and give you peace through our Lord and Saviour, Jesus Christ. We send greetings to all and remain your brother,

C.

49. Johann Cornies to Traugott Blueher. 15 February 1826. SAOR 89-1-82/8v.

Honoured Mr. Blueher,

It is several months since I last heard from you. My desire for news prompts these lines. The death of His Majesty, Tsar Alexander, has affected us deeply, particularly since His Majesty blessed our villages with a visit only a month before he died. Among others, I also had the great good fortune to attend upon our late monarch with a cup of tea in my home. You can imagine how shocked we were at the news of his death. We praise God, our keeper and ruler. His exalted will is always most excellent for us and His decisions marvellous, even though we may find His ways incomprehensible. Yet His will is holy. May He grant that we sanctify it. Praise be to God that Russia's throne is again filled by a father. As good and loyal subjects, our wishes and prayers should try to support him.

I received the box with bottles of *Lebensessenz*[8] and the book catalogues on 1 January, for which I am much obliged. I would be especially pleased if you could send me four or five similar bottles by mail. We have several invalids here, who have not been able to leave their beds for days and years. With God's help, the *Essenz* seems to have restored their health. If the mail does not accept bottles, please send them along with Mr. State Counsellor Fadeev, who will call on you to make your personal acquaintance. Upon notification, I will send payment by mail.

I advised the Khortitsa Mennonites to place their community wool with you on consignment and they are likely to do so. Their wool is better (as I reported to you last year) than that of the other community.

What about wool prices? I have heard that prices in Prussia fell, but this is probably only for less fine wool. The price for "very fine" wool is more likely to rise than to fall. I received samples of wool from France of greater fineness than any I have ever seen. Last year, this wool sold for twenty-five francs per kilogram (500 rubles per pud), washed cold.

Traces of the thieves who murdered our brethren have seemingly been found.[9] In November, the community delegated me to travel to the Romen [market] area to track down clues regarding the fate of our murdered men, but the authorities in Ekaterinoslav refused to let me go. Just at that time, a Jew was arrested in Ekaterinoslav on suspicion

8 This was probably aqua vitae.

9 Regarding this robbery and the murders, see also documents 28, 79, and 84.

of murder. He confessed that two Jewish robber bands (many or all of whose members he knew) had been in Romen at the time of the yearly market. They had intended to rob a wealthy nobleman. He had spent weeks with the thieves. They had talked about the great profit they had made in Romen, but not about the murder of the Germans. He nevertheless believes that the thieves committed the murder. One of the wagons has not been found yet, but the thieves are said to have left Romen with much money and a good carriage. No one in Romen knows anything about the robbery of a nobleman.

Although we have not been blessed with snow this winter, we have had up to eighteen degrees of frost. Most of the livestock is still out on pasture. I bought several hundred sheep to restore my flock. Only my breeding flock is not yet up to what it was. Food prices are again low: rye from three to four rubles per chetvert, wheat eight, oats three. Much hay has been harvested. The past year has been more abundant than any we have had since our first settlement.

I would be pleased to hear positive reports about Sarepta. What has happened to Mr. Stiebel, whom I met in your honoured house? Has he rethought the ideas he was proclaiming? May God grant it. How are Pastor Kohlreif, Mr. Dietrich, and Mr. Haass, and their families? Still well and contented? Please give them my greetings. Here we cannot praise and glorify the love of our Lord enough. Sincere greetings to you and your beloved wife and children. I strive to be your willing servant,

Cornies

P.S. Every year we produce a few thousand puds of butter and cheese and ship them to Constantinople by sea, where they are sold by Crimean merchants. For years now, war has impeded our communications with the Turks. It has led to smaller markets for our products and lower prices. Might these products find a market in Moscow? I would value your opinion. How might they be sold? What are present prices?

We have no German calendars in our community. Send me one if you can. Mr. Fadeev will probably not reach Moscow before April.

50. Traugott Blueher to Johann Cornies. 8 March 1826. SAOR 89-1-88/22.

My dear friend Cornies,

I take the opportunity to send you an enclosure from St. Petersburg and greet you in friendship, with wishes that this might find you well in body and in soul.

I have not yet received your reply to my letter of 12 October. A reply from you may well have gone lost, since letters from your region arrive irregularly. Have you heard anything in your community about the evildoers who murdered your members? Might there be compensation?

It is almost time for the wool trade to begin and we will see what happens. It seems, at the moment, that only a few merchants will get to your area. Without foreign demand, prices this year may well be lower than last year. Bidders may well appear later in fall, of course. But should merchants appear only in small numbers, prices remain low, and community members seek out more distant markets, I would gladly help your poorer producers of wool. To provide advances to the most needy of your producers, I would be prepared to send 10,000 rubles to the District Office in early May. I should stress that I would accept wool from smaller producers only on the condition that it be accurately sorted and sent as soon as possible. I have no idea if the Moscow market will be better than your markets, but I would assume that your producers would not be out of pocket, at the very least.

If, on the other hand, producers in your community preferred selling only locally, I would be willing to buy up several hundred puds of excellent wool bought there on my account. I would naturally desire that this matter be expedited promptly, since June and July are the best time to trade the new shearing. Finally, I must also mention that it would be useful if the wool from each animal were rolled and bound with twine so that no mixing can take place. This would simplify sorting greatly and make sales easier. Most sheep farm owners now do this work carelessly, and buyers cannot get a good overview of the wool if it is loose or mixed in balls. Purchasers much prefer lots arranged in this way. Once you get in the swing of thus packing your wool, it should not be too difficult to proceed as I have suggested.

One of the two crates of books mentioned in the accompanying communication has already been delivered. Because spring has arrived, with its bad roads, I will wait several weeks before sending it on. I hope it will reach you intact.

Through God's grace we have again remembered the suffering of our gracious Lord and His immeasurable love for us poor, sinful beings. We thank Him for His atonement of our sins in order that, washed in His precious blood and with our sins forgiven, we are permitted, without having earned it, to approach Him by his Grace.

Kindly give brother Schlatter my heartfelt greetings and assure him of my love. Tell him that Pastors Dittrich and Haas will probably leave for the Persian border in two months' time.

Finally, I send greetings to you and your dear family and commend myself to your further loving remembrance as your faithful friend,

Traugott Blueher.

Received 18 April. Answered 19 April.

51. Johann Cornies to Wilhelm Frank. 10 March 1826. SAOR 89-1-82/11.

To Mr. Frank in Ekaterinoslav,

I gather from your letter of 19 February that you have found several contradictions in the thoughts I sent you. I am pleased that you have taken the time to test them. The Bible says: "Test everything and retain whatever is good."

Let me say something about the parts you find contradictory. First of all, my lack of learning is why I cannot always express myself in writing as I would like. Secondly, I cannot recall expressing the idea that Christianity cannot be opposed, that it is incontestable, as you suggest. There is nothing on earth or in heaven so good that it could not be resisted. Thirdly, where does our will come from? In response, I ask: Where do our life, our talents, and our good intentions come from? Fourthly, we know that we are all naturally corrupt. It follows that there can be nothing good in us. Yet, good things can happen through us. That is an entirely different matter. For example, wise rulers surely think about the well-being of society. They know that to ensure peace and order, they must enact laws for their people. Good and unselfish laws must flow out of good hearts, and genuine goodwill cannot be evil if it promotes genuine good. Somewhere in holy scripture it says: "All good and perfect gifts come from above, from our enlightened Father."

Thus, if all good and perfect gifts come from above, they do not belong to man in a wider sense. They are God's, who holds man in his hand and can guide him wherever he chooses, like a stream of water. Therefore, everything good comes from God alone because He is good to us. Good only exists through Him and nothing exists without Him. Therefore, all laws are from God although they are made indirectly by humans. We must consider them as having come from God and follow them accordingly. Anyone resisting the law resists God and His order. We have been granted laws and regulations from God through good human beings who love that which is good.

Evil people intend evil things, resist everything that is good and act in evil ways. Therefore, they can give mankind no good, unselfish laws. Yet if we follow laws faithfully, then we are living according to God's will, as it says: "You shall be holy, for I am holy. You must be as one, just as your Father in heaven is one." If we follow laws in a godly way, then we also love God and our fellow man. On the contrary, if our laws are only seen to be human, we will only follow them out of fear. When we are out of sight of the authorities, we will find enough leeway to permit us to wantonly carry out evil that is contrary to our duty.

The true Christian is a law unto himself, since he only wishes to do whatever is God's will. He does nothing that does not serve his fellow man's salvation. Therefore, he does not fear punishment, because his conscience desires and does only what is good for him and for society generally. He loves everyone and lives for everyone, as God lives for everyone and loves everyone. He prays for emperors, kings, lords, and rulers because he values and loves them, and because God has selected them as leaders and rulers who rule with God on earth. They may have weaknesses and faults, but they are only human. Yet they must order and provide for a variety of things and take responsibility for them. We must love and honour them and not denounce them even if they do not always act righteously, since we do not know what their purpose and their intentions are.

The fault-finder and scoffer against authority must naturally follow the law out of fear of punishment, for he definitely does not do so out of love. Otherwise, he would not be dissatisfied and find fault with every written law. It follows that laws are made for the dissatisfied and obstinate person, but not for the person who acts on them out of love and respect, following the glance and wish of the authority over him with hope and energetic zeal, as though it were a specific order.

So much good has occurred in the thousand years since Christian authority began. In our land, we owe so much to Christianity, as compared to those countries in which the blessed gospel's light has not yet appeared, and our descendants will experience its power even more. We pray, Thy Will be done in heaven and also on earth. I believe that our earthly life prefigures every aspect of our heavenly life, and we can enjoy a foretaste of eternity here.

Paul writes to the Ephesians, chapter 2, 5, and 8: "You have been blessed by His grace, through your faith and not of yourselves alone. It is God's gift." The Ephesians lived on earth at that time, but the apostle praised them because they were contented – completely contented – with what they had received from God, and thus they were blessed. We will also be blessed as the Ephesians were, if we submit to His holy will and are contented with what He bestows on us.

If I have still not expressed my thoughts to your satisfaction, I request that you mark all points that, in your opinion, are contradictory and speak with me in person when I visit you at the beginning of April, God willing. Further discussion about the Christian's usefulness cannot continue until we agree about our opinions.

With respect, Cornies

P.S. I will bring the books I promised you when I come.

52. Johann Cornies to David Epp, Prussia. 10 March 1826. SAOR 89-1-82/14.

To David Epp in Prussia,

The School Society administrators have given me the enclosed letters to send you. I take the opportunity to include a few lines. You will have received my letter of 13 December by now. Please write me about the concerns I expressed in order that I might take appropriate steps and make preliminary inquiries with our authorities about a new settlement in Bessarabia.

I am greatly pleased that an educational institution will be founded in your area. May God bless your good and well-intentioned project and give you perseverance and steadfastness to wait for it to come to fruition, which may only come after many years. Many changes will meanwhile affect the results, yet you must learn to remain steadfast in your beliefs and not be deceived.

If our own school lasts for ten years from the time of its inception, we have a basis for believing that it will develop and endure. It has already had many positive consequences, directly and indirectly. Yet everything that glitters is not gold, so I will not be too generous in its praise. Certainly if we measure results against our Christian guidelines and confidence in the purity of our doctrines, they are still in doubt. The situation would be different if we belonged to another faith.

Our Bible Society has lost its lustre and glory, but I believe that a period of calm is useful for its growth.[10] The original enthusiasts have disappeared, but the members who started with hope remain steadfast,

10 The Russian Bible Society (of which there was a Molochnaia Mennonite branch) was closed by order of the tsar in 1824, but a Protestant Bible Society was permitted to continue.

actively carrying the daily load of their calling. Reeds do not endure as well as oak trees.

Our Bible Society's account in St. Petersburg is more than 6,000 rubles. The sale of books of holy scripture has not yet declined, which means that the Bibles are being read. Last year, sales brought in 672 rubles, 25 kopeks. Sixty-three members paid 227 rubles, 78 kopeks, and donated 29 rubles, 30 kopeks. Our membership is declining. Many individuals are apathetic because no new developments arouse their interests. Too passionate at first, they have now grown cold. In too much of a hurry then, they are now too slow. We children of Adam are like that. Our interest is immediately awakened, but then falls off. We want to accomplish a great deal but cannot endure, beginning things without completing them as we move on from one thing to another. We know a great deal but do little. It would be better if it were otherwise. Thank God, the opposite can also be found among us. The Lord knows who belongs to Him.

Our community is trying to cling to old practices and we are sinking, some more, others less. Wilfulness and fanaticism will cause our privileges here in Russia to be limited, and you in Prussia have contributed to this development. How is it possible to remain indifferent when more than 4,000 [Mennonite] souls [in Prussia] will eventually suffer temporal disadvantages because they are led by a few obstinate spiritual and worldly leaders? An important person vehemently reproached Elder J. Dyck from Khortitsa: "You are the instigators of your own dissension." I find this extraordinarily painful, because we must take the interests of our second and third generations into account. Let us do good to every man, expecting neither glory nor thanks in return.

Snowstorms last winter, 1825, caused great damage but brought us greater benefits for eternity. My loss was no less than 30,000 rubles, but I believe and feel that the Lord permitted this for my salvation. I praise and glorify Him for His goodness to His children.

My brother-in-law, Klaas Dyck, is going to visit his father in Heubuden this spring, and he sends greetings to his old father. This year's winter is a real contrast to last year's, with no snow and little wind. It is warm, with spring-like temperatures as high as eighteen degrees Reamur. Two ploughs were out today. Farewell. Please do not forget me in your prayers.

With love and honesty I remain your obliging brother in Christ,
Cornies

53. Johann Cornies to Semenov. 30 March 1826. SAOR 89-1-82/16v.

His Honour, Mr. Semenov, Deputy of the Ekaterinoslav Guardianship Committee,

Request, from J.C., resident in the Molochnaia Mennonite District:

In August 1825, I hired a Nogai shepherd, Menglak, from the Nogai village Ishebe, at an annual salary of forty-five rubles. We agreed that when he entered my service I would advance him eighty rubles to pay off a previous debt. He was to work off these eighty rubles.

Various small acts of unfaithfulness since then have forced me to keep him under watch. On 24 March, a flock of Spanish sheep was put in his care. He gave a Spanish gelding worth eighteen rubles, to Khora, a Crimean Tatar now staying in the Nogai village Ishebe, to be butchered. His excuse was that it had been carried away by a wolf. My outrider Builuck found the sheepskin on the steppe near the Nogai village of Burkut. It had been skinned in the proper fashion, and suspicion for the theft fell on the Nogai Menglak. He freely admitted giving the sheep, supposedly eaten by a wolf, to the Crimean Tatar, Khora from Ishebe.

I request that Yr. Honour have the Nogai Menglak, and also the above-named Khora, brought before the Nogai Lieutenant Mr. Baraken, and have him punished for theft according to the law.

I remain, with all esteem and respect, Yr. Honour's most obedient servant,

Johann Cornies

54. Traugott Blueher to Johann Cornies. 30 March 1826. SAOR 89-1-88/24.

My dear friend Cornies,

Since mailing my letter of 8 March to you, I have had the pleasure of breaking the seal on your letter of 15 March. Many thanks. With the last mail, I sent you a German book calendar, as you requested, and some sermons on the death of our monarch, Alexander, published by our treasured Pastor Kohlreif. I assume you will read them with interest. Please share them with our treasured brother, Schlatter.

The requested *Lebensessenz* could not be sent by mail. Liquids are not accepted. Mr. Fadeev will bring them along when he comes.

Since your community appears to be hot on the trail of the murderers, it may be possible to recover some stolen property. That is much to be wished for.[11]

You asked about the feasibility of marketing butter and cheese in Moscow. I doubt it would be profitable, mainly because of high freight rates. But both items would sell quickly in appreciable quantities, with prices at ten to twelve rubles per pud for good butter (with a little salt) and ten to twelve rubles per pud for cheese in ten funt balls, with better varieties as high as fifteen rubles per pud.

September is the best time to transport cheese, and December the best time for butter, when the hot days have passed and frosts are still light. December and January are the best months to sell butter (in lots). Moscow merchants usually buy butter on annual contracts, shipping it to other regions. There is no particular month for the sale of cheese, which is generally more limited. Several merchants assured me that willing buyers could easily be found for 1,000 puds at a time.

In my last letter, I informed you in detail about the market for Spanish wool. Trade is still sluggish, since the cold weather kept manufacturers from washing it. There is no foreign demand as of now. Prices are down about 15–20 per cent from those of last summer. Finer varieties are always in greater demand than those of medium quality. I assume that the price of the former will rise more quickly than that of the latter. The finer the wool, the more desirable it is, and its price will always be higher. Fixed prices can only be quoted with samples, since not only the quality is taken into account but also the loss of weight en route.

Life in Sarepta continues on the quiet side. There was a fair bit of construction last year and it is possible that the fire's terrible devastation will no longer be felt in a few years from now.[12] We thank God that in our house, our days are undisturbed and proceed peacefully and calmly, away from the bustle of the city.

I send friendly greetings to you and your valued family and commend myself to your loving remembrance, as your faithful friend,

Traugott Blueher

Answered 19 April.

11 Regarding this robbery and the murders, see also documents 28, 49, 79, and 84.

12 The Sarepta fire of 1823 destroyed most of the village and marked the beginning of a sharp decline in the missionary efforts of the Moravian Brethren in Russia. See Hartmut Lehmann and Hermann Wellenreuther, *In Search of Peace and Prosperity: New German Settlements in Eighteenth-Century Europe and America* (Pittsburgh: Pennsylvania State University Press, 2000), 83.

55. Johann Cornies to District Office. 26 April 1826. SAOR 89-1-82/17v.[13]

The esteemed District Office in Halbstadt,

The three Klassens, Abram, Johann, and Jacob, just visited me to excuse themselves for their behaviour.

I promised the worthy District Office not to submit anything in writing with reference to these slanderous rumours. However, since yesterday, several more letters have arrived that add terribly insulting words to the rumours already circulating about me in the District, among [German] colonists and Russians. I have no choice but to defend my honour by writing to the esteemed District Office and insisting that I be given my due in truth and in justice.

The Klassens defend themselves on the grounds that they only repeated what the Nogai Elias told them, but the law will not recognize this as a defense. They had tried to plunge me into distress on the false testimony of a swindler who is now before the courts and has admitted to various thieving tricks. This false testimony moved along in the following irrefutable manner:

1. When the Klassens were ordered to appear before the District Office on 23 April, they first visited Elias and took along P. Reimer, from Blumenort, to encourage Elias in his slander.

2. Elias visited Abram Klassen in Blumenort yesterday, 25 April. Klassen had arranged to have him repeat his calumny, wondering why he had come today instead of tomorrow, etc.

These events confirm their intention of having me declared guilty of receiving stolen horses. I told them this to their faces, in the presence of the local village officers.

The District Office must recognize that what has taken place is illegal and cannot end without a criminal proceeding. Can absurd lies be substantiated with an appeal to false testimony? This is clearly what happened here. Indeed, such a lack of evidence could lead to decisions in which an innocent person was exiled to Siberia. For this reason, I ask that this matter be handled expeditiously.

Johann Cornies

P.S. I ask the esteemed District Office to question Peter Reimer from Blumenort about his trip to Akkerman. Under no circumstances should he be absolved of his responsibility in this case.

---

13 This is the first of a series of letters that document the controversy surrounding the accusations of horse theft made against Cornies. See also documents 57, 58, and 62.

56. Johann Cornies to Andrei M. Fadeev. 10 May 1826. SAOR 89-1-82/21.

His Honour the Senior Member of the Ekaterinoslav Guardianship Committee, Mr. Fadeev,

Your Honour will graciously forgive me if I venture to impose on you. There have been reports for some time now that the landed Mordvinov estate on the west bank of the Molochnaia River at its mouth will be selling 5,000 to 6,000 desiatinas of land. I have not been able to establish the truth of this report and respectfully request that Yr. Honour kindly make inquiries by writing to the owner of this estate, Vira Nikolaievna, daughter of Admiral Mordvinov, and now wife of the Privy Counsellor Stolypin in St. Petersburg. If the land is for sale, what is the asking price per desiatina without peasants, livestock, and buildings? Also, whom should one here approach to proceed with this transaction? The soil of this land can be considered of medium quality for this region, but the lowland is saline. Since the few head of livestock and the buildings located there are in bad shape, they cannot be used in developing an estate properly and should not be counted as part of the sale.

Interested persons in our community are thinking of buying this landed estate at a low price. In my opinion, it would be advantageous for the future advancement and development of our settlements if wealthy persons were to buy land in this way. I humbly request that Yr. Honour make these inquiries as soon as possible. Please do not regard the burden this places on you in an unkindly way.

Yr. Honour's J.C.

P.S. At a public auction, the lease of the Israelite land went to the highest bidder, W. Martens, Halbstadt, for a term beginning 30 April.[14] However the rent itself was not accepted and awaits resolution by the highly honoured Committee. What can we expect in this matter? May and June provide our main income from this land, since Moscow livestock merchants require pasturage at that time. At other times, there is little other livestock here. I request that Yr. Honour inform me in this regard. With the thanks owed you, I remain Yr. Honour's.

---

14 The "Israelite land" that Cornies refers to was land set aside in 1803 (but never used) for a planned Jewish agricultural colony.

57. District Office to Johann Cornies. 15 May 1826. SAOR 89-1-21/69.[15]

From the Molochnaia Mennonite District Office,

To the Honourable authorized representative for land, Johann Cornies in Ohrloff,

In response to your communication to the District Office of 15 May, a copy is here enclosed of decisions reached by the District Office and the honourable ministerial service about the insult done to you by Jacob Klassen, Isbrand Thiessen, and Isaac Hilbrand. A directive about this matter was circulated in our local community. We hereby request that you again assume your responsibilities in regard to the Committee and the community business incumbent upon you, and complete it according to your best judgment.

In addition, you are hereby notified that the District Office has required that Johann, Jacob, and Abraham Klassen, Isbrand Thiessen, and Isaac Hilbrand appear before you shortly to offer a hand of reconciliation for the insult done you. Please inform them of your readiness for such a reconciliation.

District Chairman Klassen, Deputy Warkentin, Deputy Toews
15 May 1826

58. District Office to village offices. 15 May 1826. SAOR 89-1-89/2.[16]

To village offices in the Molochnaia Mennonite District,

An extremely insulting rumour about Johann Cornies of Ohrloff, authorized representative for surveying, has spread in the local community as well as in the Molochnaia colonist and Khortitsa communities and throughout the whole region – namely, that Johann Cornies is a receiver of stolen horses. Several people with dishonest thoughts magnified these unfounded, provocative lies. When Johann Cornies became aware of them, he felt deeply insulted. On 26 April, in written submission No. 11, he asked the District Office to refer this unworthy accusation to the courts for their judgment. He immediately withdrew from his community responsibilities to the Committee.

15 Regarding the horse thefts, see also documents 55, 58, and 62.
16 Regarding the horse thefts, see also documents 55, 57 and 62.

In keeping with its administrative obligations and duties, the District Office immediately took steps to ensure that justice is done generally and for every individual in particular. The District Office instituted a detailed examination and discovered that this unfounded insult was put forward and circulated by three householders from Tiegerweide: Jacob Klassen, Isbrand Thiessen, and Isaac Hilbrand. According to established regulations, these three must be named in this way. They also implicated the Nogai Elias, from Akkerman. It is not true that this Nogai and others reported this to the District Office. On 31 March, the Nogais Elias, Sanay, and Isthanai Adde personally reported to the District Office that Arik and Abitai, Nogais from Edenochta, and Kokan, from Akkerman, had stolen horses from the Germans. They did not report that Johann Cornies knew about this and that he had received these stolen horses. It is therefore clear that Klassen, Thiessen, and Hilbrand had no purpose other than to slander Cornies, above all because they should have given no credence to statements by Elias, who is himself before the courts for theft.

To ensure that our higher authorities are not informed about this matter, the District Office members have discussed this with the reverend church teachers and have agreed that Klassen, Thiessen, and Hilbrand, as mentioned above, be brought to repentance and reform for the insult they did to Cornies, and that the whole community be so informed. Cornies eventually agreed that this matter should be settled in this way by the District Office and the reverend church teachers, and brought to a conclusion according to their best judgment. The above-named Klassen, Thiessen, and Hilbrand admitted to the District Office and before the community that they were at fault for circulating this insult to Cornies, and that, instead of circulating something they had heard from the Nogais, they should have reported it to the District Office. They have asked for forgiveness.

The District Office and the reverend church teachers, Bernd Fast and Jacob Warkentin, have therefore decided that the District Office should inform the whole community of this matter with the warning that, in future, no one, under any pretext, must be so bold as to utter the insult mentioned above, or any other. If this is not observed, the perpetrator will not receive like treatment but will be reported to the authorities as the source of such an insult, to be punished according to the law. As a record of Johann Cornies' vindication, he is to receive a copy of this directive.

Village offices are hereby ordered to make this directive clearly known to all fullholders, cottagers, and renters in every village, and to urgently impress upon them that no one should utter this or other unfounded insults. Anyone doing so will unavoidably suffer the punishment legally required.

With this settlement, the authorized representative Johann Cornies has agreed to a reconciliation with those who insulted him – Klassen, Thiessen, and Hilbrand – and to resume all Committee and community business incumbent on him to the best of his ability.

District Office in Halbstadt, 15 May 1826

District Chairman Klassen

59. Johann Cornies to Andrei M. Fadeev. 17 June 1826. SAOR 89-1-82/23v.

His Honour, State Counsellor Fadeev,

Yr. Honour has graciously asked me to come to Ekaterinoslav to discuss various subjects before your departure. This is almost impossible for me to do at the present time. Since spring, I have devoted much time to surveying and dividing the village lands. Immediately after that was completed, I spent fourteen days with His Excellency, Mr. Contenius. Today, on the Committee's orders, I must accompany Deputy Semonov to Mr. Beselevskii's khutor in Dneprov Uezd in search of horses stolen from the colonies. I have therefore not been able to pay attention to my own establishment. Now that the hay harvest has begun, I must not lose further time.

I most humbly request that Yr. Honour regard my absence benevolently, knowing I would otherwise carry out, with enthusiasm, anything Your Honour asks of me.

District Chairman Klassen will bring the map of the villages. I wish Yr. Honour and your esteemed family a safe journey and an early and successful return.

I await Yr. Honour's kindness as Yr. servant,

C.

60. Traugott Blueher to Johann Cornies. 20 July 1826. SAOR 89-1-88/31.

Dear friend Cornies,

Your valued communication of 23 June and twenty-two balls of Spanish wool arrived yesterday in good order. The balls in both lots had lost some of their recorded weight due to the exceptional, continuing heat. We will now attempt a successful sale, which I will report to you promptly. I will be happy to work in your interest to the extent of my abilities.

Thank you for kindly reporting this year's wool sales in your region. Such sales are always of interest to me. Since your region is especially suitable for breeding sheep, it is appropriate that purposeful attention there be given to improvements.

I sent you a crate marked "C" with the carter. I include here a note informing you of its contents. I also add the following: Mr. Fadeev, who will leave from here shortly, assured me that several Sarepta products would be eagerly bought in Ekaterinoslav and in the colonies of the area. Should inspection of these goods prove that to be true, I could send these goods on commission to reliable men in Ekaterinoslav and in various of the colonies. Please notify me when it is convenient. Once this business is underway, the merchants in question might pursue the business on their own accounts.

I receive various pamphlets about Christian truths from several Christian friends abroad. These associations bear the publication costs but I pay the freight charges. Voluntary contributions for this purpose are received with appropriate thanks. Should such publications be of use in the colonies, I can send you various books, especially since their prices are insignificant when compared with other books. There is no charge for the enclosed copies.

I am unsure if you still want me to send you the book you requested, since the price has risen to 110 kopeks.

I send you and your dear family friendly greetings and commend myself to your further love and remembrance, as your constantly respectful,

Traugott Blueher.

Received 31 July. Answered.

61. Johann Cornies to Georg Guildenschanz. 21 July 1826. SAOR 89-1-82/30.[17]

Yr. Honour, Gracious Sir, Guildenschanz,

Last year, I was honoured to attend upon His Excellency, General Inzov, and Yr. Honour, providing you with quarters in my home for

17 Regarding the planned Bessarabian colony, see also documents 38, 64, 66, 80, 81, 85, 86, 104, and 148.

the night. Yr. Honour graciously spoke to me then about settlements in Bessarabia. You considered it appropriate to found a Mennonite settlement there, on vacant land available directly under the authority of the most honoured Committee, to serve as a model settlement for colonists already settled there. On 31 December, I immediately informed the entire Mennonite community in the Prussian states of this benevolent proposal. (I enclose an excerpt from that communication.)

I have received a response from the community in Prussia. The aforesaid proposal was publicized among the entire Prussian Mennonite community and to Mennonites scattered on individual farms along the Rhine River. I have been notified that there would definitely be a considerable number of Mennonites interested in settling in Bessarabia if it were possible for them first to sell their properties for cash. At present this seems impossible due to a shortage of money.

I therefore request, on behalf of my brethren in faith, that Yr. Honour might find it possible to have a parcel of unsettled land in Bessarabia designated for Mennonite settlement. Within two or three years, Mennonites from abroad will almost certainly be able to settle on this land in accordance with the august administration's wishes.

Near Culm in West Prussia, a community took over a piece of land forty years ago on a limited lease. Their contract ended this year, 1826, and they are now in a distressing situation. In accordance with an edict of 30 June 1789 affecting Mennonite life in the entire Prussian kingdom, no Mennonite may purchase property from someone of another religion unless he declares himself as a subject with government obligations. The Culm Mennonites cannot accordingly renew their lease unless they assume obligations to the government. They must vacate the land they have made arable without recompense. They will be paid only half the inventoried value of their household buildings and orchards. Nevertheless, I believe that these good, economically efficient managers will have sufficient means to establish themselves respectably in Bessarabia at their own expense.

If it is not too much to request, I would ask Yr. Honour for a small map of the land presumably assigned for settlement by Mennonites and a short description of its quality. What is the distance to the nearest cities? Where can agricultural products be sold? How far away are Kishinev and Odessa? Is wood for construction available, and if so, at what distance and at what price? What other construction materials are available? Are there rivers with flowing water? At what depth can well water be obtained? I will make it my business to explain everything to my brethren in Prussia so that the purposes of the high authorities might be favourably pursued. Several brethren are visiting here from Prussia and they intend to return home in early September. I hope to send the information I receive from Yr. Honour along with them.

His Honour, Mr. Fadeev gave me your most esteemed communication, the booklet by J. Lindl, and also his essay on economic matters. Many thanks. I am interested in trying the latter method of sheep breeding, but I cannot promise that what I observe and describe will be dependable enough to prove anything.

Yr. Excellency's obedient J. Cornies

P.S. Excerpts from D. Epp's letter dated 13 December 1825, are enclosed.

62. Johann Cornies to Daniel Schlatter. 5 August 1826. SAOR 89-1-82/31.

Sincerely beloved [*Inniggeliebter*] Schlatter,[18]

No further letters or news have arrived since you wrote me from the Crimea. Rumour has it that you travelled from Constantinople to London on an English ship, but I have not heard at which port you embarked. Our all-knowing God will accompany you on your long journey and keep your ship from sinking. May He remain in your sight and may you know that His noble intentions, which He himself has laid upon your soul, must guide your every breath and step. And should the sea claim your body, your soul would still reach the same haven as if you had stood on solid ground. My joy rests in the hope that there will be no parting for us in His realm and that, embraced by the love we share for our Lord and Master, we will experience His abundance in eternal, unchanging companionship.

Do not worry that you did not inform me about your departure by sea, because I know that we are united in spirit. You would naturally have told me if time had allowed. I bow before the throne of our omnipotent Creator and Saviour and beg Him to advise, protect, and lead you on your sea voyage and in London, to keep you healthy in body and in soul, and to keep you from submitting to the blasphemies of this world. Only in this way will you accomplish your purposes according to His will.

We praise God that our family is healthy, except for my dear wife who has been down with a fever several times and only managed to leave

18 The salutation is crossed through in the original.

her sickbed today. Envy is the root of the problems I was having in the community when you left, as in the story of Haman and Mordichai.[19] The perpetrators have publicly admitted before the whole community that envy prompted them to slander me and this has been made public in a statement with a forceful warning. I am pleased that my enemy has been defeated and pray that God may awaken his depraved conscience to an understanding that we are all sinners, subject to damnation, and each of us must question his own actions. I thank God that He has, in this way, humbled me and made me worthy of His great love despite my own depravity.

In May, Builuk sold most of his livestock at the Tokmak yearly market for more than 300 rubles, and exchanged the white horse for a mare. This he now regrets. His grain is growing very well and he has mowed quite a lot of hay. But all of this has made him arrogant and hard to get along with, as you prophesied. Fourteen days ago, it was time for the horses to be taken to the yearly market, and matters reached a crisis, just as they had in Burkut about this time last year when you were here. Kokan has certainly never spoken one word about Builuk to me, but Builuk distrusts him. He felt that what I said proved that I had greater esteem for Kokan. And so with barbed words, he turned his back on me and angrily left me and my sheep farm. I called him back twice, but he sent a message that his year was up and I should get my beloved [Kokan] to help me.

Builuk has not been in my house since, but he said many good things about you earlier: "Only now do I fully understand the help Daniel gave me. Now that he is gone I see that what Daniel told me was indeed the truth and I cannot free myself from it. It stands before me like a large mountain." Builuk had meant to buy Spanish sheep from the proceeds of the sale of his livestock, but by early July, didn't have a kopek left. He picked up the fifty rubles you left for him and borrowed another sixteen rubles from my shepherd. I have no idea what he is doing with the money. At this rate, his whole agricultural establishment will be gone in two years. Humbled, he came to me about three weeks ago and asked me to give him sheep on the same terms as those I had given Kokan and Balakai. I do not know if he will take the sheep now.

---

19 An apparent reference to the accusations of horse theft. See documents 55, 57, and 58.

I see now that keeping him in my service is of no benefit to him. But should his stormy behaviour turn into to a gentle breeze, I will do what I can to give him my support. I still doubt whether I should offer him the sheep. I pity him, but I am at my wit's end and do not know what is best for him. His wife recovered completely after the birth of a daughter. He asked me for names and I suggested Sophie, which the Mullah thought blessed, but I'm unsure if this will be her name.

Mr. Contenius was with me twice this spring, fourteen days at a time, and we often spoke lovingly of you. He has urged me strongly to go to Saxony, but I have declined in a friendly way because I am convinced that this project must originate solely from our community. It is not good for our future if we depend only on the administration to promote whatever is to our advantage. We must be watchful ourselves. Who knows for how long we will enjoy an administration that is so well disposed towards us. If we refuse to take the initiative ourselves, we would allow many advantages to slip away. In the presence of Mr. Contenius, I and Martens offered to advance, with interest, 30,000 rubles to the District Office to buy sheep in Saxony. Time will tell if our community opens its own eyes.

Now, my dear brother, I close this communication in the name of our Lord Jesus whom we share, and give thanks to Him who has bound us together through His love. May He allow us to continue to walk in His presence as members of His body, and not cease to praise and honour His Name through our works. I, my wife, and relatives send you many greetings and wish you whatever you yourself wish for in body and soul. We look forward to seeing you here soon, in our home, not for the news you will naturally bring, but to fill the gap that exists in our midst every Sunday. These lines are neither sweet talk nor a formality, but an out-pouring of my faithful heart that loves you at all times.

May Jesus be your alpha and omega, beginning and end. Pray for us even as we do not forget you in our prayers.

Your honest C.

Two letters have arrived for you, a sealed one from Moscow, and another from D. Epp in Prussia. There is nothing from Prince Reusz and Angas.[20]

20 Prince Reusz was an important patron of the Moravian Brethren. "Angas" was the Scottish Baptist W.H. Angas (see footnote 20).

63. Theodor Horwitz to Johann Cornies and brothers. Sent from Duerfelthal, 8 August 1826. SAOR 89-1-88/49.

To the brothers Cornies in Ohrloff, Molochnaia settlement, beloved friends in the Lord,

Though personally unacquainted and separated by great distances, we are close to one another as members of one body through the blood of Jesus Christ. We direct this letter to you not as unacquainted strangers, but as brethren and companions who share one hope.

Some time ago, after the Lord, in His great grace, called us out of the darkness to His wonderful light, He gave us the hope of travelling to Tavrida and the Crimea to use the talents He has bestowed on us. With the passing years, an inner voice exhorted us ever more loudly, and made us certain of our calling.

We thought that brother Molinar, Pastor of the Mennonite congregation in Crefeld, was in close communication with congregations in the Crimea and so we turned to him first. Since this was not the case, he reported our intentions to dear brother D. Epp in Heubuden, who told us to communicate our intentions and desires openly to you, beloved brethren.

I will briefly describe our Saviour's blessed guidance so that you can see where and how we might be of use.

My treasured brother, C. Hausknecht, was born in 1790 in St. Gallen, Switzerland. He dedicated himself to trade and acquired all knowledge necessary to pursue it. He was highly respected by his employer and earning a considerable salary at the time that the Lord called and illumined his soul. In 1822, animated by a deep wish to work in the Lord's vineyard, which he recognized as the Lord's dispensation, he received a call to teach and this calling served as training for his future work. He has worked unselfishly as Christ's warrior and his blessings are recognized.

As the author of this, I – T. Horwitz – was born in 1796 in Landsberg, Brandenburg, to wealthy, Jewish parents, and decided early to study medicine. After attending the gymnasium in Berlin, where I acquired basic knowledge, I studied at the university in Berlin and then in Breslau. It was here that my precious Saviour spoke powerfully to my soul, convincing me that only through Him could my soul find peace and salvation. The Lord provided me, as I was abandoned by my parents, with a refuge here in Duerfelthal where I have lived for the last three years, learning the miller's trade. I feel the joyous call within me to go forth and work for the salvation of my brethren.

Since you, beloved brethren in the Lord, stand as a beacon in a dark place, we hope you will receive us in your midst, and place us as school teachers where you believe we could be most useful to your communities and to other dearly redeemed souls, as our capabilities and gifts allow.

May He, the shepherd and bishop of our souls, Jesus Christ, yesterday, today, and the same in eternity, to whom we have committed our wishes, guide your decisions through His good and holy spirit and give you certainty and joy.

Commending you and all the brethren there to the special grace and guardianship of the Lord, we greet you with the kiss of love,

Theodor Horwitz

Duerfelthal, 8 August 1826

P.S. If possible, share the contents of our letter with H. Heese in Khortitsa. Our time is short and does not allow us to write to him personally. We long for an early answer, addressed to brother D. Epp in Heubuden or directly to us, according to the address given below. Your brothers in Christ who love you, T. Horwitz.

Received December 14.

64. Johann Cornies to David Epp, Heubuden. 14 August 1826. SAOR 89-1-82/36.[21]

Dear brother D. Epp,

Your letter of 6 June reached me through the kindness of the dear Preacher Cornelius Friesen. Sincere thanks for promptly forwarding my letter of 13 December about a new settlement in Bessarabia to all congregations. I am further obliged that you also informed congregations scattered along the Rhine.

Immediately after receiving your letter, I approached the Guardianship Committee to inform them of its main contents. I requested that, unless it is contrary to law, a quantity of unsettled land in Bessarabia be set aside for Mennonite settlement. On the basis of your letter, I suggested that good, economically advanced immigrants might be found within the next few years. Since distances are so great, I have not yet received a reply, but expect one with every mail. I also wrote to a member

21 Regarding the planned Bessarabian colony, see also documents 38, 61, 66, 80, 81, 85, 86, 104, and 148.

of the Guardianship Committee who lodged with me for fourteen days this summer along with His Excellency, Mr. Contenius, and made the same request. I will inform you as soon as I am notified.

You suggest that someone from here inspect this land with the visiting Preacher Cornelius Friesen. This is not easily done because of the distances. The boundary of the Bessarabian guberniia is 550 verstas away, but I do not yet know how far this unsettled land is from that boundary. I will inform you once I receive a reply to my inquiry.

Time rushes by as on the wings of an eagle, and soon Russia will no longer be seeking immigrants. The overcrowded population in the empire's interior is suffering a great shortage of land, and thousands stream to the southern and eastern steppes. Ten or fifteen years ago, we saw nothing but sky and steppe when travelling for several days around our villages, but now the most poverty-stricken villages of 1,000 or 2,000 souls are being established in these areas. For example, in 1815 there were some 1,500,000 desiatinas of vacant Crown lands in our Melitopol and Dneprov Uezds. Now there is no unoccupied land, except what has been assigned for Mennonite settlement, and another 20,000 desiatinas for other settlers. The same situation exists in other parts of the guberniia.

It is unbelievable how quickly a barren steppe can be transformed into a cultivated region. I can already see that measures must be taken now, at this time, to plan and develop various pieces of land for our brethren in faith. This will be much more difficult in future when good lands for settlement will not be available and the acceptance of foreign settlers will be subject to many conditions. The Russian administration does not accept foreigners simply to populate barren lands. Anyone who knows even a little about the state can easily recognize its objectives. Dependable estimates show that, on average, the population in the north and south doubles every twenty to thirty years through births alone. The state is not only interested in a large population, but must use its paternal guardianship to keep its people from suffering dearth and want. It was for this reason that it decided more than fifty years ago to bring in foreigners who know how to use land as advantageously as possible, employing various methods and economic practices. At the same time, they were to become models for the native population.

My dear friend, I do not have time to explain this subject to you completely, but, God willing, I will explain what I know from time to time. It is necessary to do this because our people are under the delusion that they were granted special privileges in Russia simply to settle uncultivated lands, with no thought to the needs and purposes of the state. If our well-meaning government were not urging us insistently to apply orderly and active methods, we would decline economically so that the economic standing of our fourth generation could not be distinguished from those of other inhabitants of this land.

Our relationship to the state is totally different from what it is in Prussia. The constitution of our communities is also completely different and no person who has not lived under such conditions can have an accurate idea of them. Here, one is justified in applying the expression, "What is a community without the state and without the general life of the society?"

I am pleased that the dear Preacher Cornelius Friesen visited you. It is regrettable that his stay could not be longer but I am completely content.

Heartfelt greetings to you and your relatives. Let us work while it is day, for the night is coming when work must end. The Lord be with you. May He grant you His peace and perseverance in your activities so that you may eventually lay your sheaves before His throne and rest from your work. May your beginning and end be blessed.

Pray for your brother Cornies.

65. Johann Cornies to David Epp, Heubuden. 14 August 1826. SAOR 89-1-82/36.

D. Epp,

Everything under the sun has its own time and hence its end, and one often asks why. Winter and spring alternate regularly, as do summer and autumn. Why? The answer is God's alone. In His omniscience, He ordered this for our welfare, just as the stagnation of the Russian Bible Society resulted from His omniscient judgment. Were one to ask why, I could give many answers and explanations, but a definitive answer would still be missing. Let us believe and hope that through Him who can see everything that is hidden, nothing can happen unless it serves our welfare and our salvation. At first, our eyes may not see what can make us happy, since God alone has decided how He will work and with what methods He needs to accomplish His exalted purpose. We must believe without seeing, submitting to His judgment like children. He knows what is best. He sees a seed sprouting in the ground and provides the blessing. Work and prayer are ours. I enclose a copy of the Russian Bible Society president's letter, and others as well.

Brother Schlatter is no longer here. He left on 19 April, o.s. [old style], in response to his own compulsions, travelling to London, England, by way of Constantinople, though at first he intended to go by way of Danzig. He undoubtedly found a better opportunity in Odessa to go directly to Constantinople by sea. If God gives him good health, he will be back with his Nogais in winter.

Please be so kind as to give the copy of *Obst und Baum Zucht* [Fruit and Tree Cultivation] to my brother-in-law, K[laas]. D[yck]., and have him pay you the amount indicated by the bookseller, Mr. Carl Tauchnitz, Leipzig.

Summer has filled our granaries with a blessed harvest, though not to everyone's satisfaction. We have taken various approaches to the wool trade. Wool sold in the community for an average of thirty-five rubles per pud, washed. About 1,500 puds were sent to Romen, but the price there was very low – twenty-eight rubles on average. I sent my own wool to a dependable trading house in Moscow on consignment, in order to establish trading connections for us in the colony. At present, our settlement has a total of 52,000 head of partly improved Spanish sheep. They have become the golden pelt, and are our only source of funds. At the last market day in Tokmak, rye sold at one ruble, eighty kopeks per chetvert (equal to four *Scheffel*) and less. The other grain varieties fetched comparable prices.

Many heavy rains each week, with thunder and lightning and heat up to thirty degrees Reamur in the shade, inconvenienced our Prussian guests greatly but, thank God, no one fell ill.

Should opportunity and time allow, please send me a few lines informing me about yourself and your region. I am always prepared to reciprocate, and consider myself your loving brother in Christ,

J.C.

N.B. My greetings to dear Preacher Sudermann – I feel deeply connected to him. Greetings to all who believe that Jesus died for the sins of the world.

66. Johann Cornies to Klaas Dyck. 14 August 1826. SAOR 89-1-82/39.

Dear brother-in-law,

I hope that your journey is over, and that you have been welcomed by your old father and your other relatives and acquaintances. After a fifteen-year absence, you will enjoy a wonderful reunion in a circle of friends, and love and joy will govern your long-postponed conversations. May loving harmony unite your hearts as though in a dream and may you respond by burying your own doubts as to whether it would be possible to return to the house where you were born.

After these experiences, you will surely be wondering what your children, your friends, and your acquaintances on the Molochnaia might be doing and wishing for. These few lines are intended to reassure you that your children are healthy and everything is well with them, as with your relatives and acquaintances. Nothing has changed and the harvest is over.

I received your letter of 15 July from Berdichev on 4 August. We are pleased that everyone was in good health and spirits, and I compliment you on travelling so economically. Continue to do so but do not become miserly. Parsimony is not good economics. You were sensible to separate yourselves from Reimer and his company. You lost little and probably gained something. As they say, "Depart from them and do not touch anything unclean." In response to the request from D. Doerksen, Heubuden, I immediately informed the families about their situation. Please pass on our greetings as you are able.

On 11 August, the carpenter's axe struck its first blows at my new sheep farm, and this is keeping me very busy. I sent my wool to Moscow, where it arrived safely, though I have heard nothing yet about prices. The wool sent to Romen by members of our community sold at prices which were ten rubles per pud lower than those they could have fetched locally. Great hopes have been frustrated, especially for people who think that all wool is the same.

I turned fifteen geldings into silver at the Novomoskovskii market. When Mr. Contenius stayed at my house and attended a general assembly of village directors, my business partner, W. Martens, and I proposed making an advance of 30,000 rubles to the community to purchase sheep in Saxony. They selected me and gave me the responsibility of travelling to Saxony to purchase sheep. I also received official authorization. This happened even though I had withdrawn completely from the undertaking. I suggested my advance of money instead. I ask you, is it reasonable to be expected to undertake the difficulties involved in using the money that one has given?

I have asked our dear friend D. E. to give you the copy of Sikter's *Obst und Baum Zucht*. Pay him with the money I authorized for your use. If the books are not bound, use your judgment as to having them bound, neatly and well. Should an opportunity arise this fall, have them packed and sent to me. Agree in advance on freight charges and handling on the road. See to it that they are not handled carelessly.

We would like to hear from you in detail (perhaps with friend Jacob Ennz), partly by word-of-mouth, partly in writing. Your house stands on its foundation at the old location, its windows and doors nailed shut. The waist high weeds that filled your orchard have now been chopped down. I don't know who did it, but he was certainly not your enemy. Our father-in-law is still in Halbstadt or with sister Bold on Klassen's sheep farm. Johann Klassen was for a long time sick with a high fever. The latter so affected his thinking that he did not know what he was saying at times. But he was not confined to his bed. He is supposed to be better now.

Since I and my wife cannot think of any other news, I will close. May the Lord be with you, may He lead your thoughts according to His sublime will. May He grant you further patience in your affairs, so a rash act does not cause you pangs of conscience later on. Fix your eyes and mind on Him who was and is patience itself. In large and small events, act and conduct your affairs as though you are followers of Jesus. Act as He acted in order that when life is done you may enjoy the results of what patience can bring. Do not allow yourselves to go astray.

Those who would send you greetings are too many to name. I therefore include them in my own greetings. I only mention my wife's greetings in particular, who wishes you what you yourself desire in body and soul. She asks you to greet her grandfather, Abram Dyck, her aunt, and Mr. Franz Klaassen and his dear relatives.

May you fare well and not forget us.

J.C.

P.S. I sent you a copy of the list of Mennonites in Russia under the *Privilegium* [Charter of Privileges], with Froese from Tiegerfeld and esteemed Cornelius Fast from Heubuden, who are guests here. Please forward it to my friend D. Epp in Heubuden, or have it copied for him if he wishes. Ask him if he has received it. It is correct and dependable.

According to published reports, five of the conspirators against the life of our blessed Monarch were sentenced to quartering. His Majesty remitted their punishment to hanging and this sentence has already been carried out.[22] Several were condemned to twenty years of Crown labour in Siberia, and to settlement there once their terms end.

---

22 Cornies is referring to the leaders of the Decembrists, military officers who attempted a coup following the death of Tsar Alexander I in December 1825.

67. Johann Cornies to District Office. [18?] August 1826. SAOR 89-1-82/39v.

To the Esteemed District Office in Halbstadt,

I received your authorization to represent you on a trip to Saxony in 1827 to purchase sheep. I am to inform the District Office whether I am prepared to accept this role in order that the authorities can be informed.

I refer to the declaration I gave the District Office members earlier. Of this you are undoubtedly aware. I return your communication and authorization as your representative. This requires no further explanation.

With all respect,
The District Office's obedient Servant
Noted for return, Authorization 7 August, No. 72.
Communication 18 August, No. 352

68. Johann Cornies to Samuel Contenius. 3 September 1826. SAOR 82/39v.

Yr. Excellency,

As prepared as I am to do anything useful and good for the well-being of the community, and although I will not shrink from any difficulties, I could not accept authorization No. 72, dated 7 August, in which I was officially authorized by all village mayors to make a journey to Saxony to buy a number of "electoral" sheep at community expense. After Yr. Excellency left my house, no one said anything more to me about the above-mentioned assignment. A meeting of village mayors chose me without my knowledge and sent the authorization to my house. I returned it to the District Office immediately.

Now, a day before the District Office members were to leave for Ekaterinoslav, they came here to ask me why I had not accepted the community's authorization. They urged me to accept it. To uphold my position in the community for the future, I was forced to reject the District Office's request.

I leave my situation to Yr. Excellency's gracious consideration,
Johann Cornies

69. Johann Cornies to Wilhelm Frank. 10 September 1826. SAOR 89-1-82/41.[23]

Highly honoured Mr. Frank, beloved friend,

I received your most welcome letter an hour ago. Suffused with feelings of gratitude for the trust placed in me, I hasten to send you a few lines. I am deeply pained that our benefactor and father is constantly burdened with sad news about us. He should, on the contrary, be pursuing the happy, sincere, and positive actions that his noble intellect has planned for our benefit. Only then, at his advanced age, might he see the fruits of his great efforts. I know that his Christian intentions, based on the gospel, keep him from wavering and taking fright. His faith is a guarantee that the fruits of his unselfish actions will, before the seat of judgment, shine as genuine gold and precious pearls. Dear God, how good you are that even now as in times of old, you scatter your blessings like salt over meat, in order that they not spoil and be destroyed.

Such feelings often tear at my heart and tears fill my eyes. Patience is needed where it is necessary, but who is so wise as to determine a proper path? I often pay for my impatience with bitter pangs of conscience. I become confused because I hurry along the right path too quickly and then too slowly. I recognize this but, as I bear my own sufferings and those of others, fail to respond day after day. Only hope and faith in Him who values me as a member of human society will lead me on my proper path, whether it is charted or still uncharted. He enables me to say, "not my will but Thy Will be done."

It is enough to say that I love you, as is confirmed by my works, but I request that you overlook my weaknesses, which can turn words into lip service. May God protect me from that.

Part of our community is building Salem, but its foundation seems like Babel. The confusion is not that of speaking many tongues; we cannot understand one another even in one. I do not depend on the multitude or on its majority, but on unity. And because unity is my goal, I cannot simply sit back quietly, but must offer my few talents to profit the general well-being, even though ingratitude is my reward. Whatever is good remains good and will bring its appropriate profit. I will

23 Wilhelm Frank was Contenius' secretary. He provided Cornies with an important source of information and influence in the Guardianship Committee.

do everything mentioned in your communication with care, altering not a single letter of the document that you have composed. Voth is making clean copies.

Please keep the tobacco I sent you until you receive news from Moscow. I received His Excellency's letter of 4 September, and will try to follow its contents promptly. I will send His Excellency a report this coming mail day. The day before they left for Ekaterinoslav, the District Office mounted a small attack on me about travelling to Saxony. It was an effort to turn against anyone who spoke the truth, to make him flee. But not everyone runs away so easily. I am not someone who abandons something just to keep the peace. That, for me, is a sin.

Many thanks for your greetings. I return them in friendship and with a wish for your well-being in body and in soul. With respect and love I sign myself as your friend,

J.C.

P.S. My new sheep barn should be ready in three weeks, though I have difficulty believing this myself. I am making every effort to move the construction along quickly. I will have 4,000 rubles less in cash. After your departure, Johann Klassen (manufacturer) was ill again for several days, but is better now.

Should you have time and leisure, please write to your friend, who signs himself as always,

Cornies

70. Johann Cornies to Wilhelm Frank. 18 September 1826. SAOR 89-1-82/43.

Honoured Sir,

All of the letters you mention have reached me without delay. I doubt Elder Fast will make the trip, since the two elders Dueck and Warkentin have made their travel arrangements on their own.

Transporting the wood and stone for the new church started immediately after the District Office members returned from Ekaterinoslav, where they had presumably received approval for the construction. It is better to remain quiet until the right time. I have not yet had the pleasure to speak to any of the members who were in Ekaterinoslav. I spend little time at home, but am at my sheep farm most of the time. I return home only Tuesday and Friday evenings to mail my correspondence.

Give your honoured father all of the tobacco and I will inform you about getting him more. I am not sure when I will visit Ekaterinoslav. It seems almost impossible for the moment without risking major losses. It is more important now than ever to provide good, planned oversight of my twenty-three workmen who are paid one and one-half to two rubles per day, now that the days are short. I hope to be able to release them soon. You can count on me. I will take care of the furs. Please write me as often as you like. I am just not sure how often I'll find the time to reply. Please do not become angry with me. My home has become a kind of inn for me and I am seldom there. I expect to hear soon about His Excellency's health and how he feels.

With the most complete esteem and love, I greet you sincerely as friend and servant. A greeting of love to your parents and family. How are they?

Johann Cornies

71. Johann Cornies to Tobias Voth. 24 September 1826. SAOR 89-1-82/47.

Esteemed and valued friend Voth,

I received various books, kindly sent by the worthy State Counsellor Schubert in St. Petersburg to be sold to interested persons in our community. Because the state counsellor has a special preference for our community, he has authorized their sale favourably at low cost. He himself says: "I feel especially compelled to send these books to you. May the Lord give you guidance, according to His will. May the main goal be to promote His kingdom and His reception in all hearts. The money is of secondary importance."

To ensure that Mr. Schubert's noble Christian thoughts are not misdirected, I have decided to ask you, my very dear, treasured brother, to take on the sale of these books. I have total trust that you will know best how to handle the matter and to keep accounts in a way that does not abuse Mr. Schubert's trust.

To prevent difficulties in accounting, I have decided not to have any of the books sold on credit. We know from experience that things run more smoothly then. Books sold in this way are not highly valued and payment is not made on time.

Should you accept my request, please pick up the books from me at my home, where we can prepare the documentation.

With the esteem I owe you and with sincere love, I remain your honest friend and servant,

Johann Cornies

72. Johann Cornies to Wilhlem Frank. 28 September 1826. SAOR 89-1-82/47v.

Highly honoured Sir, Frank,

I will make a clean breast of it! I am not at all averse to going to Saxony next spring on community business. How could I be, since it would be most useful for the community and also because our dear, estimable benefactor, Mr. Contenius, has requested it? His Excellency's wish is my command, which I seek to carry out to the best of my ability.

There is an important reason why I cannot agree with the District Office too quickly, however. Despite all the obstacles put in my way by the District Office over the past ten years, I have made great efforts to motivate the community to make its own decisions and to take positive actions for its general well-being. Our directors have the duty of taking constructive steps to initiate community actions. We should not wait for our benevolent administration to send us directives and orders.

Many hard knocks are needed to awaken us from our sleep. God is my witness that some members of the District Office used my words, intended to promote the community's general well-being, to arouse hatred against me in the community. They say I want to disrupt the peace in our community and to destroy it, a charge they know to be untrue. Otherwise, they would have called me to account. They fear that my unselfish actions in the community would reveal their spiteful activities, causing them to fall into their own trap. This is the reason the District Office members cannot bring themselves to suggest to the village mayors that I undertake this journey, and it is the reason they have not carried out their promise to His Excellency.

I do not care whether the mayors ask me to go, and I do not need their invitation to feel that it is my duty as a member of the community to do whatever is positive and useful. If only the directors were to remember their duty to the community as forcefully as they remind me of mine. Then I could undertake the commissioned journey calmly and happily. They only say, "We think you could travel" while they wait for His Excellency or the Guardianship Committee to give the order, hoping their words will remain ambiguous.

Cornies

I will send your fur, or lambskins, possibly with W. Martens, who must come to see you soon. He bought 2,250 desiatinas from Tsvicherenko and will become a shepherd like me.

73. Johann Cornies to Abram Lemke. 8 October 1826. SAOR 89-1-82/49v.

Abram Lemke,

I just got back from Ekaterinoslav today, but I learned that on 13 September, you submitted a petition to the esteemed Committee about your quarrel with your avowed wife. The contents of the petition fill me with compassion and sadness and I cannot rest until I send you my frank warning and advice. The expressions you use in the petition show that you have not remained faithful to your solemnly affirmed confession of faith. You have cast it aside in anger and agitation. Among other things, you say that by ordering the brethren not to have contact with you, the preachers are violating natural and human law.

How did this thought occur to you? Did you not confess freely and accept the jurisdiction of the evangelical ban, without having been commanded to do so? Now you disavow what you conscientiously and solemnly affirmed before God. Make no mistake, God will not be mocked. You can surely not be calm about the petition you submitted. Otherwise, your heart would be hard as stone. This I do not believe. I ask you to reflect carefully on what it means to be a Christian and on the duty owed by a member of a Christian community, a follower of Jesus, our master. If you cannot justify your position against the legal penalties of our benevolent administration, how much less can you do so before the supreme judge of this world, who sees our every deed and permits no evasion?

Your petition makes accusations against the whole community. What a disgrace! What a shame and punishment for you, since you surely know that you cannot prove what you allege in your petition and statement to His Excellency in Ekaterinoslav. Forgive me, but I must speak the truth. I am not indifferent to anyone, and not to you. I have pitied you and your situation for a long time, and particularly now when you do not understand what you have done and are doing.

Take my advice. Go to Ekaterinoslav immediately, before a decision on your petition is reached. Request that it be returned to you and ask the members of the Committee and His Excellency to forgive you your error.

You must do what you think is appropriate, but I did want to tell you what concerns me and what I feel I must say.

With the honesty of my feelings, I sign myself,

Joh. Cornies

74. Johann Cornies to Jacob Penner. 10 October 1826. SAOR 89-1-82/50v.

Esteemed District Chairman, Sincere Friend,

I hear from my brother D. Cornies that you expected to see me when I returned from Ekaterinoslav. I regret that business matters prevented me from stopping by. My orders were to make haste in discharging my own affairs and those of others. Please do not look at me questioningly because I sped past your residence as on the wings of an eagle. I did this not out of scorn but because of time and circumstance. I love and esteem you, and not because it is fashionable to do so. May God preserve me from hypocrisy.

I feel the need to discuss matters with you and believe you want to talk to me as well. Who knows why and to what purpose this may be. But God willing, it will happen eventually. With genuine interest, I esteem highly the insight and energy you show in your well-considered direction over the economic affairs of 4,000 souls for their well-being, and in keeping with the wishes of our benevolent administration. Activity of this sort will turn us into the models we should be when measured against the privileges that have been granted to us.

With heartfelt wishes for your and your dear wife's well-being, I strive to be your honest and loving friend,

Joh. Cornies

P.S. Heartfelt greetings to friend Heese and his dear wife and children, as well as to District Deputy Pauls, etc. Please, when possible, write me a few lines.

75. Johann Cornies to Traugott Blueher. 14 October 1826. SAOR 89-1-82/51.

Honoured Mr. Blueher,

In answer to your valued letter of 20 September, let me say the following: If you think that you cannot sell my wool favourably for immediate gain, or that there would be profit in storing it for a while, I would ask you to do so until 1 December, or until 20 December at the latest. I will need the money by that date. Though I appreciate your thoughtful offer of an advance, I must turn it down because my business affairs will take me away from my home, and I must settle all my accounts and business affairs before I leave to keep mistakes from being made during my absence. Treasured friend, do not interpret my rejection of your well-meaning offer badly.

I report receipt of various items you sent me this summer:

1. Eight small bottles of *Lebensessenz*, with Pastor Rosenstrauch.

2. Two cases and a package of books with Mr. Toews, Ekaterinoslav.

3. A small box of tobacco with the Russian carter. This item, handled negligently, was moistened by the rain and can no longer serve as a sample. I tried to inform Ekaterinoslav merchants of this item but they cannot be expected to carry it on consignment when there are so few people of rank to purchase it. Still, I gave this item to one of my dependable friends in Ekaterinoslav to show around to interested persons, but I have not yet heard back. In our settlement, every villager prepares his own tobacco.

Brother Schlatter wrote from Constantinople and Smyrna to tell me that he will sail to Livorno and then travel overland to Switzerland. He is well. I wonder how the respected missionaries on the Persian border have managed during the insurrection. Please send me any news in this regard.

Kindly send me a copy of the report of the investigating commission into the conspiracy against the life of the blessed monarch.[24] Address it to the District Office, secretary Gerhard Martens, Halbstadt, to be forwarded to me (because my business affairs keep me so busy and the post office is almost sixty verstas away.) The report is supposedly available at Mr. Pelzner's for five rubles per copy.

With the kindest commendation, I greet you cordially and remain with all respect and esteem,

Your —

76. Samuel Contenius to District Office. 29 October 1826. SAOR 89-1-89/1.

Copy of Directive No. 103 to the Halbstadt District office on 29 October 1826:

According to the District Office report of 9 October, I see that Johann Cornies, Ohrloff village, has refused to travel to Saxony to purchase a supply of electoral ewes and rams for the District sheep farm.

If the District Office had taken up this matter in the way I proposed, there would have been some hope for its success. But once begun from the wrong end, contrary to my advice, and accompanied with highly insulting slanders, discord, hatred, and envy, I am not at all surprised to learn that it has failed.

24 A reference to the Decembrist Revolt. See above, document 66.

I know a number of respected Molochnaia Mennonites with intelligence and insight, but they lack the knowledge and experience needed to purchase Saxon electoral merinos. This undertaking can only be entrusted to a man who is adroit, has a searching mind, is indefatigable in pursuing matters, and is endowed with a penetrating glance. Should you find such a man to take the place of Cornies in every respect, I wish you luck. If not, it would be better to postpone the undertaking under discussion until a more mature sense of discretion arises. It would, in any case, be inexcusable to gamble more than 40,000 rubles under these circumstances. I regret that the longer this project is delayed, the longer District inhabitants will forfeit an annual income of more than 100,000 rubles.

The original is signed S. Contenius.

77. Johann Cornies to Wilhelm Frank. 31 October 1826. SAOR 89-1-82/53v.

Honoured Mr. Frank,

Your valued letter arrived today. It gave me considerable pleasure to see that the court has most graciously acquitted my faithful servant J. Olinskii. I will try to contribute to his temporal and eternal welfare with helpful admonitions, and try to shape him into a useful person in human society.

It is not my fault that you, valued Mr. Frank, cannot really understand my reasoning. You believe that District Office members, and some members of the community, are enthusiastic about the journey to Saxony, speak about it constantly, and urge me to undertake it. Far from it. Since they returned from Ekaterinoslav, District Office officials only spoke to me once in a society meeting (and no one else has otherwise), and in such a lukewarm fashion that I had to refuse. When I was in Ekaterinoslav, I informed His Excellency about my reasons for declining any involvement in his wise project.

The District Office cannot say anything more in its report than what I actually told them. It does not take into account the way the District Office attempted to persuade me to travel, nor my reasons, as a member of the community, for turning down what appear to be their reasonable demands. Will such winding detours lead to the desired goal? Devious actions are as unacceptable as counterfeit coinage.

A new phase has begun with the election of a new District chairman. The votes have not all been gathered in and it is not yet definite, but one hears that Johann Klassen, Tiegerwiede, formerly District Office secretary, has about 300 votes. Even were he to receive no further votes, he would still have a majority. This is something new, but not something positive. It makes no difference to me personally, but what about the community? Cold, ice cold shivers travel down my back when I think about our general situation and weigh this against this man's character. Who knows, perhaps something will intervene to keep these fears from being realized. It never occurred to me that Klassen might be elected. I thought it would be the youngest Deputy, Toews, a completely solid man. I believe the newly elected man is known in Ekaterinoslav.

If possible, please give me your opinion about the above-mentioned election. The lambskins are still in the tannery. Construction of my sheep barn was completed eight days ago. Given good weather, I will attempt to keep my promise.

With greetings and best wishes for your success, I sign myself as always, your friend and servant,

Johann Cornies

78. Traugott Blueher to Johann Cornies. Moscow, 2 November 1826. SAOR 89-1-88/54.

Dear Friend Cornies,

The last time I had the pleasure of writing to you was on 21 September. I can now report in detail regarding your account for the shipment of your Spanish wool that has been stored here. Finally, after persistent rain, there arrived some warm weather suitable for washing wool and it was possible to fetch quite a good price for the wool. The wet weather also restored the weight that the wool had lost en route and a little more.

I have not yet found a purchaser for the small sack of better wool, since it is difficult to find a buyer for such a small quantity. I request your patience.

Enclosed, you will receive 6,220 R.B.A. Please send me a receipt to complete this entire transaction. I also request that you accept my friendly thanks for placing your trust in me.

On 20 July, I wrote that I had sent along samples of various Sarepta products. Kindly inform me if there are prospects for their sale in your region. Might a dependable man be found in Ekaterinoslav who could turn up suitable buyers?

In sending friendly greetings to you and your dear family, I commend myself to your loving remembrance as your respectful friend,

Traugott Blueher

Received 20 November. Answered 24 November.

79. Johann Cornies to State Counsellor Schubert. 6 November 1826. SAOR 89-1-82/57.

His Honour, State Counsellor, in the name of our Lord Jesus,

The report I owe you is finally arriving. Please forgive this delay for which there was a good reason. Although I received your treasured letter on 18 March, I had to wait until 28 September for the cases of books to arrive. Since I am often away from home, I did not report their arrival immediately, but I can now report the receipt of the following:

100 copies of *Biblische Geschichten* [Bible stories]
100 copies of *Wiederkunft des Herrn* [Christ's return]
100 copies of *Das Herz des Menschen* [The heart of man]
10 copies of *Messiasfreund* [Friend of the Messiah]
200 *Reise Paesse* [Travel passports]

All arrived in good condition. I will make every effort to sell them as you request. There was a demand for the books before they arrived, especially for the Bible stories. To ensure that your purpose is carried out, I have made the books available for sale through our local Society School and its estimable teacher, Mr. Tobias Voth. People who want to read them – or better said, want salvation – can purchase them at any time. This could not be done from my home because I am frequently away. We have no shortage of interested people and the books would be sold in a short time were it not for a serious shortage of money. Still, we must pray, confident that even something small can bear fruit, ten-, fifty-, and even one hundredfold. The results depend not on multitudes but on the possession of something as noble and genuine as gold, which alone cannot be consumed by fire.

Over the last four years, our region, and especially our community, has been afflicted by the almighty hand of our Heavenly Father. He calls, but they do not hear; He punishes, but they do not make amends. We belong among the disobedient peoples who now face their just reward, here and in eternity.

Since 1822, swarms of grasshoppers have caused great devastation in our area. This has resulted in a serious shortage of food and fodder for man and beast. In 1823 and 1824, virtually nothing remained: no crops on the fields, no pastures for livestock, and very little hay. When I returned home from St. Petersburg in 1824, the livestock was so thin and wasted that I could not comprehend how it could still be alive. Swarms of grasshoppers darkened the sun, there arose dust clouds as dark as the darkest rain, and fierce winds kept anyone from walking along the street. Compare this to the first chapter of the Prophet Job.

In February 1825, we had such a devastating snowstorm that all communications were cut and thousands of livestock died. The fodder shortage was so severe that many a villager removed the straw from his roof and fed it to his cattle. Because of the clouds of snow and dust, nothing could be bought at any price, even if it had been available at some distance from here. Such storms that varied in strength and duration continued from mid-February until late March. The temperature, at two to five degrees Reamur, was mild enough for the snow to stick so firmly to anything that it could be removed only with the greatest effort. The eyes of people and animals were glued shut almost immediately upon exposure to the storm.

Horses in the yard on my sheep farm were covered with such a layer of snow that one needed to look closely to distinguish the front of a horse from its rear. I too felt the rod and judgment of our loving Father, losing more than 200 horses of my breeding herd, about 1,000 Spanish sheep, and several head of cattle. The damage came to no less than 30,000 rubles. Believing that the Lord permitted all this for my salvation, I praise and glorify His goodness. The Lord has given and He has taken away. I think of what I have as His property and am happy in the knowledge that everything He does is good. May His name be praised. It was also His pleasure to again, thereafter, give me an abundant surplus. It is marvellous how He reigns, although we do not understand all of His marvels.

In our community, up to 10,000 Spanish sheep, about 1,800 head of cattle, and 1,200 horses were lost in the snowstorms. Now there is a great shortage of fodder. Our neighbours, the Nogais suffered so much that their livestock numbers fell by a fifth, and starvation led many to eat the dead livestock on my sheep farm, which is contrary to Muslim belief.

It was not much better among the Russian population. In June 1825, I was present when the area military commander reported losses to the civil governor of the guberniia. Among Russian inhabitants in the area, the past year's livestock losses during snowstorms and fodder shortages totalled 1,249,000 rubles. Yet God still loves us even if He punishes us, and His love remains unchanged.

When winter ended, every father made a tremendous effort to provide food for his family until harvest time. Money still available in the community was advanced to the needy at no interest on the condition that it be repaid within two years. To make advantageous sales of wool for the poor, four trusted men from the community were commissioned to sell almost 2,000 puds of good Spanish wool at the wool market in Romen, Little Russia. They did not return, having been murdered on the road from Romen to Poltava. The money, wagon and horses, and even the corpses of the murdered cannot be found. Nor have the perpetrators been discovered, although they are known to be Polish and Austrian Jews. The loss in money is estimated at almost 80,000 rubles.[25]

At times, such blows cause the most patient among us to feel great doubt. Nevertheless, our rock foundation remains firm though waves may overwhelm us. A Christian fears nothing for he knows that the Lord watches over him.

Now something about Daniel Schlatter. On 19 April, he travelled to Odessa and then to Switzerland via Constantinople, Smyrna, and Livorno. Like a torch snatched from the fire, he departed Constantinople two days before the massacre of the Janissaries. He arrived in Livorno after forty-two days and wrote to me from there while still under quarantine.

It is impossible to describe his love for the Tatars. He was pleased with the remarks about Ismail and Isaac in your letter, and he asked me to send hearty greetings to you and to the friends he remembers in St. Petersburg. He is making good progress with the Nogai dialect, and his letter to his Nogai employer from Constantinople caused great joy. Daniel's Nogai employer does not know how to write in their dialect, but he dictated a letter to Daniel that was sent to Switzerland in German. I take the liberty of enclosing a copy with the request that it might be given to Mr. State Counsellor Pesarovius and the merchant, Mr. Notbeck.[26] Should it be God's will, Daniel will go to London from Switzerland and then return to his Nogais.

---

25 Regarding this robbery and the murders, see also documents 28, 49, and 84.

26 Paul Pesarovius (1776–1847) was an important philanthropic figure in early nineteenth-century St. Petersburg. During the Napoleonic wars, he raised over a million rubles to help the wounded, and started and edited the Russian periodical *Russian Invalid* [*Русский Инвалид*]. In the 1830s, he was the president of the St. Petersburg Evangelical Consistory [*евангелической консистории*].

Mr. Steinmann, who was in St. Petersburg with Mr. Lindl, is pastor of the Evangelical congregation here on the Molochnaia.[27] He is their good shepherd because he has gained their trust and love by making a good beginning. Some time ago he asked me to give you his greetings. Please forgive me, sincerely beloved sir, for being so long-winded. I know that you are sympathetic to the fate of all humanity and are interested in our affairs.

Jesus is the same yesterday, today, and in all eternity. His grace fills us and unites us so that one day in His kingdom we will have the eternal joy of His presence. May God, in His trinity as Father, Son, and Holy Ghost, help us to reach this goal. Amen.

Many greetings to you and your dear consort from me and my wife. Also greet my unforgettable friends Messrs. Pesarovius and Notbeck together with their dear spouses and remember us in your prayers. Eternity will reveal my honest feelings towards you and all my loved ones in St. Petersburg.

With the appropriate esteem and respect, I remain Yr. Honour's lifelong friend and brother in Jesus,

Johann Cornies

80. Johann Cornies to Daniel Schlatter. 6 November 1826. SAOR 89-1-82/61.[28]

My dear friend Daniel,

Welcome to your fatherland, your city, and your mother's house. With my deep interest in your destiny, I am happy that you completed the journey by sea via Constantinople and then through the archipelago. We received your delightful letters from Constantinople, Smyrna,

---

27 Ignatz [Ignaz, Ignatius] Lindl was a follower of Johann Michael Sailer and Martin Boos. A defrocked Catholic priest from Bavaria, Lindl held strongly pietistic, ecumenical views. Lindl came to the attention of Tsar Alexander, who permitted him to found the German colonist village of Sarata in Bessarabia in 1822. Lindl left Russia permanently in 1823, but Sarata remained a noted pietist stronghold in New Russia, closely associated with the founding of the Baptist movement in Russia and Ukraine. Lindl was particularly famous for his fiery preaching, and a number of his sermons and reflections were published. On Lindl, See Hans Petri, *Ignaz Lindl und die deutsche Bauernkolonie Sarata in Bessarabien* (Munich: Verlag R. Oldenbourg, 1965).

28 Regarding the planned Bessarabian colony, see also documents 38, 61, 64, 66, 81, 85, 86, 104, and 148.

and Livorno. The last took only three weeks to get here. Dear brother, thank God for all His favours and blessings.

We thank God that we are all healthy and contented, to the degree that the new man has triumphed over the old. There have been no changes of importance in our community. I may be travelling to Dresden next spring. I was selected to go but have not yet accepted. I tried to explain my thinking to our old benefactor when I was in Ekaterinoslav about a month ago.

My sheep barn was completed eight days ago. Since I wanted it to be built carefully and properly, it has kept me busy since mid-August. For some time, our friend Johann Klaassen, Halbstadt, suffered a dangerous illness in his head and even fell into a coma. People feared that he might become deranged but, thank God, he is now completely recovered.

The superintendent installed Pastor Steinmann for half the community (nine villages), on the other side of the Molochnaia. They say that the old pastor will be leaving. I was not home when the superintendent was here, which I regret. Apparently he asked many questions about me. Klaas Dyck travelled to Prussia, and it seems that Epp gave him the books ordered from Mr. Tauchnitz. I had a visit from an old teacher in Prussia, and also from a hopeful young person from Tiegenhoff, not far from Marienburg. We talked only a little because he was on his way to the Crimea. Should you travel via Danzig, please make his acquaintance. His name is Eduard Friesen. Ask David Epp about him.

You will surely laugh at me when I tell you about my new hopes, but it doesn't matter; I will tell you anyway. There seems to be an increasing awareness of the Nogais, including a desire to promote their happiness, even though there are many more rascals among them than ever before. His Honour, the great and well-meaning Count Vorontsov, proposed to St. Petersburg that Nogai culture be developed through a bureau like ours. Now who is the winner? However, I will not boast about results until we can see them. May God bring this proposal to an early completion. My description of the Nogais fell into good hands. Mr. Contenius took the last copy from me, but will return it.

In response to a proposal I made, Mennonite settlers are to be accepted in Bessarabia. About ten days ago, Mr. Guildenschanz sent me an invitation to inspect the selected land in Besssarabia, about 12,000 desiatinas, but I will not go because of the bad weather. The Doukhobors are being confined to an area extending five verstas from their district, and they are not permitted to come farther. I don't know the reason, but the chief [Othodox] hierarch from Orekhov visited the Doukhobors, attempting to lead them back into the Orthodox Church. Several families have reportedly returned. I think that more than half will return to the fold if the worst comes to pass.

Grasshoppers appeared again this summer and autumn. For ten days they were as thick as snowflakes, but they seem to have done no damage among the Germans. They were not very welcome among the slow Nogais who were still busy harvesting. There is much good grain for bread this year, but it cannot be sold at any price. No one is buying anything. Several downpours of rain occurred during the summer, but no rain fell from mid-August to the end of October, which was to my advantage. Now we have had three days of heavy rain and it is warm.

Builuck worked for himself this autumn, a small wonder. He says he wants to work all the time now, which will be an even greater wonder. After he disagreed with me, we remained a little distant from one another for a while. Now everything is back to normal, but I refuse to hire him again. I feel this is better for both of us. He constantly requests that I give him sheep for the coming year. This year, his stubbornness and mine kept me from giving him any. The number of sheep that I set aside for the Nogais went to Monglut in Edinokhta, whom you know. As you requested, I read the little letter you had written in German to Builuck so that he could understand it. He weeps whenever he thinks of your leave-taking at the graveyard. It really is good that you left Burkut for a while. People there will come to appreciate you more and you will have benefitted from the change as well.

In our house we often think of you lovingly, not with fashionable exaltation and wonder, but with a quiet simplicity of heart, which God values. Our prayer is the same. What more can I say? You know us all and blessed eternity will make everything clear to you and to us. Through the grace of Jesus, we endeavour to preach with our hands and otherwise to keep silent, which is better than the opposite. My wife, with heartfelt sympathy, thinks about the joyful scene it must have been at your arrival in your mother's house, but would rather not think of your leave-taking later on. She sends your dear, faithful mother many greetings, and assures her that she will be a second mother to you in this country. I could say much more but, as you know, there is not enough space in one letter.

Permit me to make several requests. Muszhi Salos took over some Crown land under set terms (I told you about him). He arrived here with almost 400 merinos, ostensibly bought in Spain, but anyone familiar with conditions there cannot believe this. They likely came from the Canton of Geneva. Kindly make inquiries about this matter there, including the price he paid. It is important for me to know. Report to me at your convenience. Please greet any dear friends you meet on your travels, as it seems right, such as Mr. Angas and Mr. Allen in London, and the young Chunkanskii. Do not forget greetings to Messrs. Blumson and Ryhiner in Basel. Write something about your mother in your letter (I wrote to both of you in August) giving her greetings from our entire household. I also send you and your mother greetings from Builuck, enclosing his letter, which I wrote as he dictated it. He wept constantly when it was translated for him, making it difficult for me as well. May God lead the blind man to his salvation and reveal to him the unworthiness in which he is mired. He has a good heart, but is bewildered by Islamic dross and weeds. Your friends on the Molochnaia who know that I am writing this letter asked me to greet you, but I cannot list them by name for reasons of space. Travel safely, keeping God in your mind and heart.

Good wishes and prayers from your honest and faithful friend and brother,

Cornies

Adieu.

81. Johann Cornies to Guildenschanz. 6 November 1826. SAOR 89-1-82/64.[29]

Yr. Honour, Gracious Sir, Mr. Guildenschanz,

I received Yr. honoured communication of 3 October on 23 October, with the enclosed letter from Mr. Weygel. I hasten to thank Yr. Honour for the information. It will give me pleasure to explain to my Prussian brethren in faith the humane purposes of our honoured administration in settling Mennonites on 12,000 desiatinas of land. The settlers will know how to value the benefits benevolently accorded them and, united in gratitude, will prove themselves virtuous inhabitants of Russia, to the joy of their superiors and the advantage of the state.

My first invitation to all Mennonites in Prussia informed them that they will receive no advance payment and should not expect one. I will emphasize this again, to prevent any disappointment. I am

29 Regarding the planned Bessarabian colony, see also documents 38, 61, 64, 66, 80, 85, 86, 104, and 148.

enthusiastic about a settlement in Bessarabia and encouraged to hope that it will proceed according to the wishes of our benevolent government. I will be sure to inform Mennonites interested in immigrating about the purposes of government and state and have asked that a respected man in Prussia, who is entirely favourable to Russia, assist in this purpose.

I would have liked to visit you this autumn, to inspect the land set aside for Mennonite settlement, but many business matters here prevented this. Among other things, I had a proper sheep barn built, 300 fut long with appropriate facilities, that prevented me from travelling. If I am not required to make a long journey in spring, I would very much like to inspect the land in Bessarabia myself.

Please forgive me, Yr. Honour, that I have not yet returned the booklet by I. Lindl, *Mein Glaubensbekenntnis* [My confession of faith], to you.[30] His Excellency, the worthy State Counsellor Contenius, has borrowed it and when it is returned, I will mail it to you without delay.

With the most complete respect, esteem, and appreciation, I have the honour to be Yr. Honour's most obedient servant,

J.C.

82. Johann Cornies to Peter Friesen. 8 November 1826. SAOR 89-1-82/65.

Valued Mr. Peter Friesen,

I was not at home when you honoured us with a family visit to express your love and respect. Since then, my many business matters have prevented me from inviting your esteemed family to visit us and make your acquaintance.

I am not so busy now and my wife would like to send your family our heartfelt invitation to honour us with your acquaintance and friendship at three o'clock this afternoon. If you are unable to do so today, please inform us as to when it would be convenient.

With the heartiest greeting and respect, I remain your still unacquainted friend,

Johann Cornies

30 Regarding Lindl, see footnote 45. Cornies is referring to *Mein Glaubensbekenntnis ausgesprochen über 1 Cor. 3, 11 von Ignaz Lindl* (Leipzig: Tauchnitz, 1824).

83. Samuel Contenius to Johann Cornies. 11 November 1826. SAOR 89-1-88/14 & 8v.

Honoured Johann Cornies,

I thank you for sending four cheeses to my friend Steven in Simferopol.[31] I hereby remit your outlay of nine rubles, ninety kopeks, and return Lindl's pamphlet, *Mein Glaubensbekenntnis* [My confession of faith], which you lent me. I read it to my own edification and return it with many thanks. I enclose several forest-tree seeds as a token of my gratitude, with the request that you entrust them to the earth carefully, using appropriate methods.

Your local District Office reported to me on 9 October regarding the general meeting with the Wool Improvement Society, in which it repeatedly sought to persuade J. Cornies to undertake the proposed journey to Saxony for the general well-being of the community. The appeal was fruitless and, since J. Cornies declined to be involved in this business, they asked me to resolve the matter as soon as possible. I have provided the directive they requested (you will also receive a copy of the directive.)

Now that I can see how this important opportunity could indeed fail, even though it would so obviously improve the well-being of every one of your brethren in faith, I am comforted by my own conviction that I have shown no hesitation in explaining the matter clearly and in providing emphatic exhortation. Inattention will delay this useful project that is essential for each Molochnaia Mennonite and his family. Repeated postponements could result in it never coming to fruition.

I regret that my unceasing and forceful efforts to achieve the goal of promoting the well-being of every single inhabitant in the District has been fruitless, foolishly misunderstood and wasted. It is deplorable that such certain means of preventing extreme poverty among your brethren is frustrated by a lack of active love and concern regarding the well-being of so many people related in faith. If implemented, the useful results of this initiative would be revealed in time. Mature deliberation is therefore required in considering the detrimental results if this project were to fail. It is not enough to censure the neglect brought

31 Christian Steven, creator of the famous Nikitski Botanical Garden in the Crimea, was one of Russia's foremost botanists.

about by a lack of insight or by folly, conceit, or thoughtlessness that will result in damage to several thousand people.

I had hoped that obvious examples and frequent repetitions of convincing facts would make people more sympathetic to the distressing poverty of many of their brethren. I still hope that with time my efforts will awaken a determination to remedy this condition by these means. Now, hostility, strife, and a spirit of dissension results in a hardening of attitudes and the disappearance of proponents in support of such positive measures. Were this to continue, all of our efforts would be in vain. Those who refuse to accept advice cannot be helped.

Please inquire whether cloth manufacturer Klaassen will send the cloth ordered from him, and when.

Wishing you and yours a lasting well-being, I remain with all esteem, your well inclined,

S. Contenius

Ekaterinoslav, 11 November 1826

P.S. Wilhelm Martens will deliver the ten rubles, seeds, and pamphlet to you.

Received 20 November. Answered 27 November.

84. Samuel Contenius to Johann Cornies. 18 November 18 1826. SAOR 89-1-88/16.

Honoured Cornies,

The favour that you did me in sending one pud of cheese to my friend in the Crimea had the result that the rascally swindler Jacob Risto demanded, and received, ten rubles for it at delivery. When he received your letter, the state counsellor was so ill that he could not open it and read it immediately, and the swindling messenger took advantage of this circumstance to allow himself to be paid the costs of ten rubles. Through Frank, I have required of Oberschulz Rieder that he collect this money and forward it to you, dear Cornies. I ask you to buy good hams (smoked) with it, or some of the best butter, and to forward them with an honourable man (in so far as such exists) to my friend Steven in Simferopol. This miserable matter can be concluded most promptly if you will demand, by means of a few lines, the ten rubles that Rieder is to collect.

From your letter of November 12, I see that you have had the kindness to buy a horse for me at the price of 150 silver rubles, which amounts to 600 R.B.A. In my limited circumstances, this is much too expensive, so that I must ask you to do whatever can be done to free me of this expensive purchase. Did I not express myself clearly enough to you, or did you misunderstand me? My request was that you should do me the favour of informing me if a healthy, strong horse – one that is quiet and not too old – were available there, and its price in R.B.A., but not to buy it immediately. I have stable space for only two horses and must, therefore, before I can acquire another horse and give it shelter, first sell one of my two horses at the yearly market in March.

Could Jacob Warkentin perhaps be willing to take back his horse in order to help me out of my dilemma?

I am finding it difficult to write, and for this reason I close, with wishes of enduring well-being,

S. Contenius

Ekaterinoslav, [18?] November, 1826

P.S. A Jew in Kremenchuk has, praise God, admitted very recently that he is one of those guilty of the murder perpetrated against five of your unhappy brethren.[32] He accused two other criminals involved, for whose arrest in Kierworud [?] Volhynia the required measures have been taken.

Received 28 November.

85. Johann Cornies to David Epp, Heubuden. 25 November 1826. SAOR 89-1-82/65v.[33]

D. Epp,

I can now provide more information about the proposed Mennonite settlement in Bessarabia. His Honour, First Lieutenant Guildenschanz, member of the Guardianship Committee for Foreigners in Southern Russia with responsibilities for special commissions, reported to me on 3 October that His Excellency, the chief curator of the above Committee, Lieutenant General Inzov, approved my proposal that 12,000 desiatinas of usable land already surveyed by the colonial administration be reserved for Mennonite settlement. If, after the first group of 100 families have been settled provisionally, more families can be expected, then His Excellency is inclined to reserve the whole piece of land for Mennonites.

---

32 Regarding this robbery and the murders, see also documents 28, 49, and 79.

33 Regarding the planned Bessarabian colony, see also documents 38, 61, 64, 66, 80, 81, 86, 104, and 148.

To avoid disappointment, immigrants should know that they will not be given any advance funds. To give immigrants a more precise idea of the land in question, I include a short description of it, as well as a map.[34]

1. The map shows a part of the guberniia of Bessarabia. The German settlements are marked in red, the Bulgarian settlements in dark yellow. The land designated for Mennonite settlement is marked by the letters C, D, and E, and adjoins the German and Bulgarian colonies. The closest cities are correctly located on the map, in accordance with its cartographic projection. Distances to the port cities of Odessa, Akkerman, Kitiia, and Ismail are not great. The large, heavily populated provincial city of Kishinev can also be considered for internal commerce. Although it is not marked on the map, Kishinev lies not more than eighty verstas west of the settlement.

As for the development and cultivation of the land itself, I include an excerpt from a letter by Mr. Weygel from the Sarata colony, a neighbour bordering on this land. He was officially commissioned by Mr. Guildenschanz to inspect and describe it.

The prices given in this excerpt are in Turkish currency – the lion or the piaster. No constant exchange rate exists between Turkish and Russian currencies, and it is dependent upon which currency the merchants need. Currently, a silver ruble can be exchanged for eight lions. Simply expressed, one lion costs fifty kopeks, and this can rise to sixty or seventy kopeks but is usually about sixty kopeks. According to local exchange rates, 100 R.B.A. are equivalent to twenty-five silver rubles.

2. It is erroneous, and could arouse settlers' fears, to think of Bessarabia as a totally deserted strip of land, uncultivated and lying waste. To counter this, let me cite a dependable statistical summary of the German and Bulgarian settlements established there a number of years ago. German colonists live in nineteen villages with 1,958 families, or 8,681 souls of both genders. Bulgarian colonists live in sixty-two villages with 5,518 families, or 29,240 souls of both genders. These are only those settlements that are under the same administration as ours. There are also the original inhabitants [Rumanians] of the land and Russians in Bessarabian villages and cities.

34 The referenced map is not extant.

There are thus eighty-one villages of foreign colonists in the guberniia, with 7,476 families, or 37,921 souls, inhabiting an area of 692,897 desiatinas. Colonist livestock holdings are 15,491 horses, 62,285 cattle, and 140,991 ordinary sheep. There are 54,879 cultivated fruit trees and 762 mulberry trees for silk culture. 774,885 vines produce 20,950 pails of wine. This summary of the activities pursued by the present colonists makes it clear that Bessarabia is a land where every diligent, industrious individual can make good progress when using sound economic management.

Neighbours need not be feared since many are German, including the famous Sarata colony established several years ago by the cleric, Lindl. It consists of ninety-five families, or 422 souls, and is a model of morality and Christianity.

Reflect on these circumstances carefully and in detail. I have done what it is possible for me to do for my brethren, as an honourable man. Russia's state administration will not grant 12,000 desiatinas of free land without some returns. I insist this matter be considered thoroughly by anyone wishing to emigrate.

I should point out that the Dniester stream, from A and B, forms the border between the guberniias of Bessarabia and Kherson. Villages located opposite Akkerman are actually not in Bessarabia but in Kherson guberniia, and so are not under consideration here.

I must also explain the structure of the colonial organization more clearly. All colonists in southern Russia are administered under three lower colonial administrations or bureaus, namely those in Ekaterinoslav, Odessa, and Bessarabia. The bureaus are directly responsible to a Guardianship Committee located in the city of Kishinev, Bessarabia.

If anyone is considering emigration, they should elect a commission to undertake a journey to Bessarabia to inspect the land and visit the Guardianship Committee in Kishinev. They may also write to the Committee directly, requesting detailed information.

I would have gone to Bessarabia myself this autumn when Mr. Guildenshanz invited me, but I was too busy with matters here. If a long journey is not required of me in spring, I would like to inspect the 12,000 desiatinas in question and consider, on site, how settlement can best be established.

This must be enough for now. With heartfelt greetings, I remain your willing,

Johann Cornies

<u>Your travel route:</u>

From Warsaw to Brest Litovsk	196 [verstas]
to Kovel	121½
to Lutsk	71
to Dubno	47½
to Ostrog	58
to Starakonstantinov	82
to Broskurov	46
to Vinnitza	94
to Bratzlav	78
to Balta	131
to Kishinev	147
	1,072 verstas or 153 [German] miles

86. Johann Cornies to David Epp, Prussia. [25 November] 1826. SAOR 89-1-82/69.[35]

David Epp, beloved brother,

I am again intruding on your time with the Bessarabian question. I know you are only disturbed by things that are not useful, so I ask you to judge my imposition indulgently. It flows from one heart to another. I can honestly say that I know no man better able than you to deal with this matter.

Much as I would like to see a settlement of Mennonites established in Bessarabia, I must be on my guard, since any carelessness would discredit me and the settlers, and could be detrimental for us and our descendants. This is why I proposed to you a year ago that your potential immigrants choose from their midst an intelligent man to conduct a dependable correspondence on this matter. Our authorities do not accept opinions and superficial negotiations, but insist that everything be done honestly and in detail. The Crown does not want simply to attract foreigners into the country and will only be satisfied with good, upright economic managers, useful to the state.

35 Regarding the planned Bessarabian colony, see also documents 38, 61, 64, 66, 80, 81, 85, 104, and 148.

I was told the following at the Ministry in St. Petersburg: "If you do not work industriously, as you promised and for which you were granted the *Privilegium*, you are in danger of losing your special privileges. The law may change over time, but what have you meanwhile accomplished?" This is said in St. Petersburg, but attitudes are different on the Molochnaia. The thoughtful person finds that every human law is subject to change. Consequently I plan ahead to prevent anything that might arise to disturb my conscience.

In 1819, through the grace of His Majesty, Tsar Alexander, of immortal memory, 200,000 rubles of assistance were placed at the disposal of the colonial administration, granted for the settlement of Mennonites on the Molochnaia. Granted as an advance, because the flow of Prussian Mennonite immigrants was weak, they have now been largely repaid by the guberniia tax office. But some 35,000 rubles are still available – enough to assist another thirty-five to forty Mennonite families. We can expect no advances in future. Young farmers who now transfer their abode from existing communities to a new settlement must immediately pay land tax. Everything is thus subject to change, though demands are still reasonable and moderate.

Please, my very dear brother, take over this correspondence relating to the settlement in Bessarabia. Without a mediator, mistakes and misunderstandings could occur that I would find most painful.

Let me close before this becomes tedious. You need time to reflect. The Lord be with you and give you His peace. May He grant that the seed you have sown, though it may now lie covered by snow and ice, will come to fruition, and if not here, then in blessed eternity. There your efforts will be laid as gifts before the throne of God. May we meet, if not here, then united in eternity.

With the assurance of this hope, let us trust in Him who shed His blood for us on the cross. May Jesus be our beginning and our end. Amen.

My wife and I send hearty greetings to you, your dear wife, and your relatives, as I remain, with respect and esteem, your honest brother,

Cornies

87. Johann Cornies to [Klaas] Dyck. [28 November] 1826. SAOR 89-1-82/72.

Dear brother-in-law Dyck,

Friend Ennz delivered your letter of 4 October to us on 20 November. We are pleased to know that you are all well and have moved from Heubuden to Schlablau. There you are now in our aunt's circle. Thank

God that we are all healthy and doing well, as are your children. No misfortunes have struck our villages.

Margaretha has changed lodgings. She now lives with your neighbour Johann Fast. The change occurred because D. Wieb's authority was transferred to Lichtenau where a new church was being constructed. He requested that my wife have Margaretha taken from him.

Schlatter sent me interesting letters from Constantinople, Smyrna, and Livorno, but they are too scattered to quote. My sheep barn is finished. It cost not 3,000 rubles but over 5,000. I received your letter telling me that the books would be delivered with Mr. Friesen's help. You say nothing, however as to whether the books, *Der deutsche Obstgaertner* [The German fruit grower], were bound and are en route. Klaas Heide is still in Khortitsa. Perhaps you sent something along with him. Cancel the book purchases I ordered from you. The books are expensive and may not serve their purpose. What do they cost in St. Petersburg?

I would like you to bring along some dogs if that is not too difficult for you. If it is [too difficult, then] cancel the purchase. Please decide whether young or old dogs are better and how best to transport them.

You do not mention any of our other relatives. Are they all dead? Your letter would have been far more interesting if you had included news about my wife's relatives. Do not imagine that we know what you have experienced and learned. Do not be angry with me, but try to write something newsworthy in future, whatever comes to your mind, even if it is a hodgepodge, as are my letters.

My wife expressly sends greetings to Uncle Franz Klassen, to her aunt and children, and to Uncle Abram Dyck and his relatives. I also send them hearty greetings. I may be off to Saxony in spring, but do not know when. If they knew that I was writing you, many more would have sent you their greetings. You must, for now, be satisfied.

We and your dear children commend you to God's keeping. May He grant you His peace and bless your affairs so that you might return to us in good health. Keep God in mind and in your hearts, and thank Him for all His mercies He has shown and will again. Because we love you, we pray for you and send you our greetings, as do your loving children. With honesty and sympathy we remain, your well-inclined friend,

J.C.

Definite news has just arrived that the murderers who killed the four men last year have been found. They are Jews. We know nothing more that we can trust.

88. Traugott Blueher to Johann Cornies. 21 December 1826. SAOR 89-1-88/51.

Dear Friend Cornies,

Your valued letters dated 14 October and 24 October have arrived and I am pleased that you are satisfied with the sale of the stored Spanish wool.

Since I could not find the book you wanted, I had it sent from St. Petersburg. My costs were six rubles, seventy kopeks.

I thank you in advance for agreeing to arrange the sale of Sarepta products in your region. We must wait to see if anything is possible in this regard.

Wool prices here have not increased noticeably and, according to newspaper accounts, continue to be sluggish abroad as well. There is little demand from England.

Nothing has been heard from the Basel missionaries in Shushi since unrest broke out in their region.[36] We presume they are safe since the Persians who besieged the city did not take it. The Tatars robbed and destroyed the two German villages, Helenendorf and Catharinenfeldt. The people escaped with only the clothes on their backs. Colonists in the former village fled to Elisabethpol, eight verstas away. Only the four families who stayed behind were savagely mistreated by the Tatars, especially the young women, who were raped. They have since rejoined their own people. Thirty people in Catharinenfeldt were gruesomely killed and 140 souls were dragged off into captivity in the Turkish region. The Russian commander requested that they be freed, but the Turkish pasha refused. At the moment, there is no hope for them. Still, our Lord is strong enough to save our pitiable brethren who have fallen into slavery.

Here are a few excerpts from the above report:

"Who can describe the grief and distress that overcame the community in these few hours. The victims were caught with long ropes, like livestock in a noose, and driven together like a herd. Good clothes were torn from their bodies; the very old people were disrobed and cut down naked or allowed to run. The school teacher's wife was raped to death before her own door, and a pregnant woman's belly cut open and its fruit taken alive. Children were tied in pairs and hung on the sides of the horses to hasten the escape. Children who cried out were stabbed

36 Shushi is a town in Nagorno-Karabakh. It was besieged during the Russo-Turkish War of 1827–8.

to death before their parents' eyes. A valued sister, who resisted a monster who sought to haul her onto his horse, was felled by a bullet and writhed on the ground in her blood. Her suffering is mirrored in the size of the pit she clawed out with her hands. Their minister, an old man named Rohrer, was stripped and forced to circle his house until beheaded. Three fifteen-year-old girls tried to escape, but two were caught some six verstas from the village. A man, Busch, fought for his wife and three children with entreaties, pleas, and resistance, but sank down a bloody sacrifice before his wife who had sought refuge up a tree. After two children were loaded onto a horse, their mother threw away everything but her infant in order to satisfy the tyrant. The Lord helped her, but she watched helplessly as her two other children were carried off."

I send you and your dear ones heartfelt greetings and remain your honest friend and brother,

Traugott Blueher

Received 10 January.

89. Johann Cornies to Wilhelm Martens. 27 December 1826. SAOR 89-1-82/76v.

Valued, treasured friend Martens,

My family has agreed that I travel to the Kingdom of Saxony to buy a not inconsiderable number of electoral merino sheep at my own costs. According to my calculations, I need more money and turn to you with a request. If your situation permits, please give me an advance of up to 10,000 rubles in exchange for a secure guarantee of a term and interest rate agreeable to you. If this is possible, please answer me with this messenger. It is high time to proceed. On Wednesday, I will tell Mr. Contenius about my intentions. This should give the authorities enough time to make arrangements that would permit me to leave by mid-February.

Assuring you of my faithful honesty, my wife and I send you and your dear wife heartfelt greetings. I remain your loving friend,

J.C.

90. Johann Cornies to Samuel Contenius. 28 December 1826. SAOR 89-1-82/77.

Your Excellency,

The local District Office recently rejected the advance of 30,000 rubles Martens and I had proposed. It was intended for the purchase of a number of electoral merino sheep in the Kingdom of Saxony. They do not need the money because the journey to Saxony has been called off for this year.

Following discussion with my family, I have definitely decided to leave in February 1827, at my own expense, for Saxony, to buy 100–150 head of electoral merino ewes and rams of the highest quality and to transport them to this area.

I need Your Excellency's wise counsel for my intended purpose, and obediently request that you kindly give me Yr. well-meaning advice and help, including letters of recommendation for my journey and my time in Saxony.

If God brings me back safely, I hope that the journey will have been of great benefit for me and my community. My greatest resolve is to serve my brethren by positive actions and for our general well-being.

I obediently request that you give gracious consideration to my planned journey and await your early reply.

Yr. Excellency's completely obedient servant,

J.C.

91. Johann Cornies to Andrei M. Fadeev. 28 December 1826. SAOR 89-1-82/77.

Mr. Fadeev,

Since the District Office cancelled this year's journey to the Kingdom of Saxony to purchase a quantity of merino sheep for the community, I have definitely decided to leave for Saxony in February 1827, at my own expense, to purchase 100-150 merino ewes and rams for myself.

I need the necessary passes and other documents from local authorities to authorize my journey to the Kingdom of Saxony, and within Saxony itself. I do not know how to acquire the documents required, and humbly ask that Yr. Honour kindly help me in this regard so that I can conclude my purchases before shearing begins.

In the firm hope that Yr. Honour will assist me, I have the honour to be Yr. Honour's devoted servant,

J.C.

92. Johann Cornies to Wilhelm Frank. 28 December 1826. SAOR 89-1-82/77.

Honoured Mr. Frank,

The decision has now been made. God willing, I will travel from Ohrloff to the Kingdom of Saxony at my own expense in February, to buy a not inconsiderable number of merino sheep for myself. What do you say? Will you become my travelling companion? Such an opportunity to travel and to learn does not come often for a young man like yourself. Please do not spare any effort to persuade your superiors to permit you to accompany me. I sincerely wish you would. I think we would take pleasure in one another's company.

I must not make it too attractive, however. There will be difficulties on a journey of this kind. Yet I feel that no hardship or effort will be too much for me to overcome, should necessity require. I demand and expect the same of my travelling companions. Each one will have responsibilities that need to be discharged carefully and punctually. If the situation requires, one person must assist another, without objection. As to food, everyone eats exactly what I eat. The food will only be as delicate as is offered by local custom, but it must be healthy and nutritious. Grumbling and quarrelling will not be tolerated. I spare no one and punish improprieties immediately, though I do not remain stubborn or angry for long. There must generally be peace and love among us.

I will take along three travelling companions. Our party will consist of four persons: a director of the enterprise, an accountant and secretary, a shepherd, and a coachman. Your position would be that of the accountant and secretary.

If you are firmly resolved to accompany me and are able to obtain permission to come, please prepare yourself for travel. In any case, give me your thoughts with the first mail, so that I know where I stand. I have written to His Excellency, only letting him know about the trip and requesting letters of recommendation. I did not mention you. I have likewise written to His Honour, Mr. Fadeev, to obtain the necessary documents for myself.

Heartfelt greetings. I long to include you on the journey. I remain, with hope, your servant,

J.C.

P.S. I received the stamped sheet of paper that you kindly obtained for me. The Jewish tinker claims he has not been paid for the lead weights that belong on the account for section 15. When they are ready, please send them along with J. Klassen's employees. Please tell surveyor Timash to send me the map I paid for, and to complete the other ones, since I need them urgently for the trip. Please remind His Excellency, Mr. Contenius, to return the description of the Nogais.

How much will you want for the trip? I do not pay high wages but there will be a reasonable sum. Agreement in advance prevents later disagreement. Please do not fail to report all these things to me.

1827

93. Count G. Dohna to Johann Cornies. 2 January 1827. SAOR 89-1-62/9.[1]

Most esteemed friend, brother in the Lord,

Prompted by my dear, well-loved Daniel Schlatter, I am writing to express my hopes that you will visit me and also answer questions about the Saxon sheep farms you plan to visit. You will be travelling through Bohemia to Dresden. Please send a messenger from the city to me here, three hours away, and I will come immediately or have someone meet you.

I respond to your questions as follows:

1. I will give you specific information about Saxony's best sheep farms when you arrive.

2. Shearing begins in mid- or late May. The Royal Sheep Farm sells rams after 1 February every year, and ewes after Johannis [midsummer's] day.

3. Rams on the Royal Sheep Farm are priced at thirty to forty Reichsthaler per head, the sheep at fifteen Reichsthaler.

May God guide you on your long journey and send his angel to lead and accompany you. With heartfelt pleasure, I look forward to meeting you. Please give the enclosed to our dear Daniel.

With sincere love,
G. Dohna
Hermsdorf, near Dresden
Received 19 January.

---

1 This member of the prominent Dohna family was probably the grandson of Zinzendorf (see Heinrich von Treitschke, *Historische und politische Aufsatze*, 4 vols. [Leipzig, 1896], 4: 317). The Dohna family succeeded Zinzendorf as the principal patrons of the Moravian Brethren in Saxony. See also document 112.

94. Samuel Contenius to Johann Cornies. 8 January 1827. SAOR 89-1-95/16.

Honoured Johann Cornies,

Your intention to buy 100 to 150 head of electoral merino ewes and rams in Saxony has my complete approval. Regrettably, sheep in the Halbstadt Mennonite District will not be improved to the same degree as if 200 Saxon ewes and twenty of the finest merino rams were bought for the Kurushan community sheep farm, as I explained in detail. Still, it is preferable to do some good rather than none at all.

Since it is becoming more difficult to obtain passes, I am reminding you, dear Cornies, that you must not delay in sending the [Guardianship] Committee detailed information about your decisions and about the purpose of your journey (send me a copy). You will be provided with everything you need, if possible.

With appreciation, I remain your honestly supportive,

S. Contenius

95. Alexanderwohl Village Office to Johann Cornies. 10 January 1827. SAOR 89-1-21/63.[2]

Request to the authorized representative Cornies:

As you know, the Alexanderwohl community is in a sad situation in regard to the minimum of sixty-five desiatinas to which every villager is entitled. On 17 May 1826, we met with the District Office to discuss leasing 300 desiatinas of Crown lands situated on our boundary until this land is needed for settlement. With help from the District Office, we submitted a petition with this request to the [Guardianship] Committee. On 30 December 1826, the Committee informed us that all unsettled land in the Mennonite District is under lease to the Mennonite Cornies.

We therefore respectfully ask you, as leaseholder, to cede this land to us in writing. Since you are already aware of our difficult situation, we request that you, as the authorized representative, intercede on our behalf with the Committee in a way that would enable us to obtain this land at the same rate per desiatina paid by Crown leaseholders until such time as the Crown lands are settled.

2 Regarding the Alexanderwohl land dispute, see also documents 25, 26, 30, and 31.

In the confident hope that you will further our interests,
Village Mayor Dallke

96. Johann Cornies' travel journal to Saxony and Prussia in 1827 (14 February–26 September 1827). SAOR 89-1-103.[3]

15 February: We began our journey, having commended ourselves to God, said farewell to our dear relatives and acquaintances in Ohrloff, and received their wishes for good luck. We arrived safely at the home of Wilhelm Martens in Halbstadt at about 5:30 p.m., having left at 3:30.

97. From Bernhard Fast. 16 February 1827. SAOR 89-1-62/28.

May the Lord's blessing fill the hearts of all those who love the Lord Jesus from the bottom of their souls.

Three brethren from this community – Gerhard Martens, Johann Reger, and Johann Suckau – are planning to accompany our beloved brother Johann Cornies on a journey to Saxony under God's protection.

We commend these brethren to all Christian congregations of whatever position and confession they may be, asking them to provide their support in all situations that might occur. In return, we will be sure to praise and thank God, who holds all human hearts in His hand and can direct them wherever He wills, even as He does flowing water in a brook. We also feel obligated to accompany these, our brethren, in our prayers, asking God to keep them in His majesty, and to direct their hearts to show love, peace, and obedience at all times. May the Lord bless all those who perform a loving deed on behalf of these, our brethren.

This is wished by your faithfully united servant and friend in the word and service of the Lord,

Bernhard Fast, Elder of the Mennonite Community on the Molochnaia
Halbstadt, 16 February 1827

[Document bears a seal. There is also a similar document for Johann Cornies himself.]

---

3 This long journal is largely descriptive, and only a handful of the most interesting entries have been reproduced here. They are interspersed with the correspondence at their chronological date.

98. David Cornies to Johann Cornies. 4 March 1827. SAOR 89-1-62/25v.

Dear brother,

We finally received your letter on 3 March. In good health ourselves, we are most pleased to hear that everyone in your company is healthy and in good spirits. We heard about your accident with the axle. Fortunately, it was not worse, as it could easily have been. You will ask about many things, but since little is happening here I will try not to make this letter too tedious. Everything is going well on the sheep farm, which I visited yesterday. Your family, our dear mother, our family, and the family of Peter Cornies, as well as all friends and acquaintances, are in the best of health. They send you and your companions sincere greetings. Tobias Voth sends his special greetings.

Dear brother, your business must often distract you, but remain confident and courageous. Our omnipotent God will protect you if you ask His assistance. For my part, I include you in my feeble prayers.

You write about the mud you are encountering. The situation here is quite the opposite. It has been dry since your departure and the weather is warm, up to ten degrees. I close with special greetings and sign myself, your honest, loving brother, who prays for you,

David Cornies

P.S. Your wife received the books, *Der verstaendige Bauer* [The wise peasant], which seem to be very useful. I just bought fifty chetverts of rye and ten chetverts of barley, both of good quality. We broke three horses on the sheep farm, but no two-year-olds, since it seemed to me that they are really too young.

Today, every fullholder and cottager was summoned to the Village Office, and District Secretary Dyck drew up a list of where everyone attends church. Friend Martens from Halbstadt also includes a letter. Just as we were writing, Ataman Baby arrived to move his sheep onto the Israelite land. Monday, 7 March, we intend to begin ploughing, but others in our village have already started.

Received 27 March 1827 in Brody.

99. Wilhelm Martens to Johann Cornies. 4 March 1827. SAOR 89-1-62/39.

Most honoured friend,

We do not know how far you have travelled or what experiences you have had, but hope that you complete your journey safely and in good health, according to your expectations. We sincerely hope that this thin letter finds you and your travelling companions cheerful and well.

We cannot but thank our dear God for granting us quite good health. Your wife and your brother, Peter Cornies, visited us once and your other two brothers, Heinrich and David, were here today, having driven to Tokmak on business. All are well.

I had hoped you would write from Ekaterinoslav about leasing the Israelite steppe. The Ekaterinoslav Guardianship Committee notified our District Office that I must, in this regard, appear before the Committee by approximately the [blank] day of the month.

Right now the weather is so beautiful and warm that people in Halbstadt have been out ploughing their fields since Tuesday. I know of no other changes to report. More another time.

Worthy friend, please give us the pleasure of writing us a few lines very soon about your health, and about everything of importance on your journey.

My wife and I wish you and your travelling companions the best of health and commend you to God's keeping. With many greetings and wishes for a safe journey, I remain, your faithful and loving friend,

Wilhelm Martens.

Received 27 March 1827 in Brody.

**100. Johann Cornies to District Office. 17 March 1827.
SAOR 89-1-102/3.**

Sent from Michalin.

To the District Office,

I can now report on your trustful commission. After we arrived here in Michalin, Makhnovetz Uezd, Kiev guberniia, on 11 March, I personally delivered your letter to the merchant, Mr. Lenz. We had to visit the market town of Berdichev to exchange our Russian money for foreign currency before we could inspect his sheep. Once we returned to Michalin, we selected the number of sheep the District Office required of us from Mr. Lenz' flock and put down a deposit for ten of the most superior rams and ten ewes. The enclosed document shows the exact number and year for each of these sheep.

Once I receive the sheep, I will send you samples taken from each one in a sealed envelope. I hope the fineness of these animals will do honour to Mr. Lenz and be useful for the community sheep farm. I prefer them to the sheep from Tsarskoe Selo. I would particularly like to have the Wool Improvement Society form an opinion about one of the rams.

Mr. Lenz and I found ourselves in disagreement due to a misunderstanding, perhaps a deliberate one. Mr. Lenz had explicitly agreed with the District Office that the deposit should be one-tenth of the price. He now interprets the small deposit of 100 rubles, on this considerable purchase of 2,800 rubles, as an indication of the District Office's distrust and lack of esteem, and feels personally dishonoured. I gave Mr. Lenz an agreement for the money owing him. I request that, upon delivery of the sheep, this money be paid to Mr. Lenz in Banco Assignats without delay.

With the appropriate respect, I am the District Office's obedient,

Johann Cornies

101. Johann Cornies to Samuel Contenius. 17 March 1827. SAOR 89-1-102/4.

Sent from Michalin.

To Acting State Counsellor, Mr. Contenius in Ekaterinoslav,

Your Excellency, Most Gracious Sir,

On 11 March, we arrived safely and in good health in Michalin, near the city Makhnovka, among our brethren in faith (known as the Dutch). We immediately proceeded to Berdichev to exchange our Russian silver currency for ducats with the bankers Mansohn et Ephrushy. The exchange rate was unfavourable, because ducats of full weight occur infrequently here. We paid eleven R.B.A, fifty kopeks, for each ducat and all were weighed.

The bad roads impede our progress. The weather is changeable – at times rain, then snow or frost, with up to three such alterations in one day. The country roads are extremely muddy and so full of holes that we are, at any moment, in danger of being overturned.

With the most complete respect and constant esteem I remain Your Excellency's devoted servant,

Johann Cornies

102. Klaas Dyck to Johann Cornies. 19 March 1827. SAOR 89-1-62/7.

Sent from Schablau. Received 1 May in Herrnhut.

To Mr. Johann Cornies, Imperial Russian Subject, currently on a journey to the Kingdom of Saxony,

Dear brother-in-law,

On 12 March, as I walked to the parish church section of the city of Marienburg, the mailman gave me your letter of 12 January, and I learned about your sudden decision to travel to the Kingdom of Saxony. We intend to begin our return journey on 9 May, although I battled with frightful problems until last Monday when the legal documents were finally completed. My capital must be paid to me by 1 May. We have succeeded in completing the documents without court proceedings.

I firmly hope that the Lord will bring us together again in this life, and support us through good and bad experiences until we finally part. Three weeks ago, we received your letter of 20 November, somewhat late, to purchase dogs. Mr. Bichler, an honourable man, offers me some hope but needs your answer with the earliest mail. I will then leave for Loeblin on the third day of our Easter celebrations. You can depend on me to complete all of your orders punctually, as far as I can. Johann was very ill for fourteen days and my father is very ill as well. Otherwise, we are well, and so are your wife's relatives and mine, except for Aunt Franz Klaassen, who has been sickly for about three weeks and is bedridden most of the time.

Further hearty greetings from us and from Uncle and Aunt Franz Klaassen. May the Lord send his angel to accompany you on your journey, as He once did the young Tobias. I remain your loving brother-in-law,

Klaas Dyck

103. Johann Cornies to Wilhelm Frank. 21 March 1827. SAOR 89-1-102/4v.

Sent from Novoslovskaya Inn, in Saslav Uezd, Volhynia guberniia.

Honoured Mr. Frank, sincerely beloved friend,

We are stuck here in the Novoslovskaya Inn, between Labun and Saslav, about 900 verstas from the Molochnaia and have come to a halt because of the deep snow that fell last night and is still falling today. We journey much like a pilgrim who makes slow but steady progress daily (except for today). Heavy rain has turned every road into a deep quagmire and, despite our best intentions, we cannot move quickly without damage to our horses.

Local Polish towns are expanses of swampy mud and we are in danger of tipping over at any moment. The well-built and well-run inns, which do their country honour, are the only inviting feature for travellers in this region. Jews, hospitable when paid, do everything they can to make us welcome. We are glad they are here, for without them, we would suffer great discomfort and hardship.

For the first two days, the road from Ekaterinoslav was better than expected. Then it started to rain intermittently as far as Berdichev. It is impossible to describe the mud that then transformed our travel into a series of nightmares that, on many days, permitted us to cover only twenty verstas from early morning until nightfall. We left a wagon and several people with the Mennonites in Michalin and, harnessing

Mr. Lenz' horses to the other wagon, drove to Berdichev to complete our currency exchange. The trip took three days to complete. We also spent three days with the Mennonites purchasing rams and ewes from Mr. Lenz for several friends, myself, and the Kurushan community sheep farm. High winds and snow then delayed us for another day and a half.

We are quite healthy, God be praised, and are trying to make speedy progress to Brody, but one's hair turns grey on these roads. We still have 166 verstas to Brody, a three-day trip were it not for today's storm and a fut of snow. We are forced to sit quietly while time passes us by. We had hoped to see Mennonites near Ostroga this evening or tomorrow morning and pass through Saslov tomorrow (and post this letter), but only time will tell. At the moment, we have no prospect of continuing. I would advise no one to make this journey in early spring.

There should be better conditions around Saslov with its sandy soil, but we are unlikely to reach Herrnhut in six weeks. Time for us is more important than money, and we count every hour, hoping to complete the selection and purchase of our sheep before shearing time.

I regained my health in Michalin and am still well. I cannot thank my dear God enough. What good is a sick person on a trip, a burden to himself and his companions? We greet you and commend ourselves to your special intercession. With the honesty of our sentiments, I remain your devoted friend and servant.

N.B. Kindly inform my wife in Ohrloff and friend H. Heese in Khortitsa about the contents of this letter. God willing, we will write to our loved ones from Radsivilov or Brody. Please give our greetings to anyone who asks about us, especially our families on the Molochnaia and in Khortitsa.

Johann Cornies

104. Peter Friesen to Johann Cornies. 23 March 1827. SAOR 89-1-62/11.[4]

Most sincerely beloved father,[5]

We received your treasured letter No. 1 on 21 March. You can imagine the joy with which we read it. We are especially happy that you are all healthy and in good spirits. On 12 March, letters arrived from

4 Regarding the planned Bessarabian colony, see also documents 38, 61, 64, 66, 80, 81, 85, 86, and 148.

5 In later letters, Johann Cornies calls Peter Friesen his foster son (*Pflegesohn*). It was common for well-off Mennonites to foster orphans or the children of impoverished widows, and scattered references suggest that Cornies did so on several occasions.

Prussia from Claas Dyck, from David Epp, and from a certain Gerhard Dyck, Kaldowe. Klaas Dyck writes that the agreement with his father miscarried and must be negotiated again. He and his family are healthy and they intend to leave there in mid-May. He will bring along friends Schlatter, Horwitz, and Hausknecht.

Epp's letter begins as follows: "I received both of your letters of 14 August in good order. What you wrote about a settlement in Bessarabia is already in circulation. I also received the Mennonite population statistics and a transcript about the Lindl congregation in Sarata. However, the latter got wet and some of it cannot be read." I do not think it necessary to excerpt anything more from the letter.

Gerhard Dyck, Kaldowe, is a man of forty-one, his wife twenty-seven, and the oldest of his four children (a son) seven years old. Dyck, who is without means, would like to move to Russia. To earn his travel costs, he wants to herd the sheep that you intend to purchase in Saxony. He thinks he will make a living more easily in Russia than in Prussia. Epp describes Dyck as a Christian with useful skills in building machinery.

David Cornies asked me to write about our sheep farm and the rented lands. Everything is going well on the farm. Five mares have foaled. No sheep in the large flock have lambed, but they soon will. Ten chetverik of wheat have been sown, six chetverik of oats, but no barley as of now. There is enough livestock at Iushanle at present, but there are only two herds and one flock at Tashchenak. There is one flock on the Baden land and two on the Israelite land. The land Iuri leased last year is now leased by a Molokan for 650 rubles. The old eighteen-foot well at the threshing floor has been enlarged to twenty-six fut and is running well. Kochenovskii only offered 600 rubles for the land he rented earlier, but David Cornies demanded 1,100. They did not reach an agreement. David Cornies wants to rent it by sections today.

You may have received a letter from David Cornies in Brody that we forgot to number. It is sealed with glue but the envelope to Mr. Hausner, which contained your letter, was sealed with wax, but without David Cornies' seal. Your friends all send you and your companions their greetings and wish you a safe journey. Regehr's brother was here yesterday but we did not speak. He seemed well. With heartfelt greetings, I wish you a healthy and happy journey with God, and send my prayers to our dear Lord.

Letter No. 2 will follow this one.

I remain your honest son who prays for you,

Peter Friesen

Received 25 April, o.s., in Dresden.

105. Johann Cornies to Andrei M. Fadeev. 27 March 1827. SAOR 89-1-102/6v.

Sent from Brody.

Senior Member of the Ekaterinoslav Committee, Fadeev,

Your Honour, Gracious Sir,

I am privileged to report that we arrived in Brody today at noon, healthy and full of energy. Bad roads and changeable weather have kept us from making speedy progress. We hope to have overcome the worst, however, because there is a high road that leads on from here. We plan to depart tomorrow and reach Herrnhut in fourteen days' time, assuming our good health continues.

Since Russian currency cannot be taken across the border freely and we have no intentions of smuggling, we took a bill of exchange for 2,000 rubles from Radsivilov to Hausner and Company in Brody. This exchange is delaying us here today, Sunday. We humbly request that you inform His Excellency, the Acting Privy Counsellor, Mr. Contenius, about our progress. If it is God's will, we will write to His Excellency from Cracow or Breslau.

Since Brody is a free imperial city, it is more difficult to cross the border here than elsewhere, but we encountered few problems. Only the two envelopes for the honourable ambassadors in Saxony detained us for several hours, but they were returned to us and we crossed the border safely.

With respect and devotion, I am Yr. Honour's devoted,

Johann Cornies

106. Johann Cornies' travel journal to Saxony and Prussia in 1827 (14 February–26 September 1827). SAOR 89-1-103.[6]

30 March: After we had a horse shod in Tshishiska and had a drag chain made, we left at 8 a.m. and arrived in the splendid city of Lemberg [Lviv] by 10 a.m. Here, for a fee, we saw foreign animals such as a lion, two female lions, a leopard, various foreign snakes, and other similar things. Lemberg is situated in a valley and surrounded by high mountains. It is beautifully built of masonry with buildings up to four stories high. Its busy trade is conducted by many Jews, Germans, and Poles.

6 Regarding this journal, see footnote 3.

A two hundred foot (thirty-two faden) clock tower, supposedly built in 1335, collapsed in June 1826. It fell onto eleven people, and a man at the top jumped to a roof to survive, breaking his leg and seven ribs …

We wanted to travel farther today but the Lemberg police told us our passes were invalid because they should have been signed by the Ministry of Foreign Affairs and not by the Ministry of the Interior. We had to stay in Lemberg for the night to obtain a pass from the governor.

107. Johann Cornies to Klaas Dyck. 10/22 April 1827. SAOR 89-1-102/7.

Sent from Breslau.

Dear brother-in-law,

Heartfelt greetings to you, your dear wife, and little children, from Prussian Silesia. Having left Ohrloff on 15 February, o.s., as I wrote, we reached Breslau, the capital city, safely and in good health. My travelling companions are Gerhard Martens, my longtime secretary, Johann Sukau, my longtime servant, and Johann Regier, who was born in Heubuden and came to Russia three years ago. Khortitsa District Chairman Jacob Penner, and his driver and secretary are travelling with us on their own wagon. Our journey has been very slow. We were delayed almost two weeks by bad roads in Poland and in making four border crossings.

Oats are very dear, one Reichsthaler per bushel, and everything else accordingly. The Vistula rises in the Carpathians only two miles from here and forms the border between Austria and Prussia. I find it interesting to think that I am at the source of the Vistula, you at its mouth, while we are at a great distance from home and from one another.

I received the latest letter from my dear wife dated 4 March in Brody, and hope to find other letters waiting for me in Dresden. At the time of my departure, everyone was healthy except sister-in-law Boldt, who again had a fever. In three days' time, it will be eight weeks since I left home, and we have still not reached our destination. We have travelled 240 miles [1 German mile = 7.420 km.] and still have thirty to forty miles to go. God willing, we'll arrive in five to six days. Once our business is finished, we will immediately start our return march. It will be even slower than our progress to date because the land is intensively cultivated with little space left for the shepherd to graze his sheep.

Breslau, an especially large, beautiful city, is situated on a plain beside the Oder River. High towers rise amidst small groves, gardens, and narrow streets lined with houses up to five stories high. We have taken lodgings in a beautiful room on the second floor of the inn, "Zum goldenen Schwert" [At the Golden Sword], in the Goerlitz suburb. Should the development of my business affairs permit me to make a detour to Marienburg, I will, if there is time, notify you or brother Epp of our plans. Otherwise, I will come without writing. Extend warmest greetings to my dear friend, David Epp. Ask him to give Daniel Schlatter a warm reception.

Farewell and many greetings with love, from your friend and brother,

Johann Cornies

108. Johann Cornies to Samuel Contenius. 11 April 1827. SAOR 89-1-102/8v.

Sent from Breslau.

Acting State Counsellor, Mr. Contenius in Ekaterinoslav,

Your Excellency, Gracious Sir,

Yesterday evening, we arrived safely in Breslau and in good health. Although the journey has gone relatively well, the roads were bad and the border crossings difficult, with many delays. After leaving Radzivilov and Brody, we hoped to travel quickly through Galicia on the good imperial road, but were held up in Lemberg. There our passes were declared invalid for travel through Galicia because they lacked the signature of an Austrian consul. We obtained an Austrian pass after a day and a half's delay, and crossed the Austrian border above Crakow at Aszpazin. At Berun, on the Prussian side, I successfully asked the chief tax collector to accept our Austrian and Russian passes.

The Prussian high road is so well built that one horse is capable of pulling our carriage. A great variety of fruit trees line the road. Two-story-tall toll houses are spaced at intervals of two [German] miles each, and the toll is shockingly expensive – eighteen kopeks per [German] mile per horse. Oats are priced at four gulden per bushel, and other necessities accordingly.

The sheep we have to date inspected on local estates are not worth buying to take back to Russia. The best sheep farms seem to be at Liegnitz and Haynau. Since there is so little time left before sheep shearing, we have decided, once we reach Goerlitz, to separate into two groups. Penner will go through Bautzen to Dresden, and I will inspect sheep farms on this side of Dresden. We will meet in Dresden on a specific day.

We humbly ask Your Excellency to have the enclosed letters forwarded to our families, as addressed.

With the most heartfelt respect and esteem, I have the honour to be Your Excellency's most humble servant,

Johann Cornies

109. Johann Cornies to Senior Magistrate Biess. 14 April 1827. SAOR 89-1-102/9v.

Sent from Haynau.

To Senior Magistrate Mr. Biess, Petersdorf near Haynau,

Highly honoured Sir,

Your gracious reception prompts me to offer Yr. Honour my most genuine thanks. At the same time, I respectfully request that you inform me about the exact price, in Reichsthaler, of your two-year-old or one-year-old merino ewes and rams, and about the manner in which we will be permitted to make our selections – a manner that would permit us to make decisions appropriate to our purposes. We also hope that Yr. Honour will lower the quoted prices.

With the appropriate respect and esteem, I look forward to your reply and am honoured to be Yr. Honour's most submissive servant,

Johann Cornies

110. Johann Cornies' travel journal to Saxony and Prussia in 1827 (14 February–26 September 1827). SAOR 89-1-103.[7]

16 April: Departed at 6 a.m. and arrived in the city of Goerlitz at 10 a.m. This city is not large but quite beautiful and situated on seven hills. The Landeskrone, a high hill, is about a mile from the city. We occupied ourselves here until 3 p.m. and then separated from our companion, Penner, and then at 4 p.m., we crossed the border from Prussia to Saxony; specifically, into the Oberlausitz. We weren't even asked for our passes at the Prussian customs office and were permitted to drive into Saxony without delay. On the Saxon side, we were treated in the same way – not investigated at all or asked for our passes. The Oberlausitz is a very hilly region covered with forests. At 7 p.m. we arrived in Hirschfelde.

At Goerlitz, we saw Christ's holy grave in a chapel whose founder is depicted on the chapel wall. The Lord Jesus is first shown nailed to the cross, with the pieces of silver for which Christ was sold lying on a table

7 Regarding this journal, see footnote 3.

in front of the cross. Christ's prison is beside the cross. There is a break in the wall behind the cross, leading to a small vault hewn out of rock, in which Maria, the mother of God, is anointing the Saviour with spices.

Another vault represents the holy grave, and the stone in front of the door is supposed to be the size of the stone that lay before the door of Christ's grave. Three marks above the door indicate the bolts, and the other two the seals. A mark in the vault is supposed to represent the Saviour's height (on which opinions vary).

Across a valley from this vault, a tree represents the olive tree where Christ the Lord prayed during his betrayal, and a brook in the valley represents the Brook of Kidron, flowing from evening to morning. A low resting place beside the brook represents the place where the disciples slept. Finally, three linden trees beside the chapel represent three crosses, 970 steps away from Pilate's judgment seat and St. Peter's church.

111. Johann Cornies' travel journal to Saxony and Prussia in 1827 (14 February–26 September 1827). SAOR 89-1-103.[8]

18 April: Left at 9 a.m., went through the attractive little town of Zittau, and arrived in Herrnhut at about 1 o'clock. Herrnhut is small, very beautiful, and extremely clean. The houses are up to three stories high. We went into the prayer hall for evening prayers, devotions with God's word, and singing accompanied by an organ and other instruments. The cemetery is located at Hut Mountain, which is quite high and has a tower on it. The cemetery is nicely laid out and the graves go back 100 years. They are covered by stones marked with the date and place of birth, and also the date of death, of the deceased. Burials are in the order of their deaths. Large linden trees are planted throughout.

112. Johann Cornies to Count G. Dohna. 19 April 1827. SAOR 89-1-102/10.[9]

Sent from Herrnhut.
Count Dohna in Herrnhut, Most gracious Count,

Yr. Grace kindly promised to let me have the small map of South Russia for a short time. I forgot to take it with me yesterday evening and therefore humbly request that you send it to me with this bearer.

---

8 Regarding this journal, see footnote 3.

9 Regarding Count Dohna, see footnote 3.

I wish Yr. Grace and esteemed wife a safe journey and a happy reunion. May you rest in the Lord's care. Whatever He decides is always good.

With the warmest thanks, I have the honour to be Your gracious Count's most submissive servant,

Johann Cornies

113. Johann Cornies to Theodor E. Horwitz. 19 April 1827. SAOR 89-1-102/10v.

Sent from Herrnhut.

Sincerely beloved brother,

Yesterday, 30 April, after a journey of nine weeks, I arrived safely and in good health here in Herrnhut. I thank the Lord for His wonderful guidance and preservation. Your pleasing letter to me had just arrived, which leads me to say that if you place your firm hopes simply and only in Him, for whom everything is possible, you cannot fail.

When you reach the Molochnaia, approach my friend in Altonau, Gerhard Enns, whose honesty and local knowledge can serve your purposes well. Please visit my wife and give her my greetings. Give my greetings also to your companion, Mr. Hausknecht, the dear Reverend David Epp, and Klaas Dyck, my brother-in-law. I have little time now because my business is underway and I leave Herrnhut within the hour. God willing, I will return in twelve days.

From the bottom of my heart, I wish you a safe journey and a happy reunion. May the Lord be with and around you. Amen!

Your loving friend and brother in Christ,

Johann Cornies

114. David Cornies to Johann Cornies. 19 April 1827. SAOR 89-1-62/16.

Beloved brother,

I am most pleased that your letters report a safe journey. For this I thank our Lord and pray that He will continue to lead you graciously. Ploughing was just completed at the sheep farm, and sixty-two yearlings and thirty-one calves were branded. Our ninety-one mares were let out to be bred on the 14th. 950 sheep gave birth to 1,170 lambs, but seventy died. The people on our sheep farm are doing very well and send greetings, which I transmit to you with love. The old well now provides sufficient water.

The Tiege village community is pleased and grateful for your sheep purchase on their behalf. I took the letter with this information to them, and also read them your letter to me.

On the afternoon of 11 April, we had an unusual dry fog, almost like dust, that fell to the ground. When we walked through the grass, our feet turned white as though ash had been spread over the grass.

Now, my beloved brother, travel in the name of God, and may your undertaking prosper. In closing, I remain your eternally loving brother,

David Cornies

Received 13/25 May, in Dresden, and answered on the same date.

115. Theodor E. Horwitz to Johann Cornies. 24 April 1827. SAOR 89-1-62/32.

Sent from Berlin

Dearly beloved brother in the Lord,

On 1 March, we received your letter from Ohrloff informing us of your departure. By then, our dear Schlatter, who spent only a short time here, had left for London. He informed us of conditions in your area, which did little to encourage us. Had we, at that time, listened only to our own desires and inclinations, we would probably have broken off our journey. Yet we sternly tested ourselves, and the grace of our Saviour magnified His appeal to our hearts, despite the problems that threatened us. We abandoned our resistance to His summons, and believing in Him who is powerful through the weak, plan to leave Heubuden on 15 May with brother Dyck, the Lord willing. Brother Hausknecht will arrive here in eight days. He has been in St. Gallen.

A letter from brother Epp received today informs us that you are already probably in Herrnhut. He asks me to inform you that Schlatter left on the 7th, to return to Ali by way of Warsaw. It would have given me much pleasure if the Lord had brought us together to speak to one another. Perhaps we will meet in Russia, and otherwise, surely before the throne of God, cleansed through the grace of our Redeemer and Saviour, Jesus Christ. May the Holy Spirit enable us to grow constantly firmer and more sincere in our belief in Him who makes the godless righteous, so that Christ may increase his presence in our lives.

Your brother in Christ,

T. Horwitz

P.S. Should you wish to send a message or any information, kindly write to D. Epp's address.

Received 30 April, in Herrnhut. Answered 1 May.

116. Johann Cornies' travel journal to Saxony and Prussia in 1827 (14 February–26 September 1827). SAOR 89-1-103.[10]

24 April: We left Dohna at 8 a.m. and arrived at 11 in the Royal capital, Dresden, where we met Penner, our travelling companion, who had arrived on the previous evening at the Inn of Three Lindens in Bautzen suburb.

Dresden is quite a large city, but not nearly as large or as beautiful as St. Petersburg. Most of the houses along crooked, narrow streets are five stories high. The splendid bridge over the Elbe River is built of stone masonry with iron railings. At the Bautzen end of the bridge, an iron rider on a boulder depicts Augustus the Strong, the former elector of Saxony and king of Poland. Rider and horse are extremely large and look as though they are alive. The horse's veins, its harness, and its shoes all have a lifelike appearance.

117. Johann Cornies' travel journal to Saxony and Prussia in 1827 (14 February–26 September 1827). SAOR 89-1-103.[11]

On 23 April [5 May, new style], the day before we arrived in Dresden, King Friedrich August suffered a stroke and died at the age of seventy-seven. Many of his subjects, be they of high or low rank, are in tears as they mourn the death of this good monarch. They fear they will never again have a monarch as good as Friedrich August. His position was immediately assumed by the Crown Prince, his brother Anton Clement Theodor, who is seventy-two.

The city of Dresden lies in a very pleasant valley, surrounded by many beautiful villages with forest and fruit trees. Fruit trees are planted along the royal roads near Dresden and all other towns in Saxony. The architecture of the royal castle is not splendid and no more distinguished than many other buildings. Though it is five stories high, its roof tiles are just like those on other structures.

118. Johann Cornies to Inspector Zille. 30 April 1827. SAOR 89-1-102/11.

Sent from Herrnhut, to Raubersdorf near Zittau, Saxony.

Highly respected Mr. Inspector,

10 Regarding this journal, see footnote 3.

11 Regarding this journal, see footnote 3.

I respectfully request permission to again inspect the herds of Spanish sheep under your jurisdiction, especially the one- and two-year-old ewes. Were you to grant my request, kindly let me know with this bearer. I will come on Sunday morning. I am familiar with the sheep farm and know where the yearling ewes are located. We will immediately start our return march. Because my time is short, as though weighed on a golden scale, kindly instruct the shepherds not to drive the sheep far out onto the meadows.

Sir, please forgive my presumption, since not curiosity but the reliability of my business transactions demands this of me. Perhaps we can agree on a sheep purchase.

With the appropriate respect, I have the honour to be Your Honour's devoted servant,

Johann Cornies

119. Johann Cornies to David Epp. 2 May 1827. SAOR 89-1-102/11v.

Sent from Herrnhut.

Mr. David Epp, Heubuden near Marienburg in West Prussia,

Dear brother,

Greetings from the beautiful land of Saxony and, in particular, from quiet, orderly Herrnhut. Its inhabitants have given me, and continue to give me, true pleasure and inner happiness. This is my third stay here since my business led me into this region, and the worthy Count Dohna and his wife invited me to visit Herrnhut.

Your letter arrived in Ohrloff after my departure, and my friend forwarded some of its contents to Dresden on 8 May. I see that a certain Dyck wishes to transport the sheep I buy here to Molochnaia in order to get himself and his family to Russia at no cost. This is impossible because, first, my route will be through Poland (approximately fifty to sixty [German] miles distant from Marienburg). Secondly, Dyck would be of little help, because not everyone can drive sheep along such long and narrow roads. Trained shepherds are needed who know how to control sheep with dogs. Inexperience can easily result in disaster for such highly bred and expensive animals. I have brought enough people along with me and I am, additionally, hiring good, trained, and experienced shepherds here for the drive.

Should my business affairs continue to make such good progress, I am inclined to make a detour to Heubuden, to see you and buy a small number of good delta cows. I would need several qualified persons to drive them to the Molochnaia. But I cannot say anything definite yet. Man proposes and God disposes. It is always well done, however He may do it. I will accompany the sheep transport from Saxony to the Polish border. At that point, should everything be going well with the sheep and be promising for the rest of the journey without me, I will either travel ahead to Russia or visit you in Marienburg.

Once our purchases have been completed this week, we will depart immediately. We have already bought about 200 head, with more than 100 still to come. We plan to reach the Polish border three weeks after our departure and it should take a further seven or eight days to reach you. Should I fail to visit you, I will, if it is God's plan, drop you a line from the border. Prices here are very high, with expenses of six to ten Reichsthaler per day.

Farewell. Pray for me and give my greetings to all good friends. I am, as always, your loving friend and brother,

Johann Cornies

120. Johann Cornies to Wilhelm Martens. May 2, 1827. SAOR 89-1-102/12v.

Sent from Herrnhut.

My very dear friend,

Please forgive me for not writing more often. This is not as I had intended. I would gladly have communicated with you and other good friends, to whom I am also obligated, but this does not depend on my own intentions. Since I know that you love me, I am convinced that you will not be offended if I write infrequently.

How are you, your dear wife, and your little children and relatives? Are you all healthy? May God grant this. We are thankful to God that we are all healthy, full of energy, and well able to conduct our business affairs.

Yesterday, in this neighbourhood, I bought seventy good, expensive merino ewes. There are many Spanish sheep here in Saxony, and Russians could easily be badly cheated by anyone determined to do so. Fine sheep are available at prices from two to twenty-five thaler. I have always assumed that if you want something genuine you must pay genuine money, and I am being convinced of this here. Good friends are also needed to provide advice. Thank God, I have them. It is quiet in Herrnhut despite the extensive trade conducted here. Good order prevails in every corner and people are attractive, quiet, and pious. I feel very much at home.

Our return journey will begin immediately after we complete our purchases this week. We still need another 100 sheep or more, depending on the quality we are able to buy. Here, as on the Molochnaia, not everything that glitters is gold, and there are more "Metis" sheep than pure-breds.

I leave for Dresden in a few hours. Since we have divided up our business, brother Penner will buy sheep in the Dresden region. We have already bought almost 200 good, beautiful sheep, in numbers and of a quality seldom – possibly never before – purchased in Saxony. To date, everything has worked in our favour and we owe great thanks to our Creator, who brings all things into existence and lovingly smooths our way. I send you heartfelt greetings, brother of my heart, and also to your dear wife. Do not forget me, just as I often think of you and pray for you. Adieu. Give my greetings to everyone, especially to my dear wife and relatives.

Your brother who loves you,

Johann Cornies

P.S. Our main quarters are in Dresden. When we travel separately, we always set a date for our return and observe it precisely. It would be very expensive to sit around without pursuing our business – from five to ten thaler per day. The same.

121. Daniel Schlatter to Johann Cornies. 5 May 1827. SAOR 89-1-84/25.

Sent from Warsaw.

Dear friend,

Mentally and physically battered by various storms, I am finally able to write to you. You were correct when you pointed out to me that we would have difficulty in obtaining Russian passes. I sent introductions on your behalf to my friends in Saxony, but they would have supported you with advice and action even without them. I hope your journey to Dresden was a success.

I send you heartfelt greetings. I received your messages and have made the acquaintance of young Mr. Shunkovskii. If it is God's will, I will travel from here via Brody and Odessa, back to the dear Tatars. If you return through Brody, please check with Messrs. Hausner and Violand to see if I have left anything for you.

Where might you be right now? How are your companions? Hausknecht is probably travelling to Russia by now. I'm not sure what he will be doing. Made everything clear to him. Did not see friend Dyck because I did not go to Marienburg. *Aufwiedersehen,*

Your Daniel.

Received 5/17 May 1827, in Klipphausen, at the Beis home.

122. Johann Cornies to Andrei M. Fadeev. 12 May 1827. SAOR 89-1-102/15.

Sent from Dresden.

The Senior Member of the Ekaterinoslav Guardianship Committee, Mr. Fadeev, Honourable, Gracious Sir,

We are in Dresden at present, having travelled through a large part of the Kingdom of Saxony and visited many sheep farms. Penner and I purchased 440 ewes and fifty rams, with wool. We selected them from the best, unadulterated sheep on Saxon farms. This is our first day of rest in the three months since we left Ekaterinoslav. Our purchases had to be completed quickly since shearing time was at the door. It was essential to acquire exact knowledge about sheep sales, and about the sheep themselves, before we made our purchases.

Naturally, this involved great exertion, as it is almost impossible to drive forty verstas a day in this beautiful land of Saxony. Except for the high roads, speedy progress is difficult in this hump-backed world, full of large stones and hollow roads so narrow that two horses can barely walk beside one another. Roads to most of the sheep farms are almost impassable, and there is a constant danger of being overturned or suffering some other kind of damage. My wagon actually tipped over at one point and the shaft broke, but we were fortunate that the whole carriage did not plunge into the stream roaring nearby.

We have gathered 454 head of sheep from fourteen sheep farms scattered from Zittau in Upper Lusatia, on the Bohemian border, to Leipzig. We also bought several head from a sheep farm in Prussian Silesia, near Haynau. With support from important persons in the Kingdom, we were able to make favourable purchases with respect to the purity of bloodlines. The total absence of sheep buyers in Saxony this year worked in our favour as well. Never before have purchasers been permitted to choose so freely from the flocks. In making our purchases, we principally selected sheep with fine, regular wool, buying only one-year-old animals and very few two-year-olds. Our purchases created a sensation.

Now we are busy with commissions from home and making preparations for the return journey. We have already hired three shepherds, who will walk to the Molochnaia. They will be paid more than 1,000 R.B.A. In a few days, we will go to Leipzig, to receive Mr. Baron von Frank's sheep from Mr. Baron von Speck. Then we will gather together our scattered purchases and proceed on the march. We must feed the sheep with hay and oats. Even the grass in the ditches on the high road are rented out and every mouthful a sheep devours would cost a thaler.

I will attempt to fulfil Your Honour's well-disposed commissions, here and in Leipzig, and those for your honoured wife.

Your Honour will already have been in the Molochnaia. Letters I received from my wife today told me that you were expected. It would afford me much pleasure if you should have entered my house.

I send my most heartfelt thanks for Your Honour's well-disposed interest, and continue to be Yr. Honour's devoted servant,

Johann Cornies

123. Johann Cornies to Samuel Contenius. 13 May 1827. SAOR 89-1-102/13v.

Sent from Dresden.

Acting State Counsellor and Sir, Mr. Contenius,

Your Excellency, Most Gracious Sir,

I am honoured to report to Your Excellency that we have completed our sheep purchases as favourably as few buyers before us. Not many sheep buyers found their way to Saxony this year, giving us an advantage. Although prices were not low, we were given the freedom to make our selections from every herd ourselves, and to take only the number we wanted.

We used this advantage to look for sheep with fine, even wool, and took only one-year-olds, and very few two-year-olds. We did not select many from any individual herd. For example, if we were given a choice of 200 to 300 yearling ewes, we selected forty, at most sixty. The situation was the same with rams. We were assured that, in the past, no one was ever allowed to make such a free choice. Previously, sellers sold only sheep they had themselves selected.

Our purchases were made from the most superior and purest Saxon sheep herds, as the enclosed memorandum shows. The price for ewes was from fifteen to twenty Reichsthaler each, and for rams, from twenty to forty Reichsthaler. We bought nothing from the imperial sheep farms because they were selling only old, rejected ewes and a few coarse-wooled yearling ewes. We have purchased a total of 404 ewes and fifty rams. We bought all the sheep with wool because we are afraid that cold weather could be detrimental to the health of livestock accustomed to warm barns. We intend to shear them in Prussian Silesia.

After [Penner and I] separated in Goerlitz, we visited more than fifty sheep farms and sought expert advice and information from dependable, high-ranking persons who kindly gave us accurate explanations as to which of the many sheep farms have the purest breed, and which are equal to the sheep on the royal farm.

My companion Penner was on Mr. Baron von Speck's sheep farms in Litschina, where ewes were offered at five Reichsthaler each, but Penner rejected them. In two days we will both go to Leipzig to take possession of sheep from Mr. von Speck for Mr. Baron von Frank. Then we will immediately set out on our return journey. Your Excellency will see from the enclosed memorandum that our purchases were scattered across the whole of Saxony. We will begin to assemble our purchased sheep at Leipzig.

We are now making linen cribs and other preparations necessary for the return journey. We will not travel back through Galicia, but go through Niesky, Glogau, Kalish, and Ushiluk.

Everything has gone extremely well to date, thanks be to God, and we are all in good health. With the sincerest and most heartfelt respect and esteem, I have the honour to be Your Excellency's devoted servant,

[No Signature]

**124. Johann Cornies to Wilhelm Frank. 15 May 1827.
SAOR 89-1-102/16v.**

Sent from Dresden.

Wilhelm Frank, Chancery Clerk in the Guardianship Committee,

Greetings from beautiful Saxony. Spring greets us in a friendly fashion and trees are in blossom in gardens and along streets. Beautiful, well-built towns, villages, and manorial estates are set into a continuous dark green, forest-like orchard. People here always give us a friendly reception.

We thank God that we are doing well. Our sheep purchases are made and, after many hardships, we enjoyed several days of rest. Tomorrow, or the day after that, we will set out for Leipzig to begin our march with the sheep. They must be gathered from fourteen places, scattered between Leipzig and the Bohemian border.

I completed my commissions in Dresden, except for those from His Excellency, Mr. Contenius, and from Mr. Haupt. Please tell Mr. Haupt that I found only one of his friends, Mr. Laurin, but the letters sparked great joy in the whole family.

I have little time and little more to say but I know you will be satisfied with these lines. I will complete only a few orders. The Prussian border is very strict and so I will take no risks.

I send greetings to you and your family and everyone who remembers me with love, and assure you of my friendship and love, as I am convinced of yours, and call myself your friend and servant,

Johann Cornies

P.S. Our accommodations in Dresden are in the "Gasthof zu den drei Linden" [Three Lindentrees Inn], in the Bautzner suburb, not far from the Leman Baths. Our beautiful room looks out on a street lined with chestnut trees. We would feel quite at home here, if Saxony did not lack so many of Russia's beauties. Russia remains the best country in the world for me and for my travelling companions. People may prefer living in Saxony or France, but one cannot clothe and feed oneself with sightseeing. Russia may not have the variety that excites curiosity in Saxony, but it is not as expensive. A person reduced to his last penny here seldom regains a good life. This does not happen often in Russia and it is this hope that binds us to Russia's wise constitution and to our Christian duty.

125. Johann Cornies to Baron Frank. 18 May 1827. SAOR 89-1-102/17v.

Sent from Leipzig.

Baron Frank in Ekaterinoslav,

Highly esteemed Baron,

You commissioned me to take receipt of a number of merino sheep from Mr. Speck in Leipzig, and to transport them to Ekaterinoslav, at your risk, along with the sheep I purchased here. To enable Mr. Speck to make his plans, I sent him a letter with Jacob Penner, Khortitsa district chairman, as soon as we arrived in Saxony.

We arrived in Leipzig two hours ago, prepared to begin our march with the sheep we purchased. We paid our respects to Mr. Speck, and I asked him to release your sheep to us. Mr. Speck refused to do so, saying that these highly bred sheep could not be entrusted to us and he would send them to Ekaterinoslav himself.

I have thus obediently discharged your commission and commend myself with complete respect and regard, as Your Honour's devoted servant,
Johann Cornies

126. Johann Cornies to Prince Heinrich von Reuss. 23 May 1827. SAOR 89-1-102/18.

Sent from Wilsdorf.
His Honour, the sixty-third Prince Heinrich von Reuss in Klipphausen near Wilsdorf,
Most Serene Highness,

We live in changing times. A few hours ago, I left your noble house, where I enjoyed true inner joy. Now I am on the road to my distant home near the Sea of Azov and may never see you again in this life. I will live out my life in the circle of my family, as long as God wills. You remain in beautiful, well-cultivated Saxony, in quiet, romantic Klipphausen, with your dear children who have lost their mother. I feel great sympathy for you at her passing but take comfort in the words that "what God does, is done well." His will always remains just and, though I may not understand it, God has still done well.

I commend myself to your good will and your Christian intercession to our common Lord, and send greetings to you and your beautiful little children and worthy friends.

With the most obliging thanks and love, I remain Your Serene Highness' most devoted servant,
Johann Cornies

127. Johann Cornies' travel journal to Saxony and Prussia in 1827 (14 February–26 September 1827). SAOR 89-1-103.[12]

5 June: Left at 4 a.m. and, travelling through the towns Goerlitz and Bunzlau with the Gradenberg brothers, we arrived in Haynau at 10 p.m. There is a monument with German and Russian inscriptions in the marketplace in Bunzlau commemorating the death of General and Field Marshal Kutusov Smolensky in 1813 in Bunzlau. Near Bunzlau, on a hill close to a village on the way to Goerlitz, another monument marks a battle between the Russians and the French.

12 Regarding this journal, see footnote 3.

128. Johann Cornies to Samuel Contenius. 13 June 1827. SAOR 89-1-102/19v.

Sent from Steinau.
Acting State Counsellor, Mr. Contenius,
Yr. Excellency, Most Gracious Sir,

I reported from Dresden exactly a month ago today. We safely gathered all the sheep from the farms where they were purchased and left Dresden on 27 May, crossing the Prussian border at Hoyerswerda on 1 June. We then proceeded through Muskau, Sagan, and Sorau to Sprottau [Szprotawa]. Great, sultry heat set in after ten days of rainy weather, and it was necessary to shear the sheep. We sold the wool immediately, with its sweat, for thirty-five Reichsthaler per centner. This caused a two-day delay. We then resumed our journey along the road through Primkenau and Polkwitz to Steinau on the Oder, because we had been assured that there would be less sand to traverse this way than through Glogau. From here we will proceed on foot through Herrnstadt to Kalish. Our flock now consists of 446 ewes and fifty-eight rams.

We are, praise God, healthy and contented, which is also my heartfelt wishes for Your Excellency. I remain, with the appropriate respect and esteem, Yr. Excellency's most humble servant,

Johann Cornies

129. Johann Cornies to Andrei M. Fadeev. 13 June 1827. SAOR 89-1-102/20.

Sent from Steinau.
Senior Member of the Guardianship Committee, Mr. Fadeev,
Your Honour, Gracious Sir,

On 18 and 19 May (o.s.), I was in Leipzig and purchased the books Your Honour requested and the natural products your esteemed wife ordered.

I was, however, unable to complete the treasured commission from Mr. Baron von Frank. As it happened, Mr. von Speck refused to entrust Mr. Baron von Frank's sheep to me. I immediately reported this to the Baron from Leipzig and have thus completed my commission.

Mr. von Freygang, Esquire, Russian Imperial Consul in Leipzig, gave me a friendly reception, and this was a healing balm to the wound inflicted on me by Mr. Speck.

We left Dresden on our return journey in rainy weather on 27 May. We crossed the Prussian border at Hoyerswerda in Silesia on 1 June and had the sheep shorn in Sprottau, selling the wool immediately at thirty-five Reichsthaler per centner. By way of Polkwitz, we walked to Steinau on the Oder. Here we will have ourselves ferried across tomorrow and then walk to Kalish by way of Herrnstadt. If the sheep transport continues to make such good progress, I plan to travel from Kalish to Danzig by way of Thorn to purchase a number of good Dutch cows for myself and for our area. Kalish is still eighteen to twenty miles away, so this is not definite yet.

Since I last reported from Dresden on 13 May, we bought another forty-two ewes and eight rams, and the total number is now 446 ewes and fifty-eight rams. It takes a great deal of effort to move so many sheep along the very narrow roads. We live in hope that Poland will give us somewhat more room for our livestock.

Should I take a detour to Danzig, I request that Your Honour not be displeased if my reports fail to reach you. Since there is no other route than by way of Brody, I might be home just as quickly as any letters I send. This roundabout route is naturally much longer and border delays will lengthen it.

I am honoured to be Your Honour's devoted servant,
Johann Cornies

130. Jacob Penner to Johann Cornies. 22 June 1827. SAOR 89-1-62/30.

Sent from Wartha.
Beloved brother Cornies,

We have just arrived in Wartha, and I hasten to inform you about our transport and about crossing the Polish border. After we went our separate ways at the Prussian border on 19 June, we walked to the Polish border that same day but were forced to spend the night at Tchiporne, occupied by Don Cossacks, because it was Sunday. On Monday, we made our way to the main customs office in Kalish with a carnet. The customs officer advised us that, to take the sheep to the Russian border, we would have to go through Warsaw and towns and locations specified by the main customs officer, arriving at designated times. This long detour along the main road seemed too difficult and we decided to pay the high customs dues instead.

After processing by the customs office on 20 June, we resumed our march and have had quite good grazing along the road. Because it was exceptionally hot until yesterday, we have not been able to move quickly. It is cloudy and cool today, ideal for the transport, and we can keep moving all day long. Yesterday your ram from the Klipphausen sheep farm died, but I do not know why, although he had been very fat the previous day and would not eat. The other sheep are healthy, except for the usual lame ones.

Thank God we are still healthy, which I also wish you and your travelling companions. May God grant a successful conclusion to your business matters. May He keep you and us on our further travels and lead us to a joyful and healthy reunion soon.

I send many, many greetings to all of you and remain, as always, your brother who loves you,

Jacob Penner

P.S. It has just started to rain a little. God knows if this means cooler weather. That would serve us and the sheep well. At your request, Martens sent your dear wife a letter from here. The same.

Received in Heubuden, 1 July 1827.

131. Johann Cornies' travel journal to Saxony and Prussia in 1827 (14 February–26 September 1827). SAOR 89-1-103.[13]

25 June: Left at 5.30 a.m. in rain, and arrived safely at the home of Teacher David Epp in Heubuden at 12.30, having driven through the town of Stuhm and the beautiful city of Marienburg. We encountered a lot of sand through the mile-wide Stuhm forest, where it is said that robbers hide. They robbed the mail recently but seem to have been caught. The robbers are Stuhm citizens.

132. Jacob Penner to Johann Cornies. 28 June 1827. SAOR 89-1-62/5.

Potvorov, four miles from Radom.
Dear brother Cornies,

We have just arrived in Potvorov and the sheep are all safe and healthy. We intend to go through Radom tomorrow, Wednesday 29 June, and I am hurrying to write a few lines to post from there.

The weather has been cool and overcast since my last report from Wartha on 22 June. This was favourable for the sheep, and we were

13 Regarding this journal, see footnote 3.

able to make three and even four [German] miles per day. We have covered twenty-seven miles from the Polish border, and seventy and one-half miles from Dresden. Radom will mark the midpoint on our road through Poland. God willing, we should reach Ustilug on the Russian border in fourteen days' time if the cool weather continues. We have followed the marchroute you gave us as much as possible, walking through Lask, Pabianice, Volborsz, Jesvlodz, and Odszipol. We encountered a great deal of sand and some forest, but thank God, we found enough pasturage to satisfy the sheep and it was not necessary to feed them with oats and hay.

They tell us that we will encounter a good deal of sand and forest with little pasturage along the way to the Vistula (approximately ten to twelve [German] miles from here). The situation is supposed to be better for sheep on the other side of the Vistula.

If you have had a safe journey, you and your companions should be in Heubuden by now. I wish you the success you desire in your undertaking. May it be God's will that we see one another again soon. I and my travelling companions think and talk about you a great deal and hope that this is also the case with you. We send all of you many, many greetings, and commend you to the protection of almighty God. I remain, as always, your friend and brother who loves you,

Jacob Penner

Received 8 September 1827, in Karolswalde.

133. David Cornies to Johann Cornies. 5 July 1827.
SAOR 89-1-62/23v.

Sent from Ohrloff.

Dear brother,

On 1 July, we received your letters, the last from Dresden, and learned that you are healthy. With all our hearts, we wish you continued good health. We thank God that we are all well, as are your dear wife and children, and we think of you very often. Eventually, if it is God's will, we will see one another again.

There is little to write about your agricultural affairs. The livestock are healthy. The first grasshoppers appeared on 17 May and have caused great harm. They first appeared on the Altonau steppe and then, on 23 June, they began to fly in swarms at our sheep farm. We see many of them every day. They have done a great deal of damage in our district, and continue to do so. In ten villages, little of the summer crop was harvested, just as the summer crop was also devoured on our sheep farm. We did harvest 325 shocks and a little barley. The pastures on the sheep farm are dry, due to the lack of rain and the grasshoppers. The sheep were driven to the upper Iushanle, where there have been no grasshoppers yet, and also no Tatar sheep. Our horses and cattle are at home. You were correct when you wrote that K[laas] Dyck would likely arrive before your letter. He came a day earlier. He and his family are well.

All your dear friends send you greetings, and I greet you as your loving brother,

David Cornies

Martens arrived just as I finished writing. He sends many greetings. It is said that D. Schlatter travelled through Odessa and the Crimea and a case of his belongings has arrived in Altonau. Mr. Bartram was sent to Ekaterinoslav again. A special greeting from D. Penner.

Received 8 September 1827, in Karolswalde.

134. Johann Cornies' travel journal to Saxony and Prussia in 1827 (14 February–26 September 1827). SAOR 89-1-103.[14]

10 July: Mr. van der Smissen from Danzig preached in the Heubuden church. In the afternoon, Cornies, Epp, and Mr. van der Smissen drove to Santoff to visit Mr. Konvenz. From there, Cornies travelled to Curau and returned safely to Kuschilitschker, Heubuden, on 16 July, to Mr. Epp's home.

135. Jacob Penner to Johann Cornies. 14 July 1827. SAOR 89-1-62/4.

Sent from Lutsk.

Dear brother Cornies,

We reached Lutsk with our flocks at 9 a.m. and are all healthy and safe. We got to the Polish border in Luszkov at 8 a.m., 9 July, intending to cross the Russian border immediately, but were frustrated in our efforts. The officer in the main customs office at Ustilug stated that the law allows no one to bring goods or livestock across the Russian border except for merchants of the first guild. I was therefore required to authorize a merchant to import our sheep across the border, specifically someone commissioned by Aron Skulsky, Dubna merchant of the first

14 Regarding this journal, see footnote 3.

guild, or Mordka Finkelstein, Vladimir merchant of the third guild. After we spent the night on the Polish side, Finkelstein finally appeared in Luszkow at 3 p.m. on Sunday, 10 July. By then it was too late to clear that day, forcing us to stay on the Polish side another night. Early on 11 July, we received clearance from the Polish officers and made our way to the customs office in Ustilug. The sheep were cleared immediately under Finkelstein's name and, having discharged the legal customs charges for the sheep (a total of 113 R.B.A., with a receipt), we resumed our march again.

Finkelstein thought he would make a good profit from us and told other Jews that he would take 10 per cent. He did not succeed because I had presented the customs collector with one of our surplus ewes, namely, the trotter given to you. The latter kindly told Finkelstein to content himself with what I paid him, and I gave him two ducats for his efforts.

The delay at the border did not hurt our sheep. I rented good pasturage for them and they had a good feed and rest. To our great joy, the dear Lord blessed us with much rain and thunderstorms on 10 July. This dampened the dust and the grass turned a little greener and fresher. This rain did not reach very far, however, and they say that from Vladimir to Lutsk there has been no rain for a long time. The grass has been burned red by the great heat and drought, and grain has dried up on the fields. It was like this from the Vistula in Poland as well, with dry grain fields and grass burned red. It is supposed to have rained heavily recently on the other side of Lutsk. Since Radom, we have always found considerable pasture for the sheep along the roads. For the most part, it is only the so-called "Schweingras" [pig's grass] which stays green in the greatest heat and is also very nourishing for the sheep.

Due to the heat and dust since I last reported to you from Potvornov on 28 June, one ram from Oschatz and one ewe from Kleinwolmsdorf have fallen. Otherwise, the sheep are quite healthy. Since Radom we have gone through Zwolin, Pulany on the Vistula, Markuzow, Lublin, Piaskov, Krasnystov, Voyslanice, Horodlo, Ustilug, and Vladimir.

If it is God's will, you are probably already returning from West Prussia. God willing, we will be in Ostrog in five or six days, since we have about 100 verstas to go. God knows if we will meet you there.

May the Lord God keep you and us. Many greetings from my travelling companions and from your friend and brother, who loves you,

Jacob Penner

Received in Karolswalde, 8 September 1827.

136. Jacob Penner to Johann Cornies. 18 July 1827. SAOR 89-1-62/26.

Sent from Karolswalde.
Dear brother Cornies,

We arrived in Ostrog by about nine o'clock this morning. Since crossing the Prussian border, where we separated, it has only taken us four weeks and one day, and so our paths did not cross here. In any case, I doubted that they would, since it is still six days to the date we had set to meet. Only God knows if you will catch up to us in Starokonstantinov or elsewhere. Immediately upon finding quarters for the sheep in Ostrog, I made my way to Karolswalde, hoping to find letters there from home. Regrettably, there were none! Also, no letters for you had arrived at Mr. Benjamin Dirks' address. Mr. Dirks received us in a friendly manner, wishing to keep us over night. Although we assured him we could not on this occasion, I did inform him that you might take quarters with him for at least one day. Mr. Dirks only received the letter I wrote to you from Radom on 15 July. The one from Lutsk had not yet arrived.

Our journey has gone well since Lutsk, with much rain. There was nice pasturage for the sheep and the dust has settled. Another ewe died on 16 July, one from Gamig.

May God protect and lead all of you on your return journey back and may He help us to meet again very soon. Greetings to all of you, and I remain, as always, your friend and brother who loves you,

Jacob Penner

N.B. Our route will now be through Zaslov, Starokonstantinov, Cmelnik, Winitz, Bogopol, etc.

Received 8 September 1827.

137. Johann Cornies Jr. to Johann Cornies. 19 July 1827. SAOR 89-1-62/12.

Treasured Father,

It gives me pleasure to read in your letter that you are all well. May God keep you so that you can travel speedily, complete your business successfully, and return home safely. May our dear God keep us at all times for His glory. We are all healthy, except for Katarina who had a fever for four weeks. Our dear mother, and Nethen and I, all love you greatly and often speak of you.

Luetscher pruned trees here on the 8 and 9 July. He says you should bring along several grafting knives since they are hard to find here. Most of the pupils are out on the steppe while the rest of us are working hard on our studies, including Russian.

I wish you a safe journey and am, with love, your son,

Johann Cornies

Greeting from Mr. Enss in Altonau.

138. Agnes Cornies to Johann Cornies. 19 July 1827. SAOR 89-1-62/12.

Dearest Father,

It will surely give you pleasure to receive a few lines from your dear daughter as well. I often remember you with love and I suppose that you certainly remember me often.

I love you and remain, with a heartfelt greeting, your obedient daughter,

Agnes

139. Johann Cornies to Jacob Penner. 26 July [*sic*] 1827. SAOR 89-1-62/15.

Sent from Heubuden.

Dear brother Penner,

We arrived here well and in good spirits, at noon yesterday, 25 July [*sic*] and thank the Lord for this. After we separated from you the other day, we missed you a lot, although this feeling was soon gone. I wonder how you are doing?

I have a little hope that people here will sell us livestock, but I am unsure whether we will find suitable ones. Tomorrow, Monday, we will get down to business.

I don't have much to write. What is my dear Martens doing, and Regehr and everyone? Following directions? How are the sheep doing? Really, why am I asking? I must come to you in person. Reimer and the others arrived here from Prussia several days ago, but I have not yet spoken to them. Rempel and Johann are down in the yard and I am using this time to write and to reflect. May you fare well. I send the best of greetings to all of you and hope to see you soon.

Your Cornies

140. Jacob van der Smissen to Johann Cornies. 10 October 1827. SAOR 89-1-76/5.

Sent from Danzig.
Treasured, valued Sir and Friend,

The bearer of this letter is my friend and cousin, Mr. Jacob de Jager from Hamburg, who travelled to Danzig to get an emigration pass. You will hear in person what actually happened to him. I hope the District Office will agree to his remaining there since his documentation is very good. Because of my family relationships with de Jager himself, and his relatives, I consider it my duty to ask you most graciously to take my above-mentioned friend and cousin by the hand and assist him with advice and help. I do so openly, convinced as I am of your love and friendship. I know that it gives you pleasure to help and serve others. Draisma should have no further problems since the administration in his birthplace will give their consent. I would be grateful to receive favourable news in this regard very soon and to hear that you, valued friend, and your companions have arrived safely. Please commend me most kindly to your dear wife, to whom I am still a stranger, and to all your loved ones.

I again thank you heartily for the happy hours that your visit and delightful acquaintance gave me. I commend you to God's protection and blessing and sign myself as your friend who values you highly,

Jacob van der Smissen, Mennonite Preacher in Danzig

My wife also sends friendly greetings to you and your loved ones.

Received 16 April 1828.

141. Johann Cornies to District Office. 28 October 1827. SAOR 89-1-129/2.

To the highly honoured District Office,

Your well-disposed inquiry No. 1,873, of 26 October, asked me to write to you by 28 October in regard to the price for the electoral sheep that I bought for the community sheep farm this year in the Kingdom of Saxony. [As I understand matters], the complete payment cannot be made immediately because of the state of the community treasury.

I report to the honoured District Office that I am not yet in a position to specify a definite price for each individual animal because I must complete accounts for purchasing the above sheep with my business partner, Jacob Penner, Khortitsa district chairman. I have, in the meantime, gone over my own accounts, and the final price for each head should not be very different. After the costs, interest rates, and risk have been taken into account, the rams should come to approximately 160–165 R.B.A. per head, and the ewes from 100–105 R.B.A. If the payment is not immediate, I must hold discussions with my creditors before I can give the District Office definite terms of payment for 200 ewes and nineteen rams. If payment cannot be made promptly, interest on the capital should be calculated at legal rates from the day the sheep were received. Repayment of the capital sum must not occur in small amounts or on various terms.

142. District Office to Johann Cornies. 29 November 1827. SAOR 89-1-95/3.

No. 466. Communication from Molochnaia Mennonite District Office to resident Johann Cornies in Ohrloff:

In response to your communication of 27 October, the District Office asked the Bureau for Foreign Settlers to decide on the terms under which the community might purchase the nineteen breeding rams and 200 ewes you brought to this region from Saxony, and which are now at the Kurushan community sheep farm. The community's means are at present completely exhausted.

In response, the authorities sent directive No. 447 to the District Office on 15 November, stating, among other things, "that the District Office must discuss with Cornies the circumstances and estimate the amount of money that can be applied annually to the payment for the sheep he wishes to sell. A decision is to be made regarding the number of years during which the entire debt for these sheep will be completed."

Considering our circumstances, the District Office therefore finds that the payment of the debt of about 24,000 rubles, according to your communication, cannot be accomplished in fewer than ten years. According to our estimates of future income and expenditures, we do not expect a surplus that would allow us to discharge this considerable debt earlier. Although the District Office has taken into consideration the 16,587 rubles, 64 kopeks owing to the treasury, it cannot determine with any certainty what part of this debt will be repaid, or whether it can be collected at the required time in future. This is because most debtors are now too poor to pay their community taxes. Part of the total debt, specifically 9,159 rubles, 62 kopeks, is also owed by less well-off settlers who were given repayable assistance in 1822, 1824, and especially 1825.

If, however, unexpected conditions should occur making it possible to make the payments sooner, we will naturally do so. You are hereby requested to inform the District Office in writing by 6 December 1827, if at all possible, about your decision and your wishes, so that the District Office can submit the required report to the authorities before the New Year.

District Chairman Klassen, District Deputy Toews.

29 November 1827

143. Gerhard Ennz (for Johann Cornies) to District Office. 3 December 1827. SAOR 89-1-129/3.

Johann Cornies, Ohrloff, has been unable to appear at the District Office because he is ill and I, the undersigned, have been verbally commissioned [by him] to respond to the District Office's communication No. 467, of 29 November. Mr. Cornies is willing to take 200 ewes and seventeen rams purchased from Saxony back into his possession from the Kurushan community sheep farm after they have been cured of the pox and the loss has been replaced by the District Office. Duly signed and certified by the commissioned,

Gerh. Ennz

1828

144. Johann Cornies to Andrei M. Fadeev. 3 February 1828. SAOR 89-1-129/7.

Your Honour, Gracious Sir,

In response to Your Honour's kind inquiry of 22 January 1828 about my current illness, I can report that I am not completely well, but am improving daily and hope that, with God's help, I will soon have put the problem behind me. I am still too weak to go out without serious risk to my health.

At Yr. Honour's gracious request, I purchased a pud of good cheese, but have not mailed it because the cold might affect its flavour. Gerhard Ennz, Altonau, will deliver it soon. It weighs forty-five funt and costs 11 R.B.A., 43¾ kopeks.

With today's mail, I sent the Guardianship Committee a petition regarding the encroachment of the Mariupol Colonist Community on the Baden land where it has established a sheep farm that will harm us. I humbly request that Yr. Honour support our petition to the Committee as soon as you can. We seem to have misplaced our copy of the contract for the Baden land. We think our lease ends at the beginning of 1828. Please inform me accordingly.

With the appropriate esteem, I have the honour to be Yr. Honour's servant,

Johann Cornies

145. Johann Cornies to Wilhelm Frank. 11 February 1828. SAOR 89-1-129/8.

Honoured Mr. Frank, treasured friend,

The shoes, boots, books, etc., reached us in good order. Thank you for taking care of this matter. I will keep both pairs of boots. Thank you for your well-meaning concern about my illness. Your letter confirms your sympathy for me. My health improves at a snail's pace, but God knows what is best for me. Patience is a noble and precious attribute, but rare. Please keep me in remembrance with love, and convey my greetings to your worthy parents.

On another matter, your esteemed father should ask for written permission from the Society School supervisors, P. Neufeld, Ohrloff, and Abram Isaak, Tiege, to enrol your younger brother. Regulations in this regard were renewed by the Society about a month ago. The matters should follow accepted routines unless there is a better way to proceed. I can also report that your little brother is well and in good spirits. Mr. Voth, however, is ill.

Adieu, with honest feelings of love and assurances of my friendship, your faithful friend,

Cornies

146. Johann Cornies to Casper Adrian Hausknecht. 19 March 1828. SAOR 89-1-129/12v.

Mr. Hausknecht, beloved friend,

Good things do not progress by leaps and bounds. You know this as well as I do, so please do not make matters so difficult for yourself. Take my sincere advice: stick to what you have started, without regard to other concerns. Simply concentrate on spreading the good seed among the young and recognize that you will be unable to accomplish anything without opposition. Force may well break iron, but it will only harden unenlightened hearts. Still, opposition will cause noble causes to thrive and if this were not so, your move to this area would have been futile. Progress depends on individuals and the larger community. Individuals cannot always do as they like, but their sense of purpose and fervent convictions can have good results. Patient and encouraging work with maturing young minds is surely the best way to develop better convictions.

Begin by studying the attitudes and character of the community. Do not be overly critical in speaking to persons who you assume share your views. Individuals may change their minds in a split second and then speak quite differently. In that case, your frankness may well have created enemies for you. Convey the impression that you would like to remain in your school, as it is now. The time will surely come when someone in the community will call upon you to improve the schools. Then embrace the moment and move forward gradually. Assume that the community is ignorant of your noble intentions and you of theirs. You must win the trust of the community. Friendly words alone are cheap and insufficient. Only when the community is convinced of your good intentions will it accept your suggestions. Put forward only what can realistically be achieved. If you appear overly eager, you will be rejected for trying too much.

Forgive me, my dear friend, for speaking so frankly when you have not asked me for my views. If I were indifferent to you, I would not have done so. My love alone demands it. God willing, I will visit you this month or early next month on my way to Ekaterinoslav. Should I have said too much, you may admonish me. Adieu, greetings and all my love,

Your Cornies

147. Johann Cornies to Johann Sukau, Rothenbude on the Vistula. 4 July 1828. SAOR 89-1-129/16.

Friend of my heart,

Here, finally, is the account I promised you. Please forgive me for not writing sooner, as I had planned. (Man's intentions are nothing but vanity.) After I left Klakendorf on that memorable day, I approached Russia's borders day by day, step by step. We wandered happily through the Polish forests, across the beautiful, flat Ukraine, and over forestless New Russia until we reached the guberniia city of Ekaterinoslav on 6 October, o.s. I immediately attended upon my superiors, acting State Counsellor Mr. Contenius and State Counsellor Mr. Fadeev. Since I longed to see my loved ones after an absence of more than seven months, we left for Khortitsa a day and a half later. My sheep had arrived five weeks earlier and been assembled by my brother. All the sheep were healthy except for twelve head that had fallen on the march.

I stayed in Khortitsa for half a day and then we crossed the Dnieper on our way to the Molochnaia. There I found my loved ones healthy and well, except for my wife who was sickly. The stallions had survived the trip in good shape, especially the one purchased from Mr. Reimer that had grown fat. This spring, I spread them out evenly over my whole breeding herd.

[Excerpt from SAOR 89-1-129/32, Cornies to Abram Dueck, dated 9 July 1828: For every section, a special Tatar herdsman was hired so that the stallions would not hurt one another. When your stallion was driven out to pasture with his mares, he bore down, like a tiger, on the Tatar herdsman on his horse, seized him by the chest, and threw him to the ground. The Tatar came to me immediately, insisting he be released from this task or be assigned to another section. I sent in a second Tatar and the same thing happened to him. I then rode out with the third horse, but both of us were forced to flee. I soon discovered that the stallion demanded an obeisance from me before he was taken to water and returned to the pasture. He wanted to be escorted on foot and not on horseback.][1]

After being at home for six weeks, I again took control of my affairs from my brother, but then I became ill and have been sick now for four months. For this reason I did not write to you. Upon my recovery I had to deal with a year's worth of work and had no time to write to you in detail. I've received both your letters and thank you for your loving interest. I'm also grateful for the experimental grafts and trees that I kindly received from our friend Dueck. They are all growing more or less well. It was painful for me to read that you are again attacked with your old illness, but thank God that you are again better. I beg you to control your fiery temper lest you come down with a lengthy illness or even die.

Last year, grasshoppers attacked our settlement causing much damage at my sheep farm and elsewhere. I harvested nothing but rye. The grasshoppers devoured our pasture and my livestock had to be driven to grasslands twenty or thirty verstas away. They returned only in fall. The livestock plague infected another part of our settlement, killing all livestock in several villages.

Winter was hard, down to twenty-four degrees Reamur – colder than it has been since we settled here – with a lot of snow, more than a sazhen deep, especially in the south. In the Crimea, where there is usually little frost and almost no snow, it was as cold as here. A number of people froze to death. The Crimean vineyards have suffered seriously. Our Melitopol Uezd along the Sea of Azov had less snow this winter

1 Cornies wrote almost identical letters to a number of acquaintances in Prussia, recounting his trip home. We have included only the most detailed letter, but this brief excerpt, from a letter to Abram Dueck, adds additional colour.

than anywhere else in southern Russia, but a lot of snow fell on the steppes in the Taganrog region, up the Don River, and beyond the Don in the Astrakhan villages.

Much of the livestock belonging to the nomadic Kalmyks was destroyed, particularly their horses. These people possess an enormous wealth in horses and never buy a blade of hay or other fodder. They neither seed nor harvest, store nothing in granaries, and have no wagons. They transport everything on camels and oxen. Many Kalmyks have 1,000 to 2,000 horses that they move along in search of pasture in summer and winter. It is assumed that the Kalmyk steppe is 600 to 700 verstas wide, from the Don River to Astrakhan, and about 800 verstas long, from Kitar to Tsaritsyn. This far-flung land has no inhabitants except Kalmyks, who do not own a single, immoveable house. Once a pasture is consumed, they move their high carts and felt tents along like the patriarchs Abraham, Isaac, and Jacob of old did. Thousands of horses are annually driven out to the Berdichev market, where they fetch little or nothing. They are sorted and sold as Ukrainian horses to Austria, Saxony, and Prussia.

Because thousands of horses starved to death last winter, horses here are now very expensive. This spring, our settlement earned more than 20,000 rubles from the sale of horses. Otherwise, our shortage of money would have been much worse. Nomadic Tatars in the Caucasus also suffered a good deal in the severe weather. If God wishes, He can chastise and visit disaster on all peoples by such means. The prophet says: "You strike them and they do not feel. You punish them and they do not improve." Yes, that is the human way. Yet I do not believe that God's punishment is in vain, even if we do not have eyes to see and ears to hear.

I had to feed all my livestock for three months, which seldom happens, and needed seven loads of hay without straw every day. With the arrival of spring, the livestock plague reappeared in Russian villages, in several German villages, and at the community sheep farm. There are few grasshoppers in our district at the present time, but large numbers are reported here and there in the surrounding area. They are still without wings, but when these develop they will soon be upon us.

Right now, none of our products fetch good prices. Formerly, wool was the only product that kept its price, but there is no demand now due to this year's money shortage. It is acute everywhere. I sent all of my wool to Moscow immediately after the shearing, to be sold on consignment by a trading firm I know. Grain prices are very low because the army provides the only market, and it is at a great distance from us. We have to send all of our products overland to market. Eventually Russia's flag will fly along the western and southern shores of the Black Sea, as it now flies on Mount Ararat in Persia, and our region will have direct access to markets. We look forward to this prospect.

Did you receive the book about the Tatar family from brother Epp in Heubuden? I sent it to you with my travelling companions Regehr and Friesen. It is about a neighbouring nobleman and his lady. I passed samples to your sister and insisted that she send you the enclosed bill. I enclose her letter. Their situation has improved. When you have the chance, please pass on my greetings to your neighbour Mr. Westphal, my brother-in-law Mr. Jacob Friesen and his wife and children in Fuerstenwerder, Mr. Jacob Dick, Baerwalde, Mr. Fyjuth together with his relatives, as well as your brother-in-law Woelk and his wife and children. If you should find occasion to visit the Reverend Mr. van der Smissen and the merchant Mr. Haass in Danzig, please give them my hearty greetings. Please greet my friend Wall in Schoensee and give him the enclosed note.

Since I still have a little space, I should add that my youngest brother Heinrich married my wife's youngest sister this winter. They live with Mother. He will probably not be able to visit you. Mother was very ill for a few days, but is somewhat better now and sends special greetings to you, and your dear wife and children.

I have just heard that the vanguard of the grasshoppers has arrived. People are busily working, mowing field crops and putting them in storage to protect them from the huge second swarm that is sure to follow. It will not leave a single blade standing. Only someone who has witnessed similar grasshopper migrations in the past can understand such a thing. These swarms sometimes stretch out in a swath fifteen verstas wide. They are so densely packed that, as they move along, they blot out the sun for two to three hours at a time, and the noise of their whirring wings is like the soft clatter of a marching army.

In August, I intend to select forty mares and send them to an annual market 200 verstas from here.

I repeat my heartfelt thanks for your friendship and love. May you all live well with God. Yes, may He, our good father, protect you and your whole house. May He give you peace, love, and harmony. Many heartfelt greetings to you and your beloved relations from my wife, brothers, and me. With my most heartfelt thanks, I remain, with love, your honest friend.

Johann Cornies

148. Johann Cornies to David Epp. 7 July 1828 to Heubuden [abbreviated letter]. SAOR 89-1-129/23v.[2]

The day after I left Klakendorf, I took the wrong road beyond Finkenstein, and we wandered around until we got to the Rote Krug near Deutsch Eylau. There we met Gerhard Dueck and his travelling companions. We ate together and met again near Soldan, where I was having the stallions reshod. Stones had damaged their shoes. I waited for Dueck at Nicoleva on the Polish border, having decided to travel in company with him to the Russian border, which costs little to cross. I was the marshal and anybody who wanted to travel with us was required to follow my instructions. In beautiful weather, we proceeded in harmony to Ostrog in Volhynia, where we had a half-day of rain. At Michalin in the Ukraine, we passed the emigrants who had left Prussia eight days earlier. A day before reaching Ekaterinoslav, I turned left towards the city, while Dueck and his companions turned right, towards Khortitsa.

I was moving ahead at a brisk pace to again take over my own business, when I fell ill. One day while I was working to establish control over my horses, I became overheated and that evening I came down with a serious case of the chills, with violent shivering and fever. For four months, I was dizzy and weak, with spells of recovery alternating with periods of weakness. Four days after my return, Daniel [Schlatter] arrived back, suffering from a serious three-day fever that he had caught from the Nogais. He spent the winter in my house. Spring brought an end to his illness, but he was too weak to return to the Nogais. He wanted to go to Switzerland, but in early June, the two of us decided that he would spend three months recuperating in the Crimea, with its mild climate, mountains, and sea baths. Three weeks ago, he left with a Tatar. Hausknecht is in his element, living in Einlage, and is, as far as I know, healthy and happy.

Our spiritual quarrels have reached the ears of the Minister [in St. Petersburg], and a few individuals among us will do us no honour if they do not stop their wilfulness and obstinacy. The matter is soon to be examined. A Russian law prohibits foreigners from meddling in our

2 This long letter contains descriptive passages identical to others reproduced above. The repeated sections have been omitted. Regarding the planned Bessarabian colony discussed here, see also documents 38, 61, 64, 66, 80, 81, 85, 86, and 104.

quarrels, under threat of specified penalties. I would ask you to warn your elder about the situation in whatever way your position permits.

Because of the [Russo-Turkish] war, nothing can be done now about [a Mennonite settlement in] Bessarabia, nor is anything likely to come of it in future. When our army advanced on the Turkish border, the Russian Zaporozhian Cossacks, who moved from the Dnieper to Turkish areas about fifty years ago, sent their Ataman to His Majesty, the Tsar, asking for permission to return to Russia. After granting their request, His Majesty directed the Guardianship Committee in Kishinev, and our dear superior, His Excellency, General Inzov, to receive these Zaporozhians and to settle them as colonists. They say there are about 20,000 of them and that they would require a great deal of land. If there is so much unpopulated land in Bessarabia, they will surely be settled there. Still, there remains an excellent piece of unsettled land, about 13,000 desiatinas, some 200 verstas, from here. I lease it myself, but am afraid to become involved with our dear Prussian Mennonites. They seem so apathetic that I doubt that anything worthwhile could be achieved by working with them. They seem to show little concern about their future generations, when oppression and poverty will make progress impossible. Land cannot be reserved for them forever. Generally, I find they lack a community spirit and a sense of duty. This is the end of my report.

149. Johann Cornies to Jacob Penner and Heinrich Heese. 31 July 1828. SAOR 89-1-129/39.

My dear friends Jacob Penner and Heinrich Heese in Khortitsa,

I received your warm letter dated 9 July. Thank you for your sympathy and affection. Although you have neither seen nor heard from me, my business affairs alone kept me from visiting you this spring. My love remains as it was and your letters assure me of yours. Our spiritual unity will continue, even without personal contact, and would stay the same even if the distances were greater and we could meet even less frequently.

It would be terrible if we could only love people who were close to us. We thank God that He has not limited our feelings of love to such a close circle. Our love can embrace all humanity and we can act on its behalf. And the more powerfully we feel this impulse, the easier it is to understand that the whole world, with its millions, is bound together and can work actively and productively on everyone's behalf. It would be tragic if all societies existed only for themselves. Denied participation in a broader humanity, they would suffer from natural shortages produced by a lack of trade and social intercourse. We would also be deprived of our salvation and eternal blessedness. Christ, our Saviour, was martyred, died, arose from the grave, and went to heaven for the salvation of the whole world. He has prepared an eternal repose for all who love Him, whoever they may be and wherever they may live.

You inquired about selling your sheep, but I know of no one who wants to buy such a large number. In winter, a merchant asked me about the best time and place to purchase sheep from Germans, but nothing more has come of this. I will not fail to inform buyers wishing to buy sheep of the same quality as yours.

What is brother Hausknecht doing? Is his work successful? Is he in good health and happy? I can imagine that he is not always contented because he sets himself huge tasks. Rome, however, was not built in a year [*sic*] although its borders were extended over time. Time produces roses, but also thorns that should be avoided when the roses are picked. A French proverb says: "Les Malhurs et le plaisirs nef viennent jamais heuls. Avec le tems et la paille les netles Murihhent." However, "Nons avons beau faire et beau dire, la barque ne va pas hans rames." ["Misfortunes and pleasures never happen by themselves. With time and straw, nettles ripen." However, "There is no getting around it; the boat will not move without oars."] Waiting produces its own rewards and blessed are they who wait on the Lord. Please give dear Hausknecht a thousand greetings and tell him that his compatriot, our common friend Daniel Schlatter, left here yesterday for home. Because of his poor health, he does not intend to return.

Please give my heartfelt greetings to friends Lepke, D. Epp, and all of my acquaintances. Many greetings to you and your dear families. Please remember me always with love. Adieu.

Your loving Cornies

150. Agreement between Johann Cornies and Johann Bartram. 11 September 1828. SAOR 89-1-1326/47.

Mr. Johann Cornies, Ohrloff village, and Johann Bartram, Vyborg, Finland, concluded the following agreement on the date given below:

Johann Bartram undertakes to thoroughly instruct the children of Mr. Cornies in Russian language and grammar, to the extent this is possible, and in accordance with their own diligence and effort. Instruction will continue for two hours daily in winter until 1 June 1829. For this service Mr. Johann Cornies agrees to pay Mr. Bartram a sum of 100 rubles. To ensure that both sides keep this agreement faithfully, we have signed personally:

Johann Cornies, Johann Bartram
Ohrloff, 11 September 1828

151. Daniel Schlatter to Johann Cornies. Sent from St. Gall, 20 September 1828. SAOR 89-1-84/2.

Treasured Cornies,

I hasten to send you a letter from Altonau that van der Smissen regrettably did not address to you correctly. Instead of sending it to Ohrloff via Hausner & Voilland, he sent it to Switzerland. I hope that you will also have news directly from Nymegen.

There is so much that I would like to ask and to know, as you surely understand. Please write to me soon. I send a thousand greetings to you and everyone, especially in your household, your dear wife and children, your old mother, and all your relatives. Give my greetings to your wife's assistant, who took such pains with me. Greet all friends.

I have not yet had time to take up a specific profession. Please have patience with my debt, dear friend. I paid others first because they are impatient, including 400 rubles to Diezinger and 300 to Hausner for accounts here at home. I sent your writings to my friend, asking about their publication, and he sent me the following note: "The good intentions of the author are evident, as is his striving to achieve something competent, but the whole thing is not, in any way, appropriate for printing. I am firmly convinced that, as he progresses further in his intellectual development, he would personally regret having this text publicly distributed, even if many incorrect and inadmissible expressions were changed." I treasure this friend, who gave me his opinion in similar situations.[3]

3 Johann Cornies sent his description of the Nogais along with Schlatter for possible publication. Daniel Schlatter used its contents in his own book, published in 1830, without acknowledging Cornies' contribution [Daniel Schlatter, *Bruchstücke aus einigen Reisen nach dem südlichen Russland, in den Jahren 1822 bis 1828* (St. Gallen, 1830)]. Cornies' own version was ultimately published in the Russian journal *Teleskop* as "Kratkii obzor polozheniia Nogaiskikh tatar, vodvorennykh v Melitopol'skom Uezde Tavricheskoi gubernii," *Teleskop* 33 (1836). The original version is published in part two of this volume.

I cannot make this letter too long, but I would like to use the remaining space to politely ask you to send me a compact copy of the Mennonite Charter of Privileges [*Privilegium*] as soon as possible. I forgot to copy it myself and need it urgently. Tauchnitz also requests it. Address: Daniel Schlatter, to the place cited above, or in St. Gall, Switzerland, with outside cover to Mr. Wilhelm Kloeber in Brody in Galicia. I now have an account with him after closing my account with Hausner.

Thousands and thousands of greetings. Adieu! Adieu!

Your Daniel

Received 9 October.

152. Johann Cornies to Samuel Contenius. 17 October 1828. SAOR 89-1-129/46v.[4]

Yr. Excellency, benevolent Sir,

Three years will soon have slipped by since 14 November 1825, when I presented a petition to His Excellency, the Lord Chief Curator for the Colonists in southern Russia, Lieutenant General and Sir Inzov, when he travelled through the local settlements on his way to Taganrog. I then applied for inheritance and ownership rights to a tract of 3,800 desiatinas of land adjoining the agricultural establishment I started on the Iushanle in 1811. I was, at the time, motivated to do this by an announcement contained in the All-Highest Directive from the Minister of the Interior that inheritance and ownership rights for uncultivated lands would be bestowed upon those who set up landed properties to breed Spanish sheep. This is detailed in the pamphlet, "Guidance for the Improvement and Refinement of Sheep Breeding in Russia," published by W. E. Friebe, Riga, in 1809, at the request of His Serene Highness the Lord Minister of the Interior.

During seventeen years of untiring exertion on behalf of the refinement of my flocks, I have, because I lacked legal ownership of my estate, encountered serious difficulties and obstacles. Although incidents during that time may not be sufficient to command closer consideration of my concerns, I must think of the future of my agricultural establishment, valued conservatively at a minimum of 100,000 rubles. A wealth of experience has taught me not to continue on this insecure and uncertain basis for the future, but seek the establishment of my ownership to

4 Regarding Cornies' efforts to gain a permanent land grant at Iushanle, see also documents 1, 5, 177, 178, 185, 531, 535, and additional documents in volume II.

this land. I therefore make a humble and dutiful appeal, aware of the honourable, trusting, gracious, and well-meaning consideration generally given to every useful endeavour and initiative. Since I am familiar with Yr. Excellency's disposition, I request Yr. attention and consideration of my concerns in order that this matter might be brought to a desired and purposeful conclusion based on the well-known inclinations of Our High Imperial Government to act justly and to encourage reasonable endeavours.

I find that, despite the unmistakable value of Yr. Excellency's advice, given at the time of the annual inspection of my agricultural establishment, that I apply for a seventy-to-eighty-year hereditary lease from Our Imperial Government subject to specific conditions, such an arrangement would threaten me with a distant and insecure future and grave problems. As a concerned and conscientious father and provider, I must hesitate to place my descendants' future in such danger and uncertainty.

Had I not felt assured that the ownership and inheritance of the land referred to above would be bestowed upon me, I would not have made the sacrifices I did to develop it. I hope, during an indeterminate period of ten to twenty years, to move ahead with the improvement of my livestock, especially, of course, the refinement of my flock of sheep. I would similarly like to develop my garden and forest-tree plantations using the most desirable stock available, adapted to all varieties of soil and climate. I further intend to continue methodical experiments to promote sericulture as a branch of the economy. Since my own life may not be long enough to complete all of these projects, I believe that my heirs would be more inclined to continue them if they were owners of the land. For my own part, I would not want to obligate myself to such great exertions for a limited time period, if the high authorities were unwilling to bestow this land upon my heirs and descendants.

With the most trusting assurance I have the honour to remain Yr. merciful Excellency's most humble servant.

153. Johann Cornies to Traugott Blueher. 26 October 1828. SAOR 89-1-129/53.

Honoured Mr. Blueher,

My message of 19 October informed you that I had received the proceeds for the entire quantity of wool given to you on consignment this year. I enclose the receipt and thank you for your efforts. I assure you that, although the sale price was lower this year than in previous years, I know that this was not your fault and that you were not negligent. Locally, as in other regions of Russia, wool prices have fallen appreciably. Please do not worry.

Please provide us with absolutely reliable information, obtained from manufacturers in Moscow or elsewhere, regarding the handling of wool so that it can fetch its true value from manufacturers. Our sheep breeders need to know this so as to take the appropriate measures. How should it be sorted, washed, and packed? What is the best time of year to sell it? I do not shy away from the expense of acquiring highly refined rams and ewes to improve my wool so that it equals the fineness of foreign wool. As the wool improves from year to year, I also need to know about its preparation so that I am able to deliver wool to the manufacturer prepared according to this standard.

If God grants me life and health and you are kind enough to take my wool on consignment, I intend to send my wool to you again next spring. When a shipping opportunity occurs, please send me three dozen sheep shears addressed to Mr. Joseph Bissarov, merchant of the First Guild in Kharkov, to be forwarded to Mr. W. Martens, merchant of the First Guild, or to his deputy in Halbstadt, Molochnaia. Since most of the devotional literature you list is already available here, I do not know if any of it will be in demand.

Brother Schlatter left Russia forever in July. He feared serious consequences resulting from his illness. He was ill in my house for a year. Commend me to your dear wife.

I send you a thousand greetings and remain with love, your honest friend and servant,

Cornies

154. Johann Cornies to Casper Adrian Hausknecht. 14 December 1828. SAOR 89-1-129/54v.

Mr. Hausknecht, Schoenwiese,

I received your letter of 3 December only on 12 December. I will gladly give you the requested advance of 200 rubles until 1 May 1829. Your promise is my guarantee. If your letter had arrived two days earlier, I could have sent the money on immediately. Sending it by mail is difficult, because the post office is forty verstas from Ohrloff. You may depend on my sending it as soon as I find a suitable opportunity to do so. I plan to come through Einlage right after the New Year, if God grants me good health, and I will bring it myself if you can wait. May God bless your efforts and your work.

With greetings, I remain your loving Cornies.

155. Johann Cornies to Cornelius Janzen, Schoenwiese. 19 December 1828. SAOR 89-1-129/55.

Very dear friend,

Please forgive me for troubling you, but I venture to do so because of my dependence on your friendship and love. I feel greatly obliged to you for your favours and continue to be eager to serve you, although I have not yet been able to show you my honest thanks.

Dear friend, I need three or four good, healthy, honest, sober, industrious, clean, and respectable people for my sheep farm. They are undoubtedly available in the town of Aleksandrovsk. Please make inquiries about their availability and expected wages. Kindly address the answer to Wilhelm Martens, to be forwarded to me.

Your Cornies

1829

156. Johann Cornies to Wool Improvement Society. 9 January 1829. SAOR 89-1-142/2.

To the highly esteemed Molochnaia Mennonite Wool Improvement Society,

Humble submission and explanation from the member J.C.:

As a member of the Society since its founding, I have often had occasion to reflect on the fruits and achievements of our combined endeavours. Each time, I have regretfully come to the conclusion that we are not achieving our purpose of improving our community sheep farm economically and are not making genuine progress, as our supervising authorities expected when the Society was founded. The reason is that good order and complete accord are missing.

I submit the following points for consideration by the esteemed Society. I am confident that, in this way, our joint efforts and endeavours would achieve the desired results. Accordingly, I give notice that I will continue to be a member of the Society only upon the following conditions:

1. In future, all of the community sheep farm's income is applied exclusively to the advantage and improvement of the economic arrangements of this community institution.

2. The administrator, at all times, has a fund of several hundred rubles at his disposal to enable him to undertake urgent expenditures and make timely repairs. He will, naturally, account for the money spent. This matter was decided upon earlier but has not been carried out.

3. There are no exceptions to the rule laid down in the Society's directive that Society members must assemble regularly at the end of each

month at a predetermined time. The administrator must notify the members of the meeting, which should take place as scheduled.

4. A full, detailed accounting of the sheep farm's income and expenditures are provided to the whole Society and entered into its minutes, with a copy to each Society member for their understanding.

5. In addition to participating in its general affairs, every Society member is assigned, at the beginning of each year, a specific duty to fulfil and is to keep the administrator informed about its progress. When a member finds that he cannot make a decision himself, he will ask the administrator to call a meeting of the Society and make a joint decision, following appropriate guidelines.

My business affairs do not permit me to devote time to useless trips and pointless deliberations. I respectfully request that this, my humble submission and explanation, be entered into the minutes. With this I serve notice that should the worthy Society not accept and implement my carefully considered proposals, I will no longer appear as a member in its meetings and will ask to be freed of all obligations of Society membership.

With all appropriate respect and esteem, I still remain the esteemed Society's respectful,

Johann Cornies

157. Wilhelm Martens and Johann Cornies to Ekaterinoslav Guardianship Committee. 30 January 1829. SAOR 89-1-142/5.[1]

To Ekaterinoslav Guardianship Committee,
From W. Martens and Johann Cornies, holders of the beverage lease in the Molochnaia Mennonite District,
Most obedient petition:

Over the past three years there has been considerable brandy smuggling in villages where we hold the lease. It is carried on by colonists and Russians through the publicans and others. We had hoped to suppress this practice through earnest admonitions, not wishing to burden our administration with the matter. However, smuggling has increased and gained ground, and subjects us as leaseholders to grievous disadvantage. We therefore venture to bring the following three incidents to

1 Regarding the dispute described in this document over the "brandy lease" – a monopoly on the sale of distilled alcoholic beverages in the region – see also documents 158, 159, 166, 169, 201, 202, and 205.

the attention of the esteemed Guardianship Committee in the hope that the prosecution of the guilty would prevent similar transgressions in future.

1. On 28 January, Johann Rempel in Laddekopp was arrested with a barrel of brandy containing thirty pails, six quarts. A portion of this had already been tapped. The District Office was notified of this incident and is holding the seized brandy under guard. This same Rempel continues his smuggling, even with our money, and owes us 700 R.B.A.

2. Smuggled brandy was sold at night on 22 January in the Lichtenau Mayor's house by a colonist from Reichenfeld. His first name is Carl but we do not know his surname.

3. In December 1828, in Schoensee, a Russian hid six pails of brandy at the local watermill owned by Johann Toews. We do not know where this person has gone.

We obediently request that the esteemed Committee take administrative measures against such illegal acts in order that what has occurred to our disadvantage be prevented and that we might no longer suffer damage in future.

158. Wilhelm Martens and Johann Cornies. 30 January 1829. SAOR 89-1-142/5.[2]

To the Ekaterinoslav Guardianship Committee,
From W. Martens and J. Cornies, holders of the beverage lease in the Molochnaia Mennonite District,
Most obedient petition:

For many years, various publicans in our villages have been in debt to us for not inconsiderable sums of money for beverages obtained from us and then sold. Since our patience has failed to give us what is ours, we must burden our administration with a most obedient request for administrative intervention to protect us from injury to our interests. We take the liberty to enclose a record of our most delinquent debtors and the sums they owe. We further note that the debtors have used most of the money owed for their own buildings and other economic arrangements. None are in so poor an economic position that they cannot, with a little effort, repay the sums owing.

2 Regarding the dispute described in this document over the "brandy lease" – a monopoly on the sale of distilled alcoholic beverages in the region – see also documents 157, 159, 166, 169, 201, 202, and 205.

We take comfort in the hope that the esteemed Guardianship Committee will vouchsafe administrative consideration of our most obedient request and assist us in obtaining our rights.

[Followed by a list of twenty-four individuals owing amounts from twenty-four to 957 rubles.]

159. Ekaterinoslav Guardianship Committee to District Office. 12 February 1829. SAOR 89-1-141/21.[3]

Regarding the beverage lease:

Directive from Ekaterinoslav Guardianship Committee to Molochnaia Mennonite District Office:

In response to a petition from Martens and Cornies, leaseholders for the distribution of brandy in the Molochnaia Mennonite District, the Committee has ordered its Titular Counsellor Tarasovich to transport Mennonites convicted of smuggling, under guard, to this Committee for incarceration.

This District Office is most strictly ordered to cooperate fully with Mr. Tarasovich in this case and to punctually follow his demands.

12 February 1829. Identical in wording to original, translator Goern. Received 21 February 1829.

160. Johann Cornies to Johann Ambrosius Barth. 26 February 1829. SAOR 89-1-142/6v.

Mr. Johann Ambrosius Barth, Bookseller, No. 681 Grimmaischestrasse, Leipzig,

I hereby notify you that the books in your shipment from Leipzig dated 28 March 1828 have been received. Please send me another small shipment of books through Mr. Convenz, in Marienburg, West Prussia:

1. *Des peuples, et de leurs chef, ou l'organisation Societe; l'histoire et la politique du temps.* Paris, 1827. [The people, and their l*eader, or the* organization of society: The history and politics of our times]

2. *Melanges Scientifique et litteraires de Malte-Brun*, Paris, 1828, 3 v. [The blend of science and literature of Malte-Brun]

3. *L'histoire de la Russie et particulierement de Pierre le grand,* par Segur, 1829. [The history of Russia, and particularly of Peter the Great]

---

3 Regarding the dispute described in this document over the "brandy lease" – a monopoly on the sale of distilled alcoholic beverages in the region – see also documents 157, 158, 166, 169, 201, 202, and 205.

4. *Voyages et Souvenirs du Duc de Richelieu, President du Consiel des Ministers,* par L. J. d'Altsete, 2nd edition in 12. Paris, 1829. [The voyages and memoirs of the Duc de Richelieu, president of the council of ministers]

5. *Heinsius Deutsche Schaaflehre.* [Heinsius' German sheep manual]

The bill will be paid by Mr. Convenz, as before.

On another matter, Stein's *Geographie* in three parts, which I purchased from you during my visit in 1827, is missing one sheet, pages 113 to 128. Please send it with this shipment of books.

I have the honour to be, with complete respect and esteem, your servant,

Cornies

161. Johann Cornies to Traugott Blueher. 26 February 1829. SAOR 89-1-142/10v.

Honoured Mr. Blueher,

Thank you for your letter of 11 December 1828, and for your kind efforts in providing information on the preparation and sale of wool. Are wool prices currently higher or lower than they were? Friends in Prussia with large flocks of sheep sent me encouraging news that well-washed wool is selling at 100 Reichsthaler per hundredweight and higher, on the spot. Prices for very fine and medium-fine wool are rising in value, but inferior qualities are in decline.

I received the sheep shears and two copies of Tapp's *Grammatik,* all in good order. Please bill me for the latter. Also please mail one funt of good Egyptian snuff, addressed to Mr. Josef Gordovich Pritchenko in Ekaterinoslav, charged to my account.

Spring has arrived. Everything has thawed and we are enjoying beautiful weather.

May the Lord bless you and your house. Many greetings to you and your dear wife. I am, as always, your honest friend and servant,

Cornies

162. Johann Cornies to David Epp, Heubuden. 16 February 1829. SAOR 89-1-142/8.

My sincere friend,

Truth brings forth hatred and we ask: Can the closest friend of love bring forth hate and enmity? It can happen, just as the most wholesome food can harm a spoiled stomach. Jesus spoke: "You seek to kill me though I tell you the truth. 'You must die,' the embittered screamed at the preacher of truth, Jeremiah. When Stephan demonstrated the truth to the Jews, it chilled their hearts and they gnashed their teeth."

Thoughts are free before people, but not before God. Our Lord did not ask, "Why do you speak such wickedness?" but rather, "Why do you have such wicked thoughts in your heart?" When you hear the call of mercy, take hold quickly and follow the voice of the spirit, without lengthy questions and agitation. Only then will you experience this treasure in the most blessed, holy sense. Let your light shine. We can walk about carrying candles that are either lit or extinguished. We run and work with unfruitful perceptions that are not life-giving. We sit at a full table, yet die of starvation. Concise and good – genuinely biblical, but not flesh and blood – I quickly plunge ahead and may have said too much. The teaching profession is a profession of suffering.

Paul had barely agreed to serve Christ when he had to swear allegiance to the banner of the cross. The Lord said: "I want to show him how much he must suffer for my sake. It is not just that the world does evil unto you but you may thank the world for this evil for you have been called to it as a Christian." It is the Christian's duty to do good, to suffer evil and to experience injustice. If we had experienced justice, we would have plunged into hell long ago with body and soul. God's grace serves as justice.[4]

Be happy you are alive, and that God loves you. The devil himself must be working to promote our joy with his constant attacks. Do not be discouraged. If your conscience is clear, lying mouths cannot destroy you. I am pleased that you did not sign your name to falsehood. When I visited you, I knew that divisions would have to arise among you, and your experience does not surprise me. According to 1 Corinthians, chapters 11, 18, and 19, Paul was also not surprised, and recognized that it was necessary.

I received your letter of 22 November and the note from friend A. Rempel, for which I am most thankful. We had an extreme winter here, especially Ekaterinoslav guberniia, which I left eight days ago. Now the weather is spring-like. The community has taken in about 100,000

4 This is a response to a dispute that wracked the Heubuden Mennonite Congregation in 1827–8. The dispute apparently revolved around a guest sermon preached in Epp's Church, which Epp condemned for attributing "to man the good works he does with his own strength, ... contrary to the gospel." This provoked a deep controversy, in which Epp was forced to step down from his position as his community's representative to the British and Foreign Bible Society, and only retained his position as minister in the face of substantial pressure to resign.

rubles from the sale of horses. Otherwise, everything is as it was. You know that my brother Heinrich is in Ekaterinoslav, but you probably do not know that Johann Sukau has married and is moving to my sheep farm as manager. Kindly receive some books from Mr. Convenz in Leipzig, and have them sewn but not bound in order that they might be taken over the border more easily than with a binding or fabric casing. Please forward them with immigrants, but not all on one wagon. Divide them among several wagons, for delivery to Johann Klassen or W. Martens in Halbstadt, where the freight will be paid. Please send me the bill. D. Schlatter has been in Switzerland since October 1828. He could not stay here because of his poor health. Hausknecht is experiencing good and evil trials, as one usually does. I visited him eight days ago and he is well.

I visited the Crimea in November on business. Many captured Turks were still there, among them Imhoff Pasha, whom I saw at the governor's.[5] Count Vorontsov's exemplary plantations will eventually transform the Crimea into a second Italy. I regret that thrifty, industrious Christians do not inhabit the pleasant valleys of the Crimea instead of the fanatical Tatars. Only with time will it be possible to pick roses.

Kindly give my greetings to all good friends and acquaintances. Special greetings to you and your dear family, from your honest friend Cornies.

Eleven song books have been ordered, namely by Joh[ann] C[ornies] 2, P[eter] C[ornies] 1, D[avid] C[ornies] 1, Agn[es] Cor[nies] 2, Maria Cor[nies] 1, Joh[anne] Sukau 1, Pet[er] Fr[iesen] 1, H[einrich] C[ornies] 1, 1 ordinary.

163. Johann Cornies to Heinrich Cornies. 27 February 1829. SAOR 89-1-142/12v.

Dear brother Heinrich Cornies,

I arrived home safely on 15 February and found all my loved ones well. We crossed all the rivulets without trouble except for the Kurushan. I had to have a wagon fetched from home to ship me across. Spring seems to be arriving and we are enjoying beautiful, warm days. What are you doing now? Are you healthy? May God grant you contentment and good health. I discussed with Mother and brother David the gelding that died and they want to give the matter some thought.

5 Prisoners of war, from the Russo-Turkish War of 1827–8.

Dear brother, please buy some good couches and chairs for me at the market if you can find any. I need them for the sheep farm, but would probably not order chairs for my own house from Lohr. Of what use are they if they have no covers? However, if you find good, light, well-proportioned chairs suitable for my room, buy them even if they are a little expensive. They must be attractive and durable. If you do make these purchases and need money, please let me know and I will immediately send it to you by mail. If you ship the furniture with someone who is not coming here directly, please write. Make certain that you negotiate specific freight charges to avoid unpleasantness.

They are mourning at Mr. Voth's place. His second oldest daughter, Emma, died on Sunday and will be buried today (Wednesday). This is causing him much grief. Bernhard Frank is completely well and in good spirits. Please report this to his loved ones, together with a greeting from me.

Have you found a maid yet to replace Catharina? Give it some thought for spring is coming soon. It would be advantageous to keep Jacob. Offer him 200 rubles for a year. This is hardly too much for a person who looks after your entire establishment and keeps it in order. Give him my greetings, and Catharina as well. Apropos of the extra butter for which you paid me, please put this on my account.

Please give the enclosed song to the esteemed Mrs. Schmidt personally, with my greetings. Thank Mr. Pritchenko's family for their friendly reception and extend heartfelt greetings to Mr. W. Frank and Peter Reimer. Mr. Roschlau is already probably over hill and dale, but I wish him a safe journey. If Harder had arrived half a day later, he would have been stuck. Travel was cut off so quickly, but everything went well.

May the dear Heavenly Father keep you. May He endow you with truth and love, and give you His blessing now and for all eternity. Amen. Our dear mother, brothers, and all our friends send greetings. Special greetings from my wife and children, and from me.

Your loving Johann Cornies

164. Johann Cornies to Andrei M. Fadeev. 27 February 1829. SAOR 89-1-142/12.

Mr. Fadeev, Your Honour, Gracious Sir,

I cannot convince our local District Office that letters to be sent abroad must be presented to the Committee unsealed only if they are sent through the Ministry. It is their understanding that each and every private letter that is to be sent abroad by mail must be presented for inspection. I made the *ukaz* Yr. Honour kindly gave me in Ekaterinoslav available to them, but they ignore it.

Since it is now necessary for me to dispatch several letters abroad that I do not wish to present to the District Office unsealed, I most respectfully request that Yr. Honour issue a directive to the District Office for circulation to the villages stating that it is permissible to forward one's own letters by mail, sealed.

Except for a few places, all of our snow has melted, and we are having the most beautiful, warm spring days.

165. Samuel Contenius to Johann Cornies. 3 March 1829. SAOR 89-1-61/15.

Highly treasured Johann Cornies,

Since you are a diligent tree planter, I send you a package of forest-tree and flower seeds, a forage plant called *goergreka arrensis (Ackerspergras)*, and a box of *sarragate*, with the wish that everything might thrive, given thorough cultivation.

After a friendly greeting to your dear wife, I remain your Contenius.

Ekaterinoslav 3 March 1829. Received 28 March 1829.

166. Wilhelm Martens and Johann Cornies to District Office. 9 March 1829. SAOR 89-1-142/14v.[6]

To the worthy District Office in Halbstadt,

The Ladekopp Village Office had made a written declaration to the District Office that the leaseholders and the whole community heedlessly took smuggler Johann Rempel at his word, without proper evidence. They now regret their actions and ask the District Office, the leaseholders, and the whole community to forgive them. They insist that they will not again act in such a thoughtless manner. We therefore request that the esteemed District Office return their document to them.

We also request that a detailed circular letter inform the whole community that this matter was not founded on truth. The circular should

6 Regarding the dispute described in this document over the "brandy lease" – a monopoly on the sale of distilled alcoholic beverages in the region – see also documents 157, 158, 159, 169, 201, 202, and 205.

include a warning that no one should spread such unfounded slander in future. Otherwise, we would feel compelled to report such cases to the appropriate authorities.

Leaseholders Martens and Cornies

The petition submitted to the District Office by the Ladekopp Village Office:

We, members of the Ladekopp Mayor's Office, declare to the District Office, the brandy leaseholders, and the whole community that the document that gives credence to the statement of Johann Rempel is without foundation. We have no grounds to believe that what Johann Rempel asserts is true. He has demonstrated himself to be untrustworthy in the matter involving the barrel of brandy. We humbly ask the District Office, the leaseholders, and the whole community to forgive our actions, and we promise not to become involved in such unfounded accusations again. We would request that the District Office regard the document that we submitted to be invalid and to return it to us.

Johann Warkentin, Mayor; Peter Kroeker, Deputy Mayor

167. Johann Cornies to David Epp. 27 March 1829. SAOR 89-1-142/17.

To the honoured David Epp in Heubuden,

My letter in February could not be sent earlier because impediments to its dispatch had first to be settled. Ploughing began on my sheep farm yesterday. I am pleased to report that we now have one foal from the stallion bought from the esteemed Abram Wieb, Tiegenhagen, and another from Abram Dueck's stallion in Ohrloff. Almost sixty mares are pregnant from the three stallions. So far, the sheep on my properties from Saxony are doing very well and have given birth to almost 100 lambs. Johann Sukau is now living at my sheep farm.

The grass here is green and the weather warm, but sledge roads in Ekaterinoslav were still in use eight days ago. Should you have an opportunity to pay brother-in-law Franz Wieb from Klakendorf a half-thaler or more from my account, please do so with my heartfelt greetings. I am not sure what I owe him but my travel journal indicates a debt of some kind. Heartfelt greetings to everyone.

My business affairs increase from day to day. I praise God for good health and thank Him that I am well. I plan to purchase a large nobleman's estate about forty verstas from here, but would ask you to keep this information to yourself since it will happen only in the distant future. Please take care of the letter to Dirk Wiens, as well as the others.

Adieu,

Your loving Cornies

168. Johann Cornies to Casper Adrian Hausknecht. 9 April 1829. SAOR 89-1-142/18v.

I have received no letter or document from you, dear Hausknecht, except for a letter of 25 March 1829. It suggests that there was an earlier letter that you should track down in the postal forwarding station in Alexandrovsk. Other letters have been lost there before, or it was claimed that they had not been received. In such cases I searched for them myself. Friend Heese will know how best to proceed.

I am, in my own view, very busy, but do not care if people are of another view since they are not involved in my business affairs. As administrator of the property entrusted to me, I must follow the will of my Lord, knowing that sooner or later I will have to render an account.

Why should I not help you if I can? Do not be offended if I do not know your particular needs. Two people are better than one when advice or action is needed, but they must be as one if their actions are to benefit from their deliberations. For many people, action before thought has led to great grief, but one must also not be overly timid. I genuinely value good sense and real understanding more highly than I do wealth and beauty. Everything succeeds best when it is done with God.

Please write me by return mail to remind me of what you told me earlier. Adieu.

Your honestly loving Cornies

169. Johann Cornies and Wilhelm Martens to District Office. 20 April 1829. SAOR 89-1-142/20.[7]

The worthy District Office in Halbstadt,

Report from Wilhelm Martens and Johann Cornies, beverage leaseholders:

7 Regarding the dispute described in this document over the "brandy lease" – a monopoly on the sale of distilled alcoholic beverages in the region – see also documents 157, 158, 159, 166, 201, 202, and 205.

In reply to your communication No. 838, of 18 April, we report that we are not authorized to provide an expert opinion about the guilty parties who admitted their crime in our presence. The District Office can recommend remission of the punishment for the guilty parties when the Supervising Judge, His Honour, Mr. Fadeev, arrives. We leave our part to his wise resolution.

Leaseholder Wilhelm Martens, Leaseholder Johann Cornies

170. Johann Cornies to Wilhelm Frank. 20 April 1829. SAOR 89-1-142/20v.

Very dear Mr. Frank,

Your letter of 3 April arrived in good order. I am grateful for your news. A proverb says that enduring love will not gather mildew, the truth of which your loving letter confirms. I am moved and shamed that I am unable to return your services and make you, my valued friend, aware of my sincere honesty. Still, I comfort myself with the hope that you will remember my willingness [to help] at the appropriate time. I take comfort in the simple anticipation of this happening.

How is His Excellency? Is he still in good health? May God grant the dear old gentleman consolation, courage, and joy for now and a happy, blessed eternity in due course.

Heartfelt and sincere greetings to you and your dear parents. Your brother Bernhard is in good health. Adieu.

Your honest Johann Cornies

Joseph Gordovich and his wife kindly visited me at my sheep farm. Please give them my compliments.

171. Johann Cornies to David Epp. 1 May 1829. SAOR 89-1-142/21.

Dear friend David Epp in Heubuden,

Kindly have the enclosed letter delivered to its address, preferably in person, and explain clearly to Johann Mandtler that his son, who is in possession of only a travel pass, now has an excellent opportunity to stay here, as is his wish. He simply needs to acquire consent-to-emigrate documents from your government. Usually the law requires that everyone submit a security of 240 rubles to the consul in order to receive a pass that would permit him to register here as a Russian citizen. I have recommended Mandtler's son to the Chief Judge of the Guardianship Committee as a good professional and moral person.

If the emigration consent is received and presented to the authorities by this autumn, his acceptance can proceed without making various payments. Please charge expenses involved in securing this consent to my account and inform me of this in detail.

Spring is here in all its glory. In early winter, when there was still no snow, strong winds blew away much of the winter rye across our ploughed fields. There are no reports of the cattle plague, but our local region lost thousands of sheep to pox. This has now also ended.

Lemke separated from his wife. In the process, he created a most disagreeable situation for the community and its church leaders by sending various accusations against several leading officials and the whole community to the Ministry. Now, according to a Ministry *ukaz*, he is under arrest and will be deported from the country. (This is still very merciful.) His possessions have already been sold and he will shortly be taken to Ekaterinoslav under escort. In his sanctimonious way, he will eventually come to you seeking friends, but do not trust him.

Voth has resigned his job as teacher with the Society, and wants to establish himself on sixty desiatinas of land near Steinbach and develop vineyards and raise fruit trees and similar plantations, but I doubt if anything will come of this. As they say in Amsterdam, little can be done without money. I pity his family. The school position is therefore vacant.

I send greetings to you and yours. May you fare well in God.

Johann Cornies

Please mail the enclosed letter to Leipzig. Did you receive the envelopes and enclosures dated 26 February and 27 March?

172. Johann Cornies to Johann Ambrosius Barth. 1 May 1829. SAOR 89-1-142/22v.

Mr. Johann Ambrosius Barth, Bookseller, No. 681 Grimmaischestrasse, Leipzig,

Kindly send the following books, on my account, to the merchant Mr. Convenz in Marienburg, West Prussia:

1. *Gemeinnuetzige Blaetter*, second year, first volume. Halberstadt. [Generally useful papers]
2. *Oberbaurath Gilly. Beschreibung einer vortheilhaften Bauart mit getrockenten Lehmziegeln* [Description of an advantageous construction method with dried clay brick]

Johann Cornies, Mennonite village Ohrloff, on the Molochnaia

173. Johann Cornies to Traugott Blueher. 17 May 1829. SAOR 89-1-142/23.

Honoured Mr. Blueher,

Your valued message of 9 April arrived on 25 April. I welcome your news about the wool trade and am especially grateful for your kindness in agreeing to sell my wool to my benefit once you have sent samples to St. Petersburg. I have just finished washing my sheep, will begin shearing next week, and have contracted carts to transport the wool that will definitely be in transit to you by 1 June. I will mail separate samples of each variety. My wool production will about equal last year's in quantity, but the quality should be better.

Heartfelt thanks for your loving greetings. With honest love, I send greetings to you and your valued family, and call myself your obedient friend and servant,

Cornies

174. Johann Cornies to Traugott Blueher. 30 May 1829. SAOR 89-1-142/23v.

Highly honoured Mr. Blueher,

Enclosed are four whole fleeces of Spanish wool washed on the backs of sheep, as well as samples of each variety of wool that will be shipped to you next week. The first fleece is "Electa,"[8] the second "first variety," the third is "second variety," and the fourth "third variety." I would point out that these samples were taken randomly from each variety without attention to the fineness of the wool. The samples cannot be considered totally adequate and are not precise for each variety. In sorting whole fleeces, separate varieties cannot be designated precisely and combined to eliminate all variations. These samples can only provide general guidelines for the shipment ... [Eight lines illegible.]

175. Johann Cornies to Daniel Schlatter. 6 June 1829. SAOR 89-1-142/36.

D. Schlatter,

I do not know if you received my letter of 22 December 1828, forwarded through Mr. Klaeber, Brody. I wrote to Mr. Klaeber at the same

8 Probably a reference to "electoral" sheep – see footnote 25.

time, asking him to dispatch my correspondence abroad in future, but he has not yet replied. Are you still alive or have you died? I would welcome a small letter at least once a year, even if we do not exchange letters frequently. Here, everything is as you left it, except that T[obias] Voth has resigned from his school position and buried his second oldest daughter, Emma. Heese was hired in his stead. I feel sorry for the Voth family.

Much snow fell this winter and we are now having a lot of rain. Field and garden produce is growing well. My wool has been sent to Moscow. If you can find the goodwill, leisure, acquaintances, time, and opportunity to figure out a way of getting my wool to England, please do so. Prices here are falling sharply.

May God keep you and be with you on all your ways and, should you think of it, please send your sighs to our dear Lord on behalf of the friend who loves you, your brother in the Lord, who calls himself,

Your loving Cornies.

P.S. A thousand greetings to your dear mother. We also send our loving greetings to you. Builuk is alive but growing old. He would certainly send greetings to you if he knew I was writing, for he loves you very much and cannot forget you. Accept a greeting from me in his stead.

176. C. Steven, Simferopol, to Johann Cornies. 27 June 1829. SAOR 89-1-145/5.

Most valued Mr. Cornies,

I am now able to notify you that I will leave on 1 July if nothing stops me. I will spend a few days on my steppe estate, a few days in Kherson, where I have some business to transact on the Minister's orders, and hope to reach your place on 10 July. I will bring along several horses I am returning to you. A local acquaintance asked me to order a chaise from you, perhaps one ready-made that I could use with my own horses. In that way I could be of service to the person who has ordered the chaise, and the horses would not need to be sent back with a coachman. Please make appropriate inquiries for me. I was given twelve half-imperials, 252 rubles, for this purchase, and authorized to pay a further fifteen or twenty rubles if necessary. In the meantime, please accept my greatest respect,

Your most obliging Steven

Received 6 July 1829.

177. Johann Cornies to Samuel Contenius. 6 July 1829. SAOR 89-1-142/41v.[9]

Mr. Contenius, Yr. Excellency, Gracious Sir,

Today I mailed the petition graciously permitted me by His Honour, the senior member of the Ekaterinoslav Committee, for submission to His Excellency, the Head Curator for colonists in southern Russia. It requests that ownership of an area of 3,800 desiatinas that I presently work be bestowed on me. It is the area I have been using for my agricultural economy [for many years]. His Honour has given me to understand that Yr. Excellency has expressed surprise regarding my plans for plantings on ten desiatinas and my willingness to make the considerable exertion needed to do so.

I must explain my purpose. To enable me to lay out tree nurseries and to increase them properly by replanting them over time, I would like to give permanence to this plantation. This would enable me to transplant young trees and to maintain the soil in the necessary loose and clean state by hoeing and careful cultivation, as is absolutely necessary for their abundant growth. The needed expenditures would be too high for me to expend in support of this plan except on these particular ten desiatinas. To this end, I am obligating myself to plant trees on fifteen desiatinas – specifically, five desiatinas of planned orchards and five desiatinas of mulberry plantings, both of them in the low-lying area, and, finally, a five-desiatina plantation of various forest trees appropriate for planting on the high, waterless steppe, three to four verstas distance from the estate. A larger plantation of this type would limit my hay meadows overly much and result in an appreciable drop in the number of my livestock.

Submitting these circumstances most obediently to Yr. Excellency, I humbly seek Yr. active promotion of this matter. Convinced of your noble support of all generally useful purposes, I would ask you to consider this, my sincere request, favourably.

I have the honour to be, with all respect, Yr. Excellency's most obedient servant,

Cornies

9 Regarding Cornies' efforts to gain a permanent land grant at Iushanle, see also documents 1, 5, 152, 178, 185, 531, 535, and additional documents in volume II.

178. Johann Cornies to Andrei M. Fadeev. 6 July 1829. SAOR 89-1-142/43.[10]

Mr. Fadeev, Honoured Sir, Gracious sir,

Your Honour has given me permission to use your help in presenting my most obedient petition to His Excellency, the honoured General and Head Curator. I respectfully ask Yr. Honour's forgiveness that I now take the liberty of making use of this generous permission. Enclosed are two copies of the petition, identical in content. You will be so kind as to note the alterations in them. For reasons of propriety, it is extremely disagreeable for me that I could not acquire any Holland paper on which to write such a high person. I have full confidence in Yr. Honour, that you will be so kind as to intercede forcefully with His Excellency, the honoured Head Curator, on my behalf. I have also written to His Excellency Mr. Contenius asking for his kind intercession.

I again humbly ask your forgiveness for presuming to disrupt your important business on my behalf. Yr. Honour is as magnanimous as wise, and on this recognition I base my entire confidence. I know of nothing more to say, with the greatest respect, except that I do not lack great zeal for the task [of tree-planting].

Yr. Honour's devoted servant Cornies

179. Guardianship Committee to District Office. 23 July 1829. SAOR 89-1-141/12.

No. 250. From the Ekaterinoslav Guardianship Committee,
Directive to the Molochnaia Mennonite District Office:
Regarding tree plantations:

On 22 February 1829, under No. 770, this Committee ordered the District Office to make arrangements for the establishment of forest-tree plantations, without fail. Work in this direction should now already be started in the nineteen villages founded earlier in the Mennonite District. The most favourable time must not pass in choosing the necessary sites.

Weekly reports should have been made to the Committee regarding the steps to be taken in establishing this enterprise. Yet no attention has

10 Regarding Cornies' efforts to gain a permanent land grant at Iushanle, see also documents 1, 5, 152, 177, 185, 531, 535, and additional documents in volume II.

been paid to this requirement and not one single report on this subject has been received from this District Office. The Guardianship Committee emphasizes that this District Office must respond to the above order regarding the arrangements it has made.

23 July 1829. Same wording as in original, substituting translator Frank.

Received 1 August 1829. Directive given 3 August 1829.

Answered in report No. 308, 9 August 1829.

180. Johann Cornies to Heinrich Cornies. 1 August 1829. SAOR 89-1-142/48.

Dear brother Heinrich Cornies,

I only received your letter of 11 June 1829 yesterday, 31 July. It came from a Nogai and I am not sure why it was in Nogai hands. Presumably the Orekhov postal forwarding station inadvertently sent it to Count Orlov Denisov's estate on the Abitochna and the commanding officer for the Nogais sent it to me.

To prevent future mistakes, it is always essential to indicate in the address not only Ohrloff but also the Molochnaia settlement. The letter reached me too late. Otherwise I would have been willing to lend Mr. Goern 10,000 rubles, the requested sum of money, for half a year. Please let Mr. Goern know about my intentions.

We are, thank God, all healthy. Brother David and my son, Johann, will undoubtedly visit you soon. The lack of profit in the cereal mill is a painful thing, but have patience, time will bring change.

Heartfelt greetings from all of us. Live well with God. Commending myself to you as your loving brother,

Cornies

181. Tobias Voth to Johann Cornies. 30 August 1829. SAOR 89-1-90/5v.

Dear brother Cornies,

I came to take my farewell, but found you were not at home. I am therefore doing so in writing. May God, our praised and respected Lord and Saviour, bless and lead you, your dear wife and children, and the people in your house, to His honour and for your blessedness. I depart from you as your loving brother and in the hope of your love, which I value highly. I hope we can see each other often in this life, since

100 verstas is really not very far, and that we will be able to greet each other forever in heaven. May the Lord help us. Amen.

I gave the books in question to brother Heese. The account agreed with yours, except that *Die Wiederkunft unseres Herrn* [Our saviour's return] was omitted from your list. As a result, your list contains only eighty-seven titles instead of eighty-eight. This adds one ruble, eighty kopeks to the seventy-five rubles, eighty kopeks owing, and I am leaving seventy-seven rubles, sixty kopeks with your dear wife. This book accounting is hereby ended.

Again, with love, your brother Tob. Voth

Ohrloff, 30 August 1829

Notation: I had wanted to recopy this communication to give you a clean copy, since this is written in pencil, but I do not have the time. Please forgive me.

T.V.

1830

182. Johann Cornies to David Epp. 7 January 1830.
SAOR 89-1-169/2v.

Dear brother David Epp, Heubuden,

Your letter of 31 August 1829, the bill, and the books from Leipzig have arrived (the latter with Mr. Rongus). Thank you for doing this so quickly. Please mail the enclosure to Mr. J. A. Barth and send me the books when you can. I will ask Jacob Isaac to bring back the books, if possible. He is a young man from Ohrloff who plans to visit you in spring with N. Wall and his wife. J. Isaac will probably visit Tiege. I think Wall is a nephew of sister Jacob Wall in Heubuden.

Our home is much as it was and everyone is healthy, thank God. Winter set in in December, with much glare ice that turned the steppe into a sheet of glass. People skate on it, over hill and dale.

The young man you strongly recommended could earn his livelihood here if he has a good knowledge of his trade (there are more than enough fakers here). If he comes on a travel pass, his trade would probably make it possible for him to sustain himself and to win acceptance (in every case, an emigration pass is preferable). I would ask you, dear friend, that you not direct anyone to me unless he is a skilled tradesman, otherwise I will forfeit my credit with our authorities, who pay attention to the behaviour [of new arrivals] and not to what is said about them from abroad. A man must prove himself here. Should he be inexperienced, his hopes would be dashed, but if he has mastered his trade and is morally unblemished, he could receive support.

In November, I went to Ekaterinoslav with Wieb, a young visitor from Prussia who is a son of Hakenbudner Wieb from Tiege in Prussia. The superior judge in the Guardianship Committee commissioned me to write to Prussia about a new settlement of Mennonites in the Mariupol District, Ekaterinoslav guberniia, and since I was short of time, I asked young Wieb to report this to his friends. Since my space is limited, his letter to his father will provide full details. Please inquire with Mr. Wieb in Tiege.

In autumn, Tobias Voth moved to Schoenwiese where he built a large, solid house of fired bricks, about sixty fut long, with a number of rooms. He wishes to found a boarding school for [children of the] nobility, although he knows no Russian and the nobles understand no German. Heese is now the teacher in our school, under the same terms of employment as Voth. The school has twenty-five pupils.

Farewell, be content with these few lines for now. There will be more another time. How is Mr. Lange? I send him and all good friends many greetings. May the Lord be with you, may he give you His peace, Amen. Your indebted,

J. Cornies

I was very ill for fourteen days but am better now, thank God. The twenty-thaler account for Agneta Dueck, Khortitsa, is now settled.

183. Johann Cornies to Johann Ambrosius Barth. 15 January 1830. SAOR 89-1-169/5.

Mr. Johann Ambrosius Barth, Bookseller, No. 681 Grimmaischestrasse, Leipzig,

I write to notify you that the books and invoice dated 1 July 1829 have arrived. I would ask you to send the books listed below to exactly the same address:

1. Three copies of the *Conversationslexikon* [Encyclopedia], supplementary volume for the 8th edition, Leipzig, Brockhaus, 1829.
2. *Fuer Frohe und Trauernde* [For the happy and the grieving], by Friedrich Ehrenberg. Leipzig, the newest edition by Gerhard Fleischer Jr.

You will already have sent *Des Peuples* to Marienburg. I cannot give a more accurate title for *Gemeinnuetzliche Blaetter*, Halberstadt.

Your most respectful servant,

Cornies

184. Johann Cornies to Mr. Graf. 15 January 1830. SAOR 89-1-169/5.

Dear Mr. Graf,

I respectfully request that you send me the books listed below by mail. Charge them to my account. Please address them to

Mr. Gerhard Martens in Halbstadt on the Molochnaia, via Orekhov, Tavrida guberniia:

1. *Rose von Tanenberg,* by the author of Genoveva.
2. *Itha, Graefin von Toggenburg.*
3. *Die Ostereier* [Easter eggs].
4. *Das Blumenkoerbchen* [Flower basket].
5. *Genoveva,* by the author of *Die Ostereier.*
6. *Wie Heinrich von Eichenfells zur Erkenntniss kam* [How Heinrich von Eichenfells came to an understanding of God].
7. *Erzaehlung fuer Kinderfreunde* [Children's story].
8. *Der Weihnachtsabend* [Christmas Eve], by the author of *Die Ostereier.*
9. *Bluethen dem bluehenden Alter gewidmet* [Blossoms dedicated to a blossoming age], by the author of *Die Ostereier.*
10. *Fidelis v. Sigmaringen: eine merkwuerdige und lehrreiche Geschichte spaeterer Zeiten* [A remarkable and instructive story for modern times], a story by the author of Itha, *Graefin von Toggenburg.*
11. *Helanda, Herzogen von Bretagen, oder der Sieg der Tugend und Unschuld* [Helanda, Herzogen von Bretagen, or the victory of virtue and innocence], by the author of Itha, *Graefin von. Toggenburg,* 4th edition, 1st series.
12. *Die Hilfe in der Noth, oder das hoelzerne Kreuz* [Help in distress, or the wooden cross], by the author of *Die Ostereier.*
13. *Belk H. Nothburge von Rottenberg,* a story by Landhut Krull.
14. *Bertuchs Bilderbuch fuer Kinder* [Picture book for children], leaflets 181 to 184.
15. *Ausfuerlicher Text zu Bertuchs Bilderbuch* [Detailed text for Bertuch's picture book], leaflets 181 to 184.

I will send you the payment as soon as the above are received. I have the honour to be, with complete esteem your most respectful servant,

Johann Cornies

185. Johann Cornies to Andrei M. Fadeev.1 March 1830. SAOR 89-1-169/6.[1]

Yr. Honour, Mr. Fadeev,

Your esteemed letter of 24 February arrived today. I am uneasy because I did not have the privilege of speaking with Your Honour before

1 Regarding Cornies' efforts to gain a permanent land grant at Iushanle, see also documents 1, 5, 152, 177, 178, 531, 535, and additional documents in volume II.

you left for St. Petersburg. Although I considered my own situation carefully, I could not arrive in Ekaterinoslav any earlier than the day of your departure. I hesitated to distract you just as you were leaving, and therefore decided to address Your Honour in writing. I rely on Yr. Honour's affectionate consideration of my situation with respect to the desired parcel of land on the Iushanle.

Should Yr. Honour's affairs permit it, I would most respectfully request that you, during your stay in St. Petersburg, kindly introduce my petition for the parcel of land I hope to acquire. Since Your Honour knows my situation completely, I confidently submit myself to Your noble insights and benevolent intercession.

I am honoured that you should entrust Mr. Kusovnikov's horses to me, but my own arrangements do not allow me to provide substantial services for Mr. Kusovnikov. He has too few mares and so the proceeds will always be small. I cannot keep more horses, especially since my hay is adequate only for my own livestock. I strongly request that Mr. Kusovnikov take the three stallions off my hands, even if he should leave the mares with me. I will leave a settlement of this matter with Mr. Kusovnikov to Yr. Honour's wise discretion and not incur his displeasure. At present I have in my care three stallions, three mares, two yearlings and one foal, all healthy and active.

Enclosed are 100 rubles for the German books received last November.

Martens and I intend to visit Ekaterinoslav on 20 March when the lease of the Iushanle land is up for renewal. We dutifully ask Yr. Honour to commend us to Mr. Babievskii.

Wishing Yr. Honour an early return to Your esteemed family, I sign myself,

Your Honour's obedient Johann Cornies

186. Johann Cornies to Andrei M. Fadeev. 12 March 1830. SAOR 89-1-169/7v.

I have just received letters from Prussia, reporting that quite a large number of our brethren are preparing to immigrate to Russia with their families. Some have already sold their properties and will be leaving for our colonies in spring. The majority, including the wealthiest, will be ready to leave in 1831, but more affluent people face greater difficulty in selling their properties for cash because of the current money shortage. They ask whether our benevolent authorities might be willing to assign the 12,000 desiatinas of land reserved for Jewish settlement to the settlement of Mennonites instead. They ask me to intercede with the administration on their behalf.

To serve my brethren and not to fail in my duty as an honest inhabitant and citizen of Russia, I take the liberty to ask Yr. Honour whether the 12,000 desiatinas of land under the control of the Ekaterinoslav Guardianship Committee might be confirmed for future settlement by Mennonites in possession of 1,000 to 1,200 rubles cash. The money could be deposited with the Russian Imperial Consulate in Danzig and sent by the Consulate to the Ekaterinoslav Guardianship Committee as security and an advance payment for construction and land improvements. These settlements would thus have means to develop as model colonies by investing their wealth in good land thus also ensuring our High Authority's humane purpose.

Should Yr. Honour find that my request is lawful but that the 12,000 desiatinas under the Committee's jurisdiction have already been assigned for other settlements, would Yr. Honour consider designating 12,000 desiatinas of land beside that plot, which have been assigned for Jewish settlement, for the use of Mennonites?

Convinced of Your Honour's humane intentions and zeal for the welfare of the state and its foreign settlers, I do not hesitate to submit this appeal of my brethren to Yr. Honour's noble consideration. I am confident that Yr. Honour would agree to give me your kind opinion on this matter, which would enable me to inform my brethren in Prussia accordingly.

I remain, with the most complete respect and deepest devotion, Your Honour's most obedient servant,

Johann Cornies

187. Johann Cornies to Daniel Schlatter. 12 March 1830. SAOR 89-1-169/14.

Dear Daniel,

Your letter of 8 January arrived on 1 March, and has given us much pleasure. We are glad that you are still alive and remember us with love. We are all healthy and well, thank God, to the extent that this is humanly possible.

Ali and his family are living a poor, pitiful life, outwardly and inwardly, strictly following all of the commandments of Islam, but not at peace. Abdullah was circumcised about two months ago, Tashe was sick, and might still be, and Ali is afraid that she might die. To judge by appearances, he seems to be living well with her in the Nogai fashion. I cannot use him in my service, however. He does not recognize the real value of money and it provides him with no blessings. Filled with high hopes, he gets into debt and never stops speculating. His sheep are thin and will produce only low-priced wool. Each time he visits me he asks me for money. I feel sorry for him but must conceal my feelings. You know the Nogais.

As for the Nogais in general, the government is paying more attention to them than it did in the past. Some time ago our Governor, Count Vorontsov, investigated their various disagreements, especially with their commanding officer. This year the District Chairmen will be elected in the presence of an assessor from the guberniia administration and not of the commanding officer. From Simferopol, this assessor spent the night with Menglet in Edinochta. As you know, Menglet has sheep that he obtained from me. He let the sheep in for mating according to the English method (which I had taught him earlier), and when the assessor witnessed the new method, he assembled the district elders and introduced Menglet to them by asking if there was a practical agriculturalist among the Nogais in the district who was his equal. When no one in the assembly could name such a person, the assessor suggested Menglet as best qualified to be district chairman, and he was chosen.

On assuming the Chairman's position, Menglet first dismissed all the old secretaries and interpreters and warned everyone in the District not to try to bribe the Deputy Chairman, secretary or interpreter. Whatever size the bribe might be, the person would be sentenced in the presence of the whole community. This was epoch-making for the Nogais. The presence of the commanding officer has now become purely nominal and thefts have been greatly reduced.

Everything is quiet in our community. The old prejudices seem to have receded, but may be waiting to appear again. This may well happen because the small Old Frisian congregation is acquiring adherents, specifically because a preacher from Warkentin's congregation joined the Frisians. You may know him, W. Wieb from Tiege, a genial fanatic with the ability to draw adherents quickly. Balzer has settled down. His preaching is unctuous and fiery, but without much thought. He often speaks about you and admits his errors. He has not really agreed with Voth for some time (or perhaps the reverse). He no longer improvises as he preaches, nor does Isaac, and both are now coherent. The upper Iushanle area sleeps on.

Voth left our local school and, after starting too many empty projects, he used Aron Penner's money to build for himself a magnificent house with many rooms in Schoenwiese. There he plans to establish a boarding school for nobles, although he knows no Russian or French. I pity him. Penner and Ennz are there too. Voth visited me in winter. I am afraid that his hypocrisy will lead him into a [mental] institution. Heese has replaced him. The Society gave him a contract and everything is proceeding according to the agreement. There are thirty pupils, three come from the opposition and two were sent by Pastor Zelingk. My children have made great progress, especially Agnes. Voth is envious and the Society has therefore lost several members, especially from Steinbach, Alexanderwohl, Friedensdorf and up the Iushanle, except for Pastwa.

J. Sukau is manager of my estate and things are going well. God is blessing me beyond my expectations.

Hausknecht is alive and well. He and I had a quarrel because, on solid ground, I refuted some of his opinions that were exaggerations. He decided to ask for your opinion.

Pastor Foell was living with the Prussians but had to leave his house in winter and is now renting from a colonist. A ghost had appeared with much commotion and whistling, and driven the Foell family from their house. The story is that several colonists had assembled in Foell's dwelling on the last day of December where, at around 1 a.m., a din had arisen in the next room and in the attic. Then the ghost had entered the room where everyone was assembled, and there had been a whistle that had frightened everyone. No one except the Pastor's wife and a colonist, however, had seen anything. The Pastor's wife had fainted and the colonist had seen a flame darting back and forth in the room. When the flame had come close, the latter had thrown himself backwards in his chair. I think Foell might well have to leave the community if he can find a better place to be.

Lenz still lives at Lukashevich with his sheep, but is now doing better. He sold the sheep, partly for cash but most in exchange for horses and geldings. Steinmann is still alive, but that is all I know. Willert is in Friedrichsfeld and seems to want to leave for Germany in spring. General Inzov is busy with his Bessarabian colonists and working on our behalf, while Mr. Contenius, at eighty-two years of age, is still healthy. The Ministry summoned Mr. Fadeev to St. Petersburg and he left about a week ago. Surely something new is afoot. Mr. Guildenschanz is Senior Judge in the Odessa Guardianship Committee.

A preacher from Basel called Pinsel will be appointed in Hochstadt. He is presently in Odessa. This spring, 200 German colonist families that had lived in Chernigov guberniia for about sixty years will be resettled onto the Jewish land close to the Prussian settlers. Klaassen's factory is doing better, with improved cloth and sales. Herman Friesen and his whole family were very ill for several months last summer. Poor man. No news from the Crimea. Here in Ohrloff, old Penner, old Jacob Reimer, old Jacob Wieb, and Wilhelm Wiens' wife have died.

Greetings from all of your loving acquaintances would follow here, but space does not permit. Builuk, who often asks about you, was happy to hear that Fust talked to you in Basel last August and that you were well. Otherwise, everything is much as it was when you left, or however you might describe the situation. Do not worry about paying off your long-time debt. As you say, you will when circumstances permit. That was our agreement, my dear Daniel. Do not be anxious and worry unnecessarily. When you find the money send it along to Epp in Heubuden. All of us would, of course, have been pleased if your journey had taken you through Odessa and you had been able to visit us. We hope to see you another time, if it is God's will. I have written to you twice, once through Brody, on 2 December 1828, and once through Culm, Prussia, on 6 July 1829. You make no mention about having received either of the letters. It is no use for me to write if I am always in doubt as to whether you have received my letters.

Greetings to your dear mother, and many greetings to you also from me, my wife and everyone else. Live with God. From my heart,

Your loving Cor.

188. Cornelius Wall to Johann Cornies. 31 March 1830[?]. SAOR 89-1-185/21.

Esteemed friend,

The shepherd with the wethers on the Iushanle has complained that the gardener on your sheep farm this winter killed two of his dogs. Since we have suffered from a shortage of good dogs, this has done me considerable damage. One of the dogs was not worth much, but the other was our best dog, as your manager Sukau knows.

Well, this has already happened but I would respectfully ask you to forbid such actions in future, since no sheep farm can exist without dogs and a good dog is better than a poor servant.

Hoping that you do not take my request badly, I sign myself with appropriate esteem, as your devoted,

Cornelius Wall

Community sheep farm, 31 March 1830[?]

189. Daniel Schlatter to Johann Cornies. St. Gall, April 26, 1830. SAOR 89-1-84/18.

Most valued, dear friend Cornies,

You will have received my letter, sent through Brody early this year with Mr. Fadeev's assistance. My valued friend, the human heart is rich and great, clarifying much but also restricting our lives. I am often sensitive to these limits, especially when I remember my dear friend Cornies, dear Ali, and all my friends on the Molochnaia. I would love to see you again or even exchange letters with you, but I feel somehow distressed. I feel the need to submerge myself in spiritual communion with those whom I once knew and hope to see again in eternity. I am sure that such a meeting will bring forth joy and bliss and also include poor, dear Ali and his family.

My heart breaks when I think of Ali's spiritual and physical poverty and of the thousands and millions who lack the light and comfort of God's word. I know that you, my friend Cornies, have to carry a heavy and burdensome load. I sympathize with you and appreciate your insights and viewpoints that enable you to bear your sufferings. But I do not suffer for you as I do for my poor Ali. I feel closely connected to the latter and wish him an abundance of spiritual peace and the hope that he and his children will have an easier fate. What may have happened to him after I left?

Dear, dear Cornies, please give Ali 1,000 greetings and tell him that I love him, and am greatly sympathetic to his fate. I wish him blessings for his soul and being. The gratitude I feel for his love will never be extinguished.

What are the Nogais doing? And my dear Molochnaia friends? Your dear wife – please give her my best greetings? Is your dear mother still alive? How are your dear brothers? What is Voth doing? Is Enz the Oberschulz? How is your health, dear Cornies? How are your sheep and horses faring? There is so much I would like to know. And what of your dear children. How gladly would I mention the names of my many loved ones. I have not forgotten them. I am confident that you, dear Cornies, will not interpret my silence about other matters as neglect or forgetfulness.

Time is too short and postage expensive and I am busy with so many things: business at the bureau, looking after a beloved little wife at home. At the moment I am still a bridegroom, but our wedding will be in a few days. There is much here to tie me to this place that I plan to stay here. Otherwise I would have to run away again, out into the world, to my Tatars. Believe me when I say that this would not have been good for me. I prefer to stay in St. Gall. Perhaps you or your son will visit me here in Switzerland.

I often wonder how my book was received in Russia. Provided it passed the censor, were there any sales? I doubt it because it is in German and expensive. There were good reviews in the German press even though I had put it together too quickly and it contained much that was worthy of criticism and correction. The book did well in the German book trade, but I have yet to see a single gulden from book dealers or from Berlin or Heubuden, though this may soon occur. I must be patient.

My dear mother sends heartfelt greetings. Her health is up and down, but, on the whole, quite satisfactory. Earlier I wrote that my eldest brother had died. Since then my third eldest brother Soloman has also died. One after another, we all go home. I would like to spend my last days quietly and in inner peace. Still, our life, that is not meant to be free of problems and suffering, prepares us for the beyond.

Again, heartfelt greetings to dear Ali, his children and Tashe and the other Tatars I know, to all my friends on the Molochnaia and especially to you, your loved ones and the whole Cornies family.

I am eternally thankful for your love and kindness and ask for your friendship in future as well. I remain your most loving,

Daniel

190. Johann Cornies to Andrei M. Fadeev. 22 May 1830. SAOR 89-1-169/26v.

I received Yr. Honour's valued message of 16 April on 2 May. Many thanks for dignifying me with Yr. great confidence.

I wrote to my brethren in Prussia in regard to your esteemed response to my request that land for Jewish Christians be assigned for Mennonite settlement. I included in my letter the answer of His Excellency, the Director of the Department of Imperial Economy, and Yr. Honour's opinion.

I have yet to undertake Yr. commission to purchase 100 puds of kermek root for tanning, to be dug near Orekhov. The Crimean Tatars have already bought up most of the roots dug this spring. Those dug up and dried in autumn are not as good as those dug in late April and early May and dried immediately. I put off the purchase until I could get roots that are vigorous and of good quality. This I will do promptly and with care this month. I will see to it that the roots are ground, but I should mention that they can no longer be purchased for thirty rubles per thousand or one ruble per pud, as you requested. I will, however, make every effort to accomplish the matter as cheaply as possible.

Everything in the villages, thank God, is going well. The winter crops are turning out badly, but summer crops indicate hope for a blessed harvest. Grass is growing well, wool prices are low, but better than last year. Mr. Carruthors, son of the English wholesale negotiator from Odessa, is offering sixteen rubles for good unwashed wool.

With great respect I have the honour to call myself Your Honour's most obedient servant,

Johann Cornies

191. Johann Cornies to Caspar Adrian Hausknecht. 25 June 1830. SAOR 89-1-169/33v.

Dear Hausknecht,

I enclose a short description of the Molokans that could naturally be more detailed and wide-ranging, but should give Mr. Allen[2] an idea of what the spirit of these people is. I lack the time to add more detail, except for a few matters that would help to clarify their current situation. You should know that most of the constructively inclined Molokans come from among the Don Cossacks. I think particularly of a captain, a man who loves Christ more than do the others and confirms his faith through the conduct of his life. No more Cossacks will be settled here, but only along the Arxes in Karamon province, on the Persian border.

Dear Hausknecht, I would ask you to give my greetings to Mr. Allen, who knows me by name.

Please order, on my account, a dozen primers at seventy-five kopeks each from St. Petersburg. I will reimburse you for the postage upon notification. Thank you for the book catalogue, which I return. I have several dozen similar catalogues from local and foreign book dealers, but often find it hard to guess the contents from the titles alone. I made my request because I had hoped you might have practical knowledge of some of the books and find them appropriate for my purposes.

---

2 William Allen was the British Quaker who visited the Molochnaia in 1819.

Now, dear friend, keep me in your good memory. I commend myself simply as your honest,

Johann Cornies

Heese says Moliner wrote to Franz Goerz.

192. Johann Cornies to Andrei M. Fadeev. 15 October 1830. SAOR 89-1-169/42v.[3]

Fadeev, Your Honour, Gracious Sir,

In response to Your Honour's esteemed message of 10 October, I report the following regarding the reportedly high death rate in the Nogai village of Kakbas.

Since several individuals supposedly died in a short time in Kakbas, the District Office immediately sent out strict orders to all villages to cut off further contacts with the Nogais and reported this to the Ekaterinoslav Guardianship Committee and to the lower courts here. We still have no information that the neighbouring Russian villages have similarly restricted their contacts with the Nogais. I am of the opinion that no dangerous illnesses exist among the Nogais now or have existed there in the past. I will nevertheless make detailed inquires about the report of a high death rate in Kakbas and immediately inform Yr. Honour of the results of my efforts. To ease your mind, I am pleased to report that, thank God, everyone is now healthy in our district.

On 28 September I had the unexpected honour to attend upon His Excellency, the Civil Governor of this guberniia, at the noon meal in my house. His Excellency inquired courteously about the economic well-being of the villages, and was very pleased to note the good, regular construction of houses, the beautiful green of the orchards, etc., in them. Today, twenty-four post horses again stand in front of my house for the use of the Acting Governor General of New Russia. I have not

3 This is the first reference in Cornies' papers to the cholera pandemic of 1830–2, which swept through Asia, Europe, and North America, killing millions. On the Russian epidemic, see Roderick E. McGrew, *Russia and the Cholera, 1823–1832* (Madison: University of Wisconsin Press, 1965). On Mennonite reactions, see John R. Staples, *Cross-Cultural Encounters on the Ukrainian Steppe: Settling the Molochna Basin 1783–1861*, (Toronto: University of Toronto Press, 2003), 88–9. Cornies' conclusions were wrong – cholera had reached the Molochnaia district, and there would soon be high mortality rates in the Nogai villages. Regarding the cholera epidemic, see also documents 193, 198, 200, 201, 202, 204, 206, 211, 227, 231, 232, 234, 235, 236, and 239.

yet definitely heard whether His Excellency will travel through the villages. Meanwhile, I have arranged everything properly in my own home to receive and attend upon this high personage.

With all respect and esteem, I have the honour to be Your Honour's devoted servant,

Johann Cornies

P.S. A messenger has just arrived with the news that His Excellency, the Governor General, had today travelled from the village of Nova Aleksandrovsk, straight through Abitochna to Mariupol.

193. Johann Cornies to District Office. 19 October 1830. SAOR 89-1-169/44.[4]

I have the honour to submit the enclosed communication from the Nogai commanding officer regarding deaths among the Nogais. Should the commanding officer send an official document to the District Office with this same information, I request that the District Office circulate an order restoring neighbourly communications with the Nogai villages.

I have the honour to be, with all respect, the esteemed District Office's most obedient,

Johann Cornies

194. Johann Cornies to Andrei M. Fadeev. 4 November 1830. SAOR 89-1-169/44v.

Your Honour, Gracious Sir,

After receiving Your Honour's communication of 24 October on 29 October, I dispatched the requested book, *Conversations-lexicon* [Encyclopedia], well packed in waxed linen. I hope that the book will come into Yr. Honour's hands in good order.

The last time His Excellency the Chief Curator deigned to spend the night in my home, he inquired whether antiquities such as bones, stones, or similar objects had been uncovered in our settlement when the soil was dug up. He requested that if such things were found, they should be forwarded to him. I have now come into possession of two large pieces of silver, found this autumn when a cellar was dug in the

4 Regarding the cholera epidemic, see also documents 192, 198, 200, 201, 202, 204, 206, 211, 227, 231, 232, 234, 235, 236, and 239.

village of Lichtenau. They seem old, and I can make out the year 1621 on one of them. I ask Your Honour's advice on how to send these pieces of silver to His Excellency the Chief Curator.

I have not yet heard whether the kermek dispatched in September arrived in Moscow. Because communication was restricted, I fear this shipment will not produce the best results.

Yr. Honour's devoted servant,
Johann Cornies

195. Johann Cornies to Andrei M. Fadeev. 3 December 1830. SAOR 89-1-169/48.

[Mr.] Fadeev, Most Gracious Sir,

I use Yr. Honour's kind permission to send you the enclosed pieces of old silver found in the soil of Lichtenau, to be forwarded to His Excellency, the Chief Curator in Kishinev. I am especially honoured by your encouragement to me to write to the Chief Curator myself. But I am not sure what to say to His Excellency and do not want to interrupt him with my inconsequential matters. Drawing on my modesty, I humbly ask Your Honour to forward the pieces of silver on my behalf.

Please permit me to report that this autumn I started my fruit and forest tree plantation at my sheep farm. I planted 1,000 fruit trees and 2,000 forest trees, a total of 3,000 trees, planting them as they should be. This required much work and effort so that I lived at the sheep farm almost all fall. Because everything is now prepared and regulated, the work will in future be easier. To store my wool and my crops, I also built a storehouse of fired bricks, roofed with shingles, forty-eight fut (eight faden) long and twenty-four fut (four faden) wide.

In reporting the good health of my family and of the whole community, I have the honour to be Your Honour's respectful and most devoted servant,
Johann Cornies

196. Johann Cornies to Wilhelm Frank. 4 December 1830. SAOR 89-1-169/49.

I am waiting for an opportunity to hand over the *Conversations-Lexicon* to you in person. I much prefer this to using the mails, not simply to save postage but because it is always difficult to forward packages through the mails. The price is fifteen rubles, three kopeks in silver currency, including freight charges to my address. You may well be shocked by this high price, and think I have charged you a commission. The man who delivered the books had to pay three thaler when he crossed the border, one thaler for each copy, which raised the price considerably above the price charged in the store.

Since you asked me to inform you about the postage charges for the 300 rubles I sent you, I must inform you that Secretary Martens paid five rubles, sixty kopeks.

If it should not be too difficult for you, honoured Mr. Frank, please send me forest-tree seeds for my plantation. In autumn, I planted 3,000 trees, and a great deal of expense and work were involved in assembling these trees. I would like to avoid this in future by growing the trees in my own nurseries. To do so, I need seeds, especially mulberry, ash, maple, and elm seeds, wild apple and pear kernels, and whatever other shrubbery and forest tree seeds are available. I have acacia myself. Lindens, beeches, and similar trees are not worth the effort. You would oblige me with your kind services to obtain the above-mentioned seeds unspoiled during the coming winter. I will promptly repay your costs.

Time moves quickly, like the wind. Everyone, in my view, should leave behind something for the future, one person this, another that. I have decided that trees will be my purpose. To begin, I have prepared eleven desiatinas for planting and there will be more, God willing. Would you therefore kindly assist me by contributing to my project in your usual willing manner? I will not abuse your generosity, but will honour and value it, without exaggeration.

From your friend, who treasures and honours you, and who honestly calls himself your willing Johann Cornies.

197. Johann Cornies to Caspar Adrian Hausknecht. 4 December 1830. SAOR 89-1-169/51.

Valued friend Hausknecht,

I have received your letter of 10 November and thank you very much for your confidence and love, just as I have long been convinced of your honesty. I strive to love and serve God, together with all my fellow men, but this needs no further mention. We are pleased to hear that you are both well.

I settled the proposal to Kroeker with a payment of twenty rubles, four kopeks according to the enclosed receipt. I do not know if Heese is angry at you. I have never heard anything that might suggest he is and have no idea why he has not written to you. There is a right time for everything, a time for anger and a time for Christian reconciliation, so do not be surprised.

I asked around to find out whether J. Dueck might be useful to me in my business affairs and must say that he can be of no use if he does not write neatly, has no understanding of orthography, and cannot calculate percentages. I will not hear of his learning these here. I know how much effort I must take with someone whose every word must be checked. I would rather do the work myself. My business does not permit me to sit hours reviewing the work of someone who does not know how to do what is expected of him. My time does not allow this. I can get at least half a dozen here without any knowledge. My friend, I expect you to answer my letter frankly, not simply to enable you to find J.D. a position. Forgive my being so blunt and open.

What else did I want to say to you? Yes, it was about your 100 pupils, was it not? May God grant that fifty of them thrive. May he bless your efforts with these little ones and give you endurance and joy in your profession. I also wish you a happy marriage, that it might be blessed with heirs like yourselves. May the dear Lord grant you joyful thoughts, tenacity in prayer and thanksgiving before God.

With greetings to you from your loving friend and fellow pilgrim, who prays to God for you.

Johann Cornies

198. Johann Cornies to Molochnaia Mennonite District Office. 6 December 1830. SAOR 89-1-169/53v.[5]

I am not sure if the District Office knows that there have been several deaths recently in Nogai Tatar villages in the neighbouring District. These victims showed cholera symptoms and I consider it my duty to notify the District Office so that steps are taken to protect our villages by stopping traffic within the neighbourhood. Inhabitants of our District should be alerted to the problem and random contacts prevented. Only in this way can we make sure that it is not our fault if cholera is carried into our villages. Only God knows our destiny.

With every respect, I have the honour to be your Johann Cornies.

5 Regarding the cholera epidemic, see also documents 192, 193, 200, 201, 202, 204, 206, 211, 227, 231, 232, 234, 235, 236, and 239.

199. Johann Cornies to Caspar Adrian Hausknecht. 10 December 1830. SAOR 89-1-169/53.

Beloved friend,

I am deeply grateful for your letter of 1 December and its contents. Although you honestly wish J. [Dueck] success and are concerned that he be provided with means to earn a living on his own, you also showed consideration for my needs. One should in such cases always respond with truth and honesty. Be as clever as a snake and as guileless as a dove. I prefer that things be done in this way, to everyone's benefit. Love truth even though it may lead to misunderstandings and often result in lies. Truth loves light. Why fear darkness?

Thank you again. Take pleasure in everything positive, as I do. You do not need to mention the letter delivered to you. Have you written to Switzerland? Any news from Daniel? No word here.

My wife and I send you and your dear wife many greetings. I try to love you and serve you at all times so that I may honestly call myself,

Your loving Cornies.

200. Johann Cornies to Traugott Blueher. 10 December 1830. SAOR 89-1-169/60.[6]

Blueher, Esteemed Sir,

Thank you for your valued communications of 16 September and 28 October and also for the news about the cholera in our empire. I feel great sympathy and compassion for the many who must depart suddenly, before they can make appropriate preparations for a blessed eternity, but I believe firmly that the Lord desires our salvation and will gloriously guide matters to our advantage. Many people who ordinarily do not think about death are, at times like these, reminded of it in a way that draws them nearer to God. When we know that Christ is our firm hope and haven of rest and peace, storms and floods of uncertainty cannot sweep us away. We take comfort in knowing in whom we believe, in joy or in sorrow, in life or in death. Faith is a burning torch or a small, glimmering candle, but the Lord has ordained that even the faintest wick not be extinguished.

---

6 Regarding the cholera epidemic, see also documents 192, 193, 198, 201, 202, 204, 206, 211, 227, 231, 232, 234, 235, 236, and 239.

The first mention of cholera outbreaks in Moscow caused me considerable concern for the many thousands in the vast city, especially for the poor who must buy every bit of their bread each day. Where would they obtain money and courage at such a time? Would widespread starvation result? Still, while we humans make our own judgments, the Lord has power over all human hearts and directs them as He wishes, guiding them like water in a brook. In this way He also directed the loving father of our country to go to Moscow to take measures that would ease the suffering. Many others followed his lead with significant acts of benevolence and support for the poor. We give God a thousand thanks.

I admit, my beloved friend that you and your family were close to my heart as I thought about the cholera in Moscow. When I recognized your familiar handwriting on your 28 October letter, I broke it open with fear and was overjoyed to read that the dear Lord had preserved your health. Death is naturally everyone's lot and I am human enough to feel personal anxiety and think it foolish to deny my own human traits. If I knew you only through our letters, we might feel less genuine sympathy for one another. But I know you personally, having visited your home and enjoyed your love and honesty. My stay may have been brief, but it was filled with true love and an affection that awakens concerns at times like these.

Cholera has now reached our region, but not massively. Over the past few weeks, there have been about 120 deaths in four Nogai villages. Cholera broke out within four verstas of our villages and we have severed all communications with the Nogais. Our community remains healthy now, thank God. All roads are blocked and no one is allowed through without undergoing quarantine. It is impossible to thank God enough for His fatherly guardianship of our administration, which protects us through its wise measures.

Do you perhaps have news from the German colonies in Saratov, from Georgia, or from Karas in the Caucasus? I have acquaintances there, Mr. Patterson and others.[7] Is Sarepta still healthy? Please write to me.

I am sorry that the kermek did not arrive and has caused you more trouble. I fear that it may have been damaged by moisture and become unusable. Moisture may cause mould and the root, when ground, can

7 Presumably a reference to John Patterson of the BFBS, though Patterson was, by this time, back in Scotland.

lose its strength. Kindly let me know about the condition of the kermek when it arrives. It is not our fault if it spoils, but it should probably not be sent to St. Petersburg in such a condition. I cannot recommend its use in the experiment for which it is intended.

What are the prospects for next year's wool?

With genuine appreciation, my wife and I send friendly greetings to you, your dear wife and relatives, and commend ourselves to your further intercession with the dear Lord. With respect, I sign myself as your loving friend and servant,

Johann Cornies

201. Johann Cornies to Andrei M. Fadeev. 22 December 1830. SAOR 89-1-169/64v.[8]

Your Honour, Gracious Sir, Fadeev,

In my letter of 15 October, I reported that the high death rate among the Nogais was probably not "cholera morbus." I based my assumption on the Nogai commanding officer's reply to my questions, which I was honoured to be able to submit to Your Honour. I do not know whether he meant to deceive, or whether he lacked knowledge of the illness, but suffice it to say that a particularly powerful form of cholera was already present among the Nogais then and remains so today.

When we questioned the Nogais, we learned that more than a hundred persons had already died in the infected villages and that the disease had spread to several other villages. Weak supervision of the blockade enabled the Nogais to conceal the cholera. I sent three dependable Nogais in different directions into the Nogai district to obtain detailed, truthful information. They reported that the cholera was rampant in a number of villages and that the Nogais had concealed it as long as they possibly could. They claim that if they report the first cholera death to superiors, doctors will be called in to examine the buried body. Since disturbing a dead body is contrary to Islamic principles, a bribe would be needed to prevent it. After ten to twenty die, they need not fear that there will be any investigations.

8 Regarding the cholera epidemic, see also documents 192, 193, 198, 200, 202, 204, 206, 211, 227, 231, 232, 234, 235, 236, and 239. Regarding the dispute described in this document over the "brandy lease" – a monopoly on the sale of distilled alcoholic beverages in the region – see also documents 157, 158, 159, 166, 169, 202, and 205.

Despite their fanaticism, the Nogais genuinely fear cholera. Quarrels have stopped in many villages, with proper reconciliations. Black cows were sacrificed and their skins dragged around the village, their paths marked with a ploughed furrow.

On 16 December I had the special honour to attend upon His Excellency, Prince Chercheuslidsov, member of the Central Committee for Cholera, and to provide him with a night's accommodation in my house.[9] The Prince's wise regulations to check cholera, and his consideration for us despite the circumstances, gave me enthusiastic respect for this esteemed person. On the Prince's orders, the Nogai District has been encircled and is now completely shut off so that not one single Nogai can leave without submitting to the quarantine. If we follow these wise regulations scrupulously, the only thing left for us to do is to pray honestly and to submit to God's Will.

Since our community has absolutely no remedies to fight an outbreak of cholera, may the grace of God avert it. I would also humbly request that Your Honour kindly send us some of the highly recommended *Vierraeuber* [four robbers] vinegar and also chloride of lime. At such a dangerous time, with cholera only thirty verstas away, I know that the general well-being of our villages lies close to Your Honour's heart. It therefore gives me pleasure to say that everyone in our district is still healthy.

With true respect and humility, I have the honour to call myself Your Honour's most devoted servant,

Cornies

P.S. In the following, I am not animated by self-interest, envy, discord, or support for any faction. Only respect for my esteemed authorities and love for the state and community in which I live and of which I am a member, obligate me to report to Your Honour how the local District Office has dealt with the beverage lease.

The District Office ordered one of its members to visit all villages to sign up the majority of the community to support community management and sale of alcoholic beverages, under the impression that this would be more advantageous to the community treasury than leasing. Explanations given in village assemblies were often oral, not written. The position of government authorities who considered such expectations to be unfounded was ignored, as were instructions to the community to lease out the beverage monopoly again.

9 We have been unable to locate further information about Prince Chercheuslidsov.

Indeed, when the District Office delayed leasing out the beverage distribution rights, its Chairman called an assembly of mayors in Tiegerweide on 18 December, with the auction set for 19 December. Their stated purpose was to prevent bidders for the lease from appearing on such short notice. If no bidders appeared, it would be easier to persuade the Guardianship Committee that the sale of beverages should remain with the community, as the District Office wished.

The local mayor showed me the terms immediately. I am heartily tired of dealing with the chicanery of wily district chairmen, and was no longer interested in seeking the beverage lease. However, Martens sent me a message and so I went to Halbstadt to authorize our manager, who has supervised our beverage sales until now, to appear at the District Office to bid a considerable sum on definite terms for the lease in the presence of the assembled mayors. When he expressed his intention to put in a bid for us, the district chairman said the bid would not be accepted. Bidding had ended. Later, four men were named to conduct beverage sales in the name of the community.

I am indifferent as to whether I hold the lease or not, but no truth-loving person can be indifferent to intrigues and actions that run counter to government directives, or make a pretence of following them. I am sad that so many innocent persons, in their misunderstanding, follow these devious individuals.

Please accept my remarks, Yr. Honour, which I submit in confidence.

Your servant,

Johann Cornies

202. Johann Cornies to Johann Wiebe, Tiege, W. Prussia. 30 December 1830. SAOR 89-1-169/70v.[10]

Johann Wiebe, valued friend,

Thank you for kindly obtaining a number of items for me, which all arrived undamaged. Your love and friendship have become a gift for me, as have your pleasing letters. I should have thanked you before, but courtesy demands that I also share something about this region with you. To the extent that this limited page allows, I want today

10 Regarding the cholera epidemic, see also documents 192, 193, 198, 200, 201, 204, 206, 211, 227, 231, 232, 234, 235, 236, and 239. Regarding the dispute described in this document over the "brandy lease" – a monopoly on the sale of distilled alcoholic beverages in the region – see also documents 157, 158, 159, 166, 169, 201, and 205.

to take pleasure in your friendship without exploring whether I have earned it or not. I thank God for the happiness every new friend has given me and with this letter I express the thanks I owe you for your love and friendship.

As a friend, I have the duty to report my family's good health, but I must also report the death of Mr. Contenius, our benefactor and guardian, on 30 May 1830. I will send you his obituary in spring when I can. Mr. Fadeev returned from St. Petersburg in June, but there are no official reports about the business he conducted. There are no settlements yet on the land we lease. The beer brewery in Halbstadt was ravaged by fire in May and our loss was 4,000 rubles. Travelling merchants raised the prices for wool and the trade was good. My wool sold in Moscow for an average of 47½ rubles.

You acted wisely by obtaining precise information for your project and for your plans to do so in future. Do not give it up. You can definitely count on my meagre services in this regard.

Ship traffic was active on the Black Sea this summer and trade increased greatly. All prices are rising markedly, especially for arnaut wheat, which sold at twenty rubles per chetvert locally. Butter prices rose to twelve rubles per pud. Now, a sudden outbreak of cholera morbus has blocked everything. It spread from Persia to Georgia and caused many deaths in the Caucasus, Astrakhan, Saratov, Penza, Vladimir, and Kazan guberniias and among the Don Cossacks. In the city of Astrakhan alone, 12,000 individuals died in a short time, and in the city of Saratov, 300 were buried daily as long as the disease raged on. Many villages have died out almost entirely in regions where the cholera hit hardest. Cholera then moved on into Tambov, Voronezh, Kharkov, and Kursk guberniias and to Moscow itself, where a threefold military cordon was established around the city. All factories, shops and law courts were closed in the city. Once news about the cholera outbreak in Moscow reached the Tsar, he appeared personally [in Moscow] and ordered that measures be taken to block the contagion and to prevent starvation among the poorer classes. Many wealthy people followed his humane example to assist the poorer classes.

Cholera appeared in Ekaterinoslav and Kherson guberniias in early September and broke out among the Nogais not far from Pastwa in October. Many died. Our villages were cordoned off immediately, but weak enforcement in the Nogai villages allowed the Nogais to conceal the sickness in their villages. The cordon was lifted after the Nogais were declared healthy, but then cholera broke out suddenly again in several villages. The Nogai District is now completely isolated. No one is allowed in or out and guards are posted nearby. One hears that the people in Akkerman, Burkut, and Edinokhta are still healthy, but that cholera broke out in Bauerdak six or seven days ago. God alone knows what will befall us in this sad time. Our villages exist like an island in an ocean of cholera, and there is evil all around.

Cholera has the following symptoms: abdominal pain, pressure on the heart, unquenchable thirst, continuous vomiting and diarrhea, dizziness, great pain when passing urine which looks like pickle brine, arm and leg cramps that cause the feet to take on the appearance of a mummified skeleton. There is cold sweat and then death. The duration of the illness varies from one to twelve hours and sometimes lasts a few days. More than half of those infected die.

We have taken the following precautionary measures. In every village, two men visit each house daily to check on the family's health. To separate the sick from the healthy, one house has been emptied for use as a hospital. A large bathtub, etc. stands beside each Village Office.

We do not know what the future holds. Only the Eternal can see it. We must build on His grace and plead with Him to turn this scourge away from our empire and our villages. With complete faith in the wisdom of our government, we await the Almighty's ordinances without fear. May every Christian, every thinking person harbour the personal conviction that whatever comes from God will serve our well-being. May this supreme wisdom divinely illumine man's immortal spirit, created in His image, and cast light into the darkness of our earthly path.

We do not strive against God's will by using our minds in taking precautions against disease and in battling disruptive natural forces. We are using our talents from on high, submitting them to His wise counsels and thereby praising His holy name. As you know, some people here consider precautionary measures to be sinful. Others continue to indulge in frivolity, even in this depressed, discouraging time.

You ask if the Duke of Anhalt-Koethen's settlement in Tavrida is making land available for foreign settlement, and also if that land is on the steppes or in the Dnieper lowlands. In reply, I can say that the Duke has concluded an agreement with the Russian state requiring that a specific number of colonists be settled within ten years. The Dnieper lowlands are not mentioned in the terms of the agreement. The Anhalt-Koethen administrators would naturally like to attract Mennonite settlers, but what rights and privileges could they provide? Their Charter of Privileges offers them no more than what our *Privilegium* guarantees us. In their own interest, the Anhalt-Koethen administration could decide not to give its settlers all these rights directly, but grant them in stages.

In my opinion, a settler whose rights are confirmed directly by the Crown is always in the best position. Remember that foreigners brought into Russia by estate owners can only conclude twenty-year contracts. They are never considered colonists, but are always strangers who can move about Russia after their contract has ended. They receive no Crown land for settlement, nor are they under the colonial administration. They have the right to live in the empire on leaseholdings. Mennonites at Michalen, Ostrog, Dubno, and other places live under such an arrangement. When I visited St. Petersburg, they authorized me to present their situation to the Ministry and to petition for their inclusion in the colonist estate. This was not granted. It was ruled that they were to remain as free people.

I would not advise anyone to settle as a free man under the authority of a particular lord. Please, dear friend, give my advice to anyone interested in concluding a contract for Anhalt-Koethen land. They must not think that, after their contract has expired, they can move to the Molochnaia if that seems more suitable and hope to be accepted and registered among their brethren-in-faith, with the same advantages and rights. There is a wall of separation here, anchored in law, that cannot and will not be easily breached.

Kindly send this statement regarding Anhalt-Koethen to my friend Epp in Heubuden and make my excuses because I have not written to him for a long time. He must not believe that I have abandoned things I have had to postpone. Still, he is quick to forgive. Give him my greetings. I was unable to keep up with my correspondence because I was adding buildings and plantations on my sheep farm. I find myself in a dilemma as I face a mound of letters, trying to decide which friend I should answer first. I ask everyone's gracious consideration for my failure to write. Your relatives, D. Sudermann, Dirk Dueck, and P. Neufeldt all arrived here safely. Sudermann lives in my garden house and his children have often been sick. P. Neufeldt lives with the esteemed Peter Neufeldt and works at his profession, while D. Dueck lives in Pordenau. In our community there is little new to report. In the New Year the brandy lease will no longer be ours. Who will have it remains a puzzle. Peter Enns remembers you and sends you his greetings.

Please accept my long letter with love. Sincere greetings to you and your dear parents. Since I truly esteem and treasure you, I sign myself as your servant,

Cornies

P.S. I sent the Minister's exact answer about Busch-Tasch to D. Walde in Marienburg on 22 May. When C. Dueck ended his visit here, he took along a map of all the settlements I sent you. Have you received it? If unrest in Poland prevents travel in spring, I will send you our statistics. I assume you have received my son's letter. Please send me the information he requested as soon as possible. The number of students in our school is increasing and prejudice against it seems to have disappeared. The teacher is well. After some time, P. Friesen was released from my service and is now working for C. Toews. P. Neufeldt is not with me any longer as well, but both visit me and this gives me pleasure. P. Enns sold his black mare for 200 rubles. We had no winter before Christmas. There are some sledding roads now but little frost. Brother-in-law J. Klassen has built a brickworks at Ohrloff. Many greetings from D.P., P., and D. Cornies, from me and my wife. Farewell, keep God in your sight and in your heart. This I wish for you. Your honest and loving Cornies.

1831

203. Johann Cornies to Novovassilov Uezd Office. 1831.
SAOR 89-1-167a/29.

To the Novovassilov Uezd Office,

One morning last week, some inhabitants of Astrakhanka, a Molokan village in your jurisdiction, impounded my entire herd of horses that had accidentally broken into their grain fields and forced my estate manager, Sukau, to compensate them four times the true value of the trampled grain. First they demanded one silver ruble per horse, then 200 rubles, and after my manager proposed several alternatives, they took eighty-five rubles. Twenty rubles would have compensated them fully for their trampled grain.

Such behaviour shows that a greed for money blinds these owners to a fear of God. They show no restraint or love of humanity, arouse the mistrust of neighbours on their borders, and cause their community to be dishonoured. It would have been right for them to start by appointing an unprejudiced person from their community to assess the loss. Then the entire herd should have been released to my manager. I would gladly have agreed to such a decision.

This was an intentional affront to me. The herd was purposely restrained and my manager was forced to pay eighty-five rubles instead of twenty. The Astrakhanka Mayor's Office will testify to this. It is convinced that its villagers committed an injustice and is willing to provide names. These individuals immediately harvested the damaged grain, though I forbade them to do so because I claimed the grain as my property. I had paid for it at four times its value. I cannot forgive this and ask that the Uezd Office investigate this matter promptly. These

Astrakhanka inhabitants should be questioned and forced to repay the extra sixty-five rubles without delay. I rely on the Uezd Office to do this. If this money is not repaid soon, I will take the matter to court. I would be grateful to the Uezd Office for an early report outlining its actions in this matter.

1831. Johann Cornies

204. Johann Cornies to Andrei M. Fadeev. 7 January 1831. SAOR 89-1-200/2.[1]

Your Honour, Gracious Sir,

Cholera is moving from village to village in the Nogai District. Although the illness has lost some of its force, with fewer deaths in newly infected villages, the cholera cannot be expected to disappear completely among the Nogais soon, to judge by Nogai sources. No strict measures have been enforced to halt communications. The Nogais conceal this illness as much as possible. I suspect the cholera could still be hidden in Nogai villages, and even after they had been declared free of the disease, it might still be carried into our villages. I think it essential that the Committee issue a directive ordering our community to keep watch in every village for fourteen days or more after the cordon is lifted. Contacts with Nogais during this time must be avoided completely.

Cholera has broken out close to us in the villages Baurdak and Edinokhta, fifteen verstas from Altonau. On 3 January, eight people died of cholera in the former village and five in the latter. Our cordons are weakly supervised. We are negligent and let down our guard. It is essential that the Committee appoint a member of the District Office to strictly supervise those keeping watch. He must travel around personally, insist the watch be kept strictly and report to the Committee weekly. I would recommend that Deputy Regier be named to this post and ordered not to delegate authority to anyone else.

I have the honour to be Your Honour's respectful and most humble servant,

J. Cornies

---

1 Regarding the cholera epidemic, see also documents 192, 193, 198, 200, 201, 202, 206, 211, 227, 231, 232, 234, 235, 236, and 239.

205. Andrei M. Fadeev to Molochnaia Mennonite church leadership. 12 January 1831. SAOR 89-1-449a/27.[2]

Molochnaia Mennonite church leadership [*Kirchenkonvent*] copy:

I find it necessary to notify the church elders of the Molochnaia Mennonite District that their current District Office leaders have been most unwise in making arrangements for the brandy trade over the next four years. In ridiculing orders from His Excellency, the Chief Curator for the Colonists in southern Russia and the Guardianship Committee, the district chairman and District Office have shown contempt for legal authority.

The Guardianship Committee will countermand the District Office's thoughtless views, specifically the views expressed by the district chairman. Since Mennonites constitute a brotherhood, it follows that the disclosure of harmful actions taken by their members, especially by their leaders, will seriously damage the whole community.

It is my honest desire that the Molochnaia Mennonite community become more secure, that it affirm its good reputation, and that it ensure that its members are respected as peaceful and well-disposed inhabitants of Russia. This is the only way that the imperial privileges granted them can retain their firm foundation. This is also my reason for warning the Molochnaia Mennonite community to be especially cautious in choosing future [District] leaders, and in carefully observing their attitudes and decisions. The immorality of leaders, their refractory behaviour towards superiors, and the problems they cause the Ministry, have already resulted in the loss of privileges for some foreign settlers in Russia who were transferred from the administration of the Guardianship administration to that of the civilian administration. After two decades, their children curse the fathers who provoked such an outcome.

The church leadership must notify me that it has received this communication and understands its contents.

The original signed by Fadeev.

12 January 1831, Ekaterinoslav

2 Regarding the dispute described in this document over the "brandy lease" – a monopoly on the sale of distilled alcoholic beverages in the region – see also documents 157, 158, 159, 166, 169, 201, and 202.

206. Johann Cornies to David Epp, Heubuden. 5 February 1831. SAOR 89-1-200/4v.[3]

My valued D. Epp,

Your letter of 6 January just arrived and I will forward the enclosed letters to their addressees. Many thanks for taking care of my various requests so promptly. Everything was received in order, letters as well as accounts. I thank God that the cholera is on the wane and seems to be coming to an end. So far our settlement has been spared, but the assault among the Nogais was especially dire. It is still active there, but weaker now. Our villages are still under quarantine and no Nogai is allowed to travel through them.

I wrote to Mr. J. Wiebe, Tiege, with my thoughts about the Anhalt-Koethen settlement, and asked him to inform you in this regard. Do not advise anybody to join this settlement, but do not argue the point. Just state your opinion and let others make their own decisions. Grants of good Crown lands always have the disadvantage that the poor find it difficult to carry out the imposed conditions. This is not hard for the moderately well-off and the rich to do. Remember that the Russian state wants model agriculturalists who are well enough off to establish economically sound farms. They are not interested in the poverty stricken, of which the empire has more than its fair share.

Do not interpret my brief and infrequent letters as betokening an indifference to you personally. I hold you in high regard. I received a blunt reprimand from J.F.K. in Schlab[erndorf] because I wrote to others, but not to him. What should I write? "We are well" is said in three words. Do not tell him about this letter because he may then break off my already weak relations with him. I will write to him (but I don't know what). Our local school has thirty-six pupils. H. Dueck has not visited me. Winter is mild.

Fare well, and I commend myself to your dear family and acquaintances. May the Lord bless you.

Your faithful J. Cornies

H. Dueck just arrived and asked me to intervene on his behalf in order that he might remain here. For the moment I have refused to do so because we must be careful in our interventions. Without sound

3 Regarding the cholera epidemic, see also documents 192, 193, 198, 200, 201, 202, 204, 211, 227, 231, 232, 234, 235, 236, and 239.

grounds, such actions could easily misfire and invite rejection even in sound cases. For this reason, I would ask you not to send similar requests to me. Although I am inclined to help, I have to be careful lest I lose my credibility [with the authorities]. In this regard, please refer to my letter of 15 January.

207. Johann Cornies, on behalf of the District Office and Wool Improvement Society, to the Ekaterinoslav Guardianship Committee. 6 February 1831. SAOR 89-1-200/6v.

Most obedient reply from Molochnaia Mennonite District Office and the Wool Improvement Society:

In its directive No. 275, of 26 January, the Ekaterinoslav Guardianship Committee directs the District Office and the Commission for Sheep Breeding to explain why the number of lambs produced at the community sheep farm this year was so low. Only sixty-six and one-third lambs, on average, survived for every 100 ewes. The equivalent number of surviving lambs of individual farmers averaged seventy-nine and five-sixths lambs for every 100 ewes. Moreover, the numbers are much down from previous years. Those entrusted with the care of the [community farm's] sheep need to do better in order that sheep breeding might continue its progress.

We have the honour to respond as follows. Misfortunes that struck last year's lambing, with a survival rate of only 66 ⅓ percent, struck the Kurushan community sheep-farm and all private sheep-farms inside and outside our District. Despite the best supervision, some sheep breeders lost a lower, others a higher percentage of their lambs. The sheep appeared to be completely healthy and strong throughout the winter, but during lambing many dead lambs were born, and others were so weak that they died immediately upon birth. At the same time, many ewes refused to accept their lambs. Our investigations showed that they had no milk with which to feed them.

Experienced local sheep breeders attribute these unusual occurrences to the following circumstances. The summer of 1829 was generally wet and grass was abundant. Because the grass grew rapidly, its nutritional content could not fully develop. It did not absorb sufficient carbonic acid [*Kohlensaeure*], which is essential as the main source of nutrition in livestock fodder. Hay harvested this summer lost even more of its nutrients because of the frequent heavy rains. It seemed green and fresh and did not show that it lacked the essential nutrients needed by the sheep.

Why did a larger percentage of lambs of individual sheep breeders survive? With a smaller number of sheep to care for, they could alternate green feed with straw and perhaps also sheaves. Moreover a lamb born to a ewe that could produce little or no milk could survive on cow's milk while the ewe was fed with grain until her milk increased. In cases where a ewe with sufficient milk gave birth to a stillborn lamb or one that died immediately upon birth, it could suckle an orphaned lamb being maintained on cow's milk. All this cannot, however, be done when thirty, forty, or even sixty lambs are born daily, even with the best and most careful handling of a flock. This is doubly true when conditions are as unfavourable as they were in 1830. More lambs will naturally be lost than in cases where only a few sheep are under the watchful care of a herdsman.

As a result of all of these circumstances, misfortunes multiplied and the income of the community's sheep farm decreased. We are not indifferent to this situation and are disappointed that we could not solve the problem. We especially regret that we have drawn down upon ourselves the administration's suspicions of indifference and carelessness. The Sheep Breeding Society feels that it is not responsible for the reduction of lambs in 1830. Wet weather in 1829 was the reason. At the same time, the Society does not close its eyes to the difficult state of its treasury and admits that it was not conscientious enough in its devotion and care of community property to prevent abuses from occurring.

The Society esteems the administration and will seek, as never before, to fulfil its obligations in this important branch of agriculture. The members will seek to demonstrate that the community's welfare is close to their hearts and that they treasure the confidence of their humane administration.

208. Johann Cornies to Bartram. 20 February 1831. SAOR 89-1-200/8v.[4]

Esteemed Mr. Bartram,

Your honoured communication of 22 August 1830 arrived while I was away. Kindly forgive me for not replying immediately.

As you will know, your brother has not been in my house or in the local region since May of last year. The nature of his illness prevents

4 The brother referred to in this letter is presumably Johann Bartram, whom Cornies employed as a tutor for his children in 1828. See document 150.

him from occupying himself usefully and maintaining an independent position that would ensure his own existence. His behaviour suggests he is ill and his attacks of hypochondria are at times so serious that it is difficult to deal with him. Periodically his condition is accompanied by an overwhelming addiction to brandy, which increases his problems.

You acted wisely in not sending your brother support money as soon as he demanded it. Speaking frankly, he does not know how to handle money. He would not have been less of a burden if you had sent him larger sums more often.

Though I am not seeking your praise, I would say that I have treated him as a friend, and advanced him larger and smaller amounts of money for almost thirteen years as they were needed. If he had used this money economically and occupied himself with small side activities, he would have been able to live a respectable life without burdening his relatives. Regrettably, my attempts were in vain.

You will conclude from this, esteemed Mr. Bartram, that even with your benevolent support, your brother cannot be left on his own. You must anticipate that eventually you will receive extremely unpleasant news from him. Esteemed Sir, I regret having to send you such a bad report about your brother. If you had not requested it, I would not have expressed my opinion so openly.

Please accept the assurance of my esteem and respect,

Your servant, Johann Cornies

209. Johann Cornies to Andrei M. Fadeev. 24 February 1831. SAOR 89-1-200/8v.

Your Honour, Gracious Sir,

Today I have the pleasure of informing Your Honour that the kermek entrusted to carters, and sent to St. Petersburg via Moscow last year, arrived in good condition in Moscow about the middle of January. At the first opportunity, the Sarepta trading firm forwarded it to St. Petersburg, to His Excellency, the Director of the Department of Manufacture, Mr. Druzhinin.[5] The freight charges were 145 kopeks per pud. Because of the [cholera] blockade, costs were higher than those of last year. According to the account of 10 January sent by the above-mentioned trading

5 Jakob Aleksandrovich Druzhinin, director of the Department of Manufacturing and Domestic Trade, 1825–48.

firm, the carters paid twenty-five rubles for two months lodging on the River Oka. The trading firm's expenditures are 667 kopeks – thirty-one rubles, sixty-seven kopeks more than specified in my account.

The letter from the trading firm notes that the price of wool is rising in Moscow. Ordinary and medium varieties in particular sold at prices 20 per cent higher than in June and July of last year, while prices for finer varieties declined. The firm writes that this is due to circumstances in Poland.[6] Imports of Polish cloth have been forbidden and Moscow manufacturers must substitute ordinary cloth for trade to Asia. Some contracts for the Russian army have tended towards finer varieties of cloth than in the past and manufacturers must work with a content including one-half Spanish wool. It seems that these higher prices may continue.

To use this situation in the wool trade to our advantage, it is my considered opinion that the wool from the Khortitsa community sheep farm and from our community sheep farm should be dispatched to the Sarepta trading firm in Moscow on consignment. Over several years, sales in Moscow have averaged several percentage points higher than prices paid here. The Sarepta firm has sold my wool for a number of years, convincing me of this truth.

I received Your Honour's gracious communication of 12 January, but have not yet been in a position to report back anything reliable.

With the greatest esteem and devoted respect, I have the honour to be Your Honour's most devoted servant,

Johann Cornies

210. Johann Cornies to Lange. 24 February 1831. SAOR 89-1-200/11.

Yr. Excellency Lange, Gracious Sir,

I have the honour to send you the enclosed descriptions of the so-called Doukhobors and Molokans that I promised Yr. Excellency.[7] My humble request is that you overlook the imperfections in expression and composition. What little I have said about the people themselves may be imperfect, but it is true and correct.

Yr. Excellency's wisdom will allow you to understand why I do not wish to become known as its author. I flatter myself with the pleasant

6 A reference to the Polish Rebellion of 1830–1.

7 Presumably versions of the two reports included in part two of this volume.

hope that Yr. Excellency will honour us with a further visit. With a lively feeling of esteem, I remain Yr. Excellency's devoted servant,
Johann Cornies

211. Johann Cornies to Traugott Blueher. 3 March 1831. SAOR 89-1-200/11v.[8]

Most honoured Mr. Blueher,

Your valued communications of 20 January and 9 February, and the account for forwarding the kermek to St. Petersburg, have come into my hands on 23 February. I immediately mailed the 215 R.B.A. you advanced. I hereby send you my most obliging thanks for taking care of this matter.

The book written by Schlatter, our mutual friend, arrived in good condition and gives me great pleasure. Your show of affection is important to me, not simply because you sent the book, but also because you gave it to me in enduring memory of your freely given love.

You report a rise in wool prices, in which case it is possible that few buyers will find their way to our area, thus depressing local prices. You graciously offered to sell wool from our local producers in Moscow on consignment and to advance money at low interest rates to villagers in need of money.

I immediately informed several reliable men in this District of your well-intentioned suggestion, but only time will tell what the results will be. I have also acquainted the Khortitsa District with your kind proposal.

Please permit me to make a proposal, esteemed Mr. Blueher, specifically, that you have a quantity of wool bought here on your own account. I would recommend a reputable man to make this purchase, with due attention to your interests. This would give you information that would enable you, in future, to pursue the wool trade to your advantage. To assist you in such an undertaking, I will note that last year washed wool sold here at 18 to 25 rubles per pud, according to its fineness and quality of washing. Packing would be 18 kopeks for an eighteen-arshin sack, and 20 kopeks to sew a sack holding about 8 puds of wool by weight. Binding cord for 100 puds of wool might be 35 kopeks for 12 funt. A covering

8 Regarding the cholera epidemic, see also documents 192, 193, 198, 200, 201, 202, 204, 206, 227, 231, 232, 234, 235, 236, and 239.

for each wagon is estimated to cost between 5 and 6 rubles. I cannot list the exact cost of wool packing, because my own people do it for me, but I assume that it will be about 10 kopeks per pud. I would estimate the costs of the purchase transaction, storage rental, sorting, binding of the pelts, and all travel costs at about 1 ruble per pud.

Should your calculations find that my proposal could be profitable, you can send the money for this purchase directly to Gerhard Enns in Altonau, here on the Molochnaia. He has often completed such transactions to the satisfaction of those commissioning him. I spoke with him and I also give you my own guarantee for the money you will send him. Should you wish to test the wool trade in this way, you must not delay, for shearing time is approaching rapidly and the great distances here affect everything.

Please give me your views about this proposal, since an English trading company in Odessa has asked me to suggest someone to buy wool for them this spring. Granted, a number of men here are equally dependable, but they are not as experienced in wool purchasing as the abovementioned G. Enns. If you decide to ask him to make this purchase, you must inform him of the kind of wool you would like to purchase.

Thank God that everyone in our community is still free of cholera. In the Nogai District, I am told that cholera is still raging in a few villages, with ten to fifteen deaths daily.

I will, as in the past, send my wool to you should you be so kind as to accept it. Preparations have already been made for the sale of the community's wool, which will be of better quality than in the past.

I send my most obliging thanks for your greetings, and wish you the same in body and in soul. I endeavour, with genuine, sympathetic love, and best wishes for your family, to be your true friend,

Johann Cornies

212. Johann Cornies to David Epp. 23 February 1831. SOAR 89-1-200/14v.

To esteemed David Epp in Khortitsa,

Treasured friend,

Three days ago, I received reliable news from Moscow that the price of wool had risen 20 per cent for ordinary and medium varieties. However, the price for extremely fine wool, which was selling at 80 to 120 rubles in the past, is now lower. The reasons are too complicated to describe here and do not apply to the proposal I want to make.

When you did me the honour of visiting me in winter, you described your intentions to travel to Moscow in spring with a shipment of wool and to sell it as favourably as possible. With this in mind, I want to make a proposal to you, my dear friend, taking into account your interests and those of the owners giving you their wool on consignment. Please consider it carefully, weigh the circumstances and your own doubts carefully and inform me of your decision as soon as possible.

Which trading company do you intend to employ should you take a shipment of wool to Moscow for sale on consignment? I would propose that you employ the Sarepta company. I consider it to be the most respectable one there, widely recognized for its promptness and responsibility. If you have your wool sold by this trading company, you will not risk falling into the kind of distressful situation that Molochnaia colonists Walther and Kretschmann experienced. Moscow merchants put them under such pressure that they eventually sold their wool extremely cheaply and on credit against a bill of exchange that Mr. Brandenburg kindly bought for cash, but discounted it to such an extent that they suffered a considerable loss. You need not fear any such treatment from the honest trading company mentioned above.

Best of friends, if you decide to act through the Sarepta Trading Company, either by travelling to Moscow yourself or by expediting the sale of wool directly to the trading company on consignment, I could perhaps assist you by writing to the company about this matter. I would request an advance of several thousand rubles, at a very low interest rate of one-half per cent, until the wool is sold. This would cover the costs of sacks, covers, advance money for carters and such expenditures, and possibly even an advance for a few needy producers. What do you say? With this, I leave my well-intentioned advice and proposal to your wise decisions and arrangements. I await your candid response, as your devoted servant,

Johann Cornies, Ohrloff

213. Johann Cornies to Andrei M. Fadeev. [1?] March 1831. SOAR 89-1-200/16.

Your Honour, Gracious Sir,

I thank you for Yr. Honour's esteemed communication to me of 23 February requesting my opinion about settling Mennonites on 19,000 desiatinas of land along the Tashchenak under the same conditions as those offered by the Ministry to the Hungarians: forty desiatinas of land for each family, and two wells constructed in each village at the Crown's expense.

I assume that as long as Mennonites receive more and better land for settlement on the Molochnaia at sixty-five desiatinas per family, they would not choose to settle on the Tashchenak on a smaller plot of land of lower quality.

As Your Honour requests, I will cancel the order for the book *Des peuples et de leurs chef* the next time I write to Prussia.

I cannot make any definitive suggestions about disposing advantageously of His Honour Mr. Kusovnikov's horses. Horse prices are low here now, especially for mares, and naturally, Mr. Kusovnikov considers his to be of high value. As Your Honour knows, no one here will buy his stallions for breeding purposes because good offspring cannot be expected from their build. I request that Your Honour give me time to think about this matter further and to consider Mr. Kusovnikov's best interests.

I intend to visit Ekaterinoslav in April. With respect, I endeavour at all times to be Your Honour's willing servant,

Johann Cornies

214. Johann Cornies to Johann Dyck. 13 March 1831. SOAR 89-1-200/17v.

My dear friend, Johann Dyck,

As you are aware, on 4 March 1824 you signed a note for the amount of fifty-five rubles, which (in addition to the interest) is now in arrears. I have been informed that you sold your fullholding and are now in a position to discharge the fifty-five rubles owed, as well as the interest from 1824 to the present. I therefore request that you pay this amount to the bearer of this letter, in return for the note you signed. The total of seventy-four rubles, twenty-five kopeks includes the capital amount and nineteen rubles, twenty-five kopeks interest for seven years. In silver currency at 8 per cent, this is eighty rubles, nineteen kopeks.

With greetings, I remain,

Your Johann Cornies

215. Johann Cornies to Mariupol Colonist District Office. 13 March 1831. SOAR 89-1-200/17.

On 30 October 1828, with a written guarantee from the Mariupol District Office, I sold two Spanish rams to Andreas Saurin and Johann

Fleischhauer, of Grunau village, for fifty rubles. Saurin and Fleischhauer signed a written obligation to repay this sum in equal parts over three years.

Two years have now passed and the third ends this spring, 1831, but none of the above-mentioned payments have been made. I therefore request the Mariupol District Office to order the debtors, Saurin and Fleishhauer, to pay the fifty rubles owing to me by May at the latest, plus the accrued interest.

With respect, I have the honour to be the Mariupol District Office's obedient,

J. Cornies

216. Johann Cornies to District Office. 13 March 1831. SAOR 89-1-200/17A.

To the worthy District Office in Halbstadt,

On 10 October 1829, fullholder Phillipp Wiebe from Tiegerweide urgently requested an advance of 400 rubles from me. He gave me reliable assurances and explicitly promised that he could raise capital funds from property he sold in Prussia. Since Klassen, of Blumenort, was to visit Prussia in 1830, Wiebe intended to commission him to receive the outstanding money for this land. Wiebe promised to repay his debt and the applicable interest with the greatest thanks upon Klassen's return from Prussia.

With such credible promises from Wiebe, I did not hesitate to advance him the requested 400 rubles until 10 October 1830 in return for a signed letter of obligation. But when Abraham Klassen returned from Prussia, Wiebe failed to appear with his payment and I wrote to remind him of his promise. Thereupon he appeared at my residence and explained that he had forgotten the date by which his money would be paid to him in Prussia, which was 1831. He requested a further advance of 200 rubles to enable him to travel to Prussia and receive the money owed him in May 1831.

I told him that I would not make the second advance until he provided documents confirming the certainty of the outstanding claims. I then learned Wiebe did not have a single document to give creditors direction and assurance, and was forced to conclude that his report that he would get money from the purchaser of his land was not true. In fact, he had sought to defraud me with this invention.

A written declaration from the authorized representative, Peter Braun in Schoensee, West Prussia, and other appropriate written declarations from Prussia, now enable me to prove that Wiebe has no claim on any further money from the sale of his land. Moreover, with respect to the inheritance that might come his way from his mother-in-law, the documents say, among other things, that "the woman, Anna Dyck of Baerwalde, retains a capital of 3,000 thaler in cash, which is the inheritance of her two daughters (married to P. Wiebe and Aron Klassen) resulting from the division of their father's property. It is expected that the interest on this capital will be sufficient to support the former and that the two heirs will each receive 1,500 thaler upon her death. Since Wiebe received an advance payment of 800 thaler when he left for Russia, he can only inherit another 700 thaler. This is the only claim that Wiebe can make."

It should be noted that Wiebe's mother-in-law is hale and hearty and years could pass before he receives his money. The sum in any case might be held back for Wiebe's children.

Since I have been deceived in a false and cunning manner by the above-mentioned P. Wiebe, I find it necessary to humbly submit P. Wiebe's improper behaviour to the worthy District Office for its consideration. I urgently request that he be required by law to appear, that his behaviour in this matter be revealed, and that he be ordered by the District Office to repay the 400 rubles borrowed from me, plus interest for a year and a half, as soon as possible. I will not permit this deception by Wiebe to rest if the aforementioned does not occur.

With the appropriate respect I have the honour to await the District Office's resolution of this matter,

Johann Cornies

217. Johann Cornies to August Wilke. 25 March 1831. SAOR 89-1-200/19v.

To Mr. August Wilke, gardener on my sheep farm,

I hereby send you 103 copper tokens that you are to store like money and use to pay the daily labourers, each according to the time they have worked. Those who have worked uninterruptedly from morning until evening should receive a token marked with a cross. Those who have worked three-quarters of a day should get one marked with three bars: two bars for a half-day, one bar for a quarter-day.

I would like you to pay the workers with these tokens according to the exact time they have worked so that neither the workers nor I suffer any disadvantage that might otherwise lead to conflict.

I leave it to you to handle this matter according to your best insights.
J. Cornies

218. Johann Cornies to Andrei M. Fadeev. 27 March 1831. SAOR 89-1-200/20.

Your Honour, Gracious Sir,

Yr. Honour's communication of 23 March reports that the kermek roots have finally arrived in good condition at the Department of Manufacturing in St. Petersburg. The Department asks whether the root was dug and prepared in spring, in autumn, or during both seasons.

I have the honour to report that I bought the roots in Orekhov just after they had been freshly dug in May of last year. They were too fresh to be ground immediately and had first to be dried. Highly knowledgeable people informed me that the roots should not be dried in an oven or in the sun if they were to retain their full strength. I therefore had these fresh roots laid out under an airy shelter on my sheep farm, away from the direct sunlight. They could only be pulverized towards the end of July. According to the judgment of highly knowledgeable people, these roots were dug at the most suitable season of the year and were of the highest quality obtainable here.

With genuine esteem and deepest respect I have the honour to be Your Honour's devoted servant.

219. Johann Cornies to Molochnaia Colonist District Office. 10 April 1831. SAOR 89-1-200/21v.

Respectful request from the librarian of the Molochnaia Branch of the Bible Society, Johann Cornies in Ohrloff:

The Committee of the Molochnaia Branch of the Bible Society has authorized me to collect the debt for books of holy scripture owing since 1822. Count von Lieven has required the local committee to provide the names of those still in debt. This committee must answer for these debts. It is obligated to collect them as soon as possible and to send the proceeds to St. Petersburg.

I request that the esteemed District Office order the following individuals in the District to discharge their debts:

1. Johann Remboldt, Reichenfeld, 183 R.B.A.;
2. Gottlieb Gerstenberger, Karlesruh, 142 R.B.A., 60 kopeks;
3. Georg Heering, Hochstaedt, 285 R.B.A., 30 kopeks;

4. Joseph Hiller, Heidelberg, 6 R.B.A.;
5. Friedrich Widmer, Blumenthal, 6 R.B.A.;
6. Michael Maey, Reichenfeld, 60 R.B.A., 80 kopeks.

The total is 683 R.B.A., 80 kopeks.

These debts are to be paid to me at my residence in Ohrloff by 10 June at the latest. I will notify the esteemed District Office accordingly if this has not been done. The above-mentioned individuals have frequently been exhorted to pay off these debts for books sold to them on credit. The Committee has hitherto shown great patience, but is now forced to ask the District Office to insist that these individuals settle their debts by the above date.

With honour and respect, I have the honour to be the esteemed District Office's most respectful,

J.C.

220. Johann Cornies to District Office. 16 April 1831. SAOR 89-1-200/22v.

District Office in Halbstadt,

In response to the communication of 15 April, No. 1,187, I report to the District Office that neither I nor the Society School in Ohrloff have a teaching position available for the person suggested, nor are we in need of his knowledge.

With respect I have the honour to be the worthy District Office's devoted,

J. Cornies

221. Johann Cornies to Heinrich Cornies. 22 April 1831. SAOR 89-1-200/22v.

Dear brother Heinrich,

We have been told, although we doubt the truth of this report, that the Guardianship Committee intends, in May, to reopen the lease for the Bastash land reserved for an Israelite settlement and presently leased by us. Although we have seen no such public notice about this lease, the Committee seems to have designated 28 November 1830 as the last date for bidding. Since we could not appear at that time we submitted a petition to the Committee on 18 December, requesting that if no bid for the lease exceeded our annual rental payment of 610 rubles, we be allowed to lease the land for the next four years at that same amount and under the same conditions as before. We have had no response to our petition and do not know if the land will continue to be ours.

If this land is definitely to be auctioned again, friend Martens and I urgently ask you, if bidders appear, to have a document prepared, signed by me and Martens, authorizing you to act on our behalf. If bids exceed the amount of 610 rubles that we have previously paid, we authorize you to put in a bid of 1,000 rubles and perhaps even a little more, depending on the other bids. Security for our earlier leases have been deposited with the Committee.

If there is no bidding for this land, refer to our petition of 18 December. We also authorize you to conclude the contract on the previous terms of 610 rubles annually. If there is no transaction involving this land, hold back the authorization and submit no petition. However, make specific, unobtrusive inquiries, and do not miss the first and any other dates for the auction.

In our judgment, you should probably prepare two authorizations, one in which we authorize you to conclude the contract according to our petition of 18 December for an annual rent of 610 rubles, and a second one that authorizes you to bid for the above-mentioned land and to conclude the contract. You will also need two petitions, each referring specifically to the contents of the authorization.

If the Committee really intends to publicly auction the Bestash, and if no bidders appear, hold back, if you can, in submitting your authorization and petition until the last moment. If no one with a higher bid turns up, submit the first authorization and also the petition to which it corresponds. However, if other bidders submit their petitions immediately, do not delay in submitting the second authorization and petition.

Ask someone discreet, by whom I mean Mr. Frank, to prepare the authorizations and the petitions. Make sure they are done exactly according to the required format. (In passing, tell Mr. Babievskii that we will be thankful to him.) We leave the rest to your best insight and judgment and hope that you will do what is best and wisest for us. In any case, please let us know in writing about this matter. Thank you for your kind help.

Farewell, with commendations to you, your wife, and father-in-law,

Your loving brother, J. Cornies

P.S. Friend Martens told me he gave you a sealed pass for Neufeld. He did not know if you had received the new one from the Governor's Office. I urgently request that you intervene on behalf of this man and send the sealed pass to my address with brother-in-law Boldt next week.

I thank you greatly for getting the plates and continue to be your loving brother,
Johann Cornies

222. Johann Cornies to Wilhelm Frank. 22 April 1831. SAOR 89-1-200/25.

Esteemed Mr. Frank,
I am notifying you of the receipt of 300 R.B.A. you borrowed from me last year, 1830, and which you forwarded to me with my partner, W. Martens. To confirm that this account is settled, I enclose a receipt and the signed statement you gave me at that time. I endeavour to be, in all honesty, your respectful servant,
J. Cornies

215. Johann Cornies to Wilhelm Frank. 9 June 1831. SAOR 89-1-200/27.

Esteemed Mr. Frank,
In response to your letter of 2 June, I must report that I cannot, with the best of intentions, advance a loan of 2,500 to 3,000 rubles to His Excellency, the Director. I have lent all my money that I do not need for my own affairs to our local wool merchants on monthly terms. Otherwise I would most willingly have been of service, especially since I could have counted on the punctual repayment of the loan. I am sorry, treasured friend, that I am not in a position to be of help. With genuine respect and esteem, I remain, your friend and servant,
Johann Cornies

223. Johann Cornies to Johann Klassen. 22 June 1831. SAOR 89-1-200/30v.

Honoured District Chairman, Johann Klassen,
Three Doukhobors appeared at my house in Ohrloff today to notify me that one of their shepherds died near Prangenau, where the Doukhobors graze their livestock. They asked what should be done with the corpse. I am not authorized to answer this question, but am legally bound to notify you of this death. I am sending these people to you to make the necessary arrangements.

224. Andrei M. Fadeev to Johann Cornies. Received 13 July 1831. SAOR 89-1-166/1.[9]

Copy: directive to establish societies for the advancement and dissemination of forest- and orchard-tree cultivation, and of sericulture and viticulture, in the Molochnaia and Khortitsa Mennonite Districts:

The Mennonite settlements in New Russia attract more government attention than do all other foreign settlements. Morality and a clear conscience should motivate these Mennonites to prove that they are the best inhabitants of this region and carry on the largest number of trades.

The privileges the government has bestowed on the Mennonites justify it in expecting that the Mennonites meet its demands. These advantages give the Mennonites the most favoured position among all Russian inhabitants of the peasant estate, particularly their insignificant taxes, their right to include the proceeds from the beverage trade in the community treasury, their larger land allotments compared to those of other foreign settlers, and finally, the very important exemption from all military impositions, billeting, and temporary military marches through most Mennonite villages, depending on their geographic location.

Mennonite settlers already distinguish themselves from others with their special dedication to several branches of agriculture new to this area, such as breeding and refining cattle, horses, and sheep. Their villages are well arranged and are kept in good condition, as are most of the agricultural establishments in these villages. They pursue a quiet, peaceful way of life and their behaviour is highly regarded. This has earned them the praise of the government and of all visitors to the region.

The Mennonites, however, can accomplish still more by making special efforts to achieve the highest possible level of perfection. This would justify the government's expectations in the fullest measure, and demonstrate that their significant advantages over other settlers have not been given to them in vain.

Mennonite communities in general, and every individual in particular, must henceforth give preferential and continuous attention to the

9 This undated document was first received by Johann Cornies on 13 July 1831, according to the following letter. Thus, although the date of establishment of this organization has long been indicated as 1830, it does not seem to have been established in the Mennonite districts until 1831.

development of orchard- and forest-tree culture. Both of these economic branches can help lay the foundation of prosperity for Mennonites and their descendants, and visibly distinguish their villages from others.

The obligation of the Molochnaia Mennonites must rest on sacred feelings of gratitude and on their promise to establish and spread the cultivation of forest trees. In 1825, during His Majesty's last visit to the Molochnaia villages, Mennonites solemnly promised the late Tsar Alexander, of ever-glorious memory, to lay out small village woodlots in which each household would be assigned a half-desiatina plot. This vow must not be broken. Actions in this regard will assist Mennonites in maintaining their privileges on a firm, enduring foundation, and will establish their own prosperity and that of their descendants.

The cultivation of orchards and forest trees can be combined practically with viticulture and sericulture by planting grapevines and mulberry trees. Orchards and forest trees are already well established in several Molochnaia Mennonite villages. Viticulture can probably be carried on in this region with patience and care and by the attentive selection of reasonable locations and varieties of grapevines that ripen early, as demonstrated by Count Orlov Denisov's vineyard in Abitochna, near the Molochnaia villages.

There can be even less doubt about the practicality of pursuing sericulture, since this is already a successful branch of agriculture in the more northerly villages of the Josephthal and Khortitsa Districts. Sericulture may not be profitable for the present generation of Mennonites, since it is now able to use its large land allotments to achieve prosperity through their cultivation and the breeding of livestock. But these branches of the economy will undoubtedly be of greater value to future generations as the Mennonite population grows and land becomes much shorter in supply. Sericulture will, in particular, assist individuals who lack means, such as unmarried and aged persons, widows, etc. Mature mulberry trees are essential for this purpose and it is important that they be planted in increasing numbers from now on. Every thoughtful and well-disposed Mennonite will diligently strive to make the success of such plantations visible in his own establishment, inspired by the government's wishes (as expressed in the Directive for the Internal Administration of the Colonies and in ensuing government regulations) and also by his own efforts to provide a firm basis for his own well-being and that of his descendants.

Especially strict supervision is essential to the success of the policy of disseminating these branches of agriculture in the Molochnaia and

Khortitsa Mennonite Districts. Moreover, only the establishment of uniform and enduring practices can encourage and compel neglectful inhabitants, who exist in any large community, to cooperate. The most important purpose of strict supervision is to provide instructions and advice in the early stages of planting, to overcome difficulties, and to provide assistance for activities difficult for individual inhabitants to realize on their own.

The principles of the Directive for the Internal Administration of the Colonies assign responsibility for such supervision to district offices. Both districts, however, are still growing and encompass a total of fifty-seven villages. District officials are therefore kept busy with matters of administration, settlement, the collection of taxes, the keeping of accounts, and so on. Even with the best of intentions, they cannot carry out the exacting supervision required for general success and provide the necessary attention to the economic undertakings of villagers.

High authorities, acting on a proposal made by the late Acting State Counsellor, Mr. Contenius, have therefore decided to establish societies in the Molochnaia and Khortitsa Mennonite Districts on the same principles as those governing the activities of the wool-refinement commissions. They will be called Molochnaia and Khortitsa Mennonite Societies for the Dissemination and Cultivation of Forest and Fruit Trees, of Sericulture and of Viticulture. In the conduct of their affairs, these societies must follow principles confirmed by the Chief Curator of colonists in southern Russia.

Chapter I: Method and Means of Organizing the Societies

1. Each society consists of five regular members, inhabitants of the above-named districts, known for their good planning, zeal for the common good, insight, dynamism and the knowledge of all types of tree planting, as acquired through experience.

2. Of these five members, the chairman and two members in each District have been determined by the Chief Curator. Johann Cornies, Mennonite from Ohrloff, has been named chairman in the Molochnaia District, with former district chairman Gerhard Enns and Dirk Warkentin, Mennonites from Altonau, as members. In the Khortitsa District, the former district chairman Jacob Penner has been named chairman, with former district deputy Franz Pauls from Kronsweide and David Redekopp from Rosenthal as members. These three members will choose two more members with the requisite abilities from among

Mennonites in their district, according to general rules applying to free associations, and will then present them to the Guardianship Committee for confirmation.

3. In future, all members of these societies (their number can be increased), will be chosen according to this same principle by the already existing members and confirmed by the Ekaterinoslav Guardianship Committee. The chairmen will, however, be confirmed by the Chief Curator for the colonies of southern Russia upon representations from the above-mentioned Committee.

4. Society members are chosen for an indeterminate time and can only be released because of extended illness, old age, or for other reasons requiring special consideration, and upon a decision by the Committee.

5. Members of these societies are not to be chosen for any other community offices, although they can remain as members of the Wool Improvement Society.

6. Mennonite members discharge their obligations simply and solely out of a zeal to be generally useful, without a view to recompense of any kind. While they cannot make claims for remuneration of any sort, they are freed of transport duties, as are Mennonite secular leaders and religious elders. The community in question must give them transportation to discharge their responsibilities whenever this is required.

7. All orders from these societies will be executed in every village by their village offices and by every inhabitant, in the same way as those issued by the District Office.

8. Secretarial and office requirements for each society will come from the district offices. The societies may have their own seals.

Chapter II: General Obligations of These Societies

9. The societies are responsible for all aspects of the step-by-step dissemination of forest- and orchard-tree cultivation, and of sericulture and viticulture, in all villages in the Molochnaia and Khortitsa Mennonite Districts.

10. Since local circumstances vary in the two districts, the obligations of their societies cannot be the same with respect to forest-tree cultivation and sericulture. The individual obligations of each society are explained in chapters III and IV.

11. It is obvious how much all facets of orchard cultivation can contribute to the settlers' welfare and economic arrangements. Out of its concern for the welfare of these settlers, the high administration has

laid the foundation for the dissemination of orchard cultivation among foreign settlers in the Directive for the Internal Administration of the Colonies, and in subsequent regulations. In Mennonite villages, a number of good, well-disposed householders have laid out large orchards with good fruit trees. To advance orchard cultivation as a flourishing branch of the economy in Mennonite villages generally, and to distinguish them from other settlements of this region without the advantages and privileges granted to Mennonites, every householder is obligated to lay out an orchard behind his house of a size permitted by the local situation and his means. The soil must be adequately prepared and the site protected from livestock damage.

12. It is the duty of the societies to supervise this gradual but essential fulfilment in all Molochnaia and Khortitsa villages within the limits of what is possible. They must make every effort to assist householders in acquiring the needed seeds, seedlings, and shoots.

13. After their establishment, the societies are duty-bound to visit all villages in their district at a suitable time and to prepare an accurate inventory of householders who already have established fruit orchards beside and behind their houses, including the size of these orchards and the number of fruit trees in each. The lists must also include householders who have no orchards. To ensure that these orchards increase, these visits must be repeated each autumn. This inventory must be submitted to the Committee every year.

14. During these visits, society members must give advice and instruction to settlers inexperienced in orchard cultivation, and in the preparation of soils of various compositions, since this is necessary if fruit trees are to thrive and progress. To ensure that trees grow as desired, society members are to explain that the soil must be ploughed thoroughly and to a depth of two and a half to three fut, one half-year before planting. The upper part of the soil should be turned down and the lower part brought to the top. Any householder who cannot do this because of a lack of manpower should, six months before transplanting, prepare trenches no less than three arshins wide and one arshin deep. Householders must be helped to understand that without such advance soil preparation, newly planted trees will perish and their efforts will fail. Society members must give directions in a clear and kindly manner. They must explain how useful fruit orchards are, since fruit can be sold or may be used for their own and other needs.

Society members must make foreigners settling here aware that the high authorities insist they are to achieve the same level of achievement as have good peasants in Germany, who draw income from their own fruit orchards. Settlers must also be warned that anyone who is disobedient or ignores these suggestions will eventually lose his fullholding. It will be transferred to a dependable young householder, who must obligate himself to carry out the government's instructions intended for his own advantage. On the other hand, those who lay out significant plantations of fruit trees, which they keep in good condition, will receive special attention from the authorities and can be recommended for the highest rewards, commensurate with their success.

15. The dimensions of areas selected by each householder for his fruit orchard must be measured and calculations must be made to determine how many rows of trees can be planted without crowding. Every tree must be given sufficient space to grow naturally, so that roots and crowns do not eventually grow together. Experience shows orchards with trees planted too close together result in inferior trees and less fruit than orchards where sun and air can have a beneficial influence on the crown of every individual tree. (The following example demonstrates the same principle: Anyone who seeds three or four chetverts of rye on one desiatina will harvest few kernels, or none, and very thin straw.) Very dry or hot locations are exceptions, where trees must be planted closer together. Spaces between apple and pear trees should be filled with cherry, peach, apricot, and plum trees (especially Hungarian "Zwetschen"), as the most useful fruits for every husbandman on the land.

16. Experience has shown that soils vary greatly in the different locations of every region. Certain varieties of trees thrive better in one village than in another. Members of the societies must advise each village, basing their views on the evidence of experience, not on superficial inferences. If early efforts reveal that certain areas are little suited for fruit trees, it is permissible to replace them with mulberry trees, especially in the Khortitsa District, as described further under No. 35.

17. The societies should pursue similar principles in advising settlers on the planting of vineyards and in guiding individual settlers or whole villages inclined to this branch of the economy. The societies are obligated to assist in the acquisition of good, early-ripening grapevines and in teaching villagers how to plant and tend to them.

18. Societies are also obligated to pay attention to empty spaces around community buildings in each District, especially around schools and sheep farms, planting them with fruit, mulberry, or forest trees depending on the suitability of the soil.

19. Each society must maintain a library to enable society members to acquire the most complete knowledge about the cultivation of forest trees and orchards, and sericulture and viticulture, and to provide good instruction for the other settlers. It should consist of books on these subjects by the best authors, and written in a style easily understood by ordinary people. All books about these subjects presently in the district offices must be transferred to these libraries. The newest and best publications about these agricultural branches published in Germany should be acquired annually through book purchases. (These should include publications such as the useful *Frauendorfer Garten Zeitung* [Frauendorf Gardening newspaper] published by the Bavarian Garten-Gesellschaft [Gardening society].) The society's library books must be catalogued and kept in a special cupboard in the chairman's house. The books may be lent out to dependable people in the villages interested in these branches of industry, with a signature. Close attention should be paid to their clean and punctual return. If villagers do not understand everything in the books on first reading, they should be reminded of the need to review their contents carefully and thoughtfully. The annual costs of acquiring new books and newspapers are to be covered by a special fund designated for this purpose in the Molochnaia District, mentioned further in No. 26, and by the community treasury in Khortitsa.

20. Society members should assemble in the chairman's house or in another member's home on the first Sunday of each month in summer to discuss subjects requiring the rapid advancement of this area of the agricultural economy in their District. This they should do peacefully, calmly, and in an intelligent manner. Their conclusions and regulations must be entered in a special minute book and reported to the Committee. Before each meeting, one or more members of the Society should inspect, in rotation, a part of the District to assess the progress that is being made in the planting and upkeep of forest-tree and mulberry plantations, fruit orchards, and vineyards. If the seeding, improvement of ditches, extermination of weeds, etc., is needed, the Society must give orders on doing this in a timely fashion.

Chapter III: Obligations of the Molochnaia Society in Particular

21. The principal responsibility of the Society in the Molochnaia Mennonite District must be to advance forest-tree plantations already laid out, or still to be established, in each District village.

22. A directive prepared by the late Acting State Counsellor Contenius, on this subject, and regulations sent by the Guardianship Committee to the District Office since 1826, should serve the Society as guidelines. The District Office must give the Society all such records, maps, and sketches.

23. The Society must begin by investigating what work has already been done and how these beginnings can be successfully continued step by step.

24. At the end of every year, the Society must send the Committee a detailed report about progress in forest-tree plantations and about the work done the previous summer. It should also present its plans for work to be done the following year.

25. After deliberating accurately and observantly, the Society must identify those villages where further forest-tree plantations can be established, as determined by the extent to which their prosperity is well established. Such plantations must eventually be laid out in every village of the Molochnaia Mennonite District.

26. The Chief Curator has arranged that, should there be a shortage of seedlings in a settlement, all expenses for the purchase and delivery of forest-tree seeds, and also for the acquisition of books about forest-tree cultivation, etc., will be paid for from interest received on the 30,000 rubles fund advanced to Mennonites and deposited for this purpose in the Guardianship Committee office. At the beginning of each year, the Society will receive from the Committee a sum estimated for this purpose and will present a special accounting of its use at the end of each year.

27. According to the above-mentioned directive from the deceased acting State Counsellor, Contenius, and subsequent governmental regulations, mulberry trees should make up at least one-third of every forest-tree plantation. Indeed, since insects found on fruit trees will not damage mulberry plantings, half of all plantations established close to villages must consist of mulberry trees. Such mulberry plantations must be recognized for their future use in advancing sericulture. At the same time, living hedges consisting of mulberry shrubs must be planted around interior plots. The Society is obligated to follow these principles faithfully and to take timely measures to acquire as much mulberry seed as possible with the Committee's help.

28. Once a sufficient number of mulberry trees and shrubs have been planted in the Molochnaia Mennonite District, and individuals with an interest in sericulture have emerged, the Society should assist the latter in acquiring silkworm eggs and the needed instructions for this branch of the economy. It should also assist in the acquisition of a machine to reel

silk, a kettle, etc., at the cost of the community treasury, and in the marketing of silk. The Society should help in removing any problems that arise.

29. At the close of each year, the Society will identify individuals who have made progress in the planting of forest-tree plantations and of orchards near houses. These names will be reported to the Committee for forwarding to the Head Curator of colonies. The Committee requests that they be given an award of fifty rubles in imperial Banco Assignats, at the cost of the Molochnaia Mennonite community treasury. Such persons should preferably have completed the planting of their half-desiatina forest-tree plots or planted the entire area around their houses with good fruit trees, in regular rows, and kept them growing well.

[Chapter IV: Specific Obligations of the Khortitsa Society, 89-1-166, pp. 15–19v. not included here.]

It is well known how much associations directed towards the achievement of useful purposes contribute to the national well-being in many areas of Europe. Russian colonial authorities hope that the societies presently being established will be inspired by a desire to be generally useful and will embrace all efforts to accomplish this salutary end. And if they cooperate enthusiastically, firmly, and harmoniously, undaunted by temporary obstacles and difficulties, their members will surely be blessed by an omnipotent God. In so doing, they will contribute much towards the development of Mennonite Districts as models for the most remarkable settlements in the Russian Empire and establish their right to the perpetual and unshakable favour of the government.

The original was signed by the senior member of the Ekaterinoslav Guardianship Committee, Privy Counsellor Fadeev.

With the same meaning as that of the original, Ekaterinoslav Guardianship Committee translator, F.W. Frank.

226. Johann Cornies to Dirk Warkentin and Gerhard Enns. 14 July 1831. SAOR 89-1-200/31.

Honoured and worthy friends Dirk Warkentin and Gerhard Enns, Altonau,

Yesterday, I received the enclosed "Proposal for a directive for a Molochnaia Mennonite District society that will promote the establishment of forest-tree plantations and the dissemination of orchards, sericulture, and viticulture," as well as a communication from the Senior

Member of the Ekaterinoslav Guardianship Committee, Mr. Fadeev. According to the latter, we are asked to consider what, in our mutual opinion and according to our local circumstances, is missing from the enclosed directive, and might be added or changed. The thought is to ensure that when the directive is presented to the Chief Curator for confirmation it is as complete as possible.

I hereby send you the directive together with the report from Mr. Fadeev, so that we might examine and consider its contents. Kindly let me know when we might examine it together, here in my house or wherever else you wish. With respect, I sign myself as your friend,

J. Cornies

227. Johann Cornies to Heinrich Cornies. 17 July 1831. SAOR 89-1-200/34v.[10]

Everyone in our own district is healthy, thank God. There is cholera among the Doukhobors in Kisliar and among the Nogais, and it is especially strong in Nikolaievka on the Berda. May God grant that we continue to be spared. What is the situation in Ekaterinoslav? Have many died of cholera? Any acquaintances? I do not know when I will be able to see you because I have a lot of work to do. I received the two containers of yellow ochre you kindly sent me. When an opportunity presents itself, please be so good as to send me three pairs of army boots and six good chairs from the market. Please write to us about how you are doing and how everything is going in these troubled times. We are all healthy and send heartfelt greetings to you. I would be very pleased if you could send me four or five puds of packaged tobacco with friend W.M. May you and your dear family fare well.

Keep God before you and in your heart,

Cornies

228. Johann Cornies to Andrei M. Fadeev. 24 July 1831. SAOR 89-1-200/35v.

I am responding to Yr. Honour's esteemed communication of 11 July, asking for a detailed answer to the following questions about land situated on the Tashchenak:

10 Regarding the cholera epidemic, see also documents 192, 193, 198, 200, 201, 202, 204, 206, 211, 231, 232, 234, 235, 236, and 239.

1. Where can the first colony of thirty to forty fullholders be most suitably established along the Tashchenak ridge, towards the Orta Otluk, so that no empty spots or unusable land separate them?

I have made a provisional sketch for the projected colony in pencil on the map sent to me. The area for this village allows for no more than thirty fullholders, and the pencilled proposal is designed for sixty desiatinas per fullholder. In my opinion, this location is the best one for the first settlement and also provides advantages with respect to the watering of animals and of hay meadows. The rest of the unsettled land can then be settled more easily in future.

A village of sixty fullholders could be comfortably situated on the Ovrach of the Orta Otluk on land beside the first village. It is marked with red ink as 2 and 3, and has [well] water at a depth of seven fut. In this way, all land on the Tashchenak could be settled without exception. The third settlement on the Orta Otluk would have to be established at the spot marked //// with red ink and it would be for 100 fullholders.

2. Can anything else be said about this location?

There can be no better spot to locate a village along the Tashchenak [stream] than near the chumak road. It is beside Mr. Granobarskii's khutor, marked in pencil with a K. It would be necessary to redirect the chumak road as I have drawn it in pencil on the map. There would be no difficulty in changing the road in this way, since my markings show where it was located twelve to fifteen years ago. Granobarskii relocated it when he established a tavern on his khutor.

3. What would be the depth of the wells and the quality of the water?

It must definitely be assumed that wells will be four sazhen at their deepest. However, the water is salty.

4. What is the estimated cost of a proper well?

In my opinion, no wells need be dug here at the cost of the Crown. Here a village can easily exist by constructing good earthen dams which hold water all summer, as they do now along the Tashchenak, on the steppe and on the ridge. I have constructed dams which provide sufficient water for livestock. They are located on this land and can be used by the settlers. Water for household use can be obtained by every settler from his own well dug at low cost.

With esteem and respect, I strive to be Yr. Honour's most respectful servant,

J. Cornies

229. Johann Cornies to Andrei M. Fadeev. 24 July 1831. SAOR 89-1-200/37.

I respond to Your Honour's communication of 10 July and to the enclosed directive for the proposed society for plantings to be established in the Molochnaia Mennonite District. Yr. Honour graciously commissioned me, Gerhard Enns, and Dirk Warkentin, Altonau, to reflect on local circumstances and to suggest changes or additions to the directive in order that it might be as complete as possible for presentation to the Chief Curator for his confirmation.

I have the honour to report that we calmly and maturely pondered and considered the contents of this directive. After reflecting on all local circumstances, we found nothing to add to or change in the above-mentioned directive. The directive is so wisely composed with respect to all circumstances familiar to us that we accept it as complete, especially because we still have so little knowledge in this area. We may eventually think of provisions of this document that might be added to or amended.

We do, however, have doubts about No. 2, which provides for the designation of two other members by the community. If their choice should fall on someone with little sense for such activity, all the work would be left to us, creating further difficulties that would result from the presence of inactive members. We are only speculating and cannot yet say anything definite in this regard.

With the deepest respect, I have the honour to be Your Honour's obedient servant,

J. Cornies

230. Johann Cornies to Johann Klaassen. 24 July 1831. SAOR 89-1-200/37.

Johann Klaassen, cloth manufacturer,
Very dear friend,

Thank you very much for letting us know that our father [-in-law] has died. Although this fate will one day befall all of us as well, the sad news was still unexpected. You were very wise not to visit our brother, since every precaution is doubly necessary in times [of cholera] such as these. I cannot send any Bibles because they cannot yet be sold. We will not have any more [New] Testaments until autumn.

Greetings from me and my wife to you and your dear wife. I remain as always,
Your loving J. Cornies

231. Johann Cornies to Andrei M. Fadeev. 29 July 1831. SAOR 89-1-200/38.[11]

Yr. Honour, Gracious Sir,

I respectfully return the directive sent to me in waxed linen marked "Litt: H.F.," together with our opinions about it. I also include the map of the Tashchenak and my views about the proposed settlement. At the same time, I inform Your Honour of my receipt of 325 R.B.A., sent to Your Honour's address by the Odessa trading firm Meunier & Comp., to be forwarded to me. Please accept my most devoted thanks.

On 14 July, cholera broke out in Bolshoi Tokmak and by 24 July there were thirty deaths. By 28 July, there were four cholera deaths in Akkerman. One person remains sick. There were ten dead and three ill among the Molokans in Astrakhanka. In our community, everyone is still healthy, praise God, and this is also the case with the [German] colonists. One hundred and eighty souls have died in Nikolaievka, on the Berda not far from Hoffnungsthal.

May God preserve Yr. Honour and your treasured family in the best of health. With this heartfelt wish and the deepest respect, Yr. Honour's most obedient servant,
J. Cornies

232. Johann Cornies to District Office. 29 July 1831. SAOR 89-1-200/30v.[12]

By yesterday, four persons had died of cholera in Akkerman, and ten in Astrakhanka, with three still ill. To keep this evil from being carelessly dragged into our community, I feel it my duty to send the District Office this information in order that it might warn our community through

11 Regarding the cholera epidemic, see also documents 192, 193, 198, 200, 201, 202, 204, 206, 211, 227, 232, 234, 235, 236, and 239.

12 Regarding the cholera epidemic, see also documents 192, 193, 198, 200, 201, 202, 204, 206, 211, 227, 231, 234, 235, 236, and 239.

a circular that communications with Nogais and Molokans must be treated carefully or stopped completely.

J. Cornies

233. Johann Cornies to Johann Klassen. 6 August 1831. SAOR 89-1-200/40v.

Dear District Chairman Johann Klassen,

At the most recent meeting of the Wool Improvement Society at the Kurushan community sheep farm, you proposed a partial repayment of the money the community still owes me for sheep purchased [in 1827]. I am informing you that I will accept a partial repayment only if it is at least 10,000 rubles. I need this amount for a particular purpose and cannot and will not accept small sums. Otherwise, I cannot credit my accounts and fulfil promises that I have made. The bond I was given permits me to do this.

With kindest greetings, I remain your devoted,

J. Cornies

234. Johann Cornies to District Office. 10 August 1831. SAOR 89-1-200/41.[13]

I have received definite information that cholera broke out in the Wuerttemberg colonies. Eleven persons in Neuhoffnung had cholera symptoms and also on the khutor above Felsental. I respectfully inform the District Office in order that it can take preventive action, as I am in duty bound.

I remain the worthy District Office's respectful,

Johann Cornies

235. Johann Cornies to District Office. 14 August 1831. SAOR 89-1-200/41.[14]

This past week, cholera broke out among the Doukhobors in Bogdanovka, but its inhabitants conceal the illness, as is their way. I inform

13 Regarding the cholera epidemic, see also documents 192, 193, 198, 200, 201, 202, 204, 206, 211, 227, 231, 232, 235, 236, and 239.

14 Regarding the cholera epidemic, see also documents 192, 193, 198, 200, 201, 202, 204, 206, 211, 227, 231, 232, 234, 236, and 239.

the District Office in order that it might warn the inhabitants of our District against having contacts with the Doukhobors. The illness struck in Chernigovka on 2 August, and by 5 August up to eight people were dying daily.

Respectfully,
Johann Cornies

236. Johann Cornies to Heinrich Cornies. 14 August 1831. SAOR 89-1-200/41v.[15]

Dear Heinrich,

Your letter of 17 July with the sad news of our dear father's [father-in-law's] death arrived in good time. Though the news saddened us, we take comfort in the joyful hope that his departure from this temporal world means that he has crossed over into a better spiritual life where we will all eventually join him. This comforting belief in God's prophecies must be seen as a favour to us as earth-bound mortals who fear death to a degree. Faith and faith alone, though small as a mustard seed, allows us to recognize God's wonderful guidance. Our dear father's departure should not sadden us too much, knowing that what God does is done well.

It is my heartfelt hope that these lines find you all in the best of health. We are all healthy, praise God, but cholera surrounds our district. Many Molokans have died in Astrakhanka, and seven [Nogais] in Akkerman. The illness has lost some of its force and many persons have recovered with the help of remedies or even without such help, especially among Nogais who reject the use of remedies.

I will not arrive in Ekaterinoslav before September. Please speak to Madame Roode's forestry servant to prevent a long delay when I come, since I am planning to fetch 3,000 seedlings. Tell the masons that I probably will not start construction this autumn. There is cholera in Tokmak and so I cannot hire wagons to take bricks from Ohrloff to the sheep farm. I need my own wagons because our crop has turned out so well.

Has the Senior Judge travelled to Kishinev yet? Please let me know with the first mail about your well-being and whether cholera has yet ended in Ekaterinoslav and in the surrounding areas.

15 Regarding the cholera epidemic, see also documents 192, 193, 198, 200, 201, 202, 204, 206, 211, 227, 231, 232, 234, 235, and 239.

My wife and I send you many greetings. I remain as always, your loving brother, who wishes you well,

Johann Cornies

P.S. Give Mr. Frank my friendly greetings and ask him for the title or complete name of the new society established by the directive he translated. I have forgotten this and now I need it urgently. Please report it clearly with the first mail.

237. Johann Cornies to District Office. 21 August 1831. SAOR 89-1-200/43v.

I request that the District Office inform the community that German Bibles with parallel passages are available for purchase from me in Ohrloff. A copy, in a good binding, costs six rubles. Purchasers can obtain Bibles from me at any time for an immediate cash payment.

With respect, I have the honour to be the worthy District Office's respectful,

J. Cornies

238. Johann Cornies to Dirk Warkentin. 30 August 1831. SAOR 89-1-200/43.

Dear friend Dirk Warkentin,

At the next meeting of the Wool Improvement Society, I would like to discuss with you the purchase of wood this autumn for the construction proposed for next year, 1832. Decisions will need to be made. You, my friend, will be authorized to do the purchasing and to manage the construction. In all seriousness, I ask you not to decline this job. As you well know, the management will not be orderly or economical unless you take on the work that will affect our general progress. Taking your health and business matters into account, I repeat my request that you attend the meeting and accept the proposal to purchase the wood and borrow the money needed for this purpose. Any hesitation and delay in the making of building repairs will have a negative effect on our general interests. They could result in justified accusations against us of our being irresponsible.

J. Cornies

239. Johann Cornies to Jacob van der Smissen. 18 September 1831. SAOR 89-1-200/448v.[16]

Highly valued Mr. van der Smissen,

Your friendly letter brought us the welcome news that you and your family are well and spiritually active on our behalf. By interceding for all people, a Christian's prayer is of benefit to people near and far. Though he may not know them personally, he feels as one with thousands who share his salvation. He loves them without having the satisfaction of knowing that his love is returned and contributes to the sublime goal for which God created us and redeemed us through Jesus.

In reply to your request that I take a paternal interest in young C.A.Z. [Carl Anton Zimmerman], I can report that he is already under my guardianship.[17] I have found him quarters with a good, upright man. You can reassure and comfort his parents that their son is well and contented in his present conditions. He has everything he needs for an orderly life. He is happier after undoubtedly suffering harsh treatment in his wanderings, and is more motivated to live a quiet, rural life. He wants to return to Prussia next year, but his relatives, as your letter suggests, prefer that he stay here. In my opinion, his relatives should advise him strongly to remain here another year. He could thus acquire thorough knowledge of our local settlements and business affairs. This would also give him something of note, based on well-founded knowledge, to report on when he returns to his home. It would also help me to offer him some consolation, for otherwise he may fall into despair, losing every hope of again seeing his relatives. In any case, he is on a travel pass and cannot stay here forever. His relatives know him better than I do and will do what is best for him.

---

16 Regarding the cholera epidemic, see also documents 192, 193, 198, 200, 201, 202, 204, 206, 211, 227, 231, 232, 234, 235, and 236.

17 Cornies took in the mentally disturbed Carl Anton Zimmerman as a favour to Zimmerman's step father, Danzig merchant Heinrich van Steen. Though the letter of 30 June to Heinrich van Steen (SAOR 89-1-236/29v) is too damaged to provide a complete translation, clear portions indicate that, while working for Warkentin, Zimmerman attacked a fellow worker without provocation, stabbing him in the abdomen. He was put under guard and eventually transferred to an institution in Ekaterinoslav, where he committed suicide. The stabbing victim seems to have recovered after four weeks. See documents 259, 279, 280, 290, 303, 304, and 362.

Much has happened since I spent a night with you in your home near the high gate. With our dear friend D. Epp, we climbed the Karlsberg in Oliva at daybreak to watch the sun rising majestically out of the Baltic Sea, although a small cloud denied us this pleasure. Much has meanwhile changed in this world. Last year cholera morbus swept through India, Persia, Georgia, Caucasia, Astrakhan, and as far as Moscow, and also affected Nogais living near our villages. It continues to gain ground and we might well fear that it will strike all of Europe. Until now our community has been spared, although we have felt ourselves under siege since May. It seems like a miracle that we have escaped this terrible illness given that all Russian and Tatar villages in our neighbourhood have been infected. Although everyone continues to travel in every direction and to engage in trade, we are still as of today free of cholera.

Muslim worshippers see the illness in ways that trouble me greatly. They claim that it is a spirit with three heads and 500 helpers, sent by God to get rid of vicious people from this earth. Since it is part of God's judgment, they therefore think it wrong to take measures against it. Such people, they say, will die as Christians, and not share in the joys of the Muslim heaven. Although a Muslim fears cholera, he patiently awaits his fate while the priest [*mullah*] reads to him the consolations and promises of paradise contained in Arabic in the Koran, which the common man cannot even understand.

I have tried to convince Nogais that many of them could be healed. I have tried to persuade their priests to permit lay people to use medications. The problem grew worse when holy dervishes from India passing through the area on their pilgrimage to Mecca strengthened the priests in their fanaticism. Even Tatars I had taught to serve as doctors refused to speak further about their services or give out medications. It happened that in in two Tatar villages near Ohrloff, twelve persons died in one, and six in the other. At the same time, fifty persons died in a nearby Russian village, although they had used medications. This strengthened the priests in their beliefs and gave them greater respect among the Tatar people. Now they pity me for having so little faith in God's help.

Such prejudices are to be deplored. They occur not only among Muslims but also among supposed Christians. I consider no doctor to be God and no medicine as Saviour, but I firmly believe that if God does not give His blessing to our daily bread or our medications, they will neither nourish us nor heal us.

Now, my dear Mr. van der Smissen, please accept the cordial greetings of me and my wife. Kindly, when you can, give my greetings to my friend D. Epp, Heubuden. Accept my esteem, as your honest and loving friend and servant,
Johann Cornies

240. Johann Cornies to David Loewen. 19 October 1831. SAOR 89-1-200/52v.

Dear friend David Loewen,
I find it strange and do not know what to say. When you were last here on 20 August and paid down twenty rubles [on your debt], you promised to bring the rest of the money or to send it without fail the following Monday. I did not doubt your promises. By delaying payment, you are now taking advantage of my good will and I find it necessary to warn you in as kindly a manner as possible that the unpaid debt of sixty rubles must be paid within two weeks of today's date. Otherwise, it will be necessary for me to ask the District Office to intervene. This I would do with great reluctance.
Your friend,
Johann Cornies

241. Guardianship Committee to District Office. 30 October 1831. SAOR 89-1-193/32.

Directive from the Ekaterinoslav Guardianship Committee to the Molochnaia Mennonite District Office:
The Ekaterinoslav Guardianship Committee hereby notifies the District Office that in accordance with an instruction from the Head Curator for Colonists in Southern Russia, a Society for the Dissemination of Forest-tree and Orchard Cultivation, Sericulture and Viticulture, has been created for the Molochnaia Mennonite District. His Excellency has named the Mennonite Johann Cornies of Ohrloff village as its chairman, and the Mennonites Gerhard Enns and Dirk Warkentin, of Altonau village, as its first members. This confirmation is sent to inform the District Office about His Excellency's directive. The District Office is directed to inform all settlers in all Molochnaia Mennonite District villages about the creation of this Society, about its purposes, and about the members the Head Curator has named. All village offices should so inform their inhabitants, according to the seventh section of the

instructions. The District Office itself should provide the Society all possible cooperation and promptly carry out the eighth and nineteenth subsections of the instruction, which include transferring the Odessa plough to the Society and transferring all accounts for expenditures related to the establishment of forest-tree plantations that have hitherto been part of the community's accounts.

A report that this has been done must be submitted.

30 October 1831

Identical to the original, translator Frank.

[also noted:]

No. 461. Forest plantations, Received 2 November 1831. Directive given 2 November 1831.

Communication to Chairman Johann Cornies, 7 November 1831.

Communication to the Society, 27 February 1832.

Answered 27 February 1832, No. 126.

242. Johann Cornies to Andrei M. Fadeev. 1 November 1831. SAOR 89-1-200/53.

I respond to Your Honour's kind communication of 23 October in which you graciously informed me that His Excellency, the Head Curator, had confirmed me as chairman of the Molochnaia Mennonite Society for the Advancement and Dissemination of Forest Trees, Orchards, Sericulture, and Viticulture, and wished me good luck in this calling.

With profound devotion, I express my thanks for your gracious condescension and assure Your Honour that I will endeavour with genuine zeal, to the extent of my understanding and as much as lies in my power, to carry out the purposes for which I have been confirmed – to further the welfare and success of our community as our benevolent high administration intends. I only ask that Your Honour give us the time to familiarize ourselves with the obstacles that need to be cleared away if this course of action is to succeed and a durable basis established for the next generation. We need the time to educate ourselves by gathering knowledge about the planting of trees in general and for every location in particular.

If we are to be teachers and advisers, we must gather learning and experience lest we suffer disgrace and fail to maintain the authority we need to pursue this important occupation on which the well-being of such a considerable number of people depends. Despite our limitations, we are convinced that Your Honour will be patient until this has been accomplished.

I have made inquiries about the six puds of forest-tree seeds the Committee has sent to the District Office from Kishinev, as Yr. Honour asked. These seeds were immediately distributed in the eighteen older villages, with instructions for their prompt seeding according to the late Acting State Counsellor Contenius' directive. Seed allocations to bidders were not large.

I have had an improved deep-plough made for myself, which ploughs to the same depth as the one from Odessa and can be pulled more easily by eight fewer oxen. Thus far I have conducted only a small test, but I am certain that deep-ploughing will be easier with it than with the plough from Odessa. As soon as I have used the plough to deep-plough a considerable piece of land, I will report this to Your Honour and have two or three identical ploughs made for the villages.

When I visited Ekaterinoslav in September, Your Honour's highly respected wife commissioned me to bring back a sick horse you had had to leave behind on your journey through Tonki. I immediately sent a Nogai in my service to get the horse. It is now here, but thin and lame, and there is no advantage in selling it in this condition. I venture to offer 100 rubles for the horse in the hope that it will recover. I could also keep it with me and nurse it back to health for your further use. I request a final resolution of this question by Your Honour.

Respectfully and with the deepest esteem, I remain Your Honour's willing servant,

Cornies

243. Johann Cornies to Traugott Blueher. 11 November 1831. SAOR 89-1-200-/54v.

I notify you that your valued communications of 29 July, 25 August, and 29 September were received. The latter communication included a specified sales account for wool from owners D.C., N.Z., J.W., G.D., and J.R., as well as 6,345 R.B.A. On behalf of the parties concerned, I send their thanks for your efforts in selling their wool so favourably. Enclosed is their receipt.

Please do not consider me to be neglectful because I have not written to you since I dispatched the wool. My own business affairs have kept me busy and I had nothing of note to report. It was not necessary to write about the sale of my wool because, as mentioned earlier, I sent it to you for sale on consignment with my complete confidence. I am convinced that you will sell it on terms most favourable for me.

I am especially sorry that the returns from your own wool business were so disappointing. Genuinely, from the bottom of my heart, I begrudge you nothing that could be pleasing and advantageous to you. I sincerely hope that, with time, you will derive considerable profit from wool purchased in this area. It is most painful for me to find that your first purchases were so unsuccessful and scared you off from making a further purchase. G. Enns is not at fault for the poorer qualities of wool you mentioned being mixed into the sacks. In the whirlwind of this year's wool purchases, he made all possible efforts to benefit your interests. Since he could only purchase smaller quantities of wool, however, he could not sort all of it at one time. Sorting and packing must be done by several workers and this was when the wool was mixed. I can guarantee that this man is dependable and conscientious and that the mixing was not done intentionally.

Johann Klaassen, owner of the local cloth factory in Halbstadt, respectfully requests me to ask you to mail him twenty-five funt of wire identical to the accompanying sample. Through your kindness, and with the District chairman's help, he received an attachment for his wool-combing machine, but it is still too coarse for very fine cloth. It is not of the same fine size-number as the attachment he ordered earlier and he thus finds it necessary to have another attachment made here. The wire he needs must be no finer or coarser than the enclosed sample. It must be flexible, not brittle, so that it does not break when it is set. If you can find wire of this quality in Moscow, I urgently request that you remedy his great need by sending it by the next mail to Mr. Johann Klaassen, factory owner in Halbstadt. Charge it to my account.

Another request: a society, called Molochnaia Mennonite Society for the Advancement and Dissemination of Forest Trees, Orchards, Sericulture, and Viticulture, has been formed in our district and its constitution confirmed by the authorities. I have been designated as its chairman. This Society may carry its own seal. Its symbol is to consist of an oak, its branches outspread, with a grapevine entwined around it. The cable of an anchor will wind around the oak tree's trunk. The seal should be the same size as the enclosed circle. The Society's full name, possibly partly abbreviated, must be clearly and accurately engraved in brass around the seal's edge in Latin letters. Please be so kind as to have this produced. It may turn out to be somewhat dear, but it must be done well and accurate and the engraving must be clear. Mail it to me at the address of Gerhard Martens, District Office secretary in Halbstadt.

There is a small inaccuracy in the invoice of D.C. and J.R., which must have been overlooked. Both should have received 22.91 kopeks more.

Assuming your faithful, friendly sympathy, I close by reporting the well-being of my whole family. I hope that this letter finds you and your dear family well. May He bless you and give you His joy in all of your affairs.

These wishes and greetings come from your honest loving friend and willing servant,

Joh. Cornies

244. Johann Cornies to District Office. 20 November 1831. SAOR 89-1-200/58.

My request of 13 November has not been resolved and Jacob Friesen has not yet entered my service. In the meantime, Blumstein inhabitants informed me that the above-mentioned Jacob really did intend to work for me, but his previous employer, Peter Hooge, who was unable to obtain a worker, had described service for me in such unfavourable terms that Friesen had been persuaded to stay with Hooge. Hooge's allegations and excuses are thus fabrications, and the District Office cannot take them into account.

I humbly request that the District Office take this matter under advisement and, should it be legally possible, require Jacob Friesen to enter my service as soon as possible. Unfounded fabrications should not be accepted.

J. Cornies

245. Johann Cornies to Mr. Graf. 20 November 1831. SAOR 89-1-200/58.

Esteemed Mr. Graf,

Mr. Heese, the teacher, will have paid my bill for several small books sent to me during the year.

I enclose a further order for books to be mailed to District Office Secretary Peter Warkentin:

1. One copy: *Deutscher Hausschatz fuer jedermann* [German Treasury for Everyone], by Theodor Heinsius, newest enlarged edition.

2. *Rechtglauebige Lehre oder kurzer Auszug der Christlichen Theologie zum Gebrauch Sr. Kaiserl. Hoheit des Grossfuersten Paul Petrowitsch* [Orthodox doctrine, or short extract from Christian theology for use by

His Imperial Majesty, Duke Paul Petrovich], composed in Russian by Seromonakh Platon, Archimandrite of the Troitskii Monastery.

You may not have the last book in stock, but please obtain it. I will post payment immediately upon receipt of the bill.

With great respect, I have the honour to be your respectful servant,

J. Cornies

246. Johann Cornies to District Office. 23 November 1831. SAOR 89-1-200/59.

In response to my communication No. 3,644, of 21 November, I report that Jacob Friesen, whom I hired, has not yet entered my service. In accordance with this communication, I will send a conveyance to get him from Halbstadt next Wednesday. With respect, I have the honour to be the District Office's devoted,

Cornies

247. Johann Cornies to Andrei M. Fadeev. 20 November 1831. SAOR 89-1-200/62.

Honoured Privy Counsellor, Gracious Sir,

In response to Yr. Honour's communication of 30 October, I have the honour to notify you as follows: All forest-tree seeds arrived in good, fresh condition, including seeds distributed by the District Office and by the Society. All were suitable for germination. The former were all seeded, but the latter, because of frost and snow, cannot be seeded until spring. Recipients were instructed on how to prevent the spoilage of seeds over the winter until they could be seeded in spring. These seeds seem very promising.

I am not yet able to specify the exact amounts and varieties of seeds needed for spring planting, as Yr. Honour requests. We would require a considerable quantity of seeds, especially if Yr. Honour could arrange to have them arrive in time for spring seeding. I think that considerable quantities of mulberry and pine seeds should be sent.

I do not think that seedbeds should be located at the plantations, as Yr. Honour suggests. The raising of seedlings requires unceasing attention. They need to be kept free of weeds, and weeding must be done when the seedlings are still very small. If the seedbeds are at some distance from hearth-sites, this work might not be done at the right time, or could be easily forgotten. Before and after germination, all seedlings must be watered and protected from the sun's burning rays, a procedure that might also be neglected if they are located far away. The expenditure of time and money would thus be wasted.

The Society meeting of 12 November considered these circumstances carefully. It suggests to the Committee that each fullholder be permitted to raise forest-tree saplings from seed on his fullholding, where weeds can be cleared away more easily, water and shade against the sun's burning heat provided, and everything done to promote healthy growth.

On 1 November, I reported to Yr. Honour that I had an improved deep-plough made for my own use that incorporates several improvements to the Odessa plough. It ploughs to a depth of three-quarters of an arshin, the same depth as does the Odessa plough, but it moves more easily and employs eight fewer draught animals. At the time, I could not send you a detailed report because the plough had been used very little. Now two desiatinas have been deep-ploughed and the plough has demonstrated its advantages. I hope to build even lighter ploughs that will similarly plough to the required depth. Considering the work that this plough might save in the plantations, the Society decided to have three more of such ploughs constructed to prepare the soil in the forest-tree plantations. My plough cost 186 rubles without the harness, chains, and straps. The Society has submitted an estimate of 200 rubles for each plough to the Committee. I am convinced that Yr. Honour will recognize the great benefit of the plough and will accept the Society's estimates.

We welcome State Counsellor Steven's kind offer to our community of 12,000 or more year-old mulberry trees. Once we receive the Committee's directive, the Society will make arrangements to have the trees fetched from Simferopol.

On 1 November, I also reported that Yr. Honour's horse from Tonki is in my keeping. I sold Mr. Kusovnikov's horses, except for two stallions that no one wishes to buy, or can be sold only at an unacceptably low price. By year's end, I will send Your Honour the accounts and money.

It would have given me great pleasure to fill Yr. Honour's kind commission to send two puds of good, fresh butter to Baron Sudak on your account. I hesitated, however, knowing that the butter presently available is bitter and unappetizing. Once fresh milk becomes available, right after the New Year, I will, if possible, send the requested butter.

Cornies

248. Johann Cornies to Andrei M. Fadeev. [28] November 1831. SAOR 89-1-200/61v.

Your Honour, Mr. Fadeev, Gracious Sir,

Would Your Honour be agreeable to my urgent request that the Society for the Advancement and Dissemination of Forest Trees, Orchards, Sericulture, and Viticulture be permitted to have three deep-ploughs, of the same design as the one I had built, constructed here? The ploughs would be used to prepare the soil in village forest-tree plantations. An early resolution of this question would enable the Society to have the ploughs ordered immediately and constructed during the winter. If the ploughs were ordered later they would not be available for use at the right time.

Cornies

249. Johann Cornies to Andrei M. Fadeev. 25 November 1831. SAOR 89-1-200/64v.

Honourable Privy Counsellor, Gracious Sir,

Kindly permit me to explain to Your Honour why the Society (as mentioned in its 25 November report to the Ekaterinoslav Guardianship Committee) has decided to forbid villagers in our District from planting trees farther apart than one faden. The Society would cite the following advantages for each fullholder that would result from this practice.

1. If trees are planted regularly at one faden apart in quarter-plots, weeds can more easily be cleared away, especially if a machine is invented to do so with little effort. We must design such a machine that would make work easier and promote planting.

2. When the crowns of the trees grow into one another after a few years, the burning rays of the sun will no longer dry out the soil. If the soil beneath these trees is cultivated before the leaves have fallen, various forest-tree seeds can be planted. When the leaves fall they will improve the soil and provide cover for planted seeds, protecting them from frosts and promoting their sprouting. Once the seedlings sprout, they will be protected by the shade of the trees in summer. The irregular undergrowth that will then grow may, when thinned, provide pail and barrel hoops. Later thinning will provide wood for poles, ax handles, etc., and promote the growth of seedlings.

If trees are planted farther apart, villagers will not benefit from such early uses. Trees could not be felled until they had reached the thickness of a rafter and then, since there would be no young after-growth to replace the felled trees, the number of trees in woodlots would decrease. Assuming that these woodlots are to provide felled trees, we do not yet know whether, under our climatic conditions, roots will send up shoots to replace felled wood, as they do in forested regions. Therefore, for the time being, we think it preferable to seed our forest-tree plantations as proposed above.

Because of their spreading crowns, the mulberry trees ordered by the Society might, however, be planted a little farther apart than one faden. The Society has considered the uses to which mulberry trees might be put. It thinks that, after a number of years, if the trees become too crowded and their foliage, because of a lack of air and sun, becomes detrimental to silkworm culture, every other tree might be removed to provide air and solve this problem. Every villager could use this wood for his own needs.

Cornies

250. Johann Cornies to Andrei M. Fadeev. 30 November 1831. SAOR 89-1-200/66V.

Honourable Privy Counsellor, Gracious Sir,

It is my duty to respond to Yr. Honour's communication of 13 November by reporting that delays in mail service occur specifically at the Orekhov post office. I have received letters and packages held up only in this office and note that these letters and packages were forwarded belatedly, sometimes after lying around for several days.

Following Yr. Honour's instruction, we will use the winter months to acquire knowledge about the science of forestry from books in our library that would enable us in spring to apply it appropriately and in a timely fashion in each local area.

I can only report that forest-tree seeds shipped to us appear to have arrived fresh and promising of germination. The acorns were damaged because they had been knocked about in their sack and will likely not sprout.

It seems to me that it would be preferable to have mulberry trees brought from Simferopol than from Kharkov. Spring arrives here three or four weeks earlier than in the Kharkov region. This means that while our conditions are already warm and dry, Kharkov is still often stuck in snow and mud. Under these conditions, young trees are more difficult to dig up and our costs would rise accordingly. At the same time, the sudden change in temperature from cold in Kharkov to warmth here would make the sap run and the trees bud, and the trees would be ruined. On the other hand, trees could be brought here from Kharkov in autumn without damage.

My wool has not yet been sold in Moscow. Prices there, as Mr. Blueher writes, are somewhat low. Several villagers sent their wool to Moscow with mine, and it sold at fifty rubles per pud.

I do not think it necessary this year to purchase breeding rams and sheep for the community sheep farm.

I must dutifully request that Yr. Honour not agree to requests from several villages that they be permitted to transfer their forest-tree plantations to their hearth-sites. The hearth-sites have already been designated for fruit trees.

Cornies

251. Johann Cornies to Andrei M. Fadeev. 18 December 1831. SAOR 89-1-200/69.

Your Honour, Gracious Sir,

I am honoured to respond to Yr. Honour's letter of 2 December as to whether Burgdorf's book about growing forest trees is available here. Also, please permit me to explain the planting of living fences around forest-tree plantations and in the villages themselves. Hedges should enclose forest-tree plantations and hearth-sites in a manner that would render them enduring, impenetrable to livestock, and pleasing to the eye. I think we should proceed as follows:

1. Every fullholder should, before these living fences are laid out, plant nursery beds of hawthorn at his hearth-site, in quantities that will eventually provide quite a large number of hawthorn saplings. A considerable number of hawthorn saplings must be available to serve this purpose. If such hedges are not planted thickly enough, they will lack the desired durability, appearance, and other attributes. It is therefore essential to acquire a sufficient quantity of hawthorn seeds to enable every fullholder and cottager to make the needed plantings.

The Society will endeavour to obtain as much hawthorn seed as possible from Khortitsa villages, where hawthorn trees grow in large numbers. It will also not lose sight of the fact that it must advise and explain to the inhabitants of our District how much more useful and advantageous living fences are than others.

The Society will proceed promptly to provide the Radichev Village Office with a detailed description of the way in which pine seeds must be collected, sorted, packed, and stored for shipment.

Winter arrived here suddenly on 11 November with a snowstorm that destroyed much Nogai livestock. The snowstorm out of the West drowned many animals in the Sea of Azov. Mild weather soon followed, but quite a bit of snow fell again in the last four or five days.

1832

252. Johann Cornies to District Office. 11 January 1832. SAOR 89-1-236/2.

The honoured District Office at Halbstadt,

David Loewen from Fuerstenwerder had his debt of sixty rubles cash paid to me yesterday, 10 January, delivered by David, son of David Goetz. My demands on Loewen have hereby been settled. I inform the honoured District Office of this and thank it for its kind support of my request.

With respect, I remain the honoured District Office's respectful,

J. Cornies

253. Johann Cornies to Andrei M. Fadeev. 12 January 1832. SAOR 89-1-236/3.

Your Honour, Gracious State Counsellor,

In response to Yr. Honour's esteemed letter of 24 December 1831, I can tell you that Wilhelm Martens concluded a favourable agreement with the merchant Konstantinov and repossessed the iron business in Tokmak. He then immediately sold it at exactly the same price, but on better terms, to a wealthy Orekhov merchant. In this way, Martens should incur no loss. Martens is still ill and his recovery is likely to be long.

I have reached an agreement to purchase land from Granobarskii for 35,000 rubles, but, because his barrister is busy elsewhere, the conditions agreed upon have not yet been concluded in writing.[1] When this matter is finished, I intend to travel to Ekaterinoslav late in January to sign the appropriate documents.

My wool sold in Moscow at an average price of 55 rubles.

Winter continues in its usual monotonous way, with much snow but little cold weather, except for a few times when we recorded nine degrees of frost.

With the arrival of the New Year, and with the simplicity demanded by an honest heart, I take the liberty of thanking Yr. Honour for benefits I have enjoyed over the past year and commend myself to your kindness for the coming year. At the same time, I wish you and your highly respected house an undisturbed enjoyment of life. May you be blessed with everything that might embellish your days. I say this with unfeigned respect. To retain your gracious favour and to deserve it increasingly from day to day will be my most earnest desire in future, as I remain Yr. Honour's most devoted servant,

Johann Cornies

254. Andrei M. Fadeev to Johann Cornies. 12 January 1832. SAOR 89-1-232/19.

Most valued Cornies,

I did not answer your last letter because I was told that you would soon come here. I agree that you and your colleagues discuss with me what can best be done to advance forest-tree planting this year. Please decide the time that is best suited for your visit.

With respect to No. 29 of the directive, I have not forgotten the need to identify a person from your community who has achieved the most in orchard and forest cultivation in 1831, and to present him with a reward. It is self-evident, I think, that poor but zealous people should be preferred in this case.

I advise you to acquire and read a booklet sent to your church leaders from St. Petersburg by imperial decree. The title is *Das Religions, Kirchen und Schulwesen der Mennoniten, mit Verbesserungen und Vorschlaegen* [About the Religious, Church and School Systems of the Mennonites, with Suggestions for Improvements] by the Mennonite Abraham Hunzinger.[2] It is the intention of the government that our Mennonites should accept some of its suggestions, especially with respect to schools.

---

1 This purchase would become Cornies' Tashchenak estate (sometimes referred to in his letters as the "Malochna Estate"). In a letter of 23 January 1836, Johann Cornies says that the estate consisted of 3,364 desiatinas, 2,248 sazhens of land.

2 Abraham Hunzinger, *Das Religions-, Kirchen- und Schulwesen der Mennoniten oder Taufgesinnten: wahr und unpartheiisch dargestellt und mit besonderen Betrachtungen*

In my opinion, several of the author's suggestions would be useful for our Mennonites also. Your esteemed religious leaders must not miss the opportunity to make improvements in this regard without delay. For example, a secondary school might be founded in Khortitsa to properly educate village schoolmasters. It could be directed by Heese, assisted by Hausknecht.

With best wishes,

Your devoted A. Fadeev

255. Johann Cornies to J. Wiebe. 18 January 1832. SAOR 89-1-236/5v.

Honoured friend J. Wiebe,

I would be happy to give you my honest advice to assist you in your undertaking, as you request, but I am not in a position to do so now. I cannot get detailed, honest information to assist you in establishing yourself in Odessa because I have had no reliable friends or patrons there for five or six years. They have drifted away to Constantinople or to France, and several were victims of the plague.

If you came here yourself and travelled to Odessa, you would soon judge whether it would be profitable for you to forward and trade butter and cheese on consignment. If not, you could quickly find another occupation at which a clever and practical man could earn a good livelihood without needing a large capital. If you ask such questions impartially and consider them objectively before you begin, your business will prosper with God's blessing. I can say no more now, but when you arrive I may have more to say.

There is no news from here, except to say that the authorities have given me responsibility for a large enterprise to advance forest-tree and fruit-tree planting, sericulture, and viticulture. Wilhelm Martens has been ill since November. Heinrich Cornies is looking for a master to build him an oil mill. Everyone in the Peter Enns household, where Elisabeth received a marriage proposal from the son of David Hiebert, Lindenau, is fine. [Hiebert] did not succeed and things are as they were. Give your dear parents and relatives my best greetings. We commend ourselves to all of you. Your honest friend and servant,

Cornies

über einige Dogmen und mit Verbesserungs-Vorschlägen versehen von einem Mennoniten (Speyer: J.C. Kolb, 1830). The controversy surrounding this book is described in James Urry, *Mennonites, Politics, and Peoplehood. Europe-Russia-Canada. 1525–1988* (Winnipeg: University of Manitoba Press, 2006).

256. Johann Cornies to Traugott Blueher. 18 January 1832. SAOR 89-1-236/7.

Honoured Mr. Blueher,

If you have forwarded the money for my wool by the time you receive my communication of 8 January, please cover the costs of the machine fittings ordered. Mr. Klaassen will forward the amount required when the bill arrives.

I enclose samples of silk from Khortitsa, with a request that you kindly obtain instructions from well-qualified persons in Moscow on how silk should be treated. How should faulty reeling be remedied to give this silk a smoother and softer appearance? It feels hard, as though it had been sized with lime water but lime or lime water was not used. Which silk is most in demand, yellow or white? This year, the Khortitsa community has produced no more than four puds of silk. The best cocoons were selected for finely reeled silk with two, three, or four or more threads. Which silk fetches the best price, since wages are particularly high for fine silk reeling? Enclosed are samples of white, finely reeled silk (four threads) and yellow, common silk (nine to ten threads.) Please obtain the most detailed and dependable information from reputable Moscow manufacturers that might enable Khortitsa silk producers to develop their silk to its greatest perfection.

I depend on your kindness for permitting me to interrupt you in this way and hope you are not offended by my presumption. With friendly greetings and good wishes for you and your dear family, I remain your loving friend and servant,

Cornies

257. Johann Cornies to David Epp, Heubuden. 18 January 1832. SAOR 89-1-236/6v.

Beloved friend D. Epp, Heubuden,

Do not be angry because I have not written to you for such a long time or that I write so little now. Please do not think that this shows that I do not love and value you. I am happy whenever I hear that you are healthy and that things are going well.

I write to ask that you might buy a handbook and word concordance for the Bible. My friend, a Russian archpresbyter who understands German, would like one. Mr. Wiebe, Thiege, will pay you for your costs.

A thousand greetings from your friend and brother, who loves you and honestly respects you,
Cornies

258. Johann Cornies to P. Warkentin. 4 February 1832. SAOR 89-1-236/9.

Beloved friend,
I would be in your debt if you would kindly write to Mr. Petrublov in Orekhov on my behalf. Mr. Granobarskii has informed me that the trip to Ekaterinoslav to complete legal arrangements for the land purchase should occur by the first week of Lent, at the latest. This depends on Mr. Petrublov's schedule (I enclose Mr. Granobarskii's letter to guide you).

This suggestion would be fine if Mr. Fadeev had not already summoned me to Ekaterinoslav twice on official business. I would rather not come to Ekaterinoslav twice. Therefore please ask Mr. Petrublov, with due consideration, if he might arrange his business affairs in such a way that the legal matters could be completed in Ekaterinoslav next week. I would send him a good, comfortable *britchka* [trap] to call for him and take him to Ekaterinoslav.

Dear friend, compose the letter in this regard in the most flattering way, since this gentleman has a very volatile disposition. Promise the messenger a ruble to give the letter to Petrublov personally. Instruct him to allow Petrublov enough time, without being hurried or rude, to write a reply. Otherwise nothing will come of this. You will, of course, know how best to realize my purpose.

Heartfelt greetings to you, your friend who values you,
Johann Cornies

P.S. I request that you kindly return the letter from Mr. Granobarskii and send me the contents of the one to Petrublov.

259. Johann Cornies to Heinrich van Steen, Danzig. 5 February 1832. SAOR 89-1-236/10.[3]

Mr. Heinrich van Steen in Danzig, honoured friend,
On January 24, I received your valued communication of 12 January and immediately took care of the enclosures for your son and

3 Regarding van Steen's step-son, Carl Anton Zimmerman, see footnote 109, and documents 239, 279, 280, 290, 303, 304, and 362.

Mr. Warkentin. I am pleased that you are satisfied with the arrangements I made with Warkentin to accommodate your son. Meanwhile, Warkentin has done more detailed calculations and is asking for an additional four rubles per month, for a total of sixteen R.B.A. This request seems reasonable to me, taking into consideration the good, orderly treatment he is giving your son. He is patient, considerate, thoughtful, and loving in guiding him back to a quiet, peaceful life, without antagonizing him or making him more miserable. I had no qualms about agreeing to the requested increase without your prior approval.

Warkentin told me that since he arrived, your son's behaviour (not considering his silliness) is much improved. He is more agreeable, attends church services almost every Sunday, reads constructive books, etc. May God grant that he not suffer a relapse. From your letter, I gather that your son assumes that he will be returning to Danzig in spring and is already planning his departure. You must write to him soon, in detail, informing him on how long you expect him to stay in Russia. Otherwise, I may well lose the trust he has invested in me and the good influence I have over him. I will gladly cover the costs of his maintenance, even if your payment should be delayed until autumn, at the latest. I will, in any case, neglect nothing on his behalf. My supervision of your son follows from the belief that service to one's fellow man is in itself true service to God, and cannot, in good conscience, be neglected. It is written that whatever we do out of love for the most humble of men, we have done for Him.

About four years ago I decided to buy some cows in Friesland or Holland and to transport them to Russia. At the time, I exchanged letters with Mr. Gilbert van der Smissen in Altonau, near Hamburg, who secured information in this regard from his friends in Friesland and Holland. Circumstances prevented me from undertaking this business at the time, however, but I still intend to purchase cows from east Friesland. To decide money matters, I still need information about the most suitable ports in east Friesland from which to ship the cows to Danzig and about the highest transportation costs I might expect per head. I would be grateful if you, Mr. van Steen, could send me this information. Please accept my importunity in a kindly way.

I commend you and your dear wife to God's omnipotent protection. I and my wife send you friendly greetings, your willing friend and servant,

J. Cornies

260. Johann Cornies to Jacob van der Smissen, Danzig. 5 February 1832. SAOR 89-1-236/11v.

Reverend van der Smissen, treasured friend,

Your esteemed communication moves me to write these few lines to express my sincere thanks and respect. May God give you the strength and a firm foundation for your difficult but illustrious official responsibilities.

The disputes that reigned in our community about ten years ago were eliminated by dividing the congregation into two congregations. These disputes had arisen when a Bible association and a school society had been established. Both have survived the storms and have become much stronger as a result. The Bible association has fifty to sixty members, and some 2,000 copies of German Bibles and Testaments have been sold since its establishment. The school continues to thrive with God's blessing.

On orders from the Tsar, the Minister of the Interior sent a book by Abraham Hunzinger, a Mennonite archivist in Hesse, to our elders and to Khortitsa that includes suggestions for the reform of Mennonite life that might bring them closer to the state and integrate them with it. Would our local Mennonites be prepared to accept some of the suggestions, especially those relating to schools? I have not yet read the book and I respectfully request that you, Reverend Sir, do me the favour of ordering this book for me from the bookseller Mr. Johann Ambrosius Barth, at No. 681 Grimmaischestrasse in Leipzig, and also two others, for which I enclose the titles. I am personally acquainted with the bookseller, Mr. Barth, who will send the books immediately. Please pay the bill when it arrives and kindly give the books to Mr. Johann W[iebe], Thiege near Tiegenhoff, to be forwarded to me, and receive the money owing from him. I think the author of the above-mentioned book is a member of the Remonstrant Mennonite congregation. Since you will know how to obtain this information, I would ask that you share it with me.

The books are:

1. *Das Religions, Kirchen und Schulwesen der Mennoniten mit Verbesserungen und Vorschlaegen* [About the Religious, Church and School Systems of the Mennonites, with Suggestions for Improvements], by Abraham Hunzinger, Hesse.
2. *Von Hindoglu aus Kintakie in Klein Asien* [About Hindoglu from Kintakie in Asia Minor], Vienna, Beck, etc.
3. *Das Russische Dampfort* [The Russian Steam Bath].

Mr. Peter Riesen has written to his relatives that he is moving to Russia this spring and everything is ready for his departure. May his relatives assume that this is definitely so?

With greetings of friendship to you and your treasured family, I commend myself to you, as always, your obligated,

J. Cornies

261. Johann Cornies to David Epp, Khortitsa. 6 February 1832. SAOR 89-1-236/12v.

Esteemed David Epp,

From Depot Manager, Johann Cornies in Ohrloff,

Three hundred copies of the New Testament recently sent by the main Bible Society in St. Petersburg to the Molochnaia Branch have been sold and the proceeds will shortly be forwarded to the main committee in St. Petersburg. I request that if all the books, or some recently deposited with you, have been sold, you forward the proceeds to me with the first secure opportunity.

Our local committee has sent your requested order for fifty Bibles and 200 New Testaments to St. Petersburg.

With respectful greetings, I commend myself to you as your friend and servant,

J. Cornies

262. Johann Cornies to District Office. 12 February 1832. SAOR 89-1-236/13.

To the honoured District Office in Halbstadt,

I write in response to your communication No. 3,037, dated 16 September 1831, and list of debts of Phillip Wiebe in Tiegerweide. With respect to my petition of 13 March 1831, I request that the honoured District Office please credit the 400 ruble debt as a loan against Phillip Wiebe's property. Should the other interested parties not wish to make a claim on Wiebe's property, I request that a part of Wiebe's property be designated as secure collateral for the sum of 400 rubles.

The fifteen rubles owed the community sheep farm should not, however, be taken from this account. The manager has specifically been ordered to deduct this particular debt that Wiebe incurred for the purchase of hay from the income he will derive from the work he will do during the coming haying harvest.

Johann Cornies

263. Johann Cornies to C. Steven. 29 February 1832. SAOR 89-1-236/13v.

His Honour, Gracious State Counsellor Steven,

Yr. Honour will kindly forgive my interrupting your business activities with a request. As far as I know, no Crimean apples under the name of Kara Sinap grow anywhere in the Molochnaia. Their quality is supposedly very high. Since this Society is sending a man to Simferopol to take delivery of mulberry trees, I would ask Yr. Honour to advise me on where we could obtain, for cash, ten to twenty good, genuine, improved two-year-old saplings of these apple variety, as well as several of the best large winter pear trees called Con Chretien.

In the hope that Yr. Honour will not view my request unkindly, I remain, with the greatest respect, Yr. Honour's most obedient servant,

Johann Cornies

264. Johann Cornies, Gerhard Ennz, and D. Warkentin to village offices. 25 February 1832. SAOR 89-1-220/7.[4]

Regulatio No. 105 to village offices:

To seed forest-tree seeds, basic knowledge is required, just as it is required for all branches of agriculture in field, orchard, and garden. To thrive and grow, each variety of seed must be treated according to its own nature. Aware that fullholders lack opportunities to acquire elementary knowledge in the seeding of forest trees or the manner in which one should proceed in each individual case, the Society finds it necessary to describe briefly the treatment indispensable for the planting of various forest-tree seeds. Providing such instructions to each inhabitant in our settlement will ensure success in establishing the foundations of what our august state intends for us.

Seeding acorns: Acorns should, as a rule, be set out in late September or early October. The bed must be dug deeply, raked, and the acorns pushed in to a depth of one or two short inches. If the soil is dry, as is usual in autumn, it must be watered after planting. To ensure that the acorns come up well in spring, the bed must be covered with foliage, long straw, or reeds for winter so that frost will not penetrate.

4 This document is a representative example of several similar circulars distributed in the period.

Alternately, acorns can be put into a pot of sand for winter to allow them to sprout. In spring these sprouted acorns should be taken out of the pot carefully, without breaking the shoots, and put into the soil.

White beech or grove beech: Prepare the soil by digging deeply and then sow this seed in shallow grooves in early autumn, though early spring seeding is also possible. As a rule, this seed will sprout in the second year, but occasionally also in the first year. Only a few of the seeds will come up.

Red beech: Autumn seeding of beech kernels is preferred, although it can be done in spring as well. The seeds should be sown in shallow grooves in deeply dug soil. They will come up very early the first spring. Because the plants are delicate and can suffer great damage from late-night frosts, they must be located in places protected from the frost.

Birch: Depending on circumstances, this seed can be sown in autumn, or in winter when the soil has thawed, or very early in spring soon after the snow has melted. On a windless day, the seed should be scattered over a deeply dug and thoroughly raked bed. It should be watered with a watering can so that the seed sticks to the soil. Tap the bed gently with a shovel because this seed cannot tolerate a soil covering and must only be mixed with it. Take care to sow seeds thickly and evenly. Seed sown in autumn comes up in spring, and when sown in spring, in five or six weeks.

Alder: Alder seeds thrive best when put into damp soil in autumn, but can also be seeded in very early spring. Alders are seeded in the same way as birches. With autumn seeding, plants appear in spring, and with spring seeding, after four or five weeks.

Elm or maple: Maple seeds are best seeded immediately after they have been gathered in early June, but only after spreading them thinly on a clear floor. Prepare a deeply dug bed and when a rain cloud appears, seed them thickly to enable the rain to drive the seeds into the soil so that they begin to sprout immediately and come up after eight days. They will grow to a height of four to six inches by winter. If there is drought, the plants must be watered to prevent them from drying out. Spring seeding on a windless day, and no deeper than one-quarter inch, is preferred, though maples will also thrive if seeded in autumn.

White maple or Norway maple; also black maple: Autumn seeding or late March, early April seeding is done in grooves straight across the bed to a depth of a half an inch. Seeds come up early in spring, or after five or six weeks with spring seeding.

Ash: Ash seed is sown like maple seed, as described above. The plants usually appear in the second year, but if an autumn seeding is fresh, some kernels may come up in spring.

Pine: The bed for pine seed must be mixed with sand if this does not occur naturally. Seed must not be sown before April, and is then strewn into previously prepared one-quarter inch grooves across the bed. It is covered with sand, tamped down with a shovel, and watered. Since the young shoots will be damaged if the soil dries out to a depth of an inch in dry weather, a garden location should be selected to prevent damage.

Linden tree: Linden seed must be sown in October into shallow grooves across a bed of well-prepared soil. It comes up the following spring. Seed can be sown in spring and must be kept damp in order that it may come up after four or five weeks, or it will not come up until the following year.

Hawthorn: Hawthorn shrubs are well known for their use as living fences and as wood for chopping. They can be propagated through seed by the following method. Shred completely ripe, red berries by hand into a wooden container, using water. Pour fresh water over them and skim off the kernels. Mix these kernels with moist sand in a clean earthenware pot, leaving the pot in a warm room for the winter. In spring, sow them in half-inch grooves made across the bed. When sown straight into the soil without this preparation, they usually come up in the second year.

Mulberry seed: Gather the ripe berries or grapes that fall from the tree, or after a light shaking, and place them on a linen sheet, but not on top of one another or they will rot. Leave them in an airy, dry location for five or six days, then place them into a horn sieve in a barrel of clean water. Shred the berries by hand until the seed kernels have separated. Kernels that sink to the bottom are suitable for seeding. Dry them thoroughly and preserve in a cold, dry location for winter. In April, soak the kernels for two days, then sow them in half-inch grooves and cover with loose soil. The seed must be watered regularly or the sprouts may turn mouldy in dry weather.

Assumptions: Forest-tree seeds sown punctually, according to their appropriate method of cultivation, will, without doubt, sprout and thrive if watering is not neglected in dry weather and weeds are cleared regularly. It is well known that weeds dry out the soil if they are not cleared away when they are small, causing delicate young plants to dry up as well. This results in wasted effort. The raising of forest-tree seedlings must be continued until such time as the benevolent expectations of our august imperial government have been realized.

It is obvious that forest-tree seeds must be protected from the burning rays of the sun for at least a year. To enable them to thrive, all young plants must be shaded in July and August to keep them from drying out.

After village mayors have read these regulations to fullholders in a community assembly, they must make a readable copy of them and immediately send this communication on. Before sowing the forest-tree seeds described here, all fullholders should also make copies for themselves, or have the school teachers do this for them, since it is impossible to remember great detail after only one reading.

For further information about the appropriate types of soil for the cultivation of each variety of seeds and other matters, we refer to the directive from the late State Counsellor Contenius for the Society for the Advancement and Dissemination of Forest Trees, Orchards, Sericulture, and Viticulture.

Ohrloff, February 1832

Chairman Cornies, Member Ennz, Member D. Warkentin

Supplement: Spring is very near and the "Regulatio" must be publicized and copied immediately. It must not stay in any village longer than twenty-four hours in order that this information can reach everyone before forest-tree seeds are sown. After every village office has recorded the arrival and departure times on this supplement, it should be returned to the Society by the Prang[enau] Village Office.

25 February 1832, sent from Ohrloff.

Chairman Cornies

Ohrloff, received 25 February at 11 a.m., and sent 26 February at 10.

Tiege, 27 February, sent at 10 a.m. Toews.

Blumenort, 28 February, sent at 10:30 a.m. Walde.

Rosenort, 29 February, sent at 9:30 a.m. Wiens.

Lichtfelde, received 29 February at 4 p.m., and sent 1 March at 4 p.m. Riedger.

Neukirch, received 1 March at 6 p.m., and sent 2 March at 6 p.m. Neufeld.

Prangenau, received 3 March at 5 p.m., and sent 5 March, Buhler.

265. Andrei M. Fadeev to Johann Cornies. 25 February 1832. SAOR 89-1-246/21.

Dear Cornies,

I am very surprised that you have not yet been to see me. I find it necessary to discuss various matters regarding the plantations with you. Please come before the roads are entirely impassable.

A. Fadeev
Received 29 February 1832.

266. Johann Cornies to Andrei M. Fadeev. 1 March 1832. SAOR 89-1-236/14.

Fadeev, Honourable State Counsellor, Gracious Sir,

Since Christmas, Mr. Granobarskii and his authorized representative have made promises to me from week to week to appear in Ekaterinoslav to sign documents for the land I have purchased from him. Had these gentlemen originally postponed the legal transactions in Ekaterinoslav until March, I would have visited Ekaterinoslav to see you immediately after the New Year when the sledding roads were still good. Please forgive me for failing to appear, gracious Sir, and do not blame me for this long delay, which has upset my routine and temporarily impeded me from properly carrying out Yr. Honour's wishes.

I will see Granobarskii and his authorized representative again tomorrow and should be able to conclude the final agreements at that time. I will leave for Ekaterinoslav on Monday, 7 March, and make no further postponements, assuming good health and passable roads.

In the hope that Yr. Honour will not consider my failure to appear unkindly, I remain, with constant respect, Yr. Honour's most devoted servant,

Johann Cornies

267. Johann Cornies to District Office. 1 March 1832. SAOR 89-1-236/15.

The following horses appeared in my herd during this past winter:

1. a small brown mare, three years old, with a white spot on its forehead, no markings, and

2. a small mouse-coloured gelding, five years old, no markings.

They are Nogai horses but not from here, since our area has been notified that horses not belonging to me have joined my herd. I request that the honourable District Office take charge of these horses, since there may be householders who need them at seeding time. In such cases, please give them a written order for the horses' release, addressed to J. Sukau, manager on my sheep farm.

With respect,
Cornies

268. Johann Cornies to J. Regier. 31 March 1832. SAOR 89-1-236/17v.

Honoured friend J. Regier, Schoensee,

My brother, David Cornies, has informed me that you inquired about using the deep-plough built here to deep-plough your forest-tree plantation. I would be pleased to have you try the plough, since the Society is most concerned to have the first test made by someone who is without prejudice about its potential. The straps and ropes for the plough's harness are still lacking. Please purchase them at the Society's costs. I will reimburse you for the outlay, immediately after the bill arrives, with thanks.

It is generally agreed that this plough must plough no less than three-quarters of an arshin deep. Please take master craftsman Loewen along for the first test since he must make delivery of the plough once it is tested.

Report the results to me in detail. I send greetings to you and your dear wife and remain, with true honesty, your friend,

Johann Cornies

269. Forestry Society to village offices. Minutes of meeting, 13 April 1832. SAOR 89-1-220/7.

Decisions taken at the meeting of the Society for the Advancement and Dissemination of Forest Trees, Orchards, Sericulture, and Viticulture at Ohrloff on 13 April 1832:

1. Tomorrow, 14 April, the chairman, as well as Society member Gerhard Enns, will begin his tour through villages of the old settlement to inspect their forest-tree plantations. Village mayors and their deputies are ordered to be at home when the members arrive and to have a six fut (one faden) measuring device at hand.

2. Each fullholder should plough one quarter of his own plot in the forest-tree plantations with the deep-plough each year so that all quarters of the plantations will be ploughed in four years' time.

3. In accordance with section 2 of the directive to the Society, the already confirmed three members have chosen two further members, Abraham Wiebe, Rudnerweide, and Aron Rempel, Schoensee.

270. Forestry Society inspection of Ohrloff plantation. 14 April 1832. SAOR 89-1-220/8.

Remarks by Society members about the order and regularity found in every half-desiatina plot during their inspection of the forest-tree plantation:

14 April, Ohrloff. In the plantations:
1. This plot has several fruit trees
2. With irregular hedge not of mulberry trees
3. Has several fruit trees
4. Likewise
5. Very few fruit trees
6. Has several fruit trees
7, 8, 9. No plantings
10. This plot found to be regular
11. Likewise
12. No plantings
13. Regular
14, 15. Likewise
16. Among other things, a few fruit trees
17. Hedge too sparse
18. A few trees not prescribed
19. In place
20. No plantings
21. Regular

[Similar listings follow for Tiege, Rosenort, Schoensee, Fuerstenau, Ladekopp, Petershagen, Halbstadt, Tiegenhagen, Schoenau, Muensterberg, and Altonau.]

[The following note appears above the Schoensee list: "In the plantation in this village, every fullholder has four quarter-plots in four sections for a total of one half-desiatina. The first section is completely covered with willows, forest trees are planted in the second and third sections, and the fourth is still an unplanted meadow."]

271. Peter Orens Draisma, Grunau, to Johann Cornies. 16 April 1832. SAOR 89-1-223/13.

Valued Mr. Cornies,

Wishing you the best well-being, I venture to make a request. My cousin, Jacob de Jager is travelling to Hamburg this summer. I would like him to bring me back a few books. I know you are in possession of book catalogues, so I take the liberty of asking you to send me several of these so that I may make my choice.

Finally, I would ask you to lend me the book, *Beispiele des Guten* [Examples of the Good], that I would like to read. I will be sure to return the book undamaged, with thanks, at Pentecost, or eight days from now.

My friend Schoenknecht will bring me the book and give you more details about my situation. With the fondest hope that you will grant my request, I remain, with respect, your devoted friend and servant,

P.O. Draisma

Grunau, 16 September 1832

272. Johann Cornies to Kirilovskii. 19 April 1832. SAOR 89-1-236/18v.

You have put me under a great obligation by kindly accepting my son into your house for thorough language instruction and the teaching of other useful sciences.

Honoured sir, I am a father who has the well-being of his community, where he lives and belongs, at heart. I attempt to serve all of its individual members to the limits of my ability in order to achieve their well-being in every regard. My purpose is to live and work in the calm knowledge of what has been ordained as my holy duty as a man and a Christian.

This should enable you to understand the kind of education and knowledge I seek for my son. His education should develop his personal worth in order that he can become a useful and serving member of his community and of human society. I place my son in your hands, honoured sir, in the joyful awareness that you will assume the duties of a father in my place, and offer me and my wife the assurance that we have found a worthy guide and leader for our son. You are capable of directing him so that he can achieve the best results for his life and future. We are confident that our son will give you a child's obedience and that we will not need to feel ashamed for having neglected his childhood education in love, faithfulness, and obedience.

As agreed, I enclose 100 R.B.A. With confidence, great hope, and genuine respect, I commend myself to you as your devoted servant,

Cornies

273. Johann Cornies to Traugott Blueher. 20 April 1832. SAOR 89-1-236/19.

Esteemed Mr. Blueher,

I received your valued communications of 22 December and 9 February and also the remittance of 13,055 R.B.A. for the wool entrusted to you on consignment last year. The receipt is enclosed. I fully agree with your handling of this matter and thank you for this advantageous sale. Kindly forgive me for waiting so long to reply and to send you the receipt.

I was away for several weeks buying land. I bought 3,300 desiatinas of land and, if the Lord gives His blessing, I should soon be in a position to send you 600 puds of wool and more. I have already hired the old drivers to transport this year's wool to Moscow. Please sell it on consignment as you have done in the past. Down payments have already been made for much of the wool to be bought here on the spot, at thirty to forty rubles for the ordinary washed variety. Yesterday I sold the Nogai wool at an average of thirty-five rubles. You are familiar with its quality.

I received the silk you sent and thank you for your efforts on behalf of the Khortitsa community. They will be pleased to receive the accurate results you have forwarded that should enable them to prepare the silk they are producing in a way that would fetch the highest possible price.

Please send five dozen sheep shears whenever possible and charge them to my account. Maybe you could send them with the carters when they return. State Counsellor Fadeev expects that the carters will transport the monument for the departed Mr. Contenius from Moscow when they return.[5] My friend Klaassen in Halbstadt also intends to use this opportunity to obtain a shearing machine for his factory. The shears could be sent along as well, or they could be sent to the address known to you in Kharkov, addressed to Wilhelm Martens for the August annual market.

Should my friend Klaassen, the factory owner in Halbstadt, soon ask you to purchase machinery for him in Moscow, please cover the outlay and put it on my account until my wool has been sold. Then you can deduct Klaassen's cost itself and the accumulated interest from my account. Also, please inform me briefly of current wool prices in Moscow.

Hoping these lines find you and your dear family well, we send loving greetings. I thank you for your support, your friendship, and commend you to the protection of God, our Saviour. Your friend and servant,

Cornies

---

5 This monument, which disappeared during the period of the Russian Revolution and civil war, was found on a bank of the Dnieper River in 2003, and is now on display in the Dnepropetrovsk Regional History Museum.

274. Johann Cornies to District Office. 12 May 1832. SAOR 89-1-236/21.

According to your communication of 11 May, government orders require me to send people of Russian nationality working on my sheep farm to the District Office with their official papers by Thursday or Friday, 12 or 13 May. This is impossible for me to do. Most of these workers are shepherds who began the sheep drive towards Steinbach for sheep shearing a few days ago. Several yard workers were sent along to help them with this work.

It is impossible for me to send to you the few people left on the sheep farm and leave the establishment without any inhabitants at this time. I request that the honourable District Office kindly give consideration to my present situation and have the inventory required by the government prepared without requiring my people to appear at the District Office in person.

Hoping for your kind consideration,
The honourable District Office's respectful Johann Cornies

275. Johann Cornies to Heinrich Cornies. 21 May 1832. SAOR 89-1-236/21v.

Dear brother Heinrich,

I received your letter of 15 May today. Eftukhov owes the total interest from the time of his signature. Please collect it together with the principal. If you think there is no risk, lend Isaak and Redekop 5,000 rubles. Take 400 rubles of Eftukhov's interest for your own use, but let me know when you take the money and handle it sensibly. Keep the rest of the money in your safekeeping until I arrive or commission someone to get it. Please keep accurate records of all incoming money and of funds paid out.

Your loving brother,
Cornies

276. Johann Cornies to Caspar Adrian Hausknecht. 30 May 1832. SAOR 89-1-236/24.

At your request, I sent the Khortitsa silk samples to my correspondent, a friend in Moscow, and asked him to obtain appropriate information to improve the silk. A copy of the results is enclosed with three silk samples as sent to me by my friend. This should show you how the above-mentioned product can be improved. After the samples have been examined and tested to your satisfaction, please return them to me when you can.

We were able to exchange only a few words recently, even though there was so much for us to discuss. What are you and your dear family doing? I would be happy to hear that you are all healthy and in good spirits.

Among the rolls of maps left with Martens, there was a map belonging to me of colonies in southern Russia. My Leonhard forgot to keep it here and I don't know where it is now, probably in Khortitsa. Please ask about it there on my behalf and keep it until you find a good opportunity to send it back to me.

If you should get to Ekaterinoslav, please visit my son and encourage him with your well-meaning teachings and advice. You know what a young person making his first entrance into the world needs. I count on your loyalty and hope that I am not mistaken in making this request.

Sincere greetings to you and your dear life's companion, and to our friend Penner. Trust in God.

Your loving Cornies

277. Johann Cornies to District Office. 1 June 1832. SAOR 89-1-236/25.

Communication No. 1,624, dated 30 May, summons me to appear with Inspector of Colonies Pelekh on Wednesday, 1 June, at a point where three pieces of land abut on one another between Chernlovkii, the local district, and the village Petropavlovkii. The purpose would be to witness surveyor Odinzov's inspection of the boundary lines drawn and marked by the surveyor Timoshevskii. My obedient response is that I cannot possibly leave my own establishment at this time of year because I am preparing my wool production for shipment to Moscow. The carters hired are waiting to receive and load the wool. Also, I received this communication only today, 1 June.

Not only is it impossible for me to appear at this boundary point today, however, it is also not necessary. The line is so clearly marked with ploughed furrows, mounds, and ditches, that no mistake can be made.

With respect I have the honour to be the District Office's respectful,

J. Cornies

278. Peter Friesen to Johann Cornies. 17 June 1832. SAOR 89-1-233/56.

Esteemed Mr. Cornies,

I am still in the lowlands on the Molochnaia with my work force and do not know when we will finish here. Twenty rakers and six stackers are at work today. By now we have made 100 stacks, and if there is no rain, we will get at least 200 to 250 stacks this week, estimating four stacks to a load. I will need 200 to 210 rubles for Saturday and for other essentials for the week. I cannot tell how much small change will be needed, but please send whatever you can spare. Should I need more, not even a two ruble piece is available any closer to here than Kisliar.

The road from here to Apollanikii was ploughed, but a caravan of about eighty carts made its way over four furrows during ploughing without difficulty. I have not yet inspected the grass in the Tashchenak, but will when Tanai returns. From the road, it appears that there is a lot to be mowed. It will soon be necessary to separate the mowers and rakers, and so the sacks of flour are essential to enable us to cook in two spots. Should I have failed to mention something, Tanai will be able to explain.

In the meantime, I commend myself to your further good will,

Your always devoted Peter Friesen

Tashchenak, Friday noon, 17 June 1832. Answered 18 June.

P.S. A wolf attacked our herd several times at night and last night injured one lamb and possibly took another away. The dogs here are not of much help. Should I give Ullrich money for cutting manure and digging wells? He needs it badly. The well is supposed to cost eight rubles. Perhaps he will come here on Sunday. Trokhim just came, asking for food for the dogs.

279. Johann Cornies to Heinrich Cornies. 30 June 1832. SAOR 89-1-236/27v.[6]

At the end of the month, please pay the mental institution for another month's care for Zimmerman. Payment for this month was made earlier. I have not yet received the elm seeds or the chairs and couches. I heard that you received the letter late, which was brother-in-law

6 Regarding Carl Anton Zimmerman, see footnote 109, and also documents 239, 259, 280, 290, 303, 304, and 362.

Boldt's fault. Please ask Mr. Pritchenko to do me the favour of getting the Latatee root as soon as possible and forward it to me. I would be much obliged.

We harvested only seventy loads of hay on my sheep farm, but more than 200, perhaps even 300 loads, in the Tashchenak. Peter Friesen is working for me, managing the hay harvest at Tashchenak. I had to remove the Russian administrator because of his improper behaviour. How is Johann? Give him my greetings.

We are all well and send many greetings to you, adieu,

Your brother Cornies

P.S. Please send the enclosed letter with the first mail and put the postage on Zimmerman's account.

280. Johann Cornies to Heinrich Cornies. Undated draft letter. SAOR 89-1-236/30v.[7]

Dear Heinrich,

If Peter Reimer has left Ekaterinoslav by the time this letter arrives, please report to me in detail about the death of Carl Anton Zimmerman, on postal paper if possible. Also, let me know which of Zimmerman's effects, by name, were left with you or elsewhere, to enable me to report this incident concretely to his parents. I want to enclose the original you send me. Indicate also the expenses you incurred on his behalf.

If Klaassen's people order something from you, please have them bring along the chairs and couch.

Cornies, with greetings

281. Peter Friesen to Johann Cornies. 5 July 1832. SAOR 89-1-246/85.

Esteemed Mr. Cornies,

When I went through Sorokovii today, I found several people to rake hay, but the rainy weather prevented them from working. They promised to come back when the weather improves. I hope to have twenty rakers for tomorrow. I began raking today, with twenty-four men scything. I lined them up in a row and in this way we were able to do thirty stacks in two hours. Wind scattered much of the hay lying on the sward, but thank God it only rained a little and did not damage

7 Regarding Carl Anton Zimmerman, see footnote 109, and also documents 239, 259, 279, 290, 303, 304, and 362.

the hay. They say that the *Prikazshchik* [District Administrator] leaves tomorrow.

I will move the cutters to the Apollonskii boundary tomorrow where there is regrettably little grass. We already have 100 stacks here in the corner at Besruk and can definitely count on 400. I should note that the stacks are not very large.

As for the rest, I will endeavour to act in accordance with your orders and to remain your devoted,

Peter Friesen

Tashchenak, 5 July 1832

282. Johann Cornies to David Epp, Khortitsa. 7 July 1832. SAOR 89-1-236/33.

Esteemed David Epp in Khortitsa, beloved and valued friend,

I take the liberty of sending you a small number of cocoons, sincerely beloved friend, to have them reeled at four to six threads by a good reeler. Please advance the wages. I would also like to know how the reeler judges the quality of this silk.

Please accept this commission for me, dear friend, and be assured that I will make every effort to return the favour. Striving to remain your honest friend,

Cornies

283. Johann Cornies Jr., Ekaterinoslav, to Johann Cornies. 8 July 1832. SAOR 89-1-246/90.

Most esteemed Father,

I have been studying geography for some time now and need maps. I request that, at the first opportunity, you send me a large school atlas and also one of the small ones, with the supplementary booklet, or even only the large atlas. I have a convenient spot to store it here. I am now using a small atlas borrowed from Mr. Kirilovskii, but it still has the old divisions of 1790 and only includes Europe. I would like to use a more complete atlas of my own.

Enclosed with my sister's letter, received 5 July, was the reply you sent to my letter informing you that my health is now good. Your letter showed me that your mind and dear mother's regarding my illness have been put to rest. I thank God that I am really well and ask Him, who gives us all good things, to grant all of us continuing good health.

I commend myself to you, dearest Mother, and my dear sister, and remain, your devoted son,

Johann Cornies

Ekaterinoslav, 8 July 1832

Received July 15

284. Traugott Blueher to Johann Cornies. 12 July 1832 from Moscow. SAOR 89-1-232/10.

Esteemed friend Cornies,

The forty-three balls of Spanish wool mentioned in your communication arrived in good condition on 3 July. I must note that most of the balls lost some of the given weight en route. I will now make every effort to sell the wool as soon as possible and at the best possible price. I will then report further.

The carters delivered the package with fifty special lamb pelts. Many thanks for this friendly gift.

With heartfelt greetings of love to you and your dear family, I remain your faithful friend,

Traugott Blueher

Received 23 July.

285. Peter Friesen to Johann Cornies. 13 July 1832. SAOR 89-1-233/43.

Most esteemed Mr. Cornies,

I report that the provisions you sent me were received in good order, as were the twenty rubles, and I can also inform you that the harvest is progressing well. Things remain as you left them Saturday.

I continue to have the honour to be your devoted,

Peter Friesen

Tashchenak, 13 July 1832

286. Peter Friesen to Johann Cornies. Undated. SAOR 89-1-230/8.

Most esteemed Mr. Cornies,

Since I met Mr. David Cornies at the local market today, and no further messenger has arrived from you, I am forced to request most urgently that you send me wheat flour and barley porridge as soon as possible. These are almost impossible to get here or the price is much too high. This is what is most needed here for now. I do actually have many more things to ask you and I will do that soon. I have thirty-seven men cutting at two to ten kopeks each.

Commending myself to your good will for now,

Your devoted Peter Friesen

287. Gerhard Martens to Johann Cornies. Halbstadt, 22 July 1832. SAOR 89-1-246/91.

Esteemed Mr. Cornies,

Colonial Inspector Pelekh has graciously authorized me to request that, since they affect you, you sign the enclosed declarations. They are about Semen Sakharov, the Doukhobor who died in June 1831 on Crown lands near Prangenau village. Please return them to the District Office, via the Ohrloff Village Office, by noon tomorrow.

I am also sending package No. 2,321, addressed to the Garden Society, one letter, and your newspapers, all received with the last mail.

With respect, I am your devoted,

Gerhard Martens

Received 23 July 1832.

288. Johann Cornies to Johann Cornies Jr. 26 July 1832. SAOR 89-1-236/37.

My dear son,

I would have sent you the atlas earlier but opportunities to do so are limited at this time of year. God willing, I think I will bring the atlas myself in August. Your dear mother and I were very pleased to receive letters from Mr. Kirilovskii and you, especially since Mr. Kirilovskii is entirely satisfied with you.

Dear son, continue to give your teacher and your parents such joy with your pleasing, resolute character. You will find that circumstances are always better if you behave well and are able to enjoy the love of those around you. We found it no less gratifying to hear that the state counsellor gave you his attention, but do not let such signs of honour make you careless in what you do. Remember that kindness and condescension granted you by such a high person is unearned and is worthy of your esteem. If you complete everything assigned to you punctually, you will give yourself and your parents respect and joy.

Our respectful greetings to Mr. Kirilovskii and his wife, and also to your uncle and aunt. Take good care of yourself and keep God before you and in your heart.

289. Johann Cornies to Johann Wiebe. 29 July 1832. SAOR 89-1-236/35v.

Very dear friend, Johann Wiebe,

I received your gratifying letter on 18 July. I can now inform you about the future settlement of Mennonites from abroad on the parcel of land in the Melitopol Uezd. After extensive presentations by our Guardianship administration, His Majesty the Tsar confirmed that all still unoccupied parts of the 35,000 desiatinas of land intended for Mennonite settlement must be reserved for them, specifically, for 270 families immigrating from abroad, and for 270 young local families. We need not fear that this land will be given to people from elsewhere. We must conclude that only a further 270 families will be permitted to settle in Russia.

I am humbled by your favour in responding to my letters, most valued Mr. Wiebe, and I wonder what I might have done to deserve your willingness to leave your parent's home and to make a sea voyage on my behalf. I am humbled and gratified by your attitude. May God bless you and your dear parents and family. At present, I can say nothing more about the matter in question. If I do not buy more land this summer, I will be happy to make use of your offer, but my son would not go along. He is living with the Committee's translator in Ekaterinoslav for a year or two. Peter Friesen is back in my service, managing my newly purchased khutor. Nothing has changed in Ohrloff and everyone would send greetings if they knew that I was writing to you.

Very little hay was harvested this year. Had I not bought a khutor at the mouth of the Molochnaia I would be in a very tight spot for livestock fodder. The harvest is almost over and the grain is mediocre. Wool generated high prices: forty to forty-five rubles per pud of washed wool. Generally, wheat sold for up to sixteen rubles, rye for six to seven rubles, butter very cheaply.

Do not be offended if I ask you to order the enclosed list of books from the bookseller Ambrosius Barth, Grimmaischestrasse, Leipzig. Send them along with travellers or immigrants, not in packages but in single volumes to make their transportation easier. Please advance the money for me in the short term and make suitable freight arrangements, informing me of the costs right away.

I send friendly greetings to you and your dear relatives, and remain, with honesty, your true friend and servant,
Johann Cornies

1. *Polens letzte Anstrengungen fuer Nationalitaet und europaeische Freiheit* [Poland's Latest Efforts to Attain its Independence and European Freedom], Ilmenau, by Dr. Ungewitter, costs one and one-third Rthlr.

2. *Conversations-Lexicon der neuesten Zeit und Literatur, oder ein Supplement Band zu allen fruehern Auflagen* [Encyclopedia of Modern Times and Literature, or a Supplement to all Earlier Editions]. Appears as booklets of eight sheets, all good writing paper, costing eight Groshen each. The complete edition will include twenty to twenty-five issues and will be complete in one year's time. Leipzig, March 1832, Brockhaus.

290. Johann Cornies to Heinrich van Steen. 29 July 1832. SAOR 89-1-236/34.[8]

Mr. Heinrich van Steen, treasured friend,

From my letter of 30 June, you will have gathered what the situation was that forced me to send your son to the hospital in Ekaterinoslav on 15 May. I awaited your further decision.

On 5 July, however, I received the sad news from my friend in Ekaterinoslav that your son had drowned on 28 June while bathing in the Dnieper. His good behaviour in the institution had permitted him various freedoms, including the right to bathe alone at his request. Usually the patients are bathed individually by a person assigned for this purpose. Within view of this person, your son went into the water to his waist, submerged himself and did not reappear. It is assumed that he was overcome by cramps or a stroke.

The institution's inspector and doctors agree and assure me that Zimmerman did not intend to drown himself. His behaviour was calm and cheerful until the very last moment, so it is unlikely that he sought his own death. Enclosed is a document from my brother in Ekaterinoslav to authorize me to handle your son's belongings as you desire.

God's thoughts are not our thoughts and neither are His ways. In such difficult and shocking cases we must seek comfort in the blessed assurance that what God does is always done well. In hurriedly sending you

8 Regarding van Steen's step-son, Carl Anton Zimmerman, see footnote 109, and also documents 239, 259, 279, 280, 303, 304, and 362.

this brief report, I request an early communication as to what should be done with his effects. I will act accordingly and will also send you the account for expenses that I have incurred on his behalf.

With friendly greetings, I respectfully remain your friend and servant,
Cornies

291. Johann Cornies Jr. to Johann Cornies. 5 September 1832. SAOR 89-1-225/5.

Most esteemed Father,

You are aware that on August 28 I left with the state counsellor on his travels. After visiting several villages in the Khortitsa District, where I was pleased to get the news of your recovery, I returned safely on 31 August. I pray to the giver of all blessings for your continued good health.

My sister is still in good spirits and spends her time sewing and tending to little Heinrich, who is quite cheerful again, but still unable to walk on his own. If it is not too much trouble, please send the cloth for the jacket soon. I think I can have it made up here more quickly and cheaply before the yearly market begins. Uncle's oil mill will be ready any day now. There is a great demand for oils that are fresher and cheaper than those now available on the market.

My uncle and aunt, as well as my dear sister and I send hearty greetings to you, to dearest Mother, and to Grandmother. We long to hear of your safe arrival. Is dear Uncle P. Cornies still suffering from fever?

Adieu. Your loving son,
Johann Cornies
Ekaterinoslav, 5 September 1832

292. Johann Cornies Jr. to Johann Cornies. 11 September 1832. SAOR 89-1-225/1.

Sincerely beloved Father,

I received your treasured letter of 7 September and obediently seek to fulfil your wishes.

At his invitation, I accompanied the State Counsellor on his visits. He refused to accept my protest that my coming along would be troublesome, and assured me that my presence could be of some help. You will have gathered from my letter of 5 September that the trip was a pleasant one.

The state counsellor travelled through the village of Hamburg, where we spent the night with Klaas. I visited several houses with him, all quite clean. The village has several wealthy householders and we examined a number of orchards and a good mulberry plantation. The second night, the State Counsellor stayed in Khortitsa with P. Siemens, while I went to G. Penner's. He inspected the Rosenthal plantation, which has a few old fruit trees and many newly planted trees. Most of it, however, is still uncultivated. They have sold only sixty-four rubles of fruit. We took our noon meal at the home of District Chairman Bartsch. Later the state counsellor was shown several samples of silk. Pauls, of Kronsweide, has produced the largest amount of silk this year. In the afternoon, we travelled to Burwalde. The state counsellor then inspected the forested areas of Rosenthal village that were weeded and attractive. After spending the night in Khortitsa, again with P. Siemens, we returned via Einlage and examined the work of weaver Neufeldt. He intends to experiment with silk to see if it would fetch a higher price when worked over. Afterwards the state counsellor visited J. Penner, taking Mr. Hausknecht along with him. We then continued through Kronsweide, where the state counsellor dropped in on the Pauls to inspect the local mulberry plantation. He then proceeded straight to Neuenburg, where the Harders prepared a noon meal for us. From here, the state counsellor drove straight through to Ekaterinoslav without any further stops.

Heinrich Lepp and Johann Sukau left on Tuesday, 13 September, after spending three days here. They were delayed because of their passes. I was as helpful to them as I could be.

My health is still good, for which I thank the Almighty. I pray to Him for your well-being and that of dear Mother and Grandmother. I will strive to remain always, your son who loves you,

Joh. Cornies

Ekaterinoslav, 11 September 1832

293. Johann Cornies to Andrei M. Fadeev. 14 September 1832. SAOR 89-1-236/39v.

Yr. Honour,

I report the receipt of Nos. 5, 6, and 7 of the field cultivation journal, the agricultural newspaper for the months from October to February, and a book with descriptions and instructions about artesian wells. At Yr. Honour's request, I forwarded the agricultural newspaper to the Molochnaia Mennonite District Office and the book to Gerhard Dyck, Rudnerweide. The field cultivation journals were given to the local garden society, entered into its catalogue, and shelved in its library.

With the deepest respect, I am honoured to be Yr. Honour's devoted servant,
Cornies

294. Johann Klaassen to Johann Cornies. 16 September 1832. SAOR 89-1-332/59.

Very valued friend,

In response to your letter of 15 September, I write to inform you that two pieces of first quality cloth are on the loom and are being finished. One will be blue, the other black. I cannot yet give you a definite date for their completion. The blue can be finished more quickly. Cloth must be stretched up to 150 times, worked as many as fifty times, dipped five times into two or three rinses, and then stretched again. Good blue cloth will be ready by the end of the month at ten rubles per arshin, but it is not made of first quality wool.

Once the shearing machine is working and providing good service, work will move along more quickly. The machine left Moscow only on 12 August. Johann Schroeder, Josephstal, mounted it satisfactorily and delivered it to me on 12 September. He visited Mr. Blueher and his store a few times, and was received in a friendly manner wherever he went. He was told that your wool had sold for 55 R.B.A. per pud.

Gross' daughter visited the pastor secretly Tuesday morning without the permission of her parents. They were supposed to have been engaged the following day but have yet to reveal anything to her parents. The Deputy is not at home. I was in Tokmak most of Tuesday and Wednesday.

Friendly greetings to you and your dear wife from your loving, obliged brother,
Joh. Klaassen
Halbstadt, 16 September 1832

295. Johann Cornies to Andrei M. Fadeev. 19 September 1832. SAOR 89-1-236/39v.

The Forestry Society has submitted report No. 245 regarding the Committee's investigation of two individuals who deliberately grazed horses in the forest-tree plantations. At its 12 September meeting, the Society decided to punish the two, keeping in mind the need to prevent similar thoughtless actions in future. I would request that Yr. Honour kindly permit the punishment to be carried out by the local District Office before bad weather sets in and prevents completion of the work decided upon as punishment in the village plantations and on the community sheep farm.

296. Johann Cornies to Johann Cornies Jr. 27 September 1832. SAOR 89-1-236/40.

Dear son, Johann Cornies,

The interesting contents of your letter of 16 September gave me much pleasure. Continue your efforts and give us more joy, my son. I spoke with Johann Klaassen, Halbstadt, about good cloth for your coat, as you requested. A piece of fine cloth should be ready in three weeks' time. So be patient. I will forward it to you as soon as possible.

Dirk Wiens, who is married to your mother's niece, arrived from Prussia eight days ago. He is living in Blumenort for now and will be arriving soon in Ekaterinoslav to fetch trees for the Society. Please ask your Uncle H. Cornies to receive Wiens well and not to take anything from him for lodgings and fodder. Without letting Wiens know, he should put the costs on my account. Wiens is namely a poor man.

I can report that we are healthy and well. I, your mother, and Agnes send you our greetings and commend you to the care of God. Adieu. Your loving father,

Johann Cornies

P.S. I received the enclosed letter from Jacob Wiebe, a nephew of Johann Wiebe in Thiege, Prussia. He was once engaged to Johann Sukau's mother. You met him in autumn. A few days ago, his brother in Ladekopp hanged himself and no one knows why. I have left the little package in paper until you visit us.

297. Johann Cornies to District Office. 30 September 1832. SAOR 89-1-236/41.

To the esteemed District Office in Halbstadt,

The District Office is requested to kindly inform the village communities that a new shipment of German Bibles and New Testaments has arrived in the local Bible depot. They can be purchased from me at any time. The Bibles sell for six rubles, the Testaments for two rubles, twenty [kopeks].

With due respect, I have the honour to be the District Office's obedient,
Johann Cornies

298. Johann Cornies to Heinrich Cornies. 2 October 1832. SAOR 89-1-236/41v.

Dear brother Heinrich Cornies,

I request that you accept a commission from the Society to supervise the digging and packing of trees from the plantation, to the extent that your affairs permit. If the Society fails to delegate someone to do this work it may end up being done sloppily. It should not take too much of your time. Simply present the letter to the Chief Judge, explaining that you have taken on the commission, and ask him to write a few lines to the garden inspector authorizing the latter to release the trees.

Speak with Mr. Hummel to be sure he gives you a specific number of good trees. Ensure that there are least 1,000 trees, because the cost of each is then only half as much. Do not pay for the trees. The Society will mail the money as has been reported to the Chief Judge. Negotiate the amount with the inspector to make sure the accounts agree and have him write a brief note to the Society. My gardener Wilke left yesterday to fetch trees, but I completely forgot to tell him that if forest trees were not released to him, he should apply to Mr. Pritchenko, who has authority over the forest. Please get permission from Pritchenko to dig trees. I trust you will know best how to do these things and not resent my commissions. Adieu.

Cornies

P.S. The enclosed letter, which you must present to the Chief Judge personally, informs him that the Society has delegated this business to you, and requests that he kindly provide you with a communication for the garden inspector to release the trees.

299. Johann Cornies Jr. to Johann Cornies. 5 October 1832. SAOR 89-1-225/11.

I find it painful to report that my fever has come back, but not in so severe a form as to put me back in bed. I hope, if it is God's will, to recover soon with the help of the doctor. I have had only two incidents, one yesterday and one today, and have taken medicine.

Gardener Wilke arrived here Sunday, 2 October, and intends to leave Friday, 7 October. Yesterday, rain delayed his work for half a day. Dirk and Heinrich Wiens arrived here yesterday evening.

May you fare well. I send greetings to you and to dearest Mother, and remain your son who loves you,

Johann Cornies

Ekaterinoslav, 5 October 1832. Received 8 October 1832.

300. Casper Adrian Hausknecht, Einlage, to Johann Cornies. 24 October 1832. SAOR 89-1-223/18.

Honoured friend,

We have not written to one another recently because we are both busy with our daily work and have no interest in exchanging little sayings and verses as though we were children. However, if I can be of service to you and your house, I will gladly do what I can. I think that you think as I do and that I do not deceive myself or insult you in saying so.

The reason for this letter is that I need your help. I have bought a small flock of eighteen sheep. I would ask you to give me a loan of 200 rubles silver for two years in return for my signed obligation, at the usual interest rate of 6 per cent.

Can you do this? Will you do it? It would be a most agreeable service for me, since I cannot expect capital funds in this sum from home at an earlier date. David Epp, Khortitsa, would bring me the money when he returns. Think it over, do your calculations, and be assured of my devoted love and friendship.

Your fellow pilgrim,

C.A. Hausknecht

301. Johann Cornies to Khariton T. Pelekh. 2 November 1832. SAOR 89-1-236/43.

Yr. Honour, Inspector of Colonies Pelekh,

At midnight I had the honour to receive Yr. Honour's esteemed communication dated 1 November 1832. I would willingly go to the Tashchenak on 4 November, or even the 5th or 7th, in response to Yr. suggestion that I lay out the projected settlement on site.

I am, however, already entangled in business here. Please permit me to explain, my dear Sir. On 5 November, the monthly meeting of the Society takes place. Monday, 7 November, has been assigned to plantation inspections and these will take three or four days. But after this, I am at your service.

For these reasons, I obediently request that you put off the work to another time, and kindly inform me of this during the next days so that I might arrange my business affairs accordingly.

With all respect, I have the honour to be Yr. Honour's most obedient servant.

302. Johann Cornies to Peter Reimer. 11 November 1832. SAOR 89-1-236/43.

My very dear, faithful friend, Peter Reimer,

I was short of time and could not answer your communication of 23 August earlier. I also expected to see the two men mentioned in your letter, Walther and Wurzi. I would gladly help you improve your community watermill by having a master miller from here move to you there. But no good, methodical master miller will move to your community, and a bad one will be of no help. Despite my best intentions, I can therefore be of no assistance to you.

The Bibles and Testaments were packed and charged to your account, but no one dropped by to pick them up. In time I became so preoccupied with my own business that I did not write. Even today I am doing it in haste. Please do not be offended by my brevity.

Your Warkentin died in early September and I am returning the letter you sent him. We have had a dry summer – the hay did poorly, and the grain only moderately well. I hope you can be useful to the community there, and you will be, even if you cannot see or enjoy the fruits of your efforts immediately. Everything has its time. Do not despair. Roses grow among thorns. May you live well with God, and may you receive a thousand greetings from me.

Adieu. Your friend who wishes you well,

Johann Cornies

303. Johann Cornies to Wilhelm Frank. 25 November 1832. SAOR 89-1-236/47.[9]

Honoured Mr. Frank,

I received a letter from my friend in Danzig, the merchant Mr. Heinrich van Steen. As you know, his step-son, Carl Anton Zimmerman,

9 Regarding Carl Anton Zimmerman, see footnote 109, and also documents 239, 259, 279, 280, 290, 304, and 362.

was considered to be feeble-minded and brought to the Christian Benevolent Institution in Ekaterinoslav last spring. He drowned in the Dnieper while bathing.

I immediately informed his parents about the incident. I now urgently request a death certificate from the institute or whatever other appropriate source. The Prussian government requires that my friend, Heinrich van Steen (Zimmerman's step-father) produce a death certificate from the Ekaterinoslav authorities as soon as possible. It must be signed and stamped by the nearest Royal Prussian consul with the Royal Prussian seal.

I am anxious to provide my friend van Steen with the means to satisfy the Prussian government's demands and to keep him from being forced into an even more difficult situation. I turn to you, honoured Mr. Frank, and urgently request your advice. How can I acquire the death certificate and how can it be certified by the Prussian consul? If it is not too much trouble, please request Zimmerman's death certificate from the Ekaterinoslav authorities, have it certified by the Prussian consul, and forward it to me in order that I can send it along to Danzig. I will pay your expenses with my best thanks. Please let me know about this matter by return mail, and charge the postage to my account.

Please do not take offence at this interruption, but I would be greatly in your debt if you could comply with my request. I remain, with honest respect and esteem, your brother and friend who is willing to be of service,

J. Cornies

304. Johann Cornies to Heinrich Cornies. 25 November 1832. SAOR 89-1-236/48.

Dear brother Heinrich Cornies,

Your letter of 17 November informs us that my son Johann is ill and confined to bed. As parents, we are relieved to hear that the illness is not dangerous. Please let us know if he is staying with you or has his lodgings with Mr. Kirilovskii. Is he eating properly, which is the best medicine for good health? Is he taking medicine? Kindly report these matters to me and let us know if his condition is improving or getting worse. Charge the postage to my account.

Please ask friend Johann Neufeld to inquire on my behalf about the location of the late Zimmerman's grave.[10] This will enable me to fulfill his parent's wishes that the grave be properly marked when I next visit Ekaterinoslav. And please, when you can, have the late Zimmerman's belongings aired and sent to me, with a list.

With thanks for your many labours of love, we wish your dear wife and our son a speedy recovery. And please, if it does not involve too much of your time, let me know about your oil press. Specifically, how many chetverts of seeds, or how many pails of oil, can be prepared in a day? How many pails, in total, have been produced since the beginning? What are the average earnings in a day, or what is left after you deduct the labour and other costs?

Our daughter Agnes is sick with a cold, but seems to be improving. Old Mrs. F. Wieb was buried last Saturday. Winter has arrived with temperatures of ten to twenty-two degrees, sharp winds, but no snow. The weather is damaging to winter grain and gives little hope for the coming rye harvest. Livestock can graze well wherever pastures remain. I came from Tashchenak yesterday, where everything had been well prepared for the winter season. The barns can hold all of my livestock. I assume you have no information about the Rode land and do not know whether it will soon be sold. Mr. Pritchenko would probably have the best information in this regard.

I await news about my son's condition. I send hearty greetings from all of us to you and to my son. Please report my situation to him. May God keep you well. I am and remain, as always, your brother who loves you,

Cornies

305. Johann Cornies Jr., Ekaterinoslav, to Johann Cornies. 2 December 1832. SOAR 89-1-225/7.

Most treasured Father,

My letter of 25 November should have reassured you about my illness. I write these lines to let you and my dearest Mother know that I have recovered.

---

10 Regarding Carl Anton Zimmerman, see footnote 109, and also documents 239, 259, 279, 280, 290, 303, and 362.

Yesterday, 1 December, I began lessons with Mr. Haustek, two hours per day in the company of other pupils, except for Sundays and holidays. I pay twelve rubles per month. I will inquire how this money should be paid and report to you soon.

I did not buy the caps ordered for Peter Enns because they are not very good and cost four rubles, which is likely too expensive. The weather is cold. Quite a bit of snow fell this week.

I hope the dear Lord keeps all of you in good health. Little Heinrich is ill in the H. Cornies family. Heartfelt greetings to you and dearest Mother. I constantly strive to be your son who loves you with an unfeigned heart,

Johann Cornies

Mr. Frank spent about two rubles for the newspapers. He did not want to take money from me.

306. Andrei M. Fadeev to Johann Cornies. 2 December 1832. SAOR 89-1-232/1.

I was in Khortitsa on business recently and decided to take your son along with me, especially because of the holidays. He was able to familiarize himself with conditions there. I am very satisfied with him, but think that you would be well advised to have him learn more mathematics and some drawing from Haustek in autumn and during the winter. This could prove very useful to him in future.

I need concrete information about field cultivation in the Mennonite villages and request your answers to the questions below. You do not need to rush.

Your devoted Fadeev

1. Do the local Mennonites divide all their cultivated fields into three parts, or do some follow another method, and which specifically?
2. How are crops other than the grains rotated on these fields?
3. Which colonies have been manuring their fields and which have not, and with which manure? Is this always done in the same way, or does it vary according to the nature of the soil?
4. How do Mennonite implements for cultivation differ from those used locally by Russians? To what extent are they really more useful?
5. Does everyone grow his own seed-grain or do they obtain seed elsewhere?

Received 3 January 1833.

307. Johann Cornies to Dyck. 7 December 1832. SAOR 89-1-236/51.

Honoured Mrs. Dyck, Schardau,

Your son Johann arrived here Monday evening, the day before yesterday. He is well. We will now see what can be made of him. As a human being and as a Christian, it is close to my heart to do my utmost for his education, even without your justified motherly urgings. I can assure you that I will not neglect anything that would contribute to his future well-being. You may be confident of this. Please forgive me for not fetching him on St. Martin's Day. I simply had too much business to do at the time.

May you fare well. Friendly greetings from me and my wife. With esteem, I remain your friend and servant,

Cornies

308. Johann Cornies to Wilhelm Frank. 15 December 1832. SAOR 89-1-236/54.

Honoured Mr. Frank,

I must again acknowledge the help you have given me and send you my heartfelt thanks. Please note the payment of four rubles on my account. I will repay the debt when I next have the pleasure of visiting you in Ekaterinoslav. The petition to the Committee was prepared on the basis of the draft you sent me and I know you will promote this matter as quickly as you possibly can. At the moment I have nothing further to say, except to report our well-being and to commend myself to your understanding concern, with lively memories of our old friendship, which, as the proverb says, does not grow rusty. With feelings of respect and esteem, I remain, your devoted,

—

P.S. I am half intending to buy the late Mrs. Rode's estate near Ekaterinoslav when it is available, if it is not too expensive. Do you know when it will be sold? Please inquire about this matter and let me know, but do keep my intentions to yourself.

I must sadly report on developments in the German colony of Madshar on the Kuma River in the Caucasus guberniia. On 24 October, while the German men were working their fields, thirty-five Circassian men abducted eleven German children and one woman in broad daylight, shot Pastor Koenig through the arm and robbed him of all his property, killed a Russian and an Armenian merchant, and took off with three Armenians and a Kalmyk child.

309. Johann Cornies to Khariton T. Pelekh. 15 December 1832. SAOR 89-1-236/55.

Mr. Khariton Trokhimovich Pelekh, Inspector of Colonies,

Yr. Honour will kindly permit me to report that wells were opened for colonists in Orta Otluk ravine, close to the Tashchenak ridge on the land assigned for settlement. Unless it has been decided to dig these wells further, they should be closed or covered with boards and mounded earth to prevent accidents. I do not wish to be held responsible for accidents. May God protect us from them. Since I hold the lease to this land, I would be blamed for any accidents. I know that Yr. Honour is overwhelmed by many business matters, but I draw your attention to the urgency of this matter.

Counting on Yr. Honour's love of good order, I have the honour to be, respectfully and with esteem, Yr. Honour's most obedient servant,

Cornies

310. Johann Cornies to Andrei M. Fadeev. 16 December 1832. SAOR 89-1-236/57.

Mr. State Counsellor Fadeev,

Yr. Honour, I take pleasure in reporting to you the arrival today of two apprentices selected by the Mariupol District Office to learn about the breeding of Spanish sheep. I must point out that these apprentices are only fifteen or sixteen years of age and cannot be expected to acquire in three years the knowledge essential to the breeding and refinement of sheep. To judge from their appearance, they seem capable of learning, but they are not of an age to evaluate correctly what essentials must be learned. I assure Yr. Honour that I will make every effort to teach the above-mentioned apprentices about Spanish sheep breeding so that they might eventually be employed as capable shepherds, to the advantage of their community.

With the most perfect respect, I consider it my greatest pleasure to act according to Yr. noble intentions, and to consider myself as Yr. Honour's assiduous and obedient servant,

Cornies

311. Johann Cornies to Johann Cornies Jr. 22 December 1832. SAOR 89-1-236/58.

Beloved son Johann Cornies,

All your reports fill me with great joy, except for the news of 15 December that your fever had returned. I hope that, if you stick to a regular diet and restrict yourself to moderate exercise, your fever, with God's help, will soon disappear. Be careful not to take too much medicine, since, by weakening your stomach or some other organ, it may cure one problem only to cause another. I also advise you, for now, not to overexert yourself. Proceed as if you still had several years to learn the essentials. Dress properly, take several walks a day in the fresh air, but do not walk quickly. Protect your feet from the cold and especially from moisture. Wash your body with French brandy now and then since it strengthens the nerves and prevents negative effects of the weather.

I reported to the state counsellor that the juniper berries were received in good order. I enclosed the following:

1. One hundred rubles for the January quarter for Mr. Kirilovskii. I request a few lines from him.

2. Twelve funt butter in a barrel for Mr. Kirilovskii.

3. Ten funt butter in a pot for Mr. Haustek.

4. One barrel marked F. in chalk, with twelve funt butter and a cheese for Madame Fadeev.

5. The slate you requested, one shirt, four undershirts, and three neckerchiefs.

Write to me if these things were received in good order and give my respectful compliments to Mr. Kirilovskii and Mr. Haustek.

Thank God, everyone is healthy here. We still have no snow, but the frost is sharp, down to eighteen and a half degrees today. The plantations will probably force me to visit Ekaterinoslav again this winter. The cattle plague has broken out with such force in Felsenthal, Wernersdorf, Schoensee, and Tokmak that not one head of cattle survives, although it seems to have struck only individual hearth sites in the villages mentioned. If you have time and your health permits, please buy me a large, blue inkstand of the type owned by Teacher Heese.

Many loving greetings to you from me, your mother, and sister. We wish you well. Keep God in your sight and in your heart. Your father who loves you,

Johann Cornies

312. Johann Cornies to Heinrich Cornies. 22 December 1832. SAOR 89-1-236/59v.

Dear brother Heinrich,

I have nothing to report, but am asking you to kindly buy the items listed below, if circumstances permit:

1. Four individual green, thin, but large (Mechina) calf-leathers to be filled for beds, of the type that Johann sent me.

2. Six bottles of the best rum.

3. One chest bound with iron, like the one you bought for Agnes in autumn. I would prefer a larger one.

My wife sends you ten funt butter, including the pot as a gift. Please report in detail about your efforts with the oil processing mill. We wish all of you a happy Christmas and New Years. Greetings for your ever loving family.

Your honest brother,

Cornies

313. Johann Cornies to District Office. 24 December 1832. SAOR 89-1-236/60.

In response to the District Office communication No. 351, of 17 December, I have the honour to send specific accounts for the capital sum of 24,135 [rubles] borrowed from me by the community treasury on 15 October 1827, at 6 per cent interest annually. The loan was to purchase Saxon breeding sheep and rams. I have received 300 R.B.A., entered at the top of the account, which can be deducted from the 5,701 rubles.

With respect, the honoured District Office's devoted,

Johann Cornies

314. Johann Cornies to Andrei M. Fadeev. 30 December 1832. SAOR 89-1-236/60.

Mr. State Counsellor Fadeev,

I was happy to receive Yr. Honour's commission sent to me on 6 December instructing me to investigate whether 1,000 puds of wool like the enclosed sample could be purchased in this region. I must report that this variety of wool is not available in this region, especially not in large quantities. Spanish sheep breeding here has been conducted for twenty to twenty-four years, since the time when highly bred rams were first introduced into our flocks. Wool has been improved to such an extent that sheep with such wool as you describe are no longer found here. The Nogais have also improved their sheep to a considerable degree of fineness, so that coarse wool of this kind is not available there either, though a few individuals with such wool can occasionally be found. These are hardly worth mentioning, I know, since a large quantity of wool is needed.

I should explain that the Nogais and similar local peasants have never used common Nogai and Russian stock for breeding Spanish sheep. To obtain wool that sells at a better grade than common Russian wool, five or six years are required to produce second and third generation Nogai and Russian sheep mated with Spanish rams. These people generally lack the necessary patience and perseverance as well as the elementary knowledge to practise improved Spanish sheep breeding methodically. They therefore buy improved sheep from their neighbours, the German colonists. Only a few years ago, such sheep could be purchased for the same price as the common Russian sheep and immediately, with the first shearing, demonstrated their superiority. Hence, the acquisition of such [mixed breeds] freed Nogais of the need to undertake the long business of improving their own common Russian sheep.

As Yr. Honour correctly notes, two fleeces of wool from old merino sheep, at this time of the year, would still be too few to prove anything. Only in April and May does the young grass speed up the development of wool on the backs of sheep to half a vershok and more a month. Only such wool can provide a dependable sample. I would find it a privilege to provide several fleeces from genuine merino sheep to serve as such dependable samples.

I cannot be of service to Yr. Honour regarding the local price of goat hair. Goats are abundant here, but I cannot obtain any information as to whether their hair is shorn, combed or sold.

Camel hair or wool can be bought in considerable quantities from the Nogais in the Dneprov uezds, and around Perekop, Evpatoria, and Feodosia. The selling price is twenty to twenty-four rubles per pud and, in my opinion, 1,000 puds of this hair or wool could be obtained. The wool is sheared or plucked from early May to mid-June.

In our district, the cattle plague has broken out in the villages Wernersdorf and Schoensee, but only in a few places. It spreads swiftly. Generally, wherever it appears, no animals survive. It is also said to have broken out in Tokmak. The District Office has taken preventive measures to restrict the spread of the disease, but I think it would be desirable for the Committee to send strict orders to the District Office to implement more and stricter measures in this regard.

I wrote to Germany last 29 July to order the books Yr. Honour requested, but have not received an answer. I will presumably not get one before the books arrive, which could well be delayed until September, when immigrants from Prussia get here.

With the arrival of the New Year, I take the liberty of devotedly thanking Yr. Honour for the benevolence you have shown me over the past year. I commend myself to your further grace. May the Almighty grant Yr. Honour many years of undisturbed health, uninterrupted prosperity, and other pleasures and blessings. Standing under your fatherly supervision and leadership, we thank Yr. Honour for many of the agreeable conditions we have benefited from and the joys we experience.

I am especially moved by feelings of gratitude to Yr. Honour, as my son's magnanimous benefactor, for your concern about his education and progress. I cherish the hope that my son will adequately value Yr. Honour's benevolence and make every effort to appear worthy of Yr. Honour's gracious good will. May Yr. kind support of my son continue and progress. At the same time, may Yr. Honour permit a father to dutifully assure you that he will never cease to be Yr. Honour's thankful, obedient servant,

Cornies

1833

**315. Forestry Society to the Lichtenau Village Office.
3 January 1833. SAOR 89-1-251/3.**

This is an order to the Village Office to truthfully inform the Society by 5 January of the reasons why the Lichtenau village community did not follow several official orders to deep-plough its forest-tree locations last summer, as the other villages have done.

**316. Molochnaia Mennonite District Office to Johann Cornies.
5 January 1833. SAOR 89-1-258/9.**

To honourable Johann Cornies in Ohrloff,

At your request, we hereby sent ten copies of the general agricultural paper and ten copies of the German gardening paper. Once you have read them, please return them to us so that they might be sent to other householders with similar interests.

District Chairman Regier

Returned 5 November 1835.

**317. Johann Cornies to Peter Orens Draisma. 8 January 1833.
SAOR 89-1-276/3.**

Mr. Draisma, beloved friend,

I received your letter of 26 December 1832 and your poems today, and hasten to respond immediately to your request. The situation is as follows. First, filling the position under discussion cannot be postponed, much less can it be left open for a year. The alternative is to leave it occupied as it now is, and to fill the other one by April. Everything must be completely in order by April of this year. If you would like to take the first position, then you must respond with a firm and final yes, planted like a foundation on which you can build.

You have understood correctly that the community cannot give you an advance on your salary and this would not be good for you, even if it could. Otherwise, the respect and esteem a school teacher requires would suffer. I offer you an advance myself, up to 400 rubles, if you need that much, without interest, repayable in three years. This will demonstrate that your appointment is a serious matter. If nothing else keeps you from going there, take the position and commend yourself to God.

I am going to Ekaterinoslav in two or three days. When I return, I hope to find your written reply with your decision. We often fail to notice how quickly time passes by for it is a precious thing and cannot be turned back and must be taken advantage of. This you and I both must remember.

With greetings, I remain your true friend and servant,
Johann Cornies

318. Forestry Society to Ladekopp Village Office. 9 January 1833. SAOR 89-1-251/3.

To Ladekopp Village Office,

The Office is hereby explicitly instructed to ensure that cottager Heinrich Thiessen promptly fulfil his responsibilities on the cottage site he assumed from the Society on 20 December 1832:

1. By spring or earlier, Thiessen must dig a ditch on his border with Wiens, five fut wide and four fut deep.

2. A genuine fence in line with other fences and hedges along the street must be in place in April, when a member of the Ekaterinoslav Committee will inspect the villages.

3. Fruit tree beds must be prepared first thing in spring, to make it possible to plant fruit trees in autumn. The beds must have the prescribed width and depth for six apple trees plus the required number of kernel fruit trees planted between the apple trees.

If Thiessen is negligent in fulfilling his obligations, and if the Village Office has to reprove him repeatedly, the matter should be reported to the Society in detail.

319. Forestry Society to Andrei M. Fadeev. 10 January 1833. SAOR 89-1-251/5v.

Mr. Fadeev,

The Society has the honour to submit a list of fullholders in this District itemizing how much land of their half-desiatina plots in the forest-tree plantation has been deep-ploughed by each, and to what depth. It must also report why some fullholders have deep-ploughed little or no land.

A further list is included of the quantity of forest-tree seed, by weight and variety, that fullholders have again gathered up from their own forest trees and planted. Also listed are the quantity and kind of forest-tree seeds fullholders have sent to the Society in 1831 and 1832, and distributed to the local forest-tree plantations.

320. Forestry Society to Lichtenau and Lindenau village offices. 11 January 1833. SAOR 89-1-251/6.

Lichtenau and Lindenau village offices,

Upon receipt of this notice, village mayors and their deputies are required to sign their village afforestation plans at once and to return them with this messenger. This must be done promptly.

321. Guardianship Committee to District Office. 20 January 1833. SAOR 89-1-258/1.

Directive No. 26, Community Library:

Regulations issued several years ago by the late Extraordinary Member of the Guardianship Committee, Acting State Counsellor Contenius, and drawn to his attention in 1833, require him to order the *Hallische Wirtschaftszeitung* [Halle Agricultural Newspaper] for residents of the Molochnaia Mennonite District. This publication will help inform residents of new developments (newly publicized discoveries, comments, and discussions) in rural agriculture in Germany. When a secure opportunity arises, the paper should be forwarded to the treasurer and executive of the Molochnaia Mennonite District Office. The District Office should draw the attention of village offices and well-meaning householders in the District to informative articles contained in it. Articles marked by the Chief Judge should be read attentively. At the end of each year, the newspapers should be preserved in the community library and lent to dependable settlers inclined towards useful improvements. To this end, forty-seven rubles, including mailing charges, should be transferred from the District treasury to the Committee treasury without delay.

Identical in meaning with the original, translator Frank.

Received 27 January 1833. Forty-seven rubles sent to Committee with report No. 91, January 1833.

322. Peter Orens Draisma to Johann Cornies. 20 January 1833. SAOR 89-1-259/10.

Valued Mr. Cornies,

I have just received your esteemed letter and, since the mail is about to leave, hasten to reply. My decision is firm, valued Mr. Cornies. I will gladly move to the Mennonites on the Desna if you are prepared to help me with the offered loan of 400 rubles. Nothing here ties me down. With God's help, I hope to be able to administer my new position with zeal, to both my superior's satisfaction and to yours.

Dear Mr. Cornies, since I need information before I depart for the area in question, I must ask you the following questions:

1. Am I to sign the contract with the community or with the Committee, and must it be concluded for several years?

2. Does the community already have a school or does a school still have to be established? What subjects are to be taught? What is the relationship between teacher and parents, especially in regard to attendance? Does the teacher have any influence over what the children are taught at home?

3. Must the secretary be able to express himself in Russian? If so, I do not qualify because I cannot do this at all. What are the secretary's duties generally?

4. Would the journey be at my expense or will the community reimburse me? How will my salary be paid – through a collection from the community, or from the community treasury?

5. When would I have to start? My term here ends only on 1 May 1833. I am not permitted to leave earlier without authorization from the Committee.

I await your kind answer, dear Mr. Cornies, with the first mail. I give you my word that I will move to the new location. This is irrevocable. I will not withdraw unless something beyond my control is to happen. I am convinced that I can depend on you in this new position, and I will try to show my life-long thanks to you for your good intentions. May the Lord keep you and your valued family.

Expecting a very early answer, I have the honour to be, with all respect, your devoted servant,

P.O. Draisma

Grunau, 20 January 1833

323. Peter Reimer, Radichev, to Johann Cornies. 21 January 1833. SAOR 89-1-259/7.

Most esteemed friend,

I take this pleasant opportunity to send you my heartiest wishes for a happy New Year. May the dear Lord bless you and give you success in all of your many useful activities. May He grant you good health and perseverance.

This letter is delivered to you by one of my best friends, a faithful, honest man whom you can trust. He is Benjamin Decker, Deputy Chairman in our Village Office, who is travelling to visit his mother and wishes to speak to you about several subjects of concern to him. Please grant him your confidence, which he deserves.

I thank God that I enjoy personal prosperity and bear life's burdens patiently, with God's help. As you may have heard, my desire for a closer personal relationship has come to nothing, but I will endure and this may even be my good fortune. My business affairs are progressing satisfactorily and this gives me, as a positive person, real pleasure.

Please give my genuine regards to Mr. Heese and his family, and also to your brothers and your worthy family. I especially commend myself to you, most honoured friend, for your continuing good will, as your most devoted,

Peter Reimer

324. Johann Cornies to Peter Orens Draisma. 23 January 1833. SAOR 89-1-276/4.

Mr. Draisma, dear friend,

I returned from Ekaterinoslav three days ago and feel it is my duty to inform you immediately about our undertaking. After discussing this matter in great detail with State Counsellor Fadeev, I was told that you would probably not receive a salary of 400 rubles in Radichev. This is the salary Reimer receives now, but he has command of the Russian language and can represent the Mennonites there before the courts as though he were a state official. You are not capable of fulfilling this role and would be paid less. I told the state counsellor that you were unlikely to make the move if your salary were not the same as Reimer's.

This is how matters stand today. At the moment do nothing more. If things change, I will let you know. Stay in your present position for the time being, since I cannot do for you what I had hoped to do. Please forgive me for causing you anxiety about this matter. Believe me, I had your best interests at heart. Yet man proposes and God disposes.

With this, farewell and write to me soon. I remain, as always, your true friend,

Cornies

325. Forestry Society to village offices. 23 January 1833. SAOR 89-1-251/6.

To village offices in the old settlement except Fischau,[1]

Given present favourable weather conditions, village offices are hereby directed not to delay operations in forest-tree plantations, such as ditch digging around plantations. Anyone not yet digging, planting, or making enclosures must begin immediately, without fail. Next week, the Society will inspect everything that has been accomplished and determine what further work should, without fail, be accomplished under these favourable conditions.

326. Forestry Society to village offices. 28 January 1833. SAOR 89-1-251/7.

To village offices in the old settlement including Fischau,

The Society hereby informs village offices that last summer, full-holders collected nine varieties of forest-tree seeds from their own trees: mulberry, acorn, ash, maple, elm, American acacia, wild olive, hawthorn, and chestnut. The weight of seed gathered in each village is listed below:

1 In 1832, Fischau was resettled because its original location between swamps prevented development. See Franz Isaac, *Die Molotschnaer Mennoniten: ein Beitrag zur Geschichte derselben: aus Akten älterer und neuerer Zeit, wie auch auf Grund eigener Erlebnisse und Erfahrungen dargestellt* (Halbstadt: H.J. Braun, 1908), 18.

Rosenort	2 funt 18 lot. [10 grams].	Lindenau	66 funt 16 lot.
Blumenort	1 funt 2½ lot.	Schoenau	13 funt 13 lot.
Tiege	1 funt 16 lot.	Tiegenhagen	1 funt 16 lot.
Ohrloff	3 funt 28 lot.	Muntau	1 funt 30 lot.
Altonau	6 funt 19¼ lot.	Ladekopp	1 funt 30 lot.
Muensterberg	2 funt 19¼ lot.	Fuerstenau	1 funt 8½ lot.
Lichtenau	1 funt 2 lot.		
Total	108 funt 9¼ lot.		

During the coming summer, the Society encourages everyone with forest trees to gather as much seed as possible, for his own use and for that of others who do not have trees with seeds. Each person must accurately record the weight of seeds taken from his own trees, noting whether they are for his own use or for that of others. These records must be submitted annually to the Ministry.

This circular should be copied in each village office, sent on immediately and be returned by village offices to the Society as follows: Schoensee [circular] No. 16, Schoenau No. 14, Rueckenau No. 15.

327. Forestry Society to District Office. 30 January 1833. SAOR 89-1-251/9.

District Office in Halbstadt,

This was the second time that Schoensee Deputy Mayor Jacob Gossen did not appear in the Village Office when members of the Society inspected plantations in his village. He is in conflict with one or more of his neighbours, and resigned his position when the Forestry Society Chairman appeared at the Schoensee Village Office. The District Office is asked to bring about a resolution of this disagreement, as is its duty. Because of the dissension, directions from the authorities and from the Society cannot be properly implemented in Schoensee and operations in the forest-tree plantations completed, though this must be done without fail. The Society asks the District Office to restore the Schoensee Village Office to its full strength as soon as possible, as required by the directives.

328. Forestry Society to Guardianship Committee. 31 January 1833. SAOR 89-1-251/10.

Report to the Ekaterinoslav Guardianship Committee:

In conformity with No. 24 of the directive, the Society sends the honoured Guardianship Committee its detailed report about work completed last summer in eighteen forest-tree plantations:

1. To protect them from livestock, most forest-tree plantations have been enclosed within a ditch, according to regulations.

2. Last summer, one quarter of each individual half-desiatina forest plot in seventeen villages was deep-ploughed by the fullholder. Only Lichtenau could not complete this task, despite its best intentions, because of a great drought and the location of its forest-tree plantation. Consisting of meadowland, it had been moved to a new spot.

3. Fullholders in seventeen villages planted trees last autumn following the rules. A total of 2,831 mulberry trees and 17,399 individual forest trees of different varieties were planted. In total, 20,231 trees were planted in plantations.

The Society has the honour of obediently reporting this to the Guardianship Committee.

329. Forestry Society to Guardianship Committee. 31 January 1833. SAOR 89-1-251/11.

Report to the Ekaterinoslav Guardianship Committee,

In conformity with No. 24 and No. 25 of the directive, the Society met on 30 January 1833 and considered work to be accomplished in the plantations this summer. It decided to undertake the following:

1. To complete the not yet totally satisfactory enclosure of plantations with ditches according to regulations.

2. To deep-plough, to the prescribed depth of twelve to thirteen vershok, the second quarter of the half-desiatina plot allotted to every fullholder as his forest-tree holding.

3. To continue planting mulberry and forest trees to the limits of what is possible, according to the regulation No. 23.

4. To apply all possible diligence to the sowing of various forest-tree seeds in order that they might successfully sprout and develop into young saplings suitable for transplantation to forest-tree plantations. The purpose is to obtain a variety of wood suitable to the various types of soil in the plantations.

5. To prepare and lay out new forest-tree plantations this summer in three villages, namely in Lichtfelde, Pordenau, and Pastwa, according to No. 25 of the directive. This work will involve:

a. finding a location with soil suitable for forest-tree cultivation,

b. measuring and dividing it into half-desiatina quarters according to the number of fullholders,

c. ploughing the half-desiatina quarters once with an ordinary field plough,

d. surrounding the location with ditches, ensuring that these will not obstruct the making of turns by the deep-ploughing team, and

e. regulating fruit orchards in five colonies: Ohrloff, Tiege, Blumenort, Rosenort, and Rueckenau, according to No. 13 of the directive.

As the Society submits its plans for work to be accomplished during the coming summer for the approval of the highly honoured Guardianship Committee, it obediently requests that the work be approved and the required orders be sent to this Society.

330. Forestry Society to village offices. 1 February 1833. SAOR 89-1-251/12v.

To village offices in the old settlement except Fischau,

Village offices are hereby ordered to report by Saturday whether each inhabitant has finished planting and digging [ditches] in his plantation. Has he begun to do so or has nothing yet been done in this regard? This report must be forwarded to the Society by Saturday without fail. This must be observed.

P.S. If planting or digging are complete, the above report can consist of a list of plots that have been planted and ditches dug.

331. Forestry Society to village offices. 6 February 1833. SAOR 89-1-251/13.

To village offices in the old settlement except Fischau,

Each village office is hereby directed to acquire a book to record circulars and information received from the Society. The journal should be folio size, of suitable thickness, and properly bound. The cover should be labelled "Journal concerning forest-tree, orchard, silk, and wine cultivation, begun in the year 1831." Village offices not in possession of such a bound journal should acquire one by 15 April and record in it all circulars received from the Society since its founding. This must be observed.

332. Forestry Society to village offices. 6 February 1833. SAOR 89-1-251/13v.

To village offices in the old settlement except Fischau,

According to government instructions for planting mulberry hedges in half-desiatina plots, mulberry saplings without thick stems must be planted in a straight line, one fut apart. If the above regulations are followed, the hedge must, in two years' time, be cut back to soil level with a sharp knife during the month of March. It will then develop into a thick, quickly-growing hedge, neat and pleasing to the eye. The firmly rooted stems send up shoots to form a thick hedge, soon surpassing a hedge that was not cut back. This procedure will greatly assist full-holders in raising mulberry hedges quickly and easily, and must be observed.

333. Forestry Society to village offices. 6 February 1833. SAOR 89-1-251/15.

To village offices in the old settlement except Fischau,

The Guardianship Committee has set 15 February as the final date to submit the required reports listing the names of those who have completed their ditches around plantations and have planted their trees. In the coming week, village offices are strongly urged to complete all the work that was to have been done over the past year, so that no gaps exist in reports to the Committee.

If there are individuals who have not completed their ditches or their plantings, a special report to the Society must truthfully state the reasons why and what circumstances have kept them from doing so.

Villages should report on whether plantations have been enclosed completely on all sides by the prescribed ditches or by fences and barriers to ensure that they are protected from livestock. Everything must be signed by the village mayor and his two deputies.

Records with respect to ditch digging and tree planting (the format is in every village office) must be prepared and included in the reports submitted by 12 February at the latest. This must be strictly observed.

This will mark completion of the work for the year 1832.

334. Forestry Society to Blumstein. 13 February 1833. SAOR 89-1-251/16.

To the Blumstein Village Office,

The Village Office is ordered to report punctually why four fullholders, Franz Krueger, Peter Warkentin, Cornelius Warkentin, and Julius Wiens, did not plant any trees in their forest-tree plantations this year, as others have been doing since 1 October. The declarations must not consist of simple excuses, but of valid reasons. Otherwise, the Village Office will be penalized, or at least reprimanded.

To attest to their veracity, the declarations of these villagers must be signed by the mayor and his deputies and submitted by today, Monday, by 4 p.m. The declarations must be submitted by each individual fullholder. This must be observed.

335. Johann Cornies to Gerhard Enns. 15 February 1833. SAOR 89-1-251/19v.

To the honourable Forestry Society member, Gerhard Enns,

I visited Halbstadt today, 15 February, regarding Cornelius Fast's failure to complete the work assigned to him, as reported by the Ladekopp Village Office. In discussion with District Office members, we decided to investigate Fast's situation on Friday, 17 February. Please be at the District Office in Halbstadt at 10 a.m. on Friday. From there we will travel to Ladekopp.

336. Forestry Society to Blumstein Village Office, 16 February 1833. SAOR 89-1-251/20.

Blumstein Village Office,

The Society has received no reports from the Village Office about four fullholders who had failed to plant any trees by 12 February and about two who, on 14 February, agreed to undertake their plantings immediately. Has the work been done? What numbers and varieties of trees were planted? To complete the Society's records, which will be submitted to the Committee, a report must be in its hands by 1 p.m. If this order is not observed, the Village Office will be punished.

337. Forestry Society to District Office. 18 February 1833. SAOR 89-1-251/21.

A joint meeting of the Society and the District Office is required to discuss regulation No. 417 of the Ekaterinoslav Guardianship Committee, sent to this Society on 27 January 1833. The regulation is in regard to procedures that must be followed in the transfer of fullholdings. We must agree on a procedure that will achieve the purposes of the regulation, thus avoiding errors that could cause unnecessary work.

The Society graciously requests that the honourable District Office take this proposal under consideration. Assuming that the suggested time is agreeable to District Office members, the Society has scheduled the meeting for 10 a.m., 23 February, in the District Office building, Halbstadt. If this time is not suitable, the Society asks the District Office to choose a more convenient time and date. In either case, kindly notify the Society.

338. Forestry Society to village offices. 22 February 1833. SAOR 89-1-251/21v.

All village offices in the old and new settlements,

His Honour, State Counsellor Fadeev, under order No. 7, dated 24 January, has sent the Society a program of the Free Imperial Economic Society in St. Petersburg for distribution to all inhabitants of the District. Enterprising fullholders or inhabitants of this District may be interested in entering the competition in areas covered by questions two, four, five, and six. The state counsellor would gladly assist interested individuals by forwarding relevant communications to them from the Society in St. Petersburg. Prize winners may redeem their value in money instead of receiving a medal.

The enclosed program, communicated to village offices, should be made known to all village inhabitants. The latter should be permitted to copy the program, which should then be sent on. Matters respecting copies need not be entered in the village journal.

339. Forestry Society to village offices. 22 February 1833. SAOR 89-1-251/22v.

To village offices in the old settlement except Fischau,

Several directives were sent to village offices regarding the removal of fruit trees planted contrary to regulations and spelled out in orders

Nos. 10 to 12, dated 16 November 1831. Based on Guardianship Committee regulation No. 2,059, dated 20 June, these were announced to village offices by the Society in Nos. 230 to 232, on 13 August. It is the responsibility of village offices to ensure that all fruit trees are removed from the forest-tree plantations. The Society reminds village offices that if fruit trees are still found in plots during the spring inspection, a penalty of fifty kopeks will be levied against each mayor and, twenty-five kopeks against each deputy. If a village office has expressly ordered an owner to remove such fruit trees from his plantation and he has not complied, he will be penalized ten kopeks for every fruit tree remaining in his forest-tree plot.

340. Forestry Society to Andrei M. Fadeev. 22 February 1833. SAOR 89-1-251/23.

Report to State Counsellor Fadeev:

The Society obediently submits a report regarding forest-tree plantings in individual plantations in eighteen villages in 1832. It includes the names of fullholders and the number of trees each fullholder has planted. We humbly request that, this one time, six delinquent fullholders be graciously forgiven. The Society hopes that they will, in future, plant trees without delay, as the other fullholders have done, and that Yr. Honour will not need to take further notice of this matter.

341. Forestry Society to village offices. 22 February 1833. SAOR 89-1-251/23v.

To village offices in the old settlement,

In accordance with order No. 2,059, of 20 June, from the Ekaterinoslav [Guardianship] Committee, village offices were explicitly ordered to dig the ditches around forest-tree plantations five fut wide and four fut deep. The Society has learned that some ditches are narrower and shallower, a practice that will definitely not be sanctioned during the inspection. All government directives and orders must be followed to the letter. Even the slightest changes are not permitted. The Society therefore repeats its orders to village offices. It includes a gauge measuring five Prussian working feet, which is considered to be correct everywhere in the Prussian states. Village offices must keep a record of the measurements using this gauge. The depth must be measured not along the slope of the ditch, but four fut deep at its midpoint. At inspection time, anyone with ditches not of the prescribed width and depth will be held personally responsible. This must be observed.

342. Forestry Society to village offices. 24 February 1833. SAOR 89-1-251/24v.

To village offices in the old settlement,

Several village offices have drawn the Society's attention to the fact that the gauge of five Prussian (or Rhineland) feet is about four inches longer than the fut measurement commonly used here. Since all ditches around plantations were dug according to the local fut measurement, they request that the widening of ditches to the required Rhineland foot measure be postponed until spring 1834. By then, it will be possible to dig all ditches according to this measurement. The time to begin working on the land is now too close to permit agriculturalists to carry out other duties.

The Society takes into account the arguments put forth by village offices and accepts them. Therefore ditches that are five fut wide and four fut deep according to the usual fut measurement will be accepted until the spring of 1834. New ditches, however, must be dug according to the Prussian working measure. When inspected this spring, the village mayors should provide such a local measuring gauge now used for ditches. The Society asks village offices to measure the width and depth of ditches [in their village] using the local gauge of measurement. Ditches found not deep or wide enough by this measure can be corrected before the Society's inspection. This must be observed.

343. Forestry Society to District Office. 27 February 1833. SAOR 89-1-251/26.

To the Molochnaia Mennonite District Office,

In response to communication No. 136 from the District Office, of 25 February, all rules regarding tree planting in the District were read to Jacob Krause, resident in Fischau village. In a formal written undertaking, he has obligated himself to do everything required, to the limits of his ability, to comply with the rules and regulations ordered by the Society or still to be ordered by the Society regarding hearth-site No. 1 in the village of Ladekopp, for which he has assumed responsibility.

This written undertaking was entered into the journal for the minutes of the Society as item No. 1. The District Office is accordingly notified.

27 February. Same contents as above for Peter Isaak for hearth-site No. 7 in the village of Fischau.

344. Forestry Society to Village Offices. 2 March 1833. SAOR 89-1-251/27.

To all village offices,

Village offices are hereby ordered to inform all villagers that some 10,000 American acacia and 1,000 elm seedlings are available for sale from the Molochnaia colonist plantation. Prices in Banco Assignats are as follows: for acacias, five kopeks each for 1,000 seedlings, six kopeks each for 100 to 1,000 seedlings, and seven kopeks each for fewer than 100. The elms are priced at an average of ten kopeks apiece. When weather permits, interested parties can, at any time, obtain an order form from Chairman Waker of the Colonist Garden Society in Weinau. Payment must be made immediately.

A smaller number of two-year-old fragrant balsam poplars are available at the sheep farm of Johann Cornies on the Iushanle. They are four to five fut high and can be obtained from gardener Wilke for an immediate cash payment of fifty kopeks apiece.

345. Forestry Society to Andrei M. Fadeev. 9 March 1833. SAOR 89-1-251/28.

State Counsellor Fadeev,

The Society is pleased to present Yr. Honour with the enclosed first book of the atlas for nineteen villages in the Molochnaia Mennonite District. The atlas gives special attention to the location of buildings, orchards, and forest-tree plantations, etc., in each village. They were accurately sketched on site. Because Fischau village had been relocated, it could not yet be drawn accurately on the map and its page in the atlas has been left empty. The Society has the honour of reporting this to Yr. Honour.

346. Forestry Society to Andrei M. Fadeev. 9 March 1833. SAOR 89-1-251/28v.

Report to His Honour, State Counsellor Fadeev:

In accordance with Yr. Honour's oral instruction, the Society will send a vehicle to Ekaterinoslav to fetch the forest-tree seeds received at the Guardianship Committee for the Molochnaia Mennonite District. It is hoped that they might be sown at an early date.

The Society requests that Yr. Honour kindly assist our inhabitants by releasing grafting shoots from the Ekaterinoslav Crown orchard of the best winter apples and pears. They are ordered as follows:

A. Varieties of apples (enough shoots to graft 2,500 stems):
1. *Pigeon rouge* – red "Taubenapfel"
2. *Sinop-blas* – the white Sinop, best Crimean variety
3. *Rennete platte* – onion-shaped apple

B. Varieties of pears (enough shoots to graft 1,500 stems):
1. *Bergamotte de Paques ou d'hyver*, also *Bergamotte Bugi* – Easter or winter Bergamotte
2. *Bergamotte de Hollande*, also *amoselle* – Dutch Bergamotte
3. *Bon Chretien d'hyver* – winter Christmas pear

The 2,500 apple and 1,500 pear shoots (without including any other kinds of fruit in this number) should be bound together separately by variety. The name of each variety should be noted on its binding to enable the Society to require residents to keep accurate records of the trees in their orchards.

The Society further requests Yr. Honour's help in purchasing from the Ekaterinoslav Crown orchard 400 young pines, *Pinus Sylvestris*, for this District at a list price of twenty kopeks apiece.

347. Johann Cornies to Johann Cornies Jr. 9 March 1833. SAOR 89-1-276/4v.

Dear son Johann Cornies,

Peter Reimer will bring you the requested sixty rubles to cover your expenses.

Did you post the letter to Peter Reimer (who lives in Radichev), at the Ekaterinoslav post office? I have been waiting for his reply. Did you forget? This would put me in a somewhat embarrassing position. Or perhaps the letter was lost in the mail. But who would know? Please ask Mr. Frank if he can recall the subject matter of the letter he wrote to Reimer on my behalf. Then send a second letter, with roughly the same content to Reimer as soon as possible. Please report back.

We are, thank God, all healthy. The day before yesterday, your mother was not feeling well, but she is now up and about again. It would give me great pleasure to know that you have been able to help with the commissions I asked your uncle to undertake, but not at the expense of your studies. Has the presence of the Sultan in Odessa been confirmed?

Fare well with God, and give my greetings to Mr. Kirilovskii. We all send you our greetings,

Adieu.

348. Johann Cornies to Andrei M. Fadeev. 10 March 1833. SAOR 89-1-276/5.

Mr. State Counsellor Fadeev,

The Society finds that a copy of the printed directive for the internal administration of the colonies is indispensable for the conduct of its business. I obediently request that Yr. Honour have such a copy sent.

Society members arranged a meeting with the District Office to agree on procedures for the transfer of fullholdings between local settlers, according to regulations, to avoid confusion and to ensure that their purpose is correctly carried out. We then learned that during the last year, 100 or more fullholdings had been transferred without first having been submitted to the Committee for confirmation. The district chairman thought it possible that the required regulations be met through a verbal submission to Yr. Honour when you visit the Molochnaia. The district chairman may think that the Committee's orders in regard to such written undertakings are unnecessary, but this, in my view, could be damaging to our purposes.

349. Johann Cornies to Andrei M. Fadeev. 10 March 1833. SAOR 89-1-251/29v.

Report to State Counsellor Fadeev:

This is in response to Yr. Honour's communication No. 18, of 2 March, that the Society require fullholders Nos. 17, 18, and 19 in Ohrloff village, No. 9 in Schoenau, and No. 5 and 11 in Schoensee to make amends for having negligently failed to plant anything in their forest-tree plantations in 1832. They will, in future, be required to do their planting promptly and with vigor.

When the planting list was being prepared, fullholding No. 14 in Ladekopp village was investigated on site by the Society and the District Office. In keeping with the Ladekopp village community's judgment, this fullholder was removed [from his property], and in accordance with directive section 14, the fullholding was passed into the care of an able young man, who has given the Society an appropriate written undertaking regarding his responsibilities.

350. Johann Cornies to Daniel Schlatter. 11 March 1833. SAOR 89-1-276/7.

Dear, unforgettable friend, Daniel Schlatter,

There are many reasons why I have not answered your letters of 27 March 1831 and 26 February 1832. We are, thank God, well and alive, except for Ali, who died of cholera in late June 1831. He was the first of three people in Burkat to be swept away in this manner. Although cholera ravaged the area around our villages, not a single person in our community has taken sick. Tashe has married someone from the Kuban, but she has already sent him away. After Ali's death, I hired Abdula to work on the sheep farm. The boy was obedient, but his mother kept making demands for money. Since I would not give her the amounts she demanded, she took Abdula back to her home. She has now married a third time, a poor Nogai in Akuia, who knows how to rule with a whip.

The Nogais are generally happier since the New Year, when they were placed under the authority of the lower courts. Their commanding officer is the area captain for this court, and seems to be a sensible man. It is especially noteworthy that our Governor is a just and thoughtful man who holds the Nogais close to his heart. He tours the Nogai villages once a year and sometimes twice. A fruit orchard is to be planted in each Nogai village. Akkerman will be organized as a model village. Spanish sheep breeding and horse breeding are advancing quickly. Robberies and thieving among the Nogais are seldom mentioned anymore, although Nogai quarrels continue as before.

His Honour, Mr. Fadeev kindly forwarded 320 rubles to me. You seem to have paid too much. What should I do with the overpayment?

My son has been in Ekaterinoslav for about a year, lodging with the Committee translator, a moral, Christian man, who instructs him in written Russian and mathematics. He will stay there for another year. Then, if it is God's will, he will travel through Sarepta, Moscow, St. Petersburg, and Prussia, and perhaps renew our old friendship, even to you in your dear Switzerland.

I have my hands full to overflowing. In addition to my khutor, I have purchased a khutor at the mouth of the Molochnaia from Granobarskii. I was also named chairman for plantations in all our villages and installed in office by General Inzov. An office [for the Society] has now been set up in your room in the corner of my house. Secretaries now conduct business directly with the Committee from there. I am not unhappy, really more happy, in dealing with such a large amount of work.

The school is no longer a subject of dispute in our community. So many students are applying that we can no longer accept them all. Heese is the teacher and he works without stopping from early morning until late at night. The Bible Society exists. It functions so well that St. Petersburg recognizes it as the Society's second [most important] branch. It is regrettable that Voth still lives in Schoenwiese. Hausknecht lives in Einlage, has married and is treasured and loved by Mr. Fadeev. Mr. Contenius died of old age in 1831 [*sic*].[2] Mr. Fadeev is following in his footsteps, though it takes him less time.

We had unusual weather this summer. It was cold but there was hardly any rain. Now, in winter, we have no snow. It has not rained since 1 September 1832, when the rain only moistened the dust. This means we have had no precipitation for six and a half months. Not even the oldest people can remember such weather. The ground is dry and hard as a rock. The temperature has been as low as minus twenty-two degrees.

Willert returned several years ago and intends to travel to Germany soon. Bartram is in hospital in Poltava. I could report much else that is interesting, but will save that for another time. Don't expect such a long gap in my letters. I will soon write again if God grants me good health. Still, I would first like a few lines from you in reply to this letter..

Since your departure, there have been few important changes in Ohrloff and the community generally. Externally, our community's well-being is blossoming, while crafts and trade increase markedly. Wool was up to forty-two rubles, washed, on the spot last year. In Moscow, mine sold for fifty-seven rubles. Blueher is alive and flourishing. I am especially pleased with this dear man. Wheat sold for sixteen rubles per chetvert locally, and for twenty to twenty-two rubles in the Crimea.

2 Contenius actually died on 30 May 1830 – see document 202.

The Molokans would like to move to Georgia and sent deputies there on the Minister's order last year. About forty verstas beyond Shushi, land has been set aside for the settlement of all Molokans from various guberniias. None come here anymore and many local Molokans have decided to await the millennium in that new settlement as well. Some Cossacks and others are here, however, with cunning swindlers among them. Magor is still alive, and the same quiet, friendly soul.

The Doukhobors seem to be close to collapse, with some transferring to the state church. Their chief elder has drunk himself to death. Disunity, oppression and intemperance are increasing among them and they seldom keep their word. The better ones would like to send their children to our school, but the Society has still to decide this question.

During the recent war, the Zaporozhians who have, for forty years, been living in Turkey beyond the Danube voluntarily returned to Russia. Settled not far from the Prussian settlement, they include many Germans who have friends, even brothers, among the colonists. A thieving rabble was settled next to the Prussian colony. They are Germans who have lived in Little Russia for sixty-five years. They have Russian customs and some no longer understand German. It is very interesting to find so many peoples living closely together. They associate calmly and quietly with one another. As they go about their business, we observe varied customs, languages, costumes, and ways of life. I do not believe that this sort of thing can be found anywhere else in the world. Our wise Imperial government has managed to bring all of us together and provide leadership that makes all of us happy. For this we give God the glory.

The space on this page is too limited to tell you everything I wanted to. Pastor Foell is serving in Hochstadt. The Prussians have a new [pastor], Holzfreter, from Dorpat, and the community is satisfied with him. Pastor Steinmann in Josephsthal is alive, not as a living example, but as someone driven by his passions. Zoehling still glides about like a hawk, but has been discredited and will soon have to leave.

What are you doing? Your dear wife? Is your dear mother still alive? How many children do you have and what are their names? Many greetings from my wife, daughter, mother, brothers, P. Neufeldt, and Kokan, who is here at the moment. I send special greetings to you, your wife, mother, and brothers, and all friends. May the Lord bless you and your entire house. Do not forget your brother in Christ who loves you and calls himself,

Johann Cornies

351. Forestry Society to village offices. 18 March 1833. SAOR 89-1-251:34v.[3]

To Ohrloff, Tiege, Blumenort, Rosenort, and Rueckenau village offices,

The Ekaterinoslav Guardianship Committee's order No. 752, of 2 March, as well as sections 13 and 15 of the directive, require the Society to inspect fruit orchards in the villages of Ohrloff, Tiege, Blumenort, Rosenort, and Rueckenau in 1833. Fullholders in these five villages who have been less diligent than others in developing their orchards should try to catch up by working harder, more systematically, and in a timely fashion. The Society orders the village offices to ensure that further plantings of fruit trees be completed as required by the rules and orders, of 25 November 1831, of the Society.

Cottagers with their own hearth-sites must likewise be instructed to begin planting fruit trees following those same prescriptions. The number of fruit trees that cottagers should plant are as indicated and should not be changed. Moreover, orchard areas around schools should be fenced off, and if nothing has yet been planted on them, the soil should be prepared so that planting can commence this fall.

352. Forestry Society to village offices. 18 March 1833. SAOR 89-1-251/35.

To village offices in the old settlement,

According to order No. 7,522, of March 5, the Ekaterinoslav Guardianship Committee has instructed the Society to undertake the following deep-ploughing: "The second quarters of the entire plots must be deep-ploughed to a uniform depth of at least twelve vershok."

The Society orders that the second quarter of forest-tree plantation areas be fallowed and kept black this summer, so that the deep-plough can work more easily to a depth of at least twelve vershok in fall. A lesser depth is not acceptable. This is to serve as a guideline.

3 The problems in Rosenort village, first mentioned in this letter, would come to focus on three fullholders: Martin Janzen, Clas Thiessen, and Peter Thiessen. See also documents 354, 355, 361, 398, and 399.

353. Johann Cornies to Khariton T. Pelekh. 18 March 1833. SAOR 89-1-276/10v.

His Honour, Mr. Khariton Trofimovich Pelekh,

Both wells on the Tashchenak have been properly covered to prevent accidents. The last well dug is four sazhen deep and provides good water.

In reporting this to Yr. Honour, I obediently ask you to inform me whether the land on the Tashchenak will definitely be settled by colonists this year. I also ask your forgiveness if I again seek your cooperation in having money owed me by colonists for books of holy scripture reach me, without fail, by the coming month of May. With the appropriate respect and esteem, I have the honour to be Yr. obedient servant,

Johann Cornies

354. Forestry Society to Andrei M. Fadeev. 25 March 1833. SAOR 89-1-251/35v.[4]

Report to His Honour, State Counsellor Fadeev:

According to order No. 2,059, of 20 June 1832, the Ekaterinoslav Guardianship Committee ordered the Society to do the following:

In several plantations, fullholders have planted fruit trees on some of their quarters because they did not know better. This is contrary to the purpose of these plantations, and the Society is ordered to sell such trees or, if possible, transplant them into existing orchards. Dried, frozen, or deformed trees and bushes must be removed. Fruit trees already growing well and too deeply rooted to be transplanted can remain, but fullholders must undertake in writing that when these trees die, no fruit trees of any kind will be planted in their stead. In such instances, only mulberry and forest trees may be planted, according to the prepared plan. It will be the Village Office's responsibility to ensure that this, in future, is strictly observed.

The Society found ninety-one fruit trees in the forest-tree plantations in Rosenort, planted by Martin Janzen, Clas Thiessen, and Peter Thiessen, and established the fact that these trees can be transplanted to orchards without risk of their dying. Because these three fullholders had

4 Regarding the dispute over Rosenort tree-planting, see also documents 351, 355, 361, 398, and 399.

not yet adequately prepared the soil to plant fruit trees in their orchard areas, however, the Rosenort Village Office, on 7 March 1833, requested that the Society permit them to delay the transplantation of these fruit trees until fall.

The Society is not authorized to change the Committee's order No. 2,059, of 20 June, without prior agreement from the authorities. It therefore obediently requests Yr. Honour, to kindly agree to the Rosenort Village Office's request and permit Martin Janzen, Clas Thiessen, and Peter Thiessen to delay the transplantation of ninety-one fruit trees until autumn. By then the soil will have been well prepared and the trees can be kept alive.

The Society submits this to Yr. Honour's kind consideration and awaits Yr. Honour's resolution of this matter.

355. Forestry Society to Rosenort Village Office. 25 March 1833. SAOR 89-1-251/37v.[5]

To Rosenort Village Office,

In response to the Village Office's report of 7 March 1833, the Society has made a submission to the Senior Member of the Ekaterinoslav Guardianship Committee, State Counsellor Fadeev, regarding the fruit trees in the forest-tree plantation which belong to three fullholders. Permission was sought to leave these ninety-one trees in their present location until this fall. This request was made because, according to the Committee's order No. 2,059, the Society is not authorized to allow fruit trees in forest-tree plantations.

The Village Office is informed of this development and must await the further resolution of this matter.

356. Forestry Society to village offices. 5 April 1833. SAOR 89-1-251/43v.

To village offices in the old settlement,

Society members will begin their inspection tour of forest-tree plantations on 17 April. Village offices are notified in advance to ensure that fullholders might be able to complete any work still needed on the prescribed ditches and gates.

---

5 Regarding the dispute over Rosenort tree-planting, see also documents 351, 354, 361, 398, and 399.

Number stakes should be in place, and fruit trees in the forest-tree plots contrary to the purpose of the plots must be removed, to avoid unwelcome situations. Each village office should investigate its plantation just before Society members inspect it, to ensure that ditches and gates are complete, number stakes in place, and fruit trees removed. Where something has not yet been completed, the village office must admonish the person in question to do so without fail. This serves as notice.

357. Johann Cornies to Andrei M. Fadeev. 5 April 1833. SAOR 89-1-276/11.

In response to Yr. Honour's esteemed communication of 17 March, I have the honour to explain that Cornelius Fast was not able to maintain his fullholding by himself, even had he not failed to do his [tree] planting. He is almost seventy years of age and without means. The Society considered it appropriate to take his fullholding from him, using as grounds his failure to carry out orders for planting trees. A good, industrious young man was available, who was able to put this fullholding into better condition and to compensate Fast to a degree that ensures his further support. Fast and his family can live with fewer worries than on the fullholding. This can also serve as an example that negligent fullholders should more actively and industriously observe and implement whatever is prescribed for their advantage.

I am unable to report to Yr. Honour how hearth-sites have been transferred, as mentioned by the chairman in the meeting with Society members. I believe no transfers have been submitted to the Committee for several years. No one would dare to give up or take on a fullholding without the agreement of the District Office or its chairman. I therefore believe that the District Office agreed to these transfers, perhaps only until they had been confirmed by the Committee. The district chairman will presumably submit this matter to you, without being asked, during your visit here to the Molochnaia.

I am concerned that this Society's Office may be without a secretary after 15 April, because the current Society secretary, Sommerfeld, will be away in Prussia on pressing family business. Reimer has written from Radichev that he does not wish to abandon the good start he has made there, especially in the school. This makes good sense. I therefore urgently request that Yr. Honour kindly release Neufeldt, who is working for the Committee, from his responsibilities, even if only for six months. He is a young person who would fit himself into our affairs better than someone unknown to us in the area.

While I would permit my son to travel in the colonies with Mr. Haustek in spring, as Yr. Honour kindly suggests, I hesitate to leave him in Mr. Haustek's company when the latter is on his own. While my son would gain little, I am afraid that he would be opened to the community's righteous censure, as I would. To maintain my own reputation in the community and also my son's, I must forego this opportunity. Confident that Yr. Honour will not withdraw Yr. gracious interest in my son, I endeavour, with esteem and devotion, to be Yr. Honour's completely devoted servant,
J. Cornies

358. Forestry Society to Pastwa Village Office. 6 April 1833. SAOR 89-1-251/44.

If the Pastwa Village Office or mayor neglect to have forest-tree seeds, etc., picked up promptly when this should be done, in violation of the directive, the mayor will be fined one ruble and the [two] deputies fifty kopeks each. In future such fines will be assessed when, as in this case, seeds were picked up eight days later than they should have been, and in another case, when the Village Office authorized a fullholder from another village to transport seeds at his convenience and in exchange for community labour credits, which is contrary to regulations. This will serve as a first warning.

359. Forestry Society to Margenau Village Office. 7 April 1833. SAOR 89-1-251/45.

The Margenau Village Office is sternly reprimanded for not having promptly paid the Society twenty-five rubles, fifty kopeks, for sixty-five fruit trees. The Village Office should pay heed to a warning that if this money is not paid by 15 April, it will be held sternly to account.

360. Forestry Society to village offices. 10 April 1833. SAOR 89-1-251/45v.

To the village offices in Lichtfelde, Pordenau, and Pastwa,

Village offices are hereby notified that Society members will arrive at 9 a.m. next Thursday, 13 April, to inspect the sites villages have designated for their forest-tree plantations. The mayor and both deputies should be home on the above-mentioned date.

361. Forestry Society to Rosenort Village Office. 20 April 1833. SAOR 89-1-251/46.[6]

Rosenort Village Office is hereby notified that order No. 39, of 8 April 1833, from His Honour Fadeev permits three fullholders to leave ninety-one fruit trees in the forest-tree plantation until autumn, provided they are then transferred to orchards without fail.

362. Johann Cornies to Heinrich van Steen. 24 April 1833. SAOR 89-1-276/16.[7]

Esteemed Mr. van Steen,

I have succeeded in obtaining a death certificate for your late son, as you requested. I will today mail it to Odessa to have it certified by the Imperial Prussian consul. I will not neglect to forward it to you immediately upon its return. In accordance with your wishes, I have given the money received for your son's clothing to Gerhard Reimer, Ohrloff, administrator for the support of the poor in our community.

I take the liberty, esteemed Mr. van Steen, of commending to you the messenger delivering this letter, Johann Leonhard Sommerfeld. While in my employ, he was, for some time, on good terms with your son and can provide you with greater detail about your son's stay in our community than could any letters from me. Please do not view the liberty I have thus taken unkindly. I have permitted the young man, Sommerfeld, to make a visit to Prussia on family matters and thought you might find it profitable to question him about your son's stay and behaviour.

I sent money to Mr. Johann Wiebe, in Thiege, to cover several small expenses for me. If this amount should be insufficient, I would respectfully ask that you advance him whatever is still needed in this regard. It should not be more than a few thalers. Please charge it to my account and inform me accordingly.

In expectation of your further good will, I have the honour to be your friend and servant,

Johann Cornies

---

6 Regarding the dispute over Rosenort tree-planting, see also documents 351, 354, 355, 398, and 399.

7 Regarding Carl Anton Zimmerman, see footnote 109, and also documents 239, 259, 279, 280, 290, 303, and 304.

363. Forestry Society to Schoensee Village Office. 28 April 1833. SAOR 89-1-251/47v.

In response to the Schoensee Village Office's report of 16 April, the Office is directed to order fullholder Aron Schellenberg to dig up deeply with a spade the soil between the rows of trees in his tree plantation and to smooth the area well with a rake.

If Schellenberg has not done so properly by 3 May, the Village Office must report this to the Society without delay and declare Schellenberg insubordinate according to the instruction. The Village Office must also report on the condition of Schellenberg's plot and whether this work has been done well. This must be observed punctually.

364. Forestry Society to Ohrloff Village Office. 28 April 1833. SAOR 89-1-251/48.

To Ohrloff Village Office,

The report of 24 April of Society members regarding their tour of forest-tree plantations shows that the enclosure of plots with ditches and fences in Ohrloff is very incomplete. It had not been done at all by fullholder Heinrich Wieb. Several gates were missing, and some consisted of only a board. Enclosures at the ends of the plantation were especially incomplete. Two number stakes had not been painted, and one included a date, which must not be done. The tops of many trees had not been trimmed and the planting journal had not been kept up to date.

The Village Office is hereby instructed to ensure that the noted shortcomings be promptly corrected. Failure to do so will be ascribed to the Office's neglect. The Village Office must report on these matters by 3 May.

365. Forestry Society to Fuerstenau Village Office. 29 April 1833. SAOR 89-1-251/51.

The Fuerstenau forest-tree plantation is chaotic. For this the Village Office, as village leader, bears sole responsibility. Residents must follow Society regulations and if they fail to do so, the Village Office has ample opportunity to lodge complaints against them. The Office is hereby reprimanded and put on notice that it will, in future, be punished if the plantation is not developed in a more orderly fashion. Trees in plots

Nos. 1–7 have not been planted regularly. This must be corrected by autumn, without dispute. Regular ditches must be completed immediately and the trees trimmed.

366. Forestry Society to Gerhard Enns and Abram Wieb. 19 May 1833. SAOR 89-1-251/53.

To the honourable Forestry Society members Gerhard Enns and Abram Wieb,

District Office communication No. 301 informed the Forestry Society chairman as follows: On 15 May, the Chief Judge in the Ekaterinoslav Guardianship Committee, State Counsellor Fadeev, notified the Society that District Chairman Klassen had submitted a petition requesting his release from service. In the presence of Society members, His Honour authorized Deputies Regier and Driedger to carry out the District Office's business obligations.

Today, however, before leaving Halbstadt, His Honour informed the deputies that the district chairman must continue in his official duties until the Committee makes a decision about his above-mentioned petition. The District Office has notified the Society chairman accordingly and requests that the other Society members also be informed.

The Society is therefore obligated to respect the official orders and obligations of District Chairman Klassen until the Committee makes its decision.

367. Forestry Society to District Office. 6 June 1833. SAOR 89-1-251/56v.

A number of people have reported to this Society that several district inhabitants have occupied cottager plots and are building on them without first notifying district administrators, contrary to District Office and Society regulations. They have also not signed the legal written document obligating themselves to do the required planting. The District Office is requested to repeat its instructions to village offices that they should punctually carry out all standing orders, as unalterable obligations.

368. Forestry Society to District Office. 7 June 1833. SAOR 89-1-251/56v.

The District Office is respectfully requested to include plot numbers in communications relating to buildings on cottager plots. This is indispensable for the regular conduct of business. Plot numbers must also be included in the obligations signed by cottagers who are already established. Please send them to the Society as quickly as possible.

369. Forestry Society to village offices. 9 June 1833. SAOR 89-1-251/57.

To all village offices,

Each village office is hereby ordered to list every fullholder in the village by name, and the number of his plot in the forest-tree plantation. This list should, without fail, be sent to the Society by 19 June.

Village offices should also emphasize to fullholders that it is their unfailing obligation to thoroughly clear the forest-tree plantations of all weeds before the Society's next inspection tour.

370. Johann Cornies to Traugott Blueher. 10 June 1833. SAOR 89-1-276/18.

Honoured Mr. Blueher,

On 9 June, I dispatched the wool my sheep produced this year, loaded on seventeen vehicles and weighing 465 puds, seventeen funt including the sacks. Enclosed is the original copy of the contract concluded with the carters. Kindly, once you have received the wool in good order, pay the carters the remainder of the freight charges of 696 rubles from the wool account.

According to the enclosed bill of lading, you will receive forty-seven linen sacks of wool washed on the backs of the sheep as follows: Marked with J.C. is Electa, five sacks; first variety, sixteen sacks; second, ten sacks; third, twelve sacks; and special variety in four sacks marked.

I forward this wool to you for sale on consignment with the full confidence, as previously, that you will obtain the highest possible price for this product. Regrettably, however, I must note that wool produced this year has a black appearance because of unfavourable weather conditions. It is not of a poorer quality, but as excellent and unspoiled as it was last year, except that it is black with dust.

From 10 July 1832 to 12 April 1833, we had absolutely no snow or rain here at all. This resulted in a complete crop failure. In fact, in the winter frost, the soil did not harden because it had so little moisture and ditches and holes could be dug at minus fourteen degrees Reamur. Spring began with dry winds and dust clouds, and has continued on in this way until almost the present time. Wool has lost its appearance. We found it almost impossible to keep fleeces white and clean out on the pastures, especially after the sheep had been washed.

Wool from sheep on my newly bought khutor was somewhat cleaner. Unfortunately, without much thinking, I packed wool from my old estate with wool from my new. The result? When you open the sacks you will find that some fleeces are blacker than others. This may well give merchants and manufacturers the idea that the wool is unwashed. Should it perhaps be washed again using factory methods in Moscow? You are in a better position to judge. I leave the decision in your hands.

I would add, in response to your valued letter of 17 April, that wool of the quality of the samples you included is not available here. The amount of such wool might be found here or there but it is hardly worth mentioning.

I have not yet purchased 500 puds of ordinary, washed wool [for you] because most local sheep owners, still remembering last year's good prices, cannot decide to let such wool go when it fetches only thirty-five or thirty-six rubles a pud, the price you have set. The director of the Ekaterinoslav Crown cloth factory is offering thirty-seven rubles for wool produced in the local villages, without exception. Generally, few sheep were washed this year, since water for this purpose was, in many places, unavailable. I have now authorized a dependable man to purchase the desired wool from fullholders in our community and from our neighbours, the Molokans and Doukhobors. What he can accomplish is still uncertain, but I will notify you of the results as soon as possible.

I would be especially pleased if the magazine for sheep breeders were continued, particularly in German, but it could be useful even in Russian. I request that you send me the continuation of this magazine, on my account, at the appropriate time.

Johann Cornies

371. Johann Cornies to Wilhelm Frank. 23 June 1833. SAOR 89-1-276/21.

Highly valued friend,

I feel so sure of your friendly disposition that, with full confidence, I turn to you about an important matter concerning our local region. Two men of consequence arrived here just after I returned home. They were travelling on business matters, doing a reconnaissance along the coasts of the Black Sea and the Sea of Azov and the land bordering them. The civil governor, Prince Chercheuslidsov, and the merchant of the first guild, Ammaretti, directed them to me to inform them fully about the foreign settlements. For this purpose, I need the 1831 treasury lists of the colonists in the Molochnaia and Khortitsa and for Mariupul and Berdiansk. I turn to you since His Honour, the Chief Judge, is travelling and I have no other dependable correspondent to whom I can turn. I do not like to burden you with this task, most esteemed friend, but I urgently request that the mentioned lists might reach me no later than 5 July, if possible. These gentlemen plan to leave Taganrog for St. Petersburg by approximately 15 July.

372. Forestry Society to village offices. 26 June 1833. SAOR 89-1-252/59v.

To all village offices in the old settlement except Fischau,

Order No. 1,160, from the Ekaterinoslav Guardianship Committee, dated 13 March, drew attention to the following rules and regulations that the Society must establish to foster better tree growth in the villages:

1. Tree planting is done every year from the beginning of October to 10 November. Trees planted later than this will be counted as having been planted the following year.

2. Lists of the trees planted each year must be completed by village offices on 10 November and sent to the Society without fail. This concludes the tree-planting year.

3. No fruit trees outside of the established rules are to be planted in plantations. When such trees are discovered, their owners will be fined ten kopeks per tree.

4. A fifty-kopek fine will be levied against the owner of every half-desiatina plot found without a number stake.

5. To ensure that the plantations are not overgrown with weeds, the Society members must inspect them four or five times each summer. The first time a plot is found thus overgrown, a fine of fifty kopeks will be levied against the owner.

The Society orders the village offices to inform all fullholders in each village about these regulations and to insist on their implementation. This must be observed punctually.

373. Johann Cornies to Andrei M. Fadeev. 17 July 1833. SAOR 89-1-276/24.

State Counsellor Fadeev, Honoured Sir,

It was my pleasure to receive Yr. Honour's esteemed communication of 29 June from Voronezh on 15 July. I report to Yr. Honour without delay on present conditions in our community:

1. Great rain storms have transformed the arid steppeland, where livestock seemed to be starving in mid-June, into a green meadowland. Not quite adequate for large livestock, the meadows will be of great help. Ploughed fields are green with growing plants, assuring bounteous winter fodder for most of the livestock. We hope that good rain later on, after the dog days, will produce another crop of weeds on fields and further reduce the shortage of livestock fodder for winter. It is still likely that several thousand sheep will have to be driven to pastures elsewhere, but this affects principally more prosperous people. Most of the other sheep can be fed properly here.

2. Winter fodder is insufficient for the some 2,500 sheep in the community sheep flocks. A dependable man has been sent out to find fodder for them, preferably close by. The encouraging green in the Molochnaia has discouraged estate owners from offering us hay at atrociously high prices, especially when they see that our people are more optimistic than they were a month ago. Hay will naturally remain high-priced because it is also needed in so many other areas.

3. The price of rye is twenty to twenty-two rubles per chetvert, but little is available. Oats cost twelve rubles and barley is not available at all. Millet costs fifteen rubles. There is a great shortage of grain, but we hope it will be cheaper and more readily available when harvests have been completed in more fruitful regions.

Under these circumstances, the District Office has made a wise decision. It will borrow all surplus money in private hands at legal rates of interest and lend it out at the same rate of interest to persons recognized in the community as honest people who understand trade. This arrangement will make bread available, even if it is still expensive. The list of grain prices Yr. Honour sent me have made this easier to arrange. A general meeting confirmed this decision and was signed by all village offices. Today Deputy Chairman Regier is going to Ekaterinoslav to secure the Committee's quick confirmation of the decision. Although price levels will naturally be determined by the amount harvested, appropriate measures can be taken at the right time to assist community members who are totally without means. These people have yet to be identified.

4. Cattle plague is raging in nine or ten villages, with great and painful losses. However, these villagers can expect considerable compensation from the remaining villages if those manage to stay free of the disease. Other villages have offered them livestock to feed and use, enabling them to eventually replace their lost animals without great expenditures.

Still, many in our community will suffer great setbacks from this total crop failure. Yet suffering will not be as acute as feared because reasoned thought can be applied to deal with these problems. I am personally convinced that even if many suffer shortages of food, no member of our community will have to suffer real want if appropriate measures are taken. The community has adequate means to do this and the District Office is making great efforts to devise effective measures to keep our community afloat.

To my great sorrow, I will today perform my last service to my dear mother, placing her into a peaceful grave after seventy-four years of life.

May the Lord crown your journey with blessings and lessen its difficulties. I sign myself as Yr. Honour's most humble servant,

Johann Cornies

374. Johann Cornies to Andrei M. Fadeev. 22 July 1833. SAOR 89-1-276/27v.

I have just received startling reports from friends in Prussia that a considerable number of families are preparing to emigrate this year. The [Russian] consul general in Danzig, however, refuses to grant them the needed documents, basing his refusal on a prohibition he allegedly received from St. Petersburg. (Mr. Boganov replaced the previous consul who was transferred last winter.) I humbly request Yr. Honour's opinion regarding this blow that has been dealt our brethren in faith in Prussia. Has such a prohibition, forbidding Mennonites to immigrate into Russia, been made? Might the consul be using a document relating to other religions? It should be mentioned that Prussia has created no obstacles to such emigration. The consul advised Mennonites applying for exit documents to journey with travel passes instead and await developments here. This proposal would create many problems for the emigrants, leaving them without assurances that they would actually be permitted to remain here.

Awaiting your benevolent reply, I have the honour to call myself Yr. Honour's humblest servant,

Johann Cornies

375. Johann Cornies to Herman Riedel. 2 August 1833. SAOR 89-1-276/28v.

Mr. Herman Riedel in Odessa,

I received your esteemed communication of 26 July with true pleasure. Thank you for your kind offer and also for the information about grain prices in Odessa.

Our local community recently sent a deputation of four representatives to the Kiev and Kursk guberniias to buy grain, and a second deputation to negotiate the purchase of about 1,000 chetverts of bread grains in Pavlograd. The community cannot make use of your kind offer at this time, but your notification about grain prices was very welcome. I have given Mr. Klaassen the information you wished me to.

I have just received total population and crop reports for nine Russian districts of Melitopol Uezd. They will follow with the next mail. These records are incomplete and full of mistakes, but could still be of some use.

With true esteem, I am your devoted,

J. Cornies

376. Forestry Society to District Office. 6 August 1833. SAOR 89-1-251/64v.

The Society respectfully asks the District Office for information about Widow Braun in Fischau who, according to [District Office] communication No. 429, dated 18 June, wishes to build a dwelling on cottage site No. 2 in Fischau. Is she independent, able to complete the building and do the planting required by the rules and regulations, or is she under the supervision of a dependable guardian? The Society needs this information to ensure that the appropriate person can sign the required written undertaking.

377. Forestry Society to Guardianship Committee. 7 August 1833. SAOR 89-1-251/67v.

To the Ekaterinoslav Guardianship Committee,

At the Society's May meeting under Yr. Honour's chairmanship, the Society was encouraged to specifically undertake the work in the tree plantations it agreed would be done this year. The Society sought to carry out this objective, doing everything possible to advance the planting.

Now, various village communities have requested that they be relieved of work to be done this autumn after the crop failure resulting from this summer's drought has left livestock pastures in such a condition that they can barely sustain life. The villages ask whether they could defer deep-ploughing the second quarter of their plots until next year.

At today's meeting, the Society decided to tour the villages on 10 to 12 August to inform themselves personally of the situation. It will then send a complete, honest report to the Committee.

378. Forestry Society to village offices. 7 August 1833. SAOR 89-1-251/65v.

To all village offices,

The Guardianship Committee has communicated the following to the Molochnaia Mennonite District Office and the Society for the Advancement and Dissemination of Forest Trees, Orchards, Sericulture, and Viticulture:

The chief judge of the Committee, after inspecting progress in advancing orchard, forest-tree, and silk cultivation, has notified the Committee as follows:

With respect to orchard cultivation, he found considerable progress in this branch of agriculture in all villages of the five districts he inspected this year. However, he pointed out that there are a number of prosperous settlers, in possession of their fullholdings in the Molochnaia Mennonite District for an extended period of time, who should be serving as examples in advancing orchard cultivation. Instead, they have been negligent, paying no attention to this matter. Three fullholders in Friedensdorf, two in Alexanderthal, and one in Pastwa were fined one ruble each for the first offence. If they and other older, prosperous fullholders do not promptly establish orderly fruit orchards around their houses in compliance with section 6 of the directive respecting local administration in the settlements, they will be liable for heavier, more humiliating punishments.

In addition to the above, according to section 6 of the directive, the District Office and the Society are enjoined to encourage and persuade fullholders to lay out and improve their own seed and tree nurseries. Several villages have none and there are few nurseries in several villages. According to section 6 of the directive, inhabitants must be forcefully reminded not to plant trees too close together, either in the orchards (especially in new villages) or in the village plantations. They must be planted at regular intervals, two and one-quarter faden or sixteen to seventeen fut apart, alternating kernel and stone fruit trees. In the Molochnaia Mennonite villages and others situated on the flat steppe, a fullholding yard can consist of one and a half desiatinas so that the future expansion of orchards is possible without creating obstacles or difficulties. This must be followed in all villages where the local situation permits.

With respect to forest-tree cultivation: In the eighteen plantations established in the Molochnaia Mennonite District, the land for tree planting, its fencing, etc., is prepared according to established plans. This year, new sites for plantations were selected in Lichtfelde, Pordenau, and Pastwa. However, many seedlings raised during the past two years have died because of a lack of snow during last winter's frost and the drought of last spring. Therefore, larger quantities of trees should be sown.

The District Office and the Society therefore issue categorical instructions to all inhabitants of this district:

1. Older and prosperous fullholders must promptly establish proper fruit orchards beside their houses, according to section 6 of the directive for local administration, or they will be subject to punishment.

2. Fruit orchards must be planted in no other way than according to the prescribed rules and regulations.

3. Fruit-tree nurseries must be established in all orchards, and special efforts made to sow carefully a sufficient number of forest-tree seeds this year.

This must be implemented punctually.

379. Forestry Society to the Schoenau Village Office. 22 August 1833. SAOR 89-1-251/71.

To Schoenau Village Office,

Society member Gerhard Enns, Altonau, toured forest-tree plantations on 11 and 12 August. He reported to the Society that plot

Nos. 2, 5, 14, and 17 in Schoenau's plantation had not been properly cleared of weeds between trees. In plot No. 5, weeds had not been pulled but cut off, and left lying under the trees. According to the Committee's directive, a fine of fifty kopeks will be levied for each irregularity.

At its meeting of 17 August, the Society decided, for this time, to exempt the individuals from being fined for the above plots, but to impress upon them that, should these or other plots show similar negligence and disorder during future inspections, they would be punished according to the Committee's orders.

380. Forestry Society to village offices. 22 August 1833. SAOR 89-1-251/71v.

To all village offices in the old settlement except Fischau,

Village offices are hereby notified that when they receive circulars ordering that plantations are to be cleaned up, the following directives are to be precisely observed:

Village officers are not obligated to summon a community meeting when a circular announcing a Society inspection tour arrives, as several mayors have been doing. They need only to inform every household by means of a written note.

The Society is not obligated to give this advance notice. It is the duty of fullholders to keep their plots clean at all times, not only at inspection time. The day before a tour, the mayor or a deputy must visit the plantation to ensure that everything is in proper order, notify owners of anything still required, and demand that the work be done punctually.

At the same time, household circumstances should be reviewed to determine whether illness or other important obstacles have prevented the completion of all tasks required by regulations. When a Society member arrives in a village, he must be informed of, and given the names of, those unable to complete all tasks as ordered. If there is no such reason, action will be taken according to regulations.

381. Johann Cornies to Traugott Blueher. 26 August 1833. SAOR 89-1-276/29v.

Honoured Mr. Blueher,

I received your valued communications of 28 June and 8 August and also the remittance of 14,185 R.B.A. I enclose a receipt certifying that the money was received in good order. Your exchange rate for Assignats is about 1½ per cent too high, according to the local rate, but I will try to get the highest possible price for them, and then notify you accordingly. It gave me great pleasure to hear that you are satisfied with the sheep wool bought locally on your account. I trust that this business will develop favourably for you in future as well.

Should the local Banco exchange rate not rise higher by the time my wool is sold, it would be better if you sent me the remittance in gold. At present the imperial is circulating here at forty-two rubles in silver coin. Our wool sold for thirty-five rubles per pud in Romen [market] this year. The Khortitsa community wool sold for fifty rubles. This year's total crop failure, particularly in all local guberniias, is causing serious shortages. Some of our neighbours are starving. In our community, starvation has been avoided by communal efforts and arrangements we find beneficial. It is still impossible, however, for us to sustain our livestock through the winter. Because no hay and virtually no pasturage is available, thousands of animals will be destroyed. This fodder shortage extends over an area of approximately 300 verstas. Several thousand head of livestock have been accommodated for the winter in distant guberniias at the frightfully high price of four to five rubles per sheep. But where will people without means take their livestock? I have provided for the livestock on my sheep farm by buying winter fodder. To protect almost 4,000 sheep with the Nogais and on my breeding farm, I have today also sent someone out to buy feed and pasturage in the Black Sea region near Kinburn, about 250 to 300 verstas away. We look towards the future with sadness. It is an especially gloomy time for individuals who have staked all their hopes on this world alone. When it is put to ruin they have lost everything, but somebody who believes in his heart that even a crop failure can be of benefit to him, does not lose but gains something.

The price of grain is currently at twenty-two to twenty-five rubles per chetvert for rye, twenty-six to twenty-eight for wheat, and twelve to fourteen for oats. Almost nothing is available of these grains and there is no barley. We expect that when deputies sent out by the community to purchase 5,000 to 6,000 chetverts of grain return, grain will be more readily available, but not at a lower price.

I commend myself to you and your dear family, as your friend and servant who honestly values and loves you,

Johann Cornies

382. Johann Cornies to Herman Riedel. 1 September 1833. SAOR 89-1-276/31.

Mr. Herman Riedel in Odessa,

I have received the esteemed communication of 12 August from Mr. Stieglitz and Company and am able to assure you of my cooperation with respect to linseed, etc. I only regret that the quantity of linseed Mr. Stieglitz and Company seek to purchase was, by mistake, left out of the above-mentioned communication.

The current price of cowhides is six rubles, but I cannot yet report on that of sheep pelts with wool, since the wool is still too short and sales begin only in early October. Last year the price was one and a half to two rubles at the start of the season, and rose to three to four rubles shortly before shearing time, when the wool had fully grown out. Tallow currently sells for twelve rubles and is limited only by the settler's own needs.

I am pleased to provide you with the enclosed summary of production in the nine Russian districts of Melitipol Uezd. Despite my best efforts, I am still unable to obtain more complete and accurate information.

Should you need information about our local region in future, please let me know.

Your honestly devoted friend and servant,
Cornies

383. Forestry Society to Lindenau Village Office. 3 September 1833. SAOR 89-1-251/74v.

To Lindenau Village Office,

The Village Office is to summon fullholder Isaac Loewen to appear at the Society Office in Ohrloff tomorrow, Monday, 4 September at 9 a.m., to sign a written undertaking obliging him to do the regular planting for cottage site No. 2 in Fischau. It belongs to Widow Braun, of whom he is guardian.

384. Forestry Society to Guardianship Committee. 13 September 1833. SAOR 89-1-251/75v.

Report to the Ekaterinoslav Guardianship Committee:

When Society members toured the eighteen forest-tree plantations in the local district on 10, 11, and 12 August, they concluded that it would be impossible to deep-plough the second quarter in forest-tree plantations because of insufficient horse power. Because our pastures here are in such desperate shape, we have decided to keep a large proportion of our horses alive by driving them to distant localities. (Lichtfelde, Pordenau, and Pastwa are also unable to deep-plough the designated parts of their plantations.)

In submitting this report to the highly esteemed Guardianship Committee for its favourable consideration, the Society requests that deep-ploughing be deferred until next year. It also requests permission to postpone further plantings in forest-tree plantations until next year. A large proportion of trees planted last autumn have dried up. There was virtually no winter snow cover and no summer rains. It is a discouraging year. We even find that the removal of dried trees and their replacement with fresh ones will require much effort.

385. Johann Cornies to Andrei M. Fadeev. 13 September 1833. SAOR 89-1-276/34.

Your Honour, Gracious State Counsellor,

Your honoured communication of 14 August from Penza arrived on 11 September. It gave me great pleasure. Yr. Honour's good will and friendly support fill me with renewed courage to make myself ever more worthy of the honour you have shown me.

The second rain we had hoped for after the summer dog days utterly failed to materialize. The first rain, however, had helped, and plants growing on ploughed fields provided winter fodder for a large part of the ruminant livestock in our settlement. But since there was nothing for the horses, most were driven to distant pastures. At present, the steppe is so bare of grass that I cannot see how our livestock can draw nourishment from it at all. I have therefore sent my horses to winter in the Kinburn region where hay and pasture can still be found.

The winter supply of food for people is inadequate, but determined efforts are underway to ward off starvation. District Chairman Regier has shown great concern and works earnestly and actively to keep our community intact. The steppes, which were fresh and green in July and early August, have turned red and yellow. They have been dried out by great, desiccating storms that have been blowing in without stop for a full month.

This is for us, in many ways, a year of testing. Our total crop failure will set the settlers back several years. It will also force us to look into the future and consider numerous issues that will need to be dealt with if we are to prevent similar disasters in future.

The greatest blow for us, however, is the removal of the Guardianship Committee's offices from Ekaterinoslav by 1 January 1834 and its transfer to Odessa, as reported in our newspapers. Reflective and well-meaning settlers fear that through changes in our organizational arrangements, we will lose an advocate, a guardian, an advisor, and a benefactor in your person, worthy and esteemed state counsellor. Many of the initiatives that have begun well may be discontinued. Present developments could be crippled by indifference when Yr. Honour, our supervisor, who knows our character, means, and strengths, is relocated to a place far from us. It is with fear that we anticipate the hour when we will learn of the new organization and of the new superior who will lead our affairs.

Yet neither distance nor time can extinguish the thankfulness that animates all well-meaning members of the community in their feelings towards you. Every improvement in our future situation will enhance the honour and esteem in which we hold you.

I remain Yr. Honour's most humble servant,

Johann Cornies

386. Johann Cornies to Johann Cornies Jr. 22 September 1833. SAOR 89-1-276/36.

Dear son,

I send you the enclosed forty-eight rubles to cover your expenses. We are happy that your eyes are better. Do not become too tied to your glasses, but do not give them up prematurely either. The latter might again damage your eyes.

Conrad did not give me the postal forms obtained through friend Neufeldt. Enclosed is a half-imperial for Neufeldt to replace the one stolen from him. Admonish him to be careful whom he trusts and not to doze off. Give him my greetings. Your mother sent along seven silver rubles with your aunt.

We are all healthy, God be praised, and send you many greetings, also to brother Heinrich, his wife, and Mr. Kirilovskii.

Fare well with God, adieu.

Johann Cornies

387. Johann Cornies to David Epp. 26 September 1833. SAOR 89-1-276/36v.

Honourable David Epp, Heubuden, beloved friend,

Yesterday, 25 September, I received a response to my inquiry of 22 July about a prohibition against the immigration of Mennonites to Russia. The reply of 18 August came from State Counsellor Fadeev in Penza, who administers the majority of the southern German colonies. He knows of no Russian prohibition on immigration by Mennonites from Prussia. On the contrary, consent was expressly given for migration of 270 families (with acceptance of the specified conditions). Our District Office has been informed accordingly.

If those desiring to emigrate can show proof at the Consulate that they possess 800 rubles, the consul can still give them [entry] passes. The families wanting to emigrate should then come straight to this area where permissions can be negotiated, provided that the sum of money they possess has been declared truthfully, no more and no less. Each family must declare only its own possessions. Joint declarations are not allowed that would drag along someone with the family that is not part of it. Such subterfuges can cause us great harm, as have similar actions in the past. Declarations must be attested to by the signatures of the elders from Prussia.

Our local region now presents a picture of grief and misery. The settlers have been ruined by a fatal crop failure. Thousands of livestock have been sold at ridiculously low prices while the remaining animals are so emaciated that they are barely alive and will survive the winter only with great difficulty. Without any hay, there are only bad, prickly weeds that can hardly sustain the cattle. Cattle plague and the pox have killed several hundred cattle and sheep, and more are dying. The worst problem is a shortage of food, even though the District Office has made suitable arrangements to maintain the community in this regard. (District Chairman Klassen left and has been replaced by Johann Regier, an upright man.) The price of grain is high, but little is available. Where is it to be obtained? Everything is in decline and only God knows how this will end. Although there is already a great shortage of bread, I do not believe that we will have starvation in our community, but starvation will surely appear among our neighbours. Whatever God does is done well.

Adieu,

Johann Cornies

P.S. Dirk Wiens of Ellerwald immigrated last year, and is no longer in my service. He waits anxiously for letters from his friends, to whom he has written several times. He was told that his brother-in-law, Abraham Reimer of Fichthorst, whom he trusted to keep him abreast of news, is largely responsible for this situation. He makes empty promises time and again. Wiens' wife does not know what to believe about her relatives, since not one of them has gotten in touch with her.

If you can, question Abraham Reimer about this matter and scold him in Wiens' name. You might even warn him that if he cannot show greater zeal in his correspondence, there will be a reckoning. Wiens will mail him an empty envelope every two months and charge the postage to Reimer's account. Please forward greetings to him from Wiens and his wife. They are both healthy and well.

388. Johann Cornies to Traugott Blueher. 29 September 1833. SAOR 89-1-276/38v.

Honoured Mr. Blueher,

Since my communication of 28 August, the exchange rates for Banco Assignats have risen and now circulate at 12 per cent. Please adjust my account for this difference. I request also that when my wool is sold, you send the payment in Banco Assignats to the address of Gerhard Martens, District Office Secretary in Halbstadt.

I would welcome ten to fifteen dozen sheep shears. Please do me the favour of sending them on my account. They should, when an opportunity presents itself, be sent to Kharkov, to the trading firm known to you, for forwarding to W. Martens in Halbstadt on the Molochnaia.

Having benefited frequently and in many ways from your kindness in the past, I again presume to burden you with a task, highly treasured Mr. Blueher. Please be so kind as to provide a service needed by a member of our community who is seventy-five years old. A cabinetmaker by profession, his eyes no longer allow him to do detailed work. He cannot get glasses here that are suitable for his eyes. Could eyeglasses perhaps be bought for him from an optician in Moscow, or made for him? The distance at which he can see an object clearly with unaided eyes is the length of the enclosed piece of thread. When the object is closer at hand or farther away, he sees it only with effort, as in a fog. Opticians can usually prescribe suitable glasses if they know the age of the subject and the distance of his eye from the object (letters on a page, for example). Please charge the costs to my account, and send the glasses by mail to Heinrich Cornies in Ekaterinoslav.

The weather is extremely dry, as it was last year, without green grass or weeds. Everything is scorched. Whatever God does, is well done.

I send sincere, hearty greetings as your friend and servant, who honestly treasures you,
Cornies

389. Johann Cornies to Gerhard Martens. 30 September 1833. SAOR 89-1-276/41.

Treasured friend Gerhard Martens,

Again and again I send you requests and commissions, simply and only to tend to my comfort. This is the way it must appear to you. Were this actually the case, even to some degree, I would ask for your forgiveness. I am, at the present time, hard to get in touch with because I do not know exactly where my business will take me and when I will return. I have given your address to my friend Mr. Blueher, in Moscow.

Please accept all money and items for me that have been sent to your address and forward them on to me. I will repay the costs with many thanks.

Be assured of my esteem and love, your true friend,
Johann Cornies

390. Johann Cornies to Heinrich Cornies. 30 September 1833. SAOR 89-1-276/ 41v.

Dear brother,

If a small package with eyeglasses from Moscow arrives for you at the Ekaterinoslav post office, please take receipt of the package and send it on to me, sealed, even if you must leave it with Secretary Martens in Halbstadt. He will forward it to me. Make sure it is addressed to me.

We are healthy and send our greetings to Johann, and your wife. May you fare well with God. Your brother, who loves you and commends himself to you,
J. Cornies

391. Johann Cornies to Heinrich Cornies. 6 October 1833. SAOR 89-1-276/43.

Dear brother,

David Voht of Alexanderwohl still owes merchant Eftukhov in Ogren 1,298 rubles for wood. The merchant has asked me to let David Voht know that he must repay this sum at an early date. Voht is away at the moment, however, and is not expected back until ten to fourteen days from now. Please therefore ask Eftukhov to be patient until Voht returns.

With best greetings, I remain, as always, your loving brother,

Johann Cornies

392. Johann Cornies to David Voht. 6 October 1833. SAOR 89-1-276/43.

Dear friend David Voht,

On 4 October, merchant Eftukhov urgently asked me to beg you to settle your debt of 1,298 rubles with him relating to your purchase of wood. The money was due on 1 October. Eftukhov urgently needs the money to buy bread grains and cannot wait. If he delays the purchase, the Dnieper could freeze over, cutting communications and trade. Please go to Ogren immediately and settle with him.

Greetings to you and your wife. I remain your friend,

J. Cornies

393. Forestry Society to village offices. 20 November 1833. SAOR 89-1-251/81.

To all village offices in the old settlement except Fischau,

Village offices are hereby required to question fullholders about the seeds they have collected from their forest trees for personal use and for the use of others. How much of this seed did they plant? These numbers must be reported by 5 December 1933, without fail, to the Society, which must then send in a report in this regard to the Ekaterinoslav Guardianship Committee. Where no seeds have been collected, this too should be reported.

394. Forestry Society to District Office. 23 November 1833. SAOR 89-1-251/82v.

According to communication No. 756, of 20 November, from the Molochnaia Mennonite District Office, the following new mayors have been elected to office: Dirk Thun, Fuerstenwerder; Peter Wiens, Wernersdorf; Martin Dirkssen, Sparrau; and Aron Wiebe, Tiegenhagen. The District Office verifies that these men are competent to administer their village offices and recommends that they be presented to the Guardianship Committee for confirmation.

395. Johann Cornies to Heinrich Cornies. 23 November 1833. SAOR 89-1-276/46v.

Dear brother Heinrich,

Four shepherds will have completed their service with me by the beginning of the year, but I do not wish to keep any of them on any longer. Might it be possible for you to find me good shepherds in the area around Ekaterinoslav? Specifically, I need better ones than those I have been able to hire with Friesen. Butchers must have slaughtered their herds by now and released their shepherds. I am interested in shepherds who know how to feed sheep. They are to be preferred over herdsmen who have worked only with oxen. The latter, moreover, have not learned how to conduct themselves in service but continue their slovenly behaviour that can often cause damage.

Please make inquiries about such shepherds. They should be sensible, neither drunkards nor scoundrels, able to guard sheep day and night, and knowledgeable enough to fatten the sheep. They must, at the same time, be strong and healthy and more than twenty-five years of age. Younger ones tend to be less dependable and less stable. I need around four or five such shepherds for now, and probably eight to ten more by March. They should, under present conditions, be relatively cheap. I would therefore ask you to find such people for me and bargain with them. Shepherds here can be employed for their board, but to what purpose? I would pay good wages, from forty to fifty rubles and clothing. By clothing I mean cloth and fur clothing. They would have to provide their own linen shirts and pants. Look around and make inquiries, not for weaklings and youths, but for strong, vigorous, healthy persons, with some intelligence. When you feel that you have found four or five such shepherds, report to me with details about what they would expect by way of money. At the same time, ask them if they can secure annual passes relating to the matter of their [military] recruitment. Married ones are absolutely not to be hired, unless they have already been in service for at least one year without their wives. Nor do I want individuals who have not been shepherds with flocks for several years in a row. Let me know as soon as you can so that I can act in an appropriate manner.

My herds of horses and some of my sheep have been accommodated on 9,000 desiatinas of land with good pasturage, hay, and barns, on the Black Sea beside the French lands, not far from Kinburn. That is one worry less. The 5,500 sheep at my Tashchenak estate have also been provided for, as have 500 of my sheep and all of my cattle on the Iushanle. I can now face winter calmly. Jacob Klassen is my manager at Tashchenak and Mr. Golevskii is my business secretary.

May you fare really well. Give our greetings to your dear wife and to Johann. We are all healthy and greet you *1,000* times. Your brother, who loves you,

Johann Cornies

396. Johann Cornies to Johann Cornies Jr. 27 November 1833. SAOR 89-1-276/48v.

Dear son, Johann,

We have received the frame and the map of the Nizhnii Dneprov Uezd. Mother will have the bouquet you drew with your own hand put under glass in the frame, as you wished. Too bad that the frame is too large by half, but Neufeld can make it smaller. You have given us special pleasure with the map, first because it acquaints me better with the region between the Dnieper and the Sea of Azov. This is especially useful at the moment when our livestock are wintering in those regions and I will have to travel there during the winter. Secondly, you have personally drawn the map and done it much better than I had thought you would. Continue to make yourself ever more adept at useful things, and of benefit to your parents and to human society. Please take special care of the official map for the Tashchenak [estate]. Things would be bad if it were to be soiled or lost.

Mother asks you to send along two rubles worth of sour apples when you can. Is there any news about the superior judge? Give many greetings to Mr. Kirilovskii and his honoured family.

I greet you warmly and remain your father who loves you.

Johann Cornies

397. Forestry Society to Pastwa Village Office. 30 November 1833. SAOR 89-1-251/83.

To Pastwa Village Office,

In response to the Pastwa Village Office report of 22 November 1833, the Society draws to your attention the fact that the Society's order No. 308, of 2 November, pertains only to the eighteen villages in the old settlement. Pastwa has no reason to complain to the Society. The Society's orders about enclosures are intended to protect something from damage but since there is nothing to protect in the Pastwa plantation, there is also nothing to enclose. If the order had dealt with ditch digging or with fencing plantations, the Village Office would have had reasons to complain to this Society.

398. Forestry Society to Rosenort Village Office. 30 November 1833. SAOR 89-1-251/83v.[8]

To Rosenort Village Office,

Order No. 162, of 20 April, from His Honour, State Counsellor Fadeev, permitted three fullholders in Rosenort to leave in place the ninety-one fruit trees planted in the forest-tree plantation against regulations. But this was only to be until autumn when the trees were to have been transplanted into their orchards, without fail. The Village Office has not yet reported on whether this has been done. If it has not, it orders that it be done by 6 December 1833.

399. Forestry Society to Rosenort Village Office. 6 December 1833. SAOR 89-1-251/84.[9]

Rosenort Village Office must, without fail, report by 9 December about whether three fullholders have removed ninety-one fruit trees from the forest-tree plantation. Further promises cannot be accepted. If we are to appear as good citizens of Russia, administrative orders and regulations must be punctually carried out.

The fullholders have been given sufficient time to do the transplanting. If the Village Office had paid better attention, the trees would have been transplanted to their proper places long ago.

400. Forestry Society to Gerhard Dyck. 11 December 1833. SAOR 89-1-251/85.

To esteemed Gerhard Dyck in Rudnerweide,

In response to your request of 25 November to the Forestry Society for several kinds of roots and seeds for fodder plants, especially beetroot

8 Regarding the dispute over Rosenort tree-planting, see also documents 351, 354, 355, 361, and 399.

9 Regarding the dispute over Rosenort tree-planting, see also documents 351, 354, 355, 361, and 398.

seeds by next spring, we inform you that the Society has no means of procuring these seeds and is not authorized to do so by appealing to the authorities. This is the responsibility of the District Office. It has the means to make such purchases and to transport the seed, once the Guardianship Committee has approved payment from the community treasury.

401. Model form for a written undertaking. [No date.] SAOR 89-1-256.

I, the undersigned, in taking over hearth-site No. 00 in N.N. village from Mennonite N.N., in addition to fulfilling all special conditions for takeovers in the regulations, also obligate myself with this signature to follow promptly, to the extent possible, all prescribed rules and written orders issued by the Forestry Society since 16 and 25 November 1831. On the hearth-site I have taken over, I will increase plantings yearly until the whole area assigned for orchard and forest-tree cultivation is completely planted according to regulations, and the trees are growing well.

I affirm this by my signature made with my own hand.

N.N.

402. Johann Cornies to Gerhard Dyck. 18 December 1833. SAOR 89-1-276/56.

Very dear and treasured friend Gerhard Dyck,

You expressed your gratitude to me for suggesting that the chief judge approve a reward from the community treasury for your construction and the introduction of various agricultural machines of benefit to our district. No thanks are in order. My suggestion has not yet been carried out, but even if it were, I would not feel justified in accepting your thanks. I only did what I owe you and every other member of the community like you. Please respect my reserve in this matter since it is an expression of my genuine conviction.

I have taken receipt of the gelding in payment as you wished. With regard to your willing services in building cutting and seeding machines for me, I find myself in a quandary, since I am unable to set aside the needed capital funds for these projects this year. These funds have become so fragmented as a result of the crop failure that I must limit myself to only doing what is most necessary. Yet should my prospects improve over the next few months, I would be inclined to buy a cutting machine from you. I have, however, abandoned the idea of acquiring a seeding machine for the present.

With respect to your letter of 2 December requesting counsel and assistance in renting land and purchasing sheep, I can honestly not agree with you in either matter. It is now clear that our region will enter a totally new age next spring regarding land use and stock breeding. I think that land rentals may well become less desirable in a few years' time. Land owned or rented for a period of time will lie fallow and unused by livestock. At the same time, an abundance of livestock pasturage will be available at low prices, even on the village lands themselves.

I cannot provide the requested advance, my dear friend, at a time when one must think only about providing for the community's preservation. I have not found it necessary to take sheep away from the Nogais, despite the fact that some of their contracts have expired. In other cases, the Nogais still have my sheep under their care because a legal, judicially confirmed contract was concluded, and no one can deal with such a matter arbitrarily.

My dear friend, even though I have only made worrisome predictions about everything, your fortunes will not be diminished as a result and I wish you the very best. With esteem and greetings of friendship to you and your dear family, I remain your honest friend and servant,

Cornies

403. Johann Cornies to Andrei M. Fadeev. 31 December 1833. SAOR 89-1-276/59.

Your Honour, Gracious State Counsellor Fadeev,

With the passing of another year, I take the liberty to honestly thank you with respect and candour for your great kindness to me over the past year.

I also commend myself to your further kindness during the coming year and express my sincerest wishes to you and your highly treasured house for blessings that might bestow on all of you an undisturbed joy of life and everything that might add beauty and happiness to your days. These words are written not out of habit but out of honest esteem. As an honoured recipient of your gracious benevolence, I will seek to earn your favour more and more with every passing day.

I remain Yr. Honour's most obedient servant,

Johann Cornies

1834

404. Johann Cornies to Johann Sukau. 1 January 1834. SAOR 89-1-300/2.

To Manager Johann Sukau in Iushanle,

Under present weather conditions, sheep fed only on *kurrei* risk dying from the diarrhea it causes. Control their feeding by alternating straw, hay, and *kurrei*. Check on the shepherds frequently to make sure they do this in good time.

405. Johann Cornies to Inspector Pelekh. 8 January 1834. SAOR 89-1-300/4v.

Yr. Honour, Inspector for the Second Division of Colonists in southern Russia, Titulary Counsellor Pelekh in Molochnaia,

Most dutiful submission from Mennonite Johann Cornies in Ohrloff:

Estate owner Mr. Anishchenko is my neighbour at my khutor Malochna, which I bought from Mr. Garnobarskii.[1] During the two years since the purchase of this khutor, he has used my pastures and watering places for his horses, horned cattle, and sheep without my permission.

I had assumed that his herdsmen had made such encroachments on my pastures without Mr. Anishchenko's knowledge, and on the pretext that the boundary had not been clearly drawn. After I ploughed a new furrow on my side of the boundary in April 1833, there was no reason for such behaviour.

1 This was Cornies' estate at Tashchenak on the lower Molochnaia River.

In May 1833, I removed all of my livestock from the khutor Malochna, except for fifteen head of horned cattle for household use. I wanted to save the grass during the summer and pasture my sheep there in fall and winter. Little hay could be expected because of this year's extremely poor growth. Anishchenko took this opportunity to drive his livestock onto the pastures being saved for this purpose. First he grazed his livestock on the pastures on the one side, between his khutor and one belonging to Lukovich, an area of at least 600 desiatinas, and the watering places. When this area had been completely grazed, he drove his livestock onto my pasture at the opposite side, at the end of his estate, where they consumed all of the grass as well. In September, when I planned to drive my flock onto these lands for winter pasture, I saw that the damage inflicted was so extreme that no pasture remained for my sheep over even the mildest winter. Hence my dilemma. I finally had no choice but to lease pastureland for 2,000 head of sheep elsewhere that would carry them through the winter.

Meanwhile, Mr. Anishshenko's outrages and deliberate thievery have not ceased. To keep his livestock from completely devastating my pasture that I had tried to save for the winter, I had to hire first one and then two herders to drive back his livestock. In response, he first greeted my shepherds with threats and rude, intemperate words. Then, he scornfully dismissed my shepherds' complaints, arguing that neither his cattle herder nor shepherd was to blame. A third time, he angrily replied that since I had neither grain fields nor hay meadows on my land, his livestock could not possibly have done any damage. When I persisted, he armed six of his people with cudgels and told them to use force to keep his livestock in place. Finally, he claimed that after 1 October, [the Feast Day of] Pokrov, everyone was free to drive his livestock onto whatever pastures he wished.

The brutal robbery of my livestock pastures by Mr. Anishchenko forced me to summon help from the Novo Alexandrov village administration. It authorized the following four peasants to help: Andrei Batenko, Fedor Uprunenko, Mikita Katchenko, and Vassili Lutzenko. On 17 December, as a result of Mr. Anishshenko's arbitrary grazing, his horseherd was impounded in their presence, and they watched as three of Anishshchenko's horses were caught and delivered to the local administrative courts by the District Office in Halbstadt. His other horses were driven back to their home by the above-mentioned four credible men.

I therefore appeal to the evidence of the four credible witnesses mentioned above, who have spoken truthfully of Mr. Anishchenko's violent raiding of my pasturelands. The episodes have forced me to drive 2,000 head of my sheep to distant pastures leased for one ruble per head from State Counsellor Burachkov in Nizhnii Dneprovsk Uezd. These expenses have been incurred solely by Mr. Anishchenko's violation of my rights and the resulting need to hire animal drivers as described. My property suffered damage by being infringed upon daily.

Acting with consideration and moderation towards Mr. Anishchenko and his intentional attacks, I ask only for compensation of 2,000 rubles that I have had to spend on pasture for my sheep. These terms are moderate under today's conditions, as every sheep owner will admit.

However, I am ready to reduce this moderate demand by half as evidence of my peaceable intentions and claim only 1,000 rubles, provided he recognizes my forbearance and obligates himself, with his signature, to leave me in the peaceful possession of my land in future. He must also sign an agreement that specifies a penalty per head for each of his horses, horned cattle, or sheep that may stray across the boundary onto my land at any time. The same penalty would apply to my livestock that might cross the border onto his land. And should his or my livestock damage hay meadows or grain fields at any time, impartial persons would be summoned to assess the damage. Moreover, Mr. Anishchenko must undertake to keep his geese away from my watering places. They cloud the water to the detriment of my livestock, and seed land around watering places with droppings that sheep avidly consume because of their salt content. He must, moreover, stop chasing wild game across my estate, not because of their loss but because his chases threaten to scatter my sheep flocks. He must completely cease fishing in the Molochnaia River within my boundaries and not permit washing at my watering places. In short, my watering places must be kept secure and not become clouded lest the health of my livestock suffer damage.

From the above story, Yr. Honour can see how my neighbour, Mr. Anishchenko, has dealt with me and my property. I would ask that a judicial investigation into the matter of Mr. Anishchenko's arrogant behaviour be made immediately and a decision reached that would require him to reimburse me a sum of 1,000 rubles for a portion of the damage done to me. He should at the same time, be required to sign off on all of the points mentioned above. My sole purpose is to find protection from my arrogant and unjust neighbour that would leave me in the peaceful possession of my estate.

Johann Cornies

406. Johann Cornies to Heinrich Cornies. 16 January 1834. SAOR 89-1-300/10.

Dear brother H. Cornies,

I received your letter of 20 December. The four shepherds you hired arrived in Ohrloff on 10 January. Thank you for doing me this favour, especially for making the effort to choose good, healthy people of sound moral character for these jobs.

I have further requests for you. As soon as you possibly can, please send me the terms of your agreement with these four men. Are they entitled to use as much tobacco as they need? Is linen clothing on their account or on mine? How many items of fur clothing am I obligated to provide?

Kindly give the relatives of Ivan Richenko five rubles, and Martin Shurchenko's relatives fifteen rubles on my account. At your first opportunity, send the bundles and clothing they have left with you to me or to Johann Neufeldt in Halbstadt.

Please report to me whether my three shepherds from Strasropol – Yokhim Grevenchenko, Tilon Rudenchenko, and Timish Moskalenko, who have now been paid off – left behind half furs they borrowed from me for their trip home. They had promised to leave them with you. Send them to me, well wrapped, at a suitable opportunity.

I need another three shepherds like those you have sent. Ivan Richenko assures me that there are others in the village of Deevka. He noted that Stepan Olichenko, Filip Dardenko, and Prokop Senenenko are excellent shepherds and should be hired as soon as possible. This should be done before they hire on with butchers. Ivan's young brother would like to be hired as a cow herd and Ivan recommends him. Judge for yourself whether he is too young. In short, please hire three shepherds and a cowherd, which I urgently need, by 1 March. Their salaries should be no more than sixty rubles each, the cowherd naturally less. Do not agree to pay anything for linen clothing or tobacco, but give them a few rubles for this purpose, more if they absolutely insist. If they were given tobacco, other of my shepherds would feel aggrieved. Give them an advance, but do not let them take out their passes until five or six days before 1 March, so that they can arrive at the right time. A few days earlier would be better than later, which you are in a position to decide. Ivan told me I needed only to write to you when I need the people from Deevka. You should simply commission the man who recommended him to you, since he knows many people of this type.

Please write to me very soon, so that I can be absolutely certain. At the first opportunity, I will recompense you for your expenses, including the twenty rubles mentioned here.

We had flooding two or three days ago and all the lowlands were under water. Praise God that we are all healthy and well. My wife and Agnesia send greetings to all of you and to Johann. Special greetings from me, and all the best.

Fare well, adieu,
Johann Cornies

407. Johann Cornies to Johann Cornies Jr. 16 January 1834. SAOR 89-1-300/13.

Dear son Johann Cornies,

I received your letter of 30 December and the maps, all in good condition. I am very satisfied with the map you have drawn. We are pleased to hear that you are well and wish you continuing good health and happiness. We, too, are healthy and in good spirits. Please give Mr. Kirilovskii and Mr. Haustek my greetings.

This winter's heavy rain and snow soaked the ground thoroughly and gives us hope for the future. There should be a lot of grass and grain. Our livestock are doing well. Two days ago, brother D.C. went to inspect the livestock wintering near Kinburn. I had heard about a heavy snowfall at Christmastime, but it had melted within a week. Your uncle's misfortune is very regrettable.[2]

Please obtain considerable amounts of vegetable seeds on the enclosed list from Mr. Hummel. We need them in all three of our establishments. We should present Mr. Hummel with some cheeses, butter, etc. I should be able to send these to you very soon. Therefore postpone your purchases until they arrive. For now, simply ask him if he can spare the seeds and report to me. In this way we can ensure that the gift is not made in vain.

We send you many greetings. It gives us great pleasure to receive a letter from you. Fare well with God.

Your father, who loves you,
Cornies

2 This reference to "your uncle's misfortune" is the first in a series of comments about a substantial theft from Heinrich Cornies, Johann's youngest brother.

408. Johann Cornies to Heinrich Cornies. 29 January 1834. SAOR 89-1-300/14.

Dear brother Heinrich Cornies,

We were disheartened to hear of your misfortune. Can anything be done about it? Do not blame yourself for being incautious, remembering that the Lord has given and the Lord has taken away, in this case through the actions of a thief. Do not despair. He can, in some way, replace what you have lost and should He do so, remember always that the precise quantity you possess now or at any particular time is best for you. Remember too that industry, thrift, and good order must never be neglected.

I recommend that you not indulge yourself too much in fear and distress. One should never be indifferent to a small loss, and certainly not to one so considerable. Still, it is unwise to torture oneself about the loss, permitting time to slip by during which you might have accomplished something useful. Also, do not waste time and money on needless investigations and legal processes. Continue to conduct your business calmly, industriously, and with forethought. Believe me, you will definitely achieve more by doing this than by turning your loss over in your head endlessly, or by constantly making plans to regain what was stolen from you. To be sure, there is a high probability of finding the perpetrator. Explore the [criminal] act, but do not allow yourself to become entangled in scattered efforts. You will soon forget your loss, and within a short while, it will seem as though nothing had really happened. So far my advice.

I would like you to have a pair of half-boots made for our Cornelius. They should be patterned on your son's foot, but slightly larger than for Heinrich.[3] What does a funt of good, unspun cotton cost in your area? Kindly hire the people to come here as shepherds by 1 March. Write to me often about this matter, since I want to be certain about it. Because my properties are so scattered, uncertainty in the matter of shepherds creates difficulties for me and causes added costs. Take the postage costs from my account. What price are you now charging for potatoes and how many chetverts can I get from you for spring?

Please let me know how your business is progressing. What will you be doing in spring? If you should find several good, healthy, strong, quiet people as garden and barn servants for my sheep farm, please

3 It is unclear who Cornelius was, though he was apparently a young child, and Cornies would later refer to him as "my Cornelius" (see document 415). Possibly this was an orphan whom Cornies, as a guardian, took in.

report this to me immediately. I would need them before March. Several of my people will be ending their service with me at that time. Everyone is healthy here and in the homes of our brothers. Brother David left two days ago to inspect our livestock at Kinburn. Livestock holdings in our community are deteriorating badly, but bread grains are still available. May you fare well.

My wife and daughter send greetings, to which I add my warmest good wishes. Your brother who loves you,

Johann Cornies

409. Benjamin Janz to Johann Cornies. 30 January 1834. SAOR 89-1-295/9.

Very esteemed Mr. Cornies,

Please do not take it amiss if I burden you with a letter. I have been teaching in Tiegenhagen for almost two years. Now the village has hired another teacher whom they can employ for a good deal less. Since I am unsure of whether I want to stay in teaching, I turn to you with a request. Might you need someone in your establishment or on your sheep farm to write and keep books? I would gladly enter your service in April. I can assure you that, with God's grace, you would be satisfied with me. Please feel free to inquire about me with the people who immigrated from Driesen last year, Jacob Martens and Jakob Enns in Tiegenhagen, and Mr. Heese in Ohrloff. They could provide you with good recommendations on my behalf, and reassure you that my services would be useful in your business.

I immigrated from Driesen in August 1832. I do not speak Russian but am prepared to learn if I can be given an opportunity to do so. I also know something about looking after sheep since my father owned 300 head. It is a small number, I know, but large enough to give one some knowledge.

I request that you kindly reply soon. With hope, I am your willing,

Benjamin Janz

Tiegenhagen, 30 January 1834 [or 1835?]

410. Johann Cornies to Johann Regier. 12 February 1834. SAOR 89-1-300/16v.

To the esteemed Johann Regier, Schoensee,

Honoured friend,

About two weeks ago, I had occasion to speak with the Nogai District chairman for Etsherit volost. He told me that the recent general crop failure caused extreme need among the Nogais, and the total lack of food is being felt more seriously every day. Theft is a frequent problem among the Nogais.

He asked me to speak to you about our community arrangements designed to interrupt all communication between the Nogais and the Russians herding our livestock. Germans must guard their livestock, food supplies, etc., well. He predicted that as soon as temperatures allow Nogais to spend nights on the fields, thievery will become more prevalent. Good guards can restrict access by thieves, and much crime could in this way be prevented. He pointed out that contacts with our herdsmen gave thieves real knowledge about the situation in every village. They probably provided thieves with access to every household in some villages. If good guards prevent thieves from finding access to our villages, livestock that has escaped starvation can be retained for the owner's use.

Having been informed of this matter, you will know what measures to take to prevent thievery in our community. Your friend,

Cornies

411. Johann Cornies to Traugott Blueher. 14 February 1834. SAOR 89-1-300/19v.

Honoured Mr. Blueher,

I received the glasses you sent me with your communication of 14 November. They are, regrettably, unsuited to this person's eyes. He can see a point at the distance covered by the enclosed measuring thread as in fog, but nothing otherwise.

The transport drivers delivered fifteen dozen sheep shears to my brother in Ekaterinoslav in good order.

Sending you my honest thanks for your efforts, honoured Mr. Blueher, I must burden you with additional tasks. A young man in our community, thirty-five to forty years of age, an agriculturalist by trade, suffered a great loss of eyesight last August. It was without the slightest pain. None of the prescribed remedies helped and his sight has worsened from month to month, even though his eyes are otherwise beautifully clear and bright. Occasionally he feels slight pressure in his temples and eyelids, but no pain. His vision is blurred and his eyesight continues to deteriorate.

Local doctors tell him that he has a black cataract and advised him to seek out an appropriate ophthalmologist. Pastor Rosenstrauch in Kharkov suggested the Moscow ophthalmology hospital. The young man has asked me to write to you in the hope that you might make inquiries for him at that hospital, as part of your Christian duty. Is the blindness I have described known there? Does the hospital have a cure? What might the costs of appropriate medical treatment, etc., be? He asks you to advise him as to whether he should travel to Moscow this spring.

In the expectation that you might view my request as an expression of Christian love and send me a compassionate reply, I remain, with esteem and love, your true friend and servant,

Johann Cornies

412. Johann Cornies to Traugott Blueher. 15 February 1834. SAOR 89-1-300/21.

Honoured Mr. Blueher,

I can respond to your questions about the outlook for wool [sales] in this region by confidently reporting that this year will likely see a sharp decline of about one-half in the production of marketable wool. Poor pasture and severe shortages of fodder have forced many sheep owners to sell their sheep. This problem has been compounded by a rapid rise in the price of grains, up to thirty-five rubles per pud for rye and forty-five rubles for wheat. This situation has forced them to sell even larger numbers of their sheep. They harvested little hay, leaving only *kurrei* as emergency fodder. This has led to the death of even more livestock.

About a third of the community's horses are also gone. They have been sold at ridiculously low prices. A quarter of the horned cattle have died of cattle plague and, in a similarly tragic situation, pox has killed several thousand sheep.

We all face the same serious problems, because *kurrei* as a fodder is now depleted in many places. We have beautiful spring days with night frosts, but still no pastures where sheep, much less a horse or a beef cow, might eat their fill. Many additional head of livestock will be lost. God willing, I will report to you in greater detail in April. Thank God that my livestock seem still to be in good shape and that, at this date, I still have sufficient fodder.

If you wish to purchase wool on your own account this spring, it would be best to inform us in good time. Please give me the highest price you would be willing to pay locally. I might be able to make suitable arrangements for you. I expect wool prices to rise. Locally, wool of the "Silesian" quality you mention is always mixed with finer wool and is not available separately.

The situation in our community is still very difficult, but much better than that among all of our neighbours. Still, worldly treasures may come and go and so we should follow Paul's injunction: "You are to use the world as though you were not of the world." The Lord reveals His justice to us and sees us as individuals and not in terms of our possessions. We must praise God for dealing with us graciously and drawing us to Himself so wisely. We thank Him and praise His name, for He does infinitely more for us than we could ask. With real hope and faith in Christ, our Saviour, we believe our shortages not to be shortages and needs not to be needs. He may give us everything and take it away. He may also return it to us. May His will be done. We greet you and your treasured family in loving friendship, your friend and servant,

Johann Cornies

413. Johann Cornies to Thomas Wiens. 26 February 1834. SAOR 89-1-300/23.

Dear friend Thomas Wiens, Altonau,

You charged Attaman Vassily Karamanov 200 rubles for having, without your permission, driven sheep flocks belonging to my partners and me across your rented land on the Ashis Otluk. We disagree with this sum. In our opinion, you took far too much. Authorized by my partners, I therefore write to you to insist that forty rubles should be adequate. I should mention that we have been assessed compensation of two silver rubles for similarly driving flocks across like pieces of land. Since our flocks were driven over your boundary without permission, we agree to pay you forty rubles. We would ask you to return the remaining 160 rubles without objection.

In the hope that you accept this sum as a fair settlement and are prepared to be reconciled to us and remain our good friend, I expect a decision from you, best of friends, by 4 March. Greetings to you and your wife. I am your friend,

J. Cornies

414. Johann Cornies to Johann Cornies Jr. 1 March 1834. SAOR 89-1 300/24.

Dear son,

I have in hand your letter and map of 16 December 1833, both in good condition. I am much satisfied with your drawing of the map. We are pleased that you are well and wish you continued good health. We are healthy and well. Please give Mr. Kirilovskii and Mr. Haustek our greetings.

We are having real April weather, warm days with storm clouds. Should this weather continue and ploughing begin in a few days, many of our people would benefit greatly. The grass on the meadow seems to shout for joy. It has not experienced anything like this for more than two years. Joy thus follows sorrow and will be followed by sorrow again. We must take care not to become too comfortable in our present situation in order that we might avoid the deepest sorrow later on. The best course is the middle course.

Your letter of 22 February has just arrived where you mention that my letter of 26 January had not reached you. It does not really matter, since I simply acknowledged receipt of your map and asked you to request various vegetable seeds on my behalf. I have now ordered the seeds from brother Heinrich Cornies.

With heartfelt greetings from your dear Mother and sister, I greet you also as your father who loves you,

Johann Cornies

**415. Johann Cornies to Heinrich Cornies. 1 March 1834.
SAOR 89-1-300/25.**

Dear brother Heinrich Cornies,

The five men you hired arrived today. On average, they do not seem as strong and intelligent as the first people you hired for me. One of the shepherds seems especially young. In my view, a shepherd is not really of age until he has a moustache, even though the moustache has nothing to do with it. It is possible that the one who seems too young, and also the others, know their business better than I think they do. I am satisfied and mention this only to let you know what kind of fellows I would, in future, like for my service.

The garden servant seems alright, but the cowherd could be older, bigger, and stronger. I will soon need an additional cowherd, but he must be full-grown, at least twenty-five years of age, and have clean personal habits. At the right time, I will ask you to hire one more. I also need one family, or perhaps two, one for Iushanle and one for Taschenak. They must definitely be good people. Don't hire any if you cannot find such families. At the moment, I also urgently need a barn servant. He should not be a complainer but somebody who is honest, clean, of good stature, and not too young. My present employee in this position ends his service tomorrow.

With greetings, I remain, as always,

Your brother Johann Cornies

P.S. Please purchase significant quantities of vegetable seeds for me. The list of desired seeds is enclosed. Friend Enns would likely transport them. Also, please buy me one or two good bottles of Ferintz varnish. Over time, I hope you will obtain all of the things I have requested, including a pair of half-boots for my Cornelius, a little larger than for your Heinrich. Should you need money for my orders, ask the district chairman to kindly give you an advance on my account. I will repay him, with thanks, when he returns (since I am unsure when I will visit Ekaterinoslav).

List of seeds: Head cabbage, cabbage, carrots, salad cabbage, parsley, parsnip, lettuce, beets, cucumbers, early radish, sweet peas, anise, green beans, black radish, onions, large green sweet peas, watermelon.

P.S. Leonhard just told me that the cowherd at our Iushanle sheep farm ends his service on 13 March. Could you find us another cowherd who is not too young, at least twenty years of age, of good stature, quick, healthy, and clean. He must help with the milking and must do the feeding in winter. Should you find a cowherd with these qualities and also a barn servant, they could start work immediately. The current cowherd earns seventy rubles, with clothes except for linen clothing, but I would like to hire for less. Do not hire anyone who has served with the Germans. The same.

416. Johann Cornies to Traugott Blueher. 5 April 1834. SAOR 89-1-300/29v.

Esteemed Mr. Blueher,

I received your valued letter and accounts yesterday, 4 April, and also the Orekhov post office's notification that money has arrived for me.

Many thanks for your information about wool and its sale. I would be pleased to have 500 puds of wool purchased for you here. What is the present exchange rate in Moscow? Banco Assignats have fallen markedly in Ekaterinoslav (I do not know why) and are readily exchanged at 6 to 7 per cent. Perhaps this will change soon, or has paper currency fallen in value in your area as well? Please inform me about this as soon as you can.

Forgive the briefness of my letter. My herds have now returned from winter quarters and I am fully occupied with getting them back into shape. Enclosed below are details of the previous health of the blind man I mentioned. I will return the glasses to you soon.

May God keep you and your entire esteemed house. Adieu. Your servant,

Johann Cornies

From his earliest youth until 1830, this man suffered no significant illness or scabious and other rashes. In 1830, he felt chills on the soles of his feet, which crept up his knees and finally to his thighs. These chills decreased somewhat a year ago. In March 1833, however, he suddenly experienced high fever, with chills lasting eighteen to twenty hours. The attack so weakened him that he could not leave his bed for ten days. His health was then good until June, when he felt a pressure deep in the hollows of his eyes, as if the eyeballs were being pressed out from the back. He also felt pain in his forehead, above the eyebrows, with twinges in his temples and the back of his head. At the same time, his vision grew worse. In September 1833, he began to feel an itching over his entire body that would not let him sit or lie still. But there was no rash and he was careful not to scratch. This discomfort disappeared after three days.

417. Johann Cornies to Johann Regier. 28 April 1834. SAOR 89-1-300/42.

Treasured friend Johann Regier, Schoensee,

Despite my best intentions, I cannot let you have more than a mirka of the potatoes I received from Ekaterinoslav. The quantity delivered to me was not as large as promised. Please accept the smaller quantity and do not think ill of me. I assure you of my willingness but, as you can see, I could not have sent more, even with the best of intentions.

With heartfelt greetings, I remain, as always,

Your friend Johann Cornies

418. Johann Cornies to Sparrau Village Office. 30 April 1834 . SAOR 89-1-300/42v.

I have authorized Kokan, the bearer of this note, a Nogai from Akkerman, to accompany the fullholder Esau to the Nogai village Buskekle. Twenty-three sheep were stolen from Esau, and Ereshop Efende, a Nogai in Buskekle, bought the same number of sheep from another Nogai. Action must be taken without delay, before the sheep are scattered. Kokan has been authorized to make every effort to assist Esau in recovering his sheep.

If these sheep are found to be Esau's, the Buskekle Village Office or the local District Office should be so informed. The sheep must be held securely to ensure that they do not disappear while the matter is being settled.

Johann Cornies

P.S. It would be even better if Ereshop Efendi were to let Esau take the sheep along with him immediately.

419. Johann Cornies to Kirilovskii. 30 April 1834. SAOR 89-1-300/43.

Honoured Sir, Esteemed Mr. Kirilovskii,

The time has come when I must recall my son from your fatherly guardianship. Please allow me, most esteemed and treasured benefactor of my son, to express my unfeigned and heartfelt thanks for your teaching, guidance, and guardianship. These few words flow from the depths of my heart. My wife and I feel deeply moved, as we attempt to convey our great thanks for the parental support you, honoured Mr.Kirilovskii, and your esteemed wife, have given our son.

We must thank you for the immeasurable benefits he enjoyed over the last two years. May God, the giver of all good things, bless you many times over as the magnanimous benefactor of our son, who taught him and directed his education. We as parents would be mistaken were we not to hope and expect that he will value these benefits accordingly and endeavour to demonstrate, through efforts and actions, that your well-inclined benevolence and efforts were not in vain. On this, too, rests the lifelong joy of his parents.

Let me assure you that, for the rest of my life, I will not cease to be Your Honour's most thankfully devoted,

Johann Cornies

420. Johann Cornies to Johann Cornies Jr. 30 April 1834. SAOR 89-1-300/45.

Dear son Johann Cornies,

Since business affairs will not leave me time to come to Ekaterinoslav, I have asked your Uncle Peter Cornies to fetch you. Your sister Agnesia will accompany him. My dear son, take leave of Mr. Kirilovskii in a proper way. Express to him your obliging thanks for his teaching, fatherly guardianship, and care. Do the same with Mr. Hausteck. Also, take leave of the state counsellor by expressing your honest attachment to him and your esteem for the many things you were able to enjoy in close proximity to him. Ask him for his considered and benevolent advice to you in future as well. Show your gratitude to everyone.

Agree with Mr. Haustek on the money you still owe him. I may get to Ekaterinoslav within the next two to three weeks and will then pay him for everything, with the greatest thanks. Together with Uncle Heinrich Cornies, prepare a complete account of the money he has received from me, what he has bought for me, and what he has paid out for me in other ways. I really need such an account.

I just remembered that I cannot go to Ekaterinoslav in two to three weeks. Do not mention this to Mr. Haustek, however, since I do not want him to put off preparing the accounts until I arrive. I would rather that not happen. Try to encourage him to complete the accounts, even if the totals are higher than what Neufeldt and Wiebe have paid him. The amount Mr. Haustek borrowed from me need not be deducted unless he himself mentions it. Emphasize that I want his completed accounts and must be notified of our debt. Immediately upon your arrival at home, I will send the money.

Farewell, your father who loves you,
Johann Cornies

421. Johann Cornies to Wilhelm Martens. 21 May 1834. SAOR 89-1-300/48.

Dear friend, Wilhelm Martens,

I cannot lend you more than 7,000 R.B.A. for your business. Over the last eight days, local agents for Thiessen in Khortitsa have besieged me for money to purchase wool. They have taken most of my available cash with them. I literally have almost no silver currency left, which leaves me in considerable difficulty. Therefore, you will receive 7,000 R.B.A. that I will send along with your son Johann.

My greetings to you and your family. Also, when you are able, please give my greetings to my brother Heinrich Cornies in Ekaterinoslav. I wish you success in your business and also a safe journey.

Your loving friend,
J. Cornies

422. Peter Reimer to Johann Cornies. 26 May 1834. SAOR 302/28.

Sent from Alexanderwohl.
Dear and valued friend Johann Cornies,

Your letter informed me that the Nogai had brought no money. I really prefer to send someone to Ohrloff today, with a heartfelt plea that you send along another thousand rubles with my son today. I am in difficulty because I am short of money. Yesterday morning I borrowed 600 rubles from Johann Peters, Gnadenheim, but by evening there was not a single silver ruble in my house. The wool I am buying on consignment is now arriving quickly. I am at my wit's end and you are my only recourse. I request 2,000 rubles, if possible. Dear friend Cornies, please prepare a signed note for the thousand rubles requested earlier and send it along with my son. I promise to sign the note once it arrives and return it to Johann Cornies, Ohrloff, this coming Sunday, 27 May. If you are unable to fulfil my request, please forgive my insistent demands.

With greetings to you and your dear wife,
Your friend Peter Reimer
Alexanderwohl, 26 May 1834
[Marked] 1,000 rubles sent.

423. Johann Cornies to Major Mark. 15 June 1834.
SAOR 89-1-300/50v.

His Honour, Major Mark,

At your request, my friend Tobias Voth has asked me to purchase two good milk cows for you. Much as I would like to oblige, I regret to say that horned cattle have suffered greatly over the past year. Good cattle are difficult to find because cattle plague and fodder shortages have resulted in the loss of many of our best animals. Few genuine Frisian cows remain, and any still alive after these disasters are mostly in the hands of wealthy persons who would not part with them at any price. Middling and poor cows are available occasionally, especially where the money crisis has not been so acute, but these would hardly meet with your approval. I would prefer not to make authorized purchases of such cattle.

As you can see, esteemed Major, good cows cannot be bought here this year. With this I have the honour to call myself Yr. Honour's obedient servant,

Johann Cornies

424. Johann Cornies Jr. to Johann Cornies. 14 June 1834.
SAOR 89-1-302/10.

Sent from Tashchenak estate.
Esteemed Father,

Only twelve of the mowers hired earlier have arrived. Those who did come insist that some of the men, because they are afraid to work for us, were recruited to smooth [rutted] roads while others are now working for Lukovich. I will make every effort to find workers and to win their trust. Mowing has started along the border with Lukovich, where we are cutting a lot of nice hay. A large number of cutters are available at twenty rubles and they will start to bring in the hay today. Menlega was not at home. Only about 100 ash trees have grown at Atly Pasha's and a few more at his neighbour's place. I remain your devoted,

Johann Cornies
Molochnaia Estate, 14 June 1834

425. Regina Regier to Johann Cornies. 20 June 1834. SAOR 89-1-302/14.

Valued Mr. Cornies,

I write to let you know that the Nogai delivered the horses in good order. I send you and your wife many greetings, and sign myself respectfully,

Regina Regier

426. Johann Cornies to Traugott Blueher. 22 June 1834. SAOR 89-1-300/53v.

Esteemed Mr. Blueher,

On 15 June, I dispatched my wool for this year, loaded on twenty-two carts. It weighed a total of 635 puds, four funt, inclusive of sacks. The original contract concluded with the carters is enclosed. Accordingly, once the wool has been delivered to you in good order, please pay the carters the outstanding cartage charges of 1,587 rubles and charge that amount to my wool account. According to the enclosed bill of lading, you will receive wool washed on the backs of the sheep in the following grades: Electa, ten sacks; first grade, twenty-three sacks; second grade, twenty sacks; third grade, fourteen sacks. A total of sixty-seven linen sacks are marked "J.C."

In entrusting this wool to you for sale on consignment, I have full confidence that you will obtain the highest possible price for it. This sale is left to your judgment.

Treasured friend, you will receive two cheeses with the carters. I doubt that their flavour will be really good, especially the larger one, but I have none better. Please do me the favour of letting me know how you like them. If you should request anything similar in future, whatever it may be, I am at your service at any time.

The wool sample that the carters will pass on was washed by a Nogai woman. She asks whether such washed wool can be spun on machines and used to produce cloth.

I report to you that I received 944 half-imperials and twenty-eight whole imperials sent along with your letter of 22 May 1834.

Yesterday and the day before yesterday, I was honoured by visits from several illustrious persons. The most elevated visitors were Count Vorontsov, Marshal Marmont from France,[4] Prince Golitsyn, and the local Civil Governor. They all visited my khutor on the Iushanle and spent the night at my home in Ohrloff.

Weather conditions in our region this year are good, thank God. The grain in most fields looks splendid and we regret that it was not possible for many people to seed more because of a shortage of seed and draught animals. This is especially true for many Nogais, who will be again forced to survive the year on slender diets. However, I am pleased to note that these conditions should force the Nogais to reflect on their situation and to make a real effort to understand the teachings of their German neighbours. Despite a total crop failure, suffering and want have not necessarily appeared in households where good housekeeping prevails. It was also possible for the Germans to feed hundreds of Nogais.

This year the price of wool rose from thirty-eight to forty-five rubles washed, from twenty-four to twenty-nine rubles, fifty kopeks, unwashed. All payments were made in Banco Assignats, at 7 per cent and less. Silver currency has almost completely fled our area because of food shortages. Merchants arrived only with Banco and gold. No one wanted to accept the imperial, because most everyone needs the jingle of silver to buy food or repay debts made in silver. As a result, the exchange rate for the half-imperial hovers around nineteen to twenty rubles.

Wool purchases for you would have been more favourable if Banco notes had not fallen so greatly in value. Friend Neufeldt made every effort to cash your note at least a little to your advantage, but in the end it had to be exchanged without a premium.

Fourteen days ago, wool prices fell by three rubles a pud. At present, however, there is such a demand for wool that it fetches thirty-two

---

4 Auguste Frédéric Louis Viesse de Marmont, former aide de camp and friend of Napoleon, and instrumental figure in the French surrender in 1814. After Napoleon's defeat, Marmont loyally served Louis XVIII, following the King into exile in 1830. In the 1830s, he travelled extensively in eastern Europe.

rubles unwashed. No washed wool is available. The value of Banco Assignats in Ekaterinoslav has risen by up to 10 per cent, and the imperial is again selling for forty-two rubles. I will try to get the best possible price for the latter, but doubt that this will exceed forty-two rubles. There are simply no established exchange rates in our region. Every merchant sets his own.

Please, as you have done in the past, handle the sale of my wool according to your best judgment. I cannot tell you the currency in which I would prefer receiving your remittances because of great fluctuations in the base price of Banco Assignats and gold. Meanwhile, please let me know what the exchange rates in Moscow are for this month, for Banco, gold, and silver, in order that I can better assess my position.

Fodder here was consumed by April and is now unavailable at any price. The grass was scant because of the frozen ground and the cold weather, the situation dire. Straw roofs were dismantled to provide fodder. Under these conditions, villagers watched animals die before their eyes, one after another. We waited for warm weather, day after day. Eventually, only three warm days were needed to provide pasturage for the livestock.

The suffering in our own district was not as severe as in the neighbouring German colonist district. Many in our district still have sheep, though fewer than previously. In the colonist district, many are now bereft of all sheep and the situation in regard to livestock is equally dire. In May our settlement had 93,000 sheep, excluding those on sheep farms or leased land. I assume that Mennonites still have some 130,000 sheep. Numbers for other livestock are proportionately about the same. Eighteen of our Mennonite villages have again, this year, suffered severe drought, but twenty-three villages will have everything they need.

This year, I intend to allow my son to travel to Sarepta and Saratov and then come to visit you.

In sending you and your dear family friendly and loving greetings, I remain your friend and servant,

Johann Cornies

427. Johann Cornies to Gerhard Enns. 23 July 1834. SAOR 89-1-300/60.

Best of friends, Gerhard Enns,

Secretary Sommerfeldt told me of your plan to leave for Khortitsa tomorrow, Tuesday. Please take the accompanying two parcels of cocoons along and pass them on to the chairman of the Khortitsa Society.

The contents of each parcel should be reeled separately. The cocoons in "Litt: B." should first be inspected to decide if reeling their silk makes sense. If not, describe in writing what the deficiencies are and how these might be remedied. Should the silk in the deficient cocoons not be worth reeling, return them to me so that they can be forwarded to the owners with comments. Also, remind Chairman J. Penner to have the previously mentioned acorns and hawthorn seeds for our local plantations sent to us at the appropriate time.

With best wishes for your safe journey and a request to transmit greetings to all who remember me, especially to our common friend, J. Penner. Farewell, adieu, your loving friend,

Johann Cornies

428. Heinrich Heese to Johann Cornies. 23 June 1834. SAOR 89-1-302/12.

Treasured friend,

I would be most obliged if you could find the time to select twelve lamb pelts of the best variety for me. The master is presently waiting to make a cover for me. The fur blanket might then be ready for my journey to Kichkas.

Your devoted Heinrich Heese

[Marked] 12 pelts sent.

429. Traugott Blueher to Johann Cornies. 24 July 1834. SAOR 89-1-302/71.

Beloved friend Cornies,

I have received your two communications of 22 June and the three fleeces sent by post. Both shipments of Spanish wool arrived in good condition, but all of the balls of wool had lost weight because of the continuing hot, dry weather. The carters encountered only one light rain en route. The remarkably hot weather in the region around Moscow has continued for longer than any in living memory. Little hay or other field crops have been harvested, and unless there is a penetrating rain in the next few days, most varieties of vegetables will also yield little.

Your wool seems somewhat cleaner than in other years, but no buyer has yet appeared. This will unlikely happen in the next few weeks because manufacturers want first to assess price trends in Nizhnii Novgorod.

My limited examination of Mr. Neufeld's wool bought on my behalf indicates that it is of high quality. Many thanks for your kind efforts and advances, for which I await a notice from you so that I can repay the credit you gave me in advance.

Regrettably, the exchange rates for the various currencies are fluctuating to such a degree that one cannot reasonably respond to them. [Figures in text are unclear: silver rubles at 10, imperials at 21.12 rubles, 15 kopeks, both estimating the Assignat at 11.]

Thank you for the two cheeses you kindly sent. My wife assures me that their flavour is exactly what it should be. My family also sends hearty thanks.

Although I have received the wool samples, I have not yet managed to make adequate inquiries as to their washing. My next communication will include definite information in this regard.

Could you obtain 300 to 1,000 puds of Sigay wool of the quality contained in the three balls you sent me? There is a great demand for this variety by manufacturers. I would take 500 puds annually. Perhaps it could be purchased from among Tatars in your area.

Should your dear son come to Moscow, I would neglect nothing to make his stay as pleasant and instructive as possible.

With greetings of heartfelt love to you and your family, I commend myself to you as your devoted friend,

Traugott Blueher

P.S. Since I assume that your son is accustomed to a simple and plain lifestyle, it would give me pleasure to receive him in our home. A friendly reception will not be lacking.

Received 11 August 1834.

430. August Wilke to Johann Cornies. 29 July 1834. SAOR 89-1-429/59.

Sent from Iushanle.

Most esteemed Mr. Cornies,

I hereby send you the passport you forgot. I found it behind the couch while working with the seeds.

I also report that I disposed of four funt of ash seed and three and one-quarter funt of birch seed.

With all respect, I remain your devoted servant,

August Wilke

431. Johann Cornies to Tiege Village Office. 30 July 1834. SAOR 89-1-300/60v.

Ottoman Bary Zeptar Oglu has been grazing sheep herds belonging to Babio, the Karassus merchant, on my rented Crown lands on the Iushanle. He notified me that he had found eleven head of his Shuntikish breed of sheep in the Tiege community's sheep herd, also grazing on these Crown pastures. The Tiege community's shepherd declared them to be his property. Ottoman Bary can produce witnesses that the community's shepherd had earlier been holding even more sheep belonging to Bary. He demands that the shepherd's house in Tiege be searched for the pelts of such sheep. The Village Office is requested to undertake an immediate search of the shepherd's house in the presence of the village officers.

Leaseholder Johann Cornies

432. Johann Cornies to Casper Adrian Hausknecht. 31 July 1834. SAOR 89-1-300/61v.

Dear friend Hausknecht,

I received your letter of 22 July a few days ago and am sending you the answer you requested. I asked friend Heese to answer your previous letter to me, which he will undoubtedly have done. It is a misunderstanding that Schlatter sent me news of your mother's death more than a month ago, as Leyki told you. I may not have expressed myself clearly to Heese. I received a letter from Daniel in which he asked me to notify you that the money and letters you requested from your mother would be sent to you soon or, as is more likely, that you would be able to withdraw the money from an Odessa firm. This may have given rise to the impression that your mother was dead. I did not notify you immediately because my business affairs kept me away from home and because I had mislaid the letter from Daniel. I had read it only quickly and had to rummage through all of my letters to find it again.

You ask me for a loan which I cannot give you at this time. You may complain about my being hard-hearted in this matter, to Daniel or anyone else all you like, but I know my situation better and dismiss critical statements by others.

Fare well with God. With greetings, I remain your honest friend,

Johann Cornies

433. Forestry Society to August Wilke. 10 August 1834. SAOR 89-1-284/21.

To gardener Mr. August Wilke in Iushanle,

Today's meeting of the Society for the Advancement and Dissemination of Forest Trees, Orchards, Sericulture, and Viticulture, in the Molochnaia Mennonite District, decided to pay you fifty rubles per year. This is for your work with seeds that the Society will be acquiring from various guberniias. You will decide whether the seeds are likely to germinate, and take care that those arriving too late for seeding this summer retain their ability over the winter to germinate. The seeds found unsuitable for seeding should be weighed accurately, their weight and variety reported to the Society, and then disposed of.

434. Johann Cornies to Peter Neufeldt. 31 August 1834. SAOR 89-1-300/65.

Honourable Peter Neufeldt, Ladekopp, honoured friend,

I received your friendly letter of 15 August 1834. While I intend to send my son to Moscow this autumn, his sole purpose would be to perfect himself in the subjects Mr. Hausteck failed to teach him because he spent too many hours with persons of high rank. My son's reception and lodging in Moscow have been arranged. Depending on circumstances, he may travel to St. Petersburg in spring, but not to Germany. I have hired a Russian to take him to Moscow. He will do so once he returns from transporting my wool to Moscow. Arrangements should be as simple as possible. A companion would naturally be needed if this journey were to take the route you know, my friend. In that case, the offer from your step-son Jacob Kroeker would be desirable. However, for the purpose of this journey, it would be superfluous to have a companion in attendance in Moscow. He would only be bored.

I send sincerest greetings to you and your dear family, and remain your friend,

Johann Cornies

435. Johann Cornies to Inspector Biller. 4 September 1834. SAOR 89-1-300/66v.

Highly honoured Mr. Biller,

If it is possible, kindly purchase three or four funt, and perhaps more, of good mulberry seeds for our local district from settlements under your administration. I and my district would be indebted if you could provide us with mulberry seeds that are in short supply here. They could be sent to Inspector Pelekh by mail, to be forwarded to our Society. The Society will reimburse you promptly.

Forgive me for this interruption. Be assured of my continuing esteem and respect. I remain your devoted servant,

Johann Cornies

436. Johann Cornies to Heinrich Cornies. 4 September 1834. SAOR 89-1-300/65v.

Dear brother Heinrich Cornies,

Please have one or two chetverts of acorns gathered for me and for the local Society. Spread them out thinly because they can, if kept in a sack or spread too thickly, easily lose their ability to germinate in a few days. They are then useless as seed. Also, obtain two or three mirka of hawthorn seeds, spread thinly as well. If Mr. Hummel can give you white, ripe junipers capable of germinating, please purchase one garnets.

Send all the seed to me as soon as you find a good opportunity to do so. Contract the freight to Ohrloff, giving the carter a bill of lading that states clearly what, and in what quantities, he is to transport and what the price for his services is. Even if the freight charges are high, ensure that the seed is sent quickly.

This year, on my sheep farm, I have raised 92,000 young forest and fruit trees from seed and they are all doing very well. We are all healthy. Johann left for the Crimea last Wednesday and, God willing, he will leave for Moscow, etc., when he gets back. I send greetings to you, your wife and children. Farewell, adieu,

J. Cornies

437. Johann Cornies to Andrei M. Fadeev. 18 September 1834. SAOR 89-1-300/67.

Your Honour, Gracious State Counsellor,

I was pleased and greatly honoured to receive Your Honour's communication of 31 July more than a month ago. Its unexpected contents surprised me, especially since it reported that His Highness, Count Vorontsov, would deign to honour me with a visit during his journey through our villages. I am honoured and blessed by this favour, but have no idea what I have done to deserve it. I will treasure this great benevolence and seek to make myself worthy of his kindness through new diligent efforts. With deepest esteem, I thank Your Honour for your generous intercession on my behalf, and for the explanations you have given His Highness. I assure you, highly esteemed State Counsellor, that I will conscientiously make every effort to prove my gratitude through deeds.

I read with sympathy Yr. Honour's letter about your painful eyes and the difficulties you have encountered in achieving at your new residence the household comforts you are accustomed to having. Without meaning to flatter, let me say that I am confident that your love of order will, with God's help, enable you to achieve the arrangements you enjoyed while in Ekaterinoslav.

Our spring weather was exceptionally favourable this year. Rain and warm temperatures helped seeds to germinate evenly and well, giving our district considerable hope for an exceptionally good harvest. We had drought in June. In the villages from Schonesee to Altonau, and from there to Margenau, all the grain dried up at the best growing time. The villages above Steinbach, and Steinbach itself, enjoyed a very good harvest. Their surpluses will permit them to provide substantial assistance to villages suffering shortages. Potatoes and other garden vegetables did well generally, meaning that there will be less of a need for bread grains. Enough fodder was produced, with surpluses in spots, and we believe that no livestock will need to suffer. Pastures this summer were green, although the situation in some villages was better than in others. For the rest, life continues on as before. Since money is in very short supply, our money this past summer was almost exhausted. Had this year's harvest turned out generally as in the villages above Steinbach, we would have managed to make up the losses we suffered in last year's drought within two years. Now it will naturally take longer. We will continue our work in the plantations this fall.

Martens thanks you for your good wishes that I passed on to him, including your comments about his wool business with the Ekaterinoslav factory. He has always taken your advice in similar matters in the past and done what is needed to ensure his success.

The trees in our local orchards, especially the cherry trees, have suffered greatly in the two-year drought, and all of the trees have dried up in some places. Fortunately, everything in my plantation at Iushanle continues to prosper. I have raised 93,000 trees of all kinds from seed this year – mostly forest trees – and have kept them growing well.

Fortunately, I have finally hit upon an effective method to have all types of forest trees germinate from seed and grow properly in this region.

Mr. Prichenko's wife, who was in Prishib early this month, took along seven parts of the *Conversations-Lexicon* to pass on to you when she arrives in Odessa. I am informed from Prussia that this series is being issued very slowly, having only reached the letter F.

My son has managed my Tashchenak estate this summer and I have now allowed him to take a four-week trip to the Crimea. When he returns, I will send him to Moscow via Sarepta. He will spend the winter taking instruction in surveying, drawing, and mathematics. In spring, he will visit agricultural establishments around Moscow, St. Petersburg, and Riga to acquire the knowledge that will be needed for the profession I have chosen for him. Because the inspector cannot provide passes for capital cities without the permission of the Guardianship Committee, I would sincerely request that Yr. Honour speedily resolve the matter so that the inspector's submission regarding a pass for my son arrives at the Committee in a timely fashion.

In anticipation of Yr. Honour's further gracious consideration, and with esteem, I remain Yr. Honour's humble servant,

Johann Cornies

P.S. Our Guardianship administration is now at so great a distance from us that the lower courts have become much bolder in dealing with our righteous demands and grievances in a spirit that is contrary to the law. Our valued inspector presents our concerns forcefully and in keeping with the law, but the Dneprovsk and Ekaterinoslav courts have created many distasteful situations for him, misinterpreting and declaring unjust what he has investigated and found to be just. This is to discourage him in his efforts and to underline that he has no influence in their transactions and should not bother intervening. In Dneprovsk Uezd, the inspector investigated a brandy seizure from Peter Reimer and found it to be without legal basis. Last winter, I hired fifteen workers from Deevka near Ekaterinoslav for a year, all with passes for a year, and gave their families money to buy bread. In spring, five of these men left me without my knowledge before they had worked off their wages, and stole from me. The inspector demanded that these people return to my service, but the lower court took no action, except to give the inspector an incomplete answer.

I am presuming to bring this situation to Yr. Honour's attention, to request Yr. Honour's trusted, fatherly guardianship, and to assist Inspector Pelekh in his efforts, especially as these relate to the seizure of Peter Reimer's brandy.

On 15 September, I mailed 1,300 R.B.A. to your esteemed address. You will undoubtedly have received the package. Martens and I would ask you to apply 1,000 rubles of this sum, as a small token of our affection, to your new household arrangements. [An additional sum] of 300 rubles comes to you from representatives of our local merchants. We would be especially pleased if this token of our concern were not taken amiss.

With the most complete respect, I have the honour to be Yr. Honour's devoted servant,

Johann Cornies

438. Johann Cornies to Traugott Blueher. 20 September 1834. SAOR 89-1-300/71v.

Most esteemed Mr. Blueher,

I received your communication of 24 July with the information that my wool had arrived in good order. Currency prices have been stable here since the Kharkov yearly market, with a silver ruble valued at four rubles Banco, the imperial at forty-two rubles Banco, and Banco notes at 10 per cent, with no higher rates for any of these currencies. Please credit another 250 rubles to your loss on gold, which amounts in total to 5,173 rubles, 2 kopeks. I would ask you to delay sending me this money.

No flocks here produce Sigay wool – that is available only in small quantities from breeding flocks that have been neglected, or in herds where breeding has been improved for only a few generations. It is generally sold with fine wool and at the same price. Would Sigay wool, in your opinion, fetch the same price as does the usual Spanish wool?

Since you have generously offered to receive my son in your worthy house when he arrives in Moscow, I will, counting on your friendship, not hesitate to send him directly to you and commend him to your guardianship. As parents, this gives us great joy and relieves our worries knowing that our son will be well looked after. He has been away for three weeks in the Crimea, but I expect him to return within eight to ten days, when he will leave immediately for Moscow. Since it will be late in fall, I have yet to make a final decision as to whether he should make his way to Moscow through Sarepta.

With genuine Christian love, I commend you and your dear family to the protection of our universal saviour, Jesus Christ. May He keep you, may He give you His peace now and in eternity. Your faithfully obliged friend and servant,

Johann Cornies

439. Johann Cornies to District Office. 30 September 1834. SAOR 89-1-300/72v.

To the honourable District Office in Halbstadt,

I humbly request that the honourable District Office publicize at the earliest moment that I have available for sale thirty rams of genuine Saxon descent, two years of age, at fifty rubles per head, and nineteen highly bred two-year-old rams, at thirty rubles per head, all with good attributes. The head shepherd at my sheep farm will receive cash payments until 5 November.

Johann Cornies

440. Andrei M. Fadeev to Johann Cornies. 1 October 1834. SAOR 89-1-302/29.

Sent from Odessa.

Dear Cornies,

Your letter of 18 September gives me great pleasure, knowing as I now do that you and your family are well. I had hoped that you might visit us in Odessa this autumn, but you fail to mention this possibility in your letter. Thank God that at least some of your villages have had a good harvest, and it is only right that they use their surpluses to help people still in need. I hope that seeding will not be neglected in fall and spring but speeded up to ensure a good harvest.

I would ask you and your colleagues to continue your work in the plantations in order that nothing might be left undone this fall. It is a fine effort that should continue, not because authorities insist on it but because your community gave the late Tsar a promise in this regard and because authorities are genuinely convinced of its usefulness. Please describe in detail the method you employ to have all varieties of forest-tree seeds germinate and flourish. It is a matter of great interest to us.

I have received the seven parts of the *Conversations-Lexicon.* Let me know its price.

I will get a pass for your son once I receive Mr. Pelekh's submission. I would mention that you have problems in the lower courts because of your greater distance from the Guardianship Committee, a natural result of its move. We will protect you as much as we can, but when changes are made from time to time in the colonial administration there are sure to be consequences. This we have no power to change. Try, however, to avoid contact with the civil authorities as much as you can.

I too have now become a landowner by purchasing 500 desiatinas of land, with seven peasant families. It is a good location fifty verstas distance from here, with flowing water. It is not yet set up for agricultural production, but this will come. Meanwhile, my people will have food for at least a year. But what can be done? I cannot possibly live in Odessa with my crowd. For the future, at least, I plan to produce enough food to meet our needs, using a spacious eight-desiatina space to establish an orchard and forest-tree plantation. This will happen over a number of years, but should it be God's will, I will live out my old age in the shade of its trees.

Have you had any rain? We still have drought. First it was very cold and now it is again warm. There is little trade to speak of – only tallow and cattle hides are selling well. Grain prices are seventeen rubles per chetvert of rye, nineteen to twenty for wheat, and seventeen rubles per chetvert of oats. Butter sells at thirteen to fourteen rubles per pud. Is there any trade in the Molochnaia settlement?

We have so much work that neither the General nor I will be able to drop by soon, but we'll try in spring. As you can see, I am not such an idle person that I do not write, even though I am now in the city.

Fare well and my greetings to all of yours,

A Fadeev

Received 8 October 1834. Answered 26 October 1834.

441. Johann Cornies to District Office. 5 October 1834. SAOR 89-1-300/73.

To the honourable District Office in Halbstadt,

In response to the District Office's communication No. 3,149, dated 2 October 1834, I report that there are 120 old mares and twenty-one yearling mares for sale at the stud farm of my sheep farm in Iushanle. For several years I have sold my surplus mares and geldings at the annual market in Novo Vassilievka for an average price of 70 to 200 rubles per head. I report this obediently to the honourable District Office, and have the honour to be Yr. obedient,

Johann Cornies

442. Johann Cornies to David Epp. Khortitsa. 6 October 1834. SAOR 89-1-300/73v.

To the correspondent for the Molochnaia Mennonite Section of the Bible Society, esteemed David Epp in Khortitsa,

With Martin Hamm, a local Mennonite, I am sending you ten Bibles at five rubles, and twenty-nine New Testaments at two rubles, twenty kopeks, packed in a crate marked "D.E." The total cost for these books is 113 rubles, which I have put on your account.

In reporting this matter, I have the honour to call myself, with all respect and devotion, your obedient depot head,

Johann Cornies

P.S. Please inform me of the arrival of the Bibles and Testaments as soon as possible.

443. Andrei M. Fadeev to Johann Cornies. 8 October 1834. SAOR 89-1-302/31.

Dear Cornies,

Your letter of 22 September arrived and I thank you and Martens for your friendly support respecting the tradespeople. This matter was included in the new directive, to go out soon after the sixth. It will ensure that people conducting trade in the colonies will be freed of these dues.

Please ask mechanic Dueck why he has not sent me the promised model harvesting machine. How did it prove itself this summer? Please remind him that he can send the model at no cost through Mr. Pelekh.

May you fare well. I remain forever,

Your devoted A. Fadeev

Answered 26 October 1834.

444. Johann Cornies to Johann Cornies Jr. After 16 October, 1834. SAOR 89-1-300/75.

In order that your journey might be more useful for you, I send you, my son, the following precepts:

1. Conduct your devotions quietly and do not neglect church attendance. Religious devotion is a spiritual state that can only be practised when we are so disposed. It can, for example, be awakened by contemplating a religious truth or by honouring God. Listen to your feelings that have an influence over you.

2. Be cautious about the affairs of the world and the language of religion.

3. Keep a diary on your travels and read it frequently in your free time. Take notice of the way things are done in various regions and of the particular advantages of doing things differently there and better than at home.

4. Acquire the art of saving your money and always remember to put away something for a rainy day.

5. Be cheerful, happy, and lighthearted among good, joyful people, but shun those known as jolly fellows. Do not come into conflict with thoughtless companions, who may rob you if you refuse to go along with them. Do not make it obvious that you have money. Do nothing secretly or without exercising extreme caution.

6. Do not buy expensive clothes in distant lands. Be avid in observing punctuality, love of order, and cleanliness.

7. Write often to your parents in order that you may keep loving thoughts alive. Send letters in a way that ensures their safe arrival.

8. To avoid losing your way, have the road along which you want to travel explained to you carefully. Do not travel in snowstorms during the winter, for they are more dangerous than the most severe cold. Do not allow yourself to be surprised by nightfall.

9. Learn how to acquaint yourself with people, with the state of their minds, and the way they think and act. Keep your word honourably once you have given it. Try to purify your heart, preserve your virtue, and improve and refine your taste.

10. Guard against superstitions of every kind. To believe what is unreasonable is to be credulous. Avoid involvement with hypocrites, seeking out people who live and act in a Christian way. Allow them to teach you. Act in a reasonable way. Examine everything and retain what is best.

11. Be clever in your observations to ensure that you never impose on anyone or become a burden to them. Be helpful when you can, and do not fancy yourself to be too wise and too righteous. Show moderation in all that you do and observe the laws of the land.

I commend you to God. Your father,
Johann Cornies

445. Johann Cornies to Gerhard Dyck. 20 October 1834. SAOR 89-1-220/53v.

Treasured friend, Gerhard Dyck,

State Counsellor Fadeev has requested that I ask you why you have not sent him the promised model grass-mowing machine. If you did not find another way of doing so during the summer, you may forward it to Mr. Fadeev in Odessa, through Inspector Pelekh, at no cost.

To enable me to inform the State Counsellor, as requested, please report to me as soon as possible.

With a friendly greeting to you and your dear family, I remain your well-meaning friend and servant,
Johann Cornies

446. Traugott Blueher to Johann Cornies. 23 October 1834. SAOR 89-1-302/46.

Beloved friend Cornies,
I am concerned about your long silence. Because you have money coming from me, I had assumed that you would have tried to get in touch, even if a letter of yours had gotten lost.

Are you ill or have you had to go on a trip suddenly? Please write.

I sold your Spanish wool to a German manufacturer for sixty-eight rubles [per pud]. He gave me bills of exchange to his debtors in Saratov. 20,000 arrived with the last mail, a sum I will remit to you as soon as you instruct me as to the currency in which you would like it made. The value of Assignats are fluctuating from about 14 to 15 per cent, while gold and silver currencies have remained at previous levels.

I send greetings of sincere, heartfelt love to you and your dear family and remain your faithful friend,
Traugott Blueher

447. Johann Cornies to Andrei M. Fadeev. 25 October 1834. SAOR 89-1-220/38.

Yr. Honour, State Counsellor Fadeev,
It was a pleasure to receive Yr. Honour's esteemed letters of 1 October and 8 October, and to hear of your purchase of a khutor. So you have decided to become a landed proprietor. Congratulations on assuming this new role. I wish you the Lord's blessing and success. May you enjoy continuing good health, an undisturbed peace of mind and, in due course, a happy old age lived in quiet domesticity in the country.

Please excuse me for not writing to you more frequently. It is not indifference on my part but a desire not to disturb Yr. Honour with frequent letters at a time when you are burdened with such important matters. I was unable to come to Odessa this fall because of business affairs and community matters and have had virtually no spare time until now. Finally, I was away for three weeks and during that time my business affairs simply piled up.

Thank you for your kind remarks. Your interest in our affairs is a blessing and I will try to make myself worthy of your esteem.

The Forestry Society has not yet reported its activities for the year, but has not drawn back from doing what it could.

1. With good weather, deep-ploughing the soil to the prescribed depth will be completed this week. This is proceeding in the second-quarter plots of eighteen forest-tree plantations, and in the first-quarter plots of three new plantations.

2. Prior to the harvest, all ditches around eighteen forest-tree plantations were prepared to the prescribed width and depth.

3. At present, everyone is trying to plant as many trees in their plots as they can manage to acquire.

4. On its inspection trips, the Society encouraged fullholders to cultivate fruit orchards according to the received rules and directives. It has also collected records of trees that dried up last year, assessed drought damage, and encouraged villagers by issuing better instructions to them.

The Society now faces fewer difficulties than it did at its founding, but must still be vigilant lest disorder would follow if prescribed rules were not observed. Most Society activities are now of a nature that do not permit detailed reports. We are still busy giving villagers instructions and explanations that only a small minority understand at first. Everything, however, is working out better than we expected, and members of the Society seem not to be discouraged.

The good fall weather seemed to promise success, but we had no forest-tree seeds for distribution. All Society efforts in the Ekaterinoslav guberniia in this regard ended in failure and only Inspector Biller was able to acquire some mulberry seeds for us.

Fall weather, as mentioned, could not have been better. The steppe in June and July was bare, but with warm weather and soaking rains we ended up with more than enough feed for all of our livestock. Beautiful green fields seem almost to suggest that it is May, but short days and long nights remind us that it is already fall. We were able to mow a lot of hay, even in mid-September, and people who seeded winter grain cannot remember a year when the grain fields looked so good. Present prospects indicate a blessed year. May God grant it. Many villagers have already set aside much seed for spring planting. I think everyone will try to thresh as much grain as possible and ensure a sufficient supply for winter even if the results are only a moderately good harvest.

Grain prices are as they were last year: rye, twenty-four rubles in Tokmak; wheat, thirty to thirty-two; oats, ten to eleven; and barley, sixteen to seventeen. Butter sells at twelve to thirteen rubles a pud. Trade, however, is generally so weak that it is hardly worth mentioning. There are plenty of sheep on the market to buy, despite low prices of twelve to fifteen rubles for ordinary sheep. I did not sell my surplus of 2,000 ewes and have tried to follow His Excellency, Count Vorontsov's advice and lease them out to impoverished but hard-working Nogais under specific terms. Indeed, I have spread them around fourteen villages in the Nogai District.

I will send Yr. Honour the invoice for the *Conversations-Lexicon* once I have received the last issue.

I wrote to mechanic Dyck in Rudnerweide, asking him to send you the promised hay-mowing machine model through Mr. Pelekh. The machine did not function well this summer, when compared to the results of mowing by scythe. The machine works well only in half-dry, very short grass, which the scythe cannot catch, but poorly or not at all in long, green, or wet grass.

Everyone, on the other hand, praises the threshing machine. Several were built this year, not by Dueck, but as improvements on his model. With these machines, two horses and four persons can thresh fifteen chetverts of hard wheat in one day.

Since we have not seen him for a long time, we look forward to the pleasure of a visit from the chief curator. We had hoped to see him in spring, as in previous years.

I endeavour, with respect and devotion, to remain Yr. Honour's most devoted servant,

Johann Cornies

448. Johann Cornies to Traugott Blueher. 1 November 1834. SAOR 89-1-220/46v.

Esteemed Mr. Blueher,

The messenger who brings you these lines is my son. Since I count on your friendship, I am sending him on to you directly without hesitation, firmly convinced as I am that you will support him with the helpful Christian advice everyone needs, especially a young man far away from home.

My wife and I send heartfelt and sincere greetings to you and your esteemed family as your friends and servants,

Johann Cornies

449. Johann Cornies to State Counsellor Schubert. 1 November 1834. SAOR 89-1-220/52.

His Honour, State Counsellor Schubert in St. Petersburg,

The bearer of this letter is my son, whom I am sending to Moscow, St. Petersburg, and Riga to gather agricultural knowledge of value to him and to our region.

I still have lively memories of beautiful St. Petersburg, of the pleasures I experienced during my stay in the city in 1824, and especially of your friendly, Christian reception, honoured State Counsellor. I cannot thank God sufficiently for His benefits at a time when I was far away from home myself. The Lord knows what I remember and feel. He also knows the sincere Christian honour and love I experience when I send my son to pay his respects to Yr. Honour, Mr. State Counsellor, and to personally express my renewed gratitude and respect, should it be God's will that he is able to visit St. Petersburg.

I am especially moved to do so after young Mr. Rastaedt visited me three weeks ago and brought me greetings from you. I thank you for this gracious honour. Please receive my respectful request that you support my son with Christian teachings and advice. Except for the Sarepta Trading Company, where he will stay, I have no other acquaintances who could give him support in various situations that might arise. I make my request, convinced of your generous Christian disposition.

In this hope and with a heart full of gratitude, I thank you for your kindness. As long as I live, I remain with sincere respect and love, Yr. Honour's devoted servant,

Cornies

450. Johann Cornies to Traugott Blueher. 7 November 1834. SAOR 89-1-220/54.

Esteemed Mr. Blueher,

Since you will undoubtedly have received my letter of 20 September, I think I do not need to respond to your inquiry again.

Beloved friend, my son departed for Moscow on 5 November with a German driver and should, unless he is delayed by an accident, arrive there in three or, at most, four weeks. It is late fall and travel will naturally be slow. Let me start by explaining the object of his journey. Since my son has learned the basic elements of surveying, I am sending him to Moscow to perfect this knowledge through private instruction. He will also visit agricultural enterprises, examining approaches better than those we have here, with a view to having them introduced locally. He will, for example, compare the milk production of Kolmagory horned cattle with those of our local East Frisian horned cattle. Should he find the former superior in every way, he would buy twelve cows and two breeding bulls and have them shipped to our area.

If it is God's will, I would then like my son to travel on to St. Petersburg and Riga in spring, maybe in April. In any case, once he gets back to Moscow I will have to decide on his further itinerary, which will either be through Saratov and Sarepta to Molochnaia, or home directly from Moscow.

It would give us pleasure and comfort if our son could stay with you over the winter, but do not worry if that is impossible. In that case, he could naturally find lodgings nearby and visit you from time to time. I have taught him to get by on very little. I hope, in any case, that you might support him with advice and instruction in my stead. My son has learned to obey and, unless I am seriously mistaken, he will obey you as he does me. I would also ask that you provide him with recommendations and introductions to appropriate people in Moscow as well as in St. Petersburg and Riga. All of my friends in these places seem to have died or moved away.

Please keep the credit of 5,173 R.B.A. I have with you and give my son what he needs to cover his expenses. If the payment for this year's wool has not been sent to me when you get this letter, please remit it to me in Banco Assignats.

I commend myself to your further friendship and benevolence. With heartfelt greetings to you and your dear family, I remain forever, your willing friend and servant,

Johann Cornies Sr.

451. Johann Cornies to Wool Improvement Society. 26 November 1834. SAOR 89-1-220/59v.

To the esteemed Wool Improvement Society at the Kurushan community sheep farm,

I would cordially ask the Society for permission to pasture my horses and horned cattle between the Iushanle and the Kurushan over the winter, as I have done for payment in the past. Both herds are now smaller than they were, and should not cause any damage. Awaiting your decision, which I will respectfully accept, I have the honour to be your willing,

Johann Cornies

452. Johann Cornies to Andrei M. Fadeev. SAOR 89-1-220/61. 27 November 1834.

Yr. Honour, Gracious State Counsellor,

Two weeks ago, I received the two varieties of seeds I ordered more than a year ago. The eighteen funt of Swedish sandgrass seeds and sand oats arrived in good condition. I thought of offering the seeds to the Khortitsa community, but feared it might handle them improperly if it was not held accountable for them. With apologies, I take the liberty of asking Yr. Honour to send instructions to our Khortitsa friends to take receipt of the sandgrass seed from me for a payment of thirty-five R.B.A. in freight and carrying charges. I do not yet know how much the seed will cost. I will instruct the Khortitsa people about the care and planting of the seed.

Our local Society [for the Advancement and Dissemination of Forest Trees, Orchards, Sericulture, and Viticulture] has taken advantage of the beautiful autumn weather and will submit a report to Yr. Honour in December.

On 24 November, all of Friedrich Fein's buildings burned down. Thank God that no one seems to have been hurt.

With the deepest respect and esteem, I endeavour to remain Yr. Honour's respectful servant,

Johann Cornies

453. Johann Cornies to District Office. 29 November 1834. SAOR 89-1-220/62.

To the District Office in Halbstadt,

Report:

In response to your communication No. 2,993 of the District Office, dated 19 September, I hereby offer the following explanation. On orders from the former Ekaterinoslav Guardianship Committee, surveyor Timoshevskii was authorized to partition the land in our local district and mark off the boundaries with two ploughed furrows. Documents in the District Office archive contain this information.

In my opinion, Rueckenau is pursuing unwarranted complaints. They feel they have been ill done by because someone from their side was not present when the boundary line was marked. I think the village community should be asked why they failed to send a representative to the boundary when they were invited to do so. The surveyor is not permitted to send more than one such notification when a boundary between neighbours is being drawn. If no one appears, the surveyor is free to mark the boundary in the absence of such a representative. I believe that Rueckenau has the land to which it is entitled and has no further grounds for dissatisfaction, even though it lost Fuerstenwerder and Lichtfelde land that it had previously been allotted. I also believe that there is a secret enmity behind this ostensible injury. It is an issue that, should it be necessary, I will speak to at the right time.

With respect, I have the honour to be your devoted,

Cornies

454. Gnadenheim Village Office to Forestry Society. 12 December 1834. SAOR 89-1-297/2.[5]

To the Society for the Advancement and Dissemination of Forest Trees, Orchards, Sericulture, and Viticulture, at Ohrloff,

We, the undersigned, on behalf of our village community, truthfully declare that we do not accept the rude and insulting remarks of fullholder Wilhelm Born against directives of our high authorities, made in our Village Office in the presence of Society Chairman Johann Cornies. We do not accept his thoughtless assumptions that are further an insult to our entire village community. Otherwise, we might appear to share Born's opinions, which were made contrary to arrangements of the government of our country. Born was so bold as to question directives from our high authorities. We reject this act of insubordination or even a suggestion thereof. We are not prepared to treat administrative orders with indifference in any way. We have forwarded the matter of fullholder Wilhelm Born's act of insubordination to the esteemed Christian church leadership to deal with in accordance with our solemn

5 This letter is reconstituted from a draft of two items found together, written in a secretarial hand, with changes made in Cornies' hand. As the note at the end of the letter makes clear, Cornies had rejected the original letter from Gnadenheim, rewritten a "corrected" version, and sent it back to the village to resubmit.

confession of faith. This confession directs us to offer faithfulness, obedience, respect, honour, and deference to our government and all of its orders, that are not contrary to our conscience. Anyone who resists the government, acts contrary to God's ordinances and can no longer be a member of our community. We assure the Society that we will from henceforward evidence the appropriate esteem, submissiveness, docility, and obedience towards government directives, and fulfil them as punctually as possible.

The local village community requests that the Society give consideration to the crop failures, death of our livestock, and various misfortunes suffered by our village in 1833, and to delay the establishment of our forest-tree plantation until 1835.

In the hope that our above-mentioned declaration and request might be graciously received, we sign with our own signatures and in the name of our whole village community.

Village Mayor Weyer, Deputy Mayor Regier, Deputy Mayor Friesen, Gerhard Klassen, Peter Heidebrecht, Peter Krueger, Johann Wiens

Gnadenheim, December 12, 1834

To the Gnadenheim Village Office,

The report of 12 December 1834 from the above Village Office is returned because it is addressed only to Chairman Cornies. This Society deems it to be invalid and unacceptable because it is incorrectly presented. Enclosed is a draft of the report. It may be copied verbatim and sent to the Society as soon as possible.

455. Forestry Society to Andrei M. Fadeev. 15 December 1834[?]. SAOR 89-1-428/1

Report to State Counsellor Fadeev:

The Society dutifully reports that the work proposed for this summer in its 5 May report No. 61, has been completed as follows:

1. The enclosure of eighteen forest-tree plantations was completed with the required ditches five fut wide and four fut deep.

2. The last quarter section in the forest-tree plantation in eighteen villages has been deep-ploughed as far as possible, despite problems in turning teams of horses around [at the appropriate places], as the deep-ploughing record shows.

3. Dead trees in forest-tree plantations have been replaced to the extent that saplings were available, as the record of our current stock of trees shows.

4. Forest-tree seeding has taken place as recorded in the entries of "seeds received and distributed" and "seeds taken from our own forest trees."

5. In the newly established forest-tree plantations of the villages Lichtfelde, Pordenau, and Pastwa, the first quarter-sections in each forest-tree plantation were deep-ploughed to the required depth, as shown in the deep-ploughing record. Ditches on two sides were constructed to the required depth.

6. In the villages Sparrau and Conteniusfeld, the area of hearth-sites exceeds the specified regulation of one and a half desiatinas.

456. Johann Cornies to D. Neufeld. 28 December 1834. SAOR 89-1-220/63v.

Dear friend D. Neufeld,

I have found a master who can varnish wagons in the manner in which mine was varnished. He can also properly design and build a seat and framework for such a wagon that offers the same benefits. This master could instruct Wiens to build frames and seats, using the above-mentioned design and measurements. I also intend to make changes to the wagon lining. I would like to talk to you and Wiens about these matters.

457. Johann Cornies to Andrei M. Fadeev. 29 December 1834. SAOR 89-1-220/64.

To State Counsellor Fadeev,

Having received Yr. Honour's esteemed communications of 6 and 7 December, I hasten to send you a funt of sandrye seed and a funt of sandoat seed, well packed in linen and marked "Litt: A.M.F.," according to Yr. honoured request. Instructions for the planting and transplanting of these varieties of seed are enclosed.

I am pleased to accept the commission to have a proper chaise built for His Excellency, General Vorontsov, following the pattern of my chaise that I brought along from Prussia. The chaise will have a main seat, but be easier to step up into. Since the spring weather is the most appropriate time for applying the paint accurately and durably, I am not sure when the wagon will be ready.

My last letter praised our autumn weather to the skies. I must now report that the green steppe of two weeks ago is now covered in five to six vershok of snow. It fell on 16 December, and without frost or wind for three days, the soil was completely covered. No one here can remember such deep, even snow. Two weeks ago we might have felt ourselves in central Asia, but now it is as though we had been transplanted into the interior of Russia. Were it now to turn warm and rainy, the snow could melt suddenly and cause flooding in several villages. On the other hand, some villagers think there will be no flooding because the soil is not yet frozen hard and could absorb most of the water. From 18 to 23 December, it was unusually cold, with frost of twenty to twenty-two degrees, but it did not seem so cold since there was no wind.

With the greatest esteem, I remain Yr. Honour's obedient and willing servant,

Cornies

458. Johann Cornies to Heinrich Reimer and Dirk Wiens. 29 December 1834. SAOR 89-1-220/68v.

To manager Heinrich [Reimer] and assistant Dirk Wiens [on the Iushanle estate],

I hereby require you to notify me at the beginning of every month of the work to be done, whether it was started or completed, using the following format. My orders are that at the end of each month, you report again on each point of the above list: which work was started or completed, and which was not started nor completed. You are also required to report the reasons why it was not possible to complete some of the named tasks.

Johann Cornies

Notice:

Regarding work on Iushanle sheep farm that must be undertaken and accomplished during the month of January:

Work to be done. Description of work finished or not finished.

459. Johann Cornies to David Epp, Khortitsa. 31 December 1834. SAOR 89-1-220/69v.[6]

Esteemed David Epp, most treasured friend,

Your welcome letter gives me the pleasure of being able to serve you in some way. I recommended the master mason to you in good

6 This letter to David Epp, Khortitsa, regards the construction of the Mennonite mother church in Khortitsa.

conscience, knowing that you would not easily find a better mason to build your church. He has a good understanding of the elements of his work and is a faithful, believing man. As you know, this is seldom the case with a person of this sort. For three years, he has done all my masonry work, sometimes alone, sometimes with associates working under his direction.

I concluded an agreement with him to do work for me during the coming year and gave him an advance. If you want him to build your church, you should make the arrangements with him here, with an advance, so that he could hire his associates. Usually he makes advance agreements for the following summer and brings his associates with him. But if you should wait until he arrives in Khortitsa, he may not be able to undertake your project, since he may lack an adequate number of workers, or would have to hire them locally. This I do not recommend. If you fail to give him an advance, contrary to Russian customs, he may feel that you do not value him sufficiently or have doubts about the quality of his work.

The best approach for you, I think, is to write to him (as you state in your letter to me). I could then write to him, including an advance. I would guarantee the advance myself. Describe the structure to be built, set a price for laying 1,000 bricks. I paid him seven rubles cash to set 1,000 bricks. Ask him if he thinks an agreement can be reached. If your price is too low, I will keep the advance in my accounts. If he does agree, you can count on the construction going forward. You would need to make a separate agreement for the stone foundation. I provided lime, water, sand, and clay, and he looked after the rest, e.g., constructing scaffolds. I assume he would supply the bricks and stones. You would need to reach an agreement personally with him about the foundation, since this cannot be done from here.

If you agree with this proposal, instruct me as to the sum to give him as an advance. You must specify the thickness of the walls. This will determine the price per thousand for laying bricks. The church will have many windows and doors and the mason will have to take all of this into account in reckoning whether seven rubles per thousand, and some provisions, will provide adequate earnings in these times. Reflect on these matters and give me a firm decision as soon as you can so as to avoid the loss of time in sending letters back and forth. Masons usually leave home in March.

I remain, with heartfelt greetings, your honest friend,

J. Cornies

460. Johann Cornies to Johann Cornies Jr. 31 December 1834. SAOR 89-1-220/72.

Dear son,

Your letter of 10 December from Moscow gave all of us much pleasure. Jacob Wiebe returned safely on 28 December and dropped off your letter yesterday evening. I was pleased to hear that you got on well together en route. We also received your letters from Ekaterinoslav and Kharkov. We are all well. Not much has happened here or among our relatives. Since 15 December, we have had a lot of snow, five to six vershok deep, but very light. Our sledding roads are exceptionally good and the temperature was unusual, twenty degrees and colder, but completely calm and foggy. If the wind had been blowing, as it usually does in winter, this deep, light snow would have given us a storm the likes of which we have never experienced. The horses are grazing and keeping well, but the rest of our livestock is being fed.

I enclose a church testimonial. Show it to Mr. Blueher, and wherever you meet Christian individuals on your journey when it seems to be most appropriate. Do not be too obtrusive, but also not too reticent. Notify me that you have received the testimonial.

I also received a letter from Mr. Schubert in St. Petersburg. He would like you to visit him in Oranienbaum.[7] Dear son, I have made good, upright Christian friends through behaviour that is honest and decent. I hope that you will try to live by the Christian rule, "be as clever as a snake and without deceit like a dove." But do not lose sight of the apostles' teachings. Remember that whatever is genuine, honourable, righteous, modest, beautiful, and harmonious is virtuous and praiseworthy. Above all, remember that you should owe nobody anything but your love.

Give Mr. Blueher and his loving wife our sincere and heartfelt greetings. Your loving mother sends special greetings to Mrs. Blueher and asks you to find out how many children she has. You can tell us about this the next time you write.

Now, my dear son, use your time for activities that will do you honour and give us joy. This is the heartfelt wish of your parents who love you, and whose hearts want nothing but your well-being. I also wish

7 Oranienbaum was a Russian royal residence near Peterhof, on the Gulf of Finland.

you God's merciful blessings and His fatherly help for the New Year, and much courage, diligence, and effort. Amen.

May the Lord be with you. Your father who loves you,

Johann Cornies

P.S. Let me know what kind of instruction is available to you and when you can begin your studies. Who is your teacher? Is he competent and a good teacher? How much do you pay him? Are the lessons conducted in your rooms or must you go elsewhere for instruction, etc.?

I also expect from you a detailed description of the best horned cattle in the Moscow area, with respect to body structure, size, colour, and milk production, as well as price. How, in your view, do they compare to our local livestock, and would it be to our advantage to introduce them here? Take your time and report clearly about the possibility of such a purchase, as well as your views on the best and safest manner of transport. Get Mr. Blueher's advice on all of these matters and do nothing without him.

Are the livestock available in the Moscow area or from farther away? How much time would you need to make the purchase. Is it limited? Can the livestock be delivered safely from there or would I need to hire people from here for this purpose? To avoid unnecessary expenses or major mistakes, be sure not to act in haste. Letters always travel three weeks.

Cornies

461. District Office to Johann Cornies. 31 December 1834. SAOR 89-1-302/33.

To esteemed Johann Cornies in Ohrloff,

In his communication No. 2,163, dated 19 December 1834, Inspector of Colonies in the second district, Pelekh, notified this District Office that the Guardianship Committee for Foreign Settlers in Southern Russia had reviewed your petition with respect to your lease of land, sections fifteen and sixteen in the Melitopol area, for a rental of 600 rubles annually. After considering the reasons you itemize with respect to settlement, the Committee has notified the inspector that it agrees to your request with the stipulation that if settlement on the land occurs, you would leave the sites to water livestock, and the dam that you have constructed, intact without expecting further compensation. Also, you are asked to assist any settlers in searching for water and to give them all possible advice in support of their settlement.

In thus notifying you in regard to this matter, the District Office instructs you to pay the leasing charges for each period of payment in advance in order that the money can be forwarded.

District Office at Halbstadt, 31 December 1834

District Chairman Regier

1835

462. Johann Cornies to Andrei M. Fadeev. 1 January 1835. SAOR 89-1-220/67v.

His Honour, Gracious State Counsellor,

With esteem and pleasure, at the start of a New Year, I send Yr. Honour my sincere wishes for happiness and for success in your new position that has much expanded your field of activity. As foreign settlers, we are right in anticipating a prosperous future, confident that well-considered programs of development will be of advantage to us now and provide rewards for us in future.

May providence grant you good health, to the benefit of the state and its settlers, and bless you with rich rewards in this life. These wishes are sent to you by all true members of this community and represent a solemn undertaking of one particular member of the Mennonite community, for whom it has been one of the greatest pleasures of his life to deem himself, with sincere feelings of deep esteem, Yr. Honour's most obedient servant,

J. Cornies

463. Forestry Society to District Office. 1 January 1835[?]. SAOR 89-2-310/41v.

To the District Office in Halbstadt,

Communication No. 36 is hereby returned to the District Office with the observation that Clas Dyck is in no position to provide the Society with a written undertaking to do plantings in Ohrloff because he has bought a house in Rosenort where he will soon take up his residence.

In response to an order from the District Office, the [Ohrloff] Village Office explains that it has instructed Peter Mantler (not Clas Dyck), to appear at the offices of the Society on the specified date as owner of cottager house No. 5, in which he presently resides.

According to directive No. 413, of 27 January 1833, from the high authorities, no one may build a cottager house without first providing the Society with a written promise to do his requisite plantings. The cottager house was built after 1833, but no written undertaking has yet been signed at the Society Office about its location. This causes the Society difficulties and delays. The delays would appear to represent a thinly disguised rebellion against orchard and forest-tree plantings.

In asking the District Office to identify the person guilty of this defiance without delay, the Society bases its position on a directive received from the authorities. In accordance with directive and order No. 171 of Guardianship Committee member, State Counsellor Fadeev, it is the Society's duty to report ill-willed persons in the Mennonite community to the authorities, including those who submit false information detrimental to the community and contrary to what has been instituted by the authorities. Such persons must be punished to serve as an example. Under certain circumstances they may ultimately even be designated as wicked people. The ... [remainder of text missing.]

464. Forestry Society to Ohrloff Village Office. Undated [draft]. SAOR 89-1-330/69.

Ohrloff:

At its meeting of 7 January, the Society considered a report of the Ohrloff Village Office dated 4 November of last year that permitted the Ohrloff village community to fence off parts of Nos. 10, 11, and 12 in the forest-tree plantation. This would permit the construction of a road between plots Nos. 10 and 11.

Such permission is granted on the condition that the road be enclosed by a straight fence on both sides, to be built in a regular fashion and consist of at least two sawn lathes. Easily opened gateways must be installed at points where the main roads through the plantation cross this fence, and would permit unimpeded movement through the plantation. All construction must be done properly, not carelessly, and be in an orderly condition by May of this year.

The householders owning plot Nos. 10, 11, and 12 must also sign written agreements at the Village Office. The owner of plot No. 10 must agree to relinquish part of his land for this road, promising never to demand recompense in land at another spot or in money. The owners of plot Nos. 11 and 12 must agree to do plantings on areas larger than [their] one-half desiatina plots and never launch an appeal on grounds that these areas are larger than the half-desiatina plots stipulated in the imperial decree.

On 22 November of last year, Miller Gerhard Zacharias sent a request to this Society explaining that the location of his orchard is directly in front of his mill. He asks that he be exempt from planting trees in this place as the trees would hinder the flow of wind to his mill and greatly disadvantage his milling business. Society members Abraham Wiebe and Jacob Martens investigated the site and found that trees in that location would affect the functioning of miller Zacharias' mill.

465. Forestry Society to Village Offices. [1?] January 1835. SAOR 89-1-429/18.

[Draft] Organization rules:

1. According to the rules and regulations, trees in plantations must be planted in a straight line, at a distance no greater than one faden [six feet] from one another.

2. Fruit trees may not be planted in forest-tree plots, except at corners of mulberry hedges and at gateways through hedges.

3. Many different varieties of forest trees must be included in all plantings. Anyone planting unduly large quantities of a small variety of trees in their forest plot will be called to account and forbidden from planting any more trees of the same varieties in his plot.

4. Trees must be planted in dry soil and watered afterwards.

5. Trees must be trimmed back to three or four buds in the year in which they are planted. To prevent overly much sap from rising to the crown of a tree in summer, twigs that sprout from the trunk of the tree below the crown must be trimmed back to three or four buds and not close to the trunk. This will strengthen the trunk.

6. Where deep-ploughing to the proper depth is not possible, setting trenches for forest trees are to be dug one and one-quarter arshin wide and three-quarters of an arshin deep.

7. Every plot must be marked with a regulation number stake. The fine for every missing stake is fifty kopeks.

8. To ensure that weeds have been cleared away, tree plantations will be inspected four or five times each summer. Anyone found to have

neglected the weeding of his forest plot will be fined fifty kopeks the first time.

9. Tree planting must take place between 1 October and 10 November annually. During this time everyone must plant trees to the limits of his ability. Any sapling planted later will be counted as having been planted the following year. Anyone doing no planting during this time must give reasons worthy of consideration or be fined at a rate of ten kopeks per missing tree, based upon the lowest number of trees planted by an individual fullholder that year.

10. Every year, the lists of completed plantings must unfailingly be sent in by 15 November, and not one day later.

11. All trees planted in plantations according to the rules and regulations must stay in place. Dead trees must be replaced and the replacement trees will not be counted as new trees. Only trees planted in new spots should be listed as trees planted. Replacement planting must be done before a new planting is started.

12. No tree planting is to be entered in the annual record of forest-tree plantings until a circulated order to do so has been received. Records must be accurate, without erasures.

13. The gates at openings through hedges must be in good order and properly closed at all times.

14. Nothing except root vegetables should be seeded on the deep-ploughed part of a forest-tree plantation. Nothing may be seeded or planted between trees except for forest-tree seeds.

15. The required ditches must be five fut wide and four fut deep and must be kept in good order at all times to prevent livestock from getting into plantations.

466. Forestry Society to Abraham Wiebe. [1 January 1835?] SAOR 89-1-330/3.

Notes for Society member Abraham Wiebe:

1. Inspect forest-tree plantations.

2. Take note of two-year trees.

3. Mariental, about six hearth-sites.

4. Franztal should send the Society a different map marking the distance of the forest-tree plantation from the village, the length and width of fullholder and cottager plots, and the length of the plantation.

467. Forestry Society to village offices. [1 January?] 1835. SAOR 89-1-361/1.

Purpose of the trip:

1. Village offices must check that planting trenches are made at the prescribed width, depth, and distance from one another.

2. Planting trees in freshly dug trenches is absolutely not permitted. Planting may only be done in trenches dug at least half a year earlier.

3. All ditches between neighbours must be completed by November, without fail, and must be four fut wide, three fut deep, and one and a half fut wide at the bottom throughout.

4. The only trees to be considered as wild apple and pear trees are trees called "Helkii" and "Krushkii," not improved apple and pear trees that have grown wild. Planting close to fences is permitted. Where only apple trees are planted, they must be twenty-five fut apart. If both varieties are included, they can be planted sixteen or seventeen fut apart.

468. Johann Klaassen to Johann Cornies and Wilhelm Martens. 7 January 1835. SAOR 89-1-352/44.

Valued friends and patrons, Wilhelm Martens, Johann Cornies,

Your noble inclinations moved you in the years 1834 and 1835 to give me considerable monetary advances in support of the development of a [cloth] factory and to purchase the necessary wool. Although I do not wish to become overly insistent, I have requested a meeting about my situation with you several times. This meeting has not yet taken place.

My own circumstances now make it necessary to ask you, honoured friends and patrons, to kindly arrange a small conference as soon as possible that would extend a small credit to me. It is a question of whether I should permit work to continue or to stop all work until I am able to get money from Kharkov. I do not wish to abuse your kindness, but the enclosed accounts show that the capital funds on hand are insufficient to carry on production under present conditions. Unless I can make a definite sale, for which 500 or more arshins of cloth would soon be ready, I must await market days and sales here and there.

I can assure you that my situation has not gotten worse, but has improved from time to time. The amount and quality of our cloth provide proof of this, since prices have also risen during the last half year. A major part of the factory's income is consumed by expensive wool, expensive horse fodder, many expensive trips, the purchase of carders for raw wool, and many difficulties arising from two years of crop failure.

Despite various troubles, I have tried to improve and enlarge the factory and to make the work more profitable. I would like to continue on this course if only I could pay off my debts, or at least most of them.

I look forward to an early acceptance of my request and sign this, with a heartfelt greeting and great respect, as your friend,

Johann Klaassen

Halbstadt, 7 January 1835

469. Forestry Society to Andrei M. Fadeev. 10 January 1835[?]. SAOR 89-1-428/66[?].

10 January, Report No. 10:

After the Society ordered all fullholders and cottagers in this district to surround their hearth-sites with ditches of the prescribed width and depth, it finds it necessary to obediently seek Yr. Honour's agreement to a change in the measurements of ditches between hearth-sites, so that any ditches not subject to livestock encroachment need only be four fut wide and three fut deep.

This small narrowing of ditches would encourage our inhabitants anew to accomplish other similar work more confidently and willingly. It agrees with our purposes, since all such ditches will only be made between orchards. In a few years, the effects of the weather will soften the soil along the side walls of these ditches until it falls into the ditches on its own. Then, when the planned mulberry hedges are planted, the roots will have sufficient space to spread out. Ditches at the ends of the hearth-sites and along their outer edges must still be at least five fut wide and four fut deep.

In submitting this to Yr. Honour, the Society requests Yr. gracious resolution.

470. Forestry Society to Andrei M. Fadeev. [11 January 1835?] SAOR 89-1-428/67.

Report No. 11 to State Counsellor Fadeev,

Until the present time, the Society has permitted villages to plant grain on deep-ploughed portions of land in forest-tree plantations where trees had not yet been planted. It had also permitted the planting of potatoes between trees. Meanwhile, the Society has learned that such practices are extremely detrimental to trees. When seeded, soil becomes more compacted and kernel-bearing grains lose their ability to provide complete nutrition for tree roots. Especially detrimental to tree planting are weeds that have been seeded with the grain. Deep-ploughed soil also promotes their luxuriant growth.

Since potatoes need a great deal of moisture to produce their tubers, planting them between young trees dries out the soil. Potatoes draw in moisture like a sponge and remove nutrition needed by the young trees.

Taking this into consideration, the Society has decided at its meeting of 10 January to forbid grain planting on deep-ploughed areas and potato planting between trees. To avoid leaving deep-ploughed areas in [still] unused forest-tree plantations, the Society has decided to permit the planting there of potatoes, beets, onions, and similar root vegetables, which can be used for household needs. The Society's purpose is to encourage persons who feel that deep-ploughed land should not be left fallow.

The Society has the honour to obediently report the above.

471. Forestry Society to Andrei M. Fadeev. [15 January 1835?] SAOR 89-1-315/6.

Report No. 25, to State Counsellor Fadeev:

The Society found that it was desirable to invite the local district chairman, Regier, to its meeting of 10 January. When Society members and the district chairman had assembled at the designated time in Johann Cornies' dwelling on his sheep farm, the Society chairman opened the meeting with a short report of the need to eliminate abuses that had crept into our local villages. An improved order should be introduced into the work of village offices and their conduct of community assemblies.

Since this was the first meeting in the district chairman's presence, nothing definite was further decided except that meetings together with District Office members should be held more frequently in order to inform and encourage one another, work cooperatively, and make common decisions about issues affecting the general well-being.

The Society feels that it has the duty to obediently report this to Yr. Honour.

15 January 1835[?]

472. Johann Cornies to Larion Dmitriev, Master Mason. 18 January 1835. SAOR 89-1-297/7.

[Draft] Dear Mr. Dmitriev,

Most satisfied with the masonry work you have done for me, I have recommended you to the German settlement of Khortitsa as a good master mason for the building of a church [in the village of Khortitsa]. It would be built of fired brick this spring and will be eleven faden [sixty-six feet] long, five faden, two arshins wide, and two faden, two arshins high above a stone foundation. A member of the community authorized me to tell you of this project and to advance you 100 rubles should you agree to take on the job under specified conditions. Materials would be provided by the church. The church is prepared to pay seven rubles per 1,000 bricks of laid masonry bricks. You would make your own on-site agreement with the church regarding the foundation, whose exact height must still be determined.

On 15 January, I sent you a 100 R.B.A. advance payment that you should keep if you are satisfied with the [proposed] agreement. Otherwise, keep the money as an advance on the construction work you are doing for me. I would, however, advise you not to turn down this job. Accept it, if at all possible, because more brick construction will be done in this area in future. Please notify me of your decision as soon as you receive this letter and I will then inform the Khortitsa community accordingly.

18 January 1835

473. Johann Cornies to Larion Dmitriev, in the village of Gremechevo. Undated [after 18 Jaunary 1835]. SAOR 89-1-310/59.

1. On 15 January 1835, you were sent an advance of 100 R.B.A. in the event that you are prepared to undertake the building of a church in Khortitsa.

2. This church is to be built of fired bricks, eleven faden [sixty-six feet] long, five faden, two arshins wide, and, measured from the foundation, two faden, two arshins high. Openings are to be left for five doors and thirty windows. A chimney is not needed and will therefore not be built.

3. For the time being, the thickness of the brick wall to the height of the choir is to be two and a half brick-lengths deep. The middle wall

will be one brick-length deep. However the construction most appropriate to the purposes of this building is left to the discretion of the master.

4. If all necessary building materials are delivered to the site by the Khortitsa inhabitants, it is hoped that the master will undertake the masonry work at a price of seven rubles per 1,000 bricks.

5. A dwelling house will also be built in Khortitsa, and Larion might also bring along workers for this construction.

474. Forestry Society to village offices. 23 January 1835. SAOR 89-1-343/4.

[Draft] To all village offices in the old and new settlements,

Village offices are hereby again ordered to check carefully that tree-planting trenches have been made at the specified distance and depth, and to ensure that trees are not planted sooner than half a year after the trenches have been completed. Caterpillar nests in trees must be thoroughly removed until all have been destroyed. Trenches should be dug around [village] schools, according to regulations, in order that mulberry trees can be planted in them next fall. Digging of ditches around hearth-sites and cottager plots must be continued.

The purpose of this [message] is to prevent individuals from being embarrassed because they have neglected one or another of these points. The Society has received reports that some village mayors had not properly informed their residents of the above matters and have not encouraged them to carry them out. They have also not informed cottagers about these orders and regulations and are even less concerned about checking whether things ordered have actually been carried out. Deputy mayors have complained to the Society that their mayors have not informed them of such orders. Such mayors are ordered not to make themselves guilty of grievances of this kind, under threat of being held accountable for them.

475. District Office to Johann Cornies. 26 January 1835. SAOR 89-1-324/107.

To Hon. Johann Cornies in Ohrloff,

On 21 January, the Rudnerweide Village Office reported to the District Office that the manager on your sheep farm, Heinrich Reimer, as well as Peter Friesen, from Steinbach, and your shepherd, a Russian, arrived at the Rudnerweide tavern on that day somewhat under the influence of brandy. They had been driving at so rapid a speed that their horses were covered in sweaty lather. At the tavern kept by Aron Wiens, they ordered half a quart of brandy and shouted loudly as they drank, banging their glasses on the table. The tavern keeper objected, asking them to settle down, but they refused and also broke a bottle and a glass.

With the assistance of other clients, Wiens found it necessary to remove these trouble-makers from his premises. They refused, however, to settle down but rushed back into the tavern where they beat Wiens. With the help of other individuals, he removed them from the building a second time, and when they still refused to stop their violent behaviour, the Village Office found it necessary to arrest them and put them under guard.

We therefore instruct you to order your sheep farm manager, Heinrich Reimer, your head shepherd, and Dietrich Wiens to appear at the District Office next Wednesday, 30 January, at 10 a.m. You are also required to ensure that Reimer is not absent from your sheep farm on business for more than a day under any circumstances. He must appear in the District Office at any time to answer for his immoral behaviour.

District Office in Halbstadt, 26 January 1835
District Chairman Regier, Deputy Driedger, Deputy Harder

476. Forestry Society to village offices. 28 January 1835. SAOR 89-1-428/3.

To village offices in the new settlement,

The Society is dispatching its secretary, Mr. Sommerfeld, to inspect journals for forest-tree, orchard, silk, and wine cultivation in each village office to determine that each journal is in good order, as required by [directive] Nos. 215 to 217, dated 29 November. The inspection is intended to ensure that the entries for tree planting have been done. Specifically, on the Society's orders, Secretary Sommerfeld should be shown the above-mentioned journal in each village office. He will have with him copies of all notices dealing with planting directions sent out previously. At his request, these notices must be copied into each journal in order that they are widely known in every village office. A further order regulating such notices will follow later.

Village offices are likewise ordered to provide Sommerfeld with a conveyance at each location without delay and in a way that enables him to travel through several villages, not just over short distances. This must be observed.

Ohrloff, 28 January 1835
Chairman Cornies

477. Johann Cornies to Andrei M. Fadeev. 28 January 1835. SAOR 89-1-428/5.

[Draft] Your Honour, Gracious State Counsellor,

The last time I had the pleasure of personally paying my respects to Yr. Honour in Ekaterinoslav, I was assured that I could rely on you to use your influence to advance requests I might make on my own behalf and on behalf of others. I now hazard to make an appeal on behalf of three Mennonite foreigners who have lived in our community on travel passes for several years. They are the following, who wish to remain in our community as permanent residents:

1. Abraham Rempel and his family possess a respectable sum of money. He is a good agriculturalist who would distinguish himself through his considerable abilities. He has in his possession a written document from the Marienburg State Counsellor affirming that no obstacles to Rempel's emigration from Prussia stand in the way. Rempel wanted to deposit the sum of 800 rubles for an immigration pass, but the consul insisted that his superiors at the [Russian] Consulate in Danzig had not agreed to his granting such passes.

2. Cornelius Fast is a carpenter by trade and so skilled that no carpenter here can compare with him. He can and will support himself from his profession and make no claim on land.

3. Jacob Friesen, single, is a trained dyer in black and fine colours. He has scrupulously learned all of the basic elements of his craft in Prussia. While under contract here for two years as a dyer, he improved the dyeworks where he worked considerably. He will support himself through his profession and make no claim on land.

These three Mennonite foreigners would happily be accepted into the local community, not only because of the services they can provide, but also because of their good and peaceful conduct.

I humbly request that Yr. Honour instruct me as to how these Mennonite foreigners might acquire the right to stay here. Should they submit petitions directly to the Guardianship Committee, as foreigners used to do when the Committee was still quartered in Ekaterinoslav? What course of action would Yr. Honour advise to minimize the chances of taking an incorrect step?

With esteem, I am honoured to be Yr. Honour's devoted servant,
Cornies
28 January 1835[?]
Entered [into journal].

478. Forestry Society to District Office. 29 January 1835. SAOR 89-1-343/28.

To the District Office in Halbstadt,
From the Society for the Advancement and Dissemination of Forest Trees, Orchards, Sericulture, and Viticulture,

On 4 January the Blumstein Village Office reported to this Society that it had been dissolved on 31 December, when the Mayor reported his activities to the community and resigned from his position. He did so because several villagers had been involved in secret plots and slanders against him that had kept him from carrying out his duties. Under these conditions, the mayor's two deputies said they could no longer discharge their duties, stated that the accusations against the mayor were false, and pleaded that they be released from their present roles until an investigation had established the truth of the situation.

The Society asks the District Office to investigate this matter with a view to reinstating the Village Office in its functions. This will have to happen if forest-tree and orchard cultivation in the village is not to become disorganized or brought to a halt.

Once the self-respect of the District Office has been restored, it will provide the Society with accurate information about the results and make it possible for the Society to continue its mandatory work.

479. District Office to Johann Cornies. 4 February 1835. SAOR 89-1-324/99.

To Hon. Johann Cornies in Ohrloff,

On 31 January 1835, Heinrich Reimer, your sheep farm manager, Dietrich Wiens, also in residence on your sheep farm, and Peter Friesen from Steinbach, were called to account in the District Office for the disturbance they had created in the Rudnerweide tavern. Since the above-mentioned persons admitted their guilt and repented their deeds, the District Office has transferred this matter to the honourable church teachers to take appropriate action.

In informing you of this matter, we also require you to ensure that your chief shepherd (a Russian) appear at the District Office on the first Wednesday or Saturday after his return in order that he, too, can be called to account.

District Office in Halbstadt, 4 February 1835
District Chairman Regier

480. Forestry Society to Lichtenau Village Office. 7 February 1835. SAOR 89-1-330/16.

In today's report to the Forestry Society, the Lichtenau Village Office notes that, in the past, fullholdings had been transferred to unmarried individuals. By 9 February, the Village Office must submit a written notice naming such unmarried persons who are in possession of fullholdings. The Society is not well informed about such arbitrary actions that are quite contrary to government orders.

481. Johann Cornies to Johann Wiebe. 9 February 1835. SAOR 89-1-310/28.

[Draft] Much beloved friend Johann Wiebe,

You must wonder why you have not received even one letter from me for so long. Please do not jump to the conclusion that I am no longer your true and loving friend. The truth is simple: my business affairs have tied me down as have endless distractions and some little travel. Two years of crop failure have also prevented any kind of systematic correspondence. Day in, day out, people asked me for advice and help, but that too, God be praised, will soon be over. Our weather is good, we hope for an excellent harvest and you can again count on me.

1. Yes, I have received the Conversations-Lexicon and two varieties of sandgrass seed from you, for which I am grateful. I would gladly repay the favour.

2. My son is presently on a visit to Moscow to improve his mathematical skills and buy some Dutch cattle. He will be there until early May and then continue on to St. Petersburg and Riga, returning to the Molochnaia by way of Saratov. Since we must now get permission from St. Petersburg to travel abroad, it is no longer easy to leave the country, especially if it is to somewhere other than Prussia. Your cousin, J. Wiebe, accompanied my son to Moscow and made the eight-week

trip back and forth safely and in good health. My son and I are both very pleased with him.

If you can spare the time, please write to my son who would love to get a letter from you. I will enclose his address.

3. On 9 October 1833, the heirs of the late Franz Klassen in Tiege [in the Molochnaia settlement] set up a special authorization for you and Jacob Bergen [to receive your inheritance]. It was dispatched to the Guardianship Committee on 23 December 1833, to be forwarded to you. You will undoubtedly have it. I do not know the amount of the inheritance, but please hold back 100 thalers when it arrives. Give the heirs a note directing them to receive the money from me and use it to cover my expenses there. I still owe Mr. van der Steen, Langefuhr, some money, but I do not know how much. Please, when you can, repay Mr. van der Steen this money. Mr. van der Steen or Pastor van der Smissen will know the amount.

4. Our chief administrator, State Counsellor Fadeev, has asked me to look for two well-qualified Mennonite doctors who would be able to establish their competence with appropriate certificates from a faculty [of medicine]. They must be able to pass examinations at a Russian university that would qualify them to practise medicine in the Molochnaia and Khortitsa communities. I know that there are no such highly educated Mennonites in Prussia, but there might be some in Holland. I would urgently ask you, beloved friend, to discuss this matter with Reverend van der Smissen in Danzig as soon as possible. Perhaps he already knows of some such person in Holland, or might discuss the matter with friends in Holland.

We naturally need individuals with the requisite skills, but they must also be men of good, moral conduct who can win the confidence of our communities through their quiet and orderly conduct. Otherwise, the entire project would hurt us. There are enough doctors of questionable character who would gladly accept such appointments, but this we must oppose. You understand what I mean and will do what you can to help us in this regard. Please draw on my account for postal charges, etc.

In hopes of an early reply and with warmest greetings to you and your worthy family, I remain with love and honest friendship, your true friend,

J. Cornies

482. Forestry Society to village offices. 27 February 1835. SAOR 89-1-361/3.

To Lichtfelde, Pordenau, and Pastwa village offices,

His Excellency, Chief Curator for Colonists in southern Russia, Lieutenant General Inzov, has noted that reports about forest-tree plantings in our district indicate that most of our planted trees are elms, acacias, and poplars. In his order No. 4, dated 4 January 1835, His Honour, Member of the Guardianship Committee, State Counsellor Fadeev, orders the Society to ensure that maple, ash, and oak, as well as birches, pines, firs, and alders, are also planted, the latter in low-lying areas or on sandy soil.

The Society therefore orders that village offices ensure that plantings in local plantations this autumn consist of a greater variety of trees, not just a few. This order must be observed.

483. Forestry Society to Petershagen Village Office. 4 March 1835. SAOR 89-1-393/17.

In a report from the Society of 3 March, Johann Mierau is said to have dug planting trenches last autumn and planted trees in them before the Village Office could confirm that the trenches had been dug according to regulations. The Village Office must question Mierau to establish whether anyone had witnessed the manner in which these trenches had been dug. When witnesses come forward to confirm this fact, the Office must immediately notify the Society.

The Village Office must instruct the villager Jacob Krueger to appear at the Society offices without fail on the coming [date missing] at 9 a.m.

P.S. If Mierau has no witnesses, he must also be ordered to appear before the Society on the above date.

484. Forestry Society to District Office. 12 March 1835. SAOR 89-1-362/40.

Settlement:
To the Molochnaia Mennonite District Office in Halbstadt,

From the Chairman of the Society for the Advancement and Dissemination of Forest Trees, Orchards, Sericulture and Viticulture,

I enclose a sketch of the new village of Gnadenfeld made on site. In company with District Chairman Regier, we considered the need to arrange village households to everyone's benefit, and marked their locations with plough furrows. Once twenty houses have been erected on the hearth-sites, the Society will assign locations for their orchards. The Society expects no problems in this regard since, according to written instructions, all houses must be situated with their thresholds facing east, exactly at the midpoint of their hearth-sites.

Chairman Cornies

No. 150, 12 March 1835. Received 13 March 1835.

Reported to inspector on 16 March 1835.

Nos. 33, 34, 35, 36, 37, and 38, January 23, 1835

485. Abram Wiebe to Johann Cornies. Sent Rudnerweide. 13 March 1835. SAOR 89-1-356/22.

Treasured friend,

I would ask you to lend me 2,000 rubles for half a year because we have presently so much money tied up in the grain trade that nothing is left for other activities. I would also request that the interest rate be somewhat below your usual monthly rates. I would appreciate an early reply.

With best wishes and heartfelt greetings,

Your friend Abram Wiebe

486. Johann Klaassen to Johann Cornies. 29 March 1835. SAOR 89-1-356/27.

Valued friend,

I promised that I would keep you abreast of the progress of my factory from time to time. Because master workman Maentel is doing such satisfactory work, operations have been continued without interruption. I think that our wool cloth is of good quality. Its preparation too, has improved, but not as much as we would like. It seems to me that the master shearman Ehrtman is an unstable person. Although he is busy all the time, something seems missing in his attitude and commitment. Although he knows what the cloth should be like, he fails to achieve the desired quality, and matters have not been turning out as they should.

Today I counted thirty-four pieces completed on the loom. This means that the value of cloth still being worked over, but not ready for sale, is around 7,000 to 8,000 rubles. We must continue to improve our operations and the preparation of cloth. Perhaps it would give you a better picture of our operations if I were to report how much the Ekaterinoslav merchants value our cloth. Although the average price per arshin of cloth in February 1834 was seventy-four rubles, twelve kopeks it had, by February 1835, risen to seventy-nine rubles, sixty-two kopeks, and by March of the same year to eighty-nine rubles, three kopeks, all to the same merchants. These merchants have also promised to pay even more for better cloth in future. The chief administrator in Orekhov ordered 160 arshins, based on his examination of a three-and-a-half-arshin sample of dark green cloth. These prices demonstrate that our production has improved somewhat since the New Year. Prices at the Kharkov market were lower, for a variety of reasons.

My son D. writes from the Crimea that he sold his cloth for fifteen to twenty-five rubles per arshin. He insists that cloth of the quality sold to you for twenty rubles per arshin is in demand. At present, D. has more than 800 arshins of cloth with him in the Crimea and hopes to sell all of it at quite a good price. To stabilize our prices, we must improve our operations greatly.

Sales until August will be difficult for the following reasons:

1. Money in southern Russia is in short supply.

2. Large merchants, who buy to resell, forecast that a downturn in the price of wool will bring down the price of cloth to a degree.

3. Our cloth is of one kind only. Buyers demand greater variety at lower prices. My aim is to win recognition for cloth of the best quality, but there are many obstacles. I have hired more people who are being taught shearing. We should see the results of this development by month's end. But what is certain in any case is that two [trained] workers should be able to process 1,000 arshins of cloth per year. Moreover, better quality should gradually raise the prices of our production by four rubles per arshin now, and more later.

The springs on the shearing machine cylinder are worn. We placed an order for a new cylinder with Mr. Blueher in Moscow on 28 January, but I have heard nothing back from him. The money was sent through Ekaterinoslav but it has perhaps not reached him or his reply has become lost in the post. Mr. Blueher is usually punctual. If I cannot get a new cylinder, we will be in trouble once the old one gives out.

We are well and wish your dear family the same. I commend myself to you courteously and with esteem as your friend,

Joh. Klaassen

Halbstadt, 29 March 1835.

487. Johann Cornies to Johann Cornies Jr. 29 March 1835. SAOR 89-1-343/59v.

My dear son Johann Cornies in Moscow,

Your letter of 25 February, with its news that you are well, gave us great pleasure and heartfelt joy. Give Mr. Blueher and his dear family our sincerest greetings, thanking them warmly for the many good and loving benefits they have given you. Assure them of our friendship and respect.

Next Monday, 1 April, your uncle Dirk Boldt, acting as manager on my behalf, will leave for Moscow to take charge of the ten cows and two bulls that you have bought for me. He will transport the livestock back to here, assisted by Abram Reimer, a sensible young man from Halbstadt whom I have hired to drive the animals and take care of them, and by Afanasii, our cowherd from Iushanle. Martin Hamm, Tiege, will drive them to Kharkov. From there they will hire a vehicle to Moscow. It should be easy to buy a horse and wagon for the return journey. I gave Boldt 1,040 R.B.A. and 300 silver rubles – in total, 1,340 rubles. I think this amount will be enough for the journey. If this seems not to be the case, get more money from Mr. Blueher on my account. Once Boldt and his associates reach Moscow, inform me of the money needed en route [to Moscow]. I also expect a detailed report about the livestock purchase, especially the price, colour, and age of each head. Include the date of departure from Moscow, the behaviour of the animals underway, and how you were able to ensure their health. Arrange, and pass on to Boldt, a police certificate attesting to the health of the livestock. Buy four or five bottles of good wood vinegar (pyroxylic acid), which is excellent for treating infected hoofs. Instruct Boldt on the need to keep the livestock clean. It would be a good idea to buy a curry comb and brushes for this purpose.

In my opinion, it would be better to direct the transport through Kolomna and Tver, rather than through Tula and Orel. Once the livestock are underway, write to me about the money Mr. Blueher gave you and the credit remaining. I do not wish to become a burden to Mr. Blueher.

When you leave Moscow on your further travels, ask Mr. Blueher for directions on what to do in St. Petersburg and Riga should you run short of money for expenses and living costs. Do not carry much cash on you. Please discuss everything with Mr. Blueher and follow his advice. Before you leave for St. Petersburg, give me an address to which

I can address letters, and the time you expect to stay in and around St. Petersburg. Among the people you visit in St. Petersburg, be sure to include the Quaker Wihler and take notes on his agricultural activities.

Your information about our wool and its shortcomings is interesting and useful. Here everything is going well. Elder Franz Goerz in Rudnerweide died on 25 March.

All of us send you our greetings. May you fare well with God. Adieu.

Joh. …

488. Andrei M. Fadeev to Johann Cornies. 5 April 1835. SAOR 889-1-356/33.

Dear Cornies,

I received your letter of 30 March and will do whatever I can to help the three Mennonite foreigners [you mentioned] to obtain their registration documents.

As for the cows, I think I might limit my herd to six good cows and one bull. I will let you know by May.

The weather here in late March was cold. We long for rain.

Tell our good friend Dueck to stop worrying. His model arrived safely and General Inzov is pleased with it. With time, an application will be found for it.

I feel sad about Elder Goerz, but what can we do? We are all visitors here and he has gone to his home before us.

Where is your son now?

We might be able to meet in late May or in June.

Meanwhile, best wishes to you. Please give my greetings to your wife and to all of your good brethren.

A. Fadeev

Received 16 April.

489. Andrei M. Fadeev to Johann Cornies. 23 April 1835. SAOR 89-1-356/34.

Dear Cornies,

The seeding and harvesting machines, ordered by Governor General Count Vorontsov in the Molochnaia settlement with your assistance, are probably ready by now. His Honour has authorized me to ask you to have the machines transported to his estate, Novo-Vorontsova in Kherson guberniia (not far from Gronchevka). Send along a man skilled enough to demonstrate their exact use, and dispatch the chaise to His Excellency's house in Simferopol. All items should be turned over to his local managers in exchange for a receipt. However, send me an invoice (in Russian) for everything owing on these items and for their delivery, so that I can send you the money. Do it quickly, even if the amount is only an estimate, since the Count may soon be leaving for a long time.

I hope to visit you in June, if it is God's will. In the meantime, all the best to you.

A. Fadeev

Received 30 April 1835. Answered 4 May 1835.

490. Johann Cornies to District Office. 24 April 1835. SAOR 89-1-284/40.

To the worthy District Office in Halbstadt,

While moving a mill for me from Ladekopp to Tashchenak on 21 April, my workers stopped off for the night in the Arapp, close to Bauerdak village. There three of my oxen were stolen. We sounded the alarm and immediately ordered a search. Today I was notified that the oxen had definitely been sold to a Russian merchant in Prischib on 22 April, early in the morning. I request that the District Office act quickly by giving the two Nogais a Russian certificate authorizing them to take the three stolen oxen into their safekeeping as soon as they are found.

The markings on the oxen are as follows: one white, spotted five-year-old, and two white and grey six- to eight-year-olds, all branded with the marking "K" [for "Kornies"] on the left rear hoof.

Hoping the District Office will act on my request as quickly as possible, I have the honour to remain, respectfully, the District Office's devoted,

Johann Cornies

491. Forestry Society to Bernhard Fast. 26 April 1835. SAOR 89-1-361/4.

To the honoured Church Elder, Bernhard Fast,

From the Society for the Advancement and Dissemination of Forest Trees, Orchards, Sericulture, and Viticulture,

In a report dated 13 April, the Ladekopp Village Office reported to this Society that Preacher Peter Toews had dug trenches for fruit trees in his orchard that were not of the dimensions specified in the appropriate regulations and rules. Subsequently, Toews paid no attention to the refusal of the Village Office to permit him to plant trees in these trenches and, on the contrary, did so illegally. He also planted cherry hedges in direct defiance of orders from the authorities.

The Ladekopp Village Office has relinquished its obligations to the Society to take further action relating to Toews' disobedience. It notes that if Preacher Toews is permitted to continue in his disobedience, other householders in Ladekopp may well follow his example. The Society politely but urgently requests that you, honoured Elder, clothed in the authority of your office, persuade Preacher Peter Toews to carry out his obligations as a resident of Ladekopp and as owner of sixty-five desiatinas of land by obediently following all applicable orders handed down through the Village Office, as his fellow villagers do. He must also transplant trees and hedges he planted contrary to regulations. Since the sap has risen in the trees he planted, the trees cannot be transplanted now without harm. The Society will give him until October to transplant all trees and hedges planted contrary to administrative orders, with the stipulation that Toews acknowledge the obligation he owes to the Ladekopp Village Office to transplant the trees and hedges in October.

The Society expresses the hope that Preacher Peter Toews will not oppose administrative regulations in future and compel the Society to declare him a disobedient person. This would have a devastating effect on him and on the whole community.

The Society requests that you, honoured Elder, inform this Society of what you have done in this case in order that it can take whatever further measures it deems necessary.

In the Society meeting on 26 April 1835

492. Forestry Society to Tiegenhagen Village Office. [1835? Draft.] SAOR 89-1-908/15.

Tiegenhagen,

Two residents, Jacob Martens and Jacob Enns, have explained that they do not wish to provide guarantees in the case of fullholder Schellenberg, who has evidenced bad judgment and neglect in disobeying administrative orders with respect to his agricultural buildings and plantings. The Village Office must constantly push him on despite the fact that he has sufficient means to obey such orders. These guarantors fear that Schellenberg will persist in his refusal to improve his fullholding.

The Society discussed this situation in its meeting of 2 March and decided that the evidence given by the above-mentioned guarantors and in Village Office reports cast doubt on Schellenberg's intentions respecting the improvement of his fullholding as required by administrative directives. The Society has therefore decided to take action in this case itself.

The Society therefore orders the Village Office and guarantors to prepare a written statement listing the repairs and improvements that need to be made on Schellenberg's fullholding:

1. Which agricultural buildings need to be repaired or rebuilt? Are there fences that need to be repaired or erected?

2. Which conditions are contrary to directives with respect to cleanliness in and around buildings, including the need to remove manure, straw, and other objects from the yard?

3. What work has not been done as ordered in the orchard and forest-tree plantings? What must still be completed, cleaned, or prepared for further planting?

4. Are his fallow fields well kept?

The Society requires this information to ensure that the guarantors know what is needed to bring Schellenberg's fullholding up to standard. They are obligated to see that changes are implemented as demanded of them. Should they fail in this instance, the Society is required to report them to the inspector as residents who broke their word by not standing to their guarantee.

493. Forestry Society to Blumenort Village Office. [1835? Draft.] SAOR 889-1-908/17.

Blumenort,

Most villages in this district have implemented a directive sent to this Society by the head curator requiring that four or five cottager-sites in each village be set aside for young families in the tradesman class, and be marked off with ploughed furrows. At this date, Blumenort has done nothing in this respect. According to a map submitted by the Blumenort village community to the District Office on 4 April 1835, Blumenort has only three cottager-sites, each of a different size. According to the general rules, the [cottager-] sites must all be of the same size and there should be one site for every fullholding.

The Society asks whether Blumenort has designated a cottager-site for every fullholder and marked them off with ploughed furrows. The Society itself has the authority to set aside four or five cottager-sites in suitable locations, and to have them marked off by ploughed furrows early in spring.

494. Forestry Society to Schoensee Village Office. [1835? Draft.] SAOR 89-1-908/18.

Schoensee,

The map the village community sent to the District Office in 1835 shows that cottager-sites Nos. 7, 8, 11, 12, 15, 16, 19, 20, 23, and 24 are included in the forest-tree plantation. Cottager-sites 6, 9, 10, and 13 should be marked by ploughed furrows next spring. Therefore the total number of cottager-sites is now fourteen, and the village office is ordered to set aside another fourteen cottager-sites beside the village immediately. A map listing the names of all owners of old and new cottager-sites should be sent to the Society by the twentieth of this month at the latest. The Village Office must observe this order promptly.

495. Forestry Society to Alexanderwohl Village Office. [1835? Draft.] SAOR 89-1-908/18v.

Alexanderwohl,

District Office statistics show that one fullholder in Alexanderwohl does not own any sheep. Sheep provide the largest income for all households. The High Administration has expressly ordered that no one be permitted to own sixty-five desiatinas unless he keeps sheep. The Village Office is obligated to report the name of every fullholder who does not own sheep, and indicate the present condition of his fullholding. This information, truthfully reported, should be sent to the Society by the fifteenth of this month.

496. Andrei M. Fadeev to Johann Cornies. Sent from Odessa, 14 May 1835. SAOR 89-1-356/39.

Dear Cornies,

I received your two letters, dated 4 and 7 May. God willing, I hope to see you in June. Then we will talk about the purchase of cows, etc. I received money for your accounts from Governor Vorontsov, but, to save postage, will bring it to you myself. May you meanwhile make excellent progress. My good wishes for your wool sales this year. Harvest prospects here are good.

A. Fadeev

Please forward the enclosed certificate to Johann Neufeldt, as he requested.

497. Andrei M. Fadeev to District Office. Sent from Odessa, May 1835. SAOR 89-1-349.

To the Molochnaia Mennonite District Office,

The District Office is hereby ordered to submit a sketch to the [Guardianship] Committee, showing the buildings for the advanced educational institution in Ohrloff village in the Molochnaia Mennonite District, and also a detailed description of the institution's internal design and of the house that belongs to it. A building similar in design is to be constructed in Sarata in the Bessarabian settlement.

Member of the Guardianship Committee Fadeev

Received 24 May 1835. Communication to Heese Ohrloff, 24 May 1835. Another order sent 12 June 1835.

498. Ernst Walther to Johann Cornies. 25 May 1835. SAOR 89-1-324/54.

Highly honoured Mr. Cornies,

Since I was not fortunate enough to find you at home today, I take the liberty of asking whether you are still able to provide three months of summer pasturage, June to August, for 5,000 to 6,000 ewes and lambs on your Iushanle land. What would you charge per head per month? Are open watering places present? If you are prepared to accommodate such a flock, please inform me in writing in the next few days. I will gladly pay the messenger.

Your devoted servant,

Ernst Walther

Ohrloff, 25 May 1835

499. C. Steven, Simferopol, to Johann Cornies. 16 June 1835. SAOR 89-1-295/34.[1]

Very esteemed Mr. Cornies,

I have not had the pleasure of meeting you personally, but I am turning to you with a request for information about two subjects:

1 Regarding Steven, see footnote 49. Cornies had corresponded with Steven in the 1820s, so Steven's introduction of himself here is curious.

1. Have you sold your merino wool this year? What was the selling price? An estate here produces first quality wool, but is offered much less this year than last. A knowledge of prices in other regions might help to raise prices here.

2. Could you acquire a good strong hay wagon for me, one that can also be used to transport grain? I would need one suitable for use on the fields with oxen. Our local settlements get wagons from the Molochnaia, but these can only be used with horses. I would like to use either horses or oxen.

I would be very pleased to get to know you. We could exchange useful information on various subjects.

With respect,
Your devoted C. Steven
Answered 27 June 1835.

500. District Office to Johann Cornies. 19 June 1835. SAOR 89-1-356/44.

To Hon. Johann Cornies in Ohrloff,

The vice-governor of Tavrida will be travelling from Berdiansk, first to Steinbach, and then to your sheep farm on 21 or 22 June. He will also visit you in Ohrloff. This information is to enable you to make the necessary arrangements for his reception.

District Office, Halbstadt, 19 June 1835
District Chairman Regier

501. District Office to Johann Cornies. 2 July 1835. SAOR 89-1-356/52.

To Hon. Johann Cornies in Ohrloff,

In response to your report of 1 July, you are hereby informed that the body of Jacob, son of the widow Jacob Fast, in Rueckenau, who hanged himself on your Iushanle sheep farm, cannot be buried until a legal investigation conducted by the Melitopol lower court or the District Office has been done and a special permission is issued. Until that time, you are required to ensure that the body in the grave is well protected from predatory animals.

District Office, Halbstadt, 2 July 1835
District Chairman Regier

502. District Office to Johann Cornies. 4 July 1835. SAOR 89-1-352/49.

To the honourable Johann Cornies in Ohrloff,

His Honour, State Counsellor Fadeev will arrive here sometime today, 4 July. You are requested to appear in the District Office tomorrow, Friday 5 July. He will presumably wish to speak to you.

District Office, Halbstadt, July 4, 1835

District Chairman Regier

503. District Office to Johann Cornies. 5 July 1835. SAOR 89-1-356/54.

To Hon. Johann Cornies in Ohrloff,

His Honour, State Counsellor Fadeev will arrive tomorrow, Saturday 6 July, and spend the night with you in Ohrloff. Sunday, 7 July, he will take his noon meal on your sheep farm on the Iushanle. You are requested to prepare for these visits.

District Chairman Regier

District Office, Halbstadt, 5 July 1835

504. Cornelius Wall to Johann Cornies. 6 July 1835. SAOR 89-1-356/57.

Honoured friend Cornies,

Please do not be offended that I request your kind support and assistance in improving my imperfect service to His Honour [Fadeev]. I am afraid that, since I lack the necessary experience, I would have difficulty in answering any unanticipated questions. I am in your debt for the instructions you have already given me. With many thanks, I remain your humble Cornelius Wall.

Community sheep farm, 6 July 1835

505. Jacob Martens, Tiegenheim, to Johann Cornies. 11 July 1835. SAOR 89-1-356/59.

Most esteemed friend,

On 9 July, in your absence, I gave Sommerfeld the 9,000 R.B.A. in cash I owed you. As soon as it is possible and convenient, please inform me of the interest I still owe you.

Your friend Jacob Martens
Answered 11 July 1835.

506. Frantz Voht, Rueckenau, to Johann Cornies. 21 July 1835. SAOR 89-1-356/60.

To Mr. Johann Cornies, Ohrloff,

I asked you for a horse in the past, but you could not give me one. I would like to request one again, should this be possible. My team is in a very bad condition and everything is growing so quickly. I can think of no other solution than to ask you if you might be able to give me an old, superfluous horse. Please send me an answer.

Frantz Voht

507. District Office to Johann Cornies. 31 July 1835. SAOR 89-1-324/27.

To honoured Johann Cornies in Ohrloff,

While State Counsellor Fadeev was touring this district, you promised to send District Chairman Regier a map of the graveyards but no such map has yet been received. The graveyards must be supervised and you are hereby requested to provide such a map to the District Office at the first opportunity.

District Office at Halbstadt, 31 July 1835
Deputy Harder
Map given to district chairman, without written communication.

508. Traugott Blueher, Moscow, to Johann Cornies. 6 August 1835. SAOR 89-1-352/4.

Beloved friend Cornies,

In response to your communication of 10 July, I can inform you that goat wool mixed with some coarse hair (according to the sample you sent me with the last mail) can be sold here for thirty R.B.A. per pud. When separated, the coarse hair has almost no value itself and can only be sold at prices paid for mattress stuffing. However, the value of the three puds of white goat wool is 100 R.B.A. per pud when separated. Over the last few years, such wool sold quickly and was sent to France.

The Spanish wool purchased on account for this company was sold for a delayed payment, as I did not wish to risk storing it any longer.

Prices will decrease as shipments increase. There will be no problems with this payment and I am entirely satisfied.

Although it is still a long time until the next purchases must be made, I now permit myself to make a few remarks. Above all, the wool should be roughly sorted in future. If Mr. Neufeld cannot take care of this, I am prepared to pay for an assistant to do so. Combining several varieties of wool in one ball creates great disadvantages when the wool is being sold. The buyer simply does not know how to establish a fair price. To illustrate, I am sending you a sample from one such ball. Similar situations occurred with several balls. It is permissable to include coarse wool, but only if it is visibly separated, to provide a clear overview of the shipment.

Your dear son has written to us from Riga. He tells us that you would like his sister to live with us this coming winter. My wife asks me to let you know that we will welcome her in heartfelt friendship, should she be satisfied with our simple housekeeping. Thank God that love and peace reign in our family and that we are raising our children as simply as possible. How easy it is to become accustomed to comfort, but the reverse is another thing.

Greetings of friendship to you and your dear family. Commending myself to your loving memory, I remain your faithfully obligated friend,

Traugott Blueher

Received 24[?] August.

509. Andrei M. Fadeev to Johann Cornies. Undated, received 28 August 1835. SAOR 89-1-352/13.

Dear Cornies,

I received your letter of 5 August, and found the books you mentioned. When I have an opportunity, I will send the books to your district for the use of anyone wishing to read them and to follow their advice in the planting of trees.

A Mennonite woman in Schoenwiese is insistently asking to be registered here. Her husband, having immigrated a few years ago, is travelling in the Molochnaia area. She refers to Martens and his sister (Widow Dueck) and says her husband is a pious and hard-working person. If there are other such people in your district about whose good conduct and usefulness there is no doubt, please tell District Chairman Regier that the District Office can make recommendations to the

Committee that they be registered. Give Martens my greetings. When he left Odessa, he was in a rush and did not visit me on my estate. How is his purchase of land at Kinburn going? And the payments from the factory?

I must insistently ask you to take special care of the forest-tree plantations this fall, planting them well and in a pleasing manner. With all of our might, we must strive in the Molochnaia villages to establish a firm foundation for New Russia's future forests.

Wishing you good health and success.

A. Fadeev

Received 28 August 1835.

510. Agnes Cornies, Kursk, to Johann Cornies, 30 September 1835. SAOR 89-1-295/50.

Most esteemed Father,

On 30 September, we arrived safely and in good health in Kursk. If the road continues to be good, we plan to arrive in Moscow on 9 October. We intend to leave here today.

I send heartfelt greetings to you and dear Mother, and hope that my few lines might find you in good health. Uncle sends heartfelt greetings to his loved ones.

I remain your obedient daughter,

Agnes Cornies

Received 15 October 1835.

511. Christian Klaassen, Grunau, to Johann Cornies. 6 October 1835. SAOR 89-1-352/18.

Worthy Mr. Cornies,

May the Lord be with you and your whole family.

Please do not be offended at my presumption in writing to you, but I feel I must. His Honour, [Andrei M. Fadeev], a member of the Guardianship Committee for Colonists in South Russia, has instructed me to supervise our community [tree] plantations with a view to improving them substantially. Since everything in this commission is important to me, I would like to do everything I can to carry out the wishes of our high authorities. I have given careful thought to how this might be accomplished, should it be God's will and should there be no impediments. I think that a foundation for such a development has already been laid, but local authorities are lackadaisical in carrying out the orders of the established authorities. The inspector, for his part, tries to impede this project and his ill will towards me grows from day to day. In his rage, he does everything he can to create difficulties for gardener Probst and for me. In the presence of higher authorities, the inspector blames the gardener for all shortcomings, despite the fact that that his charges can scarcely be believed and the gardener is only doing his duty. As long as the inspector continues in this way, I will not apply for another gardener. The fault lies with the poor seed that he has been given, and that involves negligence of course, but the charges against Probst are unfair. He simply does what he can.

I wrote to the District Office using a numbered letter, requesting workers and the placement of a gate in front of the gardener's house to prevent roaming livestock from damaging the community plantation. The inspector summoned me, screamed at me as though I were a young boy and wrote to the District Office. As far as I am concerned, I did not need to use a numbered letter, but did it because the plantation is important to me and I wanted to ensure that everything necessary had been done. His Honour the State Counsellor commissioned me to supervise work on the tree plantation, but I know well what the inspector had in mind. He would be pleased if nothing comes of the plantation project and I and gardener Probst would simply run away. He told the gardener that he could never survive on such a pitiful income and should take a more remunerative position with the estate owner Mareus. Dear, valued Mr. Cornies, please bring all of these matters to the attention of the State Counsellor as soon as you can. Some day things around here will improve.

With respect, and in the hope of your help, I remain your devoted friend,

Christian Klaassen
Grunau, 6 October 1835

512. Karl Mathias, Hochstadt, to Johann Cornies. 6 October 1835. SAOR 889-1-352/17.

Highly valued Mr. Cornies,

I find myself without a pass and am suffering from fever. I have suffered all the time that I was travelling and still do not know when the fever will let up. I therefore enclose money in the value of 1,400 rubles in this letter, which I am sending along to you with my servant. Please notify me that you have received it. It is impossible for me to deliver it personally.

I have been ordered to eat dried plums, but I do not know where they are to be found. I have made inquiries in this regard everywhere in this vicinity. I would beg that you, highly valued Mr. Cornies, might help me out by sending me [one or two garnitz] of dried plums. Please show me this act of love, if that is possible.

With greetings to you, your wife, and children. Humbly,

Karl Mathias

Hochstadt, 6 October 1835

513. Johann Cornies Jr., Moscow, to Johann Cornies. 18 October 1835. SAOR 89-1-352/6.

Most honoured Father,

Agnes arrived here safely and in good health, as her letter reports, and I will say no more than to assure you that she likes it here very much. Since it is Mr. Blueher's wish, I will move to the Sarepta house with her. Uncle D. Boldt left on his return journey yesterday, 17 October. I sent along most of the items you ordered from me, as per the enclosed list. It is still too early to gather the seeds, nor have I found a cream tester. I did send along a crate of flower bulbs that I hope will meet your needs. I could not, however, find any fresh flower seeds.

From your treasured communication of 12 September (which I received the evening before my departure with Mr. Eger), I gather that you would like me to start my return journey through Saratov to Sarepta. I agree with this completely. I have several acquaintances there and know that I will be well received. The one problem, however, is that my passport lapses on 30 March 1836, during the trip. Please advise me. To have Agnes accompany me should not create any problems, since she encountered none on her trip to Moscow.

May God keep you and dear Mother in good health, that is my heartfelt wish. I add my childlike greetings and remain your obedient son,

Johann Cornies

2 dozen handkerchiefs, 18 rubles per dozen	36	
1/2 dozen cups	7	
1/2 dozen silver tablespoons, weighing		
89¼ zolot., at 1 ruble per zolot.	86	25
1/2 dozen penknives	18	
1 dozen pencils to write on wood	1	50
2 dozen inkwells		88
10 funt cotton at 4 rubles, 75 kopeks per funt	47	50
	197 rubles	13 kopeks

P.S. I do not yet have the list of flower bulbs or the bill. I also sent a small package from Riga with feed vetches as well as tobacco seeds and various sugar peas. The dozen pencils will please the gardener and carpenter.

With respect to the cotton, 7 funt of No. 16 and 3 funt of No. 20 belongs to D. Boldt. I received orders for the rest, actually 4 funt of No. 20 and 6 funt of No. 16. Boldt's cotton was paid for here. The same.

Received 12 November 1835.

514. Christian Wollmann, Kirschwald, to Johann Cornies. 20 October 1835. SAOR 89-1-352/28.

Highly honoured Mr. Cornies,

When I visited you, you asked me to find you a good servant. I could not say anything definite about the matter then, since the best people are always hired quickly. Due to unusual circumstances, I am now able to send you the bearer of this [letter], whose name is Georg Plivernits. He is a single inhabitant of Rosengart, who worked as a servant for Donnerstag in Kirschwalde for several years. He is an able, hard-working, faithful, and honourable person. You will find him to be dependable in whatever you require of him, even in money matters. You can take him into your service on my word.

I have the honour to send heartfelt greetings to you, your dear wife, and children, from me, my wife, and children. Wishing you well in body and in soul, I commend you to the protection of the Omnipotent. Please retain your favourable opinion of me in future. I remain with all esteem, thankfulness, and love your obediently thankful,

Christian Wollmann

220 rubles wages, home for Pentecost, washing, two rubles advance. Should Mr. Cornies not be at home, dear Mrs. Cornies is asked to break the seal on this letter and to kindly deal with its contents,

Wollmann

515. Andreas Flaming and Gerhard Kliewer, Schardau, to Johann Cornies. 1 November 1835. SAOR 89-1-324/36.

Sincerely valued friend,

On your recent tour of the villages, we spoke to you about the boy Gerhard Dyck, a minor without parents, hoping that you might take him into your care and raise him. As his guardians, we find the duty, debt, and concern of providing for his upbringing and education as a human being and as a Christian close to our hearts. We fully believe that you would treat him accordingly with concern and love. We, for our part, would enjoin him to give you his obedience and be diligent and industrious. In the hope that you might agree to our request, we remain, with the kindest greetings and commendation, your constantly loving,

Andreas Flaming, Gerhard Kliewer

516. Wilhelm Martens to Johann Cornies. 25 November 1835. SAOR 89-1-295/31.

Treasured friend,

With friend Johann Neufeldt, I am sending you the 6,000 R.B.A. you lent me, together with the interest owing on this amount and on the 18,000 rubles lent me earlier. Many thanks for your kindness.

I returned from Ekaterinoslav yesterday evening, but failed to finish my business as I had hoped I might. I am now reluctantly forced to set off immediately for Prischib to buy the hay and grain on the

Egarlitskii Kuth land. I cannot get there by November 26, the date established by the orphans court [*Waisengericht*], and the trip may well be in vain.

With wishes for you and your valued family's continuing well-being, I am, with hearty greetings,

Your friend Wilhelm Martens

517. Johann Regier to Johann Cornies. 27 November 1835. SAOR 89-1-295/52.

Valued friend,

I am hereby sending you seven copies of the instructions for tobacco cultivation, as you wished. The booklet about firing bricks cannot be found in the catalogues and books that State Counsellor Fadeev sent to the District Office with Inspector Pelekh. I seem to have been mistaken in what I remembered since you had mentioned this matter earlier.

With friendly greetings,
I am your friend,
Johann Regier

518. Andrei M. Fadeev to Johann Cornies. Undated, received 29 November 1835. SAOR 89-1-352/33.

Dear Cornies,

I thank your for your letter of 27 October and also for the four volumes of the *Conversations-Lexicon*. I was very pleased that you were able to receive several important guests. Even though such visits take a lot of time, they can also have important benefits for the settlements and for you personally. I have no doubt but that your Society will eventually reach its goal, especially with your participation. It is regrettable that there is so often no outside support. There has been no response either from Radichev or from Kiev guberniia about forest-tree seeds for the current year. Mr. Steven has also failed to answer our queries about wild chestnuts. Have you had any news from him?

We have had favourable autumn weather here as well, but then snow and severe frost descended on us on 27 October. Now winter is over again.

Will your children stay in Moscow for long? I send hearty greetings to you and your wife, and remain your devoted,

A. Fadeev

Received 29 November 1835. Answered 6 December 1835.

519. Andrei M. Fadeev, Odessa, to Johann Cornies. December 1835. SAOR 89-1-352/72.

My dear Cornies,

I find it necessary to inform you with the greatest of regrets (presumably you already know about this from the newspapers) that, at the command of the highest authority, I have been given a new appointment. It is a difficult situation for me personally that upsets many aspects of my domestic arrangements. My greatest regret, however, is that the change in my appointment means that we will no longer be able, as before, to cooperate in advancing the well-being of the Molochnaia Mennonite District. Government orders cannot, however, be changed. Perhaps I can be useful in some way in my new position as well. Eventually, I might also be able to return. The Minister assures me that I will be sent away for only a brief period and should not sell my khutor, where I intend to leave all of my personal belongings.

I just hope they will not ask me to undertake a journey at this raw time of year. I will probably be leaving in March. My journey will, in any case, proceed through the Molochnaia settlements where I expect we will see one another again. In the meantime, write to me if you have any urgent business that needs my help. After I leave, it would probably make sense for you to address your correspondence directly to General [Inzov]. I will try to arrange this.

Give my greetings to your wife and Martens. I remain forever,

Your devoted A. Fadeev

520. Johann Regier to Johann Cornies. 16 December 1835. SAOR 89-1-352/42.

Honoured friend,

For a number of reasons, I have postponed my journey to Odessa until after the holidays. One of my deputies is sick in bed and the other is required to make several trips before the holidays. I must postpone my departure until 28 December.

With friendly greetings to you and your loved ones, I remain, as always, your honest friend,

Johann Regier

P.S. I will stop at your house before I leave.

521. Andrei M. Fadeev, Odessa, to Johann Cornies. 17 December 1835. SAOR 89-1-352/38.

Dear, valued Cornies,

I read your letter of 6 December with the deepest of emotions. Yes, the future well-being of the Molochnaia Mennonite community and the giant strides made in its plantings would simply be enough to persuade me to endure patiently whatever was unpleasant in my former position in the Guardianship Committee and sacrifice all future advantages, were it possible to change the Minister's explicit decision about my new position. Regrettably, at present, circumstances and my children's well-being do not allow this.

One must submit to the orders of the administration. But I will never cease to take an active interest in your community's well-being and will promote its arrangements with continued vigor. I sent paper No. 91 to the Society. It only deals with official correspondence and with submissions requesting decisions. Until I return, should that be God's will, I will always be pleased to give my opinions, advice, and support with regard to the Society's concerns as well as dealings that your brethren may have with General Inzov and with St. Petersburg. In the meantime, tell me honestly: what can I do for you or for your family? I hope that perhaps my submissions will receive attention now, here as well as in St. Petersburg. Think about it carefully and send me a special letter.

I still do not know how long I will be permitted to stay here. I hope that matters will be delayed until spring. In any case, I hope to visit you. [In my new position,] I will become Sarepta's neighbour, and it would please me greatly to find your dear children there. When District Chairman Regier comes to Odessa, we will come to an agreement about sending Wiebe back and appointing him.

I think you have done business with the Kalmyks. Might you perhaps be interested in helping me civilize them?

May you remain healthy. Do not lose courage in promoting useful activities that will redound to the general well-being of your brethren.

After completing this letter, I received yours of 11 December. I have already arranged matters here for your Society's further direct correspondence with the head curator, and have sent the Society notification No. 91 in this regard. Avoid burdening him too frequently or with petty matters. Have more confidence in yourself as you work with your colleagues. Try to combine your different presentations into a few annual reports. Make these clear and emphatic, urgently requesting early solutions. In important matters, write to me a month in advance, if time allows, so that I can support you with opinions or queries. A few years will soon pass and we will see how God directs matters. Your relations with the inspector regarding agricultural matters will likely stay as before and I will try to arrange for this. I find your opinions with respect to the Radichev [Hutterian Brethren] Mennonites and the settlement of young families to be well founded and I will make arrangements accordingly.

Received 24 December 1835. Answer 24 January 1836.

522. Wilhelm Martens to Johann Cornies. 27 December 1835. SAOR 89-1-352/36.

Treasured friend,

In accordance with our last agreement, I am sending my son Johann to you, requesting that you kindly advance me the amount of money that you can let me have. Necessity demands that I begin my journey as far as Gruenthal today, and I cannot wait until the District Office members assemble. According to a message I received from friend Johann Neufeldt, the district chairman might not be in the District Office before tomorrow, Saturday.

With the assured hope that my request will be filled if that is possible, I sign myself with a hearty greeting for you and your beloved spouse, your honest friend,

Wilhelm Martens

25,000 rubles advanced 27 December.

523. Johann Cornies to Andrei M. Fadeev. 29 December [1834? 1835?]. SAOR 89-1-332/5.

[Draft No. 258] To His Honour, Member of the Guardianship Committee for Colonists in Southern Russia, State Counsellor, Fadeev,

From the Chairman of the Molochnaia Mennonite Society for the Advancement and Dissemination of Forest Trees, Orchards, Sericulture, and Viticulture, Johann Cornies,

Report:

Since its establishment, the local Society has several times discussed the varieties of trees that it would be most advantageous to plant in fruit orchards and along village streets. They should grow quickly and be attractive. It is particularly important that they be more enduring than poplars, willows, and similar softer varieties of wood, which do not last long. Bore-worms generally gnaw through these varieties of wood, reducing sap in the trunk when the trees are most beautiful and begin to spread their branches. As these worms gain freer access, beautiful poplars and willows dry up in a few years.

By chance, when Society members were on their inspection tours through the villages, they noticed wild apple and pear trees growing in several individual fruit orchards for more than twenty-five years. These trees are still growing exceptionally well and have reached a respectable height. Their crowns form very attractive kettle shapes in some cases, pyramid shapes in others, without any efforts to train or prune them. This led the Society to the provisional decision to plant these varieties along village streets. They offer a beautiful sight and their fruit can be enjoyed for a variety of household uses. The fact that they endure for a long time makes it especially worthwhile to plant them. Poplars, willows, and similar fast-growing trees can still be planted, but only where soil is suitable and they are more likely to survive for a longer time.

As the Society submits this proposal to Yr. Honour to plant wild fruit trees along village streets for his sympathetic examination, it requests most obediently that a favourable resolution be granted.

N. 258, 29 December [1834–5?]

524. District Office to Johann Cornies. 31 December 1835. SAOR 89-1-324/88.

No. 3,150. To honourable Johann Cornies in Ohrloff,

Based on a communication from the Melitopol lower-land court, about the death of apanage peasant Ivan Kostin, who owed you a considerable sum of money, Inspector Pelekh has informed the District Office that [Kostin's] property is under the direction of the apanage administration. The lower-land court sent the certificate [confirming the loan] signed by Kostin to the manager of apanage properties to enable you to retrieve the money owed you by Kostin's heirs. You are hereby notified that Inspector Pelekh has requested that the administrator for Novo-Grigoriev apanage properties inform him if this succeeds.

District Office in Halbstadt, 31 December 1835
Deputy Driedger

525. District Office to Johann. Cornies. 31 December 1835. SAOR 89-1-324/105.

Communication to honourable Johann Cornies in Ohrloff:

Order No. 1993 from Inspector Pelekh, dated 4 December, informs us that the Melitopol lower-land court notified the inspector that, because he gave this amount to his wife as a gift, it considers the matter of the late Molokan Trofim Ismailov's debt of one ruble, fifty kopek closed.

District Office in Halbstadt, 31 December 1835

Deputy Driedger

526. Johann Cornies to Tashchenak Manager. Undated [SAOR label says 1835]. SAOR 89-1-348/8.

Guidelines for the manager [*Prikazshchik*] I have appointed to manage and supervise my khutor in Tashchenak:

On the khutor I have entrusted to your management, you are expected to carry out the following with great assiduity:

1. All types of buildings must be maintained in the appropriate good order. If necessary, they must be daubed and whitewashed, and the roofs repaired. In general, cleanliness and good order must be observed. Ovens and chimneys must similarly be maintained in good condition and the latter swept frequently, in order that no accidents occur because of carelessness.

2. You must keep watch that all people employed to carry out all duties do so adequately and diligently, and that you do all that lies in your power to contribute to the success and improvement of the establishment entrusted to your care.

3. All work in the cultivation of the fields and the harvesting of hay must be done in the appropriate manner and at the appropriate time. The people employed must carry out the work vigilantly and industriously.

4. You must record how much of each crop was seeded and how much was harvested. Since all fields will not be threshed at the same time, the quantity threshed on each occasion must be recorded. Amounts of grain consumed and in storage must also be recorded. Pay attention to ensure that none of it is wasted for any reason, whether as food for human consumption or as livestock feed.

It is naturally assumed that careful housekeeping will prevail in storing provisions and other foodstuffs, as well as hay and straw. Care must be taken that the latter are not scattered, wasted, or ruined when the livestock is fed.

5. You must observe the increase or decrease in each variety of livestock during the course of each month and inform me about changes at month's end, including the reasons for any decline. When there are unusual occurrences you should notify me immediately.

6. All varieties of agricultural and field implements, such as wagons, ploughs, harrows, shovels, etc., as well as dishes and implements required in housekeeping, must, in all instances, be used carefully. Necessary repairs and improvements must be made immediately. Care must be taken at all times to keep [buildings and equipment] in a good and usable condition for as long as possible.

7. All varieties of household and agricultural implements such as tow ropes, horse harnesses, or wooden implements must be returned to their storage places after each use. You must absolutely not allow them to be left lying in the yard or anywhere else, which would soon render them useless. This order applies also to scythes, rakes, forks, axes, and all similar items. Livestock could easily injure their feet or sustain other damage if the implements had not been returned to their storage places after each use. Do not permit pits to be dug or traps to be set to catch rabbits or other animals, since they can also occasion accidents.

8. All people living on the khutor must take all possible care of their clothes and other belongings. You must inspect everything, and all damage must be repaired immediately. What has deteriorated and can no longer be used should, when necessary, be replaced. Workers who pay insufficient attention to the care of tools and other items entrusted to their care, permitting them to be ruined through laziness and negligence, are obligated to replace the item in question at their own expense.

9. Consider all workers on the khutor to be entirely equal in the provision of food and the assignment of jobs for which they were hired. No one should be favoured or treated harshly without cause. All should be equally encouraged to do their best, industriously and energetically. The workers must see you as a modest, loving, and serious person. The treatment of one worker with special generosity, especially if he has not earned it, will cause enmity and resentment. Others may neglect their work or do it with insufficient effort. This will place the owner of the khutor at a serious disadvantage.

10. Take care to ensure that all workers live together in amity and harmony. Only then will they support one another in their activities,

should this be necessary, and not make excuses that the work required of them is none of their concern.

Feast days should be enjoyed sensibly and wisely. No one, on such occasions, is permitted to become drunk under any circumstances. A drunken person is inclined towards quarrelsomeness and fighting, which spoils the pleasure of the occasion for himself and for others. He will be in no condition to carry out his responsibilities, and will undeniably cause his master damage. Dances and other levities are absolutely forbidden on workdays and during long evenings in fall and winter. In the evenings and in rainy weather, all workers should busy themselves with activities such as patching work clothes, repairing field implements and tools, etc.

11. When hiring day labourers, ensure that you have sufficient work on hand to keep them busy, lest they become idle. Never hire more labourers than are needed for specific tasks.

12. If you are absent from the khutor for any reason, you must leave a dependable person already in service to supervise the khutor in your absence. Explain clearly how this is to be done.

13. It is your duty to keep a stern watch to prevent people in service from entertaining outside herdsmen [tabunshchiki], Nogais, or suspicious persons. They must not shelter anyone without your approval. If anyone is caught in an act of thievery or other vile action, you are to notify me immediately. The guilty person must be given the appropriate punishment or handed over to the courts, in keeping with the measure of his guilt.

14. Care must be taken to prevent fires. Lanterns must be in good order and pipes equipped with covers. Smoking must not be allowed near grain and haystacks or during the feeding of livestock. Smoking is entirely forbidden near buildings.

15. Since it is not possible to provide orders that cover every instance, you are hereby instructed to keep my advantage in mind at all times. Implement whatever is needed for the well-being and best advantage of the khutor entrusted to you.

If undecided about an action appropriate to a specific case, notify me immediately and obtain orders from me as to the proper course of action.

1836

**527. Andrei M. Fadeev, Odessa, to Johann Cornies.
3 January 1836. SAOR 89-1-367/55.**

Dear Cornies,

I wish you happiness in the New Year, in your new position and as a member of the Statistics Committee.[1] Do not worry too much about this matter. If you write what you know about the settlements, that will suffice. Much of the information needed is included in papers on the subject now in my possession. I will send them to you with District Chairman Regier. I could not turn them over to a better man.

I have written to Mr. Pelekh, asking him to inquire whether dependable drivers with eight horses, or vehicles with four pairs of oxen, can be hired in the Molochnaia settlements. I would need them in early April to take my baggage and several individuals to Tsaritsyn or Sarepta. Please assist him in this matter and inform me of the outcome. Drivers could perhaps be found among the same people who transport your wool to Moscow.

May you stay healthy. I remain your devoted,

A. Fadeev

Received 14 January 1836. Answered 24 January 1836.

---

1 Cornies had been made a corresponding member of the new Statistics Department [*Statisticheskii otdel*] of the Ministry of Internal Affairs, created in December 1834.

528. Forestry Society to village offices. 7 January 1836. SAOR 89-1-344/1.

Village offices are hereby instructed to be punctual in informing each fullholder and cottager personally, that he must count his trees accurately and list increases or decreases in their number in the following manner:

1. Kernel fruit (apple and pear trees)
2. Stone fruit (plum, cherry, and apricot trees)
3. Mulberry trees, including those planted in orchards and hedges
4. Willows, in plantations and elsewhere
5. All varieties of other trees such as elms, alders, acacias, wild olives, maples, lindens, chestnuts, oaks, poplars, etc.

Trees that took root as runners in forest-tree plantations or in orchards, including plum and cherry trees, are not to be counted. Cherry hedges and nurseries consisting of one- to three-year-old trees are also not to be included in this count.

After each fullholder and cottager has been appropriately reminded of his responsibilities in this regard and in a timely fashion, he must submit his tree counts to the Village Office on the day set for this to occur. The Office must record these numbers according to the enclosed scheme and submit them to this Society by 20 January, without fail. The submission should be signed by the three village office members.

This circulated order must be sent on without delay to each householder and returned to the Society from Conteniusfeld.

Society at Ohrloff, 7 January 1836
Chairman Johann Cornies

529. Andrei M. Fadeev, Odessa, to Johann Cornies. 15 January 1836. SAOR 89-1-367/53.

Dear Cornies,

Convinced of your friendship, I am turning to you and our good friend Martens with a request. My unexpected change in service, the long journey before me, and the new arrangements I will have to make in Astrakhan have thrown my accounts into confusion. I need a loan of 1,500 to 2,000 rubles. Please let me know honestly if I can count on getting such a loan from you and Martens. It would be for one year, at your current interest rates. Might I receive the money when I pass through the Molochnaia colonies in March or April? Please feel free to let me know if such a loan were to create problems for you. In any case, please give me a definite answer one way or the other so that I might act accordingly before my departure.

Chairman Regier has already departed, and I sent you a description of the Molochnaia written in 1818. The numbers have meanwhile naturally changed substantially, but the information about its founding, etc., is useful. I may have more papers for you. You can obtain official information from the inspector, or from the District Office. I remain forever your devoted,

A. Fadeev

Answered 31 January 31 1836.

530. Johann Cornies to Radichev Village Office. 16 January 1836. SAOR 89-1-388/2.

I hereby notify you that I have received your communication and that [of the Odessa Guardianship Committee] informing me of your brotherhood's wish to settle on the Tashchenak in Melitopol Uezd. Before you move, I find it necessary to inform everyone in Radichev of the following:

1. I will not allow anyone to settle before local authorities have determined the actual site where the village is to be founded. This applies to householders designated as being capable of settling according to government regulations.

2. No one is to assume that they can live on my land, as some of you have suggested. Also, I will absolutely not permit anyone to live in the zemlianka [sod hut] on my land.

An orderly settlement must be founded, not a Gypsy encampment that would damage our good reputation and yours as well. You must establish an orderly organization, keep control, and not allow disorder to develop. Inform everyone of this categorically, to ensure that it is carried out in a timely fashion and maintained.

I hereby inform your village community that I will help you with good advice at all times, providing that you settle in an orderly fashion. Hoping for good results with your resettlement, I sign myself as your honest,

Johann Cornies

531. Johann Cornies to Andrei M. Fadeev. 24 January 1836. SAOR 89-1-388/4.[2]

State Counsellor Fadeev,

I have received Yr. Honour's esteemed communications of 17 December and 3 January. I and Martens will hire a team of eight

2 Regarding Cornies' efforts to gain a permanent land grant at Iushanle, see also documents 1, 5, 152, 177, 178, 185, 535, and additional documents in volume II.

horses or four pair of oxen in early April, as you desire, to take you to Tsaritsyn or Sarepta. We will keep them in a state of readiness. We have released Inspector Pelekh from this commission because he cannot hire a team as easily as we can. It is a small thing for us to do and it will give us pleasure to serve Yr. Honour in this way.

District Chairman Regier arrived here safely on 18 January and handed over the description of the settlement. I am much obliged for Yr. Honour's kindness and affection.

In accordance with Yr. Honour's wishes, I assure you that I will endeavour to occupy myself diligently, with zeal and industry, and not neglect to carry out anything useful for the general well-being of my brethren. The Society takes pleasure in the community's punctual compliance with its orders and hopes that this will continue in future. It would be appropriate if His Excellency, the Chief Curator, were to send a communication forcefully reminding all preachers that, being in possession of sixty-five desiatinas of land, they must serve in the orderly care of their plantations as examples to others in their community. And by admonishing community members to obey orders from the Society in a timely fashion, they are required to support the Society when difficulties occur.

I know only a little about the Kalmyks. [As I understand the matter,] they are easier to civilize than Nogais – more trusting, more honest, and not as sly as the Nogais, while their religion is not as opposed to their own moral improvement as is that of the Nogais. But I would be of absolutely no use as a helper to Yr. Honour in this great work. I have little of the comprehensive knowledge indispensable to the civilization of peoples, and I am also bound to this community. If the Kalmyks lived less than 200 verstas from here, I myself would naturally be interested in working with them.

Despite my sorrow, I am encouraged and reassured by Yr. Honour's kind support and permission to approach you, even though you will be far away, for your well-meaning advice and intercession in pressing cases and community matters. May God, in all His goodness, protect and guide you and your worthy family, keeping you in continued good health and true enjoyment of life under all conditions. Yes, may He strengthen you with wisdom and power to work on behalf of the poor Kalmyks, as you have lived and worked for us for twenty years.

With the most complete respect and feelings of the deepest thanks, I remain Yr. Honour's most obedient servant,

Johann Cornies

If Yr. Honour permits me to make an honest declaration of what could be useful to me and my family, and kindly extends to me your affection in using your influence on my behalf, I would make the following request of Yr. Honour. Would it be possible for me to receive, as my own property, the 4,500 desiatinas of land on the Iushanle where I now have my sheep farm and other ventures?

I am in a position to purchase the same quantity of good land around Melitopol, but my purpose is not simply to gain advantages for myself and my family. I want to be helpful to my brethren by providing an example of a good, improved establishment. I could hardly do this unless the example is close to our settlement, as is the Iushanle.

532. Johann Cornies to Andrei M. Fadeev. 31 January 1836. SAOR 89-1-388/6v.

In response to Yr. Honour's esteemed communication to me of 15 January, and to the trust you placed in us, I have the honour to reply to your inquiry about a loan of 1,500 to 2,000 rubles for one year from me and Martens. We are most willing to comply and you can definitely count on receiving it here in March or April. Martens is in Ekaterinoslav to register the land he purchased from Mr. Brodsky. I will speak to him when he returns. Should one of us depart this world unexpectedly, Yr. Honour would not have any problems.

533. Forestry Society to Gnadenfeld Village Office. February 1836. SAOR 89-1-167A/49.

[Draft]To Gnadenfeld Village Office,

The District Office and the Forestry Society have made the following decisions about the esteemed Elder Lange in the Gnadenfeld village community.[3] He is in the same position as every inhabitant with sixty-five desiatinas of land and hence obligated to assume the same duties

3 The village of Gnadenfeld was founded in 1835. The Lange mentioned here was Wilhelm Lange, long-time leader and elder of the Neumark Mennonite Congregation in Brandenburg, Prussia, and an important figure in Mennonite pietism. He immigrated to the Molochnaia in 1835, and died there in 1840. In 1836, he was already 72 years of age. The dispensations granted here were undoubtedly in deference to his age and ill-health.

as his neighbours with the exception of providing [compulsory] transport service.

It has been decided further that Elder Lange will be relieved of his absolute obligation to be present at all assemblies called by the Village Office. He is given the choice of asking the mayor or any other neighbour to inform him about every decision made by the assembled community. The Village Office must inform Elder Lange of this decision, and should not force him to appear.

The Village Office is further reminded to follow the rules it was commissioned to implement when the Society chairman and one of its members visited the Office on 12 February. It must make special efforts to ensure that peace, order, and cleanliness reign generally in Gnadenfeld village and adorn every family and household.

This order is to be retained as a document in the Village Office.

District Office in Halbstadt, February 1836

534. Johann Cornies to C. Steven. 5 February 1836. SAOR 89-1-388/7.

State Counsellor Steven,

I received Yr. Honour's esteemed communication and apologize for not informing Yr. Honour immediately when the vines, chestnuts, and 240 rubles owed for a wagon and plough arrived in good order. Although the temperature here at the time of the arrival of the vines was ten degrees below freezing, and the vines, when unpacked, were somewhat frozen together immediately above the root, I think it unlikely, since I noticed no such frost damage in the roots, that they suffered any damage. The roots were well packed and looked fresh. If it is not too difficult, would Yr. Honour, when an opportunity presents itself, kindly send me another 400 vines. I estimate that I need another 400 roots on my land, and will repay the costs immediately upon arrival of your notice.

I regret that the plough does not grip to the required depth. I have asked Thomas Wiens, a member of our community travelling to Simferopol on land registration matters, to inspect the plough and to set it correctly. Often only a small change is needed. But should it not be possible to set this plough to grip properly, I would ask that you return the plough to me when an opportunity presents itself. Please describe the type of soil you have and whether it is stony. I will then have a different plough constructed, designed to work in soil of the characteristics you cite, and sent to you.

Yr. Honour is far too kind in thanking me for carrying out the small commission with which you honoured me. I did it willingly, with the greatest pleasure and request that if my services might be of help to you in future, you take advantage of them.

In autumn, the driver who delivered the vines brought along twenty-five funt of sesame seeds for me. But I have not yet received the sesame seeds from Inspector Pelekh. I report this matter because you did not mention it in your last letter.

Please allow me, Yr. Honour, to ask for good grafting shoots for winter fruits such as apples and pears, especially for those varieties that are best suited for shipping and selling. We would like to increase such varieties in our community. If there is no good opportunity to deliver them to me privately, please send them along to the local Society by mail. I will repay the charges promptly.

A Tatar from Tashkent in Great Tartary lives here among the Nogais, and is urgently asking for seed rice. He lived on rice in his fatherland and thinks that his location on the river is suitable for rice cultivation. If it is not too much trouble, I would ask that Yr. Honour assist this Tatar by sending me seed for him.

I hurriedly gave Thomas Wiens three cheeses to pass on to Yr. Honour. I am sorry that I was not able to send first quality cheese, since I had none in stock, but the quality of these three should not be much lower.

With the greatest esteem, I have the honour to be Yr. Honour's devoted servant,

Johann Cornies

535. Andrei M. Fadeev to Johann Cornies. Sent from Odessa, 6 February 1836. SAOR 89-1-352/70.[4]

Dear Cornies,

I received your letter of 24 January and thank you for your offer to hire horses for my baggage. Please do not make definite arrangements until I notify you further or until I arrive. I am still waiting for more information and have not yet made a firm decision. Perhaps it might be more convenient to arrange transport by water up the Don [River] from Rostov.

4 Regarding Cornies' efforts to gain a permanent land grant at Iushanle, see also documents 1, 5, 152, 177, 178, 185, 531, and additional documents in volume II.

General Inzov considered favourably your desire to obtain support from your church leaders for your efforts. An exhortation was sent to them today, of which I enclose a copy. You can depend on any cooperation I can possibly provide you with since my interest in promoting the progress of forest-tree plantations and of all other plantings in the Molochnaia Mennonite District will continue. May God grant that I am able to contribute to the improvement of conditions for the Kalmyks. I do not lack good intentions, but many circumstances make me doubtful [of my capacity to be of assistance].

Johann Penner from Pastwa wants to know if he can make use of the Baden steppe until it is settled. Please tell him that the Committee does not make such arrangements at this time (which is what I told him last summer). He should apply several months before his lease ends, citing compelling circumstances. I should be reminded of this matter several weeks before he sends the petition when I will use my influence and submit a recommendation.

You must wait patiently for St. Petersburg to make a decision in regard to Count Vorontsov's petition on your behalf. When you can, send in a request for permission to lease the remaining part of the 4,500 desiatinas of land, for a period of, say, ten to fifteen years. Then, after several years, when a suitable opportunity presents itself to demonstrate how useful your efforts on behalf of the general well-being have been, the whole matter could be accomplished with God's help.

May you fare well,

Your friend A. Fadeev

Received 17 February.

536. Forestry Society. Records from February, 1836. SAOR 89-1-368/1.

1836 [File is a notebook kept on an inspection trip. Writer not identified].

Began inspection tour on 10 February, Monday, in Tiegerweide.

Rueckenau, 10 February: Would it not be better if Franz Voht's and Klaas Ennz' hearth-sites were assigned to others, Klaas Ennz because of his two vices? He had promised betterment.

Friedensdorf: Bernhard Loewen has fallen behind in his agricultural work and discussed this with the Village Office.

Gnadenheim: The subject of Peter Friesen came up for discussion at the Village Office. His house has fallen down and his debts for grain amount to more than 400 rubles. The places of Kroeker, Bernhard

Regier, and Goerzen have also not been kept up as well as they should have been. Kroeker seems a hopeless case.

Alexanderwohl: The village office agrees that Dahlke cannot manage his agricultural affairs. His property should, perhaps, be turned over to his son-in-law.

Fuerstenau: District chairman drew attention to two householders, Schierling and Cornelsen.

Peter Goerzen, Alexanderwohl, is the mayor's brother. He rented half of his land to the mayor because his children are small and his wife blind. A poor existence.

Lichtfelde, 11 February: Householders Steingart and Abram Goerzen have fallen behind in their agricultural work, the former because of his know-it-all attitude, the latter because of conflict in his household. The Village Office hopes for better arrangements now that his son-in-law [has taken over the fullholding?].

Neukirch: Deputy Mayor Doerk Epp, without the mayor's permission, drove to Halbstadt to sell his rye. Doerk Boldt has been labelled a slacker. He is addicted to drink (though he has abstained for about a year), and it would be better if he gave up his fullholding. The Village Office has more hope for Johann Bold, who has been installed in office [as village mayor?] by the district chairman.

Doerk Boldt will not, of his own accord, give up his hearth-site. The Village Office must report this to the District Office.

Schardau: Jacob Nickel and Heinrich Quiring are living in poor conditions and must give their fullholdings to others.

Marienthal: Jacob Ba[e]rg, No. 12, can hardly remain on his hearth-site any longer. He is unmotivated and has no prospects.

Pastwa, 12 February: Johann Dueck was ordered to appear at the District Office and submit a written undertaking regarding his takeover of a cottager-site from Sudermann. He did not appear because of illness.

Wernersdorf, 13 February: It is recognized that there is no hope for improvement in the farming of three householders: Kaethler, Engbrecht, and Giesbrecht. Elder Lange must be admonished for his strident way of speaking.

Fuerstenau: Would like to have its dam-site inspected, since it plans to begin construction of a dam as soon as spring ploughing is finished. Berend Enns' dwelling-place is in a hopelessly bad condition.

Fischau, 14 February: The Village Office claims it did not receive a five-fut-long measuring stick.

PART TWO

Reports and Studies by Johann Cornies

Editors' Introduction

Various tsarist administrative organs commissioned Johann Cornies to write reports about the non-Slavic peoples who neighboured upon the Molochnaia Mennonite settlement. Different versions of the resulting reports, and fragments of them, are scattered throughout his papers. Cornies produced four significant reports, published here, describing the Nogai Tatars, the Doukhobors, the non-Mennonite Germanic colonists, and the Molokans. Written between 1826 and ca. 1840, they are at once an important ethnographic source regarding their subjects, a fascinating insight into Cornies' attitude towards people of other cultures, religions, and races, and, equally, an insight into his understanding of the Mennonite situation in Russia.

Although the reports appear under Cornies' name, it cannot be said with certainty whether Cornies himself researched and composed them in their entirety, or else ordered his secretaries to do part of the work. Certainly he vetted the final product, and at their best (particularly in the Nogai report), the reports reveal their author as a reflective and insightful observer. At the other extreme, the Molokan and German colonist reports are brief and statistic-laden, while the Doukhobor report shifts oddly from praise to condemnation, perhaps indicating the work of more than one author.

These reports were written at a time when the tsarist state was increasingly concerned with identifying the characteristics that defined a loyal subject of the empire. This was a matter of vital importance. Romantic nationalism was giving rise to revolutions in Eastern Europe, and Tsar Nicholas I was developing his own reactionary policies in response. It was also vitally important for the Mennonites, because their own status as subjects with accompanying rights and responsibilities was being assessed by the state, and so their future status in the tsarist empire was at stake. In this context, Cornies' description of the rights and responsibilities of other minorities, and indeed of their status as tsarist subjects, is doubly revealing. It sheds light on what he understood to be the best strategic path for Mennonite relations with the state.

The first report, Cornies' lengthy description of the Nogai Tatar Horde, was composed in 1825 at the request of the Guardianship Committee. Cornies sent a version of this study to Switzerland with Daniel Schlatter, hoping that it might be published there, but in 1828 Schlatter reported that a friend in the publishing industry had rejected it as "in no case appropriate for printing."[1] Elements of Cornies' description appeared (uncredited) in Schlatter's own book on the Nogai two years later.

In 1836, as Cornies began to emerge as a significant figure in Russian administrative circles, the important Russian journal *Teleskop* published a revised and edited translation of the study under the title, "A Short Description of the Nogai Tatars living in Melitopol Uezd, Tavria Guberniia."[2] The *Teleskop* version of Cornies' essay is largely identical to the 1826 version published here, even retaining, for example, Cornies' references to the bad weather of "last year," referring to 1825 and not 1835. *Teleskop* deleted Cornies' section on "Geography and Statistics," along with critical comments about the government's failure to provide an adequate replacement for Count Demaison after he retired from his position of commanding officer of the Nogai in 1821. The one significant change in the *Teleskop* version came in Cornies' proposals for reforming Nogai society. The 1836 version is more willing to promote state interference in Nogai religious practices than the 1826 version.

We include the 1826 version of the Nogai report rather than the 1836 *Teleskop* article because, as Cornies' earliest substantial attempt at socio-economic analysis, it provides an important early glimpse of his attitudes and understanding. At the same time, it is unclear whether the

---

1 See document 151.

2 "Kratkii obzor polozheniia Nogaiskikh tatar, vodvorennykh v Melitopol'skom Uezde Tavricheskoi gubernii," *Teleskop* 33 (1836). By coincidence, the article appeared in the same edition of *Teleskop* as Peter Chaadaev's famous "Philosophical Letter," with the result that Chaadaev was declared insane and confined to his home, and the journal was closed. The editor of *Teleskop*, Nikolai Ivanovich Nadezhdin, would, in 1846, become the first director of the ethnographic division of the Royal Geographic Society.

changes to the *Teleskop* version were made by Cornies or his Russian editor. All substantial differences between the two versions have been indicated in the footnotes, including a full translation of the paragraph in the *Teleskop* version discussing the state's right to intervene in religious matters.

The second report is Cornies' description of the Doukhobors, a pacifist Russian Christian sect thought to have come into existence in the mid-eighteenth century in the southern regions of the Russian Empire. Competing theories link their beliefs to the *Bogomils*, a tenth-century Bulgarian heretic group, the *Cathars*, a thirteenth-century French heretic group, and, more plausibly, the teachings of the Ukrainian philosopher Georgii Skovoroda (1722–1794).[3] Archbishop Amvrosii Serebrennikov of Ekaterinoslav apparently coined the name Doukhobor, or "Spirit Wrestler," in 1785 as a derogatory epithet, implying that Doukhobors wrestled *against* the Holy Ghost, but they soon embraced the name, claiming to wrestle on *behalf* of the Holy Ghost.[4]

Doukhobors believe that the spirit of Christ dwells within every person. This means that they have no particular reverence for the Bible, because each person has direct contact with Christ. For the same reason, Doukhobors reject the authority of the state. Doukhobors are pacifists, reasoning that because the spirit of Christ dwells in all people it would be sinful to kill anyone.[5]

This account of the Doukhobors – one of several versions in the Cornies papers – is undated. The Guardianship Committee first requested such a report from Cornies in 1824, and it probably dates from after that year, while it certainly was written before 1836, because Cornies

3 Theories on the Doukhobors' origins and early history are usefully summarized in George Woodcock and Ivan Avakumovic, *The Dukhobors* (London: Faber and Faber, 1968), 17d–34. For a recent, thoroughgoing account of Doukhobor life in the Caucasus, and summary of their earlier experiences, see Nicholas B. Breyfogle, *Heretics and Colonizers: Forging Russia's Empire in the South* Caucasus (Ithaca: Cornell University Press, 2005). See also Gary Dean Fry, "The Dukhobors, 1801–1855: The Origins of a Successful Dissident Sect" (Ph.D. Diss: The American University, 1976). The most influential Russian-language account is A.I. Klibanov, *Istoriia religioznogo sektantstva v rossii (60-e gody XIX v.-1917 g.)* (Moscow: Nauka, 1965), 85–121. The latest assessment of Skovoroda's influence is Victor O. Buyniak, "Skovoroda in early Dukhobor History – Fact or Myth," in *The Spirit Wrestlers: Centennial Papers in Honour of Canada's Dukhobor Heritage*, ed. by Koozma J. Tarasoff (Hull: Canadian Museum of Civilization, 1995), 9–20.

4 Woodcock and Avakumovic, *The Dukhobors*, 19.

5 Woodcock and Avakumovic, *The Dukhobors*, 20.

makes no mention of the sensational criminal accusations against the Doukhobors and the resultant trials held in that year. While the criminal accusations were almost certainly unfounded, they ultimately resulted in the Doukhobors' exile to the Caucasus in the 1840s.[6]

The Doukhobor psalms recorded in Cornies' description are very similar to those collected and published in the late nineteenth century by Vladimir Bonch-Bruevich, and this suggests that Cornies was an accurate chronicler with access to good sources.[7] While he clearly was sharply prejudiced against Doukhobor religious and social practices, early accounts of Doukhobor life are scarce, and his observations are consequently very valuable.

The fourth report documents the conditions of the non-Mennonite Germanic settlers on the west bank of the Molochnaia, about whom much less is known than about the Mennonites. In large part, this is because the Germanic settlement did not produce its own Cornies, with his penchant for documenting and reporting. As with the Doukhobor report, this lack of documentary evidence makes the present report all the more valuable.

Cornies prepared the report on the Germanic colonists at the request of the Tavria Guberniia Statistical Committee in early 1836. It reveals both similarities and differences between the Mennonites and their German-speaking neighbours. The Germans shared with the Mennonites a level of agricultural productivity considerably higher than their Ukrainian and Russian neighbours, as well as a diversified economy with active craft production for local markets. But an important difference between the two settlements was also emerging by 1836: levels of landlessness were far higher among the Mennonites. On the surface this might seem positive for the Germans, but in fact they were avoiding landlessness by exhausting their land reserves. Soon they would face declining average yields as they placed poorer and poorer land under crops, and eventually they would resort to subdividing their land into

6 For a more thorough discussion of the accusations, see Staples, *Cross-Cultural Encounters.*

7 Vladimir D. Bonch-Bruevich, *The Book of Life of the Dukhobors*, trans. by Victor O. Buyniak (Blaine Lake, SK: Dukhobor Societies of Saskatchewan, Saskatoon and Blaine Lake: 1978). I am indebted to Koozma Tarasoff and Jon Kalmakoff for their comments on the translation, and for the specific references to Bonch-Bruevich, which they provided (Koozma Tarasoff, personal communication, 14 July 2006; Jon Kalmakoff, personal communication, 21 May 2006).

small, marginal allotments. In the short term, this staved off the social conflicts caused by landlessness, but in the long term, it impoverished the entire community. The Mennonites accepted landlessness and sought ways to employ the landless, consequently diversifying their economy and stimulating economic modernization.[8]

Cornies' description of the German settlement is brief, but it is accompanied by seventeen detailed statistical tables. In the Odessa archive, the tables – only some of which are referred to in the description – are filed separately from the description under the year 1845, but they clearly relate to the 1836 report. These are the tables reproduced here. They are probably not the tables that accompanied the original report, for the identifying table letters (entitled Tables A through R) in some cases do not correspond with the references in the description. The date and content clearly do correspond, so perhaps these tables accompanied a different version of the same report.

The description only directly refers to ten tables, while there are seventeen tables in the 1845 file. Tables G, H, and I are the principal source of confusion. There is no Table G, while the reference to "Table G" in the description clearly refers to Table H. There is no Table I, nor is there any reference to it in the description. There are *two different* Table Hs, the first one containing two parts – income and expenses – and the second summarizing the balance of the community treasury. Perhaps in a different version of the report, the two parts of the first table labelled "H" constituted Tables G and H, and the second table labelled "H" constituted Table I, but this cannot be said with any certainty. In this edited version of the report, the reference to Table G in the description has been left intact, and the first Table H has been re-lettered as Table G. This is consistent with the contents of the description. No other changes have been made to the table lettering.

Little is known of the early history of the Molokans [*Molokane*], who are the subject of the final report published here. They probably originated as an offshoot of the Doukhobors, although the Molokans claim the opposite in the early account of their history and beliefs reproduced in the report. They were labelled Molokans or "milk drinkers" because they drank milk during lent in defiance of orthodox practice, but they called themselves the "Brotherhood of Spiritual Christians." Molokans

8 The German colonists' economic condition is described in more detail in Staples, *Cross-Cultural Encounters*, 72–84.

began migrating to the Molochnaia region in 1823. At that time, the Russian state gave them permission to join the Doukhobor settlements in the region, but instead they settled on the eastern side of the Molochnaia River, closer to the Mennonite settlement.[9]

In early nineteenth-century Russian official correspondence, the Molokans are closely associated with the Doukhobors, and one splinter group is even referred to in an 1837 letter as the "Doukhobor Molokans." However, most Molokans seem to have differed sharply from the Doukhobors by their acceptance of the authority of the Bible – a fact that caused Johann Cornies to hold the Molokans in much higher esteem than the Doukhobors. As this document makes clear, there were several sub-groups within the Molochnaia Molokans. Some shared the Doukhobors' pacifism and rejection of worldly authority, but others – including the authors of the Molokan confession of faith that is part of this document – acknowledged tsarist authority even to the extent of supporting war in defence of tsar and country.

This undated description of the Molokans provides a unique early glimpse into their beliefs and practices. It is the fullest of several versions that exist in the Cornies papers. The State Archive of the Odessa Region index dates it to 1840, but there is no clear textual evidence to confirm this. The Guardianship Committee first asked Cornies to provide a description of the Molokans in 1824, and there are references in Cornies' correspondence to a description written in 1830, but the current text was certainly written after 1834 (the latest date directly referred to in the text), while the description of Molokans who migrated to the Caucasus suggests that it was written after 1840 (the year of the migration), and perhaps as late as 1845.

9 There is no good modern history of the Molokans. The evolution of their religious beliefs, and their life in the Caucasus in the second half of the nineteenth century, are recounted in Nicholas B. Breyfogle, *Heretics and Colonizers: Forging Russia's Empire in the South Caucasus* (Ithaca: Cornell University Press, 2005). A.I. Klibanov's *Istoriia religioznogo sektantsva v rossii (60-e gody XIX v.-1917 g.)* (Moscow: Nauka, 1965) views them through the lens of doctrinaire Soviet historiography. Their experiences in the Molochnaia are briefly described in Staples, *Cross-Cultural Encounters*, and their religious beliefs are discussed in Sergei I. Zhuk, *Russia's Lost Reformation: Peasants, Millennialism, and the Radical Sects in Southern Russia and Ukraine, 1830–1917* (Washington: Woodrow Wilson Center Press , 2004).

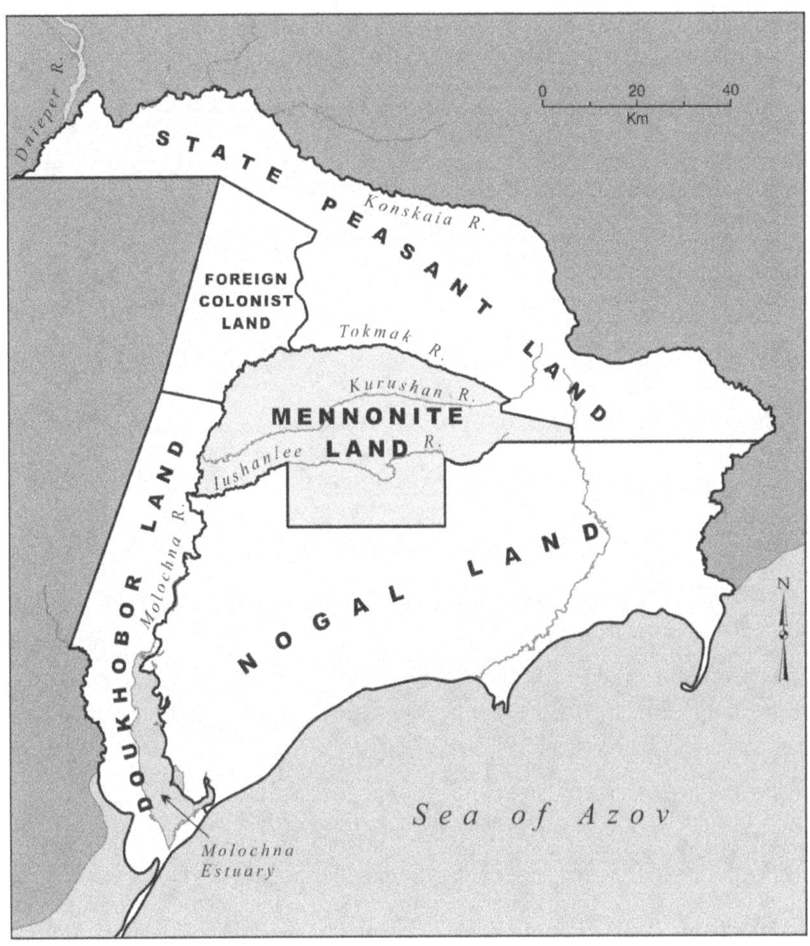

Map 3. The Nogai, Doukhobor, German, and Molokan Settlements. From John R. Staples, *Cross-Cultural Encounters on the Ukrainian Steppe: Settling the Molochna Basin, 1783–1861* (Toronto: University of Toronto Press, 2003).

I. The Nogai Tatars in Russia

SAOR 89-1-69. 1825

Introduction

Information concerning the Nogai Tatars in Russia, and especially the Nogais who were settled under the direction of Count Demaison in 1809 on the Molochnaia, in Melitopol Uezd in Tavrida guberniia; not extracts from printed works, folklore, or travel descriptions, but from personal observations of many years or from information obtained from the Nogais themselves; collected and written without intending to develop a connected or complete presentation but with suggestions and encouragement for this people.

By a neighbour of the same Nogais, 1825.

History of the Nogais

The Nogais believe that they and their fellow believers, the Arabs and Turks, are descendants of Noah's sons whom Noah blessed, and that Ishmail, Abraham's son by Hagar, is the founder of their race. Their other legends about their beginnings are quite incredible.

It seems certain that the Nogai Tatars now settled in Melitopol Uezd are a mixture of many peoples, and that they previously lived as nomads in Great Tartary, among the Yats.[1] Nogai tradition in this regard agrees with a history book entitled *Tavrik*. In Great Tartary, the Uzbeks called them "Neongai" ("may you be without good fortune forever") because of their thieving disposition and their irregular and unproductive way of life. Others with a similar disposition joined this

1 The Yats are an Indo-Aryan people widely distributed in north-west India.

horde later, though they belonged to various peoples, such as Turkmen, Bukharans, Kalmyks, and Kirghiz.

About 576 years ago, after the death of the great conqueror Genghis Khan – who is supposed to have been conceived by the sun in a young girl – a large part of this horde moved to the far side of the Volga, under the Khan Dzhanibek. They led their nomadic life there for a long time. Eventually part of the group moved towards the Caucasian mountains, to the region of the Kuma and the Terek. However, the branch of Nogais now living in Melitopol Uezd moved from the Volga under their supreme leader, Sultan Begg Beyand, and across the Don, the Dnepr, and the Dniester to Bessarabia, mainly into the region of Akkerman, where they first began to occupy themselves with crop agriculture. After they had combined some agriculture with their nomadic lives for about 32 years, Turks and Moldavians encroached upon them. Taking all their meagre possessions, they moved back to the Crimea under their leader Janmanbeth Bey, and from there, across Enikale Strait. Then disagreement caused them to divide. One section went back and settled on the flat land in the Crimea, another went to the Kuban, and another went back to Bessarabia, some by sea and others overland. Those who stayed in the Kuban divided again.

The Nogais made many treks as far as the Kalmyk horde at Stavropol and Gregorievsk, and to the source of the Kuma River. During this period their leaders were Jaum Adje, Kenje Osman, and the Crimean Tatar Kalil Effendi. The last of these led part of the horde across the Don to the Molochnaia, but died upon arrival. Kalil Effendi's gravesite is situated at the Nogai village Second Keneges, not far from Petrovska, the fort on the Berda.[2] Bey Jasitbey was their next commanding officer for 17 years, but the Russian colonel Trivogin replaced him. Captain Temeres followed for only one year and then, in the year 1808, Count Demaison (Bey Jasitbey died during the winter of 1824 on the Kalous).[3]

On their rambling migrations, the Nogais left individuals or whole groups behind so that their kinsmen can now be found on the Volga at Astrakhan, on the Kuma at Konstantinogradkaia, at Stavropol on the Kaluga and Manutez, among the Circassians at Anap, at Kisliar in the

---

2 The site of the city of Berdiansk, established in 1836.

3 Count Demaison was a French nobleman of indeterminate background who entered Russian service in 1802 and was appointed to oversee the Nogais in 1808. His complete service record can be found in the Ukrainian State Archive of The Crimean Region, *fond* 26, *opis* 1, *delo* 5509.

Kabardie, and among the Don Cossacks in the Crimea and beyond the Danube. Meanwhile, other peoples joined them on these treks, or they intermingled by marriage.

A broad, beautiful strip of land from the Molochnaia down to the shores of the Sea of Azov stood available for the Nogais' nomadic life. The people were still extremely rough and wild, uncultured and generally poor. They pursued crop agriculture in a limited way (it was restricted almost entirely to millet), in a manner that could be combined with their transient life. However, under the wise, selfless, mild-yet-stern leadership of Count Demaison, they soon made visible social and cultural progress. He restricted their nomadic life, encouraged and promoted agriculture, and forbade them to live in the moveable huts [yurts] that were so detrimental to their health. If patience and love did not bear fruit, Demaison used severity, and he placed transgressors [whose transgressions were not criminal] under supervision and assigned them useful field and garden penalties and house work in the Uezd or in the main town of Nogaisk. Such punishment was not detrimental to society in general, but was useful for the individual and his community. There was no corruption. The innocent received justice, and Demaison favoured and encouraged those who were good and industrious.

After the Nogais were formally settled under the Count's leadership in 1809, he encouraged them to build good houses, and they gained considerable wealth as agriculture spread. Goodwill, willingness to take direction, and many good attributes appeared among the Nogais. The wild or indolent were forced to follow the law and the example of others in order to escape punishment and shame, to enjoy advantages, and to insure their existence. Anyone who had not seeded at least two chetverts, whitewashed his house, etc., did not receive a travel pass. The Count was concerned that the main settlement should be enlarged and improved, taking the Nogai customs, practices, and religious requirements into consideration. He intended to establish a school. He halted peddling and wandering about by gypsies and Armenians (so damaging to the Nogai economy) with prohibitions or by settling such people in the main town.

The Nogais' religion and customs, various types of prejudice, deeply rooted inclinations towards a wild, wandering life, as well as incitements and provocations from evilly inclined and jealous Tatars and neighbours, placed great obstacles in the way of their rapid civilization, of increases in agriculture, and of all the improvements implemented by the Count. Still, it cannot be ignored that his administration resulted in a very considerable growth in prosperity and in a reduction of the wild, rude, arrogant traits within the Nogai character. He was respected by all, loved by many. Many people recognized his well-meaning intentions, and the advantages and privileges provided by his leadership and the new way of life when compared to the past.

The Count gave up his role as head of the Nogais in 1821, not because of despair with the Nogai people but due to adverse conditions and circumstances, and he was followed by a provisional successor. It was not difficult to turn many Tatars against the Count, and then many others followed only out of necessity and force. Prejudice, superstition, fanaticism, and inclination to nomadism still played a part even among better individuals. It was only necessary to awaken their memories and to draw attention to the apparent advantages of the nomadic way of life. Indifference ensued, and then discontent and dissatisfaction with Demaison, as if he wanted to make slaves of them and gave them too much work. False complaints were made against the Count.[4] Because his authority was limited he could not, even with the best will, realize his good intentions for the well-being of this people as he would have liked, according to the wishes of the Crown.

Many Nogais grew discontented in 1813, and their inclination to a wandering life reappeared as a result of reports, fabricated and vigorously spread by people of evil intent, that they were to be allowed, or forced, to move from Russia to Turkey. Calm had barely returned when one Sultan Moratkeres arrived in 1815, fleeing from Constantinople because of a criminal offence. His subterfuge was that the Great Sultan had sent him to escort the Nogais to Turkey and he was waiting only for an exit order from St. Petersburg. This matter developed to the point where many Nogais sold or traded off their cattle and tools. Speculators gained considerable advantages by promoting these rumours. Everyone sought to acquire a yurt and a two-wheeled wagon [*araba*] and prepared to move away. Eventually they realized that the rumour was groundless.

This incident set the Nogais' prosperity back considerably. They did very little seeding in that year and made no improvements to their houses. They found it difficult to give up the plan they had made, and it

---

4 The accusations against Demaison are recounted in Staples, *Cross-Cultural Encounters*, 36, 50.

required valuable time simply to return to their previous level of zeal or inclination to do agricultural work and to lead a quiet life on the land.

Since the Count's resignation, there has been almost total inactivity in their practical and moral improvement – and if it were only limited to this! Regrettably however, now (without even counting the bad years and damage from the weather which has occurred) their economic condition has *regressed*. Indolence, quarrelling, and thievery have increased considerably. There is no support or encouragement for individuals seeking anything useful. Anyone inclined towards gardening must fear damage and injury from the majority. The wicked find means to insist on their freedom and escape punishment. Roaming about, unnecessary travel to markets, frequent service as herdsmen for Armenians, Greeks, etc., damage their education and the general economy. No limits are set to peddling by Gypsies and Armenians. Very little – actually nothing – is done towards moral improvement and general civilization, even though the state is very concerned about this.[5]

Comparing briefly the *original* nomadic condition of these people, to the period of Count Demaison's leadership, to what it *is now*, and to what it *could be*, one can see that in their unsteady nomadic condition, the Nogais were a rude, proud, wild people, inclined to thievery, as revealed not only in their behaviour but also very clearly in their stature and physiognomy. Used to a roving life, and to constant change, all sustained work was repugnant to them. They disdained fieldwork and gardening. Hunting (of the previously more abundant wild animals), wandering about, riding, making music and dancing, or sitting in circles telling fables and stories about their ancestors, heavy tobacco smoking, bickering, bargaining, and bartering were almost the only occupations for the men, other than some tending of cattle. The women were left with most of the work. Almost all the necessities of life – cloth, clothing, tools, even grain, etc. – had to be bartered for cattle.

With no comprehension of the world and the state, or of countries and peoples beyond his own circle, every ignorant and proud nomadic Nogai saw himself as lord of the whole world. He used anything he wanted in the countryside and remained at any place however long he wished to be there. In an hour, he could pack up wife and children, house and kitchen utensils, as well as the house itself, on his two-wheeled wagon and move on with his livestock and all his possessions.

5 This paragraph is deleted from the *Teleskop* essay.

God, he said, had determined it in this way: He gave the Nogais a wheel when He gave others a table or a plough.

Only a few individuals were rich or prosperous under nomadic conditions, and it was very difficult to advance beyond them or even to their level. They absorbed everything for themselves; the majority remained in poverty, more or less dependent. This may have happened because of the poor majority's own faults or those of their ancestors. Indolence or imprudence caused them to yield to the more industrious or intelligent individuals, and probably also to those more audacious or wicked, and thus they became indebted or dependent on them.

The great Koshen or nomad chiefs, the Murzas or nobility, the leaders of a horde, etc. arose in this way. Injustices of all types took place. The stronger or richer man was almost always in the right. Anyone who could take revenge did so. In accordance with the teachings of Mohammed, they recognized the right to retaliation, even to the extent of death itself. Living in the round, nomad, felt yurt, nine to ten feet in diameter, was very detrimental to their health because of cold and dampness, as were the "kibitki," or earth huts, in which some of them lived in winter before their actual colonization. Large numbers of children became sacrifices to this habit.

Count Demaison's leadership seriously encouraged agricultural pursuits among the Nogais on the Molochnaia, and land restrictions forced them to practise more efficient use of the land previously used for livestock. Soon the Nogais showed increasing evidence of diligence and hard work (even if it was not yet very lasting or general), skill at agriculture, love of order, and gentler customs. They appreciated the advantages of agriculture and of good houses that protected them from wind and weather.

Population and prosperity increased. Every individual was in a position to find a good livelihood through diligence and hard work and to live an independent life. Their entire behaviour revealed much less of the former wildness and defiance. Their character became milder so that the surrounding peoples had no reason to complain about them. The circumstances of the colonized Nogais could be seen as true conditions of happiness and wealth in comparison to their brothers situated beyond the Danube and on the Kuma, who are still partly nomadic. The Nogais can thank the special attention, industry, and untiring patience of the Count for many good arrangements still to be found. It is certain that if leadership similar to the Count's had continued, the influence of colonization and agriculture on the economic and moral state of the

Nogais would soon have destroyed the inclination to a lazy, changeable, unrestrained life still clinging to them. Prejudice, superstition, and fanaticism would have been reduced, making the Nogais more receptive to moral improvement, culture of the spirit, and all institutions that contribute to the happiness of human society and therefore also to the state. If, as a *Muslim*, the Nogai did not attach himself to the Count and to the state through love, his own interests would still hold him, and demand obedience because of the protection through which he enjoys these advantages. However, if the current provisional situation is not soon brought to an end, it is certain that the Nogais will suffer a step backward in their moral and economic conditions, which cannot easily be regained.

With their intelligence and character, the Nogais must be seen as a people capable of all types of education. Under a wise, humane, but stern leader who seeks the true well-being of the state and the people in every respect, this people would soon be on equal footing with other European peoples; yes, they could soon overtake some of them.

Regional Geography and Statistics[6]

The region that the Nogais occupy in Melitopol Uezd lies below the forty-seventh parallel north. Its greatest length from east to west is about ninety verstas and its greatest width from north to south is about fifty verstas. The area consists of 300,000 desiatinas. Its boundaries are the Sea of Azov and the land of Count Orlov Denisov to the south, the German Mennonite land to the north, the land of the so-called Molokans, German Wuertemburg colonies, and Russians in Alexandrovsk Uezd to the east, and the Molochnaia lake and Doukhobor colonies to the west. The land is flat except for a few depressions and Karsak Hill or Mound. Five small rivers run through it – the Molochnaia, Abitochna, Iushanle, Keltshe, and the Berda – and also the ravines Dshekenle, Taetlekalak, Dongsla, Apanle I, Apanle II, Ashe, Kintshagai, Tshekrak, Dongslanlkoe, and Arap. The Orta and Asis Otluk ravines are on the other side of the Molochnaia where Nogais were also settled several years ago. To some extent, these [Nogais settled west of the Molochnaia] can also be considered part of those Nogais in Melitopol Uezd.

6 This section is not included in the *Teleskop* version.

The climate is generally moderate, with winter lasting three months, from mid-December to mid-March. Water is obtained from cisterns that are not very deep, and the quality is indifferent, salty or bad. In the whole area from Bessarabia to beyond the Don there are many mounds, called *mogila* or *auba*. According to Pallas, they are graves of the ancient Cumans, with the remains of stone sculptures and idols here and there.[7] Small swords, urns, and similar items have been found in these mounds.

Domesticated animals include horses, cattle, dogs, cats, and chickens. The Nogais seldom keep camels anymore because they are not useful. Among the wild animals there are wolves, foxes, rabbits, many large predatory birds and other birds, snakes, badgers, polecats, and ermine. There are many insects, and ocean and lake fish.

The flat land for pasturing cattle is called the steppe and it produces thick, high grass, and a vigorous growth of many kinds of medicinal herbs. The Nogais produce wheat, rye, millet, and salt. In the depressions there are beautiful meadows. Wood is brought from the Dnepr as there are no forests. The ground consists entirely of light, loamy soil, partly mixed with black garden soil, and is stony in several small spots. Fine white clay soil exists in the Karsak District, at Shekle village.

The land is under the guberniia government in Simferopol and under the lower courts of the Uezd capital Orekhov. The Nogais' commanding officer is directly responsible to the guberniia government. There are five district offices, then village mayors, ten-men, and elders in the villages. District chairmen are paid twenty rubles, village mayors ten rubles. Criminals are sent to the lower courts at the declaration of the commanding officer, who himself punishes small transgressions. Bargains regarding punishment are usually negotiated through the mayors and village elders. The position of the commanding officer has been filled provisionally for the last three years. He has several helpers or secretaries. In every district office there is also an extra secretary appointed by the Crown at a salary of 400 rubles per annum. The post office is a responsibility of the Crown as in every other part of the empire. Taxes stand at four to five rubles per revision soul, and these support some positions and the purchase of wood for the military in the Crimea. Military service is only obligatory for the Nogais in

7 Cornies is referring to P.S. Pallas, a German naturalist who made two lengthy trips through Russia and published an influential account of the people and places he encountered. See P.S. Pallas, *Travels through the Southern Provinces of the Russian Empire, in the Years 1793 and 1794.* 2 vols. (London: S. Strahan, 1802).

exceptional circumstances. The priests, about 500 men, and the *Murzas*, or nobles, who number approximately 200, are free of taxes. A lower class of their nobility is called *Seit*. The Murzas have the right to carry a *kenschal* (small sword) but all weapons, even the kluk or battle club, were forbidden for everyone else in 1811. Many Murzas and a few others wear medals, five of which are awarded for service. The translator Cahsi Murza holds the rank of college registrar.

The total Nogai population is approximately 17,000 revision souls. Births do not exceed deaths by much more than 100 souls. Income from the land is about 3,700 rubles, with small amounts from fishing and from pasture rented to passing nomadic groups. Nogaisk, also called "Falangash" or "Abitochna," is the main centre of the Nogai Uezd. Most of the inhabitants of Nogaisk are Armenians, who have a church there, but there are also Tatars and Jews. The chief administrator is located there and also a large, well-maintained orchard developed by Count Demaison. The planned development of a city and port on the Sea of Azov twelve verstas from Nogaisk would have drawn many whose survival is now wretched.

The Nogai Tatars divide themselves into three branches: the Jedizan, descended from the Bukharans; the Jedishkul, descended from a mixture of Bulgarians and Circassians; and the Diembuiluk, descended from the Kalmuks.

On the left side of the Molochnaia are situated:

Jedizan Villages:

Ashin and Akagu with District Office
Akkerman
Big Burkud
Little Burkud
Bauerdak
Jshibe I
Jedenochda I
Jedenochda II
Kareruga
Tulga
Jumanokus
Dschanzogur
Nikus

Jshibe II
Gantran
Tashenges
Thueshge
Emir
Tobal
Ukon-Sasseg-Togan
Ksgenaesasseg-Togan
Allshinbodai
Shaukai
Mashchir
Kamatsh I & II
Onike
Beshaul
Kakbass
Sheggle
Keneges II (or Robatai Aul)
Temergasha
Emaut Kishlik
Badai
Kolatamgale

Jedishkul Villages:

Atamgale with District Office
Altaul
Kashauglu
Kaushgale
Bodran
Durtamgale
Koturoglu

Diembuiluck Villages:

Togali with District Office
Karakursak
Kandausju
Kangurbash
Belbei
Utmek
Saraile
Kolonda-Tshkle

Arakle I & II
Kanglera
Ikon Beshkekle
Gsgnae Beshekle
Aklekasha
Orman
Aklekesha
Sashukan
Sarlar Ashungeschla
Ahielchosch
Beggburshi Argin
Shanshele

Villages on the right side of the Molochnaia, in Otluk volost:

Jedizan Villages:

Shagatai
Karashen
Tshomak
Zerbulat
Borash

Jedisckul Villages:

Asberda

Diembuiluck Villages:

Onar Kashudar
Akkus

These latter villages are also under the administrator in Nogaisk, and they rent about 25,000 desiatinas of land. They consist of approximately 1,200 revision souls who were captured during a raid by Anap. About ten years ago, 777 souls purchased their freedom at 150 rubles per soul. They pay taxes under the same conditions as any other Russian subject and have no share in the Nogai communal funds.

Religion

The Nogais are Muslims without exception. There are eleven principal mosques with minarets, or small towers, in the district, and all villages have *Mishets,* or places for prayer. In matters of religion, they are under the authority of the superior Mufti in the Crimea with a subsidiary Mufti in Emaut. Then there are Effendi Mullahs (subsidiary Mullahs) and *Kadis,* or religious judges. The Mullahs collect a tenth of the grain harvest and the fortieth piece of livestock from the people. They sound the call to prayers, pray over the sick, issue all sorts of slips of paper with spells, and are present at weddings, sacrifices, and funerals. The Effendi Mullahs prepare marriage contracts and divorces. The Mullahs and the elders arbitrate conflicts about women and the sale of wives. The Mullahs lead the schools. The Effendis and Kadis explain difficult parts of the Koran and make decisions about their meaning. A Baba (father) conducts circumcisions between the tenth and the fifteenth year; the office of circumciser is an inherited one. Priests and pilgrims who have made the journey to the Kaba indicate this by means of the Shalma, which is a large scarf wound around their caps like a turban. Sacrifice and the giving of alms can be substituted for the journey to Mecca prescribed in the Koran. In the last few years, probably because of unrest in Turkey, no passes have been given out for this journey.

In addition to the general *Kurban,* or festival of sacrifice, sacrifices occur frequently at deaths, in memory of the deceased, at weddings, before or after a trip, as a reconciliation with God when religious precepts have been neglected, etc. They sacrifice a sheep, or a cow if several families join together. It is always consumed by those making the sacrifice, together with their relatives, acquaintances, and especially the village poor. The forty-day fast during *Ramadan,* or month of fasting, is only observed strictly by older persons of both genders. They eat or drink nothing and do not smoke tobacco from sunrise to sunset; later, however, they eat and drink, often even in the middle of the night. There are seventy-one days from Ramadan to Kurban, or Easter. Every family makes a sacrifice on this festival. When fasting ends, there are three major feast days, or *Bairams,* on which there are various entertainments, and there is reciprocal visiting and gifts are exchanged.

Prayer only becomes necessary between the fortieth and fiftieth year, and the younger generation is not yet bound to it. Prayer should take place five times a day. Pilgrims, or *Hadsche,* make use of a rosary. They conduct prayer with a stiff, reverent demeanour, the face turned to Mecca, with much bowing and prostrating. The Muslim allows nothing to interrupt him. The old women pray in their houses.

Wine is forbidden according to the dictates of the Koran, but not brandy; at least the younger men do not abstain from it, drinking it when they are travelling. However, it is seldom found in their villages. The Nogais observe some prescribed cleansings. Hands are washed before and after eating, as are hands, arms, and feet before prayer. If a man intending to pray is wearing the so-called *Maes*, or morocco leather boots, a bit of water may be poured over these and this substitutes for the washing of the feet.

As Muslims, they have a great aversion to pork, and thus they cannot eat any food other than bread in homes of a different faith.

Beards are highly regarded by the Nogais. However, the old men cut off all their hair, while the younger men retain a small bunch of hair and this forces them to wear very warm headgear.

Much harm results from their acceptance of revenge, polygamy, and trade in wives. Two wives are found frequently, but seldom three. Fatalism, the poorly understood teaching of predestination, is deeply rooted. The priests nurture fanaticism. Giving alms, a principal part of the good works prescribed in the Koran, is limited almost entirely to wandering beggars, who are usually handed a bit of grain, millet, or money. However, orphans are housed and maintained by relatives or acquaintances. Institutions for the poor are not to be found. The hope for a future life is based on a belief in a heaven of pleasure, filled with beautiful girls and gardens.

Juemankun, or the seventh day, our Friday, is their day of rest, though observed mainly by the fervent old Muslims and their priests. They have many exorcists, fortunetellers, etc., and the large number of superstitious practices and opinions is indescribable.

Character and Physical Stature of the Nogais

The first thing to be noted about the character of Nogais is their great pride, rooted in their nationality and their ancestors. They reveal this pride not only towards strangers, but even among themselves. Christians are not even worthy of consideration. They speak contemptuously about the Persians (Redheads), but with somewhat less contempt about the Turks. The Nogais consider the Crimean Tatars far beneath them, though the latter can be distinguished from them for their culture, cleanliness, and more attractive physiognomy, especially the mountain dwellers. Therefore a rich Nogai would consider it demeaning to mix with them in marriage.

Definite features of the Nogai character cannot really be listed, because of the many mixtures and differences within this people.

However, in general they are endowed with a healthy, natural intelligence, and are capable of many kinds of education. Clever and well suited for field cultivation and for artistic crafts, they are a people who can make good progress with small means. When they are persuaded of the importance of an occupation that has been entrusted to them, they are especially industrious, quick, and faithful followers and performers. Even a thief is seldom unfaithful under such circumstances. Many traces of the old hospitality are still visible but usually in name only, depending upon their calculation of future returns and expectation of unreasonably large services in return. When they undertake some work, they carry it out with special speed, but they also like to sit and enjoy their repose.

It is not surprising that falsehood, distortion, quarrelling and fighting, fanaticism, and superstition reign among the Nogais due to their lack of culture, abundance of ignorance and prejudice, and a false conception of freedom and their right to exact revenge. Yet, it cannot be said that the character of the Nogais as a whole is wicked or even incorrigible when one is aware of the Nogai religion and its influences, or of their customs and their concepts and beliefs. Superstition and fanaticism can, after all, also be found among peoples known as Christians.

Thievery will disappear with a quieter life involving cultivation of the soil and the resulting improvement in well-being, especially if this is under good supervision and leadership. Indolence does not rest in the character of this people, but can be ascribed to the influence of religion and the lack of encouragement to work. Their former nomadic lifestyle encouraged indolence, but in contrast, constant riding, management of wild horses, hunting wild animals, and speedy packing up and departure with their houses and belongings also developed the skills that distinguish them now. Their level of cleanliness is much lower than that of the Crimean mountain Tatars, but they show to advantage over various other Russian peoples in their cleanliness of body, clothing, and houses, and they cannot be reproached in general for great uncleanliness.

The Nogai stature is of medium height, thick-set, and strong. Their posture is straight without stiffness and they do not have an awkward gait. There are many differences in facial features, since many different peoples joined them during their nomadic movements in the past and marriages caused numerous mixtures. Mixing still occurs today because they purchase Kalmyk, Circassian, and Crimean girls. Their Mongol origin can however still be recognized. The hair of their beards is sparse. Their teeth are straight and snow white. The beautiful gender cannot be given that name, even though one finds well-proportioned physiognomies, lively eyes, pretty noses, small mouths, long necks, especially beautiful teeth, and black hair of moderate length among girls and very young women. However, as they get older, they usually reveal only traces of earlier beauty in wasted, pale faces. The female gender wilts very early and carries the stamp of apathy, ignorance, and the contemptuous attitude towards their gender.

Nogai Housing, Dress, and Diet

Every Nogai builds his own house of mud bricks dried by the wind. An ordinary dwelling is about twelve feet wide and about thirty feet long. They use wood only for the doors and the framework for the roof, on which they lay first reeds, then brush. This is then covered with soil and finally with ashes. The cost of such a house amounts to about 100 rubles to prepare the bricks, and for wood, nails, and small windows. Many larger houses, with a floor and ceiling laid with boards, are erected at a cost of 500 rubles and even more. The usual interior arrangement is that of two sections, the bedroom and the kitchen. If there are several wives, they build a separate bedchamber for each one, and here there are mattresses and leather pillows filled with sheep's wool, a chest for the safekeeping of money and various small items, women's jewellery, etc. There is also a clay stove, rugs, and clothes. The men and women usually spend the days in the kitchen, which has a large iron cauldron, wooden bowls, spoons, water and milk containers, trays, and a butter tub. Horse harnesses and agricultural implements may be stored in the kitchen, but often also in the cattle barn or in a special section of the house. They usually whitewash the house on the outside and inside once a year.

The Nogais have few needs. Except for a cauldron and a copper water pitcher, everything is made of wood. Newer and better-built houses appear every year, but there is no noticeable increase or improvement in household and kitchen equipment. There is also very little difference between rich and poor. It is regrettable that the new houses have been built according to the tastes of the individual without considering the village's regularity.

The clothing of the Nogais is attractive and enhances their bodies, is suitable for work, and is neither as full as that of the Turks nor too tight. Summer dress consists of a small cap of fur, a *caftan*, or short jacket, of light fabric over a shirt, a linen girdle, wide fabric or linen trousers, and shoes. In winter, they don another fur hat over the small fur cap, a good fur coat of sheepskin over the caftan, and pants of fur over the linen trousers. In rain and snow storms, a *Bashluk*, or head scarf, goes over the cap and a *shegben*, or fabric coat, over the fur coat to protect them from moisture. Boots are red or black, but the *Mas*, or yellow boot-slippers, are worn in their shoes and these are also worn in the house after the shoes have been taken off.

The clothing of the women also leaves the body unconstrained, and only the head is overloaded with finery and must be held stiffly when in full costume. Without exception, the women wear a white veil to cover themselves to the eyes, but they usually throw it back completely. Under this they wear a long brightly coloured scarf, which they skilfully wind around their heads several times and then allow it to hang far down their backs. Their hair is braided. Girls attach a long white scarf to their braid, and do not wear a veil, but a large red cap instead. On it they hang small and large coins or a variety of other decorations. The caftan is worn over a white or red shirt, and a wide girdle with a large metal buckle, often entirely of silver, is drawn up around the loins. They all wear wide trousers and large red or small yellow shoes. They wear rings on their fingers, arms, and in the nose with large, heavy rings, connected by a chain, in their ears. Around the forehead, the chin, and the neck, they wear bands hung with small silver plates, polished glass, and similar items.

Fur coats, worn by both sexes in winter, are made by the women themselves and they know how to give them an attractive shape and decorate them with bands in various ways. Almost the only pleasure of the female gender is their finery, in which they enjoy showing themselves, and in which they try to distinguish themselves according to their position and wealth. Their fingernails are painted red. Many wear a wide garment of coloured fabric or silk over their caftan. The complete dress of a woman with head finery is very expensive and the most elaborate finery is worn on *Bairams*, or feast days. However, many women are dressed very wretchedly. When the ground is wet, men and women often walk with stilt-shoes to keep their feet dry and clean.

The Nogais' diet consists of horsemeat, beef and mutton, chicken and fish, milk, butter, and dishes of millet and flour. Some fruit, especially melons, is imported from the Crimea and neighbouring regions in summer. Drinks consist of mare's milk, *basa* (made from millet), buttermilk, and water.

The Nogais much prefer animal foods to vegetables. They like horsemeat better than anything else and it is very warming in winter because of the heat it contains. The meat tastes slightly sweet and they eat the intestines as well. Usually they slaughter sick, old, emaciated horses, or those marked with some fault. Often, newly dead or fallen horses are beheaded and passed off as slaughtered ones. The men prepare a national dish known as *Turama* with sliced horsemeat, and it is consumed communally as a special sign of brotherhood and friendship. No woman may touch it, in order to keep everything clean. Following a washing of hands, fingers are used to eat it from a bowl. *Kumis*, their most preferred and beloved drink, is prepared from mare's milk. It is strongly intoxicating when it has fermented but it is not so plentiful since a considerable number of mares are required to obtain enough milk.

Mutton is either boiled immediately or the whole sheep is dried in the wind after it has been skinned and eviscerated. This keeps for a long time. They are particularly skilled and dexterous in slaughtering animals and drawing off the pelts. Livestock may not be struck, but can only be cut, after which its head is turned in the direction of Mecca and the word "bsmilla" (in the name of God) is spoken. The only wild animal they eat is rabbit.

Cows' milk is first boiled, then mixed with sour milk and left to stand until it is very thick and then churned. However the butter is tasteless and unclean. In contrast, thickened milk, or *churt* [yoghurt], has a very pleasant taste, not overly sour, and is eaten with meat, cake, millet, and almost all Nogai foods. Yoghurt is also salted down in barrels and keeps all winter. Buttermilk is mixed with a great deal of water and makes a thirst-quenching drink much more palatable than the ordinary water of this region.

Millet is the Nogai's major and favourite plant food, and they prepare it in many different ways. They even take it along on their travels when it is roasted and the husks are removed and they enjoy it dry or mixed with fat. Cooked in water and mixed with yoghurt, it is a good, healthful food. For winter, they prepare a strong drink called *bosa* from fermented cooked millet. They use wheat flour less for the preparation of bread than for a variety of cakes. They bake bread in ashes but it is seldom prepared and not well liked. Since the Nogais have begun to plant rye, bread can be found more frequently. The so-called *Kalmyk chai*, or tea in slabs, is well loved when cut up and boiled in water with some milk, butter, and salt.

On the whole, the Nogai is temperate and contented if he has millet and water. He is overjoyed if he can get a piece of meat.

Diseases

Fevers with high temperatures, smallpox, scab, and venereal conditions are the main physical evils. The Nogais make no attempt to prevent or to heal these diseases. Medical help is lacking and superstition reigns. Much is viewed with total indifference and ascribed to unalterable fate, but often they consult conjurors and exorcists for advice, who recommend the strangest, most dangerous, often fatal remedies. However, the most common remedy for man and beast is a slip of paper with an exorcism, which is attached to a cap, or worn on their back or around their neck. Great healing power is ascribed to pepper, alum, sugar, and honey, and these are supposed to cure almost everything. Pressure and massage are a major remedy. They take no preventative measures against virulent, infectious diseases. Venereal evils are very frequent and are often brought into the countryside by Nogais returning from distant employment herding horses. Eye diseases are very common.

The Nogais are very patient when they are ill or await their end, submitting to fate without complaint. Generally they do not reach a high age – sixty to seventy, but very few above this. The mortality rate of the children from one to three years is out of all proportion because they are lightly clothed in wet and cold weather, and fever, colic, or consumption snatch them away in numbers. They are badly neglected and often they eat very injurious things such as earth, ash, etc., and roasted, dry millet, which their stomachs cannot digest. However, in their earlier nomadic life, and when they lived in yurts, even more children are supposed to have died than now. The number of yearly births exceeds that of deaths by little, and one does not find many strong, large families. It is striking that more boys than girls are born.

Education, Schools, and Language

The Nogais do little, almost nothing, towards education, or bringing up their youth. Only nourishment and clothing are provided for the children's animal instincts. The young grow up wild, and find no public institutions for their improvement and development. There are, indeed, so-called "schools" in all villages, earthen huts where priests teach reading and writing very wretchedly. Most of the books are of religious content, and everything pertaining to religion is usually written in Arabic, which many of the priests do not understand themselves, or at least not properly. Teaching is only an incomprehensible chattering of Arabic prayers, read, recited, or chanted by rote. School attendance is prevented by the avarice of the priests. When they are grown up, the pupils distinguish themselves by their dissolute behaviour and their vanity. These schools are usually attended only by those hoping to enter the priesthood.

These Tatars have assumed the Arabic script along with the Muslim religion. Their books are mostly copies with a mixture of Arabic, Turkish, and Tatar and a large variety of alphabets and symbols. This makes the learning of pure Tatar exceptionally difficult, and it is virtually impossible without a knowledge of Arabic and Turkish, and the use of other aids. Like the Arabs and the Jews, they write from right to left.

The Nogai language diverges from that of the Crimean Tatars, and even more from that of the Orenburg Tatar dialect. Even in the Molochnaia area, there is a remarkable difference in the Tatar languages of the different branches.

Time is divided into periods of twelve years, named after twelve different animals. The year has four main parts and twelve months, with some Arabic names and also some of their own. The year is divided according to moons, the month into weeks and days, the day by the five hours of prayer. The hours are counted from sunrise. However, many make use of the Russian division of time.

Occupation of the Men – Livestock Breeding

The predominant occupation of the Nogais is livestock breeding, and horse breeding is most favoured though it is not very profitable. It was the predominant pursuit until last winter [1824–5], during which three-quarters of the horses were lost to starvation and snowstorms. They are passionate lovers of horses, knowledgeable about them, and they ride well. The Nogais are very skilled in handling horses, and especially in taming them, including also the wild horses that join their herds. Their saddles are very good, with upholstered leather cushions. Their Kalmyk-Kirghiz horse breed is only moderately handsome on the whole, but strong, enduring, and fast. The horse is very useful because of the great distances on the steppe, but on average the value of a horse is not more than thirty to forty rubles, and of a hide, one and a half rubles. At the same time, the horse requires a larger grazing area than other livestock. Large herds of horses, or *tabuns*, stay out on the steppe for the winter where they must seek their sustenance under the snow. Since the Nogais' allotted land is not increasing anymore, as it did in the past, it could be much more advantageously used for field cultivation and sheep breeding.

The Nogais also have too many cattle to be profitable on this land, and the breed is ordinary. The value of a cow cannot be estimated at higher than twenty to thirty rubles and it gives little milk. Butter fetches a poor price.

Sheep breeding and field cultivation are most useful on this land and would be even more so if attention were given to better, improved sheep. The sheep which they now keep in considerable numbers are fat-tailed, mostly liberally spotted, and with very coarse wool which is sold at three to four rubles per pud. In contrast, the neighbouring Germans dispose of their poorest variety of wool for twenty rubles per pud. A sheep is valued at four to five rubles, the fleece at eighty kopeks. The sheep also serve as food, and their pelts become fur coats. *Tesek* (manure) is the best fuel, and to obtain it the cattle, and especially the sheep, are kept around the houses, and driven into yards enclosed by old manure, soil, and brushwood when they return from the pastures in the evening. They are also fed there during harsh weather and are somewhat sheltered from wind and cold. There are few barns and these are poor.

Sheep breeding also has a great advantage for moderating the rude Nogai customs and character, and it removes few hands from land cultivation. In contrast, horse breeding preserves and nurtures their rude and wild inclinations towards their old wandering life, with extended searches for runaways or lost horses. These searches draw many hands from land cultivation, so that farms are neglected and settled lives are disturbed. At the same time, the searcher often has no money or sustenance and comes in contact with wandering thieves, allowing himself to be misled into making common cause with them.

Cattle are also stolen or often wander from their pasture, damaging grain fields and wandering across boundaries onto neighbouring land.[8] Caught by the neighbours, they must frequently be ransomed very dearly while the poor cow is half-starved as the matter is pushed to the limit in an effort to avoid payment. All this occurs because they do not

8 In the *Teleskop* version, this paragraph is moved to the end of the section on Nogai customs.

want to keep a herdsman, or because they neglect their herds, drive them to pasture, and then go off to pursue their own interests. Damage is also caused to hay and straw as the cows are driven in and out of the village, and this must necessarily be followed by argument and strife. The irregularity of the villages contributes a great deal to the cattle's inability to find its place quickly and easily, or it prevents the herdsman from driving the cattle in an orderly manner. Also troublesome, especially for travellers, are the large packs of dogs, which howl like wild animals.

No measures exist to fight fires, but Nogais who suffer fire losses receive support, and everyone gives livestock, grain, or feed according to his ability.

Field Cultivation

Field cultivation is most profitable, but Nogais generally do not favour it, and decisions to extend and improve it are made reluctantly. Under the leadership of Count Demaison, every revision soul was required to sow at least two chetverts of grain, and at that time the total sown was about 40,000 chetverts. However, in the year after his resignation, it amounted only to 19,000 chetverts, and has decreased even more since then. The Nogais are more actively pursuing field cultivation after this last terrible winter [1824–5], which carried off many thousands of head of livestock and left people hungry. During that time they also learned to eat rye bread and planted a great deal of rye during this past year, 1825, though previously they restricted themselves to millet and a bit of wheat and barley. Also a great deal of winter seeding is evident and they are beginning to plough with horses.

The advantages of agriculture are now understood better. The women are working in the fields with the men, which was not the case before. Since they lost so many horses, and also because they cannot keep as many anymore due to the limitation on land, their unnecessary riding about, travelling, and hunting wild animals is also restricted and they accommodate themselves to field work more willingly.

The methods the Nogais use for working their fields are cumbersome and bad, and their implements are simple and rude. Were the soil not sufficiently fertile, their ploughs would not be able to cultivate enough for their own bread. For well-cultivated land, at least nine to ten oxen are needed for ploughing, while in contrast, the German colonists work three times as much land more satisfactorily with four horses. The Nogais substitute a piece of wood for the harrow, which is fastened diagonally on the right side of the wheels, its outer end attached with a rope to the yoke of the last oxen on the right side. This is dragged along with the plough across the already ploughed section. The crop is seeded on top of this and then simply ploughed under. The ploughshare and the cutting knife are the only iron on the plough.

There is no order on the plough lands. One ploughs to the east, the other to the north, and not always in a straight line, but sometimes in the shape of a half-circle, with large areas remaining uncultivated between them. The Nogais sow winter crops in October, although this should be done late in August or in early September. Harvest takes place in July and is celebrated with a festival at which the first fruits are eaten. They export only a bit of wheat. Millet, barley, and rye are for local consumption. The quality of the crops is good and their Arnautka wheat is excellent, selling for seven to twelve rubles, and it finds preference to others because the Nogais know how to clean it well.

Grain is stored in holes dug in the ground. As soon as the crop is cut, bound in sheaves and dried, it is brought home and immediately threshed with horses. Here the Nogais surrender to idleness, because threshing with horses is indeed very quick but it ruins the horses, which must find their sustenance on the steppe all year long. A long time is required for them to gather their strength again since, to do this work, the horses are also loaned from one householder to the next because of a shortage of horses (due to the decline of horse breeding).

Hay fields are not divided up according to the number of souls or of families, but the villagers measure and reconsider them every year. Therefore, every hay crop begins with brawls and strife and the best time is lost. While the fighting goes on, energetic and cunning individuals mow as much grass as they can, even using hired workmen. Often, haying begins only when the grass is dried out. The same arguments occur over transporting the hay, brought in by stacks. The wealthy and more industrious get ahead of the indolent and argumentative, and take in as much hay as they want wherever they find it. Individuals with many draught oxen and good wagons gather the most. They situate hay and straw stacks so close to their houses that the danger is greatly increased should fire break out.

Bad wagons greatly hinder the harvest. Roughly built, totally without iron, they are often obtained cheaply in exchange for wheat or other crops. Usually the worst wheels made in the Crimea find their way to the Nogais. Often they don't last even *one* year. Few persons know how to make repairs and it is often necessary to borrow wagons for short periods in exchange for payment in crops.

Mowers and other workmen must be paid very dearly, at one and a half rubles per day during the harvest, which is more than their surrounding neighbours pay. A servant for a year gets eighty to 100 rubles, and food and clothing.

The Nogai cannot yet agree to plant trees and orchards. They gather varieties of a plant called *kurrei* to feed cattle and to heat houses. Preparation of manure for fuel is done very well. Blacksmithing and wagon work is understood and carried on by only a few. Belts and saddle work are partly manufactured or simply improved. Their few mills are driven by horses and badly arranged.

Women's Occupations

Most of the work falls to the female gender. A woman with several small children is not in a position to perform all of her work without help from neighbours or friends. Nogais cannot obtain female servants unless they hire a whole family, husband and wife, since adult, unmarried women designated for sale, or already promised and sold but not yet paid for, are kept under strict observation and are not willingly allowed into strange houses without accompaniment, even for a visit. Often this is the reason why many Nogais acquire a second wife to share the work. Male servants, since they risk drawing contempt upon themselves, do not willingly allow themselves to be used for water carrying, pounding millet, and similar jobs that traditionally fall to the women.

In addition to the necessary care of their children, the women cook, wash, milk the cows, clean the houses, make butter, and also have the responsibility of whitewashing the inside and outside of the houses, gathering the dried manure from the fields, roasting millet and pounding it in a large wooden mortar, grinding millet and wheat with a hand mill, preparing bosa, and carrying water once or twice a day, often from a considerable distance. They prepare tallow candles and make soap with the ashes of a plant named *Alabata*. They tan sheep pelts and then make caps and fur coats from them for everyone in the household, and also sew all necessary shirts, jackets, etc.

The women spin sheep's wool by holding it in their left hand, pulling it out with the right hand and turning it on the spindle. They weave a brown and white fabric from this thread in a very primitive way. Also, they make various kinds of wadding and carpets from this wool, and attractive ribbons and cords are worked to decorate their clothes.

Imports and Exports

In addition to cattle, only wheat, pelts, and butter and tallow sewed into skins are exported from the Nogai district. Except for milk, butter, wheat, and the rough fabric they manufacture, everything that is needed must be bartered or purchased, such as wood for house building, wagons and field implements, and all woodenware, such as barrels, buckets, bowls, etc. All iron goods, fabrics, linen, shoes, boots, luxury wares for the women, spices, garden products, and tobacco must also be purchased or bartered for. Though salt is readily available locally, it is managed badly and must also be bought.

Customs and Practices

The Nogais retain some pleasant customs and habits, though admittedly they often retain only the semblance and not the essence itself, e.g., respect for age, and hospitality. People of other religions are well received. The hospitality for an old Muslim, or for a pilgrim or *Ashe* in particular, has something genuinely patriarchal about it. The guest is essentially master of the house and the host protects him from every disparagement or insult.

The Nogais have few games and entertainments. Recreation consists of hunting – chasing rabbits and wolves until they are exhausted and then beating them to death with clubs. On major feast days, such as the Greater Bairam, there are horse races, swings are erected, etc. Music is much loved, but their ear for music is not very refined. The Nogais play a type of lyre, a piece of wood with two or three strings, and on this the notes are always repeated in the same manner and with the same rhythm. Dances consist of a dancer who stands in one spot and makes unusual motions with his head, hands, and feet. Nogai singing is very monotonous, though they often sing as they ride along on their travels. A singer usually delights the company during drinking sessions. Tobacco smoking provides special enjoyment and the Tatar prefers to do without everything else other than this gift of God. Even aged women are as passionate about this as the men.

Marriages are usually contracted with girls from distant villages, since it is more honourable not to have seen one's bride until the day of the wedding. However, the man seeking marriage allows friends to enlighten him, especially about whether the girl is shapely, what type of face she has, and what kind of hair. If this pleases him he employs others to bargain with the father or with male relatives of the girl. Female relatives have no part in the matter. Thirty to forty cows (each valued at twenty rubles; one oxen or one horse are counted as two cows) and two to three hundred rubles cash are paid for a Nogai girl of good background and figure, while few go for less than twenty cows and 100 rubles. Young widows are cheaper and old ones are often free. Payment is either made immediately, or the agreement is written up by Mullahs and the bidder begins to pay gradually. He may not see the bride in the meantime, even if payment takes several years.

The girl's wishes do not count, though there are sensible parents who love their child more than money and consider what she desires. However, a girl is rarely asked and objects just as rarely. Completely submissive to the customs of her people, she moves towards every fate, unacquainted with the wishes and requirements with which we conduct such steps. The parents of the girl contribute, as marriage goods, clothing, mattresses, jewellery, etc. In the case of rich people, this almost equals the value of the money and cattle paid for the bride.

Crimean, especially Kalmyk, girls are less highly regarded, and poorer individuals often buy them for very little money. After being bought, the girls usually accept the Muslim religion. The Murzas have their wives paid for by the people, with gifts of cattle and other items. Crimean Tatars come into the Nogai district with their families and stay until their daughters are sold. The bargaining is done through brokers.

Good care is taken of Nogai girls but they are kept under stern supervision. One seldom meets them on the street. It is customary that children who are still in the cradle are promised to each other through an agreement between the parents. A contract is made, the father of the boy begins to pay, and by the time they have reached a suitable age, the required sum has been discharged. The young man usually does not oppose the marriage. A girl is usually married as early as thirteen to fifteen years of age. This trade in children, girls, and widows gives occasion for innumerable quarrels between parents, relatives, and children themselves, as can well be imagined, since there are no definite laws governing all possible instances. Payments already made are supposed to be returned on death, maiming, disfiguration due to illness, etc. Many difficulties arise because many things can happen between friends and parents who have concluded contracts and made payments, and over the years, circumstances turn friends into foes. The economic well-being, or the honour and respect, of a family can be lost in the meantime, and the other party looks for anything to cause dissension and to reverse the bargain.

On the wedding day, the bridegroom and the bride choose witnesses, each in a separate house. These witnesses shake hands (the first witness represents the bridegroom, the other represents the bride) and conclude the marriage. The day is passed with great feasting. In the evening, the young woman is veiled and all the women lead her to her husband's house and she sees him for the first time. Cakes and meat are distributed in the village. On this day, people from neighbouring villages appear and they are treated to *bosa* and also brandy and food (each village in a special house).

For a whole year, the young wife must refrain from speaking to anyone except her husband, parents, and siblings, and is permitted to speak with her friends only through signs and gestures. After the year has passed, a feast day is held and she has permission to speak normally. Timidity and shyness towards strangers are still prevalent among women, and the men are not pleased if anyone has frequent or long conversations with women.

The voluptuary is still able to find means to satisfy his lust, but with difficulty due to the prevailing customs and the concern which places the women under stern supervision. On the whole, the Nogai position on this point is better than in the self-consciously enlightened Occident. Artful love affairs seldom develop among them. It seems that the men are not aware that they can touch the tender chords which open to love the eye and the heart of the wife or young woman.

If a man dies, his wives are inherited by his brothers, who can keep them for themselves or sell them. A man can repudiate his wife and live separately from her. If the divorce is formally completed and the cattle paid for her are returned, she can marry again. Where there are several wives, the one married first holds the first rank within the household, but when a young wife is added to an old one, the young wife is usually preferred and rules the house. The man is free to sleep with whichever wife he pleases, but usually there are regular changes. It can be imagined that peace cannot always be found in the home under these conditions. Then, outward peace is restored with a whip.

Women live under conditions of slavery, but they do not consider themselves to be unhappy because they do not know anything better. The man is total master. A woman may never pass by a man, never visit a place of worship, nor eat out of the same bowl as a man. A man's orders and arrangements for the whole household must be followed without argument. Husbands almost always take the children's side against their mother, and this causes all true love and respect for her to be smothered in the child. To have many children, especially many boys, is considered to be a great blessing because of the hope for descendants. Girls, however, produce wealth. The first-born is privileged.

The burial of the dead is connected with sacrifice. The dressed corpse lies on straw on a bier and is accompanied to the cemetery outside the village by priests and people. Here he is laid into the grave on his right side, with his face towards Mecca. The priest reads from the Koran while the people stand forty paces from the grave. Prayers are said, several ceremonies are observed, the grave is filled in and a small mound of earth or stones is constructed. The deceased is buried within twelve hours, children probably in six hours. Many women congregate within and in front of the house of the deceased and set up a terrible *Baiwai* and howling, raising their hands to the heavens as though in despair. Mothers and widows repeat this howling at sundown for a long time. The day of death is observed annually with a sacrifice for the dead one. Women have very few claims to the goods to be inherited.

The Murzas constitute a separate people, so to speak. They have their own practices and do not intermarry with the Nogais. Proud, indolent, poor, and bad managers, they assume airs before others and take many liberties. They almost always travel with a retinue or a type of protective escort.

Obstacles to Nogai Moral Improvement with Suggestions to Deal with Them

The destructive influence of Islam is probably the greatest obstacle to moral improvement and increased civilization among the Nogais. Their indolence and indifference rest on fatalism, on their incorrect understanding of the doctrine of predestination, which acts as a deterrent to those improvements usually developed by normal human nature and intelligence. Filled with prejudices by the intolerance and fanaticism preached in the Koran, they believe that they must shut themselves off in every respect from the influence of anyone who thinks differently.

For the Nogai, man's motivation to behave morally is smothered by the promise of paradise if several outward practices or ceremonies are observed. He attempts to cover crimes and sins by performing sacrifices prescribed for sin. These sacrifices are supposed to be a substitute for spiritual merit and morality before God. The Nogai's right to retaliate is based on religious belief that permits every person to take revenge, controlled only to the extent that the government might punish him according to law. This leaves room for many quarrels and misdemeanours even if an individual does abstain from revenge to win the grace of God as a devout Muslim.

Mohammed's religion does *not* provide a basis for inner moral worth, but for an external illusion at the most. It does not offer strength and love for moral behaviour and for this reason is opposed to the prosperity and happiness of a people. Yes, the Koran even includes teachings that directly oppose a people's prosperity, and it is fatalism that causes Muslims to be little inclined to diligence and industry, to field cultivation and useful occupations. Though communicable diseases cause population and prosperity to suffer, they are not prevented, and measures are seldom taken against them. They disdain immunization to protect against smallpox. They do not consider it necessary to bury carrion. They make no effort to counter destructive natural events, nor to prevent or to ameliorate grasshopper plagues, etc. They even consider it sinful to employ measures against them. The earth is supposed to bring forth fruit with no effort. Human intelligence and strength are not considered as a gift from God to be used and applied. The Muslims include all this in the doctrine of unalterable fate, in order to serve the indolence and indifference of their nature. Shut off from good influences through the fanaticism and superstition maintained by priests, sorcerers, etc., they reject all innovations.

Ignorance leads pilgrims to the holy grave in Mecca, as prescribed in the Koran. The expensive journey to Mecca ruins the prosperity of a family, often almost forever. The pilgrim requires 2,000 to 3,000 rubles and his household is neglected for a year, or is managed by strangers for payment. He comes back self-satisfied and more fanatical, distinguishing himself before others. Proudly, he believes that he has done everything good and knows everything. He assumes an arrogant importance over others and is firmly resolved, as a faithful Muslim, to resist all guidance towards improvement and to repudiate anything new.

Polygamy and the destructive sale of wives result in unspeakable evil and discord. Also, the high price of wives robs men with few possessions of the happiness of marital life or forces them into the servant class to pay off debts or to pay the price for a wife. Polygamy is detrimental for the population and also removes livestock and money from the area in exchange for foreign girls.

The contempt with which women are treated, arising out of the teachings of Mohammed, and their degrading treatment, prevent this gender from experiencing its own strengths and a true feeling of love.

What can be born of a woman who can consider herself to be only half human according to the dictates of her holy scriptures and according to her treatment from her husband or lord? She can have no other conception of the purpose of her existence, in this life and in paradise, than to serve and satisfy crude, animal lust, in which no tender feelings of love are aroused. She is left with little more than animal instincts, which must have the most detrimental physical and moral effects on her children. What can the children experience from an apathetic mother with no feeling? Isn't the first and most important training and education of a child after its birth in the hands of the mother? What can a child receive at her breast, what can its early development be with *such a mother*, who should be laying the foundation for the child's future life and all later institutions of education? Also, what does the child learn from the way the father *treats the mother*?

With its benevolent and humane disposition, the government may not want to interfere too closely with the free practice of religion, to take severe measures against polygamy, the purchase of strange girls, and against the journey to Mecca, or against the especially great influence of the so-called magicians and priests, maintained and increased through superstition and fanaticism. It may not even want to use orders and restrictions in an attempt to hinder these practices.[9]

However, by means of improved schools and the establishment of new schools, a better foundation for the future generation could perhaps be laid, and a better sense of culture and morality promoted. Though teaching and educating the youth are difficult due to a great revulsion against pictures and figures, a beginning could be made by

---

9 This paragraph differs from the *Teleskop* version, which reads:
"These circumstances serve as obvious proof that only the constant extension of the beneficial guidance of the government can lead to the moral improvement and betterment of the material conditions of this people. Without directly violating the laws of humanity and tolerance, it is possible, it would seem, to place limits on pernicious influences that grow out of deep-rooted evil customs, such as, particularly, polygamy, the purchase of girls from other places, and the fanaticism and superstition promulgated by the sham magicians and Mullahs. The main goal might be achieved through the correction of, or better founding of, new, useful schools for the education of the young. Instruction by capable teachers of pedagogy, if not Christian then at least in conformity with natural morality, of lessons and precepts along with good examples of good behaviour, naturally softens young hearts and gives them the feeling that they are capable of making progress towards good sensibilities. From this is born respect for the qualities of humanity, and gentle, tender attitudes towards the female gender."

establishing a model school in the main centre where future school teachers could be educated. Through some knowledge and guidance towards independent thought, through living examples of teachers and those in authority, through an explanation of moral philosophy, Socratic if not Christian, etc., the intelligence and the heart of the younger males might be formed and enlightened, resulting in a different attitude and a different treatment of the females.

Without being aware of it themselves, the influence of the naturally gentler and more receptive female gender will become more effective and this gender in turn would influence the education of the children to prepare them for the schools in the most attractive way. The schools could be used to work towards the worth and destiny of man, of the human race in general, and especially of the female gender. Other, better conceptions of marriage could be awakened and rooted in the heart, and not simply *apparent* and *temporary* but *enduring* good will could then be established.

Through institutions of education, the fanaticism, fatalism, superstition, and the overwhelming influence of priests and all evils of Islam can be mitigated. Speedy, visible effects cannot be expected from these institutions as means for moral education because of the many deeply rooted prejudices, the aversion to so-called unbelievers, the fear of proselytizing, and the generally great influence of religion. As drawing, geometry, mathematics, etc., are taught in schools, the Nogais will be led to the conviction that, while man can be guided to religious feelings and considerations by viewing an actual subject or picture in nature or in human art, he can also learn other useful things from it. They will see that not every image is a holy picture, as many of them think, that it is actually nothing but *paper,* and that it is not necessarily a sin not to honour every *image,* since it may not represent *Him* whom they must honour.

The total absence of educational institutions is definitely a major cause for stagnation in Nogai culture and morality, as well as their fanaticism and superstition, and their lack of attachment to the state under whose protection they enjoy so many advantages and liberties. Schools could counter one of the greatest obstacles to their improvement – namely the stupid, detrimental posture of their inherited pride in nation and ancestors, kept alive by ignorance, and always an obstacle to accepting improvement. Proud of their name, of their inherited customs and practices, the Nogai Tatars see themselves as the foremost people of the world, and their own branch of the Nogais as the most superior and the most famous among the Tatars. The individual Nogai considers himself wise and clever, his physical stature excellent and beautiful, and the arrangement and conduct of his household the best and most praiseworthy, despite all experience and all superior knowledge: "We do not need to know or learn anything more, we do not want anything more and nothing other than what our fathers had. What others do may be good but they are not Nogais and are therefore to be considered as less."

Pride in their birth and ancestry divides the Nogais among themselves and runs from the three above-named main branches into many subsidiary branches, and down to single families, in which one part despises another more or less, so that marriages usually occur only with considerations of birth, descent, and branch.

The Nogais are disposed to a nomadic life, to continual change and gadding about, and this has not yet been rooted out. They are a people who, from time immemorial, not only moved as nomads within a specific country, in search of a change in habitation and pastures, but wandered in large numbers from one land to another and often to lands at a great distance and back and forth again. This detrimental inclination will increase if they are left to their own devices without wise leadership to encourage and convince them of the advantages of peaceful country life, of working field and garden, of handicrafts, and of culture in general. It can be assumed that probably more than three-quarters of them would joyfully leave house and field to renew their old life, and to wander either into Turkey or further into Asia.

This destructive disposition towards a wild, rude life, gadding about without ties – yes, even with an impulse to thievery – is further nurtured and cultivated by Nogai service as *tabunshchiks*, or horse herdsmen, outside their region, with Armenians, Greeks, etc. When these herdsmen return to their community after shorter or longer time spans, they are almost always wild people, unqualified for any work, very often practised thieves who maintain themselves by hanging around and stealing. Their restlessness supports purposeless wandering about to markets, an interest in haggling, and a passion for thievery and quarrelling. Frequent absences throw their household and family circumstances into confusion.

Hunting is even more detrimental to the economy and to morality, causing an aversion to steady work, and nurturing a raw sense of pride. It provides an occasion for thievery. Often the hunters return after several days with matted and ruined horses, though the quarry they have run to death only consists of rabbits and wolves. If they were lucky, they may have destroyed a wild animal and possibly gained a ten-ruble reward for a wolf pelt, or one ruble for a rabbit, which bears no comparison to the damage done to their horses, to the neglect of their farms, and to the time wasted. The avid hunter is usually also disinclined to field cultivation, to diligence, and industry.

Horse breeding leads thousands into a wild, wandering life, nurturing a delight in indolence and disinclination towards field cultivation. They pay little or no attention to the improvement of the breed. Horses of any value require large pastures, and this land itself could be used much more advantageously for increased and improved sheep breeding and field cultivation.

Wandering Armenian and Gypsy peddlers are also harmful to the Nogai district. The Armenians bring linen, fabrics, shoes, and other items of clothing, ribbons, spices, and similar things. Mainly wares of bad quality, they are bartered at high prices for cash payments, grain, millet, livestock, butter, furs, etc. The Gypsies work with metals, make or repair field, house, and kitchen implements, and also carry luxury wares such as earrings and nose and arm rings, buckles, buttons, and similar things. They cheat in the most shameful manner, and stay with families in a village for long periods of time. Their women act as fortune-tellers.

The absence of an administrator concerned about the true well-being of the people is an obstacle to developing civilization and moral betterment, as are arrangements and laws which pay too little attention to specific Nogai peculiarities, character, customs, and religion, and the contempt with which the Nogais are often treated by lower officials. This is the reason improvements begun by Count Demaison have not been continued and cannot be maintained.[10]

A good supervisor is necessary to enable all institutions and means for Nogai improvement to thrive. He must promote, support, and protect them. It is to be hoped that the provisional situation may soon end and, in the interests of the well-being of the peoples of Russia, the position of a supervisor may again be entrusted to a man who treats the Nogais with love, trust, respect, and seriousness, and who conveys the same to all lower officials and requires it of them.

10 Instead of lamenting Demaison's retirement, the *Teleskop* article lists Demaison's accomplishments, which, "little by little," led to the end of these evils.

The arrangements put in place must be specifically designed with Nogai customs and religion in mind. They are Asiatics, attached to a religion with a zeal that is also partly political, and this penetrates their social life, customs, and usages. One can hardly differentiate the actual teachings of the Koran from its interpretations, and what can be attributed to the influence of religion, or to other causes. Their attachment is to a religion which very much flatters human desires and passions, and it becomes so solid and extensive that the people who have surrendered to it are fettered to it in indifference and indolence.

If people surrounding the Nogais become aware of efforts being made for their improvement, and that they are respected by the government and treated with love and respect by lower officials, this would lead to respect for the Nogais. It will then encourage and drive the Nogais to win respect for themselves through their own good performance that will even put many of their neighbours to shame. A well-disposed leader will win their love and devotion for Crown and fatherland and they will no longer be heard to say so insolently, audaciously, and unthankfully that they only recognize the Turkish emperor. All their perverse sense of pride, ignorance, and roughness can only be remedied permanently and fundamentally with patience and love under a good leader.

In particular, schools are needed, even if they are introduced under compulsion. A main school could be established as the first step, in accordance with Count Demaison's intentions, and this would lay a foundation and make a beginning. Good subjects would surely soon emerge from the school, who could be appointed as teachers and district supervisors. To the extent that it can be done without detrimental effects, the school should be arranged according to the wishes and concepts of the people and conducted with regard for their requirements and religion. Reading and writing of Tatar, Arabic, and Russian, as well as arithmetic, geography, general world history, and natural history, etc., should all be taught. Special emphasis must however be given to morality and to a thorough knowledge of the Koran and its interpretation.

A printing press could be connected to the school, or it could be a lithographic facility to save expenses and accommodate more closely to the tastes of people who respect handwritten texts more highly than printed ones. Small texts of moral, historic, or geographic content could be prepared in the dialect of the people and distributed, since there are quite a few who can read. Should the government wish to send several young Tatars on travels or to be trained in educational institutions in Russia or in foreign countries, it could probably find Tatars who would allow their children to take part, providing there were no expenses for them and there was no intention of making proselytizers of them.

Could not the Nogais be urged and encouraged to seek more employment in field and garden work with neighbouring Russians and Germans? This would increase neighbourly love and friendship, and they would become acquainted with one another's opinions and customs.

Handicrafts and trades are almost totally lacking and this prevents prosperity. Wood and iron wares, woven fabrics, luxury articles, and almost all needs except furs and food must all be bought from foreign Armenians or at Russian and German markets. There is an insufficient number of mills in the area. Those that do exist are badly set up, driven by horses, and can produce very little flour. Most of their milling is done at German or Russian mills for the price of the tenth part.

Because the Nogais totally lack garden products and tree fruits, a not inconsiderable sum of money in the form of cash, or in millet, grain, etc., finds its way to the Crimean Tatars or neighbouring Russians for apples, pears, nuts, and, particularly, for a large quantity of tobacco and watermelons. No matter how much the Nogais enjoy certain garden products, and especially tobacco, they cannot bring themselves to do the planting. Here and there someone may have started to do this, but there were usually enough malicious persons who soon destroyed or stole the plants. The Nogais did not tolerate planting in order to prevent the practice from becoming general and eventually a requirement for everyone. The absence of potatoes is especially regrettable. Even though they enjoy eating these as guests in other places, they will neither buy nor plant them.

A director concerned about the well-being of these people in accordance with the state's purposes will certainly – by means of wise regulations and laws to encourage and require field and garden cultivation, improvements in sheep breeding, and training in the trades – soon achieve visible and lasting good in respect to their economic conditions. Also, the industrious and hard-working should be treated with consideration and rewarded, and the wicked punished appropriately. Schools should be established. Introducing protection against pox will contribute much to the population, as will effective regulations to prevent other communicable diseases and the too-hurried burial of corpses. Carrion must be covered, and supervision is needed so that sick livestock is not butchered and eaten. The Nogais should be encouraged to carry on sheep breeding, field and garden cultivation, and useful handicrafts. Limitations should be put on external service as herdsmen, on hunting, and on anything that nurtures and strengthens an inclination to a changing, unsteady, rude, wild life. Anything to restrain and soften a rough character would lead the human being to a quiet life and to continuing work, and this will gradually eliminate the old inclination to a nomadic life. Their moral condition will be improved, even without taking into account the educational institutions to be established.

Nogai feelings of pride could be shaped by arranging folk festivals to establish affection for sovereign and country. Everyone who distinguishes himself through education and moral behaviour should be acknowledged, considered to advantage, and rewarded. Religion should be respected. Positive aspects of the Koran should be stressed and given consideration in political arrangements and in schools, while detrimental aspects should be countered indirectly. Good examples demonstrated by officials will be most effective. The more a supervisor penetrates into the spirit of Islam, into the character of the people, and into their individuality, and is able to utilize this knowledge, the more he will be respected, find entrance into hearts and souls, and accomplish the purpose and effect of established institutions and arrangements.

Skilled tradesmen should be attracted to a settlement in the main centre and peddling by Armenians and Gypsies should be limited. The Nogais will then be able to obtain better and cheaper wares, and sell grain, furs, butter, etc. Frequent shortages of grain can be remedied by building storehouses. Conscientious management of salt found on the land will provide a major advantage.

Service as foreign herdsmen must be halted. Every person who wishes to travel should be required to seed at least two chetverts of grain so that very few will find an advantage in having others tend their fields. This was done under Count Demaison's leadership. At that time, Armenians and Greeks paid 500 to 600 rubles for the *Ottoman*, or first herdsman, though now they can be hired for 150 rubles and even less.

The director will pay attention to the building of good mills, or the improvement of existing ones in the district, to regular and purposeful laying out of villages, and to the exterior and interior construction of houses, which must be well maintained. Rules will be provided for dividing hay fields, pasturing livestock, and using ploughlands. The Nogais will be required to plant gardens and trees. Criminals will be severely punished. The director must be an example to the people with his own household and establishment and ensure that his subordinate district supervisors also serve as good examples in their area. By travelling around the district frequently, he will learn about and see the conditions of the people and the land.

If the projected establishment of a city and port on the Sea of Azov in the neighbourhood of Nogaisk should not come about, would it not at least be possible to enlarge and increase the population of Nogaisk and to provide it with a main school? Would it not be possible to form a model colony in the district with a portion of the poor but industrious and willing Nogais, all aspects of which could serve as an example to the other villages?

Would it not be possible to set up a sheep farm with improved sheep? With time, it could provide large increases for the community funds through wool sales, and would also give the Nogais good, well-bred rams. There are still unused Crown lands in the Nogai district which are not good for settlement because of a lack of water. They could be useful for sheep farming since the sheep could be watered in neighbouring villages. To cover the main investment until it produces more income as prosperity grows and population increases, the Nogais, with their low taxes, would not find it difficult to initially pay the community fund *one* or *one and a half* rubles annually for every revision soul. This would produce an annual income of 17,000 to 26,000 rubles. The proceeds from the fish catch, the income from nomadic groups passing through, etc., could be included. Resources would not be lacking if the director had the will and energy to use his power.

The Nogai lands are in an important location on the Sea of Azov and this deserves the greatest attention. How this strip of land is used cannot be insignificant for neighbouring peoples and for the whole of southern Russia itself. Should the state's good intentions in improving the well-being, the moral and economic conditions of the Nogais not be attainable, it would be very desirable that this people be allowed to move on to the wide steppes of eastern Russia in accordance with their wishes. Then this beautiful piece of land can be given to others who would make better use of it, to their own and to the state's advantage.

Conclusion

It is the duty of every human being, in whatever condition and in whatever position he may find himself, to employ all powers he has been given for the best of the human community and for the general well-being, and to use all means available to him for this purpose. Any well-intentioned inhabitant of Russia will also have an interest in the condition of one of the peoples of this realm itself. With joy he will grasp every opportunity presented to him, as unimportant as it may seem to be, to assist in some degree in spreading education and external prosperity among a people still retarded in some aspects when compared with others. To dare to say something about the current conditions of the Nogai Tatars might also seem less presumptuous and clumsy coming from someone living in Russia whose purpose it is to serve as an economic and moral model for these his neighbouring people. He must therefore watch in pain as efforts to contribute to the well-being of this people are frustrated because their supervisors are not always inclined to support such efforts, and they act in a manner contrary to the interests of the state. Seeking only their own interests, they concern themselves little with the well-being of state and people.

What joy it is, however, when a friend of the state and its peoples, especially of the Nogai Tatars, is encouraged by his own superiors to write something about these people and to explain their current conditions. This neighbour has for many years stood in close connection and communication with them, and is sufficiently convinced that they are capable and qualified for every development. He is convinced that this deficient and imperfect explanation will nonetheless be kindly received and will not remain completely disregarded. It was not his own personal interest that motivated him or led him as he wrote, but the fulfilling of a pleasant duty towards the state and his superiors, who hold the well-being of this people close to their hearts.

With the plea that the imperfect form and language in this presentation not be considered, but that it be received as the expression of a heart beating for truth and human well-being, I remain with deepest respect,

Your obedient servant, Johann Cornies

II. The Doukhobors of the Molochnaia Area

SAOR 89-1-396. Undated [after 1825, before 1836]

During the second half of the last century, a group was discovered in Russia whose existence seemed impossible under the conditions existing in the empire at that time. In the midst of a people who were largely unenlightened, conforming only to the outer pretence of religion and with no knowledge of its spirit, there suddenly appeared people who not only rejected all practices and dogmas of the Greek Church, but did not even accept formal baptism with water or the Lord's supper.

Naturally, such people could not be left in peace by their neighbours or by the government, especially because no one understood their spirit or their basic beliefs. They suffered almost constant persecution from all directions. All meetings with clergy and with police officials led to investigations and imprisonments. Terrible abuse and insults accompanied every encounter with neighbours and all their actions made them seem monstrous disturbers of the general peace. Higher governments judged them largely on the basis of reports from lower officials, frequently sentencing them to exile as state criminals.

Only the gentle, peaceful regime of Tsar Alexander I freed these people, who, by 1788, were known as Doukhobors. In the year 1801, Senator Lopushchin instituted an investigation in Slobodskaia Ukraina guberniia. On his recommendation, His Majesty was persuaded to designate a special, separate place for their settlement in the Molochnaia.

The first thirty families settled in the Molochnaia in 1801. In 1804, sectarians in Tambov and Voronezh guberniias requested the same resettlement and this was also permitted. They were collected from various parts of the Russian Empire and from exile, without consideration of the variety of their religious convictions but *simply* because they agreed on rejecting the veneration of saints and other ceremonies and sacraments of the Greek Church. They considered themselves to be spiritual beings born of the spirit and spiritually enlightened, and this is the meaning of the name "Doukhobors."

They call those who do not belong to them "people of the world," but also "darkness." They claim that they descend from three disciples, Hananiah, Asharelah, and Michael, who suffered because they would not venerate the picture of Nebuchadnezzar.

It was difficult to declare the Doukhobors as unbelievers as long as they still lived among the peasants, scattered in the various guberniias of Russia, appearing as upright and virtuous people, avoiding drunkenness and sloth, and concerned untiringly with their own economic affairs. Their conduct appeared to be highly moral. They fulfilled imperial tax and other communal obligations to the other peasants promptly in order to escape harassment of all sorts, and professed a belief that seemed to be Christian, affirming it with verses from the holy scripture. Thus, it was difficult and doubtful to declare them to be unbelievers in Christ, the Son of God, who was born and taught, suffered, died and ascended to heaven for the sins of this world, and who will come again to judge the living and the dead.

However, since they have been left to themselves, living together in several villages on the Molochnaia, and not prevented from practising their religion peacefully, it can be concluded more clearly that they only call themselves Christians, and that they deny Christ's power. They explain the basis of their beliefs as follows:

> We pray to God in spirit and in truth. We avoid all outward pretences because they are not necessary for salvation. We are the law of God, the belief in Jesus Christ. *Memory* is God the Father, *reason*, God the Son, *will* is the Holy Ghost. The *Father* is our God, the *Son* our life, the *Holy Ghost* our resting place. The *Father* is the height, the *Son* is the breadth, the *Holy Ghost* is the depth. The *Father* is high and no one is higher, the *Son* is the breadth of wisdom, the *Holy Ghost* the depth that no one can fathom. Everything contained in the gospels is accomplished in us. In this manner, Christ was received in us, was born, grew up, taught, suffered, died, was resurrected, and rose up to heaven. Christ is the word and this is written into our hearts. Without God and His Christ there is no other salvation, and if we do not appeal to God with a clean heart, He cannot save man. Human salvation requires an unquestioned belief in Christ, together with good

works, for without good works faith is dead. It must be, however, a living faith and this is the acceptance of the gospels.[1]

They say that they are baptised in the name of the Father, the Son, and the Holy Ghost. Baptism occurs when man repents and seeks God with a pure heart. Then his sins will be forgiven and he will think of God and not about the world. The works of the new man are the evidence of birth from above, through baptism.

Baptism has seven qualities:

1. Abandoning sin;
2. Anointing or acknowledging peace;
3. Expressing God's word or His sense;
4. The last anointing or the consecration by prayer;
5. Spiritual confession;
6. Spiritual communion;
7. Cleansing by the blood or humility. Blood means the Word of God.

These seven steps constitute union with God. Anyone who has attained union with God through these seven steps, which are spiritual baptism, or the new birth, is already living in God and can see the angels with spiritual eyes. The Christian is given *two* names: a mortal one at birth, and a spiritual one with which God has named him at his spiritual birth, and which corresponds to his works. Sins are confessed to God, the Heavenly Father, in prayer. To call oneself a sinner is boastful and false humility. When a man falls, he must immediately get up again, ask God for forgiveness with a humble heart, and strive not to sin again.

With respect to Holy Communion, communion occurs at all times by avoiding sin through the holy, life-giving, and undying secrets of Christ and through the inward reception of the Word of God, which is Christ, and penetrates reason, bones, and brain. Bread and wine are received through the mouth as food and do not benefit the soul. Fasting consists in avoiding debauchery. Though they do not venerate the saints, they must imitate them, and in this way they appeal to the saints. They

1 For the Bonch-Bruevich version, see Vladimir D. Bonch-Bruevich, *The Book of Life of the Dukhobors*, trans. by Victor O. Buyniak (Blaine Lake, SK: Dukhobor Societies of Saskatchewan, Saskatoon and Blaine Lake, 1978), xviii, 89.

remember the dead with good works and conduct no other ceremonies for the dead. God himself remembers the just in His kingdom. They do not pray for the dead because they see this as unnecessary. The Christian's end is not death but a transformation. Therefore they say that their brother has transformed himself, not that he is dead.

They say that the body of the first man was of the earth, his bones of stones, his veins of roots, his blood of water, his hair of grass, his thoughts of the wind, and his beauty of the clouds. The human soul is strength, and strength is God and God in man. Wicked children come of wicked parents, but the sins of the parents do not prevent the salvation of the children. Everyone must give a reckoning before God to attain salvation. The blessed state of the just is paradise and the kingdom of strength. Paradise is in the Word. No torment occurs for the souls of the just in the Kingdom of God. Hell consists of malice.

Souls after death can no longer repent. Man is justified by works and condemned by works. Judgment of the righteous and sinners is left to God, as is resurrection of the dead. They do not speculate about the revelation of mysterious things with people whom they do not know well or who have a different faith. This is based on the declaration of the Saviour: do not throw pearls before swine. Likewise, if asked how soon they expect Christ's arrival, they only say that this must occur soon if one judges by the actions of the world. Only works lead to salvation and it is only necessary to know the way of the Lord. It is the Christian's duty to conduct himself and live in a clean and tidy manner.

When the Doukhobors still lived secretly in Russia, necessity forced them to follow the practices and decrees of the Greek Church in outward appearances. Because they had absolutely no respect for these practices, but did not want to betray this attitude, they gave everything belonging to outward religious practice special spiritual meanings. For example, the days of the week were assigned the following meanings: *Monday*, all God's works must be told; *Tuesday*, man's second birth; *Wednesday*, the Lord calls mankind to salvation; *Thursday*, praise God, you who are His blessed; *Friday*, sing and praise His name; *Saturday*, fear the judgment of God so that your soul is not destroyed in falsehood; *Sunday*, arise from dead works and come to the Kingdom of Heaven.

The seven Doukhobor heavens represent the seven evangelical virtues in the following manner: submission is the first heaven, repentance second, abstemiousness third, brotherly love fourth, compassion fifth, advice sixth, and love seventh. God also lives there.

The Doukhobors depict twelve Christian virtues as *twelve friends:*[2]

1. *Truth* frees mankind from death.
2. *Cleanliness* brings mankind to God.
3. Where there is *love*, there also is God.
4. *Work* honours the body and helps the soul.
5. *Obedience* is the quick road to salvation.
6. *Exculpation* brings mankind to salvation without effort.
7. *Contemplation*, the most honourable of all virtues, is the absence of condemnation.
8. Satan himself trembles before *compassion*.
9. *Victory* itself is the work of Christ our God.
10. *Prayer, together with fasting*, unite mankind with God.
11. No law or command is higher than *penance*.
12. *Thankfulness* is agreeable to God and his angels.

Any person possessing these twelve friends is represented by the angels and they carry his soul into the Kingdom of God.

The Doukhobors conduct assemblies under open skies in two circles, one circle of men and one circle of women, and they recite prayers, one after another, and sing psalms. They do everything by memory. When they enter the assembly, they greet each other, the men with the women and the women with the men, in this manner: they grasp each other by the right hand, make *three* bows to each other and kiss each other *three* times, while each one recites prayers. These *three* bows and *three* kisses represent God's Trinity, while the grasping of hand to hand is a sign of the covenant of love, of good tidings, of recognition of truth, and *the recognition of the hidden God inwardly within themselves*. They have no particular days set aside for this. All days are the same and every free day is a day to assemble. They keep church and state holidays because they could be harassed or brought to trial for violating the laws of the land.

---

2 For the Bonch-Bruevich version, see *The Book of Life of the Dukhobors*, 160, 282. The following differences appear in the Bonch-Bruevich version: 6. Non-condemnation (instead of exculpation); 7. Reasoning (instead of contemplation); 8. Prayer (instead of compassion); 9. Gratefulness (instead of victory); 10. Mercy (instead of prayer); 11. Humbless/humility (instead of penance); and 12. Confession/repentence (instead of thankfulness).

Analysis

It is simply their reputation for being spiritual and possessing perception that gives the Doukhobors a separate existence. In general, they show the greatest ignorance in spiritual matters. They know how to present an appearance of upholding religious principles when they actually have no definite forms of belief and do not know what they actually believe or accept. With their conceit of enlightenment, they assume superiority over anyone who thinks differently and give themselves an outer bearing and demeanour that distinguishes them from the Russian peasants in their vicinity.

Though assiduous in following the morally acceptable external demeanour necessary for distinction from others, even this sense of honour must soon disappear. A lack of knowledge is becoming more evident among the Doukhobors because their young people receive absolutely no education and religious instruction. As spiritual beings, they imagine that they do not require teachers for themselves or for their children, and their young people do not even learn to read and write. Parents limit themselves to teaching their children the questions and answers they must know so that they can always give an evasive response to anyone of different belief who asks what they actually claim to believe. They only use holy scripture for the purpose of affirming their answers. They do not believe they need the revealed Word and insist that no Bible can be found among them. If the total absence of education and religious instruction for their young people continues, the next generation's decline to an actual pagan state must be feared.

Anyone who has an opportunity to get to know Doukhobors, not just superficially but more closely, will already find great immorality as an inescapable result of their irreligiosity and their deistic principles. Lack of belief and superstition are closely related. Heathens know that there is a God, but do not know how to find Him and so pray to stone and wood. On this earth, human beings are always affected by their senses and feel a need for sinful viewpoints and outward actions. If they delude themselves that they are spiritual without actually being spiritually disposed, they fall into unbelief and then very easily into superstition. Thus, one should not be surprised to see a people without religion sink into actual idolatry.

The large majority of Doukhobors say approximately this:

> There is a God. He is spirit but He is not in heaven, He is in us. We are God. This spirit or God in us enlightens and teaches everything. We do not need the teaching profession. We explain the Bible through this spirit, not

> according to the interpretations of the Greek Church. Spirit predominates over the Word. We approve of the moral philosophy in the scriptures. The remainder is allegory which only has spiritual meaning, and even historical events must be interpreted in this way, e.g., the deluge is a spiritual flood, and the passage of the Children of Israel through the Red Sea must be understood in this way, etc. *Christ was God's Son* but we are not his children. Our elders know more than Christ. Ask them.

Their spiritual head is highly respected and he is approached for counsel and dispenses advice. Though they claim to uphold the principle of non-resistance, they do not pray for enemies.

After his death, the soul of a good person goes into the body of another good person or is born again in another individual, while a wicked one migrates into a wicked person. They say that they are not in the world, though they are still in it. Their children do not call their parents father and mother, but elders. Parents speak of their children not as "mine" but as "ours." Everything belongs to everyone. However, the early Doukhobor practice of holding property in common has decreased constantly and now remains only in the community herd.

In recent years, several families of Doukhobors have returned to the Greek Church and have moved away. What motivated them to take this step cannot be determined, but certainly the absence of a purely spiritual perception, and the need for a meaningful veneration of God, played a part. More would probably withdraw now if fear were not holding them back. Fear of the large ruling group also prevents the better ones from speaking freely and candidly about what they and those who are differently disposed actually believe. Anyone who does not embrace the spirit is in danger of being slandered and if nothing can be discovered against him, he is quietly and severely oppressed.

Principal Doukhobor characteristics cannot easily be listed because they have assembled from so many regions. On the whole, one can say that simplicity, sobriety, and a sense of honour are present. In particular, they are hard-working, business-like people. Livestock raising and field cultivation are their principal means of support and their fields and livestock are well cared for and maintained. Their clothing is very clean and so are their houses, which are often very attractively built. On the whole they are well-developed, well-proportioned people with beautiful facial features. Polite and hospitable towards strangers, they are not the best at keeping their word in business dealings. Much frivolity and immorality, hatred and quarrelling occur in their midst. Gold seems to be their god and they find insufficient means of obtaining it.

Not much that is absolutely reliable can be said about the details and varieties of religious opinions among them and about their actual main principles, since they so often speak falsely and secretively in ambiguous terms. Also, they often contradict themselves. This is made more difficult because they make it a principle not to compose anything in writing about their religious opinions. Basically, it could actually be called atheism rather than deism. It is not too much to say that, on the whole, they are a people without religion and without institutions to maintain and propagate morality and the common well-being.

It can be concluded that the Doukhobors, through their irreligious deviation from the genuine truth of the holy scriptures, can be regarded as true heathens, who deny the genuine worship and reverence of the Trinity and blaspheme the holy Word of God. Naturally, like all idolaters, they have their own idol, and in this they deviate from all previously known types of idolatry. They themselves are the subject of their greatest veneration, and in them resides the whole existence of God. They apply to themselves everything that is written in holy scripture about God the Father, the Son, and the Holy Ghost, and all powers and actions of this Trinity. In this way, everything that is written in the scriptures about salvation and about the heavenly realm is fulfilled in themselves. They have no need of any external Word of God, because in them exists the Holy Spirit and they possess the living strength of God inwardly, in themselves. This point of view must be considered in order to understand their deceptive ways of speech, their secretive interpretations and their contempt for other people.

The psalms and prayers they compose in enthusiastic strains must also be understood in this sense. The following are examples:

Psalm (Doukhobor Psalm in Prophetic Sense)

John and no other is the new Moses, who was born of the incorruptible virgin out of the Word of God. About the salvation of humanity, the new Moses says that God spoke with much wisdom. The flesh will be crucified and man will be saved. It was necessary for eternal salvation that the Son of God, Jesus Christ, became man and that we believe and confess that our Lord Jesus Christ is the Son of God and human. The Lord speaks with a human mouth: Hearken, now there is a realm, look to the east where the Mountain of Zion is, and go there and contemplate it. Springs flow out of the middle of the mountain and wash off the impurity of the sons of the daughters of Israel. The heavens located on the Mountain of Zion are covered with benefactors. Oh! Children in white vestments, in vestments decorated with fiery stars. The same heavens proclaim the glory of God and sound on the whole earth. Their voice also reaches the ends of the world. When the end of the world occurs, then the heavens will open, the voices of thunder and lightning will show themselves, terrify humanity, and the realm will be set in motion. Then, all languages will assemble in a land which is the realm of the White Tsar; there will be revealed the throne of the new David; there will be great terror, where the Lord in the form of an archangel with the trumpet of God, will come down from heaven and sit on the throne of the new David and judge the living and the dead. Then, the Archangel Michael will trumpet, will begin to battle the old snake, and will overthrow the snake. Habel will destroy them with the living scripture, throw Satan from his throne and destroy the throne; also his majesty will be destroyed. Then the Lord will say "amen" and open the heaven as well. The Lord will rule in his heavens from everlasting to everlasting.

Interpretation of the Contents of this Song

What is a Doukhobor but one who represents John, Moses, and Christ? Whatever is said about Christ's assuming the flesh is fulfilled in that Doukhobor. Divinity lives in the flesh, which is the Word of God, through which God speaks and articulates great wisdom. Though the flesh is tortured on earth by humanity, the inner being will go into a better body through the transformation at death and will be saved thereby. For it is necessary that this high being, yes, this Son of God, Jesus Christ, take the fleshly form and also become a human being, for God speaks with a human mouth. The realm of the east and the Mountain of Zion are inspirational terms describing the Doukhobor community. The middle of the mountain means the divine human among them, fortified with the greatest wisdom and power. The spring of joyous salvation for His believers emanates from Him, whose virtues are covered with good deeds and are magnificently adorned with gleaming white. These virtues broadcast their glory among worldly people, whose existence will come about. They, however, will step forth forcefully with terror for humanity. The head of the Doukhobors will then be the only honoured King. Everyone will assemble around Him. However, before this happens, distress and want will cease for the Doukhobors, but they will sing and will overpower the world with their hand. The battle will be great but they will be victorious and will ascend the throne of the highest honour from one transformation to another.

Prayers Recited in Assemblies

1. To whom shall I go from You, my Lord, to whom shall I flee from your countenance? Were I to go up to heaven, You are there; were I to go down to Hell, You are there. Were I to take the wings of the rising sun and let myself down on the furthest ocean, so there Your hand will teach me and Your right hand will hold me. To whom do I go, to whom do I turn, eternal Life, except only to You, my Creator? Where do I take refuge and with whom else do I find solace, joy, refuge, and rest for my soul? To whom do I go from You, my God? You are the word of eternal life, which is in me. You are the source of my life, the giver of all good things. My soul thirsts for You, my heart thirsts for You, God of my life. Let us be refreshed by Your holy name, by You, our sweet Lord Jesus. My soul, my heart are wounded. Nothing in my whole life would be more beautiful for me than Your most sublime spirit. Your words will be sweeter than honey to my gums and my mouth; Your vindication Lord, will be of more value to me than gold and precious gems and much sweeter than honey.

2. To whom shall I cry out, whom shall I love as I do You, my Lord, my God? For You are my life. You are my salvation, my honour and glory. You are my wealth, You are my eternal protector, You are my hope and expectation. You are my joy, my eternal rest. Should I love a frivolous, an unknown, a perverse, a perishable, a false object more than You, my true life? You are my life, my salvation. On You alone I pin my hope, all my trust, all my wishes, all my supplication.

Lord, I seek You with my whole heart, my whole soul and all my strength. From the depths of my heart I call to You. My heart empties itself to You alone. I will be totally in You and You in me. I call out and recognize in me the one, genuine God whom You have sent, Jesus Christ. In your light we recognize the light of the grace of your Holy Spirit.

These Doukhobors live on the right bank of the Molochnaia on the Tashchenak ravine, on the Molochnaia Estuary and on the Sea of Azov, in ten villages that are completely and exclusively inhabited by them:

1. Bogdanovka
2. Troitskaia
3. Terpenie
4. Spaskaia
5. Tambovka
6. Radivonovka
7. Sasekelovka
8. Efrimovka
9. Garela
10. Gamilovka

There are 3,820 souls: 1,894 males, 1,926 females.
Within this total are the following:

	Males	Females
Nobility	1	4
Discharged soldiers	11	7
Citizens and guild members	83	95
Apanage peasants	62	60
Odnodvortsy[3]	1,248	1,282
Ukrainian Cossacks	23	25
Military colonists	43	35
Economic and other state peasants	428	418
Total	1,894	1,926

3 Odnodvortsy, or "one-homesteaders," were a class of free peasant landowners. By the late eighteenth century, their distinct legal rights were rapidly eroding. See Jerome Blum, *Lord and Peasant in Russia from the Ninth to the Nineteenth Century* (Princeton: Princeton University Press, 1961), 478–9.

III. Survey of the History and Conditions of the German Colonists Settled on the Right Bank of the Molochnaia River

SAOR 89-1-375. Undated [probably 1836]

According to Herodotus, the colonists on the right bank of the Molochnaia River and in Edikuren Valley have settled where nomadic Scythians once lived. The colonists emigrated from various regions of Germany and other places, specifically from Nassau, Swabia, Wuerttemberg, Zweibruecken, Darmstadt, Alsace, Prussia, Brandenburg, Saxony, Pomerania, Mecklenburg-Schwerin, Mecklenburg-Strelitz, Mainz, Baden, Bavaria, and regions of Poland.

In part they were gathered by commissioners Zuegler and Escher, who were sent abroad by the Russian government between 1803 and 1809 to recruit immigrants. They were also recruited through missions and consuls. A few emigrated on their own later. Forty-two of the 100 families from Poland settled near St. Petersburg in 1809, found it very difficult to clear forests there, and resettled to the Molochnaia.

Overcrowding made these colonists receptive to leaving their fatherland. It was impossible for them to support themselves in Germany because of land shortages, and there was also the unceasing devastation of war and conscription, of which they are free in Russia. Most of them arrived at their site during the years 1804 to 1806. In accordance with the general rules for colonists, they received money for the journey, for sustenance, and for the establishment of their households until they harvested their first crops. Repayment of these loans was extended for several years because of crop failure and illness. At the present time, they live in twenty-two villages within a radius of 100 verstas bordering on the colonies of the Mennonites on the Molochnaia and the Crown village of Bolshoi Tokmak in the south, the Doukhobors and the Crown village of Mikhailovka in the west, the estate of General Popov in the north, and the town of Orekhov in the east (see Table A).

The entire area assigned to the colonists consists of 67,131 desiatinas of usable and unusable land. Each family is assigned sixty desiatinas, with a tax of twenty kopeks for every desiatina. In addition, the Crown has further determined that young colonists be settled on 19,000 desiatinas in the Tashchenak ravine (see Table B).

The German settlers' land is convenient and fruitful. Most of it is black humus soil, sandy only in some spots along the Molochnaia, with brushwood on the slopes. There are only a few saline deposits in the villages Gruenthal, Friedrichsfeld, and Reichenfeldt, but the water is wholesome everywhere, for humans as well as for livestock.

Frequent outbreaks of the cattle plague [*rinderpest*] can without doubt be ascribed to the Great Drought [of 1833–4], because the livestock ingested a great deal of dust and suffered from a shortage of drinking water. The main contagion was from external livestock travelling through with the *chumaks* [wagoners and traders]. Ignorance often played a not insignificant part in the loss. Instead of isolating the sick livestock and burying the cadavers, the disease was given free reign due to superstition, ostensibly in order to avoid acting arrogantly in defiance of God's judgment, but actually out of thoughtlessness.

All of the villages have quite pleasant sites but those settled on the steppe in Edikuren Valley have a greater advantage and are more suited for agriculture than the nine villages on the banks of the Molochnaia. By comparing present circumstances with those of the past, it can definitely be assumed that this district will achieve considerable significance. The settlers arrived on the site generally poor and lacking knowledge of agriculture, unaccustomed to the frugality, orderliness, and effort of good household management. In spite of this they have so far overcome all difficulties that stood in the way of an orderly life on the land. Having degenerated in their moral impulses during their lives as soldiers – or through the evil examples of foreign armies in their fatherland – many could not give up their habits easily, and it should not be surprising that even now occasional incidents occur that indicate coarseness (see Table C). Accumulated from all the nooks and crannies of Germany and other states, they lack the spirit of unity and mutual cooperation necessary for success. Given the unhappy absence of spirit in their church practices, it was simply and only the fatherly vigilance of the Guardianship Committee that led them to the well-being that was their goal.

In spite of these unfavourable circumstances, their conditions have improved markedly in physical respects and, to some extent, also in moral respects. Morality has been promoted by the establishment of a second parish in the Lutheran congregation and the appointment of a genuinely spiritual leader. His truly spiritual sermons do not fail to make an impression, and his exemplary life gradually awakens a zeal for imitation. Believers of the reformed confession also belong to this congregation, and this is a preferable situation to that of the Catholics.

More attention is also now bestowed on the schools than in the past (see Table E). The late Acting State Counsellor Contenius bequeathed a fund of 12,000 rubles from his estate to train local school teachers, and this goal can be achieved soon by the establishment of an already-planned central school.

Thus the second generation, accustomed to the climate and to diligence, having the advantage of better religious instruction, and already more closely integrated through family relationships, will be able to progress much more vigorously to ultimate well-being under continuing guardianship.

The agricultural establishments of the settlers have improved more than their good habits. The proximity of the Mennonite community and the necessity of close communication laid the foundation for current conditions. The Germans lived with the Mennonites until they were settled and this provided guidance for the settlers and acquainted them with thrifty household management and purposeful field cultivation. More importantly, however, poverty forced them into several years of employment with the Mennonites which accustomed them to sound arrangements.

Field Cultivation

The land of the German settlers is particularly suitable for field cultivation. With the exception of the hills along the Molochnaia, the land is flat and even. Most of it has black humus soil to the depth of one faden [1.83 meters] and produces a ten- to twelve-fold grain harvest in fruitful years. Grass grows luxuriantly and the grasses consist mostly of cereal grasses or "Guackel" (*Tritieum repens*). Cultivated fields and hay meadows have been divided among the owners of 60-desiatina fullholdings. However, their fields are not cultivated on the four-field system but according to local custom, and they also do not fertilize their cultivated fields. Therefore, because yields are based on the maintenance of the land's fertility, much depends on the succession of grains, or the so-called rotation. In addition, correct knowledge of the soil is necessary, and also the time and extent to which the soil must be worked to put it into a condition to grow the largest number of agricultural plants and also to produce those of the best quality. However, most of these people possess no knowledge of this. Also, since they still annually break new soil or plough virgin meadowland, they have not found it necessary to arrange regulated field cultivation, and such a practice can only be expected of them when finally the limitation of their land due to increased population forces them into it.

Their field implements consist mainly of one plough and one harrow, manufactured by themselves according to the Mennonite type and pattern. Some have purchased these implements. The field hoe and the roller have not yet been introduced here. They build their grain and hay wagons like the Mennonite wagons. They mow and treat the grain with scythes, as is done by the Mennonites. They thresh grain mostly by hand, but also by treading it out with horses. No threshing machines have yet appeared. They have also not yet introduced systematic cultivation of potatoes. Several settlers pursued tobacco cultivation particularly strongly before 1833, the year of crop failure, and it found a good market, but the years of crop failure destroyed its importance (see Table D).

Livestock Breeding

The German settlers' horses, kept only to work agricultural establishments, are of quite a good breed but otherwise nothing special. Their cattle are a mixture of Ukrainian and Frisian breeds but there are also quite a few pure Ukrainian cows, whose production of butter and cheese is very low (see Table F). Admittedly, the housekeeper's lack of knowledge in preparing cheese and butter can be blamed not a little for this.

The Germans prefer sheep for commercial breeding (see Table F). They began Spanish sheep breeding with a gift from the Crown of twelve pairs of sheep, and they have already developed an important community sheep farm from this breeding stock, using it to improve the common local sheep. Situated at Gruenthal Village and managed by a community society, it provides breeding rams for all private herds in their villages. The income from this community sheep farm flows into the general treasury administered by the District Office (Table H indicates its extent).

Tree Planting

The late Acting State Counsellor Contenius established tree planting on a firm foundation in the district by laying out a community tree plantation at the village Alt-Nassau. He did this in order to arouse an inclination towards tree planting among the settlers. Tree plantations prevent the problems of bringing trees from distant regions, since they suffer and are often damaged during transport, or develop diseases and do not make progress. Contenius also wanted to show that the soil on the settlement's land is suitable for growing trees.

Tree planting can make no progress in the countryside if the man of the land sees no examples of larger plantations of trees before his eyes to challenge him, and if he does not learn how to plant trees. For this purpose, Contenius founded a thirty-two-desiatina community plantation in 1810, and a trained gardener was hired for a specific wage from the community treasury. The plantation started with nurseries from which the colonists were to obtain the trees they needed, so that every young tree to be planted in the district could be taken from this plantation. Every owner of sixty desiatinas of land was obligated to work in this plantation for two days a year to give him the opportunity to receive practical instruction in the very simple art of raising a tree from seed, or of improving it and transplanting it. The plantation has completely achieved its purpose. The settlers saw and learned how trees must be raised, improved, and transplanted, and soon they had a will and desire to see trees around their houses, so that now one already finds that many settlers have beautiful, fine-looking orchards with various types of fruit trees bearing fruit. Smaller orchards or individual trees, all growing well, are generally found at every house. They all owe their existence to the community plantation. The plantation itself is in a thriving condition (see Table J). The colonist garden society has the responsibility of supervising and carrying out planting, and especially of maintaining the mother plantation at Alt-Nassau.

Viticulture

Even though wine is the favourite drink of the colonists, they have little inclination to plant vines and pay little attention to the small beginnings of viticulture, even though the hills found along the Molochnaia are very suitable for vine planting and growth if sites are correctly chosen and subsequently treated (see Table K).

Bee-keeping and Fishing

Bee-keeping is of little importance, with 386 beehives in the whole district, and fishing deserves even less notice.

Character, Customs, and Practices

The specific character traits of the settlers cannot be depicted precisely, since the settlers come from such varied regions of Germany. One finds that they are good-natured, decent, and honourable, but on the whole they evidence no enduring perseverance. They make decisions quickly, but they also quickly and negligently abandon them. They are inclined to be disputatious, which often results in great coarseness. The immoral examples of the old immigrant colonists and the ignorance of the school teachers could not help but be detrimental for the second generation. The results would have been even more detrimental if the eye of the Guardianship Committee had not watched over them and been concerned for their well-being through its philanthropic but stern guidance, and if poverty had not forced them to seek service among people where they saw and heard better habits for a number of years and eventually experienced it themselves.

Quite a few of the settlers distinguish themselves for their exemplary establishments, and their orderliness and cleanliness. The style and arrangement of their buildings is comfortable and orderly, and living rooms are neatly furnished. Convinced of the real bliss of peaceful household management, greater gentleness and decorum now reign in their domestic concerns.

Field cultivation and livestock raising are the main supports for their livelihood, though many of them also occupy themselves with trades and handicrafts. Potteries have particular value in manufacturing ordinary, glazed earthenware dishes for local use. Builders and carpenters still lack skill and sense of proportion in order to excel. Shoemaking and tailoring are at a better level. Fabric manufacturers and weavers only make cloth and linen for household needs. Most of the implements for field cultivation are purchased from the Mennonites. About 100 persons work as weavers, cloth shearers, fullers, pressers, spinners, and other similar jobs in the Mennonite cloth factory in Halbstadt.

Houses are generally constructed of clay, but by now newly built ones are arranged more comfortably and in better taste (see Table P). The settlers show more variety in clothing. The more well-to-do settlers, especially those of the feminine gender, like to differentiate themselves from the poorer ones with their clothing. Because of a defective upbringing, they betray an inclination to luxury, and a tendency to exceed the balance for their class and income, by wearing bright colours and showy finery. The feminine handicrafts, such as spinning, sewing, and knitting are still at a very low level, no less than the art of preparing food, since in addition to the usual gruel, only a few kinds of vegetables and potatoes are commonly eaten.

The language in use is a corrupt High German, with a mixture of various dialects among which the Swabian has predominance. Its idiosyncrasy is that almost constantly "d" is mixed up with "t," "g" with "k," and "b" with "w." Even when reading, they use *kunk* instead of "genug," and *Torf* instead of "Dorf." Also, their spoken language is made very unpleasant by the customary rough endings consisting of curses and oaths. Inclinations and characteristic tendencies to riotous shows and festivals are essential parts of weddings and christenings. Their immorality is displayed most wickedly at the annual festival called *Kermis*, when such conduct is excused as a permissible pleasure. The results are not less damaging to their morality than the frolics of colonists in the free states of North America.

Otherwise, the settlers are hard-working and diligent people. Their health is firm and enduring, evidence that the climate has a beneficial influence on them. In general, their economic position is good and quite a few of them are wealthy. On the whole, only a conciliatory and communal spirit are lacking among them for exemplary behaviour and actions. Even though many settlers have better insights and want to become useful to the community, they still lack the courage and determination to create a foundation and to establish that desired objective, namely the well-being of the community.

The German settlers in the Molochnaia are morally much superior, and their economic arrangements are better, than those of the settlers in the Crimea and around Odessa. On the average, the Molochnaia settlers are more diligent and behave in a more orderly fashion, not being as addicted to drink. They are better and more respectably dressed, and their houses are bigger and better arranged. Also there are more agricultural side buildings, wagons, and implements for cultivation, showing that they are better agriculturists, and their livestock is better and is also maintained better.

The German settlers only lack community spirit and religion – true heartfelt religion – because they have not been fortunate enough to receive purposeful religious education in their youth. Experience teaches us, and the history of all times demonstrates, that the well-being of a community, of a people, or a state is founded securely and exists and blossoms simply and only on religion.

Table A Families and Population

	Village	Families With Land	Males	Females	Total Pop. With Land	Families Without Land	Males	Females	Total Pop. Without Land
1.	Molochnaia	45	196	169	365	70	244	211	455
2.	Hoffenthal	20	94	95	189	7	13	15	28
3.	Alt-Nassau	40	175	157	332	11	34	35	69
4.	Weinau	36	154	137	291	4	14	11	25
5.	Durlach	12	50	40	90	2	7	9	16
6.	Karlsruh	36	165	155	320	8	25	26	51
7.	Kronsfeldt	31	144	127	271	0	0	0	0
8.	Reichenfeld	41	185	161	346	12	46	37	83
9.	Kostheim	35	124	113	237	1	1	1	2
10.	Leitershausen	48	197	181	378	3	5	7	12
11.	Wafsrau	26	126	112	238	8	14	21	35
12.	Neu-Nasau*	28	111	104	215	2	6	4	10
13.	Hochstadt	39	166	155	321	11	26	26	52
14.	Friedrichsfeld	63	267	231	498	21	63	39	102
15.	Grunthal	10	39	41	80	3	12	7	19
16.	Rosenthal	31	153	130	283	4	14	10	24
17.	Neu-Monthal	28	122	104	226	6	19	16	35
18.	Heidelberg	92	308	330	638	13	34	34	68
19.	Blumenthal	48	191	187	378	7	23	21	44
20.	Tiefenbrun	29	112	95	207	5	13	17	30
21.	Waldorf	27	100	102	202	7	18	22	40
22.	Alt-Monthal	31	134	133	267	3	13	8	21
	Totals:	796	3,313	3,059	6,372	208	644	577	1,221

* Incorrectly listed as Neu-Wafsrau in the original.

Table B Land Distribution

	Useful Land		Not Useful Land		Total	
	Desiatinas	Sazhens	Desiatinas	Sazhens	Desiatinas	Sazhens
Total Settlement Land	61,712	1,533	5,418	2,013	67,161	1,146
Allocated to Individuals					50,175	2,000
Allocated per Family					60	
Community Land					8,856	893
Church Land					360	
Land Reserved for New Immigrants	2,320	1,040			2,320	1,040
Land Reserved for Children of Original Settlers					19,000	
Land Located in Melitopol Uezd				9,527		

Table C Community Statistics for 1835

Persons over 80 years of age:	4
Blind persons:	2
Deaf persons:	3
Insane persons:	1
Incurably ill persons:	6
Children born illegitimately:	0
Persons who contracted smallpox:	147
Sudden deaths:	0
Drownings:	0
Violent deaths:	0
Suicides:	1
Persons found guilty of arson:	0
Persons subjected to investigations and law suits:	8
Persons convicted of burglary:	3
Persons convicted of counterfeiting:	1
Persons found guilty of other crimes:	15
Persons exiled to Siberia for crimes:	2

Table D Crops Sown and Harvested

Winter Crops:	Chetverts Sown	Chetverts Harvested
Wheat	¾	2
Rye	810–5/8	10,245–1/8
Summer Crops:		
Wheat	1,469–1/4	8,446–5/8
Rye	1–3/4	0
Buckwheat	15	7–1/2
Oats	964–7/8	3,784–1/2
Barley	872–5/8	7,100–5/8
Millet	89–1/4	656–5/8
Potatoes	670–5/8	2,405–5/8
Peas	18–3/4	55–7/8
Beans	34–1/8	23–5/8
Flax	61–1/8	110–3/4
Hemp	17–1/4	20
Total	5,025	32,858–7/8
Average of 796 fullholders	6.31	41.28
Yield from rye, wheat, and barley	1.00	7.18
Hay harvested in stacks [Birken]		643–1/2

Table E: Number of Schools and Students

			Students		
		Schools	Males	Females	Total
1.	Molochnaia	2	65	54	119
2.	Hoffenthal	1	25	21	46
3.	Alt-Nassau	1	45	37	82
4.	Weinau	1	36	42	78
5.	Durlach	1	12	6	18
6.	Karlsruh	1	38	38	76

		Schools	Students		
			Males	Females	Total
7.	Kronsfeldt	1	29	27	56
8.	Reichenfeld	1	43	29	72
9.	Kostheim	1	26	21	47
10.	Leitershausen	1	31	34	65
11.	Wafsrau [?]	1	40	21	61
12.	Neu-Nasau	1	25	22	47
13.	Hochstadt	1	46	35	81
14.	Friedrichsfeld	1	54	52	106
15.	Grunthal	1	10	9	19
16.	Rosenthal	1	34	28	62
17.	Neu-Monthal	1	35	19	54
18.	Heidelberg	1	60	55	115
19.	Blumenthal	1	30	33	63
20.	Tiefenbrun	1	22	18	40
21.	Waldorf	1	17	7	24
22.	Alt-Monthal	1	32	28	60
	Total	23	755	636	1,391

Table F Livestock

		Number	Breed
Cattle:	Total	4,733	
	Average per Household	5.95	
	Stud Bulls	36	8 Russian 28 Freisland
Horses:	Total	3,455	
	Average per Household	4.34	
	Stud Stallions	25	6 Russian 19 Mennonite
Sheep (Merino and Refined):	Community Fold	6,320	
	Privately Owned	39,843	
Pigs:		1,327	

Table G Community Income and Expenses*

Revenue					Expenses					
	Per Unit		Total							
	Rubles	Kopeks	Rubles	Kopeks			Rubles	Kopeks	Rubles	Kopeks
79 horses	57	40	4,534		**Taxes**	Local	31,958	43		
173 cattle	40	72	7,126			Crown	4,115			
2162 sheep	7	16.37	15,488		**Subtotal of taxes**				36,071	43
5303 1/5 puds wool	19	54.85	103,669	47	**Salaries**	Mayors and Secretaries	1,821			
227 puds butter	8	72.82	1,981	30		Office Supplies	317	60		
3 1/2 puds cheese	10	57	37			Clergy	1,700			
9 puds smoked ham	5	23	47			Teachers	4,047			
199 trees		58.54	116	50		Shepherds	8,916			
Grain			26,261	7		Pastoral Expenses	528	25		
Hay			658	72		Organists	125			
Potatoes			454	60	**Accident and fire insurance**		441	50		
Honey			199		**Subtotal of salaries and insurance**				17,896	35
Fruit			552	60	**Total Expenses**				**53,967**	**78**
Total			**161,125**	**26**	**Surplus [income less expenses]**				**107,157**	**48**

* This table is labeled "Table H" in the original. See introduction.

Table H Status of the Community Treasury

	Subtotal		Total	
	Rubles	Kopeks	Rubles	Kopeks
Balance on 1 January 1835	9,484	49		
Income in 1835	47,341	20		
Subtotal			56,825	69
Expenses in 1835			31,791	80
Balance			25,033	86
Miscellaneous payments to the community treasury for debts incurred in the years 1830–4			27,179	65
Total on 1 January 1836			**52,213**	**51**

Table J Trees

In community plantations	Fruit-bearing fruit trees	4,681	
	Young, non-bearing fruit trees	15,649	
	Total		20,330
In private orchards	Apple	14,508	
	Pear	7,773	
	Plum	9,003	
	Cherry	24,315	
	Peach	202	
	Apricot	4,592	
	Total		60,393
Mulberry Trees	In the three mulberry plantations	3,459	
	In private gardens	3,681	
	Total		7,140
Forest trees			20,433
Total			108,296

Table K Viticulture

Vineyards	4
Land employed as vineyards in desiatinas	10–1/2
Vines	2,236
Vines planted in 1835	1,040
Families with vines planted in the four vineyards	90
Families that have produced wine in the past year	0

Table L Trades

Dyers	1
Oil mills	5
Flax Looms	158

Table M Craftsmen

Wagonmakers	8
Carpenters	13
Bricklayers	9
Blacksmiths	23
Nailmakers	1
Locksmiths	0
Knifemakers	1
Hoopers	3
Potters	20
Tanners	0
Joiners	20
Glazers	2
Lathers	3
Soapmakers	1
Shoemakers	44
Tailors	22
Clothmakers	4
Linenweavers	35

Ropemakers	1
Hatmakers	2
Millers	11
Bakers	3
Butchers	4
Bookbinders	2
Total	**232**

Table N Status of the Orphans' Fund

	Rubles	Kopeks	Rubles	Kopeks
Capital and interest on 1 January 1835	25,141	75		
Income in 1835	8,841	91		
Subtotal			33,983	66
Expenses:				
Paid to adult orphans	955	32		
Paid for the maintenance of orphans	330	55		
Subtotal			1,285	87
Capital with interest on 1 January 1836			32,697	79

Table O: Religion

Congregations		3
Members	1st Congregation	2,766
	2nd Congregation	2,963
	3rd Congregation	1,864
Confessions	Roman Catholic	1,864
	Evangelical	5,729
Clergy	Catholic Priests	1
	Catholic Deacons	0
	Evangelical Priests	2
	Evangelical Deacons	1
	Total	4*

* Total in original reads "3."

Table P Buildings

Public Buildings		
Churches		1
Bathhouses		2
Pastorages		3
Schools		26
Residences for district inspectors and secretaries		4
Sheep barns		1
Residences for community gardeners/foresters		2
Silkworm barns		1
Community mills		3
Private Buildings		
Houses:	Quarried stone	9
	Brick	1
	Milled wood	0
	Mud bricks	221
	Timber	79
	Clay	485
Total		795
Watermills		0
Windmills		15
Gristmills		0
Earthmills		0
Total		15

Table Q Births, Deaths, and Marriages

		Births minus deaths
In 1835		
Births	378	
Deaths	144	234
Marriages	82	
In the last 10 years		
Births	2,583	
Deaths	1,658	925

Table R: Community Grain Reserves

		Chetverts	Chetverik	Garnets
Grain warehouses	19			
Additional warehouses needed	5			
Grain deposited in 1835		3,357	6	0
Grain given out in 1835		1,586	5	6–3/4
Grain reserves remaining		1,771		1–1/4
Grain reserves required based on 2 chetverts per revision soul*		14,780		
Grain reserve shortfall		13,008	7	6–3/4

* This amount was mandated by law.

IV. The Molokan Sect in the Molochnaia

SAOR 89-1-548. Undated [after 1833].

These people are called Molokans because they do not observe fasts and they partake of milk and meat on all days of the week. They call themselves true spiritual Christians. They were banished from Tambov and Vladimir guberniias in 1823 and settled in Melitopol District between the lands of the Nogais and the Molochnaia Mennonites.

At present three villages belong to this sect, which includes many Don Cossacks. Some of these Cossacks served the fatherland for a long time and wear the honours of their service openly, including those who were officers. The sect's origins are unknown even to its members. They only know that they originated long before the Doukhobors and that the Doukhobors originated when they separated from the Molokans under the influence of an overly excited leader, a Molokan named Sava Kapustin.

The first Molokan families that were banished to the Melitopol District arrived in 1822, and were supposed to be settled among the Doukhobors on the Molochnaia. However, the Doukhobors did not accept them because their religious views diverged too much. Molokan principles agree more with the main points of faith of the Russian Orthodox Church. Holy scripture is the primary guideline for their beliefs. It is the Word of God revealed for humanity. They recognize Christ, the Son of God, as God revealed in the flesh, who died on the cross for the sins of the world. They believe in the continuing existence of their own being after death, and not, as do the Doukhobors, in a migration of the soul. However, the Molokans and Doukhobors both give baptism and communion a simple, spiritual meaning, not practising them through outer signs and symbols. They reject the depiction and honouring of saints, as well as the remaining ceremonies of the Orthodox Church.

They have no priesthood and no institution for the education of their young people.

Otherwise, the Molokans have nothing in common with the Doukhobors, are not secretive as the Doukhobors are, do not live under any religious coercion from elders or superiors, and speak freely and openly about religious matters among themselves and to strangers. The majority seem to love goodness and want to follow the Word of God, but they have no comprehension of the actual spirit of Christianity. Instead they live by the rules of law, and divide and separate over their interpretation of and attitude towards several items unnecessary for salvation, forgetting *love*, which is the fulfilment of the law and unifies everyone and is bound up with everyone who loves Christ.

Some Molokans observe Sunday so strictly that they are not even permitted to make a fire. Some eat pork, others enjoy brandy, and others enjoy certain types of fish, etc., while all this is forbidden and sinful for others. Because of this, they have three, four, or five separate assemblies whose members do not consider the members of the other assemblies as brothers in faith. This saddens the better people among them.

Some of the Don Cossacks of the Vladimir Molokan assembly are troubled that they cannot maintain order and unity among their members since, contrary to their will, many individuals have been settled in their midst who did not want to stay in the Orthodox Church or who could no longer be tolerated by it. It may also be that there are quite different attitudes to many points, so that it is not surprising that they are divided among themselves and that among them there are currency counterfeiters, forgers of passes, and many similar criminals, who had to leave the Orthodox Church. Assuming a pretence of piety to show that they were better than others, these criminals were banished among the Molokans. In addition to this, one section of the Molokans holds the religious principle that their three villages are the free cities of Numbers, chapter 36, verse 6, where every criminal and vagabond is accepted and finds shelter. They believe that it would therefore be sinful for them to hand such criminals over to the courts.

Field cultivation and livestock breeding are the Molokans' principal means of support. On the whole they are very hard-working and industrious and, in an economic sense, they are prospering very well. They have constructed and arranged their household buildings quite well, but, except for the Don Cossacks, their lifestyle is very simple and dirty. They are cunning, deceitful, and seldom keep their word.

The commandments of Moses are closer to Molokan hearts than the clearest pronouncements of Christ and his apostles, and instead of enlightening the old, literal phantoms with the new spirit of the gospels, they stress the validity of the letter more than the spirit, and the shadow more than the being itself, so that they are sanctimonious and often seem to hold foolish beliefs.

The Molokans strip Christianity naked of its order and customs and dress it anew with patched leftovers of old Judaism mixed with their own opinions. They dream about and live in expectation of a genuine, visible thousand-year kingdom of peace on earth, and they read about, and investigate with the greatest eagerness, all reports that appear to indicate this or relate to it. They expect an Antichrist. The Molokans possess the writings of Stilling, read them industriously, and especially look for those references describing a thousand-year kingdom of peace. These references flatter their expectations.[1]

In 1833, a certain Terenty Belogurov, impatiently expecting that the thousand-year kingdom would dawn imminently, was moved to see himself as specially designated and felt called upon to preach repentance to the Molokans.[2] He came forward suddenly and, in accordance with prophetic proclamations, introduced himself as the Prophet Elijah sent by God before the dawning of the thousand-year kingdom. Terenty preached repentance and conversion, and required the Molokans to believe that the thousand-year kingdom would definitely begin after two and a half days had elapsed. He advised the Molokans not to work or conduct their business, but to occupy themselves entirely with singing and praying. He determined the time when he would ascend into heaven, alive and before their eyes. Terenty's ascension day dawned. He stepped onto a wagon, but when he intended to ascend he crashed to the ground onto the large number of Molokans standing around him and hurt a woman.

---

1 A reference to Johann Hienrich Jung-Stilling (1740–1817), the prominent German pietist writer. Stilling's millenialist writings had an important influence on the chiliastic Mennonite group, led by Claas Epp, that founded a colony in Turkmenistan on the Aral Sea in the 1880s.

2 Belogurov's arrival in the Molochnaia is dated at 1836 by Sergei Zhuk, *Russia's Lost Reformation: Peasants, Millennialism, and Radical Sects in Southern Russia and Ukraine, 1830–1917* (Baltimore: Johns Hopkins University Press, 2004), 114.

Molokans with different beliefs immediately took him away and reported the incident to the courts. Until they delivered him to the courts, Terenty remained steadfast in the assertion that he really was the God-sent prophet Elijah and that the chains hanging on his feet were his most certain proof. On his return from prison, Terenty stuck with his assertion that the thousand-year kingdom must soon appear, but during his incarceration he had soon forgotten that he was Elijah.

Terenty died a natural death, but he left a considerable number of followers who remained assembled day and night, singing and praying. Several of these became inspired and expressed themselves in their assemblies by means of strange and unusual behaviour. They stamped their feet, stretched their limbs out in a stiff and cramped manner, and snorted through their noses expelling a mass of filth, especially when someone who did not belong among them appeared in their assembly. They held their possessions in common.

These degenerate ecstasies could not be maintained for long. These Molokans became disunited and, with permission from the authorities, a portion of them emigrated to Georgia in the hope of waiting there for the thousand-year kingdom. The portion of this sect that stayed here gradually became quieter and smaller, so that one never hears anything unusual about them anymore.[3]

Confession of Faith and Description of Practices

The better members of this sect, the Don Cossacks and those from Vladimir guberniia, claim the following confession of faith and practices:

We believe with our hearts and without doubt in the Word of God, which was spoken by the prophets in antiquity and by the saviour of the world, Jesus Christ, and by the apostles as it is written in the Holy Bible. We accept with reverence all of the books of the Bible unaltered, and teach its contents with all our strength for our genuine salvation, because we accept it as the Word of God and because we base ourselves upon it. We believe and confess with our hearts that God is one being but is indivisible as Father, Son, and Holy Ghost. This Trinity is not dependent upon anyone, not begotten by anyone, but exists of Himself,

3 This may refer to the Molokans who voluntarily joined in the Doukhobor exodus to the Caucasus between 1840 and 1844. If so, it would date the document later than the 1840 date assigned by the Odessa Regional State Archive cataloguers.

and is the source of all created beings. God is eternal, inscrutable, and an invisible spirit. God dwells in an inaccessible world, knows everything, sees everything, rules everything; everything is permeated by Him. He is comparable with no one and with nothing.

We believe further that this Trinity has created from one of God's words the heavens and the earth, and also all spirits without flesh, and in the same way, has created the visible world with all its creations. We believe that everything created by God was good and perfect, but several spirits became proud in their perfections, misused them and, for this, were thrown from heaven by God and have become satans and devils. The others remained perfectly submissive to their creator and removed themselves into bliss for eternity, so that these now cannot sin and are called cherubim, archangels, and angels.

We believe that the first human being, Adam, was created in the image of God, but this image and exact likeness did not consist in what was created out of the womb of the earth, but in his immortal soul, which received its existence from the inscrutable holiness of God. This created, immortal soul in Adam had material reason and purity, gifted with the clear perception of God. Adam did not know evil; he had a holy freedom which strove to God, the only Creator.

This first human being, Adam, caught by the cunning of the devil in the guise of a snake, misused his freedom and, violating the command of his creator not to touch the tree of knowledge of good and evil, ate the forbidden fruit and fell. Adam destroyed his image and exact likeness of God, was deprived of his blessed condition, and was cast out of the beautiful paradise onto the cursed earth where, for his sin, he was sentenced to work, to suffer illness, to live in misery and distress, and eventually to die. However, God, the Trinity, saw Adam's poverty and his tears over the loss of his blessed state, took pity on him, and promised to send him a saviour out of the seed of his wife who would crush underfoot the head of his seducer, the snake, and restore to him his lost image of God. The saviour was none other than the only born Son of God, who, after the fulfilment of the time prescribed by God, left heaven and came to earth, received the Holy Spirit unfathomable for us, was born of the virgin Mary, became God incarnate, dwelt visibly among the occupants of the earth, received baptism from the hand of His predecessor at the predetermined time, and then assumed His position as a teacher.

The salvation of fallen humanity and the pure truth of Jesus' teaching were sealed by His sufferings and by the spilling of His holy blood on the cross for the redemption of the world. Eventually He tasted death. Arisen on the third day, He appeared to His apostles for forty days and taught them the heavenly truth of salvation. Then, in view of all of His apostles, He ascended into heaven, and there sat down at the right hand of God for the inexpressible honour of our salvation.

Soon after His ascension to heaven, Jesus sent His apostles the Holy Spirit, which goes forth from the Father, and with this He founded and confirmed His holy church, which is an assembly of true believers. This church of our Christ is enlightened with His Holy Spirit. When the end of the world nears, Jesus Christ will return to us in all His glory with all those who are holy and with the angels, and with His strength will awaken the dead who have died since the beginning. He will transform those who are still living and turn them into incorruptible beings, then will justify the holy and those who believe the truth, sanctify them, and lead them into the heavenly kingdom of His father until eternity. The unbelievers and the sinners forgotten by God will be judged and cast down into hell and eternal torment.

We believe without doubt that the Word of God contained in the Holy Bible is also actually holy, so we accept with our hearts the laws of God, which are written in the ten commandments and were given by God to the prophet Moses on Mount Sinai. We appeal to the saviour of the world for help and we endeavour to uphold them in all their meanings, such as the following:

1. We consider it to be a terrible sin to love with our whole hearts and cling to something in this world that is not of God. We love and venerate with all our hearts only God in three persons, Father, Son and Holy Ghost, and deify and pray to no one other than Him.

2. We abhor all idolatry, because it is very sinful to pray to any creation other than God or anything similar, neither to anything that is in heaven nor anything that is on the earth or under the earth, because it is written: "You must not make yourself any likeness which has been carved by hand, and are not to raise any image to which you pray." The holy apostle Paul said, "Even though we are in God's image we are not to assume that the deity is the same as the golden, silver, and stone images made by artists by means of human thoughts." According to the declaration of this same apostle, in this way they have confused also the glory of the eternal god with mortal man, birds, four-footed animals, and worms. Because of this we keep no pictures in our homes which are intended to represent the deity and are made by human hands, for we see no salvation in them and consequently do not pray to them. This

has been forbidden by the most high God through the prophets and apostles in many places in holy scripture, threatening painful and eternal punishment. Therefore we look to our Jesus as lord and fulfiller of our beliefs, in whom we have an inestimable example. The holy apostle writes about him: "He is a likeness of the invisible God, the first-born of all creatures, for He has created everything in heaven as well as on earth, the visible and the invisible, the thrones, the rulers; the governments and the principalities are all created through Him and for Him. He is above all and everything exists in Him."

3. We take care not to use the name of God in vain in any form or way, i.e., frivolously, according to habit, without reverence, and not to swear by God, especially in falsehood and deceit. We use the name of God only in our prayers, pleas, and expressions of thanks, and keep with reverence the holy oath to the Tsar, and in other cases where it is required of us to acknowledge the truth and not falsehood. According to the commandment of our Lord Jesus Christ, "Do not swear, whether by heaven or earth, nor any other oath. Your speech be *yes, yes, no, no.* Whatever is beyond this, that is evil." Also, we salute with a kiss the word of our saviour Christ in the holy gospel of John at the beginning of the first chapter.

4. We believe that, in addition to the Saturday of the Old Testament on which God commanded through Moses that the blessed should refrain from all work and occupy themselves with works agreeable to God, Sunday, the day of Christ's resurrection, should also be acknowledged as the New Testament commands, as should the day of resurrection and all other established holidays. On these days, we set aside all work except for what is absolutely necessary and assemble in the house of prayer or in the outer temple to cleanse with many prayers our inner selves, our souls and hearts, of abominable sins. In spirit we pray according to the prophecy of the apostle Paul: "Become full of the spirit and edify yourselves with psalms, songs of praise, and holy songs. Sing and pray to the Lord in your hearts." At this time, we read the Holy Bible and strive to understand God's commandments and the orders which they contain for our own salvation.

5. We honour our parents, father and mother, according to God's commandment and the confirmation of Jesus, son of Sirach: "Whoever honours his father will live longer and whoever obeys the Lord will be a consolation to his mother. Fear God, honour your father as your lord, and serve your parents. Honour your father and mother in deed and word and you will find blessing." According to the order of the holy

apostle Paul: "Children, obey your parents before God, for it must be so. Honour your father and mother; this is the first commandment with the prophecy that 'then things will be well with you and you will live long on earth.'" We honour the tsars and the government in following the prophecy of the same apostle Paul, who says, "Every soul must be subject to higher government, for there is no such government which is not made and established by God, and because of this, he who opposes his government works against God." Also we must be obedient and pay taxes not only out of fear of punishment, but we must act conscientiously, for our rulers are the servants of God and are called to this service. Therefore we become subject, for God, to every human decree, to the tsars as also to the high authorities and the rulers, as if they were sent from Him for the punishment of the criminals and the education of those who do good. For this reason we obey the tsars and their power and gladly subject ourselves to them.

6. We consider it a terrible, fatal sin to kill a human being and to spill innocent blood. There are two types of deathblows. Firstly there is the killing of the flesh, when life is taken from someone with violence, whether with a weapon, with poison, or in any other form, except when there is a war and it is necessary to protect the throne, the Tsar, and the fatherland, and one is obligated by oath to defeat the enemy. In this case, killing cannot be considered a sin. Secondly, there is the killing of the spirit, when someone is led away from the real truth by seductive words and is led astray into sins that bring him to eternal destruction. Also we consider it to be a deathblow when someone insults, persecutes, and hates another, for according to the words of the intercessor Johanni, "everyone who hates his brother is a murderer of that man."

7. We hate and abhor lewdness, adultery, and every sinful impurity according to the evangelical word: "Whoever divorces himself from his wife and marries another, he commits adultery, and if the wife divorces herself from her husband and marries another, she also commits adultery." We understand adultery not only in a physical but in a spiritual sense, when there is contemplation of a woman with the secret wish of desiring her, for as it says in the words of Christ, "whoever looks at a woman in order to desire her, he has already committed adultery in his heart." Also in this sense, an adulterer is someone who treasures this world and its quickly passing pleasures. The apostle James says, "Adulterers and adulteresses! Do you not know that the friendship of the world is enmity to God? And that whoever is a friend of the world becomes God's enemy?" To prevent physical as well as spiritual

adultery, we try to live temperately, guard ourselves against drunkenness and intemperance, and flee from devilish company where people learn to lead a sinful life.

8. Following the eighth commandment of God, we distance ourselves as much as possible from outward theft and embezzlement, highway robbery, plundering along the roads, burglary, theft from fields, and theft of other things. Further, we avoid all violent acts, deception, trickery, and fraud in measurements when buying and selling, because we also consider these to be great sins.

9. We follow the ninth commandment of God: "You shall not speak false witness against your neighbour." We distance ourselves from such reports, gossip, insults, mockery, and flattery, for these, as well as visible deception, stratagems, and unjust accusations, come from the father of all lies, the devil.

10. The tenth commandment prohibits us from desiring anything that belongs to someone else, such as a neighbour's wife, wealth, and everything that a neighbour has. Therefore we strive with all our strength to tame all our passions which war against our spirit, such as envy and hate. We try to calm our own inclinations towards these and blot out the secret cravings of our hearts, because they lead to trespassing against the commandments of God and to eternal damnation.

Finally, we know and believe that these ten commandments of God consist of two main points, namely the love of God and of one's neighbour. The first four refer to the love of God and the last six to the love of one's neighbour. The entire law consists of these two commandments and of the prophets who assure us that Jesus Christ is the Son of God.

We believe and profess that whoever keeps and fulfils these ten commandments of God to their complete extent will be saved. According to the Word of God, "I gave them my commandments and taught them my laws, through which the person who keeps them will live." We also believe that no human being, after the fall of Adam, can fulfil these commandments with his own strength, because we know, as the apostle says, "the law is spiritual and I am flesh, which has been sold to sin, and I myself know not what I do." Therefore, the prophet David professes before God: "As You, Lord, will avenge sin, Lord who then will prevail?" Because of this he pleads: "Do not go to court with Your servant, because before You no living person is just."

We believe that it is necessary for human beings, in order to do good works and to keep the commandments of God, to believe in Jesus Christ, the only begotten Son of God, who came into the world as flesh for our salvation and became man out of love for us lost sinners for whom he revealed the holy gospel, and who suffered for us, tasted death on the cross, arose on the third day, and then ascended to heaven to intercede with God the heavenly Father for us. This faith, which is necessary for our salvation – yes, this true faith – we must seek nowhere but in the Word of God, which can be read in the Holy Bible. We believe that the Word of God engenders faith in us, which makes us capable of receiving God's blessing.

The Sacrament of Baptism

We know that Christ had Himself baptised by John in the Jordan so that He became manifest in Israel, and that He came there to be baptised with water. We also know that the apostles baptised others in water, like Phillip the eunuch at a spring in the field. However, according to the word of John the Baptist, "human beings cannot take anything that is not given to them from heaven." The apostle Paul declares: "Christ has not sent me to baptise but to preach." We believe that baptismal water is not normal water that washes only the body and not the soul, but also living spiritual water, which is the belief in the Trinity, Father, Son, and Holy Ghost, and does not contradict submission to His holy words. As the Saviour says, "anyone who believes in me will have streams of the living water flowing from his body." He was speaking about the spirit, which those who believe in Him must accept. Therefore, we understand the sacrament of baptism not only as a fleshly, but also as a believing, spiritual, cleansing from the sins of our spirit, and the destruction of the old human being and his works in us, in order to be newly clothed. Anyone who is renewed in this way will understand and recognize the image of He who has created him, through His precious, blameless life. Even though we wash off the actual uncleanness of a child after its birth, we do not accept this as any form of baptism. We give a child its name according to the book of prayer out of the Psalms.

The Sacrament of Anointing

We do not accept external anointing, but believe that if we are convinced of Christ in our hearts and keep his commandments we have a spiritual anointing from above, in accordance with the words of John, who was instructed by God: "You have the anointing from Him who is holy and knows everything, and the anointing which you have received from Him stays with you and you do not require that anyone should teach you. Rather, as the anointing teaches you many things, this is truth and not a lie and as it has instructed to you, so remain with it."

The Sacrament of the Lord's Supper

We understand that this sacrament is in accordance with how, on Easter day, the day when the Easter lamb was to be sacrificed, our saviour Jesus Christ sent his disciples to prepare a specially arranged place where they would be able to eat the Easter lamb. When the hour of the Lord's supper arrived, He sat down with his disciples, took the bread, gave thanks, broke it and gave it to them, as He spoke: "This is my body which will be given for you; do this in my memory." It was also the same when he took the cup after the Lord's supper and said, "This is the cup, the New Testament in my blood, which will be spilled for you." The devoured Easter lamb is to the memory of God's miracles and the leading of the Children of Israel out of Egypt, and the bread and the cup are to the memory of the death of Jesus Christ.

The New Testament became the salvation of humanity as the apostle Paul has declared in his Epistles: "What I have given you I have received from the Lord, for the Lord Jesus, in the night when He was betrayed, took the bread, gave thanks and broke it, saying: 'take it, eat it, this is my body which will be broken for you. Do this in my memory, and the same with the cup, for as often as you eat of this bread and drink of this cup, you will proclaim the death of the Lord until He comes.'"

According to the words of the gospels, there is also a spiritual death. Human beings live not by bread alone, but also by every word of God, as Christ the Son of God says about himself, "I am the living bread which has come from heaven, and whoever will eat of this bread will live unto eternity. It is the spirit which gives life, the flesh is of no use. The words which I speak, they are spirit and they are life." According to the words of the apostle Paul, "anyone who has once tasted the material gift and become part of it is of the Holy Ghost and has tasted the benevolent Word of God and the powers of the future world. For that human being, the Word of God is an imperishable seed from which he is born from natural life into a life full of blessing. Without the Word of God, human beings are dark, hungry, thirsty, and spiritually dead."

The Sacrament of Repentance

This sacrament is in accordance with the words of King David when he confessed to God, "I have uncovered my sin to You, and have not hidden my fault; I said: 'I confessed my crimes before God the Lord, and You have taken the debt of sin from me. According to the teachings of the apostle Paul, admit your sins to each other and pray for each other that you become healthy, for the prayer of the righteous is capable of much if it is in earnest.'" For this reason we admit our sins to each other and to the reverent elders and pray for each other to the intercessor Jesus Christ, the Righteous, who is the atonement not only for our sins but for those of the whole world.

The Sacrament of the Priesthood

We acknowledge the person of Christ as bishop and high priest, who also became a priest in eternity for the Hebrews according to the order of Melchizedek, and sits at the right hand of God, that is, the Son of God, according to the declaration of the apostle Paul: "Because we have a great high priest, Jesus, the Son of God who has ascended to heaven, so let us remain with this belief; for we do not have a high priest, who could not have sympathy with our weaknesses, for He is not a man but He tends the holy possessions and the genuine tabernacle which God has raised." And He designates some as apostles, others as prophets, others again as evangelists, priests, and teachers for the fulfilment of holy merit and the building up of the body of Christ, whom the apostle Paul exhorts: "Tend Christ's flock, as you are commanded to do, and see that you are not forced but do it willingly, not for shameful profit but from the bottom of your heart, and do not rule over the people, but become models for the flock. In the same way, the young are to be subject to the elders. Collectively, be subject to each other and hold fast to humility, for God opposes the arrogant but he shows grace to the humble." According to the apostolic declaration mentioned above, we have chosen well-meaning men leading God-fearing lives, who are called elders and occupy themselves with the reading of the Word of God and other of our requirements, and whom we honour spiritually and obey, according to the apostle Peter.

The Sacrament of Marriage

Marriage is concluded in the presence of impartial persons, men and women from our community and the honourable elders who have been chosen for their offices. The bridegroom and bride who wish to marry are both asked if this is their wish, if the groom, and also the bride, have made a commitment to anyone else, and if this commitment has been forced on them by their parents or by someone else, or if they are related to each other. After this, if they give their voluntary agreement, the marriage is concluded. It is written in the book of the prophet Tobias, when Raguel said, "'My child has been given to you, take her according to the law,' and he took the hand of the daughter and put it into the hand of Tobias to be his wife and said, 'take her according to the law of Moses and take her to your father.'"[4]

After they have promised each other to stay in lifelong unseverable marriage, they fulfil the words of the holy apostle Paul in the Epistle, where not he but the Lord decrees "that the wife not separate from the man and the man, when he is joined to a wife, shall seek no separation." He must seek no other if he has separated from his wife. With this, the newlyweds confirm their marriage with the evangelical oath upon which we pray to God, sing psalms, emphasize God's commandments to the newlyweds, exhort them to lead a blameless life in the maintenance of their home, and to honour the elders and government. At the end of these promises, however, there is a reading from the apostle's book, the Epistle to the Hebrews, chapter 5, beginning verse 231 [*sic*], and from Colossians, chapter 3, beginning verse 259 [*sic*], and from Paul's first Epistle, chapter 3.[5] Afterwards, the newly married are confirmed as man and wife by those who are present, and they see themselves as such, bound together as long as they live, according to the law.

The Sacrament of Anointing

We do not carry out anointing, even though we know from the Word of God that the apostles healed many sick people with oil. The Apostle James commanded that the priests of the church be called together in order to pray over him, after which he received anointing in the name of the Lord. We interpret the oil as a heartfelt, fervent prayer by the faithful for sick people, and for this we go to the sick in our midst and pray for the recovery of their health.

---

4 The document refers to the "Book of Tobias," but the verse is from the *Apocrypha*, Book of Tobit, chapter 7, verse 13.

5 The verses cited here do not exist in any conventional version of the Bible. However, other versions of the document in the Cornies papers cite the same verses, suggesting that this is not simply a typographical error.

About Burial of the Deceased

Burial is accomplished in the following manner: when the soul has left the body, the elder brothers and sisters of the deceased read psalms. At the time of burial the deceased is accompanied to the grave by weeping and the singing of psalms, following the example of the followers of Christ as written in the Acts of the Apostles: "Stephanus, however, was attended by God-fearing men and they lamented over him" (Acts, chapter 8, verse 2). We remember them in the same way, and pray for their release from their sins and their summoning into the Kingdom of Heaven. We give alms for them and do good deeds for the poor, for which we find an example in the Bible, 2 Maccabees, where the Israelites pray for the sinners fallen in battle. The prophet Baruch also prays: "Almighty Lord God of Israel, hear now Israel's prayer for those who are held by death's revenge and the prayer of the children who have sinned before You and have not listened to the voice of the Lord, their God." We believe that even after death we will live. According to Esther, judgment will come after death and we will live anew. Then the name of the just will come forward and the works of the unjust will show themselves, and the unjust will move into eternal torture and the just into eternal life.

About Fasting

We observe fasts at various times according to the Word of God because we imitate the lives of the disciples of God, the old prophets, and the evangelists. Christ and the prophets fasted: Moses and Elias observed fasts of forty days, and Esther and Daniel of three weeks. In the same way, our brotherhood of spiritual Christians observes fasts before Christmas and before Easter.[6] Some among us, when they are able to do so, fast for two to three days or even for a whole week. In this time, the fasters offer prayers to the Lord God and sing psalms. They eat and drink nothing at all, as Jesus Christ our Saviour taught those who followed him and as the holy gospel illustrates: "When you fast, anoint your head and wash your face so that you do not shine before people with your fasting, but only before your Father who is hidden; and your Father, who sees what is hidden, will reward you openly."

6 A footnote in the original text reads, "The Tambov sect mentions nothing about this fasting."

About the Church

By the Church we understand an assembly of true believers, in accordance with the words of our saviour Jesus Christ: "Wherever two or three are assembled in my name, there I am among them." In the same way, it says in the Epistle of the apostle Paul, "You are the temple of the living God, as God says: 'I will live in them and walk in them and will be their God and they will be my people.' When you assemble, each of you must have psalms and each must have one teaching, witness, revelation, or interpretation, and must let everything happen for the better." According to the words of the apostle Paul, "do you not know that you are the temple of God and the spirit of God dwells in you? For the temple of God is holy and this you are and not only of yourself, for you have been dearly bought. Therefore, praise God with your bodies and in your spirit, which are of God." The apostle Peter calls the Church the temple in the assembly of believers, who believe without doubting in Jesus Christ, the cornerstone: "And you also, as the living stones, build yourselves as a spiritual house, to sacrifice spiritual sacrifices. So let us also sacrifice through Him, God's continuing sacrifice of praise. This is the fruit of the lips that confess His Name and are pleasing to God through Jesus Christ." Even though God ordered that Solomon was to build a house of God, we still see in the gospel, in everything that has happened, nothing pleasing to God. As it is written in the Acts of the Apostles, the Saviour says: "My house shall be called a house of prayer." Solomon built God a house, but the Almighty does not live in temples made by hands, for as the prophet says, "heaven is my seat and the earth a stool for my feet. What sort of a house do you then want to build, says the Lord, and where is my resting place?" In the Acts of the Apostles, it is also explained that "God, who has made the world and everything that is in it, since He is Lord of heaven and earth, does not live in temples made with hands." He is also not tended by human hands, since He Himself gives each and every one life and breath. In the Acts of the Apostles we see how the disciples of Jesus prayed, and when they came into the chamber, they climbed to the loft and were constantly together, of one mind, praying and pleading. In the same way, in the house of Mary, mother of John, the church diligently prayed to God about Peter. Also, Paul preached in the room and continued his words until midnight – yes, even to the breaking of day. Following the example of our Lord, Jesus Christ, when He prayed to His heavenly Father with bent knees, words and spirit coming from His lips in every place, and also of His disciples who prayed to the one God in chambers and in their houses without imagining in any way that they might be equal to the God-head, so we also have assemblies of men, women, and children in our rooms on Sundays and holidays, where the Word of God is read and heard carefully to fulfil the holy commandments. We also sing psalms and bring prayers to God the creator. We believe that God accepts a heartfelt prayer in the temple as well as in a house, for David said, "He rules in every place; bless my soul, oh Lord!"

About Prayer

We pray with heartfelt emotion and bend our knees just as Jesus Christ prayed on His knees in His time to honour the heavenly Father our God, the Tsar unto all eternity, the incorruptible, invisible, unified, wise. In the same way, the apostle Paul bent his knees and prayed together with many others and tears were spilled in abundance. The apostle Paul said, "I ask you to pray about everything, entreat, and plead. Be thankful for all people, for the Tsar and all superiors, so that we can lead a peaceful life, and to enable us to walk in honesty and fear of God at all times, for this is a good activity pleasing to God." Our prayers when we worship God are those prescribed to us by our saviour Jesus Christ, "Our Father who is in heaven," etc., and also prayers of the apostles and prophets. We also have psalms, for according to the words of the apostle Paul, "Pray constantly in all circumstances with entreaty and pleading in the Spirit." At the time of entreaty and pleading in our assemblies we stand, each facing the other, before the Spirit of God. Therefore pray to him in spirit and in truth. According to the words of our saviour Jesus Christ, the true honouring of God is in the spirit and in praying truthfully, because the Father seeks such worshipers. God is a spirit and those who worship him must do it in the spirit and in truth. This prayer and honouring we fulfil with all punctuality because we call ourselves spiritual Christians.

We consider burning incense to mean the presentation of heartfelt prayers, the true belief in the God of the Trinity, in accordance with David's words: "My prayers must be worthy before You like a smoking sacrifice before Your face." With this David means that the prayers of the holy are the incense.

As well as the holy sacraments, we take to heart the Word of God and our inner beliefs. In our confession of faith we do not consider ourselves to be without sin or holy, but we work for our salvation with fear and trembling in the hope that it can simply and only be attained through belief in Jesus Christ, the only begotten Son of God, and fulfilment of the commandments of the Lord. We do not have our own strength for this, but take it from the living faith of our sect in our intercessor and saviour, Jesus Christ.

The Molokans live in three villages which are occupied only by them:

1. Novo-Vasilievka
2. Astrakhanka
3. Novo-Spask

The population of these villages consists of 1,350 males and 1,447 females, 2,797 souls of both genders. Included in this number are three male and two female nobles, four male and four female foreigners, four male and three female discharged soldiers, eight male and thirteen female merchants, twenty-five male and thirty-five female citizens and craftsmen, 178 male and 196 female Crown peasants, 820 male and 853 female odnodvortsy, 308 male and 341 state and other peasants.[7]

7 Apparently the file originally included a table of economic data, as indicated by the following footnote in the original text: "It should be noted here that in the years of crop failure, 1833 and 1834, more than half of the number of livestock were lost because of a lack of feed and that field cultivation also suffered considerably for this reason, and not even half of what was seeded in earlier years could be seeded."

Appendix I
Genealogy of Johann Cornies' Immediate Family

[Appendix I is based on the twenty-two-page unpublished Genealogy of the Cornies family compiled by Jacob Kornelius Toews in 1953. It was accessed through http://cornies-genealogy.blogspot.ca/.]

Johann Martin Cornies (1741–1823), father of Johann Cornies

Maria Klassen (1760–1833), mother of Johann Cornies

Johann Cornies (1789–1848)

Anganetha Klassen Cornies (1792–1847), wife of Johann Cornies

Peter Cornies (1791–1847), brother of Johann Cornies

David Cornies (1794–1873), brother of Johann Cornies

Heinrich Cornies (1806–?), brother of Johann Cornies

Johann Cornies Jr. (1812–1882), son of Johann Cornies

Agnes Cornies (1819–1870), daughter of Johann Cornies and wife of Philip Wiebe, secretary of Johann Cornies. After Johann Cornies' death in 1848, Wiebe succeeded him as chairman of the Forestry Society.

Appendix II
List of Correspondents

Barth, Johann Ambrosius, bookseller, No. 681 Grimmaischestrasse, Leipzig

Bartram, Johann, Viborg Finland, sometime visitor to Molochnaia Mennonite District

Biess, senior magistrate, Petersdorf, Saxony

Biller, inspector

Blueher, Traugott, director of the Sarepta Merchandising Firm in Moscow

Contenius, Samuel, curator of Guardianship Committee in Ekaterinoslav

Cornies, Agnes, daughter of Johann Cornies

Cornies, David, brother of Johann Cornies

Cornies, Heinrich, brother of Johann Cornies, with business in Ekaterinoslav in the 1820s and 1830s

Cornies, Johann Jr., son of Johann Cornies

Dmitriev, Larion, master mason living in Gremelsteva village near Peremishl

Dohna, Count G., Herrnhut (also Hermsdorf, near Dresden), grandson of Count Zinzendorf, who was the founder of the Pietist Moravian Brethren

Draisma, Peter Orens, Grunau village in Molochnaia Colonist District

Driedger, deputy district chairman in 1835

Dyck, Klaas, a brother-in-law of Johann Cornies

Dyck, Gerhard, Molochnaia resident who designed and constructed various farm machines

Dyck, Johann, debtor

Enns, Gerhard, Forestry Society member

Ennz, Gerhard, employee of Johann Cornies
Epp, David, Heubuden near Marienberg, West Prussia
Epp, David, Khortitsa Mennonite District
Fadeev, Andrei Michaelovich, senior member of Guardianship Committee
Fast, Bernhard, Halbstadt, church elder in Molochnaia
Flaming, Andreas, Schardau inhabitant
Frank, Wilhelm, employed as translator, clerk, etc., with Guardianship Committee
Friesen, Peter, described as his foster son by Johann Cornies
Goerz, Franz, church elder in Molochnaia
Graf, bookseller
Guardianship Committee, originally in Ekaterinoslav, later in Odessa
Guildenschanz, Georg, senior judge in Odessa Guardianship Committee
Hahn, Peter von, son-in-law of Andrei M. Fadeev
Harder, deputy district chairman of Molochnaia Mennonite settlement in 1835
Hausknecht, Caspar Adrian, teacher in Mennonite village schools
Heese, Heinrich, teacher in Mennonite village schools
Horwitz, Theodor E.
Inzov, Ivan Nikitic, head curator of Guardianship Committee
Janz, Benjamin, teacher in a Molochnaia village school
Janzen, Cornelius, resident in Schoenwiese village
Khortitsa Mennonite District Office
Kirilovskii, translator for the Guardianship Committee in Ekaterinoslav and tutor for Johann Cornies Jr.
Klaassen, Christian, Grunau village in Molochnaia Colonist District
Klaassen, Johann, cloth manufacturer in Molochnaia Mennonite District
Klassen, Johann, Molochnaia Mennonite District chairman
Kliewer, Gerhard, Schardau village inhabitant
Koshani, manager at Tsarskoe Selo sheep farm
Lemke, Abram, inhabitant in Molochnaia Mennonite District
Loewen, David, debtor
Mariupol Colonist District Office
Mark, Major
Martens, Gerhard, employed by Molochnaia Mennonite District Office
Martens, Jacob, Tiegenhagen village inhabitant

Martens, Wilhelm, wealthy Mennonite settler, one of wealthiest Mennonite estate owners in the Molochnaia area, and business partner of Johann Cornies
Mathias, Karl, Hochstadt village in Molochnaia Colonist District, debtor
Molochnaia Colonist (German) District Office
Molochnaia Mennonite District office
Neufeld, D., Molochnaia inhabitant
Neufeld, Peter, Ladekopp village inhabitant
Novovassilov Uezd Office
Pelekh, Khariton Trokhimovich, inspector of colonies
Penner, Jacob, Khortitsa District chairman who later moved to Molochnaia District
Radichev Village Office, Hutterite community
Regier, J., Schoensee village inhabitant
Regier, Regina, Molochnaia inhabitant
Reimer, Heinrich, employed as manager of Iushanle estate in 1834
Reimer, Peter, employed by Radichev Mennonites (Hutterites)
Reuss, Prince Heinrich von, Klipphausen near Wilsdorf, Saxony
Riedel, Herman, merchant in Odessa
Schlatter, Daniel (1791–1870), independent Swiss missionary to Nogais, author of 1830 book on Nogais
Schubert, state counsellor in St. Petersburg, involved with Bible Society
Semenov, Member of Guardianship Committee
Sieter, inspector for Molochnaia settlements
van der Smissen, Jacob, Danzig
Steen, Heinrich van, Danzig
Steven, C., Simferopol, agricultural office administrator
Sukau, Johann, Mennonite resident in Rothenbude on the Vistula, West Prussia
Sukau, Johann, employed by Cornies
Tihlmann, Johann, Mennonite settler
Village offices
Voht, Frantz, Rueckenau village inhabitant
Voth [or Voht], David, Molochnaia inhabitant
Voth, Tobias, teacher at Ohrloff Society School
Wall, Cornelius, Molochnaia community sheep farm manager
Walther, Ernst
Warkentin, Dietrich, Mennonite settler

Warkentin, Dirk, Forestry Society member
Warkentin, P., Molochnaia inhabitant
Wedel, Peter, church elder in Molochnaia Mennonite District
Werner, Rosenthal village in Molochnaia Colonist District
Wiebe, Abraham, Forestry Society member
Wiebe, Abram, Rudnerweide village inhabitant
Wiebe, Johann, Tiege, later Neuteich, West Prussia
Wiens, Dirk, assistant manager at Iushanle in 1834
Wilke, August, gardener on Cornies' sheep farm
Wollmann, Christian, Kirschwald village in Molochnaia Colonist District
Zille, inspector at Raeubersdorf near Zittau, Saxony

Appendix III
Glossary

Arshin: measure of length equal to 71 cm or 28 inches

Chetverik: dry measure, also called mirka, equal to one-eighth of a chetvert

Chetvert: dry measure equal to 2.099 hectolitres or 5.95 bushels

Cottager or *Anwohner*: a landless village inhabitant with a house on a half-desiatina garden and orchard plot

Desiatina: land measure equal to 1.092 hectares or 2.7 acres

District Office or *Gebietsamt*: headed by elected chairman, or *Oberschulz,* and two assistants

Fullholding or *Wirtschaft*: Mennonite family farm, normally with sixty-five desiatinas of land, consisting of house and farm buildings on a one-and-a-half-desiatina home and garden plot in a village, a half-desiatina woodlot, and plough, hay, and pasturelands in common fields around the village

Funt: weight equal to 0.41 kilograms or 0.9 pounds

Fut: English foot

German mile: equal to 7,420 metres

Guberniia: major administrative division, a province of the Russian Empire

Khutor: an owned or leased individual farm or group of farms outside of villages

Orphans administration or *Waisenamt*: a district body with executive authority to administer and enforce Mennonite inheritance practices

Pud: weight equal to 40 funt, 16.38 kilograms, or 36 pounds

Renter or ***Einwohner*****:** a landless village inhabitant, often young and recently married, who occupies rented rooms in a village

Ruble: monetary unit, equal to 100 kopeks; in 1839, the value of one silver ruble was fixed at 3.6 paper rubles

Sazhen: length equal to 2.134 metres or 7 feet

Uezd: administrative district

Versta: length equal to 1.065 kilometres or 0.633 miles

Village Office or ***Schulzenamt*****:** village administration headed by elected village mayor, or *Schulz*, and two assistants, or *Beisitzer*

Volost: administrative subdivision of the peasantry comprising a number of villages; the equivalent of a Mennonite District before 1871

Appendix IV
Chronology

1789	First Mennonite settlers from West Prussia settle in Khortitsa, southern Ukraine, founding Mennonite Old Settlement
1789	Johann Cornies born in Baerwalde, West Prussia
1789	Start of the French Revolution
1792	Treaty of Jassy concludes Russo-Turkish war, extending tsarist control over larger areas of southern Ukraine
1803–4	Founding of Mennonite Molochnaia settlement in southern Ukraine
1804	Cornies' family immigrates to southern Ukraine. Oldest son, Johann, works in brandy distillery in Old Colony
1805	Cornies' family, including sons Johann, David, and Peter, settle in village of Ohrloff, Molochnaia Mennonite settlement
1806	Youngest Cornies son, Heinrich, born
1805–7	Franco-Russian war ends with Treaty of Tilsit, 1807
1812	Russia acquires Bessarabia
1812	Napoleon attacks Russia
1812	Johann Cornies establishes leaseland estate on Iushanle river along southern edge of Molochnaia settlement
1817	Johann Klaassen, Rosenort, establishes Halbstadt cloth factory

1817	Johann Cornies appointed Molochnaia Mennonite settlement land surveyor
1818	Johann Cornies appointed member of Mennonite Land Settlement Commission to oversee immigration and establishment of new settlers from Prussia
1818	Tsar Alexander I inspects Molochnaia settlement
1822	Pioneering post-secondary school established by Ohrloff School Society, chaired by Johann Cornies
1824	Johann Cornies travels to Moscow, St. Petersburg, and Tsarskoe Selo to purchase pure-bred Merino sheep for Molochnaia settlement
1823–6	Molochnaia Mennonite settlement ravaged by inundation of grasshoppers, devastating snowstorms, and other scourges
1825	Tsar Alexander I visits Molochnaia settlement shortly before death in Taganrog
1827	Johann Cornies leads purchasing mission to Saxony to purchase pure-bred merino sheep for Molochnaia settlement
1828–9	Russo-Turkish hostilities end with Treaty of Adrianople that extends Russian control along the Black Sea coast
1830	Samuel Contenius dies (30 May 1830). His office as head of the Guardianship Committee Regional Office in Ekaterinoslav had been assumed by Andrei M. Fadeev in 1819
1831	Tsarist state establishes Molochnaia Mennonite Forestry Society [*Verein zur foerdersamen Verbreitung des Gehoelz, Garten, Seiden und Weinbaues*] with Johann Cornies as permanent chair
1832	Johann Cornies purchases Tashchenak estate
1835–6	Johann Cornies Jr. journeys to Moscow, St. Petersburg, Riga, Sarepta, etc.
1836	Field cultivation and crafts and trades added to the Forestry Society's responsibilities. The words "Improvement of Agriculture and Development of

	Trades" added to Society's title of the institution now popularly known as "Agricultural Society"
1836	Andrei M. Fadeev pays farewell visit to Johann Cornies on journey to new position in Astrakhan
1837	Guardianship Committee for Foreign Settlers in Southern Russia, with offices originally in Ekaterinoslav, later in Kishenev and Odessa, and regional offices and inspectorates throughout southern Ukraine, is transferred from the jurisdiction of the Ministry of Internal Affairs to the Ministry of State Domains (responsible for Russia's state peasants, non-serf peasantry, about half of the total peasantry. Mennonites were legally part of this social stratum)
1837	At Fadeev's invitation, Johann Cornies travels to Astrakhan and Sarepta
1838	Johann Cornies appointed member of Learned Committee of Ministry of State Domains
1842	Disputes between church leaders and Johann Cornies in Molochnaia Mennonite settlement temporarily resolved through forceful intervention of new head of Guardianship Committee, Evgeny von Hahn
1843	Hutterites (also known as Radishev Mennonites) settled in environs of Molochnaia Mennonite settlement and placed under direction of Johann Cornies
1843	Guardianship Committee expands responsibilities of Johann Cornies and Agricultural Society to include development and supervision of schools in Molochnaia Mennonite District
1846–8	Johann Cornies exercises authority over Khortitsa Mennonite settlement
1846–7	Crown model plantation established under Cornies' direction
1847	Anganetha Cornies, wife of Johann Cornies, dies
1848	Johann Cornies dies
1848	European revolutions

Index

www.ingramcontent.com/pod-product-compliance
Lightning Source LLC
LaVergne TN
LVHW010354080826
844660LV00015B/963/J

* 9 7 8 1 4 4 2 6 4 5 0 6 6 *